Historical Perspectives

on Business

Enterprise Series

A History of Accountancy
in the United States

The Cultural Significance of Accounting

GARY JOHN PREVITS
and BARBARA DUBIS MERINO

OHIO STATE UNIVERSITY PRESS

Columbus

Copyright © 1998 by The Ohio State University.
All rights reserved.

Library of Congress Cataloguing-in-Publication Data

Previts, Gary John.
    A history of accountancy in the United States : the cultural significance of
accounting / Gary John Previts and Barbara Dubis Merino.
        p.   cm. — (Historical perspectives on business enterprise series)
    Includes bibliographical references and index.
    ISBN 0-8142-0727-8 (alk. paper). — ISBN 0-8142-0728-6 (pbk. : alk. paper)
    1. Accounting—United States—History.   I. Merino, Barbara
Dubis.   II. Title.   III. Series.
    HF5616.U5P724   1997
    657′.0973—dc21   97-24109
                                                                                         CIP

Text and jacket design by Nighthawk Design.
Type set in ITC New Baskerville by G&S Typesetters, Inc.
Printed by Braun-Brumfield, Inc.

The paper used in this publication meets the minimum requirements of American National
Standard for Information Sciences—Permanence of Paper for Printed Library Materials.
ANSI Z39.48–1992.

9 8 7 6 5 4 3 2 1

To our families

Contents

Chapter 3   *1827–1865*   63
The Beginnings of Corporate America

Chapter 4   *1866–1896*   103
Accounting in the Gilded Age

Figures

Tables

Preface

In the late 1970s when we wrote the first edition of this project in concert with the U.S. bicentennial observation, the history of accounting, as an academic field, was in its infancy. Concerns of historians then were principally technical and descriptive, not contextual and analytic. Our work in 1979 was an early attempt to incorporate the latter. Today, many historians of accountancy, with the support of nonhistorians, address contextual aspects of historical inquiry and consider a broader interpretation of the history of our discipline's role in society. Our revised interpretation of our discipline's role in the social order is directed to students of history who are not already familiar with the basics addressed by our study.

Furthermore, the world order and the context it provides for consideration of our society have changed. The end of the cold war, the democratic reforms being considered widely throughout Europe, and the aftermath of the Persian Gulf war have prompted some political scientists to assert that humanity is approaching "the end of history of political systems." Indeed, following World War II, some writers were skeptical that the United States represented a civilization in terms of recognized historical theories (Lerner 1957: 58). However, as the end of the twentieth century approaches, there may be less scholarly skepticism and more acceptance of the notion that the United States represents a culture and a civilization. Described as "the world's largest land mass lying between latitudes conducive to energetic human activity" (Martin 1984: 1), that part of the continent that became the nation of the United States of America differs from all others in the history of humankind. The story of accountants and accountancy in the context of this nation, its culture and geography, as well as its economic and political activities is a story of the "cultural significance of accounts."

There are, of course, limits on our ability to interpret and relate to the past; a historical maxim reminds us that "history is an argument without end." We acknowledge history to be a child of its own times and therefore attempt to understand the past on its own terms. In this way we expect that our effort will assist others in relating what "was" the past to what "is" the present and in anticipating what "ought" to be the future. We have adopted, for purposes of style, the views of Norman Cousins (1991) in that

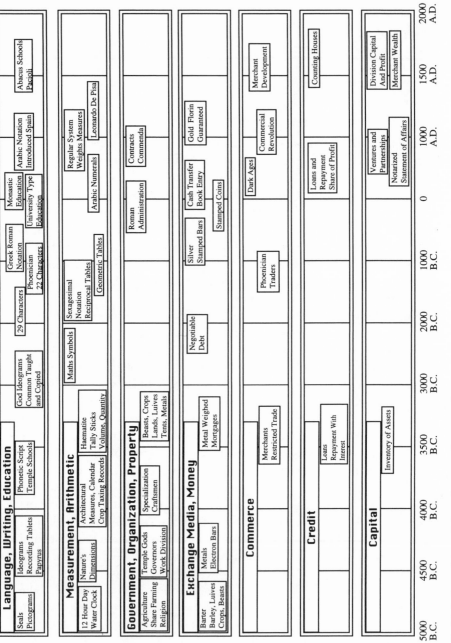

Pref.1 A view of the origins of accounting over time

we realize that the general use of the term "man" or "his" when applied to humankind is imperfect for persons who prefer "his or her" or "persons." To the extent we adhere to traditional terminology we intend no disrespect.

Our revision has benefited from many insights provided by readers and reviewers over the years since the initial edition was published. We wish to thank our correspondents and students for their interest and support, which encouraged us to undertake this revision. Our rewriting began in earnest in 1990, although we had planned a revision for the past decade. Allowing for the consecutive years when we were distracted from the project (Merino spent a Fulbright year in Poland; Previts served as president of the Ohio Society of Certified Public Accountants), we are concluding our efforts very close to schedule.

We have also benefited from the dedicated and able assistance of our student research assistants. Gary Previts thanks those at Case Western Reserve University, including Jennifer Byron, Kevin Carduff, David Crichton, and Eric Lin. In addition, Previts acknowledges the important intellectual colleagueship provided by Eric Neilsen and David Hammack, with whom he has shared teaching the Weatherhead School graduate course on the History of American Industrial Enterprise these past five years.

Finally, we are mindful of the ambitious scope of our work and expect that many opportunities for criticism will therefore arise. We welcome open debate as a stimulus to understanding the role of history in our discipline and our profession.

Abbreviations

AAA	American Accounting Association
AACSB	American Assembly of Collegiate Schools of Business
AAPA	American Association of Public Accountants
AAUIA	American Association of University Instructors in Accounting
AECC	Accounting Education Change Commission
AETBS	American Express Tax and Business Services
AIA	American Institute of Accountants
AICPA	American Institute of Certified Public Accountants
APB	Accounting Principles Board
ARB	Accounting Research Bulletin
ARS	Accounting Research Study
ASB	Auditing Standards Board
ASCPA	American Society of Certified Public Accountants
ASOBAT	*A Statement of Basic Accounting Theory*
ASR	Accounting Series Release
BCCI	Bank of Credit and Commerce International
CAFR	Comprehensive Annual Financial Report
CAP	Committee on Accounting Procedure
CAPM	capital asset pricing model
CAR	Commission on Auditors' Responsibilities
CASB	Cost Accounting Standards Board
CFM	certified in financial management
CFO	chief financial officer
CIA	certified internal auditor
CIO	chief information officer
CMA	Certificate of Management Accounting
CPI	consumer price index
CRO	chief reporting officer
DOD	Department of Defense
DOE	Department of Energy
EDGAR	electronic data gathering, analysis, and retrieval
EITF	Emerging Issues Task Force
EMH	efficient market hypothesis
EPS	earnings per share

ESOP	employee stock ownership plan
FAF	Financial Accounting Foundation
FASB	Financial Accounting Standard Boards
FCC	Federal Communications Commission
FCPA	Foreign Corrupt Practices Act
FEI	Financial Executives Institute
FERF	Financial Executives Research Foundation
FIFO	first in, first out
FRB	Federal Reserve Board
FTC	Federal Trade Commission
GAAFR	*Governmental Accounting, Auditing and Financial Reporting*
GAAP	generally accepted accounting principles
GAAS	generally accepted accounting standards
GAO	General Accounting Office
GASB	Governmental Accounting Standards Boards
GPO	Government Printing Office
HLT	highly leveraged transactions
IASC	International Accounting Standards Committee
ICC	Interstate Commerce Commission
IFA	International Federation of Accountants
IIA	Institute of Internal Auditors
IMA	Institute of Management Accountants
IOSCO	Interntional Organization of Securities Commissions
IPO	initial public offerings
ITC	investment tax credit
LIFO	last in, first out
MAS	management advisory services
MFA	Municipal Finance Association
MFOA	Municipal Finance Officers Association
NAA	National Association of Accountants
NACA	National Association of Cost Accountants
NASBA	National Association of State Boards of Accountancy
NCCPAP	National Conference of Certified Public Accountant Practitioners
NCGA	National Council on Governmental Accounting
NJSCPA	New Jersey Society of Certified Public Accountants
NYSE	New York Stock Exchange
NYSSCPA	New York State Society of Certified Public Accountants
NOL	net operating loss
OMB	Office of Management and Budget

OSHA	Occupational Safety and Health Administration
PE	price earnings
PICPA	Pennsylvania State Institute of Certified Public Accountants
RAP	regulatory accounting principles
ROI	return on investment
SAB	Staff Accounting Bulletins
SAP	Statement on Auditing Procedure
SEC	Securities and Exchange Commission

Introduction

We begin this new edition of our work by (1) providing a perspective on our views, (2) establishing premises related to the origins of double entry, the role of capital markets, and accounting, and (3) reviewing the notion of property rights in society.

Columbus and the "Novus Ordo Seclorum"

Alistair Cooke observes that the object of Columbus's venture, which would lead him to the American continent, was twofold: "For Gospel and for Gold" (Cooke 1973: 32). In short, Columbus sought to be a missionary and a prospector. Yet he came to fame as a discoverer. Some, including Samuel Eliot Morison, the naval historian, say that Columbus "did more to direct the course of history than any individual since Augustus Caesar" (Shaw 1991). To this day, paper currency of the United States bears the motto "Novus Ordo Seclorum" (New World Order), which reflects the course of this influence.

We know now that Columbus was not the first person to make contact with the American continent. But his was the immediate prelude to an age of sea venturing, exploration, and discovery by Europeans. After he landed in the Bahamas in 1492, there were subsequent ventures to other parts of the Atlantic by Cabot, Ponce de León, Verrazano, and de Soto; and in the Pacific by Balboa. In the next century, discovery was augmented as colonies and outposts were established by Dutch, Spanish, French, and English explorers. These activities stretched across vast regions, from the French claims north of the Saint Lawrence River to the Spanish and Portuguese territories in the South (beginning with Florida) with English areas in between these.

1

About the Origins of Double Entry

Writing in 1956, Peragallo asserted: "The earliest known double-entry records, fragmentary though they be, are the 'Massari Ledgers' of 1340 of the Commune of Genoa, which date a century and a half earlier (than Pacioli's *Summa*)." Earlier, in 1930, Murray cited Kheil (1898), noting that "indeed it is argued that Spain was the original home of book-keeping by double entry" (467). These origins, if so, have not been confirmed. Mills (1986: 65) notes that the earliest-known Spanish accounting literature is found in *Tratado de Cuentas,* written by Diego del Castillo in 1522.

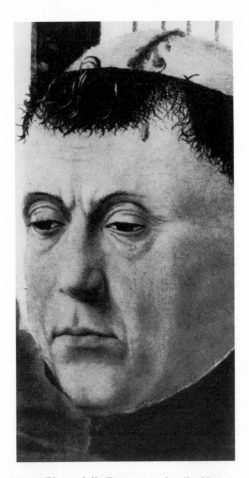

Intro.1 Pierra della Francesca, detail of Luca Pacioli from Brera altarpiece, Virgo and Child with Saints, Brera, Milan. Reproduced by permission of the Ministero per i Bene Culturali e Ambientali.

Kataoka (1989: 131) tells us: "According to . . . Wolfgang von Stromer (1968: 126), the Nürnberg merchants introduced . . . double entry book-keeping from Venice into south Germany in the 15th century for the first time." He further asserts that "Jacob Fugger went to Fondaco Tedeschi in Venice in 1473 at the age of fourteen in order to study commerce, and he introduced the accounting system of Venice to [the] Fuggers." Lee (1972: 58) reports that while "the bankers of 1211 had certainly not achieved double entry . . . the paragraph form of account was historically no bar to the gradual recognition in Tuscany of the essentially two-sided nature of all business transactions. What is certain," Lee continues, "is that by 1300 some Florentine firms at least, while still using the paragraph layout, had begun meticulously to cross reference all entries . . . thus attaining to double entry, or something remarkably near it."

Antoni (1977: 17) presents evidence about the origins of bookkeeping per se (not double entry), arguing that "we are now able to back date the origin of bookkeeping by almost a century through the fortunate discovery of a specimen drawn up at the end of the 11th century or in the first decade of the 12th century by a Pisan shipbuilder to record expenditures incurred in the building or repairing of a galley." Lee (1977: 89) affirms that "with the doubtful exception of the Fini ledger [1296] . . . evidence for full double entry before 1299 is tenuous."

Of course this lack of certainty does not deter speculation or research about prior accounting and double-entry developments, nor should it. Even though Robert (1957), writing that Roman citizens kept accounts, notes that "no longer is it possible to believe that the Roman methods were a near approach to our own, or that they had anticipated many of the advanced techniques on which accountants pride themselves today," others are less certain. Most (1976), in his comments on the research by German historian Barthold Georg Niebuhr on the history of Rome, investigated Niebuhr's claim that "the system of bookkeeping by double-entry, so far from being the invention of the Lombards, is as old as the Romans, and was used by the Quaestors in their accounts." Most presents a rationale that attempts to link the notions found in pre-Christian accounts of Rome but does not offer a determining argument, leaving the opportunity for future consideration.

The First Published Book on Accounting

Hausdorfer (1986) asserts that Benetto Cotrugli, a merchant and man of learning, born in Ragusa in southern Dalmatia, consul for Ragusa in 1458, and minister to Ferdinand, King of Naples, in 1462, included a section on bookkeeping in his *Della Mercatura et del Mercante perfetto,* presumably some thirty-one years before Pacioli's treatise was printed in 1494. However, Cotrugli's effort, written shortly after the invention of movable-type printing presses in the 1430s, did not appear in print until several decades after Pacioli's *Summa* was published. Whether or not Cotrugli's work contained "double entry" remains a speculation. Inoue (1982) tells us that in 1518, when nothing but Pacioli's *Summa* was known to be in print, Matthaus Schwarz, a bookkeeper of the Fuggers, had printed his own manuscript on bookkeeping called "Threefold Bookkeeping." This work and the many that would follow (e.g., Grammateus, Manzoni, Ympyn, Pietra, Stevin, Oldecaste, and Mellis) throughout Europe and capital market nations have been discussed by Geijsbeek (1914), Kheil (1906), Murray (1930), Littleton (1933A), and many others.

Accounting and Capitalism

The propositions of Werner Sombart in his 1924 *der moderne Kapitalismus* have received attention in recent decades and have continued to serve as a useful debate ground for historians seeking to understand the role of our discipline in society. We review the principal aspects of this debate without necessarily intending to resolve it.

Yamey (1964) is critical of Sombart's assertion that bookkeeping aided the rise of capitalism, and that double-entry bookkeeping made possible the separation of a business from its owners. In short, accounting claims too much if it claims to be a cause of capitalism. Most (1972), however, observes that accounting may be considered a conceptual framework for planning and control, which in the context of the technology and developments of the times (Arabic numerals, the clock, the printing press, and the use of gunpowder in arms) provides support for Sombart's views.

Another view of the relationship between accounting and capitalism can be found in what Edwards (1991) identifies as the "demand/response" theory of accounting development, which views accounting as a "social technology," continually responding to changes in business requirements. In this respect, prevailing economic conditions, the nature of business organizations, and the willingness to innovate combine to dictate, to a large extent, what accounting practices will develop.

Viewed with care, one might consider Sombart's propositions to preclude a "demand/response" explanation. Is accounting a cause or an effect (response) in capital market activities? We prefer a more accommodating interpretation, consistent with a pragmatic view of history that considers the development of accounting thought and practice as not exclusively consistent with either Sombart's view or Edwards's. We contend that both are correct. Double entry is unique: it renders into objective, quantified terms the concept of capital as claims against listed resources. It became a necessary condition in forming increasingly large amounts of capital for ventures and, later, administrative entities and control of these entities' activities and costs. In explaining *the cultural significance of accounts,* DR Scott claimed that the vernacular term *bottom line* was axiomatic of the "make a buck" culture of the United States. In the sense of this "bottom line" role, accounting plays more than a technical informational role in American culture—it portrays it.

Therefore, our identifying and assessing the role of accounting in the context of a variety of eras of contemporary capital market development will reflect an interactive view of accounting as a "condition" affecting and affected by market evolution.

On the Evolution of Terminology

An example of the consistency of double entry and the manner in which it evolves can be seen in the solution to a modern bookkeeping mystery, which might be called the "Case of the missing R." Students understand today that *Cr.* can be related to the word *credit,* but how does *Dr.* relate to *debit?* In short, where does the "r" come from in the abbreviation *Dr.?* Sherman (1986) establishes that the language link comes from the use of the words *debtor* and *creditor.* Indeed, in chapter 11 of *Summa,* Pacioli uses the terms *debitore* (debtor) and *creditore* (creditor) in a manner consistent with Sherman's observations; thus, *debitore*/debit/Dr. and *creditore*/credit/Cr.

Capital Market Eras and Accounting Practice

In each era of capital markets, accounting's role may be portrayed through attention to the contributions of accounting practitioners and authors. For example, Pacioli's *Summa* (1494) is most probably the contribution that best represents a synthesis of accounting in the age of *venture capitalism.*

As venturing explorers gave way to colonial trading activities, the age of *mercantile capitalism*—first based in general trade and then in specialized trade of natural products such as timber, fish, and fur—ensued. This was supplemented by trade in agricultural products, including tobacco, rice, and indigo. The writings of John Mair, *Book-keeping methodiz'd . . .* (1763) and *Book-keeping moderniz'd . . .* (1768), afford a benchmark for accounting practice of the time.

The development of manufactures following upon the specialization of production foretold the industrial revolution and the age of *financial capitalism*, typified by the activities of persons such as Vanderbilt, Morgan, and Gould (Galambos and Pratt 1988). Writers, beginning with Cronhelm in England and Thomas Jones in the United States, provided new accounting treatments for this era, culminating in the algebraic notation of Sprague (1880).

The separation of owners and managers in a corporate economy, as described by Berle and Means (1932) and studied by Chandler (1977), established an identity for *managerial capitalism*. Drawing from the powerful simplicity of Sprague's (1908) accounting equation (Assets = Liabilities + Proprietorship), Hatfield, Paton, and Littleton, among others, established a classical form of accounting through *financial statements* to serve this period.

Since the 1970s, following the impact of the Wheat and Trueblood reports, standard setting in the private sector has been guided by the Financial Accounting Standards Board (FASB) Conceptual Framework. This framework sought to produce *financial reports* to assess cash flows. More recently, a committee chaired by Edmund Jenkins has developed a *business reporting* model that expands and transcends the financial transaction tradition of accounting and firmly roots "accountancy" as a business information discipline.

As global capital markets emerge and individual investor involvement in market trading declines, the role of professional fund managers in the capital market has come to dominate and signal the emergence of the present age, *investment fund capitalism* (*Economist*, May 19, 1990). Today, accountants remain faithful to an intellectual habit, viewing transactions initially in terms of the orthodoxy of Sprague's algebra. His equation, albeit increasingly challenged by the broader view of database and information disclosure considerations of accounting, provides a classificatory basis for teaching transaction treatment and quantitative manipulation.

Given that accounting/double entry facilitates information and is a factor in the private enterprise capital marketplace, we shall review the role of property and individual property rights in these settings.

Accounting and Property Rights

Chatfield (1974: 15) notes that Littleton sets "private property" as one of the preconditions for the emergence of systematic bookkeeping, "since bookkeeping is concerned only with recording the facts about property and property rights." This precondition is understood to represent the right of

Accounting Knowledge		Technology
Comprehensive Disclosure — TQM International Accounting Standards — Program Controls Environmental Consequences — Value Added Activity Costing — Long Future Accruals Markets / Transactions Costs — Principal - Agent Internal Auditing Controls — Economic Consequences Internal Auditing — Non-for-Profit Entities Information Contents of Financial Statements Human Behavior / Social Accounting Manpower Values Intergovernmental Relations Governmental Auditing Standards Total Systems Planning	**1990**	World Wide Web (WWW) Compact Disc Interactive 3500 Satellites Launched by this Date Personal Computer Parallel Computing First Local Area Network Created (Ethernet) Electric Pocket Calculator Development of the Internet Microprocessor
Effectiveness Auditing — Organizational Models Management Auditing Concepts — Organizational Planning Management Concepts — Decision Theory Interdisciplinary Applications — Cost - Benefit Analysis Systems Auditing Concepts — Cost Standards Effectiveness Auditing Standards / Analysis Information Systems — Total Systems Review Planning, Programing, & Budgeting Systems Management Processes — Cost - Revenue Analysis Management Sciences Program Accountability Deficiency Findings Management Auditing Management Planning	**1970**	First Global Telecommunications Satellite (Intelstat) First Commercial Copier Sold by Xerox Sputnik Launched in USSR Shawlow and Town Patent a Laser Integrated Circuit Optical Fiber Color Television
Tax Planning Principles of Financial Reporting Tax Advising Planning and Control Systems Tax Accounting Management Accountability Management Services Management Accounting Cost Analysis Auditing Standards Appropriation Control Governmental Accounting	**1950**	Punch Card Records Electronic Digital Computer Automatic Digital Computer Transistor Xerox Patents Copier Technology Hewlett Packard Company Founded Frequency Modulation (FM Radio)
Cost and Production Statistics Uniform Statements Tax Records Cost Accounting CPA Certification Examination	**1930**	Merger Creates International Business Machines (IBM) Mechanical Computer Mechanical Recording Tape Laser Theory Proposed by Einstein Computing - Tabulating - Recording Co. Founded (IBM)
Audits of Records and Statements Financial Auditing Income Statement Emphasis Balance Sheet Emphasis Bookkeeping (Single Entry) Financial Accountability	**1900** **19th Century**	Cash Register Cathode Ray Tube Adding Machine Stock ticker Telephone Telegraph Typewriter Color Printing Printing Press

Intro.2 Chart comparing accounting knowledge and technology

individuals in a society to own and control "productive" property, not only personal property.

Littleton (1933A: 13) notes that private property represents the power to change ownership. Tawney (1926: 35), in *Religion and the Rise of Capitalism*, comments that "private property is a necessary institution, at least in a fallen world; men work more and dispute less when goods are private than when they are common. But it is to be tolerated as a concession to human frailty, not applauded as desirable in itself." Tawney adds that Saint Thomas Aquinas insists on the idea that property is "*stewardship*" (216; emphasis added).

During the seventeenth century, social unrest in England brought the matter of property rights into conflict. "Confiscations, compositions, and war taxation had effected a revolution in the distribution of property, similar . . . to that which had taken place at the Reformation" (Tawney 1926: 213). Groups that had taken the lead in the struggle against the monarch's power over property identified with the theory expressed by Locke when he described property as a right anterior to the existence of the state and argued that "the supreme power cannot take from any man any part of his property without his own consent" (Tawney 1926: 214). But Locke only put into a philosophical frame ideas that had become established in the context of political struggles and that were then already common for groups of landowners and merchants.

It was Aristotle who argued that the principles of private property, private families, and self-interest are so deeply ingrained in the nature of most persons that eradication is impossible (Levy and Sampson 1962: 521). As Cochran (1959: 39) observes, "the Constitution drawn up at Philadelphia in 1787 was a triumph for all men who wished to safeguard private property and stimulate trade and manufactures."

Lerner tells us that property ideas in the American colonies were deeply influenced by Locke and that the structure of American society up until the end of the nineteenth century provided substance for his theory. The components of that property idea were "that a man had a right to the things with which he had mixed his sweat, that his property was linked with his craft and job and therefore with his personality, that you could no more deprive him of his property than of his freedom and individuality, that in fact his individuality was linked with the property which made him self-sufficient and self-reliant, and that he could do what he wishes with the property that was his—these elements of the property idea had force in a social setting where almost every man owned a piece of land or hoped to save enough on his job to start a small business" (Lerner 1957: 298). In the

United States, private property became the constitutional basis for the economic organizing of a culture.

Opportunities to acquire land holdings and other forms of private productive property attracted immigrants to the American colonies. Beginning with the effects of the industrial revolution, land holdings, manufactures, and commercial activities aggregated increasingly over time.

The merchant class, who were propertied and who operated as owner-managers, evolved into a separate class of professional managers and inves-

Intro.3 Portrait of Elijah Borden, Connecticut accountant and merchant, with his accounting materials. By Ralph Earl, 1789. Courtesy of The Metropolitan Museum of Art. Bequest of Susan W. Tyler, 1979 (1979.395).

tors. Investors initially viewed their stock shares as ownership, evidence of a retained propertied status. As investment patterns aggregated, small individual shareholders found themselves comparatively powerless to influence their investment. Because of the relative size of portfolio investment, they were nearly as powerless as earlier unpropertied classes. As early as the 1950s it was estimated that as much as 80 percent of new venture capital was supplied to the organized capital market through institutional sources (Lerner 1957: 299).

Smaller businesses involved in goods or services with national market potential became threatened or supplanted by larger enterprises. With increasing attention paid to accumulation of private personal property (homes and automobiles) and the indirect use or absence of power over private productive property, the notion of property rights was in need of clarification.

Speculating on the present state of "investment fund capitalism," the *Economist* (May 19, 1990) noted that the principal option exercised by a disgruntled institutional investor was to "vote with his feet"; that is, to sell off as opposed to participating in the management, as had been done by investors in preceding generations. After all, the institutional investor, as fiduciary agent for those whose funds are entrusted to his care, has a duty to avoid involvement in the management of investee operations. Involvement would represent a potential conflict of interest, if not a misapplication of talent. In a society driven by property rights incentives, this paradox of duties, frustrated by investment fund conflicts, underlies present concerns about the status of such rights, traditional stewardship or agency relationships, and access to information and reports for investors and investment managers.

If, as many have observed, old ideas never die, then the idea of property rights and their role in our economic system certainly appears to be endowed with long life, albeit with a changed meaning. For as one writer noted, "the position of property in America is neither private nor pure. In a dynamic economy . . . the bundle of legal claims called 'property' never remains stable; . . . a new invention in technology or managerial practice, a depression or a war, may give new value to claims hitherto ignored or diminish others hitherto cherished" (Lerner 1957: 299).

This view on property rights, and its inherent implication for disclosure, following upon a consideration of the evolution of accounting and capital markets, suggests the direction our *History of Accountancy in the United States* will take.

Chapter 1 1492–1775

Accounting from Discovery to Revolutionary Times

> There were forty men . . . aboard the flotilla including a surgeon
> and the royal controller of accounts, sent along to keep tabs on
> Columbus' swindle sheet when he started to figure the cost of
> gold and spices he would accumulate.
>
> **—Alistair Cooke, *America*, 1973**

Alistair Cooke, a popular media host, journalist, and author, points out that when Columbus set sail, among the select members of his crew was an accountant designated by the Spanish monarchs to supervise the "books" of the venture. On this note, our study of the cultural significance of accounting begins.

From a Continent to a Country

In this chapter we address some of the multinational contextual influences in effect during the period of venture and development before the revolt by the thirteen colonies against British rule. In so doing, we discuss the role and cultural significance of accounts during the era.

The vast new American continent promised many opportunities for Europeans. "By 1500 Europe had developed well armed ocean vessels the rest of the world simply could not match. As power moved from East to West in the first five centuries, so it journeyed from South to North in the next two. With even better vessels and stronger domestic economies, the Dutch and the English wrested foreign trade from Mediterranean Europe. . . . Spain used its vast imports of American gold and silver in the sixteenth century to import goods and services from other European countries. By failing to develop its own manufacturing and commercial capacity, Spain declined in the seventeenth century" (Duggan 1979: 140–41). New England's major attractions were its many good harbors, its narrow coastal plain, and its short, swift rivers. The promise of the sea for survival was attractive, and it offered fishing and trade from which the colonial New Englanders could develop their settlements and nurture businesses. The middle colonies became the "bread colonies" because of their wider coastal plains, better soil, and moderate climate. Ultimately, agricultural surpluses provided a trade basis.

Southern colonies had navigable but sluggish rivers adjoining a broad and very fertile rising coastal plain. These served the developing large agricultural form of the plantation and such crops as tobacco, rice, and indigo, as well as ordinary foodstuffs that were produced abundantly in the longer growing season.

Because colonial America was heavily forested along the eastern coast, settlers cleared the land for acreage with a disregard for conservation. Wood was their essential material, and it was used for everything from building to household and farm implements. Wood as fuel warmed homes and provided cookfires. Ships were built and forest products exported (Dykema 1976).

English settlers provided the major source of population growth in the 1600s. In the eighteenth century, this influx diminished with the expansion of the industrial revolution in England. New York had a substantial Dutch population, but during the 1700s the Scots, Irish, and Palatinate Germans were the most numerous immigrants. To the South, black slaves numbered nearly 500,000 by the time of the Revolution, replacing the need for indentured servants there. The indentured workers system persisted among Germans coming to Pennsylvania and often resulted in attracting persons with industrial skills. Although the colonial population at the start of the 1700s was not more than 400,000, it was more than 2.5 million by 1776.

The Ideology of a New World Order

The origins of the colonies that became the United States can be traced back to many cultures and countries, including the Netherlands, Spain, France, Scotland, and England. Yet the history of colonial America chiefly reflects the common law, language, and culture of English settlements, as the marketplace of Adam Smith and the property rights views of John Locke were transplanted to the American continent. The tenets/principles of education were also defined by tradition; for many years to come, schools would teach that recorded history began with Genesis.

The work ethic of Puritanism and the religious revolution of the sixteenth century nurtured the economic system that would ultimately discard the condemnation of usury, to the extent that being involved in an undertaking for profit would become not only an advantage but a social duty; that is, "The good Christian was not wholly dissimilar from the economic man" (Tawney 1926: 210).

The Pilgrim pioneers who founded the New World Order (Novus Ordo Seclorum), which evolved into our present system of capital markets, practiced those tenets of their faith that were consistent with the pursuit of economic gain. Religious intolerance as experienced by the Quakers and the Catholics led in turn to the spread of similar pursuits in colonies such as Pennsylvania and Maryland.

The Dutch had come primarily to trade furs rather than to colonize. In the early 1600s, Henry Hudson spent a month up the river that now bears his name, exploring to a point just below the present city of Albany, but he did not find the much-sought-after Northwest Passage. Disappointed, he retraced his steps, stopping in England because his crew was a mix of English and Dutch sailors. Hudson dispatched a report of his voyage to the Amsterdam Chamber but was prevented from going himself, because the English—betraying the keenness of mercantilist rivalries—claimed he was considered in their service and not that of the Dutch.

In 1653, some dissenters from Virginia took refuge in the Tidewater region of the Carolinas, and by 1670 English capitalists made contributions to support a group of proprietors developing the area around Charleston.

"In 1658 the Puritans of Massachusetts took political control of 'Falmouth' their name for the present towns of . . . [Maine]. The locally unpopular annexation was motivated by military considerations on the part of Massachusetts, whose leaders saw Maine as a convenient buffer between Protestant New England and Catholic New France" (Barry 1982: 7). By 1664 the English had succeeded the Dutch and had gained control of New York. The Georgia colony was founded in 1733 by James Oglethorpe with the similar intention of creating a buffer against the Spanish in Florida (Shannon 1951: 16).

For the pioneer Pilgrims, Puritans, Quakers, Catholics, and others who dissented from the limitations of established orders, life was not easy. Their new homeland was a vast wilderness that did not reveal its full wealth. Entrepreneurial effort and joint venturing, which often undertook activities of considerable risk over great distances, formed the basis for colonial economic life.

"The founding of colonies was a notoriously unprofitable activity" (Morgan 1958: 35). The New Netherlands Company, composed of four merchants, sent fur-trading voyages into the river named after Henry Hudson. Each of the four merchant companies held equal one-quarter rights to the

Dutch charter for three years from 1614, but "it appears likely that none of the four companies involved derived any profit from this venture" (Condon 1968: 21). And in New England economic stability was achieved by immigration per se: "What principally sustained the colony . . . and indeed brought it prosperity during the first ten years of its existence was neither fish nor fur nor any other staple, but immigrants." For "in spite of the woeful tales about the expiring condition of Massachusetts, God's wrath in England seemed to many a more imminent danger" (Condon 1968: 66).

Immigrants had been a mixed blessing in the Jamestown colony's experience a few years earlier in 1608. In summing up his scorn for the impractical instructions coming to Captain John Smith from the London Company, Vaughan notes that "adding to the colony's woes was the odd assortment of new recruits. They were not the blacksmiths and carpenters and 'diggers up of trees' that Smith needed; instead he got twenty-eight gentlemen, [and] fourteen artisans of the wrong kinds. . . . The company gave top priority to the adventurers' profits . . . [while] Smith had to keep the settlers alive. . . . An excursion to the west (in 1608) . . . which . . . commandeered 120 of the best men [from a total population of 200], found neither the South Sea nor precious metals" (Vaughan 1975: 42).

The demand for tobacco would finally provide the "gold" that British adventurers sought. Settlers, including forebears of Thomas Jefferson, "wrested land from the wilderness small parcels at a time, turning it into productive acreage. [And t]o their descendants, they passed along what has been called 'that feel of all with which Nature concerns herself'" (Blackburn 1975: 33).

Early planters and merchants also found that disputes could be troublesome. "Legal historians 'marvel at the appetite for litigation' throughout the colonies. Neighbors sued over boundaries; merchants, over debts; heirs, over wills; politicians, over elections" (Blackburn 1975: 15).

By the mid-1700s, another, more notorious form of seafaring venture was also prospering. In 1760 the thirteen colonies had about 400,000 slaves. Northern shipowners were not slow in taking part in the trade, since after 1700 it had become an important part of a broader and multifaceted shipping economy in the colonies. At the time, such trade carried little social stigma. In simple terms, this part of economic trade was a triangle: rum shipped out of New England was traded for slaves on the African coast; slaves were in turn traded for molasses and gold in the West Indies; molasses was taken home for use in distilling rum. As Shannon notes: "When every conceivable item of cost was accounted for, the owner of a £300 ship expected to make more than its value out of the voyage" (Shannon 1951: 38–39).

The Joint Venture and Capital Formation

Writing in 1768, Mair tells us that "the most ancient trading company in Britain is the Hamburgh company, . . . first incorporated in the reign of King Edward I, anno 1296" (391). It was involved in woolen goods first in Antwerp, then in Calais, and finally Hamburg. Mair continues that during the reign of Queen Mary, the next company incorporated was that of the Russian merchants, followed by other companies trading in Polish Prussia and in Turkey/Levant. Accounts of an English merchant, John Smythe of Bristol, for the period of 1538–50 offer a glimpse of contemporary accounting practices. The Smythe books fall into one of three groups: "voyage accounts which show his exports, commodity accounts which show his imports, and personal accounts of his factors, servants, customers and suppliers." Further, "There is a rudimentary but incomplete profit-and-loss account; but no cash account. . . . Some of the accounts are left unbalanced, . . . but the main features if not the precise volume of his business are clear enough" (Fisher 1976: 151).

Yamey (1976) advises that these accounts were not in double-entry form but says that "whether one calls it 'incomplete double entry' or single entry is a matter of taste. I would not use a description including the words 'double entry.' But it is not 'single entry' either, if one implies by that a system. Incidentally, there is no capital account in the ledger, and no indication that there was a secret ledger with such an account. The ledger is interesting for its quantitative entries in the merchandise accounts."

According to Winjum, the Gresham journals of the years 1546–52 are the earliest-known extant English account books in double-entry form. Winjum concludes that "Gresham, like so many of the merchants of his era, was primarily concerned with the detailed record-keeping and control aspects of his accounting system; he was either uninterested in, or unaware of, double entry's unique ability to determine simultaneously enterprise progress and status" (Winjum 1971: 149, 155).

It was shortly after this period, in the early seventeenth century, that English capitalists begin to turn their attention to the American continent. In 1600 the East India Company was empowered by Queen Elizabeth to trade exclusively with all companies east of the Cape of Good Hope (Mair 1763: 391). These adventuring English trade companies sought to expand trade routes and bases of resources, setting the stage for exploration and settlements in North America, first in Roanoke (1585), which failed, and then in Jamestown (1607), which survived.

Once the *Mayflower*'s contingent of 102 men, women, and children had embarked upon their journey, problems of an accounting nature arose.

Williard Stone notes that at least as early as 1620 the Pilgrim fathers were concerned over the matter of finances and suggested that their treasurer, one Mr. Martin, had not fulfilled his duty: "Mr. Martin saith he neither can nor will give any accounts; he crieth out unthankfulness for his pains and care, that we are susspitious of him and flings away, and will end nothing." Less than a year later Governor Bradford received a request from the London financier-merchant Thomas Weston to "give us accounts as perticulerly as you can how our moneys were laid out" (Stone 1975).

Before 1692 Massachusetts consisted of two private joint stock companies, the Plymouth Colony and the Company of the Massachusetts Bay. When King William of Orange assumed the British throne, he folded Plymouth into Massachusetts, forming a single colony. The first job of the treasurer of the new colony was to take over the asset balances from the separate treasurers of the Plymouth Colony and the Massachusetts Bay Company.

In 1628 the Massachusetts Bay Company had received its charter from King Charles I. The founding "undertakers" then spent two years raising money, then recruiting emigrants, buying provisions, and making arrangements for ships. They appointed a governor, a deputy governor, and a treasurer to handle these affairs. The records of the governor and company for June 17, 1629, include the following: "Auditors appointed for auditing the accompts, vis Mr. Symon Whetcombe, Mr. Nathaniel Wright, Mr. Noell, Mr. Perry, Mr. Crane, Mr. Clarke, Mr. Eaton, and Mr. Andrewes; these 8, or any 4 or more of them, to meete at a convenient time & place to audite the accompts." The meeting of the General Court held in London on July 28, 1629, goes on: "The business treated on at the last meeting was now read; and therupon the accompts of Mr. Gounor, Mr. Deputie, and Mr. Trer, being now psented to this Court, the Auditors, form'ly appointed for auditing the Comp accompts, were now desired to meete & puse & audite these accompts; Weh they have agreed to doe tomorrow in th' afternoone."

Plans were then made to establish the company in Massachusetts and to transfer the government to New England, including some of the principal merchants involved in the project. Money continued to be collected and spent as the sailing date approached. In the record of a meeting held on October 16, 1629, the following appears: "But for that there is a great debt owing by the joynt stock, it was moved tha some course might bee taken for cleering thereof, before the gouvmt bee transferred; and to this purpose it was first though fitt that the accompts should bee audited, to see what the debt is; but the business not admitting any such delay. It was desired that Mr. Gounor & Mr. Trer would meete tomorrow & make an estimate of the deby & prepare the same against a meeting to bee on Monday next, to determine this question." This businesslike approach to the venture appears to have been retained in the New England settlement. The records for March 3, 1636, include the following: "Mr. Hutchinson & Mr. Willm Spences are deputed to take the accompts of Mr. Simkins & to returne the same into the nexte Court." The procedure of "taking" the treasurer's accounts was followed regularly thereafter.

Regular audits, of course, were not annual audits. Not until more than a century later, in 1752, was it enacted by Parliament that the first day of January was to be acknowledged as the beginning of the year, and thereby a basis was established to make accounts annual.

The financiers of the New England Pilgrims were not alone in experiencing difficulties with the colonists' accounting. In April 1651 the Dutch directors of the trading companies involved in New Amsterdam engaged Johannes Dyckman as "Bookkeeper in New Netherland." One year later, the directors wrote that since they were "not properly informed of prizes captured, ships sold, and so forth," they had sent over another man (Committee on History, 1949A).

There is evidence of accounting not only within colonial joint venture trading companies but in the records for businesses as well. For example, extant account books of the seventeenth-century Boston merchant John Hull indicate the practice of credit transactions. In 1660 Hull sold eight bushels of wheat on "three months tyme" to John Winthrop Jr., son of the first governor of Massachusetts.

Early evidence of the use of double entry by colonial Puritan merchants is found in *The Apologia of Robert Keayne* (1653). Keayne's will cited his accounts kept in double-entry form. He noted that, of the three books of accounts he kept, "the third is bound in white vellum, which I keep constantly in my closet at Boston and is called my book of creditor and debitor, in which is the sum of most of my accounts contracted wherein there is [*sic*] accounts between myself and others with the accounts balanced on either side and also an account of my adventures by shipping with their returns and also an account of what debts I owe and how far they are discharged" (Bailyn 1964: 68). As to his statement of position, Keayne continues: "There is also in my closet a long paper book bound in white parchment which I call my inventory book, which I do yearly [commonly] cast up my whole estate. It is a breviate of my whole estate from year to year and shows how the Lord is pleased either to increase or decrease my estate from year to year."

By 1667 the Boston *Town Record* reveals the availability of account-keeping education and the practice of auditing the town accounts:

1667: "Mr. Will Howard hath liverty to keep a wrighting school, to teach children to write and to keep accounts."

BOOK-KEEPING MODERNIZ'D:

O R,

MERCHANT-ACCOUNTS by DOUBLE ENTRY, according to the ITALIAN Form.

WHEREIN

The THEORY of the ART is clearly explained, and reduced to PRACTICE, in copious SETS OF BOOKS, exhibiting all the Varieties that usually occur in Real Bufinefs.

To which is added,

A Large APPENDIX.

CONTAINING,

I. Defcriptions and fpecimens of the Subfidiary Books ufed by Merchants.
II. Monies and Exchanges, the nature of Bills of Exchange, Promiffory Notes, and Bills of Parcels.
III. Precedents of Merchants Writings, peculiar to England, Scotland, and common to both.
IV. The Commiffion, Duty, and Power of Factors.
V. A fhort Hiftory of the Trading Companies in Great Britain, with an account of her exports and imports.
VI. The produce and commerce of the Sugar Colonies; with a Specimen of the accounts kept by the factors or ftorekeepers; and an explication of wharf and plantation accounts.
VII. The produce and commerce of the Tobacco Colonies; with a fpecimen of the accounts ufually kept by the ftorekeepers.
VIII. The method of keeping accounts proper for Shop-keepers or Retailers.
IX. The method of keeping the accounts of a Land-eftate.
X. A Dictionary, explaining abftrufe words and terms that occur in merchandife.

By JOHN MAIR, A. M.

The SIXTH EDITION.

EDINBURGH:

Printed for BELL & BRADFUTE, and WILLIAM CREECH; And fold by T. LONGMAN, G. G. J. & J. ROBINSON, T. CADELL, and C. DILLY, London.

MDCCXCIII.

Figure 1.1 Title page of John Mair's *Book-Keeping Moderniz'd*, 1768

March 10, 1689/90: "At a publique meeting of the inhabitants of Boston Voted that Mr. Peter Sergeant, Mr. Benj Alford and Mr. Samson Sheafe be desired to Audit the Townes Acct with ye Selectment for the two years past."

Even as noted a historical event as the Salem witch trials of the 1690s begat accounting records. Accounts from the Boston and Charleston jailers evidence payment for locks, chains, irons, and wood to nail their jails "witch tight," plus noting the charge of 2s. 6d. per week per witch in custody (Holmes 1975A). So complete is the series of records that investigation reveals that in 1697 the Boston jailer had still not been paid for his expenses. He petitioned the General Court to redress his grievance and submitted his accounts, thereby causing the court to decide the following:

Province of the Massachusetts Bay:

At a Session of the Great and General Court or Assembly at Boston, by Prorogation

March 13th 1699/700

in Councill

Resolved,

Theat the accompts annexed be referred unto an Auditor Committee to Examin the same; And that Elisha Hutchinson, Peter Sergeant and John Walley Esqu be a Committee of this Board, to joyne with John Leverett Esqr, Capn Andrew Belcher and Mr. Samuel Phips named a Committee by the Assembly to Examin and Audit the sd Accompts: and to make Report thereof unto the General Assembly at their next Session.

Isaac Addington Secry.

These anecdotes are more than curiosities, they are early evidence—certainly not unexpected—that merchants, joint ventures, political bodies, and courts, as well as trading merchants, kept accounts, found them subject to audit as a matter of course, and offered them as evidence for action to recover payment. This establishes the customary role of accounts in the economic and social culture of colonial North America.

Early Writings and Education Affecting the British Colonies

By the late seventeenth century double-entry bookkeeping "seems to have become the centerpiece in the education of young men and women in the trading classes. . . . If the Enlightenment was not a bourgeois project, it is nonetheless clear that there was a bourgeois Enlightenment, one which was centered in the counting house" (Hunt 1989: 155, 157).

This view of accounting as a social instrument, as a device that enabled humans to better comprehend and control the world of business, made it a symbol of rational utility in an ever more complex world. Seen in a larger context, along with time management and broader skills in literacy and mathematics, accounting enabled businesspersons to quantify, summarize, and interpret (albeit imprecisely) the abstract processes of business that could be evidenced by transactions and captured within the double-entry system. What we consider today, for example, as the "language of business" was beginning to emerge in these early days of mercantile capitalism.

The notion of accounting as a centerpiece of education for both men and women is confirmed by the comments of Benjamin Franklin, who in chapter 4 of his autobiography recalled that although he could get no report on the agreement of partnership from the man who was his partner, "on his decease, the business was continued by his widow, who, being born and bred in Holland, where as I have been informed, the knowledge of accounts makes a part of female education, she not only sent me as clear a state as she could find of the transactions past, but continued to account with the greatest regularity and exactness every quarter afterwards, and managed the business with . . . success" (Murphy 1975: 49).

Several works on double-entry bookkeeping are known to have been published in English, and in other languages as well, during the sixteenth century. These include Oldcastle (1543), Peele (1553), Weddington (1567), and Mellis (1588) (Eldridge 1954). All are direct or indirect translations of Pacioli's *Summa* (1494). After this time, original English works on double-entry bookkeeping began to appear, and books on double entry started to be published with frequency, the authors being for the most part schoolmasters or teachers.

James Peele, the author of a 1553 work and a "practizer and teacher" of bookkeeping, provides a sense of the cultural significance of accounts in English business during those times: "For emongest althynges nedefull in any nacion, touchying worldly affaires, betwene man and man, it is to be thought that true and perfect reconyng is one of the chief, the lacke whereof often tymens causeth not onely great losse of time and empoverishement of many, who by lawes seke triall of suche thynges as neither partie is well hable to expresse, and that for lacke of perfect instruccion in their accompt, whiche thynge might, if that a perfect ordre in reconyng were frequented of all men, might well be avoided."

Mepham (1988B) and Pryce-Jones and Parker (1974) point out that the first Scottish book on accounting was published in 1683; subsequently there were four significant Scottish accounting authors: Malcolm, Mair, Gordon, and Hamilton. Their lifetimes spanned the period 1685 to 1829. Of these, Mair's *Book-keeping Methodiz'd* (7th ed., 1763) and *Book-keeping Moderniz'd* (6th ed., 1768) enjoyed great acceptance and included chapters on accounting in the Tobacco Colonies, Maryland, Virginia, and the Sugar Colonies, such as Jamaica (see figure 1.1).

Bookkeeping was made popular as a term following its adoption by Colinson (1683) on the title page of his Edinburgh volume *Idea Rationaria or The Perfect Accountant . . . containing The True Forme of Book-keeping.*

Green (1930: 32) thought that the first American text was probably written by William Mitchell in 1796. However, both Sheldahl (1985A, 1989) and McMickle (1984) have shown that earlier works were written or printed in the colonies. Sheldahl notes: "More recent research has generated only one additional title ("exclusively or primarily" on the subject) prior to 1796, *An Introduction to the counting house* (1789) by Thomas Sarjeant. Chapter-length contributions by . . . British writer George Fisher (Philadelphia, 1737) . . . and New England author Samuel Freeman have also been noted" (Sheldahl 1985A, 1989: 2).

Accounting Instruction

Records indicate that in 1635 Plymouth Colony engaged a Mr. Morton to teach children to read, write, and cast accounts. Casting accounts, as such, did not involve double-entry bookkeeping but "casting up the value of merchandise, tare and tret, interest rule of barter, fellowship, equation of payments, exchange"; in short, those subjects that constitute commercial arithmetic (Haynes and Jackson 1935: 7).

Learning via apprenticeship, namely, working and gaining experience in a "compting" house, was perhaps the singular most practical route to obtaining a skill and earning a living for the young settler, or for the indentured servant, once freed from the provisions of paying for the cost of transport.

American "writing schools" can be traced to as early as 1709 in New England. George Brownell of New York advertised as a teacher of "Merchants Accounts" in 1731. These schools taught reading, writing, business math, and some form of bookkeeping. By the turn of the century, there were any number of books authored by Americans with titles like the *Schoolmaster's Assistant.* Such commercial textbooks usually contained a section relating to business or practical arithmetic, reflecting the widespread existence of grammar schools in which arithmetic, handwriting, and bookkeeping were

A

NEW AND COMPLETE SYSTEM

OF

BOOK-KEEPING,

BY AN IMPROVED METHOD

OF

DOUBLE ENTRY;

ADAPTED TO

RETAIL, DOMESTIC and FOREIGN TRADE:

EXHIBITING A VARIETY OF TRANSACTIONS
WHICH USUALLY OCCUR IN BUSINESS.

THE WHOLE COMPRISED IN THREE SETS OF BOOKS;

The laft Set, being a copy of the Second according to thofe fyftems
moft generally in ufe, is given in order to exhibit, by a comparative view, the advantages of the fyftem now laid down.

TO WHICH IS ADDED,

A TABLE OF THE DUTIES PAYABLE ON GOODS, WARES
AND MERCHANDISE, IMPORTED INTO THE
UNITED STATES OF AMERICA.

THE WHOLE IN DOLLARS AND CENTS

By WILLIAM MITCHELL.

Philadelphia,

PRINTED BY BIOREN & MADAN.
1796.

Figure 1.2 A title page from an early U.S. accounting text, 1796

taught. In 1774 Byerley and Day of New York advertised to teach "book-keeping after the Italian method and the practice of the most regular counting houses." Similar references to grammar schools and early commercial education have also been found in Philadelphia and Charleston in the early 1700s.

Capital Markets, Speculations, and Early Public Stock Ventures

The corporation as a common business form ceased to exist in the British colonial empire after 1720, when Parliament, in response to the widespread speculation and losses accompanying the collapse of stock values associated with the South Sea Company, passed the so-called Bubble Act. This act required the personal approval of the monarch for all corporate charters.

The South Sea "Bubble" had burst when, over the course of a single month, from August 25 to September 28, 1720, the stock value of the South Sea Company, which had once reached a peak of 1050, fell from 900 to 190. The company, originally organized to convert the large floating debt of the state into a funded debt, was to take over about ten million pounds sterling of unfunded debt, which at the time was worth around 70 percent of par. Holders of the unfunded debt could convert it into South Sea Company stock at par. The objective was to organize a corporation to monopolize foreign trade with the islands of the South Seas and South America. This franchise was the principal asset of the company.

As the company developed outposts, directors of the company circulated rumors of the great possible profits in the South Sea, and in 1720 they planted a story that a 60 percent dividend would be paid at Christmas. As one authority stated, "The nation was so intoxicated with the spirit of adventure that people became prey to the grossest delusion." It was not only South Sea stock that was purchased in the blind, but stock for hundreds of other new ventures. Poor and rich alike talked of little else; the paper profits they were making were used in turn to purchase other new stock. The market began to tremble when it was recognized that the supply of money was not large enough to meet the installments on the securities purchased on margin as they came due or to absorb defaulted stock at existing prices if it were thrown on the market. Pressure was applied by the South Sea Company through its purchased influence in Parliament to investigate non-chartered or improperly chartered rivals with a view to having their stock taken off the market. Holders of these "questioned" securities, fearing they would lose all, sold out and prices tumbled. Speculators who had bought on margin were caught and sold their South Sea stock to cover their position. This triggered a run and the failure of the South Sea Company (Hasson 1932).

Trading ventures, formed among joint partners, and even well-established credit risk firms collapsed. The "Bubble" caused a financial panic in the British Empire and its colonies that touched almost every investor or consumer; the actions involved so many stock issues that almost everyone had experienced market losses. Businesses and individual ventures failed at alarming rates.

Accounting Practice and Some Early Public Accountants

The English trading companies described above had grown in public acceptance from 1600 until 1720. Public investor speculation and the 1720 failure of the South Sea Company, formed in 1711, resulted in a sharp decline in similar promotions until the early nineteenth century. Such speculative collapses were not limited to the English. At the same time that the South Sea Bubble burst, a similar promotion in France, the "Mississippi Bubble," also led investors to ruin in speculations over the land in the Louisiana Territories and the development of areas around New Orleans and other French land concessions in America, offered through John Law's *Le Compagnie d'Occident* (The Western Company) (Minton 1976: 96).

In reaction to the South Sea Bubble, as subsequent business undertakings became more conservative, a role for modern public accounting in the English-speaking world was born. Public agitation demanded an investigation, which got under way in December 1720. One of the directors of the South Sea Company, Jacob Sawbridge, and his partners in the firm of Turner & Co. were particular objects of public wrath. Their estates were confiscated and one of the partners, Sir George Caswell, was imprisoned in the Tower of London. Charles Snell, a "Writing Master and Accomptant," was apparently retained to investigate the accounts of Sawbridge & Co.[1] His undated report, probably prepared at the end of the year 1720 or early 1721, is a document that many consider to be more an example of special pleading than independent inquiry. Nevertheless it represents an early example of modern "public" accounting investigation and reporting. (Snell's report was later challenged in an anonymous editorial. If public accounting among our forebears was to set a precedent, one might have guessed it would have been conceived in the midst of controversy and subjected to criticism.)

As noted by William Holmes, we know too that in the American colonies, as early as 1718, Browne Tymms had advertised a public accounting practice in Boston newspapers: "Mr. Browne Tymms Living at Mr. Edward Oakes, Shopkeeper in Newbury Street, at the South End of Boston, Keeps Merchants and Shopkeepers Books." It seems appropriate to acknowledge Holmes's conclusion that Tymms was an early public accountant, perhaps the earliest known to have practiced in America.

The evidence that Tymms of Boston had been "advertising" as early as 1718 and that he kept merchants' and shopkeepers' books, coupled with the activities of Snell in London, suggests that public accounting, in the sense of individuals involved primarily in the specialty occupation of keeping and interpreting others' financial records, performing audits, and providing other expert services, existed at the start of the eighteenth century in both England and her American colonies, albeit in a fashion and in an economic environment far different from those of today. James Don Edwards notes that, at a later time in this pre-Revolutionary period, Benjamin Franklin engaged James Parker to perform functions that were those of a public accountant, namely, to make an inventory and evaluation of equipment and materials and to present a report on the state of the accounts (Edwards 1960: 44).

In meeting the constantly increasing needs for records being created through trade expansion in the early 1700s, Carl Bridenbaugh observes: "The increased sums of money and larger number of items handled made it necessary for merchants to maintain staffs of clerks in their counting houses. Bookkeeping by 'Double Entry, Dr. And Cr. the Best Method' came into wide use everywhere . . . by 1733 and schools gave instruction in shorthand and the Italian method of keeping books. Accountants offered their services in all the larger towns" (Bridenbaugh 1966: 359).

Mercantile Capitalism

The era of mercantile capitalism, a period of enterprise characterized by the market system of the "invisible hand" described in Adam Smith's *The Wealth of Nations* (1776), portrays the late-eighteenth-century economic environment of the British Empire trading and plantation seacoast colonies in North America (Samuelson 1962). The merchants' and planters' accounting systems of the period required few of today's methods. The comparative absence of speed in transport and communication was such that the detailed information about infrequent transactions was recorded and transmitted quite differently.

Transaction evidence exists in the form of "waste books" or "day books," since the "paperwork" trail that provides evidence for journal entries today is not usually found, owing to the scarcity and expense of vellum papers. Journals and ledgers of the period enable accounting and business historians to assess the economic state of activities in the early colonies. The financial records of the famous New England Hancock family businesses from 1724 to 1775, such as those detailing the loss sustained on the voyage of the ship *Lydia* in 1764 (Baxter 1945: 181–82), provide a basis for conclusions about some colonial accounting practices. Accounts of other voyages during the 1740s establish the existence of similar profit and loss calculations, although "it appears that the interpretation of the Profit and Loss Account was quite difficult, as it included a hodge-podge of amounts" (McMickle and Vangermeersch 1987: 57). Planters, including George Washington, are known to have kept personal ledgers. From the age of fifteen (1749) until his death in 1799, Washington kept records that were "ruled like a cash book and contained his cash accounts with debits on the left-hand page and the credits on the right-hand page" (Cloyd 1979: 88).

The lack of sound monetary systems required that accounting be not only multidenominational but multinational, accommodating guineas, doubloons, and Portuguese johannes, as well as items of value from flour to salt that might be bartered in exchange. With this complex of value bases serving as the medium of exchange, it is appropriate to regard the time as a period of "barter accounting," which remained in effect until the nineteenth century, when cash became sufficiently stable and accepted in daily use to permit the development of a customary basis for "realization" of a transaction.[2]

Eighteenth-century colonial accounting was rooted in the seaport cities, but other studies note that typical practices for account-keeping by merchants and planters were used throughout the colonies. The waste book of Henry Laurens, an early Charleston merchant and landholder, for example, contains profit calculations developed during the 1750s. And store records of the colonial merchant William Prentis, for the years 1733–65, have been studied, as have the memorandum-style account books of Thomas Jefferson, containing entries kept from 1767 to 1826 (Coleman, Shenkir, and Stone 1974).

The diversity of Jefferson's enterprises, which included his plantation and a small nail factory, and the completeness of the Prentis accounts, reflect the new sophistication of colonial commerce, including forms of management compensation, "dividend" policies, and the account-keepers' greater familiarity with the process of maintaining financial records (Shenkir, Welsch, and Baer 1972).

North of Virginia, several important accounting developments were taking place. On more than one occasion, Benjamin Franklin of Philadelphia is known to have relied on account information to assist in winding up his business affairs. In Maryland, the Ridgely Account Books, which continue through the eighteenth and nineteenth centuries, were kept in double entry. The records of Robert Oliver, a Baltimore merchant, suggest how profit and loss and certain other impersonal accounting techniques were performed. In Newport, in the early 1700s, the John Stevens Shop kept double-entry records through the 1720s. A New York paper in 1729 carried an advertisement noting that "any merchant or others that want a bookkeeper or their accounts started after the best methods, either in private trade or company may hear of persons qualified . . . by inquiring at the post office or coffee house." In the 1730s the Brown family of Providence, Rhode Island, had at least one member, Obadiah, who "taught himself accounting methods using for this purpose *A Guide to Book Keepers According to the Italian Manner*" (London 1729).[3]

There were, of course, other texts on the Italian manner (i.e., double entry) available in the pre-Revolutionary colonies. Scotland's John Mair, noted earlier, thought to be the first popular author of a series of texts, published his first work, *Bookkeeping Methodiz'd*, in 1736. Subsequent editions were published through 1765 and a revised edition, titled *Bookkeeping Moderniz'd*, was completed in 1768. Some assert that Mair's book was probably one of the most widely read on the subject during the era. Mair's *Bookkeeping Methodiz'd; or, a Methodical Treatise on Merchant-Accompts According to the Italian Form Wherein the Theory of the Art is Fully Explained* was attentive to the mercantilist accountant, in that chapter 7 (7th ed., Edinburgh, 1763), dealt with "the produce and commerce of the Tobacco Colonies [i.e., the American colonies], with a specimen of accompts usually kept by the storekeepers."

Cost Records and Accounting

To some, cost accounting is synonymous with the industrial revolution and an age of manufactures. Perhaps less interest or attention has been focused on early cost-keeping in our development era because manufacturing, although it existed on a smaller scale, was not sufficiently common to permit general study. Furthermore, as Garner states, there is an interest in tracing the beginnings of cost accounting to that period of capitalism when production began to be substituted for domestic enterprises such as putting out (piecework) and handicraft activities. So, although cost-keeping in post-medieval periods can be found in proprietary settings, little has been found in published books of the times (Garner 1954: 3, 25). Some suggest that this was to keep the proprietary advantages of a particular cost system secret. Others say that systems were so unique to proprietary concerns that it would not have been useful to teach them in a general fashion.

The Smythe accounts from the 1550s, cited earlier in the chapter, are an example of developments in the cost-keeping for clothmaking. "The ledger is rich in information about prices, about the charges for dyeing and dressing cloth, and about the costs of shipping" (Fisher 1976: 151). More recently, Edwards, Hammersley, and Newell have asserted, based on a study of records (1597–1633) for a copper works, that "a number of modern accounting concepts and procedures were in use by c. 1600" (1990: 62). This new evidence and the research effort it represents are hopeful signs that additional information about pre-industrial era cost accounting may soon be sufficient to permit informed generalizations about the role that cost information played in management and production processes during this period. Until then, cost accounting in the precolonial and colonial periods of the United States remains in need of better definition.

Government Accounts

Pilgrim ventures at early stages included self-contained government auditing functions as early as 1620 (the Mayflower Compact) and thereafter within the Massachusetts Bay Company. As early as 1644, New England colonists had been provided with the services of a government official, designated the auditor general, whose duties were prescribed on three pages of script. This position was known to have lasted until about 1657. In the Plymouth colony after 1657, "the treasurer was charged with maintenance of all financial records of the colony and with periodic reporting of his stewardship of public funds. The treasurer's accounts were reviewed annually by an audit committee chosen by the General Court" (Holmes, Kistler, and Corsini 1978: 38).

As historians have observed, "seventeenth-century towns had dual identities: they were both private, commercial organizations (associated with the speculators who had developed them) and public, communal institutions. The shareholders in town projects controlled the local government, and residents who were not investors were typically denied participation in civic affairs" (Perkins 1989: 166). Cook refers, for example, to seventeenth-century Springfield as a "company-town," founded by the Pynchon family, who attracted propertyless men by offering wages for their labor. Much remains to be learned about accounting in such settings (Cook 1984: 434).

Other studies of Plymouth also indicate that annual reports of the audit committee of that colony commenced in 1658. The statements reveal the imposition of fines as a form of governmental restraint on community behavior and a tax system that included an excise tax on real estate and personal property. Public expenditures were used to pay salaries and expenses of officials and to provide military protection. Printed copies of the treasury accounts for the period show payments for a "marshal" and a fine for sei ing a "pistell to an Indian." Apparently the relationship with the Narragansett Indians following the Pilgrim expedition against the tribe in 1645 had still not stabilized.

By the first quarter of the next century, financial statements for government enterprises were being prepared. For example, reports for the initial year (1732–33) of the Georgia Colony were drawn up in a charge/discharge form as a type of stewardship reporting. An epitaph on a tombstone in the old church graveyard in Jamestown, Virginia, is further evidence of the early colonial accounting of governments: "Here lies the body of Philip Ludwell who died the 11th of January, 1720 in the 54th year of his age. Sometimes auditor of His Majesty's revenues and 25 years member of the council" (c. 1666–1720).[4]

The Ludwell epitaph suggests that a system of governmental auditing existed in the English colonies. Ludwell's identity as a "sometimes" auditor of revenues is consistent with the fact that until the 1760s it was more common for Parliament to consider the colonies as entitled to "home rule," with control of affairs being conducted in town meetings and the influence of the Crown remaining remote. New England towns, for example, maintained their own highways, cared for their poor, supported public schools, regulated business in a minor fashion, and served as the unit of control for the assessment, collection, and audit of government revenues.

Taxation

By the 1680s the Massachusetts colony had developed an effective budget process and a system of levying taxes on each town. The tax rolls suggest that in 1686 Scituate was the wealthiest community.

Ignoring for the moment the broader political issues related to mercantilism, navigation acts, and the Boston Tea Party, taxation policy was a subject of interest in colonial times. Several forms of levies were imposed by colonies, from quit-rents (a type of feudal tribute land tax); to tonnage duties (port fees charged to incoming ships); poll and property taxes; excise taxes on tobacco and liquor; and even a composite tax that Crum asserts was a form of "value-added" taxation (Crum 1982: 28–30). These levies appeared in Virginia and other colonies as early as 1619. Limited archival research exists to date to help us understand if or how tax accounting was involved in the administration and evaluation of colonial tax policies.

Kozub describes the frequency of use in the colonies of various types of taxation (Kozub 1983: 101). Little is known, based upon extant tax records, about the accounting processes involved, with the possible exception of information such as that provided by Holmes, Kistler, and Corsini on the Plymouth Colony tax levy of 1666–67; their book details rates and revenues from a levy on the colony towns (Holmes, Kistler, and Corsini 1978: 52–53).

The Cultural Significance of Accounts before the Revolution

A notion has been proposed that identifies the period roughly between 1500 and 1800 as one of little change from the methods found in Pacioli's treatise; that is, that it was a period of "accounting stagnation" (Winjum 1970). The state of accounting technique in America and the issue of stagnation need to be separated. This is not to suggest that a knowledge of accounts was prerequisite to survival in the American colonies. But it does seem that by the time of the Revolution, double entry had become important, if not necessary, to the merchant and trader who had experienced the commercial expansion of the 1700s. The general populace, being limited in their ability to write and compute, were not likely to involve themselves with any formal system of accounting. Yet when education was introduced as early as 1635, schools were teaching the fundamentals of "casting accounts." To the educated colonial, therefore, accounts were a useful adjunct to personal record-keeping and provided important information as commerce became more complex.

Contemporary views of colonial accounting include the following: "Accounting in 1760 was essentially what it was to Pacioli—a set of arithmetical techniques to assist the businessman to conduct his affairs in an orderly, purposeful, and well-informed fashion. There was no theory, and no deeply felt need for any; its only immediate use would have been to lighten the labour of mastering double entry in books or in school by substituting knowledge of principles for the hard grind of learning detailed rules by rote, and such consideration for the student was a thing of the future" (Lee 1975: 6). And it has been suggested that this was "a time of elaboration upon the basic double-entry techniques of the 14th and 15th centuries" (Levy and Sampson 1962: 401).

William Baxter contends in his analysis of colonial accounting that its development was a function of merchant specialization (Baxter 1946).

Briefly, the more specialized the culture, the more the need for accounts. Although the bursting of the South Sea Bubble delayed the popular advent of the medium of the corporate entity to amass capital, colonial businessmen were able to create joint ventures to provide sufficient capital to undertake new, relatively specialized, and often risky ventures. When joint ownership increased, the adoption of early double entry and the requisite proprietary accounts expanded. As specialized colonial trade and commerce increased, Adam Smith's theory of economics, which noted and accommodated the necessity and efficiency of specialization, came to be acknowledged. Accounting in America appeared to be thriving.

As a final observation, we quote a passage by Mair, a popular voice of this time: "Though this method of *Debtor* and *Creditor* be of a very general nature, and may be used to good purpose in most kinds of accounts, I propose to explain it here chiefly with a view to merchant-accounts; . . . And after a learner comes to understand the general principles of the art and has seen the application made in such an extensive manner as merchant-accounts admit of, it will be no hard task for him to digest other accounts in like form, and so extend the application of the art to the accounts of the national revenue, to public banks, to manufactures, to estates, farms, or families" (Mair 1768: 4).

Chapter 2

The Formation of a National Economy

> The importance of Accomptantship is so generally known, and its
> utility so universally acknowledged, that any commendation will
> be unnecessary, further than to observe, that a thorough knowl-
> edge of the art is essential to the character of a Man of Business.
> —**Chauncey Lee,** *The American Accomptant,*
> **Lansingburgh, N.Y., 1797**

Political and Economic Context of a New Nation

King George III ascended to the English throne in 1760. His reign
marked the beginning of the end of the British rule over their coastal
American colonies. Under his rule a series of political decisions, resulting
in taxation and regulation that the colonials deemed intolerable, would
force a conflict of arms and the birth of the United States of America. From
these events would be occasioned sacrifice, bitter defeat, and, finally, victory
for the colonies. These outcomes are well known, and the popular understanding of them is such that this reference will suffice as a basis of remarks
about the setting of the Revolution.

Our purpose here is to consider the transformation and accounting consequences of this period as the new nation formed its business customs and
developed systems of trade. One of the most significant developments of
this era, from the perspective of long-term impact on the subject of accounting, is to be found in the writings of a moral philosopher thousands
of miles removed from the turmoil of the American continent. His book
The Wealth of Nations (the shortened title being most popular) predicted the
age of industrial specialization and described the "invisible hand" of marketplace enterprise, the precepts of which the United States would manifest
in its economic system. Adam Smith's work, published in 1776, was a declaration of independence from mercantilism, an economist's reaction to the
heavy-handed influence of the state in setting markets. In Smith's view, the
market should be determined by the collective force of individuals following their own self-interest.

This economic theory of individual supremacy and the recognition of the need to accommodate the efficiency of specialization in matters of economic conduct, when linked to the political system and doctrines of personal liberty and contract responsibilities set forth in the United States Constitution (which took effect in 1789), provided direction for the new nation's government and policies, and for its economic progress (Pemberton 1976). Individuals were free to pursue their own ends; indeed, they were encouraged to do so in this new, albeit unsettled and hostile, environment that was teeming with resources and potential for trade. The "promises" of individual wealth had already begun to be fulfilled by 1774; by then colonials already had as great a wealth per capita as any people in the civilized world (see figure 2.1). A significant class of wealthy individuals, constituting about 10 percent of the population, did exist, but more important, some 40 percent—representing independent small farmers—had also attained a reasonably successful status. A merchant class also had established itself. Personal wealth per capita in 1776 (in mid-twentieth-century terms) has been estimated at about $4,000. This distribution and dispersion of wealth would require the development of a social vehicle to accumulate large amounts of savings and capital from the multiple individual sources. This vehicle would be the corporate form of entity.

The laws affecting an individual's property rights, that ingredient of Locke's political philosophy which fueled Adam Smith's economic ideas, were significantly stabilized, particularly with respect to contracts for the purchase of land, in a Supreme Court decision of 1810 (*Fletcher v. Peck*). Chief Justice John Marshall and his court ruled that under the Constitution

Figure 2.1 Continental dollar, minted 1776

the right of contract prohibited the Georgia legislature from repealing a grant that had in turn conveyed private property rights to "innocent third parties" (Swisher 1958: 13).

Similar property rights issues were identified by Chief Justice Marshall. In the famous case of the Dartmouth College contract decision in 1819, he noted: "It is a contract for the security and disposition of property. It is a contract, on the faith of which, real and personal estate has been conveyed to the corporation" (Hudon 1969: 88). In its decision the Court reasoned that charters of private corporations, as distinguished from public corporations, such as towns, etc., were contracts and that such charters were protected under the contract clause of the Constitution. This enhanced the attractiveness of private (corporate) charters to serve as pooling entities for investment resources and for operations (Swisher 1958: 16).

Taken together, the corporation would accommodate expansion of business and meet the needs to accumulate capital and in turn provide a form of business entity that reflected and respected the rights of property through shareholder stock rights. In turn, as these institutions matured, they would create increasing demands for accountability, control, and reporting of corporation assets and activities—and thereby establish the demand for services and techniques provided by accountants.

The Commercial Structure of the United States

In 1776, almost all (95 percent) of the estimated 2.5 to 3 million American settlers lived on farms. The population hugged the seacoast and waterways in order to expedite the transportation and trade needed to sustain its relationship with a Eurocentric world.

A census of the United States in 1791 is included in table 2.1 as found in Gallatin's book, cited below. The commentary beneath the population schedule explains the column totals. Gallatin mentions the "North-West" territories, including what is now Ohio and areas to its west. The physical area of the United States would increase dramatically not only as these territories were settled but as further acquisitions were made, including the Louisiana Territory purchased in 1803 during Jefferson's first term, which spread westward from the Mississippi to the Rocky Mountains.

Through the 1790s and 1800s, thousands of businesses took form in the wake of the ruin of many others tied to old London merchant houses. The latter had also failed at substantial rates (seventeen in 1781, twenty-five in 1782, and thirty-eight in 1783), especially after Holland entered the war against Britain in 1780. British leaders claimed that "the liberal credits granted by London houses to the U.S.A. had bankrupted three-quarters of them" (Chapman 1979: 218).

As the turmoil of the American Revolution and the War of 1812 was replaced by a stable political environment, Americans set out to restore their trade and expand their holdings of new lands west of the Allegheny Mountains. Technical inventions and their labor-saving efficiency tended to reduce costs. As turnpikes, canals, and then railroads appeared, new markets were opened for goods that, in turn, induced specialized manufacture and early forms of mass production. Industry and commerce had become rooted in the midst of a predominantly rural society.

"The industrial revolution came to southern New England villages in the form of textile mills near the end of the War of 1812. . . . '[E]arly nineteenth-century American industrialization bore no single face.' Contrary to the tendency of many historians to equate industrialization with urbanization, [other historians] argue that more than half of Massachusetts' antebellum textile industry was located along rural waterways" (Smith 1984: 429).

Individualism and opportunity were accented during these years by a surge of expanded trade, commerce, and manufacture. Industrial technology made an impact in the Northeast in the form of labor-saving, mechanically powered devices. A national economy and capital market came a step closer to realization, although the influence of state banks and regional capital markets was to remain important if not dominant. "The initial development of a transport network is noted from the fact that 55 turnpike companies were chartered in Pennsylvania between 1793 and 1812, along with 57 in New York and 105 in Massachusetts. Canal construction from South Carolina through Maryland and Virginia and up through New York required nearly $3,000,000 in capital by 1807. That amount it should be remembered would be many times greater in terms of today's prices" (Callender 1902).

Accounting, based as much on barter as on cash (which was in short supply and of unstable value), reflected payments that came in the form of rum, beef, butter, and other forms of commodity money. Merchants kept their records in a series of accounting books beginning with the waste book (a financial diary) from which journal entries were made. Apprenticeship in the accounting house or "compting house" of a merchant was the usual means of learning about financial records. Young men, mostly from well-to-do families, were thus apprenticed before being sent into business (Previts and Sheldahl 1977).

TABLE 2.1

Schedule A, U.S. Government Receipts and Disbursements, 1789–1793

(A)

A General View of the Receipts and Expenditures of the United States, from the eſtabliſhment of the preſent Government in 1789, to the 1ſt of January 1796.

RECEIPTS.

Years	1789 to 1791 Dols.	Cts.	1792 Dols.	Cts.	1793 Dols.	Cts.	1794 Dols.	Cts.	1795 Dols.	Cts.	Dols.	Cts.	Dols.	Cts.
Balances of Accounts which originated under the late Government, viz.														
Cash in hands of Commiſsioner in Holland,........	132,475	31									132,475	31		
Other balances paid at different periods,..........	11,001	11	4,702	82	8,448	58	693	50	5,317	97	30,163	98	162,639	29
Revenues, viz.														
Duties on imports and tonnage..........	4,399,472	99	3,579,499	06½	4,344,358	26	4,843,707	25	5,588,961	26	22,755,998	82½		
Internal duties,........			72,514	59½	248,654	00	231,447	65	337,255	36	889,871	60½		
Postage of letters, ...					11,021	51	29,478	49	22,400	00	62,899	00		
Exceſs of dividends on bank bank ſtock, over intereſt payable on bank ſtock loan, ...			8,028	00	38,500	00	55,500	00	66,233	34	168,261	34		
													23,877,030	77

Incidental, viz.

	1789 to 1791 Dols.	Cts.	1792 Dols.	Cts.	1793 Dols.	Cts.	1794 Dols.	Cts.	1795 Dols.	Cts.	Dols.	Cts.
Fines and forfeitures for crimes,	311	00	118	00	660	00	570	00	600	00	429	00
Fees on patents,	8,962	00									1,830	00
Sales of arms,			4,240	00							13,202	00
Profits on remittances, &c.	238,661	7	134,210	90	67,701	14½			28,670	91	469,244	02½
Mistake in treasurer's accounts,												10
		12½		10							484,705	
Loans, viz.												
Foreign loans in Amsterdam and Antwerp,	5,420,000	00	2,380,000	00	400,000	00	1,200,000	00			9,400,000	00
Domestic do. obtained in anticipation of revenues,	246,608	81	556,595	56	600,000	00	3,200,000	00	2,500,000	00	7,103,204	37
Other domestic loans,	2,000,000	00	2,000,000	00			200,000	00	800,000	00	3,000,000	00
											19,503,204	37
Total of Receipts for each Year,	10,457,492	29	8,739,999	4	5,719,342	4	9,761,396	89	9,349,438	84	44,027,579	55½

EXPENDITURES.

Years	1789 to 1791 Dols.	Cts.	1792 Dols.	Cts.	1793 Dols.	Cts.	1794 Dols.	Cts.	1795 Dols.	Cts.	Dols.	Cts.
Civil List,*	706,720	29	368,319	86	334,263	29	431,999	47	352,233	36	2,193,536	27
Pensions, Annuities, and Grants, viz.												
Pensions to military invalids,	175,813	88	109,243	15	80,087	81	81,399	24	68,673	22	515,217	30
Annuities and grants,	13,102	96	5,597	72	5,329	51	33,921	87	2,970	20	60,922	26
											576,139	56

TABLE 2.1
Continued

	1789 to 1791		1792		1793		1794		1795			
	Dols.	Cts.	Dols.	Cts.	Dols.	Cts.	Dols.	Cts.	Dols.	Cts.	Dols.	Cts.
Military Establishment, viz.												
Army and militia, magazines, &c.	630,499	65	1,092,920	96	1,130,249	08	2,597,047	93	2,422,612	31	7,941,361	30
Indian department,	127,000	00	13,648	85	14,340	06	13,042	46	81,773	50	123,823	16
Fortifications,							42,049	66				
Naval armament,							61,408	97	410,562	03	471,971	00
											8,537,155	46
Intercourse with Foreign Nations, viz.												
Diplomatic department,	1,733	33	78,766	67	89,500	00	74,995	00	15,005	00	260,000	00
Extraordinary expenses,	13,000	00					56,408	51	897,680	12	967,088	63
											1,227,088	63
Sundries, viz.												
Light-houses and navigation,	22,591	94	38,976	94	12,061	68	37,496	36	29,861	30	140,987	64
Mint establishment,			7,000	00	17,366	00	23,153	12	22,400	00	69,919	61
Contingent and miscellaneous,	28,343	15	28,856	65	5,527	65	34,174	99	46,825	41	143,727	69
											354,634	94

Years	1789 to 1791		1792		1793		1794		1795			
	Dols.	Cts.	Dols.	Cts.	Dols.	Cts.	Dols.	Cts.	Dols.	Cts.	Dols.	Cts.
Charges on Public Debt, viz.												
Interest on foreign debt,	947,862	12	669,359	08	719,252	88	746,564	37	769,523	38	3,852,561	83
Do. on domestic debt,	1,140,177	20	2,313,049	82	2,005,199	67	2,383,015	84	2,193,031	16	10,034,473	69
Do. on debt due to foreign officers,			33,657	87							33,657	87
Do. on domestic loans,	2,598	12			18,753	41	48,694	44	149,333	33	219,379	30
Commissions and brokerage in Holland,	222,800	00	125,000	00	17,948	28	54,062	20	4,480	00	424,290	48
Premiums paid on the old Dutch loan,	36,000	00			40,000	00			48,000	00	124,000	00
											14,688,363	17

Principal of the Public Debt, including Arrears of Interest to 31ſt Dec. 1789, viz.

	Dols.	Cts.	Dols.	Cts.	Dols.	Cts.	Dols.	Cts.	Dols.	Cts.	Dols.	Cts.
Payments on the French debt,	2,238,527	83	1,777,554	42	1,172,265	09	380,700	31	301,352	66	5,870,400	31
Do. on the debt due in Holland,					400,000	00	400,000	00	400,000	00	1,200,000	00
Do. on the Spaniſh debt,					241,681	95					241,681	95
Applied to purchaſes of the domeſtic debt,	699,984	23	318,347	88	408,807	98	172,840	76	18,955	19	1,618,936	4
Payment of two per cent on fix per cent ſtock,									515,972	72	515,972	72
Payments on debt due to foreign officers,			30,696	92	39,000	47	44,752	35	11,883	68	126,333	42
Reimburſement of anticipations,			246,608	81	556,595	56	1,100,000	00	1,400,000	00	3,303,204	37
Do. of other domeſtic loans,					200,000	00	200,000	00	200,000	00	600,000	00
Unfunded debts paid in ſpecie,	298,479	94	136,877	84	7,120	29	3,855	86	61	59	446,395	52
											13,922,924	33
Subſcription to the Bank-Stock of the United States,			2,000,000	00							2,000,000	00
Loſſes on remittances,							13,779	03½			13,779	03½
Total of Expenditures for each Year,	7,451,843	45	9,147,374	05	7,515,350	99	9,035,862	74½	10,363,190	16	43,513,621	39½
Balance in caſh on 1ſt January, 1796,											513,958	15½
											44,027,579	55

Balances of accounts which originated under the late

	Dols.	Cts.
Government, as per Receipts, ...	162,639	29
Loans effected during the above period, ...	19,503,204	37
	19,665,843	66

	Dols.	Cts.
Principal of Public Debt paid during the above period, ...	13,922,924	33
Subſcription to the Bank Stock of the United States, ...	2,000,000	00
Balance in caſh on 1ſt January, 1796, ...	513,958	15
Exceſs of Expenditures beyond the Revenues received, ...	3,228,961	18
	19,665,843	66

* Compenſation for: President 85,827.83; Vice-President 14,000; Judiciary 79,491.48; Legislature 364,559.08; Public Offices (e.g. Treasury; State; War; others) 146,611.33; Government of Territories 16,230.57; Total: 706,720.29. See Schedule X, Gallatin for detail.

Source: Gallatin's *Sketch of the Finances of the United States,* published in 1796. Typeset in the original archaic style.

Capital Markets

One of the most important events in the economic development of the new nation occurred in New York on May 17, 1792. A group of merchants and auctioneers gathered on Wall Street to fix a daily meeting time to carry on the trading of a heretofore scattered market for government securities and for the shares of banks and insurance companies. They had recognized that the unorganized and irregular fashion of the coffeehouse auction impeded the trading of securities, and they decided to meet daily at regular hours to buy and sell securities under an old buttonwood tree on Wall Street, only a few blocks from the present site of the New York Stock Exchange.

These first brokers handled the public's buy and sell orders in new government securities, as well as in shares of insurance companies, Alexander Hamilton's First United States Bank, the Bank of North America, and the Bank of New York. This step toward an auction-based capital market, regularly scheduled and located in a principal trading and commercial center, evidenced not only the logistical benefit of a convenient capital marketplace but also the realization of businessmen that the raising of capital for ventures had reached substantial and public proportions. Although not a "national" capital market as yet, it would one day overtake the more clearly regional character of investment interest at that time. Effective, timely, and reliable communication systems of course were lacking, and no systematic financial information or reports were available. Periodic reporting was only beginning to achieve acceptance and was far from the regular statement-based reporting of today. Traders therefore depended on their knowledge of the situation, their local sources of information, and their expertise and command of local business prospects, all of which would tend to govern the scope of their capital investments. Nevertheless, the seeds of modern capital markets and a genesis of the demand for external financial reporting can be traced in the actions of the twenty-four founding members of this exchange when they commenced regular trading.

By 1793, the brokers moved indoors into the newly completed Tontine Coffee House at the northwest corner of Wall and William Streets. By this time shares in larger banks, as well as state and federal debt issues, were regularly traded. During the remainder of the decade, 295 chartered companies were formed, most of them banks, insurance companies, dock construction ventures, road companies, and mining firms. Although the public was not trading in all of these firms, the pattern for trading and the regular and ready recourse to the market enhanced the value of shares as well as their liquidity. Private financial activity was checked for a time by the War of

1812, but peace brought the formation of new enterprises, and New York State bonds, issued to pay for the Erie Canal, joined the issues traded on the exchange.

In 1794, sixteen state-chartered banks were operating to serve a diverse and growing economy. In contrast, in the British Isles only five incorporated banks were to be found (Klebaner 1979: 528). "These first American banks were chartered corporations, but in the old sense of privileged, monopolistic entities" (Sylla 1985: 110). From 1795 to 1803, the Massachusetts legislature effectively created an open banking incorporation practice, granting eight more bank charters, but permitting no more than one bank in any town except Boston. By 1829, it had granted fifty-one charters.

The free banking movement spread to other states, principally to New York and Pennsylvania; it is what some have interpreted as a democratic move to remove the Old World forms of limited bank incorporations that bestowed power and privilege. By 1825, when the New York legislature enacted the first general incorporation laws, bank failures were beginning to raise concerns over whether the system of free bank incorporation, which limited liability, had reached its limits. "Are the one hundred and sixty-five chartered banks that have failed in America to go for nothing?" said Gilbart, writing in 1837 (Sylla 1985: 115).

From 1812 to 1831, one of the most successful financial entrepreneurs of the era was Stephen Girard. His bank, the largest private bank of the time, was controlled completely by Girard himself. His Philadelphia institution issued notes and acted as a commercial bank, maintaining an intricate "network of correspondent bank relationships . . . [which evidenced that] . . . the capital market was more developed than one might have supposed for the time" (James 1979: 135). Girard operated profitably in an environment competing with chartered institutions in Pennsylvania and "Western" bankers in new cities such as Cincinnati and by serving as a director of the Second Bank of the United States.

Banks employed accounting personnel, of that there is little doubt. For instance, the Manhattan Company, incorporated by the state as a utility to supply water to New York City, was permitted by its charter to use its "surplus capital" in any legal enterprise, and soon entered banking (including branch operations) and gave employment to a number of bookkeepers designated by title from first bookkeeper to fourth bookkeeper at a variety of locations (Hunter 1985: 68–69).

The cotton textile industry, able to boast of only a few mills in 1804, was operating half a million spindles by 1815. The tempo of business quickened as the country headed into a boom following the War of 1812. By 1827, the stocks of twelve banks and nineteen marine and fire insurance companies, the Delaware & Hudson Canal Co., the Merchants' Exchange, and the New York Gas Light Company—the nation's first public utility—also were traded on the exchange.

New York was not alone, of course, in providing a capital market for ventures. Regional capital markets were a key attribute of early enterprise in the United States because they afforded the added assurance of being convenient to both investors and sources of information. It is important to remember that Boston, Philadelphia, Baltimore, and Charleston, each a major seaport, also had local capital markets operating. Indeed there was a rivalry of some degree between the Chestnut Street brokers of Philadelphia and the traders on Wall Street. This competition was accentuated when the Bank of the United States was formed in 1791 and headquartered in Philadelphia. The Philadelphia Bank's stock market price influenced brokers in other cities, particularly in their trading of bank stocks. But New York remained the home of risk capital, where the speculators and equity holders were to be found, and it was in New York that many early stock ventures, which included the right to assess shareholders on a pro rata basis for new equity needs, were used to underwrite high-risk "industrial" undertakings.

Also marking this era were general incorporation laws, such as that enacted in 1825 in New York. Why did the corporation come into prominence in the United States (there were some three hundred charters by 1800) when France and England, the acknowledged leading business nations, had only a small number each?

Corporations arose because of their capacity to support expanding markets and enterprise operations at levels of competitive efficiency called for in a nation where the tasks and risks were large and the sources of wealth and capital not highly concentrated. There was also the need to use scarce skills, both technical and managerial, wisely. The high cost of scarce labor encouraged use of machinery and therefore begat relatively larger investment outlays (Cochran 1959: 41, 55). The appetite of such operations for capital would influence the shape of the money markets and the industrial revolution that overtook the American economy in coming decades.

Public Projects and Taxation

Business historians observe that state aid for the construction of canals and turnpikes during this period is an example of government involvement in public works and commercial activities and that states indirectly subsidized agriculture in much the same way. Before 1830, corporations had difficulty raising large amounts of capital without government assistance. This was in part because of the high degree of risk of some ventures or, in the case of manufacturers, because domestic investors sought the assurance of a strong government to protect infant industries.

Overseas investors wanted additional evidence to judge those situations far removed from their own environment and sought a promise of the faith and credit of a governmental agency to further ensure the potential of a proposed enterprise. For this reason, very few American corporate securities were well known or traded in Europe before 1830, except those related to the United States Bank itself.

A complex set of duties and taxes existed in the wake of the federal government's assumption of state debts. The schedules provided in Gallatin's *Sketch* (table 2.1) suggest that taxes also included a system of excises on liquors, on snuff manufacturers, and on stocks and bonds, as well as a stamp tax on legal documents.

Jefferson did away with the excise taxes and relied upon tariffs as the principal revenue source, but the excises returned to finance the War of 1812, being thereafter repealed once again after the war. The tariff thereafter remained in place as the principal federal revenue producer until the Union levied an income tax during the War between the States several decades later (Carter 1986: 26).

In 1819, a decision of the U.S. Supreme Court served to further establish direction for tax policy in the United States. *McCulloch v. Maryland* (1819) not only addressed the implied powers of the federal government over state powers in bank charters, but also held that a state may not tax an instrumentality of the federal government (i.e., the United States Bank) (Swisher 1958: 23).

Federalist Policies

Having only recently acknowledged their interdependence, the thirteen "United States" ratified a Constitution, which took effect in March 1789. The general weakness of the confederation in establishing provisions for monetary unity became a serious impediment to trade and the movement toward an economy unified by a national market. The value of paper money, in particular that of the Continental Congress, was suspect. Each state jealously guarded its right to issue its own coin and currency.

The need for a unified monetary system became apparent to George Washington when he became president. Washington appointed Alexander Hamilton as secretary of the treasury. The act that created the Treasury Department in 1789 charged the treasurer with the responsibilities of (1) preparing plans for the improvement and management of the revenue and support of the public credit; (2) preparing and reporting estimates of the public revenues and public expenditures; (3) superintending the collection of the revenues; (4) deciding on the forms of keeping and stating accounts and making return; and (5) granting under prescribed limitations, warrants for drawing money from the treasury. Hamilton's brilliance can be credited for three significant events that took the colonial economy from a barter system to sound financial exchange with a unified and stable monetary unit:

1. Establishment of the Bank of the United States. From its headquarters in Philadelphia and through its eight branches the bank provided monetary stability and established a precedent for advancing federal notes as currency in place of money.
2. Development of the Coinage Act of 1792. Two precious metals, gold and silver, underwrote the new monetary unit of the United States, the dollar. The act provided that all public offices and all proceedings in the court of the United States had to be kept in conformity with the new coinage regulations, thereby ensuring that the new coins and the dollar-decimal monetary system would take precedence over competing state units.
3. Federal funding of foreign and domestic war debt. This strengthened the fiscal and credit posture of the new republic. All features of this were included in a single act passed in August 1790.

Hamilton and the Federalists hoped that notes of the United States Bank would circulate as currency and thereby serve as a substitute for the paper money the public had come to mistrust. Meanwhile, state banks, which had been actively multiplying, set forth hundreds of issues of paper currency, creating confusion and ultimately a panic when, by 1837, more than 8,000 issues were outstanding. Of course a much more involved political story lies behind the Federalist movement and the history of banking in the new republic, but this period marks the initiation of a monetary system based on federal note issues of sufficient stability and general acceptance to warrant the use of "cash" accounts in ledgers, thereby noting the beginning of the end of the "barter" economy prevalent up to this time.[1]

Accountants in the New Nation

There are few similarities between the routines of today's financial accounting systems in modern multilevel international enterprise and the accounting records of the colonial citizens, aside from their foundation in the system of double entry. Business historians note that by the time of the Revolution the use of double-entry accounting was widespread. Harrington reports that "most" wholesale houses in New York appear to have used double entry by the eve of the Revolution. Of course, this does not mean that double entry information was used in the same fashion as it is today. In this era of the merchant capitalist, one made use of accounting primarily as an internal administrative device, and statements of accounts as such were not widely prepared, circulated, or published as they are today.[2]

William Weston, an English author of bookkeeping texts, was among the first to be in a position to influence American accounting practice as to the "annual" taking of balances. In 1754 Weston wrote a book for young Englishmen who were going to America to become plantation managers or factors. In his text of 260 pages, he prescribed (reflecting Parliament's edict of 1752) that books were to be balanced once per year and were to be proved by adding all the debit entries and all the credit entries in the ledger (Sampson 1960).

Many of the bookkeeping texts of the period also supported this trend toward annual "reckoning," as noted in the observation of the author William Gordon in 1765: "Merchants generally, at some fixed period, once in the year, balance or close the Ledger not only because the space allotted for account may be for the most part full, but likewise to show the true state of affairs and to determine what increases or diminutions his capital has suffered by last year's transactions" (Brief 1964: 18). This emphasis on determining changes in personal capital was a significant development and perhaps the major informational "output" of books kept for business during the period of merchant capitalism. It was common for texts written after the Revolution up to the turn of the century to note this information. For instance, in 1796, E. T. Jones, an accounting text writer from Bristol, wrote: "Once a year, most persons in trade have a statement of affairs made out, by taking off the balance of every account in the ledger."

Our Forefathers' Accounts

As described in the previous chapter, Washington's expense accounts and his plantation accounts indicate he had a working knowledge of accounting. One writer has speculated: "One of the most perused books in his private library was *Book-Keeping Moderniz'd,* a standard work of Scotland's John Mair which would have been well suited to Washington's needs as it included chapters on methods and accounts for plantation owners in the colonies" (Palmer 1976). For example Washington's accounts show that from August 3, 1775, to September 1783, he received a total of £80,167, or about $400,000. Washington tried to figure his profits from the above but apparently found the task dismaying. Finally he settled his accounts with his manager in terms of produce instead of money. Additional evidence of his account "rigor" is found in his December 31, 1769, balancing entry, which reads: "By cash lost, stolen, or paid away without charging £143,151.2." Washington's business and household accounts, including accounts in the Bank of Alexandria, from 1763 to 1799, were kept at Mount Vernon. Additional records, including his personal expenses ("Ledger A" and "Ledger B") maintained during periods of public service, are in the collection of the Library of Congress. John Hancock inherited a business fortune from his uncle, Thomas Hancock, the Boston merchant. John might have been less blessed had it not been that "Thomas knew as much about his own affairs from an accounting standpoint as was possible" (Bruchey 1958).

In a more critical review of the qualities of Washington and Hancock, Kitman relates, perhaps a bit tongue in cheek, the following after reviewing Washington's expense accounts and Hancock's ambitions to have headed up the Continental Army, which Washington led:[3] "The few extra dollars Washington may have picked up on his expense account was penny ante stuff compared to what an accomplished smuggler and insurance man like Hancock made out of the war. . . . George Washington, as it has been pointed out for centuries, was willing to make every sacrifice for liberty. Except one: reducing his standard of living [*sic*]. Even here he may have sincerely been unaware of the incongruity of his actions" (Kitman 1970: 281–82).

George Taylor, who signed the Declaration of Independence as a representative of Pennsylvania, came to America as an indentured servant bound to the owner of an ironworks. He was sent to work as a furnace coaler but it was thought that he was too weak for the job. Because he had a better education than most youths, he was given a job in the business office handling transactions and accounts. Indeed, Taylor had an accountant's flair for opportunity and when the owner of the works died, Taylor married the widow and thereby became the new owner (Previts 1976b).

The wealthiest of the signers, Charles Carroll of Carrollton (because there were at least three other Charles Carrolls in contemporary Maryland, he signed himself "of Carrollton"), is known for both his longevity (he survived until 1832, the last of the signers to succumb) and for his keeping of "meticulous books" (Cadwalader 1975).

Thomas Jefferson also maintained extensive financial records, as was customary for plantation owners, including an entry in his account books for July 4, 1776, noting a purchase of two items and a donation to charity (Shenkir, Welsch, and Baer 1972).

Another signer, Robert Morris, was instrumental in aiding the revolutionary cause by providing the means of financing for the new Congress. Morris, later acting as superintendent of finance, administered the funds for Congress and, with the backing of Haym Salomon, is noted to have "introduced system into financial accounting" related to the new government. Salomon, called the "Good Samaritan of the Revolution," lent more than $200,000 to the United States. He died at the age of 45, and the loan was apparently not repaid (Morris 1975).

Henry Laurens, president of the Continental Congress in 1777 and a signer of the Treaty of Paris, used accounts to maintain a record of his personal financial affairs with the state government of South Carolina during the 1770s; and his neatly drawn "Statement of Account with the United States," dated January 20, 1780, provides evidence of the customary importance placed on such records in early government transactions.

Robert Livingston, who along with Franklin, Jefferson, Adams, and Sherman constituted the committee to draft the Declaration of Independence, was absent at its signing because of his need to attend to affairs in New York. Livingston operated many enterprises and used double-entry accounts. The extent and the effectiveness with which Livingston's enterprises employed double entry caused them to be labeled "models" of double entry by business history writers (Johnson 1976).

The Counting House

How widespread and how well developed was the practice of keeping accounts during this era? What institution represented the locus of its practice? How significant was accounting information to those who developed it?

Perhaps more than any other element of its age, the development of the merchant counting house was both a force and an effect in the maturation process of account-keeping in this country. From the pre-Revolutionary period through the first legal recognition of public accountancy in 1896, the counting house supplied a central environment for early accounting functions. The colonial counting house was the "records center" of the merchant; it was also the established center for educating aspiring young businessmen and merchants. Training of this type was common throughout the colonies. John Hancock and Henry Laurens, two signers of the Declaration of Independence, were both schooled in counting houses.

Account keeping per se, as it was practiced in the counting house, reflected increasingly ingenious steps to simplify and routinize "processes." The columnar arrangement, the order and form of entering the information in double-entry style, and the techniques of learning suggested by the books of the period all claimed to advance and to simplify the method. The principles of economic measurement and consistent reporting that underlie our third-party-oriented accounting methods of today do not appear to be matters of concern then, perhaps because the merchant kept accounts primarily to suit his own, and not third-party, needs. Nineteenth-century merchants had elevated their account books to a place of special prominence, physically keeping them separate in what has been described as a "throne room": "In that throne room lay the bookkeeping records which made it possible for all the strings of diverse enterprise to be controlled by the hand of the resident merchant" (Bruchey 1958).

Thus, from the early eighteenth century to a later, more advanced stage in the mid-nineteenth century, we can presume that a significant popular knowledge about the benefits of accounts for purposes of controlling business came about through the apprenticeship system of the counting house. That is to say, based on apprenticeship training in rendering accounts, merchants became aware of and dependent upon financial records. As trade and business expanded following the War of 1812, a stable currency medium was provided, and thus a monetary basis to underlie transactions was established that enabled efficiently summarized and comparable accounts to be prepared so that rapid evaluations could be made. This development was to make it more necessary for the many, not just the few, to become knowledgeable in accounts. As account-keeping became a requisite skill, and counting houses handled larger volumes of transactions, they became less well suited as a learning place and source of apprenticeship. Instead, textbooks and teachers of accounts began to make their presence felt in the larger towns (figure 2.2).

Education of Accountants

At the start of the nineteenth century, private institutions of accounting education, operated in many instances by textbook writers, had begun to offer specialized courses, first in the home of the authors and then gradually at locations in the commercial district. During this period the proprietary business colleges and schools were beginning to develop to replace an apprenticeship system. While schooling did not fully overtake "clerking" or apprenticeships in the counting house for many decades, it was the itinerant educator of the early nineteenth century who would pioneer the development of free-standing entities for business and accounting education. These early private commercial colleges were links in a chain of evolution to today's graduate business programs and accounting schools at universities

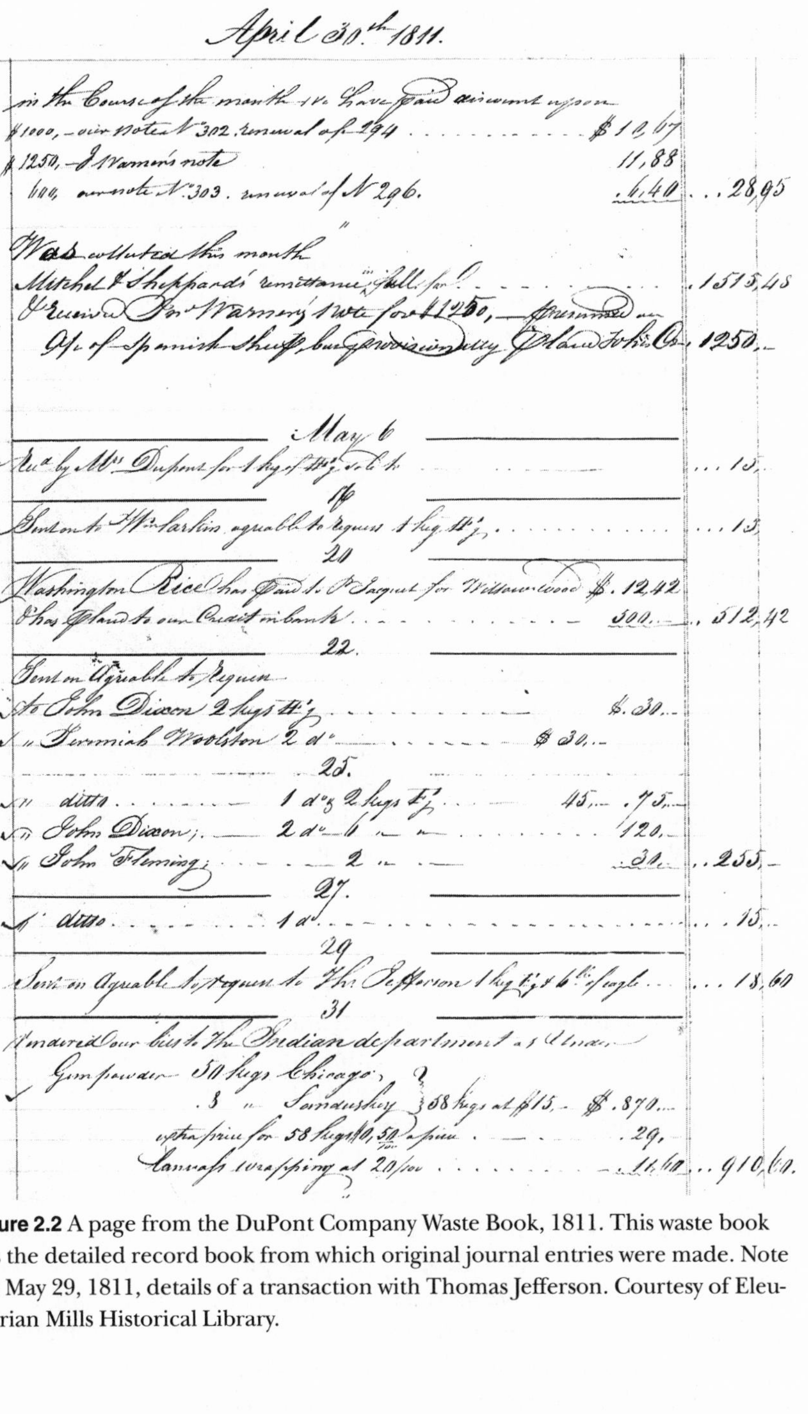

Figure 2.2 A page from the DuPont Company Waste Book, 1811. This waste book was the detailed record book from which original journal entries were made. Note the May 29, 1811, details of a transaction with Thomas Jefferson. Courtesy of Eleutherian Mills Historical Library.

(Reigner 1958: 73). James Bennett, noted for his textbooks, the first published in 1814, was listed as a "teacher of bookkeeping" in the New York City *Directories* through 1835. The twelfth edition of his text provides a testimony that Bennett had instructed thousands, "many of whom, prior to their attendance in the Author's lecture, possessed no knowledge whatever of accounts." Bennett further noted that he had "instructed persons from thirteen different nations of the earth" (Holmes 1974). The "Balance Chart" (see figure 2.3), which appears for the first time in his 1820 edition, "was a teaching innovation which made use of the technique of connecting entries in the accounts by flow lines to indicate related debit and credit sides of a transaction" (Stone 1982b: iv).

Another American identified as an early educator and author was Thomas Turner, of Portland, Maine. Turner's 1804 text shows a set of books for an individual proprietorship and for a partnership and states that a "senior school boy can within a few months obtain a foundation of the principles and a perfect knowledge of the method."

The techniques of Bennett and Turner contrast the varieties of accounting instruction emerging at the start of the 1800s.[4] Turner emphasized the need to teach the "school boy" as it had become common to teach the methods of accounts in New England from early times; whereas Bennett's lectures were a type of forerunner of the business colleges that would emerge to educate working-class students. In each case there was a response to the growing need on the part of business people to have an understanding of accounts because of the increase of commerce in the country and the unbounded field open to them for specialties and commercial prospects.

Early Textbooks

As detailed in chapter 1 the origin and authorship of the first American text on account keeping by double entry can be traced, arguably, to before the time of the American Revolution. However, Sheldahl's research asserts that Sarjeant's 1789 book is the most appropriate candidate (Sheldahl 1985A). While ordinary in its brevity, Sarjeant's work is reportedly a complete treatment of the traditional Italian approach.

This era's innovative works include William Mitchell's 1796 volume, *A New and Complete System of Bookkeeping* (Philadelphia), and Benjamin Workman's *The American Accountant,* which went into at least three editions. The first appeared in 1789, and the third, revised and corrected by R. Patterson, appeared in Philadelphia in 1796. Thomas Dilworth's *Young Book-Keeper's Assistant* (Philadelphia 1789) is another early text (Haynes 1935: 11–13).

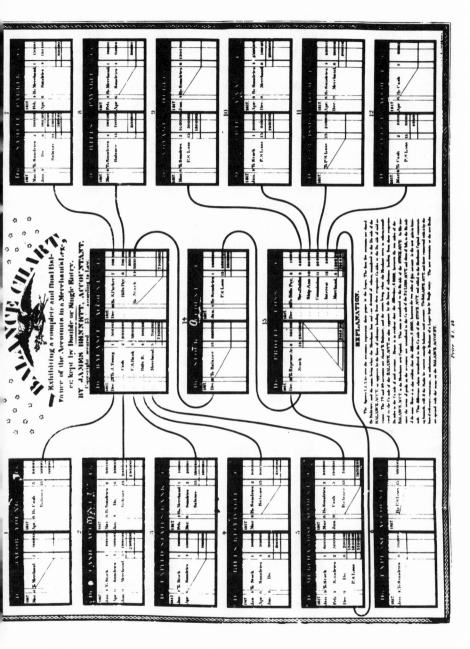

Figure 2.3 The American system of practical bookkeeping by James Bennett, 1820

Benjamin Booth's book *A Complete Service, etc.*, published in London in 1789, was nonetheless considered to be an American work. Chauncy Lee's *American Accomptant*, which contained 297 pages and was printed in Lansingburgh, New York, in 1797, was the first "serious" work on the subject by an American; it reflected an innovation of "The Italian Mode of Bookkeeping agreeable to Gordon's system of accomptantship." Gordon's works were written in Great Britain and went into several editions. They were in widespread use in the three decades before the end of the eighteenth century.

In his 1789 text, Booth's introduction related the effects of the Revolutionary War on his own life: noting on the title page that he was "Late of New York, and now of London, Merchant," he laments further "being cut off, by the late war, from the friendships formed in my youth; and prevented by the peace that succeeded it, from pursuing the line of business to which I had long been habituated."

This disconsolate remark by the expatriate author suggests that merchant account-keepers were as vulnerable then as now to the process of politics and the pains of war. It may have been that Booth had Tory sympathies and was thenceforth banished from the colonies when the new nation took form. Yet in his efforts to make himself "useful to society," he responded to the creative task of writing a complete system of bookkeeping from the viewpoint of an American now functioning in England. Booth's contribution may be all the more significant because it flows "against the grain," in that the major texts had been coming to the colonies by way of Britain before the Revolution, and now shortly thereafter, an American writer was introducing his system to the English as noted in his remark: "It is surprising, that, in a commercial country like this, there should not be one treatise on this subject, which when applied to a large scale of business, can be reduced to practice. Those I have seen, appear to have been written, either by persons who have not the ability sufficient for the undertaking, or by such as never had the opportunity of bringing their theories to the test of experience."

Booth emphasized the need to present effectively summarized transactional data, noting that several firms had failed because they could not cope with the extensive business of the house, which reflected the expanded scale of business markets in general. Whether or not we should recognize the uniqueness of Booth's "summary" approach remains to be determined. But his comments testify to the state of commercial expansion and the increased scale and complexity of business, wherein business failure could be traced to the lack of adequate accounts and summaries.

Cronhelm acknowledged Booth as "the first English work illustrative of the *modern* Italian Method" (1818: xiii). The modern method reflected that in practice, the three principal account books (waste book, journal, and ledger) were often either abridged or supplemented according to the requirements of business (Yamey 1978). What the "modern Italian" method demonstrated was the adaptable aspects of the process, such that writers began to incorporate some of these real-world advantages, such as specialized books of original entry, compound entries, and subsidiary books.

Frederic Cronhelm was another member of this "modern" school of early nineteenth-century writers. His *Double Entry by Single* (1818) can be credited with several important elements:

1. He defined bookkeeping as: "the art of recording property, so that as to shew at all times and value of the whole capital and of each component part" (Cronhelm 1818: B). This definition began his work in a chapter using the term "Theory of Book-keeping," suggesting an appreciation for the abstract capacity of the subject.

2. He included a chapter on the "Principle of Equilibrium" (note use of the term "principle"). In this chapter he introduces the notions of positive and negative property and a general proposition in the form of an equation. As an explicit mathematical notation it is an achievement of significant dimension. Later, in 1880, Sprague's writings would expand from similar equational notions into a comprehensive system, The Algebra of Accounts. Yet Cronhelm's book seems to have been limited in its impact. Perhaps because the premises of the publishers were destroyed by fire "shortly after its publication . . . and nearly the whole edition was consumed" (Yamey 1978). Writing in 1933, Littleton recognized its significance stating: "The fundamental relationship between the accounts of double entry bookkeeping is symbolized by Cronhelm's equation: *Positive properties − Negative properties = Proprietor's stock.*"

The "modern Italian writers" such as the American expatriate Booth and the Englishman Cronhelm captured in their works the capacity for this system to expand and adapt to encompass more complex entities. They also appreciated and utilized abstract terms and notions in a manner that makes plausible the assertion that a new age, one of theoretical sophistication, was at hand. "This progress in theory is one of the principal factors which indicate the expansion of bookkeeping into accounting" (Littleton 1933A: 203).

Mitchell, an American author, writing in 1796, was also critical of the traditional Italian form so popular in the colonies in the wake of Mair's influential books (Sheldahl 1985A: 7). "Mitchell particularly criticized Mair's book for being overburdened with rules, problems, and cases, causing the aspiring bookkeeper to become bewildered. . . . He termed the use of the classical 'Italian method' . . . as being too difficult" (McMickle and

Vangermeersch 1987: 81). Mitchell then proceeds to suggest simplifications. Mitchell's work does not appear to have been commercially successful, as there were no subsequent editions. It provides testimony, however, to the increasing attempts to modify the traditional form of bookkeeping.

Few American texts (eighteen in all) are identified as appearing during the years 1796 to 1826 by Bentley and Leonard (1934–35: 1:6). Even with the known restrictions and limitations of their listings, this number is less than a third of any decade's total volumes thereafter. It suggests that the few works that were initiated and achieved commercial success during this period are important. This would include Bennett's *The American System of Practical Book-Keeping* (1820), which continued through forty-one editions until 1862 and was known to be used in his lectures for several years prior to the first edition. Hitchcock's *A New Method of Teaching Book-Keeping*, which enjoyed several editions through the 1850s, would also be included.

Little is known about the relationships, if any, that may have existed among these writers and others of their peers. Some interchange can be hypothesized, and Stone (1982A: iv) has developed some linkages between Jackson, Mair, and D. Dowling. *Jackson's book-keeping; adapted to the coin and commerce of the United States* first appeared in 1801 and represents "an interesting opportunity to trace bookkeeping methods and techniques from England to America" (Stone 1982B: iv).

Stone tells us that Sheys's *The American Book-Keeper; etc.* (1818), published in New York, may be the earliest U.S. accounting text to address bank bookkeeping, preceding C. C. Marsh's 1856 effort (Stone 1982E: iv). Sheys devotes only 15 percent of his text to explanations; the rest is example material. He distinguishes among three types of accounts: "Real, consisting of property; Personal, consisting of persons with whom one deals; and Fictitious, which are 'invented accounts' such as Profit and Loss, Interest, etc." (Sampson 1960: 462). In these "modern Italian" writings of Anglo-American origin we begin to discern traces of what a few decades later would become clearly established by Thomas Jones and others as distinctions between nominal and real accounts. This further supports Littleton's contention that "the nineteenth-century saw bookkeeping expanded into accounting" (Littleton 1933A: 165).[5]

Accounting Practice and Disclosure

Businesses of various sizes from small, merchant groceries to the first full-scale, large manufacturing enterprises operated during the period studied in this chapter. In addition, despite the political tensions reflected in the

War of 1812, much of the everyday merchandise was imported through England and the transactions records were mostly denominated in English currency up through the start of the nineteenth century. Barter transactions were also commonplace, and complicated, although merchants did not seem unwilling to undertake such activities (Stone 1979: 41).

The linking together of sources of capital via a regular auction, price-setting market mechanism was a major step in the emergence of an American economy that was slowly divesting itself of regional prejudice and supplying capital to enterprises located beyond the realm of customary travel and kinship. It is perhaps difficult to perceive the significance of this development in light of the global capital market structure of the late twentieth century, but it should be apparent that the movement toward a national capital market required increasing use of reliable financial summaries in evaluating the prospects of a distant company. At the same time, it is worthwhile to recognize that the information needs of these early markets were not met by what we would identify as financial statements. The English East India Company did prepare a form of balance sheet and supplementary information as early as 1756, but this was not thought to be common practice (Baladouni 1981: 69). Financial information of the sort deemed useful for investment decisions of this age was only beginning to take the form of summary reports. In some religious congregations, financial data appeared as early as 1814, but it would be many years before regular reports were prepared (Swanson and Gardner 1986: 61).

References to British auditors' visits to the colonies and to investments that likely would have caused such visits are commonly referred to in the history of accounting.[6] But public accounting listings in directories are few and public newspaper announcements by accountants such as one found in the *New Jersey Journal* of July 8, 1795, were probably rare. An apt conclusion for this time is that the public practice of accounting seems to have been combined with teaching and writing on the subject of bookkeeping (Edwards 1960: 45).

The ledgers of Robert Oliver, a merchant of Baltimore (1796–1806), indicate that accounts and periodic trial balances were prepared, not for the purposes of disclosure but solely for compiling the balances of all open accounts in order to determine bookkeeping accuracy. These early trial balances condensed into a few pages the financial information from as many as five hundred pages and grouped debtors and creditors as well. A modern trial balance could have been constructed from Oliver's trial balances, but no evidence of a more advanced form has been found. Although it is quite likely that proprietors were learning the value of a systematic and effectively summarized set of books, there is no clear evidence that as entrepreneurs, owners expected, demanded, or relied upon financial information set forth in such a conventional and convenient fashion (Bruchey 1958).

In Baltimore, as in Boston or Philadelphia, the merchant was likely also to be a major shipowner or investor. And, "to be heavily involved in the shipping of one's own cargoes and those of other merchants (on commission) was, at best, a risky affair" (Gilbert 1984: 17).

What this information provides is a sense of the importance of accounts in an era when merchants were the principal agents of our national commerce. The coastal trade of this era, and the related growth and commercial success of the seaport cities, was not only import- but export-based. Trade tariffs provided a major source of government revenues and provided a basis for funding infrastructure and educational development.

Cost/Management Accounting

Since the shopkeepers and merchants were prime users of account records at this time, one might also wonder about the early industrialists' uses of account data in ventures and barter. If account books aided the memory of the trading merchant, were they not as necessary in the complex transactions of manufacturers in cotton mills, iron foundries, and construction firms? Information about early American industrial cost-accounting practices is sparse. The major industries of the Western world were located in and effectively protected by the trade patterns and policies of Great Britain. U.S. manufacturers, though on the rise, were clearly in their infancy (Bruchey 1965: 86). It was not until 1820 that manufacturers' associations came into being under the leadership of the National Institution for the Promotion of Industry. A newspaper, *Patron of Industry,* was also introduced to inform and influence public and political opinion in favor of a protective tariff to aid developing industry (Cochran and Miller 1942: 17). It is perhaps necessary then to distinguish that although *cost* accounting came into evidence only after 1800 and developed during the American industrial revolution, industrial bookkeeping practice and techniques were of earlier origin.

Fleischman and Parker argue that the accomplishments of the period have been perhaps undervalued, and are noteworthy, based on their review of context records of twenty-five British firms during the years of the industrial revolution in Britain. It was not until "scientific management" overtook these early cost techniques that the shortcomings were highlighted and judgments of their inadequacy were formed in hindsight (Fleischman and Parker 1990: 24). They consider that industrial cost accounting was identified by the following:

- Only rarely did manufacturing costs flow through the general ledger accounts.
- There was no meaningful integration with financial reporting.
- The accuracy of product costing became increasingly suspect as the magnitude of indirect costs grew.
- The orientation was . . . toward rational price-setting rather than utilization of cost as a control tool.

Among firms in the shipbuilding industry, excerpts from account books around the time of the Revolution indicate a very rough-and-ready type of receipts and expenditures system, with no clear view of accounting for overhead allocations or the loss of fixed asset value via depreciation.

Reports of accounting for iron manufacturers of the period indicate that double-entry records were modified to accommodate inventory information. These records were sufficient, if employed by a person with knowledge of accounts, to afford the basis for estimating costs of production, although information such as cost of production was not clearly set out or summarized as part of the record-keeping procedure (Gambino and Palmer 1976: 18–19).

The rudimentary nature of cost systems during the period is also born out in the case study of the Providence merchant partnership of Almy and Brown. Formed in 1789, before Samuel Slater began to revolutionize the textile trade with his system, the partners attempted to consolidate spinning, weaving, and finishing, which occurred at a variety of locations, by taking advantage of the looms, spinning jennies, carding machines, and spinning frames available to them. The partners attracted skilled craftsmen to Providence to build jennies, to serve as master weavers, and so forth. Yet by 1794, "Almy and Brown was about to fail . . . [because of] the merchant capitalists' inability to determine operating costs" (Conrad 1984: 15). This view is consistent with the interpretation of Chandler's ideas about management in this era overall, namely that "the traditional forms of business organization, in both commerce and production before 1840 . . . were little changed from those of fifteenth-century Venice, with business generally being carried out by small, family oriented enterprises" (Eichner 1978: 99). This apparently stemmed from the lack of cost-keeping techniques capable of representing the larger scales of activity and the technology that was rapidly affecting productivity. The need to take full advantage of technology was made most apparent by the concern over availability of workers and mechanics. "I find," said the superintendent of the Springfield Armory in 1822, "the rage for manufacturing cotton prevails to such a degree and there is so great a call for first-rate workmen that I am apprehensive I shall lose some of our most valuable workmen except I am authorized to raise their wages according to circumstances" (Habakkuk 1967: 16).

Roxanne Johnson's work on the formative years of E. I. DuPont de Nemours & Co. from 1800 to 1818 reveals that "decision makers required a record-keeping system which would provide information on the financial position of the firm for themselves as well as shareholder-investors and creditors with financial interest in the enterprise" (Johnson 1987: iii). While she cautions that this level of sophistication should not be considered the basis for a generalization about the time period, we now have some compelling evidence that more capable and sophisticated management had such "systematic procedures."

Later businesses displayed similar capabilities. "The Boston Manufacturing Company, beginning in 1817, had a rudimentary cost-accounting system that allocated overhead to the cost of manufacturing, and, in 1818, a system of 'Semi-Annual Accounts' that calculated the cost of cloth by type. By 1822, repair costs, but not depreciation, were taken into account" (Lubar 1984: 24). Thus, as large-scale industry appeared in the early nineteenth century, costing systems were in use at Boston Manufacturing.

Johnson and Kaplan assert that the appearance of new accounting techniques in textile factories abetted centralized management control within these organizations since decision-makers sought to develop pricing that the market and transaction information could not supply, given that the "transactions" were internally generated (Johnson and Kaplan 1987: 22–23).

British writers, including Hamilton (1777–79) and Cronhelm (1818), had provided extensive materials and examples of manufacturers' books, but "there was no consideration of cost accounting in any English language text, until Garke and Fells produced their *Factory Accounts* (1887)," which was more than a century after Hamilton had given impetus to the ideas (Mepham 1988A: 68). This explains why some writers contend that, given the times, systems such as the one at Boston Manufacturing were by the 1840s "arguably superior" to costing methodologies found in extant texts on the subject, such as Cronhelm (Porter 1980: 3). Yet such systems appear to have been unique, peculiar to each company, and ad hoc, versus incorporated, into the double-entry system of records.

Garner suggests that one reason that may have deterred the public dissemination of such cost systems through texts is that it would have compromised an advantage. "The handling of a firm's accounts in an especially advantageous way was considered personal, a secret not to be let out to rival firms" (Garner 1954: 30).

Nonprofit Management Accounting

A unique episode in the application of double-entry accounting to the business operations of a religious commune (1814–24) is told by Flesher and Flesher in the recounting of the Harmonists' community. A more sophisticated system of information was developed to meet the demands of a form of common ownership during a period when single owners or partner-owned entities dominated. The community's records relate the operations of the shoemaker, the saddler, the blacksmith, the hatter, the weaver, the potter, and many others. The system of the Harmonists provided internal reports "showing selling prices allocated on a percentage basis to material, labor and profit. . . . Forecasted income statements and budgets were used for purposes of planning and managerial decision making" (Flesher and Flesher 1979: 301).

Government and Accounting

Considering the many problems encountered in constructing a new national fiscal system to include the assumption of prior debt, the levying of taxes, and the establishment of a central government bank, there were major innovative developments in what would now be recognized as a pioneer era of national (macro) accounting.

One of the most valuable sources of information about the financing of the early federal government is Albert Gallatin's *A Sketch of the Finances of the United States* (1796). Gallatin's work provides narratives on the revenues, expenses, and debt of the federal government and a set of nineteen statements (for example, see table 2.1) that detail financial sources from the start of the Constitutional government in 1789 through January 1, 1796.

Gallatin (1761–1849) came to America from Switzerland and served in the House of Representatives where he led the fight for congressional control over the "purse strings" of government. In part because of his efforts, the forerunner of the House Ways and Means Committee was established. In 1801, he became secretary of the treasury under Jefferson and served for twelve years.

Gallatin's *Sketch* is important, for it classifies and sequences government accounts. Earlier tabulations of federal government receipts and expenditures, which were not much more than lists of single-entry transactions, had been publicly available. However, Gallatin summarized the entire period of operations from 1789 to 1796 in his statements and thereby developed a single source of information as to comparative amounts of revenues and costs. The detail for each line in statement A is then further explained in statement X in Gallatin's book.

The problems of financial record-keeping at the local level may have been less complicated, since incorporated municipalities were not common or especially large. At the time of the Revolution, only about fifteen cities had been chartered, ranging from hamlets to urban centers such as New York and Philadelphia. Since states tended to maintain control over a city's fiscal destiny, the system of financial accountability responded to whatever system prevailed in state government, which had evolved from either a monarch-colonial responsibility system, or a town meeting–peer accountability system.

Some of what we have learned about municipal accounting during this period is related to studying Freeman's *The Town Officer,* first published in 1791. Freeman, active politically and a supporter of the American Revolution, devoted sections of each edition (there were eight editions in all) to town accounts. He explains Forms (a Journal), accounts for monies unappropriated, and uses a collector's account as part of fifteen accounts in all. McMickle and Vangermeersch state that "his purpose in describing [inventing?] municipal accounting was certainly to enable better control and to help assure that monies voted by the town and collected through taxes were expended to the purposes for which they were collected" (McMickle and Vangermeersch 1987: 70).

The Significance of Accounts in a New Nation

During the period of the Revolution and the establishment of the new Republic, American lifestyles changed in response to the politics and economics of self-interest and modern capitalism found in the writings of Adam Smith. An 1819 Supreme Court decision heralded the advent of the corporate era in American enterprise when Chief Justice Marshall's *Dartmouth College* opinion provided a legal foundation for modern corporate capitalism, recognizing the distinct quasi-personal contract attributes of the corporate form.

The economy and the populace were still rural in form and agrarian in substance. The industrialization of the economy and urban concentration were only beginning to be experienced. To have attained a formal education was a privilege reserved for the well-to-do. Account-keeping was performed customarily in the merchant's counting house, where it was learned as an essential management skill—and where it would continue to be relied upon in ever-increasing subtlety as the system was streamlined for purposes of managerial use.

As the need for financial data began to expand, in response to the growing commerce of the new era, instruction in accounting became a separate activity and American teachers, often using the title of "professor," offered public lectures and courses to those seeking a future in the business world.

There was marked competition among American authors to provide "the" complete system that was most fitted to the commerce of the United States and most useful to management. In the main, instruction was geared to accounting in a rote form. Abstract discussion of value in the economic sense was not emphasized since it was not deemed the province of the bookkeeper to be concerned with the *nature* of value, only the *quantity* of value, be it the cash or commodity at hand. The merchant or proprietary party was the individual believed to be sufficiently skilled in the notions of the values of his trade and competent in the skill of numbers produced by his account books to fuse their meanings into successful business decisions.

The era of the corporation was destined to change much of this. The proprietor's managerial function would soon have to be discharged at a higher level: the engine of corporate capitalism would begin to generate demand for expert financial and accounting advice as owners employed managers to orchestrate the multiple activities of these enterprises.

The close of this era marked the beginning of the end of mercantile capitalism and the related dominant use of merchant accounts in the realm of personal enterprises. Partnership and corporate ventures would increasingly demand that accounting techniques be adapted to their needs. It was the dawn of the era of the corporation and an age of financial capitalism. John Jacob Astor, a merchant and fur trader whose legendary wealth was accumulated during these changing times, had anticipated the "imposing and formidable" imagery of the corporation and acquired a New York state corporate charter for the American Fur Company, with capital of $1 million, in 1808. His petition stated "that an undertaking of such magnitude would require greater capital than any individual or unincorporated association could well furnish" (Chandler and Tedlow 1985: 63). In 1811, New York legislated an incorporation law limited to manufacturing entities (Cochran 1959: 115). New York then passed the first general incorporation law in 1825, establishing availability for widespread use of the corporate form to all businesses.

A fitting scene to depict the transition from family enterprises to corporate entities occurred in 1826, when Charles Carroll, whose personal estate and wealth were legendary, came to lay the cornerstone of the first station house of the Baltimore and Ohio Railroad, a line he had helped to finance. As the nation passed out of the hands of our Revolutionary forefathers, and what they represented, it was to pass into those of the corporate promoters, of which railroads were a symbol.[7]

By the close of this next era, companies that were predecessors to the giant railroads were being formed and beginning operations (Chamberlain 1974: 58–72). The railroads, as corporate creatures, would spawn supporting industries, lead to a rise in the markets for industrial securities, change the role of the capital markets, and instigate a demand for a professional class of accountants to service the business information needs of managers, owners, investors, government, and society. To some, these corporations would be the agents of national unity, resolving the issues of national expansion that a modern transportation and communication system had imposed. The implications for accounting in this setting are the next subject for consideration.

The Beginnings of Corporate America

> It is not disputed, that however well the principles of bookkeep-
> ing may be taught, each student in applying it to practice, will ex-
> hibit some peculiarity in the disposition of the details; . . . but if two
> men were to write on the same subject with the same sentiments,
> would they not construct their sentences differently? . . . Both may
> write grammatically, yet one may greatly excel the other.
>
> **—Thomas Jones, *Hunt's Merchants' Magazine*, December 1842**[1]

The Economics and Demographics of Antebellum America

From the start of the second quarter of the nineteenth century through
the period bounded by the events giving rise to the start and end of the War
between the States, Americans experienced the flush of westward expansion incited by gold discoveries in California, technological change, massive
immigration amid political hostility relating to a "state's right" to be "slave"
or "free." During the 1840s the first writings of Darwin on the subject of
evolution were being presented to academic audiences.

The tone of the times is reflected by the following: "Men's lives are determined chiefly by habits formed in daily activities. In the United States
each year after 1800, more and more men spent their days in factories and
mines, on canals and railroads, tending machines, locomotives, and steamboats, *keeping accounts,* selling commodities, digging coal, copper, lead, and
iron, drilling oil and natural gas" (emphasis added) (Cochran and Miller
1942: 1).

According to the 1840 census, seven principal employments included,
by number of persons employed: agriculture; manufactures; commerce;
learned professions and engineers; navigation of the oceans; navigation of
canals, lakes, and rivers; and mining. These occupations accounted for the
activities of 35 percent of the population (*Hunt's* 1843: 53).

"Real per capita income rose some 30 per cent between 1800 and 1840; . . .
a major force behind this growth was the 'business revolution'" that had
occurred by 1840 (DuBoff 1980: 459).

A significant example of economic growth was to be found in the cotton trade. In 1791, total U.S. production of cotton was listed at two million pounds. By 1840, the number had increased 250 times to five hundred million pounds. It was supposed that at that point, the United States provided three-fourths of the cotton trade of the world. Indeed, cotton was king! (*Hunt's* 1841: 218).

By 1840, the U.S. population was more than 17 million, including 14 million white, 400,000 "free colored," and nearly 3 million "others." This number was greater than the population of England and Wales. Fourteen of the states and two territories (Wisconsin and Iowa) were "free," while twelve states and two territories (Florida and the District of Columbia) were slave (*Hunt's* 1841: 281, 343).

The factors of production, as among technology, capital, land, and labor were in such balance that the United States had quite different incentives than Europe: in the United States, land was abundant and labor was in short supply. "(S)ince there was so much land to cultivate, Americans . . . had a very strong incentive to develop machines which would enable farmers to cultivate a larger area. The alternative was to leave the land uncultivated. It was said of Illinois in 1857 all grain is here cut by machine. Cradles are out of the question. . . . If grain is too badly lodged to be so gathered it is quietly left alone. . . . This work done by machinery is not very much cheaper than it could be done by hand, but *the great question is—where are the hands to come from?*" (emphasis added) (Habakkuk 1967: 101). Other formidable and unforeseen challenges were to face the young nation in the coming decades. Between 1850 and 1890, the forces of change would fashion a marketplace that would grow from 25 to 60 million consumers. By 1850, eastern port cities, such as Baltimore, New York, and Philadelphia, were competing to extend their sea lanes inward as landlanes of steel raced westward forming an east-west trunkline. This transportation net also worked its way north and south, from Mobile and the Gulf north, and from the Great Lakes south.

During the 1860s when the Civil War raged, the northern states continued their industrial and market development, causing the historian Shelby Foote to observe, "The North fought the War with one arm behind its back" ("The Civil War," PBS television program, 1990). The war, one of carnage and misery, has been interpreted in countless volumes. Some versions argue that it was about emancipation: stated in moral terms, the need to eliminate a system that placed economic property rights, where one person held another as property, over individual liberty. The war was an atonement in blood for the evils of slavery. Others saw it as a test of states' rights within the Union and the federal system. It was for these reasons and it was for far more.

The war forced people to think in terms grander than the boundaries of their state, at a time when travel was still limited. It caused thousands to experience vast distances and different places, yet all within one nation, one continent. The end of the war produced, even when grudgingly, a sense of nationhood such that persons said "The United States 'is', not The United States 'are'" (Foote 1990).

The political consolidation following the Civil War, the market expansion begun by the establishment of a continental transportation network, and the development of the factory system transformed the United States rapidly and relentlessly. The economic consequences of the war will be debated without end. Did the war retard or accelerate industrialization? The paucity of national income statistics prior to 1869, the year Kuznets begins his estimates, accounts for such fertile debate. We shall not enter the fray but recommend that those who do consider Andreano (1962) and Gilchrist and Lewis (1965) as initial readings.

The Politics of Jackson Democrats

A blaze of democratic nationalism, kindled during the era of Andrew Jackson's popular prominence, consolidated the voting strength of the small farmers of the new West and the laboring classes in the growing urban centers of the East. The precious belief in an idyllic republic, fostered by Jefferson—a land to be kept for the husbandman and kept from industrialism—was not to be.

Property Rights and Political Structures

Alexander Hamilton had cast the political philosophy of our nation's new industrialism during the turbulent period that followed the War of Independence. By joining the Bank of the United States through its offerings of debt to business and propertied classes, Hamilton created a "national debt" from which the political wisdom of business and wealth was afforded a permanent basis of influence. Talleyrand, the brilliant yet cynical European statesman and cleric, was a friend of Hamilton, having spent several years in America. He is reported to have said, "I consider Napoleon, Pitt, and Hamilton as the three greatest men of our age, and if I had to choose between the three, I would unhesitatingly give the first place to Hamilton" (Fuller 1977).

The cornerstone of Federalist political philosophy required that the propertyless masses be kept from obtaining dominant power through popular suffrage. With property and political power joined, extending the vote to those without property would likely damage that linkage, one that was predicated upon developing an alliance of business and government into the industrial America envisioned in Hamilton's celebrated *Report on Manufactures.*

Although political scientists may argue about the particulars of Federalist and neo-Federalist policies, in fact the alliance of property and politics at this stage of the economy's formation was essential in order to gain exposure from the press, the pulpit, and the courts. Such exposure was necessary for this version of the "American system," which acknowledged, protected, and rewarded those who were successful in accumulating private productive property. Such a socioeconomic philosophy would underwrite the aspiration of ambitious young Americans—both native-born and immigrants—as they sought to transform an agrarian land rich with industrial resources into a cornucopia of the goods produced by workers and machines in urban factories. In the 1830s it was not clear that the technology, capital, and talented labor required to achieve such a marked transition from Jefferson's landowner's state were to be found.

The political competition and separation between the voting but unpropertied segment of the population and those who had money, power, and control of the physical means of production initially and ultimately provide an explanation of the need for financial accounting and reports. This need is made more obvious when voting power, resource control, and resource ownership themselves are separated in a society.

Personal traits and the ideals of thrift and hard work (famed as the Puritan work ethic) became blended with the curious American propensity for mechanical tinkering (Yankee ingenuity) and the pursuit of property wealth. This was to become the "American way" and it was to be achieved through an industrial system.

There were fewer than 20 million Americans in 1840, but by 1875 that number would grow to approach 30 million, including more than 1.5 million immigrants from the United Kingdom alone who represented nearly one-third of the total immigration for the period 1840–60. As settlers pushed into Ohio, Missouri, and the Dakotas, more and more urban centers formed as transmission points for goods once imported but now being manufactured along the seacoast city complex of the North and East. The economy of the antebellum era was also blessed with at least one other essential industrial technology: the production of textiles in New England.

Only the South persisted in a landed-gentry lifestyle, reflecting a commitment to the way of life Jefferson had foreseen. The economic power of agriculture, however, was linked to its cotton crop and for the most part to foreign markets. In the final test, the power of industrialism and corporate manufactures would subdue the plantation agrarian system, end the use of blacks as slaves, and generate an even more interdependent lifestyle.

During the decades before the resolution of these social philosophies and throughout the Civil War, American industrialism was becoming centered on the economics of railroad development. Traditional commerce remained dependent upon water-based travel, but as the new West was settled, internal east-west trade became significant. The political policies of Jackson, who opposed the rechartering of the Bank of the United States and identified himself with the small farmer and urban worker, awakened the hopes for popular suffrage and kindled the ambition of those who saw opportunity for "easy money" to buy the farmlands of the new West.

More than any other sole phenomenon, the "iron horse" presaged the birth of American industrialism. The railroads' capability to provide relatively cheap and rapid transport across a seemingly vast land, to stitch together expanding markets by linking suppliers and users of commodities at places where waterways were unknown and other transport was impractical, was a technological and economic feat of unprecedented importance. The corporate form of business served as the essential vehicle for railroad capital formation. It established a demand for legions of other corporate entities and a multitude of supporting industries and skills including coal mining, steel milling, and civil engineering, such that huge sums of capital would be needed to finance each new venture. Capital markets, money men, and accounting information were to become important in the planning and production of the hard goods and services that railroading would bring forth.

In the midst of this blooming of the iron flower of the railroad came occasional panics in the capital market, as occurred in 1857. The business practices of the period, as under most adverse circumstances, drew criticism from many quarters. The practices were the result of no single factor, unsavory or not; in the United States, during the period following 1840, businesses promoted dynamic change. "A national economy replaced a localized one, the size of the representative firm increased, and the nature of competition altered. . . . One of the outcomes of this vast change was that some . . . schooled in one age lived to dominate another. Many of them thus carried the ethos of the old school and were not aware that some of their practices were no longer considered ethical. The new code had not yet stabilized sufficiently to provide them with a fixed reference point. . . . With the rapid economic change occurring during the 1800s, the individual was left to define the rules for himself" (Engelbourg 1980: 3–5).

By the 1850s, New York and Boston had been linked by electrical telegraphy. This made it possible to provide immediate communication among the financial centers of the eastern seaboard: Baltimore, Philadelphia, New York, Boston, and Charleston. As well, it expanded the network of potential financial contacts and agencies beyond the regional framework relied upon to accumulate and supply capital. Previously, a part of the Winchester Repeating Arms Co. of New Haven was organized in 1855 at a capitalization of 6,000 common shares at $25 par value each. The forty backers were chiefly from New Haven and nearby towns. "Seven were clockmakers, three carriage makers, two bakers, two grocers (and) Oliver Winchester, then engaged in the manufacture of shirts" (Williamson 1952).

Telegraphy's influence grew rapidly. "By 1851, only seven years after the inaugural pioneer Baltimore-to-Washington line, the entire eastern half of the U.S. up to the Mississippi River was connected by a network of telegraph wires that made virtually instantaneous communication possible" (Yates 1986: 149). This meant reductions of communication in terms of "days" from what had been required just a few decades earlier—when, for example, the Battle of New Orleans had been fought two weeks after the War of 1812 had been ended because the message had not reached General Andrew Jackson.

U.S. cities grew at rapid rates, as evidenced in table 3.1. Cities in turn served as the bases from which railroads would stretch west, expanding each port city's role and rivalry with its neighbor. Canal and river port cities including Buffalo, Cleveland, and Cincinnati in the "West" also experienced substantial growth. But the canals were limited in their ability to operate after freezing conditions set in, such that their cost advantages in competition would be overtaken by the year-round operations of the railroads. New

TABLE 3.1
Growth of Cities in the United States, 1830–1840

City	1830 Population	1840 Population	% Change
New York	202,589	312,710	54
Philadelphia	188,797	258,037	36
Baltimore	80,620	102,313	26
Boston	61,392	93,383	52
New Orleans	49,826	102,193	105
Charleston	30,289	29,261	−3
Sixteen cities	770,479	1,164,189	51

Source: Hunt's Merchants' Magazine, 1844, p. 462.

Orleans, not a rail city but a river city, fared best of all, experiencing the highest rate of growth from the expansion in cotton exports.

The clipper ship expanded trade because of its speed. Speed in transport and communication—in any form of action for that matter—became the new American way.

The masses of new immigrants, combined with corporate railroads spreading westward, created the growing belief that anyone could be successful in America—where acquiring property was proof of success.

The Capital Markets and Financial Disclosures

By 1850 a few railroad securities began to appear on the New York stock market. A following of trends led observers to comment that stocks were depressed in 1837 and 1842. The panic of 1837 was due, at its source, to the orgy of speculation and overexpansion through which the nation had been passing. More accurately, it was a hard currency, banking, and land speculation adjustment as opposed to a stock market–induced plunge. Even given all of its industrial expansion, the United States' wealth was tied to the use of land (i.e., to agriculture) and would be for decades to come. In this case, a rise in the price of cotton in 1835 caused thousands of southwestern planters to buy slaves and lands on credit, in the expectation of paying for them out of their profits. Banking controversies and the requirement that only hard money (specie in gold and silver) and not bank notes be accepted in payment for government lands led in turn to banks calling loans to accumulate money to meet their obligations. As poor crops were reported in 1835 and 1836 and as cotton merchants began to fail, New York banks suspended operations or failed. The aftermath of the panic, which was muddled through in a political fashion not unlike the 1980s savings and loan bailout, would not be resolved until the matter of banking system integrity was addressed independently from the politics of selecting lucrative depositories for public funds, a role that was standardized in "pet" state banks (Hockett 1936: 541).

The next panic, in 1857, triggered by the failure of the Ohio Life and Trust Company, was due to excessive importation of foreign goods and also to the rapid construction of railroads, to a large extent on borrowed capital. The effect of the crisis on the majority of Stock Exchange properties was ruinous. Prices fell 50 percent in a few days, and many members of the board of brokers were obliged to go into involuntary liquidation (Clews

1887: 6). Only a new wave of popular bold speculation and the expansion westward with more railways (not to mention the impact of the Civil War) would help the market.

The source of much of this postcrisis fixed capital and working capital was England. "The United States have always obtained the use of much English capital, by means of debts contracted by their citizens to the merchants and manufacturers of Great Britain; but of late the amount has been greatly augmented, by means of loans made on the credit of the individual states or by the sale of stock of the chartered companies" (*Hunt's* 1840: 449).

Although the center of international finance remained in London, the New York Stock Exchange had been located permanently by 1863, denoting the establishment of a logistical pattern and a headquarters for American capital market activity. Boston-bred banking houses such as George Peabody and Junius Morgan's had already become a powerful rival to the Rothschilds', with Junius's son, J. Pierpont, basing his operations in New York City.

The capital requirements of the railroad versus the textile corporation were different and reflected changing attitudes regarding the manner of financing various forms of enterprise. Textile capitalism was regional, centered in the financial district of Boston and throughout the relatively close environs of New England. It relayed capital among families of established generations of New Englanders, bound in a common trust based on regional and personal acquaintance. The closely held, family ties of textile capitalism sharply contrasted with the sprawling, ever-westward-moving demand of railroad capitalism, which was linked with the coal, steel, and lumber suppliers across their routes and involved shippers and passengers, whose patronage would ultimately decide the outcome of their venture.

The origin of the financial reporting requirements of this era is based upon the assumption that creditors as well as investors and institutional sources of capital wanted to know financial information relating to their holdings. Furthermore, when equity and debt holders were both foreign (chiefly British) as well as domestic parties, the form and content of disclosure tended to respond to the needs and expectations of those parties. The British investor had come to appreciate the vagaries of the parliamentary direction of company law, beginning with the repeal of the "Bubble Act" in 1825, making limited liability company charters available, although with limitations and scant encouragement (Edwards 1980: vi). But by 1855, clear legal access to the limited liability form was available to Britons. British investors, since the provisions of the 1844 companies act, had begun to expect "a 'full and fair' balance sheet . . . to be presented at each ordinary meeting of shareholders . . . [and that] . . . auditors were to be appointed and their report on the balance sheet was to be read at the meeting" (Skinner 1987: 15–16). But though "legislators . . . believed, if we may take their words and actions at their face value, in the merits of accounting disclosure, they omitted to define in any clear way the form or content of the accounts that were to be prepared, or the valuation principles that were to be adopted. Nor were the duties of the auditors laid down in any detail. [And while several sound reasons existed for this open approach . . . t]here seems little doubt that it was an easy matter for the unscrupulous to violate the spirit of the legislation" or for the ignorant to avoid it (Edey et al. 1956: 356).

Widespread domestic ownership interest also spurred intrastate regulation of railway companies, creating, as never before, a need for internal auditing, annual reporting, and capital accounting.

In 1848 legislation in New York providing for the "formation of corporations for manufacturing, mining, mechanical, or chemical purposes" contained a limited, almost perfunctory, financial publicity-disclosure requirement in section 12, specifying the following:

> Every such company shall annually, within twenty days, from the first day of January, make a report which shall be published in some newspaper, published in the town, city or village, or if there be no newspaper published in said town, city, or village, then in some newspaper published nearest the place where the business of said company is carried on, which shall state the amount of capital, and of the proportion actually paid in, and the amount of its existing debts which report shall be signed by the president and a majority of the trustees; and shall be verified by the oath of the president or secretary of the said company, and filed in the office of the clerk of the county where the business of the company shall be carried on; and if any of said companies shall fail so to do, all the trustees of the company shall be jointly and severally liable for all the debts of the company, then existing, and for all that shall be contracted before such report shall be made. (*Hunt's* 1848: 440)

Significant litigation, if any, brought about by this law has not received attention, at least by accounting historians. What has been of more interest to litigation researchers relates to early dividend laws (e.g., capital maintenance and prohibition of dividends from contributed capital) and later, toward the close of the century, on the matter of depreciation and similar provisions in determining profits, dividends, and taxes (Reid 1988). Littleton reminds us: "In trying to understand the accounting ideas of the past century, the balance sheet theory of profit . . . may be further examined in its relation to the type of business enterprise concerned. The words of the courts' definitions of profits are better suited to the calculation of partnership than of corporation profit. Usually, in a partnership or single proprietorship, any undivided profits remaining at the end of the fiscal period are transferred to the capital accounts of the persons concerned. Thereafter, when another period has elapsed, the 'balance' of the balance-sheet measures current profit, because past profit has previously been merged with contributed capital" (Littleton 1933a: 217).

As to the legality of corporate capital and dividends, Kehl notes that "up to 1850 there had been scarcely a score of adjudicated cases dealing with the legality of corporate dividends. Yet . . . the fundamental concepts of modern dividend law had . . . already crystallized . . . in many American states" (Kehl 1939: 65).

For the multiplicity of reasons alluded to, railroading also created a demand for new business and management skills, including the services of an emerging class of accountants and auditors. In order to secure credit information about local merchants who visited New York from the Northeast and new West, a "mercantile agency" was established in New York in 1841. This agency was the forerunner of what was eventually purchased by R. G. Dun (*Dun's Review,* first published in 1893, and namesake of Dun and Bradstreet) and is regarded as having gained sufficient stature to have "influenced the direction and volume of . . . credit" (Moody 1980: 141).

As the joint-stock railroad company became an accepted institution for economic progress, the government poured 50 million acres of public domain into its pathway to augment development. Telegraphy and railroads provided a "one-two" communication-transportation punch that rocked the agrarian base of the nation and finally tumbled it firmly into the arms of merchants and manufacturers, who now had access to a national market being swelled by immigration and led westward by "manifest destiny" and the forty-niners in their quest for gold.

The financing of railroads required not only federal grants of land and investor equity but also loans and bank credit. Railroad bonds were sold by the millions, often without any promise that financial accountabilities would be provided. The capital markets, such as they were, whipped themselves in a railroading frenzy that was only outdone by state legislatures and local politicians who lent their influence in exchange for a part of the shareholdings. Lobbyists dispensed railroad securities to placate judges, legislators, mayors, governors, aldermen, or whoever may have represented opposition (Jenks 1944). Popular speculation in and uncontrolled distribution of these securities, together with the failure of many of these poorly conceived rail ventures, ultimately cast a pall over the markets, contributing to the panic in 1857 which, in the absence of the Bank of the United States, was unprecedented in severity. New York banks had acted to provide reserves in the absence of the national bank, but as the western inflow dried

up and western depositors began to call their reserves, New York speculators found that their money and margins had gone, and they were forced
to liquidate securities to repay called loans. Stocks were sold at any price. In
a week, thirteen leading issues dropped 40 percent; the best bonds were
down 10 percent. In six weeks, four major railroads had failed and the market was in collapse, as were the banks, for they had depended upon rail
securities for their own collateral.

Southern agriculture and the cotton crop survived the disaster; in fact
they had provided the economic stability to overcome the crisis. Yet even
after the market recovered, suspicion as to the motives and strategies of
northern industrialists remained among southern capitalists. Southerners
felt scorned because of the slavery issue, and resented their dwindling political influence. Popular suffrage was carrying political power away from the
South to the urban Northeast. The wealth of cotton was being displaced in
terms of control over the economic destiny of the country. The seeds of
suspicion and dissension were being sown (Schmidt 1939).

Accounting Education and Practice

These were novel times. Some writers would be satisfied with assigning
this period the title "Accounting in the Railroad Age" and in that context,
preparing an explanation of accounting. But this approach might not treat
accounting as a discipline itself. Therefore it is more to the point to discuss
the intrinsic elements of accounting during this period; namely, the methods of instruction, the state of thinking, and the types of practice, with railroad accounting as a consideration among the latter.[2]

The role of education, as viewed through the teachers and texts then will
be considered first, within the context of the higher educational system of
the time. Then financial accounting, auditing, and management accounting will be addressed, as well as instances of nonprofit accounting.

Proprietary Schools

Accounting and business education had not yet achieved acceptance in
university settings in the antebellum period. Instead, it met its demand
through proprietary private schools, first offered by individual entrepre-
neur-authors, and then by collections of business schools operating in commercial centers, made legitimate by their acceptance in the marketplace
and by national organizations (figure 3.1) that championed and identified their educational mission. Foster operated a "commercial school" in

Figure 3.1 *Harper's Weekly* Profile: Members of the International Business College Association, 1866. *Source: Harper's Weekly* (October 13, 1866: 653).

Boston from 1834 to 1837, moving then to New York City and opening "Foster's Commercial Academy" at 183 Broadway. Bartlett operated out of Philadelphia and later Pittsburgh; Thomas Jones, in New York City; Comer began his "Institute" in 1849, and others mentioned below added to the commercial school movement through the decades up through the Civil War (Reigner 1958; Stone 1986).

Changes in traditional collegiate education were opposed by some faculties and fostered by others. An 1828 report of the Yale faculty noted, for instance: "The course of instruction which is given to the undergraduates in the college, is not designed to include professional studies. Our object is not to teach that which is peculiar to any one of the professions; but to lay the foundation which is common to them all" (Day 1829).

Education norms during this period were described by a writer in *Hunt's* in 1843. One in every eight persons had a primary education; one in every ninety had a grammar school–academy education and one in every 900 had achieved schooling in college (1843: 54–56). Mercantile education was deemed incomplete and shallow and reflected attitudes such as: "I wish my boy to learn arithmetic and writing; but I do not care about his studying any foreign language, or to take up time with history; for I am going to make a merchant of him" (*Hunt's* 1844: 143).

Teachers and Textbooks

In the East, teachers and writers on the subject of accounts already had been active for several years. Among the most notable were C. C. Marsh, E. G. Folsom, Thomas Jones, Benjamin F. Foster, H. B. Bryant, H. D. Stratton, and S. S. Packard. Perhaps the most notorious and mysterious author of the period was John Caldwell Colt, brother of Samuel Colt, namesake of the Colt revolver. J. C. Colt was convicted of murdering the publisher of his accounting book and then died mysteriously (some alleged he disappeared) before his scheduled execution (Ross 1974; Goldberg and Stone 1985).[3]

Thomas Jones is arguably the most important; Benjamin Franklin Foster of Boston, New York, and later London, the most colorful and controversial, was a competitor and imitator of Jones (Hughes 1982). The most successful in terms of recognition and influence may have been Bryant, Stratton, and Packard. Their chain of business colleges, some of which continue as proprietary schools today, influenced generations of young people, as did their texts. Other important proprietary school leaders include R. M. Bartlett of Philadelphia, George Comer of Boston, Peter Duff of Pittsburgh, George Soulé of New Orleans, and E. K. Losier of Baltimore.[4] In the 1860s the owners of proprietary schools were meeting on a national basis, providing a basis for interchange and for comparing educational norms.

By the 1840s, Colt, Jones, and Foster and many others had brought forth several editions of their works on double entry as part of the wave of text-books being used by the masses of students enrolled in business and commercial colleges. Stone refers to Jones as the author of the first book worthy of being called an *accounting* text (Stone 1982C).

The decade of the 1850s represents an important initial point of commercial education in the "new West." On May 9, 1851, E. G. Folsom, professor of the science of accounts, incorporated his Mercantile College to be opened in Cleveland. Among Folsom's first students were H. B. Bryant and H. D. Stratton, who later acquired the Folsom College and developed an international chain of more than fifty commercial colleges, leading the growth movement in business education from 1853 to 1866 (Corfias 1973).

The relationships established among Soulé, Stratton, Bryant, Folsom, Packard, and others were furthered by their participation in national organizations such as the International Business College Association. They also made use of one another's names in the context of assigned problem materials in their individual texts, undertook joint authorship of books and co-ownership of business colleges, supporting a view that this group of teachers and authors constitutes an antebellum school of American accounting writers (Previts and Sheldahl 1988). Examining their writings establishes that they were aware and critical of many of their peers' works, from Bennet(t) to Marsh to Jones, whose innovation of a real and nominal account system gave rise to processes such as columnar worksheets and summaries, which in turn facilitated the regular preparation of statements (Hatfield 1977; Homburger and Previts 1977).

Practice Issues

Correspondence among the newly developed community of commercially trained accountants was beginning to surface in the form of articles and reviews appearing in business magazines. *Hunt's* contained many commentaries and problems related to bookkeeping and accounts. An 1850 issue included even the following:

The Poetry of Bookkeeping

Attentive be, and I'll impart
What constitutes the accountant's art.
This rule is clear: what I receive
I debtor make to what I give.
I debit Stock with all my debts,

And credit it for my effects.
The goods I buy I debtor make
To him from whom those goods I take;
Unless in ready cash I pay,
Then credit what I paid away.
For what I lose or make, 'tis plain,
I debit Loss and credit Gain.
The debtors' place is my left hand,
Creditor on my right must stand,
If to these axioms you'll attend,
Bookkeeping you'll soon comprehend,
And double-entry you will find
Elucidated to your mind.

An early problem printed in *Hunt's* was submitted by Thomas Jones and represented an attempt to test the skill level of accounting readers. *Hunt's* also contained reviews of new accounting texts. In an 1839 number, for example, a detailed, laudatory review of the fourth edition of J. C. Colt's *The Science of Double-Entry Bookkeeping* was included, a portion of which stated: "In a commercial community like ours, the scientific mode of keeping accounts is a study of surpassing interest. For many years it has attracted attention commensurate with its importance. At the present moment, when our mercantile concernments are so widely extended, and when consequently the qualifications for success must so far exceed those formerly demanded, the mysteries of Bookkeeping have excited such increased notice, that the press swarms with commentators." This anonymous review of Colt's book notes that the work provided a number of "practical models" for keeping books that had never been given by any writer before Colt.

Hunt's was also a forum for the early views of nineteenth-century American accounting theorists. Thomas Jones, for example, who is acknowledged by Henry Rand Hatfield and others as being perhaps the first American to distinguish clearly between real and nominal accounts, wrote a series of articles in *Hunt's* on education and instruction on the general principles of the discipline that was becoming fundamental to the emerging industrial style of life. Thomas Jones pointed out: "The object is not to make every man a bookkeeper, but to make him competent to understand whatever accounts may come under his notice, and to detect and expose erroneous results, however ingeniously they may have been drawn" (Jones 1842). Another instructive episode relating to the state of practice is reflected in the outcome to a challenge problem prepared by J. W. Wright for the July 1844 issue of *Hunt's*. The problem involved a partnership dissolution and the remaining partner's inability to close the books. In September 1844, Wright wrote the editor, stating: "Sir—the receipt of forty-three communications, ineffectually attempting to solve my 'Question for Accountants,' in your last number, has placed me in possession of the absolute existence of facts, with which I have long since been but partially impressed, namely, that the generality of our public teachers of bookkeeping, and, as a legitimate consequence, our private accountants, are lamentably deficient in a thorough knowledge of the theoretical laws and practical adjustments of complex accounts, . . . How strange that no two of your correspondents agree, either in details or aggregate results!"

The public instruction of accounting and the commercial college movement criticized by J. W. Wright received a major impetus from the efforts of Bryant and Stratton, the two young men who studied under Folsom in Cleveland. Their chain of schools, numbering close to fifty by 1865, and the texts they supplied became the mechanism for a uniform manner of instructing the "uneducated" about accounting.

The task of writing the premier text for the chain was undertaken by Silas S. Packard, a proprietor of one of the franchise schools. Packard lived to become acknowledged and celebrated as one of the most influential business educators of the nineteenth century. His *Counting-House Bookkeeping* became a standard work abroad as well as in America. It was an ambitious and highly practical undertaking, not unlike the intermediate textbooks of our contemporary programs, but of course, designed to function in the discipline of a nineteenth-century environment. Packard's *Counting-House* covered a breadth of topics, describing the principal books of account and discussing dividend policy for joint stock companies within the 350-page content. There was also material related to "specialized" accounts including farms, banks, and commission houses as well as proprietor, partnership, and agency accounts.

Jones and Foster

The teaching and writing careers of Thomas Jones and Benjamin Franklin Foster coincide over nearly four decades, beginning in the 1830s. Jones is considered to be the first modern American accounting text author, because he sought to abandon the "rote and rule" approach to education, insisting that financial statements, rather than ledger balances, were the purpose of the account-keeping process.[5]

Jones's attention to statements is evident in the examples shown below in his 1859 work, *Bookkeeping & Accountantship*[6] (see figure 3.2). Jones's system of focusing on the financial statements plus his emphasis on the "merchant's position" affords him the unique role of being a leading, if not the

PART I.

SECTION I.

EXEMPLIFICATION.

BOOK-KEEPING implies a systematic arrangement of mercantile transactions, the purpose of which is to afford at all times ready access to the Resources and Liabilities of the party whose operations are recorded, thus :

RESOURCES.		LIABILITIES.		
Cash	5,850	*Bills Payable*, outstanding		3,000
Bills Receivab e	3,800	*I owe James Blackwell*		1,000
George Irving owes	1,000	*Total Resources,*	11,150	
Ira Perego "	500	" *Liabilities,*	4,000	
		My present worth is		7,150
	$11,150			$11,150

Each particular item of the above forms the subject of an *"account"* (see definitions), thus there is one account of Cash, another account of Bills Receivable, another of Bills Payable, another for James Blackwell ; so that the statement of Resources and Liabilities can at any time be drawn up by reference to the book of accounts called the Ledger, and the whole art of Book-keeping is merged in the peculiar arrangement of this book.

There are but two methods of Book-keeping in use, the one called Single, and the other Double Entry.

Single Entry affords only the above statement ; but when accounts have been arranged by Double Entry, they enable us, by additional accounts, to draw up another statement, viz. of the Profits and Losses resulting from the same operations, for example :—

LOSSES.			PROFITS.	
On *Railroad Stock*		850	On *Merchandise*	1,950
Business Expenses		579	" *Bank Stock*	500
Total Gain	2,579		" *Exchange*	129
Total Loss	1,429			
Net Profit		1,150		
		$2,579		$2,579

Capital at commencement	.	.	.	.	6,000	
Net Profit	.	.	.	.	.	1,150
	Present worth	.	.	.	$7,150	

Figure 3.2 Initial text page from a nineteenth-century bookkeeping text by Thomas Jones of New York

first, expositor of proprietary accounting per se in the first half of the nineteenth century. Jones, like his peers, including C. C. Marsh, contributed to the transition from traditional merchant accounts "toward an accounting system better suited to (the) emerging industrial and corporate economy" (Sheldahl 1988).

Benjamin Franklin Foster acknowledged "borrowing" Jones's ideas. (He "confessed" to having copied the principal feature of his own system from Jones in a letter to Jones dated August 1, 1838, and published on the back page of Jones's 1859 edition of *Bookkeeping & Accountantship*.) Foster marketed the system to the far corners of the North Atlantic community, for he was a prolific writer. Foster probably carried the Jones technique to more people than would have otherwise been done and thereby advanced the state of the art, albeit with dubious credit.

An Early History

Foster made a useful archival-type contribution in his 1852 volume, *The Origin and Progress of Bookkeeping*. As are most inveterate accounting writers, Foster was a bibliophile, and his pride in having amassed an impressive collection of early works probably caused him to write this slim 54-page work, which was an annotated bibliography and a listing of the books in his personal collection plus several he had not collected but had reviewed. The work is of value because it provides a unique and important historical reference point, listing more than thirty texts written in the first half of the nineteenth century by American authors, and providing a total list of 156 books for the period 1543 to 1852.[7]

Steamboats and Stagecoaches

Americans have seemed, at least for the last century or so, to be fascinated with the means of transport and the speed with which distance, any distance, can be covered. Perhaps because such a vast continent lay before them, it was not unusual to have such a preoccupation with distance and speed. And then as today, transportation businesses required a specialized accounting.

The steamboat was the premier means of transport for Americans until it was eclipsed by the flexible and speedy service of the railroad. Among the early publications on steamboat accounts were *The Steam Boat Clerk* (1839) by Stone and *The Western Steamboat Accountant* by Peter Duff, which appeared in 1846 (Flesher, Soroosh, and Givens 1986). The book included "a new and complete system of bookkeeping; arranged and practically adapted for the use of steamboats navigating the great western rivers and lakes, exemplified in one set of books kept by double entry . . . designed for the use of schools, bookkeepers, steamboat masters and owners." It seems reasonable to assume that this book and a subsequent revision, *The Steamboat Accountant,* were developed as part of the curriculum of Duff's Mercantile College, which had been established in Pittsburgh in 1840, offering instruction "in mercantile and steamboat bookkeeping" (Givens 1980).

Among early transportation company reports are those of the 1864 operations of Wells Fargo, then a stagecoach and express company. The frequent mentions of holdups and loot recovered from bandits, along with rewards and arrests, paint a vivid picture of the "Old West" by means of the 1864 income statement (see figure 3.3).

By 1840, a total of $150 million already had been invested in railroads in twenty-four states or territories. Fueled by anthracite coal, first mined in 1820 (365 tons) and at levels exceeding 800,000 tons per year by 1840, steam power would be the energy form of the age of the iron horse.

Early railroad accounts such as the Utica & Schenectady report of 1841 (table 3.2) were cash basis summaries with an overtone of statistical operating information. Previous historical research in the matter of early railroad reports suggests that, in part because of this emphasis on reporting and analyzing cash from operations, eventually the "funds" statement and the statement of cash flows developed (Rosen and DeCoster 1969).

By 1842, the Utica's report (table 3.3) is reflective of the "where got–where gone" cash analysis format (Boockholdt 1977). The 1842 report covered the entire period of the company's operation and follows an arrangement believed to be fairly standard for the next several decades. Another example of the general receipts and expenditures format, as commonly found before the middle of the century, is supplied in the 1846 report of the South Carolina Railroad (table 3.4). This report, as the others, was published in a financial periodical, and employs a single receipts and expenses aggregate format for each semiannual period of operation.

Evidence of the development of accrual accounting is also found in the accompanying property statement for the South Carolina Railroad (table 3.5). Note the final item in the credit portion of the statement before the totals.

Audits and Early Annual Reports

The geographic dispersion of railroad operations made it desirable to have traveling auditors conduct purely financial audits for the principal

Other Credits

Overland Mail Co., rent and commission	$ 900.00
Special contract, Virginia City	1,777.77
Revenue taxes	12,000.00
Washoe robbery, bullion recovered	3,430.79
Claim against insurance company for genl. avge. St. Oregon remitted to Treasurer for credit of California	4,042.82
Express earnings for year	188,255.10
Total Credits	$210,406.48

Charges

Robbery, express box. A. Austin		$ 1,522.34
Genl. Avge. Str. Oregon [?]		4,042.82
Reward for arrest and conviction of Fiddletown robbers		1,000.00

Coulterville robbery:

Willowman Bros. Company	$ 306.00	
Sullivan & Cashman	1,100.00	
D. N. Field	248.00	
Expenses--July	44.00	
Reward to sheriff	500.00	
Expenses--August	565.00	
Expenses--September	175.00	2,938.00

Washoe Road robbery:

Donahoe & Ralston Co.	534.85	
Levy & Company	700.00	
J. C. Dagley	50.00	
No. Kee & Company	236.00	
H. Kohn & Company	500.00	
F. Garasche	2,240.00	
Reward for post[age?] recovered	2,179.30	
D. B. Sullivan	70.00	
Owens M. Co.	140.00	
Rewards--July	1,790.73	
Expenses--August	702.50	
Reward for robbers killed at San Jose	1,500.00	
Sheriff, expenses	263.08	
I. C. Goods--Lawyer	645.00	
Attorneys in cash Washoe	1,175.00	$ 12,726.46

Old padkages sold for charges	$ 783.35
Silver Bar lost, Washoe stage	1,944.08
Robbery, Aurora express	645.00
Hanford arrest--excaped convict	105.00
Total Charges	$ 25,707.05
Balance Profit and Loss Account	$184,699.43

Figure 3.3 Wells Fargo's 1864 Income Statement. "The profit and loss statement for 1864 . . . shows considerable attention to robberies. Apparently the bookkeepers could find no account in which they could enter the cost of robberies. One thing seems obvious from this statement: Wells, Fargo & Company did not hesitate to spend money to track down robbers or to recover stolen treasure. Also, it is interesting to note that, with silver at roughly $1 an ounce, that particular bar of silver weighed about 125 pounds. One wonders what happened. It should be hard to *lose* a 125-pound bar of silver." (Noel Loomis, *Wells Fargo* [New York: Crown, 1968]. Copyright © 1968 by Noel M. Loomis; used by permission of Crown Publishers.)

TABLE 3.2
Utica and Schenectady Railroad, Report of the Treasurer, 1841

THE CAPITAL OF THE COMPANY IS 20,000 SHARES		$2,000,000
THE TOTAL COST OF THE ROAD, FROM ITS COMMENCEMENT		
TO THE 1ST JAN. 1841, INCLUDING THE RIGHT OF WAY,		
$322,470, AND THE PURCHASE OF THE MOHAWK TURNPIKE,		
$62,500, WAS		1,901,785
THE CALLS ON STOCKHOLDERS HAVE BEEN	$1,500,000	
DITTO, DERIVED FROM DIVIDENDS	300,000	
		1,800,000
THE AMOUNT RECEIVED FROM PASSENGERS, THE MAIL		
AND ALL SOURCES IN 4 YEARS AND 5 MONTHS, FROM		
COMMENCEMENT OF ROAD TO 1ST JAN., 1841		1,618,517
THE TOTAL EXPENSES DURING THE SAME PERIOD		552,598
NETT EARNINGS, 71 PER CENT ON 4½ YEARS		1,065,919
THE DIVIDENDS DECLARED TO 1ST JAN. 1841,		
BEING EQUAL TO 13½ PER CENT PER ANNUM		
ON THE CAPITAL FO $1,500,000, DURING		
4½ YEARS		917,000
THE TOTAL COST PER MILE OF THE 78 MILES		
INCLUDING MOTIVE POWER, RIGHT OF WAY AND		
TURNPIKE, IS		
	$23,580	
OFF RIGHT OF WAY AND TURNPIKE	4,934	
		18,446

Source: Hunt's Merchants' Magazine, May 1841.

TABLE 3.3
Utica and Schenectady Railroad, Report of the Treasurer, 1842

AMOUNT RECEIVED FOR INSTALLMENTS OF STOCK		$1,800,000.00
" TRANSPORTATION OF PASSENGERS		1,864,691.53
" " U.S. MAIL		83,047.10
" TOLLS OF MOHAWK TURNPIKE		22,834.78
" INTEREST ON MONEY DEPOSITED		10,226.87
" FROM MISCELLANEOUS SOURCES		49,134.71
TOTAL RECEIPTS FROM ALL SOURCES TO DEC. 3, 1841		$3,829,934.99
DEDUCT EXPENDITURES FOR ALL ACCOUNTS UP TO DEC. 31, 1841, VIZ:		
ON CONSTRUCTION ACCOUNT	$1,968,022.17	
ON TRANSPORTATION ACCOUNT	709,230.12	
ON DIVIDEND ACCOUNT	1,017,000.00	
TOTAL EXPENDITURES	3,694,252.29	
BALANCE, BEING EXCESS OF RECEIPTS OVER		
EXPENDITURES UP TO DEC. 31, 1841		$ 135,682.70

Source: Hunt's Merchants' Magazine, November 1843.

TABLE 3.4
South Carolina Railroad, General Statement of Receipts and Expenditures for the
Year 1846

GROSS RECEIPTS FROM ALL SOURCES IN FIRST HALF YEAR	$251,741.36
ORDINARY CURRENT EXPENSES FOR THE SAME TIME	193,592.21
NETT PROFITS FOR THE FIRST HALF YEAR	$58,149.15
GROSS RECEIPTS FROM ALL SOURCES SECOND HALF YEAR	$337,340.16
ORDINARY CURRENT EXPENSES FOR THE SAME TIME	224,578.96
NETT PROFITS FOR THE SECOND HALF YEAR	112,761.20
NETT PROFITS FOR THE YEAR 1846	$170,910.35

Source: Hunt's Merchants' Magazine, January 1848.

TABLE 3.5
South Carolina Railroad, Property Statement, December 31, 1846

DR.

TO STOCK—FOR $75 PER SHARE ON 34,800 SHARES		$2,610,000.00
" INSTALLMENTS FORFEITED		312,417.65
TO SURPLUS INCOME		40,708.52
TO BALANCE OF INDEBTEDNESS		2,765,090.74
TOTAL		$5,728,216.91

CR.

BY PURCHASE OF CHARLESTON AND HAMBURG RAILROAD, EMBRACING ROAD, MACHINERY, & C.	$2,714,377.50	
BY PURCHASE OF LAND ATTACHED THERETO	59,741.30	
" NEGROES	11,963.19	
		$2,736,081.99
BY CONSTRUCTION OF COLUMBIA BRANCH		2,863,654.49
BY LANDS PURCHASED SINCE JAN, 1844	5,083.83	
BY LESS TO CREDIT AIKEN LANDS	35.35	
		5,048.48
BY NEGROES PURCHASED SINCE JAN, 1844		800.00
BY SUSPENSE ACCOUNT		8,490.00
BY RAIL IRON PURCHASED		15,773.97
BY IMPROVEMENT OF DEPOTS		8,680.29
" PROPERTY		30,437.49
BY SHARES IN THE RAILROAD		40.00
BY AMOUNT DUE ON PAY-ROLLS AND BILLS NOT CHARGED, BUT FORMING PART OF BALANCE OF INDEBTEDNESS		9,210.60
TOTAL		$5,728,216.91

Source: Hunt's Merchants' Magazine, January 1848.

purpose of verification of the mathematical accuracy of accounts at branch locations. Methods of basic auditing included recalculation, comparison with standard railroad rate cards, ticking and checking of totals and cross totals. During the antebellum years, railroads performed many novel accounting tasks within the financial framework of the modern industrial corporate form of business (Boockholdt 1977). They dealt with the problems of expensive, widely dispersed rolling stock, "Round House" plant and maintenance costs, stock subscriptions, capital costs during construction, obsolescence from technology, and problems of long-term construction contracts. In their attempts to solve the complexities of these issues, accountants (or consulting accountants, as the more successful practitioners chose to call themselves) attained status as important advisors and experts on reports.

Cash-basis reporting was commonplace in these early corporate systems as evidenced in the prominence of cash statements, with reference to financial transactions of railroads being stated in terms of January 1 beginning cash balances and column details of cash receipts and disbursements leading to the December 31 cash balance.

Railroad Accounts

Mid-nineteenth-century New England railroad records provide several examples of reports and railroad auditor reports. In part to overcome the problem of control, railroads created divisional sections with superintendents in charge of each. A division had its own "accountants" who reported to a central treasurer's office. An auditing function existed for purposes of reviewing the treasurer's activities and reporting to the directors. It was common to find audit reports included in the annual report to shareholders in the years before 1860 (figure 3.4). In fact using the Massachusetts Western Railroad Corporation's annual report as a base, one finds an abundance of apparently well designed and meaningful detail on the operations of the corporation. The annual report of the Boston & Worcester Railroad for 1857 included a four-page auditor's report that was not only an "auditor's report" on the treasurer's accounts but an early form of an auditor's management letter on weaknesses, combined with recommendations for improvement, and indicative of a sophistication not found in accounting texts of the times (see figure 3.5). The auditor of today can point to this traditional involvement in an advisory role to identify important precedents for contemporary advisory services.

The widespread appointment of internal auditors among the railroads by the mid-nineteenth century has also been established. Special audits in

Auditor's Report

To the President and Directors
of The Western Rail Road.

GENTLEMEN:
In discharge of my duties as Auditor, I have once each month during the past year, thoroughly examined the Books of the Treasurer, ascertained that the amount of moneys received and paid out, were correctly entered upon his books from the proper vouchers in his possession, and that the balance represented to be on hand by his cash book, was actually on deposit in various Banks, as shown on the first day of each month by their accounts current and books of deposit.

A statement of transfers made and a balance sheet of the Stock Ledger has been handed in to you monthly by the Treasurer, examined and certified by me as correct. Having been engaged in making up the Dividends for the past three years, I can with confidence assert that the whole number of Shares issued by the Western Rail Road Corporation on which Dividends have been paid is 51,500.

The accounts of the Treasurer have been compared with those of the Cashier at Springfield and found to agree.

The books of the different Departments at Springfield and at the Stations on the Road are well kept, and written up to the end of the year.

Annexed you have a list of the uncollected freight at Stations for the year ending November 30, 1855, showing the amount unpaid on the 15th day of December to be $448.92.
Yours, Very Respectfully,

WILLIAM RITCHIE, Auditor.

Boston, Dec. 27, 1855

Figure 3.4 An auditor's report, 1855. *Source:* William Holmes, "Accounting and Accountants in Massachusetts" (part 3), *Massachusetts CPA Review* (May/June, 1975: 17).

cases where management employed external accountants to investigate internal frauds, such as that of the New York and New Haven in 1854, were also apparently commonplace (Boockholdt 1983).

Income Determination, "Net Income," and Disclosure

Antebellum accounting writers characteristically recognized a form of profit and loss account in their texts, but directors seemed to focus on the balance sheet. Littleton reports that the "method" of ascertaining net income in the middle of the nineteenth century, as found in railway reports and court cases, was to derive "net revenue" or "profit" as the residual amount or by product of balance sheet reports. He quotes a court case that asserts "it is only on that sort of statement (balance sheet) that you can draw

An Example of an Audit Comment Letter

Boston & Worcester Railroad,
Auditor's Office, Jan. 14, 1857

To the President and Directors:

Most prominent among the duties of this office, is that of examining and approving all the bills, pay rolls, or other claims against the Corporation, prior to their payment by the Treasurer.

In order to perform this duty satisfactorily, the Auditor ought to know personally the value of all articles purchased, or services rendered. . . .

As an additional protection against error, and to insure the means for immediate reference to the original account which has in any case been allowed, I have adopted a plan by which all the bills are retained in this office, and in their place a certificate sent to the Treasurer, which describes each one in a few words, and upon being receipted serves every purpose as proof of payment.

These certificates, as well as all other vouchers in the Treasurer's hands for charges on his books, have been examined both by the Auditor and Committee on Accounts, and found uniformly correct and satisfactory. . .

Another and important portion of an Auditor's duty should be to inform himself as to all the courses of revenue, and see that each produces its proper amount.

Passengers

The amount to be received from Passengers and Freight constitutes the great bulk of income on all roads, and is affected primarily by the schedule of prices charged, that being determined by the Directors through the Superintendent.

Each of the departments is in charge of an efficient head, and in their respective offices it is ascertained whether the several agents on the road account for all the tickets or the freight bills with which they stand charged.

So far as the sale of tickets is concerned, there is no difficulty in imposing a sufficient check. But all passengers do not purchase tickets, and I believe their number increases year by year, and that the rule which has been made in regard to such is either of no use or not enforced.

In this respect I think there should be a change.

Figure 3.5 An example of an audit comment letter, 1857. *Source:* William Holmes, "Accounting and Accountants in Massachusetts" (part 3), *Massachusetts CPA Review* (May/June, 1975: 17).

continues

Freight

The quantity and price of freight to each station having been properly billed, and the agent is charged therefor, and then as the several sums due are collected and returned, they are checked off and the charge cancelled. . . .

It is very clear that a short road, at the terminus of a long line, cannot afford to incur large risks in the collection of monies of which so small a portion comes for its own service.

Such risk should either be avoided altogether, or shared by other parties to the same business.

Mail, Rents, etc.

The amount received for mail service is determined by contracts with the government, and requires but little notice.

The income from rents is becoming more and more important, and requires constant care.

A schedule of all property under rent is kept in this office, with which the collections are from time to time compared.

Sales of Old Materials

These sales are made only by the Superintendent, or under his direction.

The amount is returned through this office to the Treasurer, and by him credited to the proper accounts.

Transfers of Stock

All stock certificates signed by the President, are recorded in the Auditor's office, and copies kept of all transfers of stock by the Treasurer.

The stock ledger and dividend books have been carefully compared and found correct.

I annex the Treasurer's trial balance at the close of the month of November last, and a condensed statement of the financial condition of the Corporation on that day. . . .

All which is respectfully submitted.

David Wilder, Jr., Auditor

Figure 3.5 *Continued*

any rational conclusion as to whether or not there is a profit" (Littleton 1933A: 216). An example of another approach dates from as early as 1833 when the Baltimore and Ohio Railroad published a statement of receipts and expenses that concludes in a "bottom line" identified as "net revenue" (see table 3.6).

Even in England, where much of the capital for future U.S. expansion would be found, income reporting was not well established at this time. Generally no separate computation of net income was required. However, probably one of the more important reasons for the lateness of the acceptance of the income statement is the difficulty experienced in defining net income. As late as 1856, the Joint Stock Companies Act in Britain contained no compulsory requirements concerning the statement of profit and loss (Hein 1978).

Net profit or loss, gain, net revenue, earnings, and similar terms reflecting various practices were used to convey the notion of net income. Insurance companies, engaged in life assurance or maritime business, frequently employed the term "net loss" or "net profits." The July 1841 issue of *Hunt's* described the following related to fifteen Boston-based maritime insurance companies:

Amount Insured	$ 344,661,909
Nett premiums thereon,	$ 5,701,582
Actual losses,	$ 5,778,288
Showing a clear nett loss of	$ 76,706

The search for a standard term to represent the "net results of business operations" would continue for decades to come, and the discourse could be found even in the 1862 Congressional Record as to a basis for taxation, viz:

Mr. Dixon: I wish to ask the Senator if he understands that in making up the income the amount of the debt is deducted?

Mr. Fessenden: Certainly.

Mr. Dixon: Then why not say in the outset of the bill "net income"? You do not say that.

Mr. Sherman: I would not say any thing about it. "Income" is a word that has received a definite construction, not so much in the laws of the United States as the general and commercial law, and especially the law of England. . . . If you said "net income" that would mean income after paying personal and household expenses. . . . The purpose, I understand, is to reach a man's

TABLE 3.6
Baltimore and Ohio Railroad Co., Receipts and Expenses, 1833

General Statement of Receipts and Expenses of the Baltimore and Ohio Rail Road Company, from the 1st October, 1832, to the 30th September, 1833.

Expenditures			Receipts	
Expenses of Transportation—			Revenue from Tonnage,	$112,446.48
Amount disbursed by the Superintendent of Transportation, for this account,		$83,880.75	do. Passengers,	83,233.26
Repairs—				$195,679.72
Amount disbursed by the Superintendent of Machinery, for repairs of Coaches, Wagons and Locomotive, and for use of same;—for cost of Oil, together with salary of said Superintendent,	$15,450.57			
Amount disbursed for repairs of Railway, during the 1st, 2nd and 3d quarters of past year, by the Superintendents of Construction; and during the 4th quarter, by the Superintendent of Transportation,	$31,553.04	47,003.61		
Estimated wear and tear, &c. of Horses and Harness, together with salary of Superintendent of Transportation		7,600.00		
Net Revenue		57,195.36		
		195,679.72		$195,679.72

Source: Adapted from R. Vangermeersch, Academy of Accounting Historians, Working Paper No. 38, Richmond, VA, 1979.

income. That embraces everything he receives, deducting what he pays out for interest and the like—everything he receives from his property, without making deduction for personal expenses. (Langenderfer 1954: 284)

In the United States, this lack of standard terminology across the spectrum of practice foretold significant concerns given the forthcoming change from owner-manager/closely held operations to larger enterprises.

However, as sources of capital diverged geographically, moving from regional to national, and as competition for capital began, the use of a "net income type number" became more frequent. The usefulness of such a "net income type number" to serve as a capital allocation feature, in factors such as return on investment (ROI), price earnings (PE) ratios and, later, in earnings per share (EPS), would also begin to emerge. While it would not be until many years later that individuals like Moody standardized the analysis of railroad performance measures to assist in investment review, the early New England railroads, such as those represented in table 3.7, had already begun to be compared at regular intervals on the basis of net income with results being reported in periodicals such as *Hunt's Merchants' Magazine*. The use of the specific term "net income" in New England railroad reports can be dated to as early as 1842. It is evidence of the beginnings of the "bottom line" orientation of financial reports in the United States (*Hunt's* May 1843).

Antebellum Management Accounting: Silent, Dynamic Years

Given the political, economic, technological, and educational changes of the period, it could be expected that management accounting, in the demand/response sense, would also change rapidly, developing heretofore unknown properties. It was the advent of the modern business enterprise, and then the availability of the corporate form in manufacturing, that would establish the continuing need for internal accounting information for decision-making and control by using records and accounts to ascertain the direct labor and overhead costs of converting raw material to finished product (Johnson 1981). Garner (1954) provided a watershed work in *Evolution of Cost Accounting to 1925*, and in recent years, accounting historians have provided increasing information about nineteenth-century cost-accounting developments. Since the conclusion of Garner's research, the findings of many others have assisted in developing understanding of the evolution of cost processes as found in antebellum enterprises, such as textile mills. When the economic significance of the antebellum cotton

TABLE 3.7
Massachusetts Railroad Report, 1852

OPERATIONS OF THE RAILWAYS OF MASSACHUSETTS, 1852.
COMPILED FOR THE MERCHANTS' MAGAZINE BY DAVID M. BARFOUR, ESQ., OF BOSTON
FROM THE ANNUAL REPORTS TO THE LEGISLATURE.
In the following table, "Interest" and "Amount paid other Companies in tolls" for passengers and
freight, are not considered as running expenses, and are therefore deducted from the total of
expenses; and the "Amount paid other companies in tolls," and the amount received for
"Interest," are deducted from the total receipts.

| | Length in miles | | | | Receipts. | |
| | Of main roads. | Of branches. | Double track & sidings. | Cost. | From Passengers. | From freight and gravel. |
Names of railways.						
Worcester	45	24	59	$4,845,967	$424,714	$314,943
Western	155	..	62	9,953,759	615,481	685,063
Providence and Worcester	43	..	13	1,731,498	129,044	118,566
Worcester and Nashua	46	..	5	1,321,946	88,435	67,212
Fitchburg and Worcester	14	..	1	312,229	16,212	12,900
Connecticut River	50	2	8	1,801,946	124,788	93,237
Pittsfield and North Adams	19		1	443,678	17,532	21,963
Berkshire	21	..	..	600,000	.....	.....
Stockbridge and Pittsfield	22	..	..	448,700	.....	.....
West Stockbridge	3	..	..	41,516	.....	.....
Providence	41	12	23	3,546,204	256,423	155,029
Taunton Branch	11	1	1	307,136	46,648	27,985
New Bedford	20	1	1	520,476	73,544	31,914
Norfolk County	26	..	..	1,245,928	28,992	20,557
Stoughton Branch	4	..	1	93,433	6,371	5,534
Lowell	26	2	40	1,995,249	157,170	222,004
Nashua	15	..	17	651,215	48,901	73,201
Lawrence	12	..	2	346,063	28,446	8,495
Salem and Lowell	17	..	2	362,672	20,640	33,054
Stony Brook	13	..	1	265,813	.....	.....
Boston and Maine	74	9	46	4,092,927	422,868	220,595
South Reading Branch	8	..	1	236,227	15,326	7,949
Fitchburg	51	17	66	3,633,674	253,371	311,778
Vermont and Massachusetts	69	8	5	3,451,629	74,205	99,607
Harvard Branch	1	..	..	25,701	.....	.....
Lexington and West Cambridge	7	..	..	237,328	.....	.....
Peterboro' and Shirley	14	..	..	263,540	.....	.....
Eastern	55	20	21	3,621,874	384,798	69,974
Essex	20	1	3	609,007	21,082	10,076
Newburyport	15	..	1	255,614	14,283	4,036
Old Colony	37	8	17	2,293,535	209,122	93,496
Dorchester and Milton	3	..	..	124,718	.....	.....
South Shore	11	..	..	428,831	.....	.....
Fall River	42	..	5	1,050,000	132,907	88,556
Cape Cod Branch	28	1	2	633,907	40,487	18,685
Grand Junction	6	..	3	1,282,073	.....	3,000
Total	1044	106	407	53,076,013	3,641,790	2,819,409

Receipts			Expenses. Of					Net income
From mails, & c.	Total.	Of road-bed.	Of motive power.	Miscella-neous.	Total.	Net Income.	p.c. on cost.
$19,162	$758,819	$69,153	$71,386	$269,201	$409,740	$349,079	7.20
39,329	1,339,873	158,988	122,598	375,092	656,678	683,195	6.86
6,081	253,691	13,783	14,956	85,437	114,176	139,515	8.06
6,462	162,109	11,982	12,581	59,266	83,829	78,280	5.92
2,291	31,403	3,167	2,302	12,993	18,462	12,941	4.14
10,980	229,005	25,408	22,459	95,287	143,154	85,851	4.76
900	40,395	5,028	2,277	10,782	18,087	22,308	5.03
. . . . .	42,000	. . . . .	. . . . .	. . . . .	560	41,440	7.00
. . . . .	31,409	. . . . .	. . . . .	. . . . .	. . . . .	31,409	7.00
. . . . .	1,827	. . . . .	. . . . .	. . . . .	22	1,805	4.35
18,032	429,484	40,280	34,717	141,862	216,859	212,625	6.00
1,591	76,224	9,138	9,498	33,188	51,824	24,400	7.94
2,456	107,914	13,842	10,689	39,592	64,123	43,791	8.41
907	50,516	423	5,122	21,555	27,100	23,416	1.88
115	12,020	. . . . .	. . . . .	. . . . .	4,102	7,918	8.46
8,934	388,108	54,216	45,257	155,820	255,293	132,815	6.66
9,768	131,870	12,912	18,747	49,373	81,032	50,838	7.81
4,838	41,779	3,093	2,824	12,404	18,321	23,458	6.78
. . . . .	53,694	27,479	. . . . .	19,769	47,248	6,446	1.78
. . . . .	13,536	. . . . .	. . . . .	. . . . .	. . . . .	13,536	5.09
15,538	659,001	88,208	43,960	191,138	323,306	335,695	8.20
7,073	30,348	. . . . .	. . . . .	. . . . .	22,111	8,237	3.49
9,425	574,574	65,758	52,980	216,849	335,587	238,987	6.58
44,867	218,679	35,229	24,128	73,155	132,512	86,167	2.50
. . . . .	5,853	. . . . .	. . . . .	. . . . .	6,831	. . . . .	. . . .
. . . . .	7,480	. . . . .	. . . . .	. . . . .	450	7,030	2.96
. . . . .	16,102	. . . . .	. . . . .	. . . . .	2,150	13,952	5.29
44,201	488,973	33,883	39,785	145,329	218,997	269,976	7.45
5,560	36,718	6,320	3,959	24,258	34,537	2,181	0.36
. . . . .	18,319	205	1,343	11,758	13,306	5,013	2.00
6,184	308,802	39,118	24,114	132,069	196,301	112,501	4.95
. . . . .	7,630	. . . . .	. . . . .	. . . . .	42	7,588	6.00
. . . . .	24,680	. . . . .	. . . . .	. . . . .	. . . . .	24,680	6.00
7,476	228,939	27,014	25,391	77,451	129,856	99,083	9.44
1,571	60,744	6,218	6,071	18,398	30,687	30,056	4.74
. . . . .	3,000	857	. . . . .	16,270	17,127	. . . . .	. . . .
273,801	6,885,517	751,702	597,144	2,288,296	3,674,410	3211107	Av. 6.05

Note: Reproduced from the original by David A. Ozog, 1993. In reproducing this table, several footing and cross-footing errors were discovered on the orignal. This table shows the numbers as they appeared in *Hunt's Merchants' Magazine* in May 1853.

markets is contemplated, we begin to appreciate that cost-accounting practice in the mechanized ginning, spinning, and looming of cotton textiles was an early example of accounting in a high-technology, mass-production, capital-intensive industry, as the United States began to stir from being a rural-agrarian society to one of an urban and industrial character.

Integrating Cost and Financial Accounts

Writers have also found important evidence of early systems that pioneered integration of the cost and financial records in these mills. The import of this combination is held to be nearly as significant as the origin of the system of double entry itself: it represents a response to industrialism by development of a capacity within the double-entry system.

Cost procedures at the operations of Josiah Wedgwood and at Charleton Mills, both in England, provide examples of calculations and cost systems similar to those used in New England operations at about the same time (McKendrick 1970; Stone 1973). Johnson has noted that the Boston-based Lyman Mills operations used a double-entry cost-accounting system, integrating a work-in-process account, as early as 1856. By the end of this period, manufacturers' cost-accounting practices had matured into systems for purposes of inventory cost and prime cost collection.

Today, scholars study the origins of nineteenth-century cost managerial practices, perhaps especially those practices whose relevance is now challenged. In recent years, the writings of Kaplan (1984) and Johnson and Kaplar (1987) have raised interest in the subject. It now seems appropriate to interpret evidence that nineteenth-century cost-keeping was sophisticated, to the point that it assisted management control practices, included departmental cost allocations, and aided, in Britain, for example, in decisions about selections of technology (Tucker 1981; Fleischman and Parker 1991).

Costing procedures continue to be discovered in a variety of industries and entities from the Massachusetts ice trade (Kistler, Clairmont, and Hinchey 1984), to southern logging operations (Flesher and Flesher 1980), to Chickering's piano manufactory (Kornblith 1985), to paper and textiles mills (Lubar 1984; McGaw 1985), all in the private sector, and in arms-making in the government sector. Costing at the armories at Springfield, Tyler, and West Point was considered to be among the most sophisticated applications prior to 1840, but the systems at these locations were not as yet an established part of the managerial process (Hoskin and Macve 1988; Tyson 1990).

"It is . . . a striking fact that cost literature of this period is very scarce"

(Garner 1954: 29). If antebellum management accounting did not achieve an established state, it may have been due to the lack of such literature and institutional opportunities for sharing knowledge, perhaps because of the proprietary nature of applications. If such matters were kept "secret" to avoid providing techniques that would assist rival firms, the lack of published works is to be expected. Yet, even when early cost practices were described in texts, this exposure was not found to be influential (Mepham 1988). The silence, then, should not be taken to mean that cost accounts were not being kept in a progressively improving fashion. But the silence suggests that, in the antebellum era, industrialism was second in significance to mercantile interests, and accounting attention was still focused on the latter. A comment in the first issue (January 3, 1857) of *Harper's Weekly* supports this view:[8] "We are a nation of shopkeepers, and none the worse for that. . . . It is very important, then, for us to sustain a good commercial name; and to do this, we must take care that the debit does not overbalance the credit account in our ledgers. If we allow too large a margin for our expenses, we shall be sure, whatever may be the profits of dry goods and hardware, to fall short in the final account with our creditors."

Yet research suggests that cost accounts were becoming an important part of the nascent American system of manufacturing in which interchangeable parts in cleverly designed products, such as clocks, could also be adjusted as an integral part of the manufacturing process (Hoke 1989). This was indeed a dynamic period of experimentation and development in cost accounting throughout the economy. The attention to cost-keeping found in the variety of industries for which studies now exist suggests that regular cost-keeping, albeit specific to each entity, was a general practice in those nineteenth-century American businesses that were the forerunners of modern enterprises.

Taxation, Governmental Accounting, and Nonprofit Accounting

With the advent of Federalist policies and national government control over a public debt, the role of accounting in the public sector continued to expand, particularly with the passage of a personal income tax to fund the cost of the Union effort during the Civil War. Financing the war through taxes and controlling public expenditures were problems creating unique demands upon those who were trusted with public accounts. States and their growing municipal subareas faced the problems of providing regulatory controls over public utilities, including railroads and other transport operations. As the need for government activities grew, so did the need for tax bases from which to draw revenue. Although there was a traditional dislike among people and politicians toward "internal" taxation, sole reliance on tariff duties for revenue was proving to be inadequate.

Taxation

Under the Federalist leadership of Alexander Hamilton, an early internal tax was levied on whisky but was repealed by the opposing party when they came to power in the political aftermath of the Whisky Rebellion. Nevertheless, an important precedent had been set, and the federal government had made clear its power to levy internal duties in case of need. The rising trade and its positive effect on custom collections, supplemented by public land sales and ultimately the sale of public debt via treasury notes, as originally devised by Hamilton, afforded the central government the funds to survive the periods of need during the War of 1812, the panic of 1837, and the Mexican War. When the Civil War commenced with the firing on Fort Sumter on April 12, 1861, the Union forces met several early setbacks, and a need for internal taxes became inevitable in view of the changed expectations regarding the duration of the hostilities.

The program of Lincoln's treasury secretary, Salmon P. Chase, was to finance the war through direct taxes on income. The tax bill passed by Congress was intended to bring $20 million and was assessed on free and slave states alike, to the amount of 3 percent on all income over $800 (Langenderfer 1954: 106). This established a precedent for keeping personal records and signaled the birth of tax accounting. Carter tells us that:

> The 1862 act adopted two rates of tax on residents, three percent on annual gains, profits or income between $600 and $10,000, and five percent above. A withholding tax system was imposed on civil and military government salaries, and on dividends and interest paid by railroads, banks, trust companies and insurance companies. . . . $37 million was collected in six months. . . . [A later] act increased the rate to 10 percent with great progressivity. The original act had allowed deduction for federal, state and local taxes. Later acts increased the number of deductions to mortgage interest, repairs and losses from the sale of land. A deduction for house rent was extended to all persons whether paid or not.

Further,

> The Act of 1862 taxed estates on the transfer of personal property in excess of $1000. . . . Anticipating another later rule, the Treasury decreed that the tax applied to transfers intended to take effect after death. (Carter 1986: 26)

Governmental Accounting

For the most part, industrial cities in America were an entirely new phenomenon. The financing and fiscal administration of the growing cities and towns during this period is less than well documented. Political "bosses" in many of the eastern cities were in control of the ballot mechanisms necessary to ensure their power. Municipal governments were ill prepared to construct administrative safeguards to ensure a proper measure of public safety and welfare. In the four decades spanning the pre–Civil War era, the new Midwest's urban population increased from about fifty thousand to more than a million persons (Dodd and Dodd 1976). The previous methods of government and taxation seemed inadequate and corrupt under the spoils system and "machine" politics. In part, city governments failed because they lacked a "doctrine" that could serve as the basis of appeal for recognition from the legislature and the courts. Lacking the vehicle of widespread municipal incorporation and a budgetary process, municipal executives were unable to act effectively, for they had no basis to coordinate planning, control, and execution. But although municipal governments were unsound, it would be nearly a generation before their situation would become so chaotic as to render reform essential.

Nonprofit Accounting

Congregations, such as the Shaker communities at Pleasant Hill, Kentucky, maintained complete systems of accounts over the period 1830 to 1850 (Kreiser and Dare 1986). The concept of auditing within these organizations was also found in community covenants, although audit records have not been located (Faircloth 1988). While Shaker accountability over their temporal affairs was modeled in double-entry form, it differed importantly from commercial accounting since no individual property was held, and property rights resided in the community as a whole.

Antebellum Accounting Theory

Economic historians summarize some of the accounting issues of this period as follows: "The industrial revolution . . . had much the same impact on business record keeping . . . as did the earlier commercial revolution. . . . To facilitate the raising of funds, the corporation form of organization was widely adopted. . . . The corporation's continuous life, as well as the limited liability of its owners, required that great care be taken to distinguish between invested capital and earned income. . . . If income and capital (were) to be kept separate, production cost during each accounting period must fairly accurately reflect the depreciation . . . of fixed assets" (Levy and Sampson 1962: 397).

Addressing matters related to accounting for fixed assets was a common issue found in early railroad reports and trade journals. The 1833 annual report of the Baltimore & Ohio devoted a section of its annual report to considerations of renewal cost of trackage, given an estimated life of twelve years. The annual provision was expressed in terms of an annuity "reckoning compound interest at 5 per cent." A Reading Railroad report in 1839 noted "Repairs and depreciation of engine and tender estimated at 25 per cent on cost, $8,000" (Mason 1933: 211). Depreciation accounting, as we would know it, was not accepted practice, however. Many railroads, such as the Boston and Providence, adopted the retirement method of accounting for fixed assets, which was the most widespread theory from the mid-nineteenth century until the early twentieth (Boockholdt 1978). Accountants by midcentury commonly used specialized books and columnar analysis sheets, abetted by the emerging technology of paper products, which made supplies of innovative stationery products readily and cheaply available (Sheldahl 1985B: 139).

During this age, variety was a by-word in accounting practice. As noted above, solutions proposed to the challenge problem in *Hunt's* resulted in dozens of proposals, causing one writer to comment, "How strange that no *two* of your correspondents agree either in details or aggregate results!" (*Hunt's* 1844: 259). To which Heriot, the grandson of noted colonial accounting author Benjamin Booth, responded: "Books may be correctly kept in various ways, and the same transaction may be properly stated under different forms" (*Hunt's* 1844: 446).

Young people and immigrants aspiring to business and accounting enrolled at metropolitan proprietary business colleges to learn the ways of commerce. One such young man, later called "a bloodless . . . bookkeeper" by a wildcat oilman he had visited, was trained in the points of scientific accounting at Folsom's Business College in Cleveland in 1855. When a group of money men from Cleveland sent this prim twenty-one-year-old bookkeeper, John D. Rockefeller, off to assess the prospects for the commercial future of oil in Pennsylvania, a chapter of American history was begun (Cooke 1973: 259).[9]

Businessmen were not alone in their interest and exposure to accounts. Inventors and philosophers too felt the touch of accounting on their lives. George Eastman, the genius of modern photography, was born in Rochester in 1854 and began working as an insurance office clerk and ultimately became a junior bookkeeper in the Rochester Savings Bank.

BALANCE SHEET, LEGER, SET II.

Philadelphia, February 28th, 1852.	Leg.	Face of Leger.		Profit & Loss.		Stock.		Balance.	
		Dr.	Cr.	Dr.	Cr.	Dr.	Cr.	Dr.	Cr.
Stock	1		1,190 00				1,190 00		
Cash	1	6,561 92						6,561 92	
Merchandise	1	1,855 38		1,855 38					
Reading Rail-Road Stock	1	1,250 00	1,100 00	150 00				1,100 00	
Bills Receivable	1	3,340 64						3,340 64	
V. C. Burrell & Co.	2	596 50						596 50	
Bills Payable	2		7,680 00						7,680 00
Charles T. Mayland	2		2,300 00						2,300 00
Burgess & Pinkerton	2		565 56						565 56
Levi Williams & Co.	2		960 44						960 44
Evans, Peters & Co.	3		1,150 50						1,150 50
Profit & Loss	3	225 11		225 11					
Allen Thompson	3	18 75						18 75	
Discount	3		1 80		1 80				
		13,848 30	13,848 30						

By Stock, for Net Loss | | | | 2,228 69 | 2,228 69 | | |

| | | 2,230 49 | 2,230 49 | | | | |

Net Insolvency | | | | 1,038 69 |
| | 2,228 69 | 2,228 69 |

Total Resources and Liabilities | 11,617 81 | 12,656 50
Net Insolvency, as pr. Stock | 1,038 69 |
| 12,656 50 | 12,656 50 |

Figure 3.6 An example of a corporation worksheet, 1852. *Source:* S. W. Crittenden, *An Elementary Treaties on Book-Keeping by Single and Double Entry* (Philadelphia: W. S. Fortescue, 1877).

Books and ledgers of account were also becoming standardized in style in part because of the increasing availability of inexpensive paper account books and perhaps because of the influence of standardized instruction through widely marketed texts and chain-type proprietary business colleges.

The rote-work load of the bookkeeper was eased by improving the systematic approaches to recording journal entries in preprinted columnar books and by teaching various series of "recording rules" via textbook cases (see figure 3.6).

Commenting on the changes from a British perspective, one writer observed: "They began in the counting house as firm after firm found it necessary to adopt more sophisticated and accurate book-keeping systems, but by the middle of the nineteenth century questions of pure accounting came into prominence, as businessmen and legislators grappled with the problem of providing sufficient financial information for investors in public utilities and other joint stock companies" (Etor 1973: 38).

The vast array of commercial transactions sought out a form of quantification, summarization, and standardization that would assist in communicating the essentials of each business. It was a supreme challenge and opportunity for accounting teachers and practitioners to address.

With the advent of railroads and corporate stewardship, annual financial reports were becoming used for public summary reporting. Evidence of accrual accounting concepts in financial statements of railroads and in the texts of popular authors was also beginning to appear. Peter Hain reports that of some fifty texts published between 1788 and 1899, about one in ten mentions accrual or other balance sheet–type adjustments. Bryant and Stratton (*National Bookkeeping* 1861) show an item labeled "Interest payable on mortgage" and call it "a somewhat novel feature" (Hain 1972). This attention to the principle of accrual suggests that practicing accountants had stepped away from memorized and rote techniques when faced with complex transactions and unique economic consequences. Holmes supplies a lighthearted example of such early "conceptualizing."

> Interest and rents have been accrued for a long time, but other prepaid and deferred debits and credits are of comparatively recent origin. The earliest example I have been able to find in an American textbook is in Mayhew's *Practical Bookkeeping*, first published in 1851 out of Michigan. Many of Ira Mayhew's examples in his book are naturally related to farming. In one of his examples he charges the current year with only ¼ the expense of manuring, . . . because the land was permanently enriched, and the benefit will probably be realized in the next three crops to as great an extent as in this. It is hence apparent that but one-fourth of the expense of enriching should be debited to this crop.

> I find it entirely apropos that perhaps the first account to be thus deferred in America and spread from year to year should be Manure. (Holmes 1976)

Cochran's *Agricultural Book-keeping*, published in Detroit in 1858, indicates that specialized texts had come into being by the eve of the Civil War. Cochran used market price to value field crops at harvest time and supplied well thought out "time-tables" for recording labor and horse-team hours and cost to various farm enterprises (Stone 1982D).

Marsh's *The Theory and Practice of Bank Book-Keeping, and Joint Stock Accounts*, published in a series of editions in 1856 and after, is another example of specialized accounting texts of the period. It featured sample books of accounts for a bank, including teller cashbooks, general cashbooks, collection registers, and sample balance sheet and profit and loss statements. Reviewing, as a historical case study, the operations of an antebellum bank's accounting system in the 1840s, Razek concluded that the processes used represented a "rather sophisticated financial reporting system" resembling "those in use today by small financial institutions" (Razek 1987).

Accounting's Social Impact

Entrepreneurs such as Cyrus Field, the man who linked England and America with the Atlantic cable, had found in the meaning of accounts a message of fulfillment. By his use of an accounting expression perhaps we can begin to understand how deeply "accounts" had begun to affect the American lifestyle. As the story is told: "Field traveled tirelessly in the British Isles, selling his idea to financiers. Lord Clarendon, the British Foreign Secretary, was among many skeptics. 'Suppose you make the attempt but lose your cable on the ocean bottom? What will you do?' 'Charge it to profit and loss and go to work to lay another,' Field replied" (Fleming 1974).

Early nineteenth-century mercantile businesses also found guidance in their counting house records, and owners took pains that their journals and ledgers were kept secret and apart from the other business records. "Prior to the rise of the railroads, America's first truly big business, it was the owner who operated almost every business enterprise"—that is consistent with the popular perception that throughout this period, in most businesses, owners managed and managers owned their businesses. The end of the post–Civil War period would be the eve of "managerial capitalism," the rise of a professional management class and the separation of owning and managing (Tedlow 1985: 312). By the 1840s, specialization, the focusing upon a single function or product, had begun to affect even individually managed companies.

"By the time of the Civil War, salaried middle and top railroad managers—the first representatives of this new economic group in this country—had created organizational and accounting methods that permitted their enterprises to coordinate and monitor a high volume of traffic at a speed and regularity hitherto unknown" (Chandler 1977: 122). Chandler also asserts that by the 1850s, another major organizational change was under way in that internal business operations of larger organizations had replaced "the activities and *transactions* previously carried out by many small units" (Chandler 1977: 123). It was to be the cost accountants' challenge to address the vexing problem of sorting out these internal transactions with the same meaning and convention that had become accepted in accounting for the external transactions of businesses.

Harry Clark Bentley (1929), a twentieth-century New England accounting educator and author, contends that the developments and contributions by accounting writers during the first half of the nineteenth century surpassed those of the second. But Pilcher, writing in 1935, says, "The period 1860–1895 from the point of view of intellectual adventure is the most productive period of American accounting history" (Pilcher 1935). And it might also be argued that the two periods are intertwined and that a strict comparison may no longer be useful. The post–Civil War period, as a separate but related episode, will be considered in the next chapter.

Chapter 4   *1866–1896*

Accounting in the Gilded Age

> As more details are learned about the 1880's and the 1890's it
> becomes ever clearer that a great many occurrences in the last
> double decade of the nineteenth century played an important
> part in making it possible for accounting in the twentieth century
> to be what it is.
>
> **—A. C. Littleton (1946)**

The Political and Social Environment in the Gilded Age

Many consider the post–World War II period as a time of unprecedented
growth and change in American life. A study of the changing economic,
social, political, and technological environment of the post–Civil War era
indicates that these years were also ones of high opportunity, intense activity, and national achievement. A critical view of the "Gilded Age" infers
a corruption of the American dream by so-called robber barons, the rise of
giant businesses, new financial empires, and the immense profits from oil,
steel, and railroads. It suggests that the United States grew rich before it
became of age, and that its years of confidence came before its years of
maturity (Lerner 1957: 7, 200). Commentators of the time, such as Charles
Dickens, observed that there had never been an equal to American money-
mad materialism.

It was also an era of national fulfillment, of manifest destiny, signified
by joining East and West in 1869 at Promontory, Utah, by the driving of
the golden spike completing the first transcontinental railroad. The Gilded
Age witnessed a growing unity among farmers of the Great Plains with the
birth of the grange movement. In the East, it was a time of capital-intensive
industrialization and urbanization as steam and electric power and machinery brought about changes in the demand for labor. The South,
numbed by the consequences of the Civil War, underwent a period of "reconstruction."

World power was on the horizon as the American nation moved away
from a century-long tradition of isolation in global affairs. Inventions such

as the motion picture camera, first used on Broadway in 1894; the incandescent light, patented by Thomas Edison in the 1880s; and the telephone, first used in Boston in 1876, heralded consumer and communication changes of unparalleled dimension. It was also the era of Scott Joplin's ragtime, Mark Twain's humor, P. T. Barnum's showmanship, of depressions and panics in 1874, 1884, and 1893, of Victorian morality, and the birth of American golf, with the first membership club forming in New York City in 1888.

Youth found inspiration in "Horatio Alger" success stories about young people who turned pennies into fortunes through hard work and unceasing application of their talents in the marketplace. It was all at once the age of unbridled competition among vast, new enterprises and business trusts that sought to dominate the national market for goods, services, and power. Accounting came to be used as a "control over efficiency as well as a means of balancing books" (Cochran 1959: 63).

Cities swelled with the waves of Ellis Island immigrants, who had viewed the Statue of Liberty as they entered the New York harbor. The statue had been dedicated in 1886 as a gift from the people of France. In the thirty years spanning 1860 to 1890, America's population doubled from 31 million to 62 million (Schlesinger 1939: 132). By 1880, some business historians suggest, Americans had become a metropolitan economy, although the population had not shifted to a predominantly urban pattern and would not for another thirty years.

The ills of the age were many, despite the fact that the average per capita income for the populace of the United States had by the 1880s surpassed that of Britain to become the highest in the world. The concerns were depicted by those such as utopian author Edward Bellamy (*Looking Backward 2000–1887*). Bellamy foresaw a social order directed by one overarching trust operated and owned by all. This system would address the inequities he saw, as illustrated by his writing in 1887 as to the news of the world and the nation, as follows: "Foreign Affairs.—The impending war between France and Germany. The French Chambers asked for new military credits to meet Germany's increase in her army. . . . Great suffering among the unemployed in London. . . . Monster demonstrations to be made. Home Affairs.—The epidemic of fraud unchecked. Embezzlement of half a million in New York. . . . Clever system of thefts by bank teller: $50,000 gone. . . . Speculators engineering a great wheat corner at Chicago. . . . Large failures of business houses. Fears of a business crisis. . . . A woman murdered in cold blood for money in New Haven. . . . A man shoots himself in Worcester because he could not get work. . . . Startling growth of illiteracy in Massachusetts" (Bellamy 1887: 309).

Social Philosophy

During these decades before the turn of the century, businessmen were relatively unencumbered by government involvement. Americans held to a view of laissez-faire, the right of citizens to be left alone in their economic activities. This posture, combined with the rapid industrialization and growth of businesses, seemed justified in the hope of the benefits anticipated from economies of scale. Yet small firms, too, were growing rapidly. Firms of all types were increasing in number twice as fast as the population.

The model for the modern integrated industrial concern developed from the post–Civil War railroad merger movement, one of the most notable amalgamations being the creation of the New York Central System in 1867. Such combinations, it was argued, made it possible for faster service. Travel from New York to Chicago had been cut from fifty to twenty-four hours as a result of Cornelius Vanderbilt's consolidation of the Central. With the opening of the West, after completion of the transcontinental railroad in 1869, it became possible to benefit from the superior efficiency of large-scale rail operations. Passengers now could travel coast to coast in a week versus months by ship. But an indirect price for this speed and efficiency included abuses such as corruption of public officials involving grants of rights of way and manipulation of securities in unregulated stock markets. Furthermore, the incentive for improvement lay, not in the goal of service to the public, but in the achievement of monopoly over basic forms of transportation, goods, and services, which assured businesses a freer hand in setting prices in markets.

After the Civil War, the rise of a professional managerial class began to effect a transfer of business control from the owners to the managers of corporations. "In a word, top management determined the long-term objectives of the enterprise and allocated the resources in men, money, and equipment needed to carry out these goals" (Chandler 1977: 145). The major corporation acted to internalize activities previously provided by those outside the entity by smaller, less efficient units, thereby increasing operational efficiency.

The potential for growth and the prospects of unlimited business opportunity supported the popular sentiment for unrestricted individual freedom in business (Cochran and Miller 1942: 122–23). "From the late 1860s through 1893 the American economy grew at an unusually high rate. . . . These years were the heyday of the entrepreneurial firm" (Galambos and Pratt 1988: 26–27). The entrepreneur's role was nearly inviolable. This role and its ability to develop the promise of new ventures set the tone of the time. Schumpeter, writing many years later, described it as follows: "We have seen that the function of entrepreneurs is to reform or revolutionize the pattern of production by exploiting an invention or more generally an untried technological possibility for producing a new commodity or an old one in a new way. . . . To understand such new things is difficult and constitutes a distinct economic function . . . to act with confidence beyond the range of the familiar beacons and to overcome that resistance requires aptitudes that are present in only a small fraction of the population and that define the entrepreneurial function. The function does not essentially consist in either inventing anything or otherwise creating the conditions which the enterprise exploits. It consists in getting things done" (Schumpeter 1942: 132).

Despite the growth of and abuses related to big businesses, Americans initially eschewed direct government involvement in the conduct of business. Before the century ended, misdeeds identified with big business and laissez-faire such as cut-throat competition and the creation of trusts and monopolies would popularize a movement for a countering system of government regulatory controls over utilities and other major businesses that affected the interstate domain. Yet these early government powers, once attained, would not be widely applied to check the abuses of corporate power until the early years of the twentieth century. The relationship between business and government and the role of this relationship in American history would, however, become a principal ingredient in addressing the conflict between businesses' consolidation of control and the property rights of individuals in a democracy.

In January 1882, the Standard Oil Trust was formed and a new vehicle for combining corporate interests and operations was initiated. The trust device was the brainchild of Samuel C. T. Dodd. After considering and discarding several forms wherein the Standard Oil Corporation could devise a legal structure to incorporate all its operations, Dodd recommended to Standard officials that they create a corporation in each state in which Standard had a major investment. Superimposed on these state corporations would be a "corporation of corporations," a trust that would be, in terms of control, the only important vehicle. The trust would hold the voting stock of the subsidiary companies; trust certificates would be issued to the companies on a percentage basis according to the amount of stock contributed; and the management of the entire organization would reside in the trustees of the trust. The trust afforded Standard the opportunity to develop complete vertical integration of operations, including barrelmaking, pipelines, selling agencies, storage facilities, and byproducts merchandising (Gressley 1971: 5).[1] Railroads, followed by more oil and then steel companies, were organized along the lines of the trust. Trusts also were formed in tobacco, sugar, and coal. Trust certificates attracted the eager attention of New York speculators. "The trade in sugar refining certificates alone, by the late 1880s, averaged 150,000 shares a week—in contrast to 2,000 in Pullman shares" (Navin and Sears 1955: 115). Federal legislation ultimately banned the trust vehicle, but large corporations were to be integrated using modified legal frameworks, such as corporate holding companies, facilitated by a New Jersey law passed in the 1880s permitting one corporation to own another. On April 1, 1901, the first billion-dollar "super consolidation," the United States Steel Corporation, was formed.

The Constitution, Corporations, and Labor

The Fourteenth Amendment, enacted in 1868 primarily to establish the civil rights of the recently freed slaves, also afforded the means for expanded federal involvement in the regulation of corporations. Corporations were "legal persons" and the Fourteenth Amendment restricted states from discriminatory regulation against such corporate persons. In substance, states were preempted from regulating interstate corporations.

In 1888, the Supreme Court affirmed that the protection under the due process clause of the Constitution was not, like that of the privileges and immunities clause, confined to citizens, but extended to all persons, including corporations. This decision reflected an earlier court ruling that recognized the corporate entity as an "artificial person," thereby extending the civil rights of the corporation to a point of practical advantage. Even smaller business operations began to adopt the corporate form. Prior to this, the corporate form had been of benefit mostly to financial institutions, insurance companies, railroads, and a few major industrials, with a major segment of American enterprise conducted in the partnership or proprietary form.

All told, this decision, when combined with the passage of the Fourteenth Amendment and the subsequent enactment of the Interstate Commerce Act (1887) and the Sherman Antitrust Act (1890), brought into effect the federal movement to regulate interstate corporations.

Urban workers and labor organizations grew in number and strength during this period. The long span of the post–Civil War period (1865–90) saw hourly wages rise by nearly two-thirds. Because of the continuing drop in the price level (deflation), "real" wages therefore increased even more. Labor groups combined to form the American Federation of Labor (AFL). At first numbering approximately 150,000, AFL membership would increase to more than 500,000 by the turn of the century and represent 90 percent of the skilled labor population. This increased strength of organized labor sparked popular concern about shifts in power just as did the rise of the corporate trust structure.

The 1890s were marked by violent strikes, including the Homestead Steel Strike in Pennsylvania and the bloody Pullman strikes in Chicago where workers seeking redress on wage reductions confronted government troops in the streets. "Whether the workers were organized or not, however, the employer's relations with the work force tended to be adversarial. To a considerable degree the workers and employers had different interests. The businessman was under pressure to hold down labor costs, and indeed the entire move to the factory was in large part a means of substituting capital for labor in a manner that would reduce the cost of production" (Galambos and Pratt 1988: 21). It was also the time of Europe's labor unrest and the rise of the urban working class. Concerns over labor conditions and worker rights were the focus of civic and religious institutions. The need to improve them was the theme of writings such as Pope Leo XIII's social encyclical of 1891, "Rerum Novarum."

Politics, Panics, and Populism

A panic originating in the European money markets spread to the United States in 1873, causing corporate credit to crumble. This, when combined with the rumors of corruption in the federal government, brought about major economic disturbances (Fels 1951).

More than 5,000 concerns failed, and losses mounted to $220 million, a significant amount in those days. Three million workers were unemployed, and farmers found that their grain could not be sold on the wheat markets. Conditions were aggravated by the revelation that several members of President Grant's administration held stock, for which they had never paid, in the Credit Mobilier, the holding company that had constructed the Union Pacific Railroad.

By 1884, following another panic in the economy, a Democrat was returned to the White House for the first time since the end of the Civil War. This reflected perhaps the public disenchantment with an administration tied to the Credit Mobilier and may have indicated a new populism. Nearly simultaneous with the changing mood that brought the Democrats into power, there was a decline in the use of the trust as a device to direct the growth and expansion of corporations. Although trusts continued in existence through the turn of the century it was in the mid-1880s, perhaps in response to the panic of 1884, that the consolidated holding corporation began to emerge as an alternative to the trust as an operating and control mechanism.

The panic of 1893 was touched off by the bankruptcy of the Philadelphia and Reading Railroad. But its causes ran deeper. It reflected unrest about "ten-cent corn and ten per cent interest," which troubled the farmers of Kansas, just as six-cent cotton infuriated the South. Miners in Montana and Colorado suffered from the decline in the price of silver. Populists in the West and South felt bound by the speculators and financiers of the East, who controlled the supply of money and limited coinage (Schlesinger 1939: 193). It was an intense contraction, one of the most severe depressions in U.S. history, reflecting overinvestment in industrial and rail enterprises and fear of a silver inflation in the face of the eroding gold reserve. Unemployment rose to levels exceeded only by the Great Depression of the 1930s.

The cloud of popular mistrust created by scandals within the federal bureaucracy and related panics was to linger until the election of 1896. The 1896 election was one of the most intensely fought in American history. The East saw William Jennings Bryan as a threat to society. His platform championed the free coinage of silver and opposed the gold standard. The election of 1896 resulted in a significant political realignment. Two years earlier, in 1894, the Republicans had secured control of the House with the largest gain in a congressional election in the nation's modern history. In that year, the Democrats failed to return a single member to Congress in twenty-four states. The presidential race of 1896 revealed equally strong shifts in sentiment that favored the Republicans. An analysis of this change, although complex, revealed that it was caused largely by workers and immigrants who had blamed the Democrats for the severe depression sparked by the panic of 1893. Urban workers were suspicious of the economic interests of the farmers and organized western political elements (Hoffman 1956).

Although there may be dispute as to whether the 1880s or the 1890s was the period during which the economic momentum shifted from agrarian to industrial, it is important to recognize that these decades together provide the formative influence for our culture in industrialized America.[2] For example, this era witnessed the birth of the modern city. Census data reveal that the number of cities with 8,000 or more inhabitants increased from just 280 in 1880 to more than 500 by 1896. Many cities doubled in size and some, such as Chicago, showed spectacular rates of growth.

In the West, under the sponsorship of the Homestead Act, the population was drawn to farming and ranching. Horace Greeley's advice "Go West, Young Man" created the West's version of a corporate buccaneer, namely, the cattle baron. Ambitious ranchers underwrote the series of Indian Wars and fought to free the land from native influence. Investors were attracted to the cattle industry in large numbers by the late 1870s. Subscribers to the stock in cattle companies were of varied ages and backgrounds: Boston dry goods merchants, land speculators, and southern landowners (Gressley 1971: 71). Mining speculation also attracted Eastern investors, including stockbrokers and other merchants from the Midwest (Brewer 1976).

The Capital Markets, Railroads, Industry, and Wealth

By 1869 thirty-eight railroads, with $350,000,000 in capital stock, were listed on the New York Stock Exchange. Railroads and their financing were the center of attention in the capital markets. The funds for railway construction came from bank credit and foreign exchange supplied by European investors. Every new burst of railway construction was met by a corresponding burst of investment from abroad, including England, Holland, and Germany. A boom that lasted from 1866 to 1873 was fueled by such investment; and when the depression of 1873 struck, it took a heavy toll of foreign investors. By 1887, another depression had hit. English investors sold off to American investors at greatly reduced prices, the result being that Americans gained ownership in the railroads at a small portion of the original investment. It was established that foreign investors had lost heavily, perhaps more than $250 million on railroad bonds alone, a number that would be several times that in equivalent amounts today.

After the 1870s, the failure of the gold supply to keep pace with money growth demands generated by industrial expansion enhanced the position of the investment banker who was skilled in managing and providing both cash and capital. Bankers controlled important power to determine and direct major economic decisions affecting capital flows, structure, scope, and the very existence of developing businesses. Investment banking during the period between 1873 and 1884 in particular was characterized by the actions of J. P. Morgan. Initially in partnership as Drexel and Morgan, the operation was renamed J. P. Morgan and Co. in 1895. Morgan's first successful major venture was in 1879 when he became involved in marketing overseas stock for the Vanderbilt family to provide capital for the expansion of the New York Central, while preserving control for the family. In exchange for his services he was appointed a member of the New York Central Board of Directors. Morgan's influence over this period through the year 1900 provides a guiding thread to the elements that affected the capital markets.

The House of Morgan survived the economic panics of the 1880s and 1890s. This survival itself enhanced its reputation and prestige. During the failures and panic of 1893, Morgan's money, expertise, and organizational abilities aided many shaky railroad capital structures. Morgan put into effect reorganization plans that permitted many of the railroads to survive. The essence of his "morganization" plan was to scale down bonded debt and exchange it for preferred stock. If bondholders were unwilling to exchange their bonds for stock, they were persuaded to take bonds of lesser yield (Chamberlain 1974: 173). No one has ever revealed the essence of Morgan's genius. However, it was his steadfast commitment to the opportunity he saw in the country's economy that directed him once to state: "Never sell America short!"

An anecdotal view of the competitive nature of the times can be glimpsed from the following, spoken by C. B. Stickney at an 1890 meeting of fifteen other prominent railroad executives called by Morgan. "I have," said Stickney, "the utmost respect for you, gentlemen, individually, but as railroad presidents, I wouldn't trust you with my watch out of my sight" (Matthews 1981).

The names Morgan, Vanderbilt, Gould, Drew, Stanford, and Fisk may still evoke a certain popular resentment. Josephson, who coined the term "robber barons" in a book of that name, electrified and outraged readers with what appeared to be indisputable data about these buccaneers of capitalism. The public capital markets were becoming a "golden trough," feeding the ambitious and the speculators. Yet historians note also that the perceived predatory acts of these individuals were accomplished only through collusion with and assistance from government officials.

Railroad companies had received substantial subsidies from state agencies. The Erie Railroad organizers including Gould, Fisk, and Drew made their fortunes through secret stock manipulations only because the New York legislature was dominated by public representatives whom the Erie group was known to control. Central Pacific Railroad's control over the legislature in Sacramentò, California, ultimately led to that state's government granting monopolies over certain prize routes.

Yet not all of the railroads or their entrepreneur promoters were embroiled in this type of government-sponsored chicanery. Unprotected and competitive railroads, such as those owned and controlled by Vanderbilt and Hill, grew without government-aided monopolies and were also known to be as profitable to their stockholders and probably less costly to their shippers. Although the eastern roads did not depend on illicit subsidies financed by taxpayers, they were characterized by sharp and often vicious competition for routes, in turn achieving for these roads the benefits of a legal monopoly without having to obtain the sanction of the government.

A post–Civil War investment publication, *Commercial & Financial Chronicle,* commented in 1867 on railroad management that "in too many cases their affairs are administered in the interest of the directors rather than of the stockholders at large. . . . This species of management is of a piece with the selfishness and dishonesty with which political affairs are managed by our legislators and office holders, and is one of the many indications of the debasement of official morality which disgraces our times. Is it surprising that when our railroad corporations are thus engineered with a view to rendering the value of their stocks as unstable as possible (to the advantage of insiders who speculate) that the public should shun such investments?" ("Railroad Management," 1867: 520–21).

As noted by Daniel Drew about the insider: "To speculate in Wall Street when you are not an insider is like buying cows by candlelight" (Kroll 1987). One form of stock watering that was commonplace is noted by Greene (1897) in his volume *Corporation Finance:* "The tendency of corporation managers, under the pressure of public protest against high dividends, to water the capital has been much accelerated by the financial law that stock-watering actually increases market values. . . . If a company's stock is quoted at sixty, and a stock dividend of fifty per cent is declared, the quotations will not fall to forty as they ought . . . and . . . now the company (increases by fifty per cent) the number of its shares and continues to pay (6⅔%) . . . (t)he original holder, while receiving the same aggregate dividends as before, finds his principal increased in value. . . . This fact . . . has always been a strong incentive to stock-watering" (140).

One of the most noted scandals of the age was that of the already mentioned Credit Mobilier, the financial holding company that built the Union Pacific Railroad. The Mobilier scandal was brought to light by members of the House of Representatives. One of the House investigators summarized the situation by saying, "With absolute fairness we have striven to obtain the truth and in the sentence I declare in all the history, I never saw a scheme of villainy so profoundly arranged, so cunningly carried forward, so disastrously executed as this one disclosed in the report now submitted to the House." The corruption reached into all branches of President Grant's administration and into the offices of various members of Congress (Green 1959). Clews tells us that "it was composed of stockholders of the railway company, and had a capital of $3,750,000. Profits were large and the stock was quoted at 400. Certain Congressmen were given stock at par on their personal notes, the object being to gain their favor in case adverse legislation was proposed" (1887: 514).

To assess the developments in this period, marked by the birth of many rail and industrial empires, it is important to consider that it may have been impossible to raise the large quantities of scarce capital required by such operations had it not been for the intense promotion of early entrepreneurs. The economy's appetite was almost boundlessly growth-oriented. The success of investment bankers in early corporate promotion is suggested by statistics that by 1893 there were 1,250,000 shareholders out of a population of 62 million people in the United States. (This can be contrasted with ownership for post–World War II in figure 8.7.) The strong will and tactics of this early group of "captains of industry" in large part accounted for the establishment of an efficient corporate form of enterprise in a period when any other form of organization, given the nature of the market, might not have similarly provided for growth.

In 1889 the daily *Wall Street Journal* began publication, assuring a comprehensive source of investment news to supplement other weekly published sources. Charles Dow, one of the *Journal*'s founders, expressed this comment in an early editorial: "Nobody who plants corn digs up the kernels in a day or two to see if the corn has sprouted, but in stocks most people want to open an account at noon and get their profit before night" (Kann 1989).

By 1890, tickers and telephones were commonplace and it was possible to transmit stock-trading data instantaneously to points far beyond Wall Street. By the turn of the century, New York's Wall Street was about to emerge as the leading location of international finance, surpassing London's Lombard Street. This rise in the influence of American capital markets had come quickly and at the hands of but a few men, with little or no governmental regulation. These men virtually controlled America's business life: Morgan in banking and finance, Rockefeller in oil, Vanderbilt in railroads, Carnegie in steel. These were the titans amidst the tycoons, men whose annual incomes were in the millions when there was no income tax, and whose control over organizations and battles with one another for the whole industrial empire is one legend (Sobel 1965: 158). A colorful insight into this group is found in an early biography of the Vanderbilt family. Commodore Vanderbilt had a personality about which no single statement could be more revealing than the following, found in the text of a letter the old commodore sent to a competitor. " 'You have undertaken to cheat me,' he wrote; 'I won't sue you for the law is too slow. I'll ruin you.' And he did" (Campbell 1941). In 1880, Rockefeller was worth an estimated $18 million. The former bookkeeper, whose meticulous ledgers showed that in 1864 he had paid 5 cents for an apple, $1 for a haircut, and on his honeymoon, 75 cents for a view of Niagara Falls, had become a household word in America. His name meant wealth. In 1913, Rockefeller's fortune peaked at $900 million (Mio 1991).

A portion of Rockefeller's fortune, as that of the old commodore and of Carnegie, served to fund several of today's major private universities. Carnegie's wealth was also donated to support public libraries across the nation. These acts of philanthropy abetted the folklore that tycoons considered their wealth a form of "stewardship" for others, a view not often appreciated (Wren 1983).

The economic environment of this era was also influenced by the fact that throughout the post–Civil War period there was a gradual but steady increase in the purchasing power of the dollar brought about by general price deflation. Furthermore, the economy was beginning to change character. By 1880, the United States had entered into a metropolitan-style economy characterized by the growth and significance of industrial urban areas as key points of demand, distribution, and political influence.

It is important to recognize that in addition to the East's industrial cities and capital markets, in this era of manifest destiny crops, land, mining, and cattle also played an important role in the functioning of the American capitalistic system. Both eastern and European investors were attracted to western mines, ranches, and cattle as investments. Furthermore, the abundant American wheat harvest of 1879 offset the disastrous European crop failures that had resulted from poor weather. This led to the export of millions of bushels of wheat per day and served as the source of an agricultural boom that finally led the American economy out of the serious depression that had lingered since 1873. Without these western investments and the strength of American agriculture, it is difficult to explain how our economy would have had a balanced attractiveness to investors at home or overseas.

The history of eastern investments in western mortgage companies, land, and cattle is interesting and involved. The conservative lending policies of major eastern capital sources led them to protect their customers from sustaining substantial losses in western investments. However, because they did not venture into high risk/return situations, the involvement of the conservative New York money sources did not in itself account for the entire capital of western ventures.

As the westward movement gained momentum after the Civil War, the demand for mortgage credit grew rapidly; at the same time, credit funds also grew rapidly in the East and in Europe. Important amounts of these funds were attracted by the temperament and potential of the West. Perhaps it was in part that the eastern investors were enchanted by the potential of the cattle industry, although researchers suggest that investments in cattle arose because eastern investors had originally made investments in other areas of the West, usually mining, railroads, or real estate. As such, investment in cattle was a part of an "associative spirit." Investors in the cattle industry included merchants, bankers, financiers, and industrialists, although there was also a small group of professional men. Names commonly found include those such as Marshall Field (the Chicago merchant), Teddy Roosevelt, August Busch, and David Goodrich.

By the end of the 1800s, both the western manager and the eastern investor had learned a modicum about the economics of the cattle business. Expenses were closely scrutinized and curtailed, dividends were postponed as necessary, and improved procedures of operation were being adopted. Only when these business procedures were followed did cattle companies show an accounting ledger–based profit. Intensive investment in the cattle industry from 1882 to 1885 represented the high point of activity. The low point came from 1886 to 1888, followed by a short period of recovery and a much larger resurgence form 1898 to 1900.[3] Thereafter, the cattle industry in the plains underwent a radical change wherein ranching became increasingly locally controlled.[4]

With the creation of the Interstate Commerce Commission (1887) and the passage shortly thereafter of the Sherman Act (1890), the days of laissez-faire were coming to a close. Section 1 of the Sherman Act prohibited any contract, combination, and conspiracy in restraint of trade. Section 2 prohibited monopolization, attempts to monopolize, and combinations or conspiracies to monopolize "any part of the trade or commerce among the several states or with foreign nations." These actions communicated a message that the federal government would respond to popular political pressures to curb the abuses of unrestrained competition and corporate monopoly. It would not be, however, until the second decade of the twentieth century that the provisions of these laws would be interpreted by the Supreme Court under a "rule of reason" so as to permit enforcement to curb widespread abuses and monopolistic practices.

Accounting, Reporting, and Analysis

Financial reports before the turn of the century reflected the influence of the railroad corporation, the trust form of business, and the large manufacturing corporation. This section considers the format, content, and influence of financial reports of the period, including regulatory and legal aspects, the role that accounting systems played in internal administration of large organizations, and attempts by the private and public sectors to establish uniform accounts.

> In America as in England the balance sheet was the primary statement— but for different reasons. The British balance sheet developed as a report to stockholders on management's stewardship of contributed funds. Nineteenth-century American corporations had no comparable history of large losses from stock speculation and were not as closely regulated, nor was incorporation considered a privilege which created reciprocal disclosure obligations. American corporations . . . drew most of their capital, not from stock sales, but from short term bank loans. Their balance sheets were directed mainly toward bankers . . . (and) . . . related more to the conversion of inventory into cash than to earning power. (Chatfield 1974: 72)

Increasing public interest in understanding railroad reports gave birth to financial analysis before the turn of the century. Beginning with the post–Civil War period, the analytically prudent investor became acquainted with statements of financial information as the object of financial reporting and disclosure systems. Among the pioneers of credit and financial analysis were Peter Earling, Thomas F. Woodlock, John Moody, and a proponent of the need for publicity of corporate accounts, Henry Clews. It was Clews, head of a respected banking house, who suggested that expert accountants in the private sector could provide the requisite service needed for appropriate publicity of corporate accounts. He stated that publicity could be accomplished by the employment of skilled accountants because certified results of their examinations would be accepted as conclusive.

Earling's introduction to analytics was the turn-of-the-century treatise *Whom to Trust: A Practical Treatise on Mercantile Credit,* written in response to requests for information about his methods of credit-granting practices. "Prior to and concurrent with Earling's ideas, the amounts of credit to be granted had been estimated from statements submitted by the borrower, but the analysis of the statement appears to have gone no further than a careful reading of the figures and investigation of their accuracy" (Brown 1955: 11). Earling's work illustrated an approach and gave birth to a much more analytical method. He investigated asset valuation and recognized the variation of financial data among industries and also expressed relationships or proportions between assets and liabilities and net worth. This was the dawn of the era of modern security analysis.

Thomas Woodlock's *The Anatomy of a Railroad Report* was published in 1895 and acknowledged by others, including Moody, as a popular and authoritative presentation on the subject matter of railroad operations and financial reports. Analysis of financial statements by banks, credit establishments, and other institutions was an activity that affected the entire economy.

Moody, a pioneer financial analyst, noted concern over matters of secrecy. In *How to Analyze Railroad Reports,* Moody observed that until the early 1890s, balance sheet secrecy was a distinctive characteristic of financial statement disclosure by railroads. In 1867, the *Chronicle* commented that "information upon the finances of the roads is suppressed, and accounts are falsified." During the 1870s and 1880s, the New York Central Railroad rendered no annual reports to its stockholders. Also, in responding to an inquiry from the New York Stock Exchange for financial information, the Delaware, Lackawana, and Western Railroad, whose stock was also traded on the Exchange, responded that "the Delaware, Lackawana and Western Railroad makes no report, publishes no statements, and . . . (has) not done anything of the kind for the last five years" (Sobel 1965: 85). Other corporations were similarly tight-lipped. For example, between 1897 and 1905, the Westinghouse Electric and Manufacturing Company neither published an annual financial statement to its stockholders nor held an annual meeting (Hawkins 1963: 137). The secrecy surrounding financial affairs was cited in a 1900 government report on the subject. The report noted that "while the chief evil of large corporations is a lack of responsibility of the directors to the stockholders . . . the directors . . . practically never make reports to the individual shareholders for periods."

Another common feature of accounting systems of this age was the use of the "private ledger," which was an account book equipped with a lock and key wherein were kept the capital expense accounts, the record of officers' salaries, controlling accounts of sales and purchases, and any other cumulative accounting information the firm desired to keep confidential (see figure 4.1). A partner or trusted employee posted the essential figures from the usual accounting records, and only this person saw the trial balance and knew the condition of the important accounts (Roberts 1975). A statement by J. P. Morgan about Teddy Roosevelt's "trust busting" ways suggests secrecy was the mode. "If he had his way," said Morgan, "we'd all do business with glass pockets" (Jackson 1983: 237).

The public's concern over disclosure was evidenced in a passage that appeared in the *Railroad Gazette:* "The annual report of a railroad is often a very blind document and the average shareholders taking one of these reports generally gives up before he begins" (January 6, 1893). In more remote locations, shareholders relied on audit committees to obtain information about the financial condition of rail companies. The East Tennessee

THE READING RAILROAD COMPANY'S BOOKS.

(Concluded.)

THE following is a copy of the last report made by the President and Managers for the information of stockholders, which was submitted January 12th, last past :

Dr.   GENERAL BALANCE-SHEET OF THE PHILADELPHIA AND READING RAILROAD COMPANY, NOVEMBER 30, 1879.   Cr.

CAPITAL ACCOUNTS:		
Railroad	$6,318,877.58	
Depots	4,194,711.89	
Locomotive engines and cars	9,855,442.24	
Real estate	7,688,844.25	
Philadelphia, Reading and Pottsville Tel. Co. stock	20,730.00	
East Pennsylvania Railroad Co. stock	949,356.18	
Reading and Columbia Railroad Co. stock	232,480.00	
Allentown Railroad Co. stock	320,562.99	
East Mahanoy Railroad Co. stock	247,295.61	
Mine Hill & Schuyl. Haven Railroad Co. stock	175,297.75	
Phila. and Reading Coal and Iron Co. stock	8,000,000.0	
Phila. and Reading Coal and Iron Co., bond and mortgage, July 1, 1874	29,737,965.58	
Phila. and Reading Coal and Iron Co. bond and mortgage, December 28th, 1876	10,000,000.00	
Steam-colliere	39,737,965.58	
Susquehanna Canal coal-barges	2,561,245.24	
Schuylkill Canal coal-barges	23,872.80	
Schuyl. Navigation Co. works and franchises	437,840.70	
	1,000,000.00	
		101,365,544.16
Add:		
Schuylkill Canal new barges	23,410.44	
Less:		
Balance of installments Susquehanna Canal new barges	4,494.35	17,986.09
		101,288,530.25

CAPITAL ACCOUNTS:		
Total mortgage loans *		
6 pr. c. $ debent'e loan, 1862-68, coupon	1,196,500.00	
7 " " $ deb, conv " 1870-90	98,000.00	
7 " " $ " " 1873-93	10,499,900.00	
4 " " $ " " 1878-98	596,600.00	
Script, 1877-82		$7,303,877.94
6 pr. c. deb. and guaran. $3,470,025.00		
6 " " " " frc't' 2,948.10		
6 " Gen mtg. gold $ or £ 1,733,980.00		
6 " Perk. "guar" 99,180.00	5,305,733.10	
Loan of Schuyl. Nav. Co., matu'g 1895	1,200,000.00	
" " " " 1918	756,650.00	
" " " " 1915	681,600.00	17,646,733.10
Loan of E. Penna. R. R. Co. mt'g 1888	2,578,250.00	
	495,900.00	3,074,150.00
		77,994,761.04
Common stock	32,726,375.28	
Preferred stock	1,551,800.00	
		34,278,175.28

LIABILITIES:

ASSETS:

Cash on hand			228,929.94
Bills receivable			24,691.00
Freight and toll bills receivable in December, 1879			778,561.36
Stocks and bonds held by the Company	1,082,408.39		
Materials on hand	7,083,811.43		
Debts due to the Company:			
Sundry branch roads	735,599.99		
Philadelphia and Reading Coal and Iron Co.	1,730,398.05		
Sundry accounts	5,177,919.78		
	1,658,207.19	8,561,425.02	
			17,962,734.85
Funded coupons not yet matured:			
Phila. & Reading Railroad Co. coupons	2,244,889.00		
Schuylkill Navigation Company	128,001.00		
Susquehanna Canal Company	230,195.00	2,602,084.00	
Discount, commission and expenses of general mortgage loan, 1874—1908, issue of $10,000,000 in January, 1875		500,000.00	
INCOME ACCOUNTS:			
Loss, per report November 30th, 1878	1,041,440.99		
Add loss year ending November 30th, 1879	1,063,421.73	2,104,862.72	
		123,853,215.80	

Floating debt		
Debts due by the Company, including rentals, and principally for current business		7,550,079.54
Wages, materials, drawbacks, and connecting roads for November business		1,572,565.48
Coupons and interest on registered loans to December 1st, 1879, inclusive		870,911.18
State tax on capital stock and gross receipts		805,240.85
Sinking fund loan, 1886-88		98,165.71
Sinking fund Schuylkill Navigation Company improvement bonds		164,070.45
Credit balance of insurance funds	298,000.00	
Credit balance of renewal fund	847,298.65	
	11,847.57	
		11,050,571.48
		123,853,215.80

* We have omitted the items which make up this amount, deeming it necessary only to give the aggregate of mortgage indebtedness.

Figure 4.1 Capital accounts and assets and liabilities of the Philadelphia and Reading Railroad Co., 1879. *Source: Book-Keeper* (August 17, 1880: 37).

and Western North Carolina Railroad Company, a planned thirty-four-mile line formed in 1868, utilized a committee of the board of directors to provide financial audits (McKee 1979).

Concerns over public companies' accounts and disclosure are depicted in the pages of *The Commercial & Financial Chronicle*. In 1888, for example, the Atchison Topeka and Santa Fe applied to the New York Stock Exchange to have its 6 percent sinking fund secured bonds listed, publishing the listing application in the financial press on March 24. After the economic troubles of the early 1890s, the road fell into difficulties and the following report was given in the July 28, 1894, edition of the *Commercial & Financial Chronicle* under the title "The Atchison Disclosures."

> The committee in charge of the reorganization of (the Atchison Topeka & Santa Fe) has given out a statement based on investigations into the books and accounts of the concern, made by Mr. Stephen Little, the expert accountant, which seems to point to startling irregularities in the reports of the company's income. In brief the charge is (we quote the exact language used in the committee's statement) that "during the period from July, 1889, the date of the last reorganization, to December, 1893, the date of the appointment of the receivers, the income of the company has in his (Mr. Little's) opinion, been over-stated in an aggregate amounting to $7,000,000. . . .
>
> It is unfortunate from every standpoint that the public has absolutely no facts or information as yet upon which to base a judgment concerning this startling announcement. ("Atchison Disclosures," 1894: 135)

Subsequent details included the following:

> Summarizing these various amounts, we find that in addition to the $7,285,621 of over-statement of earnings reported by Mr. Little for the Atchison system last August . . . , he has made in his present report the following further deductions: $1,201,050 for equipment destroyed or worn out; $1,131,912 for income from investments bad or doubtful and $642,917 for increase of interest on the unfunded debt, giving a grand total of $10,261,500. ("Atchison Disclosures," 1894A: 854)

These passages, and the complete text surrounding them, suggest both incompetence and culpable errors on the part of the management of the road. Given the size and significance of the railroads, and the state of disclosure evidenced by this episode, one might infer a chaotic reporting process existed. Yet this would be an unfair surmise. The pages of the *Chronicle* were regularly filled with the reports of other major roads, such as the Baltimore & Ohio, the Chesapeake & Ohio, and the Northern Pacific, for example.

General Electric (see table 4.1) was an exception to the pattern of unaudited statements. It provided an auditor's report with its statements before the turn of the century. However, by the late 1890s, a voluntary and unaudited form predominated, for example: "The quarterly returns of the New York Central Railroad, issued with so much promptness, have left no one in doubt as to what kind of a showing the company would make for its fiscal year ending June 30. The annual report has now been issued, permitting us to see how the results for the year were reached and what have been the chief features of the year's operations" (October 3, 1896: 580–82). Or, as in the Lake Erie & Western Railroad Co.'s Ninth Annual Report, addressed to the stockholders, which appeared in complete text on pages 826–27 of the May 2, 1896, issue of the *Chronicle*. It contained a lengthy statement that in contemporary disclosure terms would be an example of what the Securities and Exchange Commission today calls "management discussion and analysis."

Similar coverage was given to the recapitalization of the American Bell Telephone Company in September, October, and November 1899 issues of the *Chronicle*. The practices of quasi-public enterprises, including these transportation and utility companies, were profoundly influenced by the legal arrangements based upon cash receipts less cash disbursements notions of reporting and profit. As such, many investors sought information that would assist in establishing and corroborating the "dividend value" of a stock. Such a value-based approach equated bond (namely "income bonds") and stock investments in terms of their cash payout via interest and dividend payouts at a time when each of these two forms of corporate securities was being celebrated by unprecedented listings on the New York Stock Exchange.

"Dividend value" and other value-based approaches would serve to underlie the formulation of approaches to measurement and policy for years to come. This was true particularly with regard to the belief of early regulators that all accounting information could be rigorously and perfectly prescribed in the form of a cashlike "operating statistic." This, remember, was an era when corporations were not concerned with the consequences of taxation and tax effects on dividend payouts and on interest paid for bonds and debt (see table 4.2).

Since the early promulgations of the Interstate Commerce Commission (ICC), accountants and businessmen have become increasingly sophisticated as to their notions of value and techniques of measurement in attempting to determine the proper basis for establishing an adequate and fair system of measuring and reporting return on investment. Today, historians argue "that the nature of the accounting and statistical tools used by

TABLE 4.1
First Annual Report of the General Electric Company, 1893

General Electric Company - CONDENSED BALANCE SHEET --- JANUARY 31ST, 1893

ASSETS.

INVESTMENT ACCOUNTS:

STOCKS OF UNDERLYING COMPANIES:

Thomson-Houston Electric Co.	$8,416,851.78	
Edison General Electric Co.	8,693,208.46	
Thomson-Houston International Electric Co.	1,212,000.000	18,262,000.24*

REAL ESTATE:

Edison Building, N.Y. City	410,804.62	
Less Mortgage thereon	200,000.00	
	210,804.62	
Other Real Estate	87,922.12	298,726.74

STOCK OF UNITED ELECTRIC SECURITIES CO.:

Preferred (Par, $454,300.)	408,870.00	
Common (Par, 825,500.)	825,500.00	1,234,370.00

STOCKS OF MANUFACTURING AND OTHER COS.:

Canadian Gen'l Elec. Co. (par, $1,000,000.)	1,000,000.00	
Excelsior Electric Co. (par, 6,000.)	1,300.00	
Ft. Wayne Electric Co. (par, 704,700.)	352,350.00	
Northwest Gen'l Elec. Co. (par, 155,000.)	155,000.00	
Miscellaneous Companies (par, 481,033.)	71,566.00	1,580,216.00
		$21,375,372.98

OTHER ASSETS:

STOCKS AND BONDS OF LOCAL COS.:

Stocks (par, $11,362,011.65)	$5,722,622.80	
Bonds (par, 4,858,380.00)	3,400,629.07	$9,173,251.87
CASH		3,871,033.58
NOTES RECEIVABLE		5,151,950.64
ACCOUNTS RECEIVABLE		7,078,879.15
INVENTORIES	2,307,225.13	
Less 10%	230,722.51	2,076,502.62
		2,207,982.75
		29,559,600.61
		$50,934,973.59

LIABILITIES.

CAPITAL STOCK:

Common	$30,426,900.00	
Preferred	4,236,900.00	$34,663,800.00

5% GOLD COUPON DEBENTURE BONDS,	10,000,000.00

OTHER LIABILITIES:

Accrued Interest on Debenture Bonds,	$83,333.32	
Dividends Declared but Unpaid	668,538.00	
Notes and Accounts Payable	4,554,347.68	
		5,246,219.00
SURPLUS JANUARY 31st 1893 . . .		1,024,954.59
		850,934,973.59

* See Page 8

STATEMENT OF PROFIT AND LOSS --- JANUARY 31st, 1893.

EXPENSES.			EARNINGS.		
Interest and Discount	$89,513	42	Net profits from the business of the eight months, over and above all expenses, deductions for bad debts, etc	$3,356,593	10
Interest on Debenture Bonds	152,917	17			
Dividends paid and dividends declared but not yet paid	1,971,056	50			
Patents, now charged off	118,51	42			
Surplus carried forward	1,024,954	59			
	$3,356,593	10		$3,356,593	10

E. & O. E. — April 11, 1893.

L.P. ORD *Comptroller*

Note: Adapted from the original.

TABLE 4.2

Listings on the New York Stock Exchange, Bonds and Stocks, 1885–1890 (in millions of dollars)

Year	New Issues	Old Issues New Listing	New Issues Replacing Old Issues	Total
Bonds				
1885	103.8	27.7	65.7	197.2
1886	81.6	47.3	109.1	238.0
1887	180.4	16.3	146.7	343.4
1888	262.0	11.8	237.2	511.0
1889	206.8	6.0	176.8	389.7
1890	198.1	105.2	381.5	684.8
Stocks				
1885	17.8	3.7	35.4	56.9
1886	54.0	67.2	208.2	329.4
1887	98.7	32.6	138.7	270.0
1888	62.4	10.4	175.4	248.2
1889	69.7	9.9	179.9	259.6
1890	164.4	10.5	263.0	437.9

Source: "Listings on the New York Stock Exchange in 1890," *Commercial & Financial Chronicle,* January 3, 1891, p. 6.

the ICC (as reflecting the ideas of Henry C. Adams) had an impact on the regulatory process, specifically that the difficulties encountered in the development of accurate and relevant railroad statistics often undermined the agency's ability to achieve its regulatory goals" (Miranti 1989: 469). Adams wanted rigidly uniform reporting formats and methodologies (Miranti 1990B: 184). This was accountancy's first rendezvous with bureaucracy. Later, the debate would encompass whether or not the right of any accounting association to professional status and privilege was a worthwhile cost to society. It was a prelude to the profession's future experience in establishing its place in a capital market's society and in the culture of the United States (Galambos 1983: 471, 487).

The new federal bureaucracy as found in the ICC was abetted by a judiciary that supported the notion of substantive due process in the reasonableness of rates under regulation. In cases decided in the 1890s, "the Supreme Court became a super-legislature to review the reasonableness of rates in all regulated industries. For example, the Court invalidated Nebraska's regulation of railroad rates. The distinction between confiscatory and unreasonable rates disappeared. The Court asserted that: 'What the company is entitled to ask is a fair return upon the value of that which it employs for public convenience'" (Conant 1974: 126).

To this day, this century-old concept of an accounting information system with an objective of providing a surrogate "cash statistic" attempts to establish "fair return." Of course, other "value" measurement notions challenged that idea, perplexed the profession, and led to controversy and contradiction. The cash statistic process with origins in America's early industrial age does continue to influence our regulatory practice and thinking. Is the notion that accounting information should be contained in a cashlike statistic if it is to be useful for measuring return on investment relevant in light of advances in popular economic knowledge? Similarly the basic accounting equation developed by Sprague (Assets = Liabilities + Proprietorship) continues to appear in textbooks as a means of depicting relationships among accounts. Perhaps no two other notions, products of this era, so fully dictate our current practice as the early cash statistic and Sprague's equation (Previts 1984).

Before long, uniform listing requirements of stock markets would emphasize the need for filing of financial statements by corporations trading their securities. The need to attract capital, along with the increasing attention given by businessmen and legislators to the problem of providing sufficient financial information, would provide dual justification for the unprecedented growth of public accounting practice and periodic financial disclosure.

British-trained accountants in America had a convenient and authoritative set of examples that could be modified and applied to the American scene from such sources as the British Companies Acts. A replacement method became widely adopted, under which the asset cost remained as book value, without regard for depreciation. An expense account was used to even out the differential in charges resulting from costs of renewal and maintenance. The Remington Arms Company, for example, showed no depreciation in their financial statements until after the turn of the century (Williamson 1952: 120, 402). Another factor affecting the development of an appropriate method for valuation of fixed assets in quasi-public corporations was the occurrence of a general price level decline in America. During the period of 1875 to 1900, there was an increase in purchasing power such that the historical cost values assigned to fixed assets, if not adjusted in book value for "wear and tear" or other loss in value, were in effect being *written up* by deflation. In addition to matters of technical accounting, political considerations significant to the relationship between a regulated industry's rate for securities and the capital asset rate base caused the issue of fixed asset accounting to be prominent.[5] The view of the railroad as a quasi-public corporation, and the concern over the result of government influence on rate setting and return on railroad investments, focused attention on the value of capital assets and appropriate methods of accounting for the same. At first, the courts had not recognized the rights of regulated corporations or public service corporations to deduct depreciation in the determination of their rate base. By 1876, the Supreme Court did acknowledge the right of railroads to take depreciation, yet it was not perceived to be an expense, in the sense of an expenditure, for railroad accounts were kept primarily on a cash basis. Later courts, in a fashion reflecting the 1898 Supreme Court decision *Smyth v. Ames,* indicated that a "fair return to regulated industry could be based on the 'present value of the property,'" as opposed to historical cost as often used in early uniform systems.[6]

Without a depreciation expense concept, companies incurred costs for wear and maintenance, charged the amount to surplus accounts, and avoided income statement disclosure. This practice was popular in those years when companies suffered falling profit margins. Moody described the practice as follows: "In the past, especially, many railroads followed the policy of keeping down their current operating costs including maintenance but at the same time spending the necessary money on their properties and then at the close of the year deducting from the surplus shown above charges in the amounts currently spent but not currently charged up. So in the final result they would have no surplus at all, and the item 'surplus above charges' or 'surplus above dividends' would simply be a bookkeeping entry" (Moody 1916: 170). Moody goes on to say, "It is one of the strong arguments in favor of uniform accounting requirements that railroads coming under the jurisdiction of the interstate commerce commission cannot do this any longer. They are now required to charge to maintenance the items which properly belong there and can only put in improvement or betterment accounts the actual expenditures of such nature" (see figure 4.2).

As early as 1880, business periodicals reviewed the subject of compulsory regulatory accounts. In 1889, an issue of *Office* magazine reported the speech of George Ramsdell, president of the Western Gas Association, regarding the lack of uniformity of gas company accounts and announcing the appointment of an association committee to investigate the lack of systematic accounting. These references suggest an awareness on the part of practitioners and businessmen for self-regulation of accounting practice.

Concern over the fairness of reporting as indicated by Moody in part explains the justification for the creation of the Interstate Commerce Commission in 1887. This act evidenced the birth of regulatory agencies, the fourth branch of our modern federal government. In 1894, the commission established a system of accounts entitled "The Classification of Operating

1893

FIRST

ANNUAL REPORT

OF THE

UNITED STATES RUBBER CO.

———

March 31st, 1893.

FINANCIAL STATEMENT

UNITED STATES RUBBER COMPANY, MARCH 31st, 1893.

ASSETS.

Cash on hand and in bank.	$56,194.02	
Notes and Accounts Receivable.	2,846,163.50	
Value of Rubber and other Mdse. on hand, estimated,	674,011.51	$3,576,369.03
Furniture and Fixtures: New York and Boston,	$4,587.18	
Investments,	25,267,833.69	25,272,420.87
TOTAL ASSETS,		$28,848,789.90

LIABILITIES.

Preferred Stock,	$13,388,800	
Common Stock,	13,984,800	27,373,600.00
Bills and Accounts Payable,		925,251.02
TOTAL LIABILITES,		$28,298,851.02
Balance,		$549,938.88
Less April Dividend,		536,004.00
SURPLUS,		$13,934.88

Figure 4.2 First annual report of the U.S. Rubber Company (UNIROYAL), 1893

Expenses." [7] With this focus on the classification of operating expense, it is evident that earning capacity was becoming, in the words of John Moody, the factor that should be studied "*in advance of everything else*" (Moody 1916: 18).

How were the accountants to provide leadership in this complex area of regulation and legal precedent? Would they be relegated to the status of "busy examiners of detail"? As these early pressures manifested themselves, the emerging accounting profession was poorly organized in terms of institutions and literature to cope with public demands for financial reporting. Yet interesting and important precedents were being established. For example, consolidated accounts were prepared for the American Cotton Oil Trust in 1886, and Maurice Peloubet notes that consolidation accounting developed in the United States before it did in Great Britain. In Great Britain, the appropriate disclosure for holding companies involved adjusting and amplifying the parent holding company investment account, whereas in the States, there was a growing custom to take a consolidations approach, that is, to present a picture of the enterprise as if it were a whole (Peloubet 1955: 31). American accountants were able to benefit from the expertise of the British professional and at the same time to innovate, adapt, and progressively determine new and different schemes of disclosure in light of the different environment of the American capital market.

The great merger movement in American business that swept the manufacturing sector of the United States beginning in the 1890s was one of the environmental factors conducive to accountancy's development in the "demand/response" sense. The mergers were the product of a particular combination of circumstances: a capacity to generate capital; "the development of capital-intensive production techniques; a spurt of rapid growth in a number of heavy industries . . . ; and the panic and depression of 1893. . . . [T]his sequence of events produced an episode of abnormally severe price competition that manufacturers finally turned to consolidation to alleviate" (Lamoreaux 1985:189).

As the trust and holding corporations gained headway (table 4.3), popular writers and prominent authorities predicted that such businesses would fail. Their belief was founded upon the view that no one person or board of directors could successfully master such large organizations in a competitive environment. In 1900, Collier surveyed the evolution of the business trust. A summary of his findings suggests the substantial financial structure and the diverse nature of this industrial device. However, accounting administrative control systems being developed during this period provided the information and means of direction to place at the disposal of management data relevant to operations. Steel companies, rubber com-

TABLE 4.3

The Structure of Pre-1900 American Business Trusts (capitalization in millions)

Product/Process	Number of Trusts	Year(s) Established	Common Stock	Preferred Stock	Bonded Debt
Food	14	1887–99	252	105	84
Distilling and Brewing	10	1894–99	123	49	29
Tobacco	5	1890–99	106	79	4
Paper	6	1898–99	123	53	26
Textiles	6	1896–99	160	56	16
Leather and Rubber	5	1892–99	154	143	10
Wood	3	1892–96	100	—	1
Glass and Clay	5	1890–99	84	17	—
Chemicals, Oils, and Paints	11	1882–99	274	96	5
Iron and Steel	18	1887–99	408	287	55
Machinery and Hardware	8	1893–99	122	105	—
Electrical Manufacturers	11	1891–99	140	40	10
Minerals, Metals, and Coal	6	1891–99	121	47	4
Printing	1	1892	3	3	—
Warehousing	2	1895–97	20	8	18
Cement, Munitions, and Other	7	1889–99	119	43	—
			2,309	1,131	352

Source: W. M. Collier, *The Trusts: What Can We Do with Them? What Can They Do for Us?* (New York: Baker and Taylor, 1900), pp. 8–13.

panies, munitions works, transportation, sugar, and refining companies provide examples of the success of such internal management accounting system operations during this period for such large-scale enterprises (Wildman 1914).

Sophisticated techniques such as an estimated bad debts treatment of uncollectible accounts were described as early as 1880 in the nascent literature of accounting. Other examples of internal innovations include the development of loose-leaf and columnar books. These types of records, when compared to bound inflexible-style book sets, made it possible to sequence, amend, and control information. The voucher system also came into use as a method of controlling cash payments and for determining liability and working capital requirements.

Disclosure

With the settling of the West, the Winchester rifle had become a symbol of the times as a weapon in both hunting and war. The role of accounting information in the mass manufacture of arms at the Winchester Repeating Arms Company is in part portrayed in the rudimentary balance sheets reconstructed by Harold Williamson (1952). The activities sketched by these statements portray some of the important financial events of the company over the period of its early development and growth. The content and structure of the statements suggest the fundamental role of balance sheets in communicating financial information and reveal a step in the evolution of financial reporting and disclosure in America.

As noted in a previous chapter, the writings of Thomas Jones of New York mark the beginnings of the modern period of financial reporting. Jones's instruction emphasized the financial statements as the end result of the system of accounts. In the post–Civil War period, the ledger had begun to lose its preeminent position in the system of financial accounting. External capital interests required statements that periodically synthesized the results of changes in the asset position of the firm. This betrayed the increasingly important role played by external capital sources in the financing of large enterprises. As businesses became more widely held and financed, statement extracts of the journals and ledgers were required in concise, uniform, and understandable form.

Another observation regarding the widespread use and importance of financial information in records of this time can be found in Gressley's *Bankers and Cattlemen.* Gressley points to the fact that his ability to compute the dividends paid by successful land and cattle companies was based on the information on the ledger sheets available from the companies for the periods during the 1870s and 1880s. He determined the average declared dividend as just over 8 percent and thus concluded that few eastern investors found a pot of gold in the West. It is appropriate to observe that since it was possible for Gressley to determine this information one century after the fact, it is likely that such information was used immediately for similar evaluations.

Gressley's research additionally reveals that a small percentage of early land and cattle companies did show excellent returns. For example, Marshall Field and Levi Leiter reaped dividends averaging 11 percent on their stock investments over a ten-year period in the Pratt-Ferris Cattle Company. Financial records provided a means for the eastern financier to determine the profitability of investment. More research is needed as to the implications of such records, yet they serve as examples of the likely influence of accounts on investment in nonmanufacturing enterprises.

Across a wide spectrum of companies, from arms manufacturers to cattle companies and railroads, examples of increasingly sophisticated accounting disclosures and information are found. Railroad statements provide landmark examples because of the dominant position of railroads in the capital market. Railroad reports of the period contain the forerunners of the concept of working capital and funds flow disclosures. Statements based on this type of information can be found as early as the 1870s. Thus, by 1893, it was common to find statements entitled, "Statements showing resources and their application during the Year," the purpose of which was to show changes in the solvency position and the effects of some interentity transactions. To the extent that noted corporations were unresponsive to demands for financial data, regulatory agencies began specifying classifications of accounts relative to legal decisions that affected the basis for the evaluation of assets and the determination of a fair return.

By 1899, the New York Exchange initiated steps to require financial statement reports on a regular basis from listed companies (Sobel 1965: 177).

Origins of an Accounting Profession

It is generally considered that the American accountancy profession traces its formation to this period of history, during the age of national capital market formation. "The last quarter of the nineteenth century in America marked the beginning of a period of substantial economic change which provided the environment conducive to the establishment of the new profession of public accountancy" (Miranti 1986: 30). Questions come to mind about these early professionals and their practice. Who were they? What were the elements of their practice? What was the nature of their education? How did they contribute to the overall formation of professional associations and to the legal recognition of accounting? Seeking answers to these questions provides the basis for a better understanding of the birth of modern public accounting.

Littleton's survey on early public accountants, published in 1942, reveals that in 1850, nineteen accountants' names were listed in the city directories of New York, Chicago, and Philadelphia. Considering this low number it would be difficult to support the view that public accounting practice or accounting practice per se was widespread at this time. Consider also that even as late as the 1870s, it was common practice for teams of stockholders to make periodic visits to corporate offices as a means of attempting to verify reported information. Stockholders' verification of this type was perhaps practical because of the limited size and regional locale of corporations. As late as 1875, it was still difficult to find a manufacturing company with $10 million in assets, whereas more than one hundred companies had assets exceeding $150 million by the close of the second decade of the twentieth century (Newman 1967: 40). The rapid growth in the size of corporations indicated by these statistics suggests that the demand for public accounting services would now begin to mount.

Accountants were called on to assist in a wide variety of matters. They became involved in the preparation of disputed cases for arbitration or suit. They were hired to detect improper entries and fraud as well as to discover errors in the books and records of companies. Defalcations, breaches of trust, irregularities, and swindling schemes were matters of daily occurrence in this environment. As one practitioner stated:

> The professional accountant is an investigator, a looker for leaks, a dissector and a detective in the highest acceptation of the term; he must have a good knowledge of real estate, machinery, buildings and other property. His business is to verify that which is right and to detect and expose that which is wrong; to discover and report facts as they exist, whether they be plainly expressed by clear and distinct records or whether they be concealed by the cunning knave or hidden under plausibly arranged figures or as is frequently the case omitted from the records entirely. He is a reader of hieroglyphics, however written, for every erasure, altercation [*sic*], interlining, dot, dash or character may have a meaning. He must interpret, rearrange and produce in simple but distinct form self explanatory and free from mysteries of bookkeeping, the narrative of facts, the relation to each other in results. He is the foe of deceit and the champion of honesty. (Keister 1896)

Accounting practice was the province of men, although records reveal that, after the turn of the century, several women were admitted to practice as certified public accountants.[8] Clews, the investment banker, portrayed the chauvinism of his day in a more telling report: "As speculators, women hitherto have been utter failures. They do not thrive in the atmosphere of Wall Street, for they do not seem to have the mental qualities required to take in the varied points of the situation upon which success in speculation depends" (Clews 1887: 436, 514). One need only remark, however, that "power" in the all-important social circles was clearly in the control of women. Few persons were successful in challenging Mrs. John Jacob Astor for social supremacy, except perhaps the Vanderbilt women (Vanderbilt

1989). The vagaries of each area, speculation and society, were perilous and enforced by what we today could call "networks."

Expert consulting accountants provided skills and had the experience needed to ensure results; as the investment community and general public began to recognize the need for special talent and training, the demand for accountants' services grew. Yet there were too few statutory disclosure laws, professional associations, or publications to assist in the exchange of ideas or development of techniques to meet this new demand.

By 1885, cities and their directories began to reflect an increasing number of persons offering services as expert accountants. The city of Louisville, Kentucky, located at a distance from the financial and commercial centers of the East, listed the services of five practicing accountants. The city directories of New York, Chicago, and Philadelphia indicated a rapid growth in the numbers of public accountants, from 81 in 1884 to 322 in 1889. As Ernest Reckitt, an early Chicago practitioner, observed, there was some turnover within these numbers, that is, persons who started and then withdrew from practice. Therefore the total number of individuals who had undertaken to practice publicly would be even greater than indicated. Littleton's study revealed that for the three major cities noted, during the period from 1850 to 1899, some 1,370 different individuals appeared in listings as accountants and 662 of these appeared only once. Despite the high number of nonrepeaters in the listings, the number of those that did repeat, in relation to the total population, suggests that this period can be identified as having witnessed the birth of modern public accounting practice.

This period also witnessed an unprecedented wave of corporate mergers that peaked in the 1890s. These mergers fueled the demand for accounting services that involved more than the review of clerical accuracy or the detection of fraud. The breadth of accounting services now expanded from the testing of values, financial advising, and various audit services, to include report writing, even though statutory disclosure requirements did not exist. In the 1890s, the forerunners of at least three of the national public accounting firms were established, and on April 17, 1896, the first state legislation recognizing and establishing the title of certified public accountant was enacted in the State of New York.

Prior to the merger wave of the 1890s, accountants and auditors, particularly those who had come from Great Britain, benefited from the brewers' boom of the 1880s. During this period, British capital was attracted to America especially for the purpose of investing in breweries. In such farflung locations as Saint Louis, Chicago, San Francisco, Baltimore, Milwaukee, Denver, Springfield, and Indianapolis, brewing companies were formed; as a consequence, accounting investigations and subsequent audits of considerable length were required.

James T. Anyon (1925), an English-bred early CPA leader, suggests that the "back parlor" (moonlighting) nature of many American accounting practices raised doubts among the public about the quality, ability, and character of early native accountants. He noted that accountants were viewed as "men of figures"—those who dealt in and loved figures for themselves, who calculated balances in accounts, prepared elaborate statements, and looked for errors. Accountants were viewed as the type of persons who thought figures, sometimes juggled them, and always wrote and talked them.

If this image betrays a lack of popular appeal, perhaps it is well to explore the reasons for this perception. During this period, accounting work was identified with musty drudgery. The bulky old bound ledgers in which records were kept were complicated affairs. It was quite impossible when starting a new ledger to determine with any accuracy the number of pages that an account might require before another ledger was opened. It was common to forward accounts as they filled up pages such that an account starting on page 10 might be forwarded to page 99, then to page 150, then to page 209, and so on. Unless the account was indexed by page, an outside auditor found it quite difficult to follow. Not until the loose-leaf ledger became practical to employ around the 1880s was the cumbersome bound ledger replaced. About the same time, special journals and voucher journals were achieving wide attention and use. Thus, they provided an additional reduction in the repetitive and needless duplication of entry information. Accounting reports rendered during this period were prepared and submitted in longhand, since the popular acceptance of the typewriter did not occur until the mid-1890s. One of the requisite skills of the accountant was to have "an accomplished hand" in penmanship and a modicum of patience: when multiple copies were required they had to be produced in the same tedious and exacting longhand.

Some accountants, then as now, were skeptical as to the advantages of new office technologies, such as the typewriter when it first appeared. "Why should I pay $125 for a machine when I can buy a pen for two cents?" some asked. Other accountants thought typewritten correspondence impersonal and offensive, likening it to receiving a printed public handbill (Reckitt 1953: 9).

Auditing techniques of the period included the following: vouchering all cash disbursements, checking all footings and postings, and tracing the ledger to the trial balance and the trial balance to the financial statements. As much as three-fourths of the audit time was spent on footings and postings. Experience showed, however, that about three-quarters of the defalcations were hidden by failures to account for income or cash receipts. Frequently, books would have been out of balance for months or years and locating errors was a terrible task.

In 1869, *Auditor's Guide,* by H. J. Mettenheim, appeared (Moyer 1951). Only sixteen pages, it was hardly adequate for the times but it suggested techniques for preventing fraud, including that all entries be clear, full, and explicit, that money columns be ruled to prevent slovenly work, and that the cashier be required to use a voucher for every payment. In 1881, Selden R. Hopkins's *Manual of Exhibit Bookkeeping* dealt in part with auditing matters. In 1882, G. P. Geer's *Science of Accounts* contained significant sections on auditing, including that proof should be sought outside the books in attempting to verify statements of debtors and creditors. Geer went on to specify certain internal control requirements that should be established in corporations, for example, that obligations of the corporation should be authorized by the vote of the directors and that all payments of large amounts should be made by check or draft on a bank of deposit. Geer also noted that when receipts or disbursements passed through the hands of a treasurer and cashier, and different collecting or disbursing clerks, the accounts of each should be arranged so as to check and prove each other (246).

Considering the techniques and the auditing theory of the period, it becomes clear that such early audits were effectively audits of the bookkeepers. The primary targets were error and fraud. Two out of three new audit engagements during the 1890s were likely to reveal defalcations. Such statistics do not come as a surprise in light of the fact that there had been no prior audit; fidelity bonds were not in existence; and few if any internal controls, including the division of duties, existed (Moyer 1951).

All of this suggests that the type of services and the qualifications of the individuals practicing public accounting during this period probably varied widely. There was little to prevent someone from advertising as follows in public directories or newspapers: "Complicated, disputed and confused accounts; also accounts with executors, trustees and estates in assignments investigated and stated. Books opened and closed. Suspected accounts confidentially examined. Partnership settlements made" (Moyer 1951: 4). Such pronouncements were not restricted to public directories and newspapers. Expert account cards were also circulated referring to similar services being offered to include expert work with joint stock companies, banks, and other corporation accounts.

The Institute of Accounts of New York, formed in April 1882, is the earliest recognized professional accounting organization in the United States.

Its aims during its first decade were almost wholly devoted to education for accountants and providing accounting literature. At institute meetings, technical and professional subjects were discussed. Subsequently the institute published *Accountics,* a periodical that combined news items and professional materials. The institute required a full test of qualifications before admission. Unfortunately, little is known of the operations of the institute after the turn of the century as its records have not been located and only a few of its examiners were known. Yet for a quarter-century, from 1882 until about 1908, the Institute of Accounts provided a professional association that admitted members from public as well as commercial practice. Its membership in 1884 numbered eighty persons and over the years included such notable members as Charles E. Sprague, Selden Hopkins, Charles Waldo Haskins, Farquhar MacRae, and Henry Harney.

Between 1874 and 1889, twelve other societies with identities related to accounting activities were formed in cities including Kansas City, Memphis, Saint Louis, Boston, Chicago, San Francisco, and Cleveland (Webster 1954: 10). Among the most active of these groups was the Bookkeepers Beneficial Association of Philadelphia, which was organized in 1874 with thirty-five members and grew to a membership of nearly three hundred by 1888. This association celebrated its fiftieth anniversary in 1924 but was dissolved sometime thereafter. It is not clear that this association acted as did the Institute of Accounts to screen membership by a set of rigorous examinations.

Several accounting periodicals serving these organizations also appeared during this period. The *Book-Keeper,* edited and published by Selden R. Hopkins and Charles E. Sprague, appeared in July 1880 and continued until 1883. Other publications included the *American Accounting Room* and the *Treasury.* These were succeeded by the *Office,* published by A. O. Kittredge. Each of these reported a circulation of 3,000 or more, and extra editions of 10,000 issued as samples were sent out widely to accountants and others.

Topics of Institute of Accounts speeches for the period from 1883 to 1887 included the following: "Costs Accounts in Metal Factories," by A. O. Kittredge; "The Unlearned Profession," by Silas S. Packard; "Documents as Related to Accounts," by Charles E. Sprague; "Account Keeping of Telephone Companies," by Charles Dothan; "Prices and Profits," by Joseph Hardcastle; and "Mechanical Consolidation Items," by Captain Henry Metcalfe. At the meeting of December 15, 1886, Charles Taller, a member of the institute, gave an address entitled "French and American Account Keeping Contrasted." This is the first known professional address on international accounting matters in America. Later during this meeting, a signal event, leading to the formation of an association that was to serve public accountants exclusively, occurred. As an interesting sequel to Taller's speech on French and American accounting, Edwin Guthrie, FCA, guest

James Yalden, first president, American Association of Public Accountants

W. Sanders Davies, first president, American Institute of Accountants

Charles Waldo Haskins, cofounder of Haskins & Sells

Edwin Guthrie, cofounder of Barrow, Wade & Guthrie

of the evening, gave by request a description of the Institute of Chartered Accountants in England. Guthrie had come to the United States at the invitation of James T. Anyon, who had arrived in October of the same year (Webster 1954).

British auditors had begun to reside in America as London firms found it less expensive to provide services on an extended basis by establishing resident offices in major U.S. cities. As business increased, the English firms were slowly Americanized by taking on staff of either British-born naturalized Americans or native-born Americans. Prior to 1888, such British firms serviced primarily British capital investments in fire insurance, railroad, and mortgage companies via monthly audits. With the subsequent "brewers' boom" mentioned above, British firms became involved in the audits of American breweries in several distant points in the United States.

The British contingent also served as a nucleus to influence the founding of the American Association of Public Accountants (AAPA). In addition to having known many British practitioners, Anyon had become acquainted with several American accountants of prominent stature, including William Veysey and John Heins. The history of the AAPA, which after several reorganizations and mergers ultimately became the American Institute of Certified Public Accountants (AICPA), is well documented in John L. Carey's two-volume *The Rise of the Accounting Profession*. These volumes detail many of the particulars of the early formative matters that were addressed by the AAPA.[9] American-born accountants as well as those from Britain composed the movement (Miranti 1990A).

The certificate of incorporation of the American Association of Public Accountants was filed on September 20, 1887. The first president was James Yalden, an Englishman. The vice president was John Heins, an American-born accountant. The secretary was James T. Anyon and the treasurer was William Veysey. The most formidable obstacle facing public practitioners at this time was a lack of formal legal recognition of their public practice. Carey noted that the existence of the AAPA did little to change things immediately. Both the Institute of Accounts and the AAPA began via separate routes to investigate securing legislation to achieve such legal recognition. Norman Webster and George Wilkinson have provided us with a legacy of details and information regarding the pre-1900 CPA movement. Although some historical essays on the subject of these early years suggest that a noble "onward and upward" spirit existed between British and American accountants, other interpretations do not support this view. The early AAPA was a hybrid of the English club–medieval guild pattern of the Institute of Chartered Accountants. It did not become an "American" organization for several years. Part of the evidence of its lack of acceptance by native Americans before 1900 is found in the fact that it had fewer than 100 members at the turn of the century and these were predominantly English-born residents of New York. Accountants from other states were noted in Association records as "non residents." Early professional activities were marked by the existence of these two camps, the British and the American. Although harmony would be forthcoming, it is important to note that, in addition to the problem of lack of legal recognition, the professionals themselves had not yet achieved a sense of unity and self-identity. As long as practitioners were thus divided, it would be difficult to achieve legal recognition (Wilkinson 1928).

A dozen years before the 1896 Certified Public Accountants Law of New York was passed, the Institute of Accounts issued certificates to Fellows who passed strict, practical, and technical entrance examinations. The prerequisite of technical competence as a basis of self-regulation therefore had been established prior to the existence of a law.

But the professional associations lacked the power and complete authority to control the growing ranks of all practitioners. Therefore, in 1895, an initial attempt to obtain CPA legislation was made by both organizations (see figures 4.3, 4.4A, and 4.4B). During the winter of 1894–95, a rough draft of a bill providing for a professional examination and a distinctive title was prepared by Henry Harney, president of the Institute of Accounts. Many years before, Harney had committed to paper some ideas along this line. He appointed Charles E. Sprague to convey the draft to Albany and see what could be done toward having it enacted into legislation. Sprague was a friend of Melvil Dewey, secretary of the Regents of the University of the State of New York. Dewey advised that the enforcement of the law be put under the jurisdiction of the Regents of the University of the State of New York, which had the capability to conduct such examinations. Furthermore, he pointed out that this would give the measure something of an educational character. The legal designation Certified Public Accountant was agreed upon at this time.

In the meantime, acting independently, several members of the AAPA prepared a draft for a bill providing that no person shall practice as a public accountant after the passage of the act unless he be licensed by the Regents of the University of the State of New York. No distinctive title was sought under the AAPA bill. This bill was introduced in February 1895, before the New York State Senate.

Two weeks later, the institute's bill was introduced in the New York State Assembly. The institute's bill contained two features clearly disadvantageous to the large British-born membership of the AAPA. First, it required that CPAs be citizens of the United States; second, it provided that only certified public accountants of the State of New York should be appointed or employed to act as examiners of accounts, expert accountants, or paid auditors by court administrators, receivers, state, county, or municipal officers.

A meeting was called in March 1895 to attempt to reconcile the two bills and the rival organizations by means of creating a special committee (the

[58 Vict.]   *Accountants.*

A

B I L L

TO

Amend the Law relating to Accountants.   A.D. 1895.

WHEREAS the profession of accountant has attained such a
position that it is advisable in the public interest that the
Legislature should exercise some control over the same :

Be it therefore enacted by the Queen's most Excellent Majesty,
5 by and with the advice and consent of the Lords Spiritual and
Temporal, and Commons, in this present Parliament assembled,
and by the authority of the same, as follows :—

1. After the *passing of this Act* no person shall describe himself   Restriction
as an accountant, or as a public accountant, or use any name,   of the use of
title of
10 title, addition, or description or letters indicating that he is an   public or
accountant by profession or a public accountant, whether by   professional
advertisement, by description in or at his place of business or   accountant.
residence, by any document or otherwise, unless he is registered
as a public accountant in pursuance of this Act : Provided always
15 that this section shall not extend to or affect any salaried officer
employed as an accountant exclusively in or under any Government
department or corporate body, or in any bank, society, association,
or institution incorporated by Royal Charter, or by or under any
Act of Parliament, or constituted by any articles of association or
20 other deed of constitution.

2. No person shall describe himself as a member, or fellow, or   Restriction
associate, or student of any of the corporations, institutions, or   of the use of
the title of
societies mentioned in section four of this Act, or use any name,   member, or
title, addition, or description or letters indicating that he is a   fellow, or
associate, or
25 member, or fellow, or associate, or student of any such corporation,   student of
institution, or society, whether by advertisement, by description in   certain
or at his place of business or residence, by any document or other-   bodies
wise, unless he be a member, or fellow, or associate, or student of
such corporation, institution, or society respectively

[Bill 133.]

Figure 4.3 A copy of British legislation relating to accountants

"Committee of 14") to resolve the differences. Two members of the committee representing the AAPA were Anyon and Yalden. Among those representing the institute were Harney and Charles Dutton. There were also
nonmember representatives, including Silas S. Packard and John E. Hourigan. The committee lost little time in determining that the association's bill

proposing a license should be dropped and the institute's bill proposing a title should be pushed. The committee also determined that an attorney should be retained to watch the progress of the bill before the legislature. A subcommittee of the "Committee of 14" retained E. G. Whittaker to represent the committee at the Assembly, and the subcommittee met with the Assembly's committee on general laws to advocate passage of the bill. The subcommittee was unable to influence the legislation. Assemblyman Wylds, who had introduced the bill, could not be persuaded to report it favorably to the House. Meanwhile, in the Senate, the bill that had been substituted for the institute's version failed to receive a majority vote.

The AAPA quickly followed up to reintroduce the provisions of the bill in the following year's meeting of the legislature. Perhaps because the AAPA represented the practicing *public* accountants and not a mixed group of accountants, it was deemed most appropriate for them to pursue the passage of the bill in the next session. Frank Broaker became the chairman of the association's subcommittee. He turned the bill over to Senator Albert Ray of Brooklyn, who introduced the bill in the Senate in January 1896. It was referred to the Committee on Judiciary. During the same period, a bill under the same title was introduced in the House by Assemblyman Marshall. The bill passed the Assembly on April 3 by almost unanimous vote, passed the Senate on April 7, and was approved by the governor on April 17, 1896.

A significant single amendment to the bill, made as a result of apparent cooperation between the rival professional groups, assured its passage in 1896. The amendment provided that the certified public accounting designation was available to any citizen of the United States or *person who had duly declared his intention to become such a citizen*. The success of the 1896 legislation may have hinged upon that provision, which opened the way for many British chartered accountants and other non-Americans who had not as yet secured their papers as U.S. citizens. Without the amendment, a split in the support for the bill between American and British professionals might have developed because of the restrictive provisions in the act regarding state-directed accounting engagements. When the bill did take effect, many British chartered accountants who chose to retain their British citizenship moved to other states to set up their practice.

In the years 1896 and 1897, 112 certificates were awarded, 108 under the waiver that had been established by the Board of Regents to grant the CPA certificate to those who could prove they had been in reputable practice as public accountants since January 1, 1890. These certificates were awarded in alphabetical order. Frank Broaker received the first CPA certificate. The first examination under the new law was given December 15 and 16, 1896.

THE SOCIETY OF ACCOUNTANTS & AUDITORS.
(INCORPORATED 1885)

4. King Street,
Cheapside.

London 26 July 1895
E.C.

TELEPHONE Nº 345   TELEGRAPHIC ADDRESS, IMPERSONAL LONDON

J. Cullen Roberts Esq.,
American Association of Public Accountants
56 Pine Street, New York.

Dear Sir,

I am much obliged for your letter of the 16th inst. and for the accompanying draft of an act which you have recently endeavoured to pass in the Legislature. The matter is of course of much interest to us as we are endeavouring to obtain legal recognition of the Status of accountants here. I enclose you draft of our Bill which has been read a first time in the House of Commons. The recent dissolution of Parliament has of course prevented further progress with it for the present.

Yours faithfully,
[signature]
Secretary.

Figure 4.4 Early CPA legislation. (A) Letter.

Only three of the four who passed this examination are known; they were Edward C. Charles, Joseph Hardcastle, and William H. Jasper (Wilkinson 1903: 9).

The typical American-born CPA candidate who sat for the exam at the turn of the century was about thirty years old, attended public schools for grammar education, and worked as a commercial or government clerk or

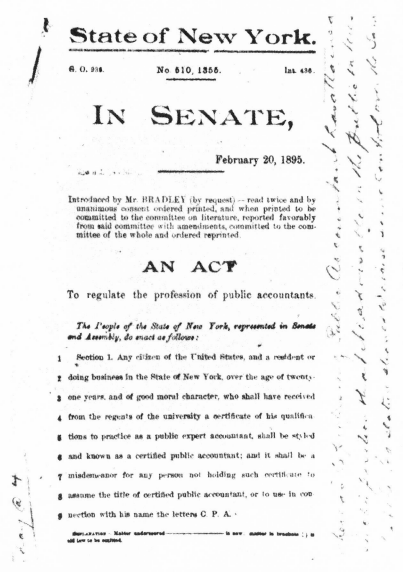

Figure 4.4 *Continued* (B) Draft.

bookkeeper before engaging in the public practice of another accountant and/or returning to teach at a commercial college. Thereafter upon setting up practice in his own name, he would take the CPA exam and commence his professional activities. A college education would not become a requirement for decades; at this point a high school equivalent education was specified.

State Societies and Legislation

In response to the initial passage of CPA legislation, several states soon followed in obtaining similar statutes. Pennsylvania's CPA law was enacted in 1899. Maryland passed a CPA law in 1900; California, in 1901; Washington and Illinois, in 1903. CPA legislation would be in place in all forty-eight states by the mid-1920s (tables 4.4 and 4.5).

The CPA certificate served as a kind of university professional degree. The fact that the CPA law in New York was supervised by the Board of Regents furthered this perception. It was common then for persons to refer to having obtained a CPA "degree," alluding to it as a type of formal education at a time when entry requirements for qualifying generally did not include collegiate education.

CPAs now began to form separate professional associations. John Hourigan of Albany appears to have been an important catalyst in the formation of the New York State Society of CPAs, whose initial meeting was held at the Hotel Waldorf on March 30, 1897. Earlier, Hourigan had solicited via a letter the interest of accountants in the state to form a society similar to those of physicians, architects, and civil engineers. Hourigan served as an incorporator of the New York society and became its first vice president (Committee on History 1953A).

Although the New Jersey law was not enacted until April 1904, public accountants in the state organized their society in January 1898. This society, through one of its members, Richard Stevens, New York CPA No. 29, practicing in Newark, was instrumental in eventually overcoming the opposition of the New Jersey legislature to achieve passage of the CPA bill.

Pioneers of the American Profession

The many early CPA movement leaders, including Anyon, Hopkins, Sprague, Harney, Broaker, and MacRae, reflected a diversity of backgrounds. Hopkins, for example, had contributed a section to the book *Dollars and Sense*, written by the famous showman Phineas T. Barnum. Hopkins's section, "Money, Banks and Banking," focused on "where money came from and where it went." In addition, Hopkins was editor of the *Book-Keeper*, published in the 1880s, and wrote books on the subject of bookkeeping practice. In 1888 he had written a "Horatio Alger" type novel, *A Young Prince of Commerce*.

In 1883 Barrow, Wade, Guthrie & Co.—considered to be the first "national" accounting firm—organized in the United States. The formation of other U.S. accounting firms proceeded apace (Wise 1982: 1, 2). James

Thornley Anyon (1851–1929) emigrated to the United States in 1886 and joined the staff of Barrow. He became a partner the following year (Zeff 1988: x).

Charles Ezra Sprague can be assigned much credit for gaining the instrumental support and advice of Melvil Dewey, a prominent New York education official, to secure passage of the CPA law. Sprague was a man of many talents. By vocation a banker, he had an interest in foreign languages and also had been involved with Hopkins in the publication of the *Book-Keeper*. Long active in affairs of his alma mater, Union College of Schenectady, he was also the author of the "Algebra of Accounts," a lengthy series that first appeared in the issues of the *Book-Keeper* in the early 1880s. Sprague achieved fame after the turn of the century as having made a major contribution to the theory of accounts through his algebraic demonstration of the systematic concept of "Assets equal Liabilities plus Proprietorship" ($A = L + P$) (Sprague 1908: 20). A Union veteran of the Civil War, he had been wounded at the Battle of Gettysburg. Sprague's southern counterpart was Henry Harney. Henry Harney, born in Baltimore about 1835, had been the chief accountant of the Bank of Richmond from 1856 to 1861 and had distinguished himself in the Civil War at the Battle of Bull Run/Manassas on the side of the Confederacy ("Major Henry Harney," 1897). He became a member of the Institute of Accounts in 1886 and served five successive terms as president. It is interesting to note that two adversaries in the Civil War, Sprague and Harney, served effectively together as leaders of the CPA movement, which transformed the accounting community.

Frank Broaker, the holder of Certificate No. 1, was born in Millerstown, Pennsylvania, in 1863. He was the son of John Strawbridge but took his stepfather's name. He worked for John Roundy, a Scottish accountant, from 1883 to 1887 and then worked in his own name before entering partnership with Richard M. Chapman (CPA No. 2 under the provisions of the 1896 act). He was active in the American Association of Public Accountants as vice president from 1892 to 1896 and president and ramrod of the legislative efforts in 1896.

Broaker was involved in a controversy relating to the publication of *The American Accountants Manual,* a book he had prepared in 1897 based on the first CPA examination questions. The manual contained recommended solutions to the examination and sold for three dollars with the proceeds going to his private account. Further, Broaker had been charged with forming a society of accountants with himself as president. It was alleged that he had urged accountants to join the society and that they were led to expect that if they did so, the Regents might be induced to waive the examination as was provided in the law for a person possessing the necessary experience qualifications. In response to complaints about Broaker's actions with regard to the *Manual,* the State Board of Regents effected a reorganization of the State Board of Examiners of Certified Public Accountants by appointing James T. Anyon to replace Broaker and by appointing Charles Waldo Haskins and Charles E. Sprague, who had served on the first board of examiners for the Certified Public Accountant certificate. A published comment in an 1897 issue of *Accountics* notes that the summary dismissal of Broaker for allegedly violating the precedent for treatment of revenues from such a manual was severe and perhaps unwarranted.

In June 1898, Christine Ross successfully passed the New York CPA examination. After she passed the examination, her certificate was withheld while officials decided whether or not a woman should be certified. Such were the times. The minutes of the Board of Regents meeting of December 21, 1899, stated: "Voted that the full CPA certificate be granted to Christine Ross, who successfully passed the professional examination in June 1898." She was awarded Certificate No. 143. Ross, a native of Nova Scotia, began practicing accounting in 1889 and thereafter practiced from offices at 17 Battery Place (*Introducing Women Accountants,* 1958).

Farquhar J. MacRae, a native of Brooklyn born in 1862, worked for Selden Hopkins and Henry Harney and was listed as a public accountant in the New York *Directory* of 1892. MacRae became a member of the Institute of Accounts in 1890, secretary in 1892, and a member of the executive committee in 1897. He served four terms as vice president. He later became active in the state society and the Federation of State Societies of Public Accountants after the turn of the century. MacRae and others advertised their services regularly. For example, an 1894 advertisement for the audit company of New York noted: "examines and reports on the accounts and financial condition of corporations, copartnerships and individuals and examines and reports on the physical condition of railroad, manufacturing and other properties. Its services are of value to investors, financial institutions, borrowers of money, directors of corporations, merchants, firms, and purchasers of properties." Such ads were common fare. As early as 1872, individuals, including William H. Veysey, were placing "tombstone" advertisements in the classified section of the *Commercial & Financial Chronicle* which claimed: "Complicated and disputed accounts investigated and adjusted" ("Tax Relief," 1872: 234).

Another interesting profile is that of Ferdinand W. Lafrentz. In 1873 Lafrentz immigrated to the United States from Germany and lived in Chicago. Subsequently, he moved west, working in Ogden, Utah, and serving as a member of the Wyoming legislature in 1888. In response to the request of a friend who was traveling to the West Coast, Lafrentz became familiar with the activities of the American Surety Company and was employed as an accountant in 1893. He subsequently became president and chairman of that organization. At the same time, he had established a practice in his own name, F. W. Lafrentz and Company. Later, Lafrentz's organization was formalized into the American Audit Company, with offices located in the Waldorf Astoria. The American Audit Company became F. W. Lafrentz & Company in 1923. Lafrentz continued his service to the American Surety Company past his ninetieth year. He was a poet, having authored a book of poems called *Cowboy Stuff* and a book in German about his boyhood days in Fehmarn, an island in the Baltic Sea just north of the German mainland.

TABLE 4.4
The First CPAs

New York Certificate Number	Names
1	Frank Broaker
2	Richard Chapman
3	Leonard Conant
4	William Sanders Davies
5	Rodney S. Dennis
6	Charles Waldo Haskins
7	Brownell McGibbon
8	Frederick Manuel
9	Charles J. Mercer
10	E. W. Sells
11	C. E. Sprague
12	Frank Irving Stott
13	Arthur W. Teele
14	Alfred Percy Walker
15	Andrew Allen Clarke
16	Robert L. Cuthbert
17	Arnold Davidson
18	Henry Harney
19	John Hourigan
20	Ferdinand W. Lafrentz
21	Fergus Lamb
22	James A. McKenna
23	Farquhar J. MacRae
24	Andrew B. Martin
25	Clarence A. Martin

Source: Accountics, June 1898, pp. 72–73.

TABLE 4.5
Legal Recognition of Accountants

Year Law Passed	Number of States	States
1896	1	New York
1899	1	Pennsylvania
1900	1	Maryland
1901	1	California
1903	2	Washington, Illinois
1904	1	New Jersey
1905	2	Michigan, Florida
1906	1	Rhode Island
1907	3	Utah, Colorado, Connecticut
1907	3	Ohio, Louisiana, Georgia
1909	5	Montana, Nebraska, Minnesota, Massachusetts, Missouri
1910	1	Virginia
1911	2	West Virginia, Wyoming
1912	1	Vermont
1913	8	Oregon, North Carolina, North Dakota, Nevada, Tennessee, Delaware, Maine, Wisconsin
1915	6	South Carolina, Indiana, Arkansas, Kansas, Texas, Iowa
1916	1	Kentucky
1917	4	Idaho, New Hampshire, Oklahoma, South Dakota
1919	2	Alabama, Arizona
1920	1	Missippi
1921	1	New Mexico
1923	1	District of Columbia

Note: Reproduced from Eric L. Kohler and Paul W. Pettengill, *Principles of Auditing* (Chicago: A. W. Shaw Company, 1927).

Lafrentz received some of his accounting training at a Bryant and Stratton Business College. He was a member of the American Association of Public Accountants and held Certificate No. 20 in New York State. He also lectured at the New York University School of Commerce, Accounts and Finance.

Despite achieving legal recognition of accountancy, market forces adjusted at their own pace. Speaking many years earlier in 1881 from the perspective of Canada, William Anderson, president of the Institute of Accountants of Ontario, said: "It is our regret that we must say that there is far too little value place[d], by the business community of Uncle Sam's dominions, upon the services, skill and knowledge of competent and practical accountants" (Anderson 1881: 114).

Many community leaders of the era supported the notion of legislation designed "to keep or cause to be kept authentic and properly adjusted sets of accounts." However, they did not yet support that such reports "should be made public property" or that disclosure or auditing be mandatory. The editor of the *Book-Keeper* continued, "But we entertain the conviction that accurate business records should be kept, so as to be produced whenever the welfare of the public or the interests of the Government may demand their examination" ("Demand," 1881: 120).

The "keystone" of a professional accountant's role, objectivity, was recognized in statements such as: "It must not, for a moment, be forgotten that the position . . . , is one of confidence, trust and often grave responsibility. . . . And further, sound principles of accountancy will not allow [one] . . . to make important entries in his books until he is furnished with such authority, that in case the entry should, in the future, be questioned, he may readily produce evidence necessary to establish his professional integrity, and, if need be, protect his honor and uprightness" (*Book-Keeper* 1881: 168, 169).

As the business world moved into the twentieth century, economic theory, the legal system, and society all were shifting their attention toward growth of large enterprises under the system of capitalism. The need for a trained corps of public accountants was becoming recognized and addressed through the passage of CPA legislation and the formation of professional accounting associations. The problems and the challenges were many. For one, the associations of practitioners were not growing as rapidly as key members believed they should. In part, this may be attributed to the fact that the rules of admission were rigorous and restrictive. Although some early writers have stated that American public accounting was not in existence before the 1880s, it would be more appropriate to say that public accounting was viable before 1880 but not visible until after 1880. Evidence supplied by Littleton and Webster indicates that accounting activity prior to the 1880s was prerequisite for the establishment of the widespread qualified, competent, and professional discipline that began to emerge in the 1880s and the 1890s.

During these years before the turn of the century the full energies of this small group were devoted to:

1. Organizing at the state, local, and national levels.
2. Securing passage of laws and initiating appropriate administration of such laws.
3. Initiating attempts to establish university programs of accounting.

In light of these tasks, this young professional group was not sufficiently large to be extensively engaged in matters of developing uniform technical standards, and it would be unfair to blame these pioneering CPAs for not making headway in the area. After the turn of the century, a "federal" form of professional association, one that utilized both state and national organizations, would be discovered to be the most effective approach to advancing a program of unity, standards, and professionalism for certified public accountants (Miranti 1990A: 179).

Higher Education for Accountants

Business was beginning to require a type of training that existing schools, both high schools and universities, did not provide (see figure 4.5). In some ways, the attitude of businessmen discouraged universities from undertak-

Figure 4.5 A classroom scene typical of the post–Civil War era. *Source: The Countinghouse Arithmetic* (Baltimore, 1889).

ing business education on a widespread scale. For example, Andrew Carnegie commented that "college graduates are not successful businessmen," stirring up a controversy that lasted well into the 1890s. The old ironmaster thought that young men destined for business ought to be mingling with men who did business.

Prior to 1875, bookkeeping was perhaps the only subject that could be classified as a business topic regularly taught in high schools. Even after 1875, formal business education was still unknown in universities. Evidence suggests that Robert E. Lee, then president of Washington College, recommended the establishment of a School of Commerce there in 1869; Lee died, however, before any action could be taken (Ruml 1928: 246). It was not until 1881 that the University of Pennsylvania, upon receipt of $100,000 from Joseph Wharton, established a school for "imparting a liberal education in all matters concerning Finance and Economics" (Sass 1982: 21).

In the face of the growing demand for individuals trained in business procedure to assist large corporations and other developing business enterprises in the conduct of their affairs, business colleges sprang up throughout the country during the post–Civil War period to provide trained personnel. As noted earlier, chain schools such as the Bryant and Stratton Business Colleges and pioneering business educators including Silas S. Packard, an accountant and later president of the Institute of Accounts, were among the important names in the business college movement of the pre-1900 period. Packard's view of the bookkeeper's function, written in 1881, was as follows: "What I would have every book-keeper be, is not a poor routinist, but a good one; not a theorist only, but severely practical; not visionary and esthetic, but sound and solid; being able not only to 'keep' books, but to tell what they contain" (Packard 1881: 132).

In 1883, the initial offering of what would be a sustained accounting course series at the collegiate level was undertaken at the Wharton School of the University of Pennsylvania, which had started only two years earlier. The content of the courses, which included two terms of instruction, involved several technical requirements, as well as a series of lectures on "The Theory and Practice of Accounting." According to the recollections of one of the first students, there were twelve pupils in this first collegiate accounting class. The course textbooks included Selden Hopkins's *Manual of Exhibit Bookkeeping* and C. C. Marsh's *Bookkeeping and Joint Stock Accounts* (Lockwood 1938).

In the decade preceding the passage of CPA legislation, some professional leaders including Broaker, Yalden, and Stevens formed the New York School of Accounts "to provide for young men special means of training and of correct and practical instruction in the knowledge and science of modern accountancy and finance" (Slocum and Roberts 1980: 65). The venture failed because of insufficient enrollment, the requirements of which included that the applicant be a graduate of a college or university registered by the Regents of the University of the State of New York. At the time, collegiate education was a sufficiently exclusive achievement to substantially limit the pool of prospective students.

Just before the turn of the century, the University of Chicago authorized the establishment of a College of Commerce and Politics (renamed the College of Commerce and Administration). In its initial academic year, 1898–99, ten students were registered and within three years there were eighty-nine students in total. Henry Rand Hatfield recalled that accounting at the University of Chicago, where he taught, relied upon the early writing of Professor J. F. Schar of Germany, who had written on the matter of single and double entry during the 1890s. The lack of suitable textbooks no doubt hampered the effectiveness of accounting at the university level. However, as early as 1886, Wharton faculty member Charles Gilpin had authored a textbook, *Theory of Double-Entry Bookkeeping* (Pilcher 1935: 141).

The pioneering efforts of the Wharton School, the University of Chicago, the Amos Tuck School at Dartmouth (1899), and, after the turn of the century, the School of Commerce, Accounts and Finance at New York University, provided important first steps in collegiate education in accounting.[10]

Proprietary Education

While university business programs developed toward the end of the era, the bulk of the training and education of businessmen and accountants during the period came by way of the proprietary business colleges. At a banquet for Silas S. Packard on the occasion of his seventieth birthday in 1896, toasts and testimonials acknowledged his important role in the business college movement. Packard had organized and conducted a general exhibit of the American Commercial and Business Schools at the Chicago World's Fair. For over fifty years, Packard had taken upon himself the work of commercial teaching and the promotion of business education. His students became known as "Packard boys and girls," a trademark word representing young men and women who had a sound business-practices education. Packard, born in 1826 and raised on the Ohio frontier, was a type of Horatio Alger success story. As one put it, "inspired by poverty in youth he had learned the necessity for labor and for struggle" (*Testimonial Banquet,* 1896).

Packard wrote texts on accounting and bookkeeping for the chain of business colleges that he established. These books in revised form were still in use through the 1900s. Packard's books are recognized to have had an influence beyond the United States, including Canada and Japan. Before 1876, William C. Whitney, an American business school proprietor, had journeyed to Japan and established a commercial school at the invitation of the Japanese minister to Washington. Whitney had operated a Bryant and Stratton Business College in Newark. He took with him to Japan texts that dealt with the science of accounts. Two such texts in use during the evolution of Japanese accounting during the late nineteenth century included Packard's *Manual of Theoretical Training in the Science of Accounts* (1868) and Folsom's *Logic of Accounts* (1873). It has been difficult to determine their significance, given that to date Japanese accounting historians have focused mostly upon the notion that "the Japanese assimilated British accounting practices to Japanese features" during the modernization that occurred in the last half of the nineteenth century (Chiba 1987: 13).

Packard's writings provide useful evidence in another area: "value theory." Writing in 1868, he "clearly equates the value of unsold property to replacement cost, stating, 'The value of unsold property is not necessarily measured by its cost nor its selling price; although in ordinary cases the cost standard is adopted in taking account of stock, the proper standard of value is the cost of the good in the purchasing market; or what it would take to replenish them'" (Martin 1979: 9).

Packard had taught at various places before opening his own commercial college as a part of the Bryant and Stratton chain. In 1867, he bought out the interests of his partners, abolished the Bryant and Stratton affiliation, and founded the Packard Business College. This was a step toward terminating chain-system influence in business education and laid the foundation for independently owned schools. The franchise movement of business schools faltered after the initial success of the Bryant and Stratton system partly because of internal weaknesses involving changes in policies as well as the lack of uniformity with regard to the practices of individual schools under local leadership.

Just as Packard was the patriarch of business education in the East, George Soulé was a patriarch of education for business in the South. New Orleans, which had flourished in the post–Civil War years, also experienced an acute need for persons trained in business subjects. Soulé authored successful and widely used accounting texts. Soulé's book was introduced in 1881 with subsequent editions through the early 1900s.

As business colleges began operating on a proprietary and profit basis, they grew rapidly. The membership of the International Business College Association, profiled in figure 3.1, suggests the basis from which proprietary business and accounting education commenced. In 1889, Packard described business colleges as strong in number and financially prosperous. Response to the success of these colleges included some public school competition to meet the demands heretofore served by the private business colleges. Cities recognized that business college subjects would pay their own way. Nonetheless, private business colleges filled the educational void for a significant period.[11]

Textbooks and Teaching

An examination of the textbooks that were used to teach account keeping during this period reveals the standardization of the worksheet step of the accounting cycle (see figure 4.6). In this step, the pro forma worksheet based upon the unadjusted trial balance through to adjusted profit and loss and balance sheet columns was used much the same way as we find it in the accounting cycle of today.[12]

A common weakness of the general financial accounting texts of this period was the lack of technique for dealing with corporation accounts. Even late editions of Soulé's *Science and Practice of Accounts* were oriented to proprietary ownership rather than to capital stock companies, although a few editions did treat opening entries and techniques for capital stock companies.

It would seem that the experience of the practicing accountant in the handling of corporate accounts was not flowing readily into the classroom. Business practice, not academic achievement, guided the technical innovations then disseminated through popular textbooks.

Origins of "Preclassical" Theory

During this period several attempts to conceptualize accounting practice were initiated. Most notable was the appearance of Charles E. Sprague's series of papers entitled "Algebra of Accounts" in 1880. This was the forerunner of the proprietary theory presented in his *Philosophy of Accounts*, published shortly after the turn of the century. Sprague's writings precede the development of classical historical cost and matching notions that emerged during the period following World War I, hence the term "preclassical."

Sprague's writing in the "Algebra of Accounts" evidences a capability for abstract and axiomatic approaches in accounting thought well before such ideas were popularly recognized. His early works provided a classificatory and deductive framework for the proprietary equity notions being widely

Carlton & Fowler's Balance Sheet. Set V.

L. Folio	NEW YORK, MAY 31st, 1876.	LEDGER BALANCES Dr.	LEDGER BALANCES Cr.	PROFIT AND LOSS Losses.	PROFIT AND LOSS Gains.	H. L. CARLTON Dr.	H. L. CARLTON Cr.	GEO. R. FOWLER Dr.	GEO. R. FOWLER Cr.	STATE OF AFFAIRS Assets.	STATE OF AFFAIRS Liabilities.
1	H. L. Carlton,		20,100 00				20,100 00				
1	George R. Fowler,	1,164 99						1,164 99			
1	Cash,	2,432 90								2,432 90	
1	Bills Receivable,	1,852 13								1,852 13	
1	Bills Payable,		2,917 50								2,917 50
1	Merchandise,	14,847 01	17,241 88		2,394 87					17,241 88	
2	Interest and Discount,	152 33		152 33							
2	Fixtures and Expenses,	284 50		284 50							
✓	Personal Debtors,	2,896 08								2,896 08	
✓	Personal Creditors,		612 44								612 44
		23,629 94	23,629 94	436 83	2,394 87				652 68	24,422 99	3,529 94
				1,305 36			1,305 36		512 31		20,893 05
				652 68					1,164 99		
				2,394 87	2,394 87	21,405 36	21,405 36	1,164 99	1,164 99	24,422 99	24,422 99

Total Losses and Gains,

H. L. Carlton's, ⅔ gain,
Geo. R. Fowler's, ⅓ "

Firm's Net Gain $1,958.04

Net Capital,

Net Insolvency,

Total Assets and Liabilities,

Firm's Net Capital, { H. L. Carlton's Net Capital, $21,405.36.
Geo. R. Fowler's Insolvency, 512.31.

Figure 4.6 Textbook example of financial reports, 1876. *Source:* John Groesbeck, *Practical Book-Keeping, Single and Double Entry* (Philadelphia: Eldrege & Brother, 1884).

discussed in the publications of the time and linked early accounting notions to mathematics and economics.

Sprague began his exposition by noting that accounting "is a history of values." His basic accounting equation, Assets = Liabilities + Proprietorship (A = L + P), appeared in the 1880 series stated as, "what I have plus what I trust equals what I owe plus what I am worth," which was written symbolically as H + T = O + X (Sprague 1880). From sets of derived equations, he provided the reader of accounts a logical and systematic approach to developing a transaction cycle for accounting. Rather than requiring that one memorize an endless series of rules, Sprague emphasized that the keeping of accounts involved certain equations in which addition and cancellation of uniform value determine net wealth.

"Annals or chronicles merely relate facts which have occurred; but true history groups together facts of the same tendency in order to discover if possible the cause of happiness and misery, prosperity and ruin; so true bookkeeping, being a history, should group together similar values in its equations to discover the causes and effects of Loss and Gain" (Sprague 1880). He concluded, "In the equation of accounts the answer sought or 'unknown quantity' is what am I worth? This we will represent by the letter X." Although Sprague's exposition did not go beyond the proprietary model, the forty-two paragraphs of this early treatise included notational operations for balancing and measurement that were suitable for more than proprietary operations. Paton would later develop the theory to address corporate entities.

Sprague's accounting equation (Assets = Liabilities + Proprietorship) was destined to become the starting point of today's approach to accounting education as well as the focal point of subsequent modifications. In this way, Sprague's axioms have become recognized as the essence of a preclassical school of American accounting theory. His writings were evidence of the unique and essentially complete theory from which modern American accounting developed. It was within this framework that conceptual concerns over issues such as costs and value, income and outlay, inventory and depreciation, would be argued. Decades later, both H. R. Hatfield and W. A. Paton, prominent early leaders among accounting university professors, would acknowledge Sprague's work as providing an important impetus to their own (Previts and Sheldahl 1988).

The influence of Sprague on the writings of later and equally eminent thinkers may be inferred from the remarks about Sprague by Paton, who was born in 1889 and was influenced to pursue accounting because of the writings of the former:[13] "It was these writings that aroused my interest in accounting, and without this spur I am quite certain that I would never have shifted from teaching economic theory to a career primarily in the accounting field. . . . Above all, he pushed the door ajar to a realization that accounting constitutes the outstanding approach to a pervasive understanding of business enterprises" (Paton 1972: iii, v).

As has been noted earlier, this was also a crucial time in the debate over the appropriate treatment of what is now recognized as the depreciation of fixed and wasting assets. *Accountics* ("Reorganization," 1897) reported on the importance and state of the issue, noting a speech given at a regular meeting of the Institute of Accounts in New York on Thursday evening January 14, 1897, by Frederick W. Child, a member of the institute. Attended by a large audience, Child's address focused on depreciation of plant, tools, fixtures, and so on, and the plan he recommended for managing the accounts respecting the same. He proposed that such accounts as machinery and tools, buildings and similar things should show the total cost of those items or the amount of the capital invested therein and that the amount written off for wear and tear, depreciation of value, and so forth, should be credited to special reserve accounts. "Thus," he noted, "if tools and machinery which cost $27,000 were in the estimation of the managers of the enterprise, depreciated in value by reason of use and other causes to an amount at a certain time equal to 10 percent, then the amount of depreciation ($2700) instead of being credited to tools and machinery account, should be passed to a credit for reserve on tools and machinery." This represents one of the earliest reported public discussions in America of the use of an account to accumulate and report depreciation reserves.

Under Child's approach, successive percentages, the results of which were entered during a term of years, would be credited to the reserve account. He urged that the allowance for depreciation be regarded as an expense in the factory account and be spread over the goods produced. He did not believe that satisfactory results from the accounting point of view were ever obtained by carrying the amount of depreciation of machinery and plant into the loss and gain account directly; depreciation of plant was part of the cost of the product.

The pages of *Accountics* in the same year reveal another discussion on the subject of goodwill. Although the article focused upon court cases, particularly those in England, it did, after thorough discussion, indicate that the accountants of the period were involved in debating the issue. Other conceptual concerns were also evidenced. Several years earlier, at a meeting of the Institute of Accounts in October 1889, Sprague had delivered a lecture on the subject of "income and outlay." He clearly suggests that the appropriate treatment was tied to the principle of *periodicity:* "The artificiality of profit and loss and its tributaries results partly from their relation to time.

The reciprocal action and reaction of outlay and income are continuous, but for convenience we treat them as periodical. We are compelled to cut them into even lengths for purposes of comparison" (Sprague 1889).

In this lecture, Sprague distinguished between losses and expenses, indicating that if the bookkeeping is that of a business concern then expenditures made under such headings as insurance and so forth are in no sense losses as the title profit and loss suggests. They are, he concluded, business outlays, deliberately made for the purpose of producing income that (it is hoped) will exceed outlay.

As early as 1880, the literature contained subjects of modern interest including a discussion of a treatment of extraordinary versus ordinary items of expense. In the writings of Soulé, we find descriptions of the use of suspense accounts, in particular, a type of allowance for doubtful accounts as a device for treating accounts of receivable values. It is also interesting to note that the term "principles" was employed in the description of the methods applicable to accounts as early as 1890.[14]

Two notable expositions on the theoretical and valuational aspects of accounting during the post–Civil War period were published before Sprague wrote his important series. The 1868 work of Silas S. Packard entitled *Manual of Theoretical Training in the Science of Accounts* was a forerunner in this preclassical era. In 1875, E. G. Folsom, proprietor of a business college in Albany, New York, published *The Logic of Accounts,* which had been written in 1873. The book focused on "valuation" problems in accounting (figure 4.7). He classified value initially under two headings, commercial value and ideal value. As he observed: "With the view of reducing double entry accounts to an exact science we begin with value as a generic or universal term applicable alike to all things and divided, first into two distinct classes; then each class into species of its own, until ultimate simple values are reached, as shown by the analysis" (2).

It may have become apparent that his notions were not useful or operational in practice, for his message appears to have had no great following. It was not until Sprague's writing that a clear point was made about the value of an asset and that such value could be measured in services given or the cost incurred. Sprague saw both the supply and demand aspect of value. Folsom probably saw the distinction between value in use and value in exchange much earlier but only from the supply side. He valiantly tried to incorporate it as the core of his accounting system but his method apparently failed to gain distinction.

As evidenced by frequent references to it in the *Book-Keeper,* early U.S. accountants made use of the British publication the *Accountant* as an important resource for ideas. Therefore, it should be added that the theoretical

TOPICAL ANALYSIS OF VALUE.

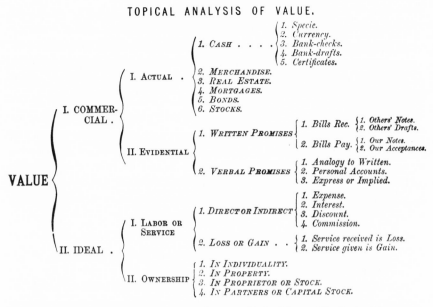

Figure 4.7 Folsom's "value theory chart." *Source:* E. G. Folsom, *The Logic of Accounts* (New York: A. S. Barnes, 1873).

developments of the age were not occurring in a vacuum, but with a linkage to the United Kingdom and, again referencing the *Book-Keeper*, with Canada.

The contents of the *Accountant* were of interest to North American readers, and items such as Cooper's paper of 1888 very likely drew attention. Titled "What is Profit of a Company," it provided a rationale that addressed the many differing opinions of the day. Cooper stated that "profit is the surplus of assets over the liabilities, including with the liabilities the paid up capital, and that the amount of profit is arrived at by ascertaining this surplus, after fairly estimating the value of all assets and liabilities" (Cooper 1888: 746).

This quarter-century of American professional accounting was marked by attempts to establish the role and function of the practicing accountant. Accountants devoted considerable editorial and manuscript attention to what public accounting *was* and what the public accountant *did,* or to responding to such rhetorical questions as, "What is an accountant, as distinguished from a bookkeeper?" or "What is an auditor?"

The passage of the New York CPA law and the exposition and influence of Sprague's theory of accounts provided the basis upon which to solidify a native U.S. accountancy profession and theory. The legislation affected the attest function and established the essential social franchise for the profession. In the background, influencing the acceptance of the professional movement was the experience of the chartered accountancy profession in the United Kingdom, which had established a social role for auditing as part of a process for "guarding . . . the interests of . . . Shareholders" (Pixley 1881: 151).

In this period, in part due to the notion identified with Sprague, it became possible to represent the activities of accounts in a notational and axiomatic fashion that facilitated abstraction and modeling of accounting transactions. Without these achievements, the developments of the first thirty years of the next century would not likely have come to pass, particularly in terms of the accounting techniques needed to communicate the financial data and statements that characterized the growth and complexity of the corporation.

Toward Managerial Accounting and Economies of Scope

During the 1850s, Paul Garner has noted, industrialism was beginning to have an impact on the character of account-keeping (Garner 1954: 42–43). By "1880, managers in complex metal-working firms demanded information about more than the efficiency of internal processes. These firms attempted to achieve success through economies of scope—gains that result from jointly producing two or more products in one facility" (H. Thomas Johnson 1987: 6).

The post–Civil War steel industry boom was a response to the demands of the westward drive of the railroads. For the first time, many text writers began to consider accounts related to factory and production costs. John Fleming's *Bookkeeping by Double Entry*, published in Pittsburgh in 1854, included several changes to reflect cost-accounting considerations. Fleming changed the name of the merchandise trading account to "factory account" and also attempted to determine the appropriate treatment for factory buildings. By the late 1880s, textbooks on the subject, such as that by the English authors Garke and Fells, recommended a strict "tie-in between the cost accounts and the general accounts" (Newlove 1975: 40). The basic principles of French and German cost systems were also in place by the 1880s (Nikitin 1990: 89; Coenenberg and Schoenfeld 1990: 96). Also about that time, Andrew Carnegie was pioneering the introduction of cost accounting in his mills and maintaining a considerable staff in his cost department. He insisted that his financial success was in part due to his ability to know his costs in the steel industry (Reckitt 1953: 18).

Before the 1880s, commercial text writers regularly paid only modest attention to industrial accounts at the very time that industry was being revolutionized by the factory system, widespread use of mechanical equipment, and devices for rapid communication and transportation. Perhaps a lack of firsthand experience and expertise in this generation of management accounting authors explains the lack of writing. One can also speculate that prior to 1885 the lack of detailed writings about the methods used by management and factory accountants was assignable to incomplete knowledge, or at another extreme, to a desire to retain the advantage of their knowledge by keeping it a secret. Several small societies of accountants and bookkeepers existed prior to 1880, as professional circles through which this information could have circulated. However, there were few professional accounting magazines prior to 1880, and this lack of communication may have impeded the transfer of knowledge. There is also the possibility that while developments were achieved in the area of cost controls, at this point, there was still not a sufficient basis of practice to lend credibility to generalizations about the value of a given approach or system.

Historical research by Fleischman and Parker, as well as Johnson and Kaplan and others, focuses upon the pre-1880 period and considers factory records themselves as a device for determining the true state of management accounting prior to 1880. Their research indicates that the systems in existence were much more sophisticated than could be determined from the literature and textbooks of the time. Johnson has observed that as the vertical integration of large complex businesses occurred (such that from source supply to consumer, a single organization was involved in transforming the raw material to the final product), it was necessary that an organizational structure and an accounting system be developed to integrate the entire effort under a unitary form of managerial accounting that featured independent departments as well as central office communication and control features (Johnson and Kaplan 1987: 64).

Railroads, however, in the view of Galambos and Pratt (1988) were the first large enterprises to develop a rationale that would support distinctions of fixed and variable costs. They identify Albert Fink of the Louisville and Nashville Railroad as the "Father of Cost Accouting" (48).

A Critical View

Not all business writers were content with accounting or the persons who practiced it. Wells (1970) found Kirkman, for example, writing in *Railway Expenditures* in 1880 as follows:

> When I was very young I remember to have been much cast down at the evident want of interest which railway managers manifested in statistical lore. I can recall, now, that my ideal officer was a man of delicate physical structure,

of towering intellectual front, with pale, weak eyes and sickly complexion withal, his shoulders bowed with study and the contemplation of the subtle phases of railway polity. My ideal was, in fact, not a manager at all, but a statistician, a clerk, an accountant. I had not then learned that the class of men I had in mind were never leaders in the affairs of life, but the followers only—the pack-mules, so to speak. The managers of our railways are never of an active statistical turn of mind, and as I said before, it is perhaps fortunate for the owners that this is so. (pp. 22–23)

He then notes:

The rapid growth of the railroad interest has developed everywhere embryo accountants in more or less profusion, whose greatest delight seems to have been to introduce in connection with the property with which they were identified all the new and strange forms and observances that occurred to them. In the progress of their work what was before luminous such men make wholly incomprehensible; with them the dawn is ever succeeded by eternal darkness. In this gloom it is their happiness to live; it does not, however, retard their development or decrease their numbers. They multiply indefinitely like bats in a cave. Everywhere they will pursue their theme with industry and enthusiasm, but it will be the enthusiasm of the bigot, born of ignorance and fostered and perpetuated by ignorance.

It is the happy privilege of such a class to believe that they possess the divine power to create. Having no capacity or room for additional knowledge they are consequently insensible to their manifold deficiencies; disregarding that which is, they exercise their circumscribed minds in producing something that does not exist and that ought not to exist. (31)

Kirkman's critical view of the inflexible mode of "statistical" accounting that typified railroad financial reports was not unique; it was held particularly among harried railroad managers who found themselves bound by a chain of ledgers and a rote litany of debit and credit passages that seemed to have little to do with the "cash basis success" of the business. Again, quoting Kirkman: "The balance of cash that remains in the treasury after collecting the earnings and paying the operating expenses of a railway company, constitute its net income. . . . Herein lies the essence of accounting; this is the goal; every thing else is collateral to it. Bookkeeping was an afterthought, a device adopted for the purpose of recording and classifying affairs and preventing roguery" (Wells 1970: 2).

Progress in Cost-Management Accounting

In 1885, there was a turning point in the maturity of American literature in the field of cost accounting. That year, Henry Metcalfe, an American army ordnance officer, published a book entitled *Cost of Manufactures*. Metcalfe's work and his position as an authority were recognized in professional circles; during the 1880s, he spoke at a meeting of the Institute of Accounts in New York.

In the period 1883–87, other lecturers at institute meetings often dealt with topics on the subject of management accounting, including accounting for branch stores, account-keeping for telephone companies, and cost accounts in metal factories. The institute was not restricted to public practitioners but included among its members company and managerial accountants.

An overview of the practice of cost and managerial accounts as indicated by the records of businesses and by the contents explained in the leading textbooks of the period reveals the following types of cost accounting systems and terminology:

1. *Overhead:* The term burden, or overhead, as we know it today, was noted as early as 1862 in the writings of Nassau Senior, an English economist who had developed a theory to distinguish between fixed and variable overhead cost. Overhead was called various names— including "on cost." "On costs" were manufacturing costs which were to be added "on to" the total of labor and material in arriving at total cost.

2. *Depreciation:* Williamson's study of the Winchester Company indicates that its internal accounting practices did not consider depreciation. He also indicates that the first cost controls appear to have been installed in the late 1880s in reaction to competition in the industry so as to determine where costs could be reduced. Mill owners and railroad operators faced unprecedented information needs about the manner of allocating costs of large capital assets. In many mills, "accounting practice continued to treat machines as expenses rather than as depreciable assets" (McGaw 1985: 708). This rationale was justified, some historians argued, because the rate of obsolescence was high, given the rapid rate of technological development and therefore, from an internal performance view, "(d)epreciation accounting offered no help to managers when buying or replacing machines" (McGaw 1985). By the late 1890s, however, the majority of legal decisions recognized an allowance for depreciation for reporting purposes (Reiter 1926: 126). George Terborgh, writing in 1954, may have best summarized the issue by saying, "the practice of making regular periodic charges for capital consumption is a development largely of the last fifty years. Prior to this development many enterprises had no systematic procedure whatever, especially the smaller ones" (quoted in Brief 1964).

3. *Interest:* Certain writers of the period argued for the inclusion of interest on capital employed as a burden cost or cost of manufacturing. Economic theory had not clearly defined whether or not such was appropriately treated as a division of profits or a payment for a factor of production.

4. *Cost Flow:* Studies of the Shelby Iron Works records for the periods from before the Civil War through the 1880s indicate that the management of the firm was able to determine a broad cost of production via aggregative summaries of costs. (The management of Shelby was able to determine cost per ton of pig iron as early as 1847.) There did not appear, however, to be any recognition of cost flow. Their aggregative method of determining cost per ton was essentially an averaging approach and was still used as late as 1887 (Cauley 1949).

By the turn of the century, even the all-purpose American accounting textbooks widely used in business colleges began to refer to cost accounts. This, and the development of auditing as a special area, marked the birth of teaching specialty subjects within the field.

Cost accounting as a subfield would not mature for decades, following on the wave of corporate mergers and of a unitary form of organization. In railroading, paper, and textile mills, it could be observed however that through the late nineteenth century "industrial accounting records supplied the information needed by 19th century technological innovators" (McGaw 1985). And, in many ways, cost systems had become more sophisticated. The railroads and mill industries represented forerunners of the form of future manufacturing and corporate organizations: a 1874 report of the Atchison, Topeka and Santa Fe Railroad included as an exhibit a table of distribution of operating accounts, that is, overhead expense in proportion to revenue from freight service and passenger service.

There also was skepticism about the accuracy that could be obtained from cost accounts. Although integrating commercial and cost information was becoming more common, still there was controversy over whether or not to integrate cost accounts and financial records. In a speech given in 1897, Frank Broaker suggested the use of a double-entry technique of integration based on a consumption journal. Such attempts to describe the basis of integration indicate that a generally accepted approach was not yet achieved.

Another important influence on cost accounting during this period was the appearance of "scientific management" techniques. The influence of efficiency engineers, such as Frederick Taylor, George L. Fowler, and Harrington Emerson, began to be felt toward the close of the century, as the drive to a form of "national efficiency via systematic activity" (Okano 1985). "The drive for efficiency was primarily, although not exclusively, an American phenomenon" (Wells 1978: 93). From 1860 to the 1890s, factory "systems" became increasingly "scientific," using sophisticated forms of organization for production. Historians, including Epstein, further assert that "standard cost accounting arose to provide information needed by engineers engaged in scientific management pursuits . . . , thus add[ing] credence to the view of other historians (namely, R. H. Parker and Murray Wells) that economists or engineers, not accountants, originated most of the concepts and practices associated with modern management accounting" (Johnson 1979). Before 1900, Epstein argues: "Businesses did not see the necessity of having an accountant working in the company. The mechanical engineer took his place in helping to determine the allocation of overhead costs, which was of major concern in this time period," in part because of the substitution of machines for labor, reflected in the constantly rising fixed capital investments of the time (Epstein 1973: 31).

In 1890, J. Slatter Lewis's *The Commercial Organization of Facilities* indicated the use of staff-and-line techniques, which had become formalized as part of overall management systems. In 1895, Frederick W. Taylor, the father of scientific management, suggested a revolutionary approach to labor costing with the introduction of the piece-rate system. This was the start of what was to be scientific labor time and motion efficiency in manufacturing.

The new systems emphasized "standards" instead of "estimates." Both terms and processes were arbitrary allocations, but the former were "scientifically" determined whereas the latter were simple extrapolations (Wells 1974).

Under this theory of systematic management, the "system" maintained the operation with the aid of the accounting and production records. The logic of processing and supply at each workstation therefore dictated the process of the factory's system. Scientific management added the study of efficiency of effort at each station and at each motion of operation, thereby affording the ability to establish standards of performance. The existence of the systematic and scientific management of industrial operations created a need for cost accountants who could develop "price tags" for operations in order to make monetary comparisons within this system of standards.

What is known about cost accounting in small businesses during this period has been contributed in recent studies by Tyson and others. There is evidence to suggest that the systems in place were taken to fill needs in a demand/response sense of accounting development. In the case of one company, operated by owner entrepreneur J. Henry Rushton, it can be said,

"business conditions . . . stimulated Rushton to undertake . . . formal costing procedures as a basis for rational managerial decision making. These
conditions include[d] increased competitive pressures, market development strategies, catalog and special order pricing decisions, and profitability concerns" (Tyson 1988: 29).

Taxation

Popular support for income taxes waned after the end of the Civil War.
An editorial from the *Chronicle* in January 1871 summarized public sentiment: "It has ceased to be necessary; . . . [u]pon no point has there ever
been a more general agreement than there now is, that this superfluous
taxation should be stopped" (*Chronicle* January 7, 1871).

The postwar income tax fell upon "280,000 persons, who have born the
whole burden, the rest of the nation going free." Of these 280,000, about
100,000 persons paid $20 or less. If the tax was criticized as being unjustly
levied on the few for the benefit of the many, it certainly did not seem to be
a heavy burden. What was the principal complaint? "The chief cause of . . .
discontent among us was rather . . . the vexatious and inquisitorial methods
of levying the tax [not] the large amount or the wide pressure of its burden.
The oaths it administers caused frequent perjury. . . . By all means let us
abolish all unnecessary taking of oaths, in every department of our revenue
system. . . . A second change is the prohibition of publicity. To have stopped
the publication of income lists in the newspapers is one step in the right
direction. . . . The lists might be kept secret instead of being open to public
inspection" ("Mr. Boutwell," 1871: 102–3).

Tax on Corporate Dividends

Congress had passed an act of "July 14, 1870 which provide[d] that the
sections of the old law which impose a tax of five per cent upon the dividends and interest paid by the corporations referred to [in the act], 'shall
be construed to impose the taxes therein mentioned to the 1st day of August 1870, but after that date no further tax shall be levied . . . .' The same
act imposes 'for and during the year 1871 a tax of two and one-half per
centum' on interest paid upon the bonds of such corporations and upon
their dividends and undivided profits." The companies subject to the tax
included "banks, trust companies, savings institutions doing a general banking business, insurance companies, railroad, canal, canal navigation and . . .
water companies." The Commissioner of Internal Revenue, Mr. Pleason-
ton, also noted that "the individual holder of the stock or bonds will be

liable for the tax on all that portion of the dividends and interest upon which the corporation has not paid the tax" ("Internal Revenue Tax," 1871: 403).

Taxes, such as the income tax, corporate, and inheritance taxes, were repealed or permitted to lapse in the early 1870s with high tariffs, revenues from land sales and other sources being used to produce income for the Treasury. The federal income tax would, of course, return on the eve of World War I and become increasingly significant.

The administration of the tax acts, such as the corporate tax, gave rise to disputes then, as now. In 1872, for example, the New York Central applied for relief from the 5 percent tax on a $23 million dollar scrip dividend of 1868. The Central claimed the dividend represented undivided earnings "on the road during a period of fifteen years." The commissioner accepted the view of the Central and "treat[ed] the dividend as if it had been accruing for the past 15 years, and exempt[ed] it from assessment until 1862, when the income tax law was first enacted" ("Tax Relief," 1872: 278–79). This episode is instructive in that it provides an operational example of scrip dividends and the concept of accrual. Furthermore, it can be appreciated that in order to provide the information necessary to administer such a tax, the accounting information and records available in subject corporations would have had to be sufficient to support contested filings.

Tax issues were not limited to the federal level. In 1888, Mayor Hewitt of New York urged remission of taxes on personal property in order to attract business to New York. He proposed that taxes be levied on real estate or be derived from corporate franchises. The damage done to a city's economy by property taxes was due to the impact upon "the mobility of capital [which] is so great that a very slight difference is sufficient to determine the place of investment" ("Theory and Objects," 1888: 213).

State and Local Government Accounting

By the mid-1890s, American cities were growing at a rate about three times as fast as rural areas. By 1920, the census would show that the urban population of America exceeded the rural population. With this unprecedented expansion of cities, the demands for services such as water supply, property protection, and public health became apparent. Certificates such as that shown in figure 4.8 for the City of Baltimore were issued in the larger municipalities. This certificate is evidence of the debt used to fund expansion of a water supply system. Issued in 1874, it was scheduled to mature in 1894.

In the face of this growth and the need for cities to begin to finance their

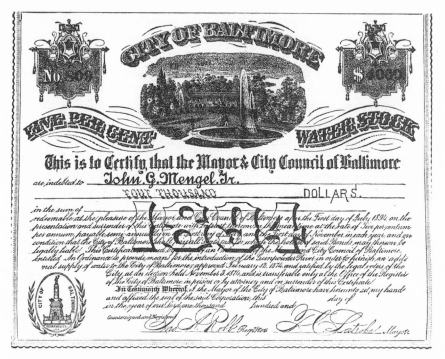

Figure 4.8 Water stock for the City of Baltimore, 1894. *Source: The Countinghouse Arithmetic* (Baltimore, 1889).

increasing system of services on a larger and more complex scale, there was a need for uniform accounting and supervised reporting for state and local entities. As early as 1878 and 1879, the states of Minnesota and Massachusetts enacted legislation that affected county administrations, specifying activities that would enhance the efficiency with which county officials fulfilled their duties. The Minnesota act provided for the appointment of a state examiner to be named by the governor and required that the examiner should be a skilled accountant. The examiner's duties included the inspection of state accounts and the accounts of county officials. He was also charged with enforcing a correct and uniform system of bookkeeping. The Massachusetts act also focused on the financial administration of county officers such that by 1887 the scope of this supervision included the establishment of the office of comptroller of county accounts (Potts 1976: 50).

The influence of these early precedents flowed down to the municipal level and served to define the duties of appropriate officials. Although it was uncommon for cities to issue financial reports prior to the twentieth century, certain examples, notably in the cities of Boston and Milwaukee, do exist for years prior to the turn of the century.

An early American treatise on the subject of governmental accounting, a booklet entitled "Public Accounts," written in 1878 by E. S. Mills, dealt with the keeping of state and municipal accounts (Potts 1976: 47). This twenty-seven-page work described a double-entry system for county treasurers, whom Mills viewed as acting as general business managers for the people. The Mills system was designed to report the following by way of a proposed comprehensive financial system:

1. Cash on hand at the beginning of the period
2. Delinquent taxes due at the beginning of the period
3. Total collections of the past year
4. Receipts from state funds, fines, licenses, and other receipts
5. Expenditures for the past year
6. Abated taxes of the last year
7. Delinquent taxes due at the close of the year
8. The cash balance at the end of the period

There is no evidence that Mills's scheme was widely used or regarded. Nevertheless, it presented an early systematic attempt to deal with the perceived problems of municipal accounting. Not until after the turn of the century was a comprehensive municipal accounting system developed, including budgetary accounts. Frederick Cleveland's dual system is recognized as the first of this type.[15]

Concern over the adequacy of financial disclosure of municipalities served as one cause for the formation of citizen groups that initiated movements to reform city government administration. The era of "Boss Tweed" and excessive political patronage that followed the Civil War was felt most sharply in the large Eastern cities and now reached a point where the public had become restive and was dissatisfied with city administrations. In 1891, James Bryce wrote, "There is no denying that the government of cities is one of the conspicuous failures of the United States." New Yorkers took it upon themselves to slay the Tammany tiger. In 1894, the National Municipal League was formed, and in 1897, the Citizens Union was formed, representing leading citizens who acted together to bring about better government. By the time the National Conference on Good City Government was held in 1896, some 245 organizations were functioning. The concern of city dwellers about municipal government served to influence the type of financial and accounting systems that would be forthcoming after the turn of the century (Dahlberg 1966).

An initial audit of one major city's financial accounts that took place before the turn of the century conveys an example of the state of affairs. Ernest Reckitt was invited by R. A. Waller, the controller of the City of

Chicago, to make a "spot" audit of the books of the City of Chicago in 1898. For a fee of $2,500, an amount not nearly sufficient for the size of the operation to be undertaken, Reckitt agreed to start the audit. He immediately employed twelve men for the assignment, which took three months. Among the irregularities Reckitt found was a deficiency of about a half million dollars in the special assessments fund as well as an overall chaotic condition with respect to the payments of city bonds and coupons.

Reckitt recalls that when he requested to examine the actual bonds and interest coupons for one of the periods, he was taken to a vault where all the bonds and coupons paid during a number of years were lying in a disordered array. He observed that it would have been virtually impossible to put the bonds in numerical order so as to commence any audit, and it was therefore impossible to verify the control over the bonded debt and the interest payments of the city.

The reported deficiency in the special assessments funds raised considerable public interest, particularly since the investigation had only touched the "high spots" and was specific only with respect to the listing of the balances of all assessments from 1871, the date of the Chicago fire. All prior records had been destroyed in that fire.

As a result of Reckitt's audit, the city government commissioned the detailed investigation of all assessment records in both the controller's office and the city clerk's office. The firm of Haskins & Sells (now Deloitte & Touche) was selected, having submitted the lowest bid. Sells later informed Reckitt that the audit had resulted in a considerable financial loss to the firm. However, on an overall basis, in part due to the fact that there was a fee generated from detailed investigations of other city departments, the firm was given an opportunity to recover some of the large loss that it had suffered on the original contract. Such service by public accounting firms within city government resulted in the inauguration of improved systems of accounting so that future audits could be more intelligently and inexpensively conducted.

A financial view, provided by the Census Office, of all United States municipalities having populations exceeding 2,500 was released in 1891. The attention paid to this information in the financial press was to construct a type of balance sheet statement for a typical city of one hundred thousand inhabitants for an average year, which "on the whole . . . may be taken as typical of the financial operations of the large American City" ("Municipal Finances," 1891: 35–36). This report provided a portrait of the sources of revenues and services considered appropriate for a city of the period (table 4.6).

A federal budget report of sorts was provided each year, as required by

TABLE 4.6
Model Report for a City of 100,000 Persons, 1891

Receipts

Taxes	$1,114,267
Special assessments, streets and bridges	106,368
Special assessments sewers	11,041
Licenses, liquor	94,292
Licenses, other	29,292
Fees, fines, and penalties	21,716
Water works	150,610
Interest on deposits	4,600
Income from funds and investments	86,820
Miscellaneous	103,040
Total ordinary receipts	1,720,012
Loans	674,821
Funds and transfers	147,053
From state or county	43,552
Cash on hand beginning of year	286,757
Grand total	$2,872,195

Expenditures

Libraries	$6,546
Schools	209,585
Fire	93,923
Health	18,243
Lighting	61,978
Police	142,539
Charitable objects	57,335
Streets and bridges	268,642
Sewers	55,548
Buildings and improvements	77,721
Parks and public grounds	101,380
Salaries	94,668
Waterworks	152,694
Interest on debt	258,003
Miscellaneous	277,208
Total ordinary expenses	$1,877,013
Loans	475,905
Funds and transfers	226,643
Cash on hand end of year	292,634
Grand total	$2,872,195

law. In 1867, for example, the secretary of the treasury supplied an "unusually voluminous . . . balance sheet for the nation" detailing that the total debt of the United States was $2.3 billion, and discussing the loans and funding processes in place to address the nation's public debt "whose burden and pressure were made heavier . . . by a large increase of . . . gold bearing bonds" ("Mr. McColloch's," 1867: 709–11).

In 1891, the Treasury "issued an extra statement of assets and liabilities." In evaluating the new statement, the editor of the *Chronicle* observed: "This arrangement of figures does not change the facts as to the Treasury situation at all. The old form and this new method are one in that particular. We do not need to say that book-keeping never added a dollar to any man's balance or to any nation's balance. It can give accounts a new twist and can conceal what every reader wants to know—but that is obviously the limit of its power" ("Treasury Figures," 1891: 697).

A few months later, the same editors protested changes in the monthly Treasury Report format, including the dropping of a liability item for "accrued interest." The editors note:

> The Treasury Department is not a private or an isolated affair, but it is such an extensive collector and disburser of cash that there is no industry in the country which is not more or less under the influence and within the control of its daily and monthly transactions. This alliance too with the money market and with the commerce of the country is rapidly becoming closer year by year, as the Government becomes more entirely the source and centre of our currency supplies. These exhibits then are intended to display as fully and as clearly as possible every detail in Government receipts and disbursements, so as to guard against stupidity or dishonesty in official methods, and to prevent ignorance or mistake on the part of the public. Under such circumstances it is hardly necessary to say that accrued liabilities, where they can be fixed and known, are a material and desirable part of the information given out. ("Treasury Statements," 1891: 4–5)

The criticism had no effect on the Treasury, which continued to omit the accrued interest, as noted in its June 30, 1894, statements published in the *Chronicle* ("Debt Statement," 1894).

Beginning in the 1890s, "the public was so thoroughly aroused to the need for governmental economy that the budget idea was suggested for adoption in the . . . [federal] government" (Theiss 1937: 45). But many years would pass before budgeting would become a part of the federal process and governmental accounting would achieve a level of sophistication approaching the importance of its dimension in the economy.

In 1893, in response to public concern, Congress created a joint commission (named after its chairman, Joseph Dockery), consisting of three members of the Senate and three members of the House, to inquire into and examine the organization and operation of the executive departments of the federal government as to all aspects of efficiency, compensation, and public service provided. This commission would probably have accomplished as little as countless other committees of investigation, were it not for the insertion in the act of a practical, new idea. It occupied only a half-dozen lines but it meant everything for the success of the work: "Said Commission is authorized to employ not exceeding three experts, who shall render such assistance as the Commission may require" (*Charles Waldo Haskins,* 1923: 20–21).

The experts selected, Charles Waldo Haskins and Elijah Sells, were successful in their duties with the commission and would thereafter form the public accountancy firm that today has evolved worldwide into Deloitte & Touche.

The Cultural Significance of Accountancy in the Gilded Age

The year 1877 marked the end of the period of reconstruction following the Civil War. It also marked the start of the era of big cities and big business and of the frontier town of the West. It was a colorful time, gripped by changes of a scale and type unique to our history. And yet viewing accounting then is to consider what was only a century ago.

Among the important accomplishments of the Gilded Age was the profession's ability to initiate forms of self-identification and legal recognition. Formal education, standardized textbooks, and a system of accounting principles were yet nascent or nonexistent. But municipal accounting was being shaped by the demands of citizen groups, and initial audit engagements in large cities were beginning to provide information that would lead to the passage of legislation to require a more uniform system of accountability. Accounting writers, too, were beginning to express in their works an understanding of accounting's underlying "principles" as being broader than those relating to technical aspects alone.

Writing in 1880, Albert Gallatin Scholfield in *Essay on Debits and Credits* "noted that the deepest social roots of accounting are (1) in the institution of private property, (2) in the moral obligation which comes into existence when the legal property is loaned, and (3) in the conventional practice of recording the exchange of possession of property" (quoted in Pilcher 1935: 141). Scholfield also advised his pupils at his Rhode Island Commercial Schools that "between yourself and the business to which you aspire, is the counting room with its multitudinous demands, details and results; legal, prudential and financial; and you cannot effectually and successfully reach the one without the other" (Scholfield 1890: 4). The cultural significance of accounts had extended, then, from the counting room to the business itself. The connection between accounts and business success had been forged.

By the turn of the century, the economy was recovering from the severe depression of 1893 and had turned to a policy of "sound money" in the election of 1896. The important role of accounting was being recognized in the financial and business community, that is, beyond the business itself, as corporations began to hire expert auditors to replace the annual audit visit of shareholders. The "Advantages of a Professional Audit" were extolled in British books, to include that a "professional auditor . . . will act impartially . . . , will be able to suggest improvements in the system . . . and [will help avoid] lamentable muddles in the affairs of public companies" (Norton 1894: 281). Popular history of the profession may suggest that 1896, the year in which the first CPA law was passed in New York, marks the birth of the accounting profession in the United States. Closer examination suggests, however, that the post–Civil War era, the Gilded Age per se, marks the origins of professional accountancy. The birth of modern accounting societies, including their activities and publications, initiated the profession in the United States, culminating in the passage of CPA legislation. These organizations reflect the significance of accountancy in this period. Their existence and influence give testimony to the changes in accountancy in the United States' first industrial capital market era.

The Formation of an Accounting Profession

> A society which considers wealth or property as ultimate, whether under a conception of "natural" rights or otherwise, is setting the means above the end, and is therefore, unmoral or immoral.
>
> **—Dewey and Tufts (1908)**

As noted in the previous chapter, the post–Civil War period in the United States was marked by a series of dynamic economic changes. Technological advances had expanded production possibilities, a nearly complete railroad network permitted mass marketing, and communication improvements facilitated consolidation of industry.[1] Henry George's influential *Progress and Poverty: An Inquiry into the Cause of Industrial Depression and of Increase of Want with an Increase of Wealth* (1879) marked the beginning of a debate over the growing disparity between the nation's increased productive capacity and the poverty of many of its citizens.[2]

The 1890s have been called the watershed of American history (Commager 1950). During that decade, the United States made the change from agrarian simplicity to industrial complexity and the corporate form began to dominate American industry. Corporations employed more than 70 percent of those working in manufacturing and produced 74 percent of the value added by manufacturing. From 1880 to 1900, the increasing concentration of wealth and economic power ushered in a dynamic reform movement. Hofstadter (1963: 2) argues that "toward the turn of the century, it became increasingly evident that the material growth had been achieved at a terrible cost in human values and in the waste of natural resources"; therefore, progressive reformers emerged who sought to "work out a strategy for orderly social change."

The Progressive Movement

Progressivism is best understood as an eclectic term for an attitude that incorporated such elements as pragmatism, moralism, fundamentalism,

175

socialism, and prohibitionism. Progressive thought embraced "a faith in democracy, a concern for morality and social justice" and expressed an "exuberant belief in progress . . . and the efficacy of education" (Thelan 1969). Fond of speaking in abstractions, progressive reformers drew support from a broad spectrum of the public, including businessmen.[3]

Progressivism, as used here, is not meant to connote "liberalism." The movement did not articulate a single, unified philosophy nor did all progressives embrace a single common cause. Several progressive movements existed simultaneously. These diverse movements often are combined and described as "the quest for social justice."[4] Progressive reformers used the popular press to mobilize public opinion. They focused on political corruption, social injustices, and economic exploitation arising from concentration of wealth.[5] They questioned the basic foundations of individualistic economic theories, raising serious concerns about the viability of continued reliance on laissez-faire economic policies.

Classical economics had provided the English-speaking world with its fundamental economic model. The individual was at center stage. A competitive market, guided by an automatic mechanism, "the invisible hand," translated individual self-interest into societal well-being. Americans long had accepted the notion that "commerce had been the world civilizer" and that the interests of both society and the private entrepreneur could be simultaneously promoted by permitting the maximum amount of freedom to the individual.[6]

During the Progressive Era, pragmatists, institutional economists, and political reformers contended that industrial concentration had rendered "old-fashioned" market competition inoperable.[7] Those who controlled the nation's trusts, they contended, could exact a tribute by limiting production and administering prices.[8] The federal government initially responded to the growing threat consolidation posed by urging states to pass antitrust legislation to restore competitive forces. The passage of the New Jersey incorporation law in 1889 that permitted holding companies (i.e., corporations) to own stock in other corporations removed a formidable barrier to industrial combinations.[9] The federal government responded with passage of the Sherman Antitrust Act in 1890.[10] While the legislation did little to curtail consolidations, Galambos and Pratt (1988) note that it was eventually politically effective.[11] The law quieted critics by providing symbolic reassurance to the public, thereby enabling politicians to avoid a direct confrontation with financial capitalists.[12]

Since passage of antitrust legislation did not curb concentration of power, the traditional American "creed" no longer appeared plausible to many of the nation's citizens. Reformers continued to demand that policy-makers address the question of how to cope with the growing implausibility of the nation's public philosophy and its economic structure.[13] Progressive activists' demands for political, corporate, and tax reform, combined with their faith in efficiency and reliance on "experts," facilitated recognition of the accountancy profession.

The Efficiency Movement

Hofstadter (1963) concludes that the distinguishing characteristic of the progressive reform movement was its activism, the conviction that time would *not* take care of social evils and that the reformers must energize the citizenry to action by exposure of evils through publicity.[14] Pragmatism provided philosophic justification for progressive activism. Charles Pierce, William James, and John Dewey defined truth in relation to its practical consequence. Dewey (1922) rejected what he called "the spectator theory of knowledge"; he demanded that human agents use their knowledge (critical intelligence) to promote social reform. Pragmatists believed that experience and education should enable people to design and control their economic system; pragmatism provided philosophic justification for the reliance on experts so evident throughout the Progressive Era.[15] Reformers turned "to the expert as a disinterested person who could divest himself of narrow class or parochial" interests (Grantham 1964: 245). The independent public accountant, the disinterested expert, would become central to implementation of many reforms. Progressive reformers' demands for increased efficiency in government and industry, regulation of large businesses, and passage of an income tax law to equalize wealth, created the opportunity for accountants to gain professional recognition in the United States.

Demands for Governmental Efficiency

Independent accountants first gained visibility and national recognition through their work in the governmental sector. Accounting practitioners joined progressive reformers in asserting that corruption and inefficiency lay at the root of social ills in the public sector.[16] In this area, the profession was in the vanguard of the reform movement. Because they concurred with the idea that public officials needed close scrutiny, independent accountants willingly worked to develop new monitoring systems to curb expected abuses.

The profession increased its national visibility by serving as advisors to various federal commissions that sought to increase the efficiency of federal agencies and by designing uniform accounting systems for state and local governments. With Charles Waldo Haskins and Elijah Watt Sells receiving Senate commendation for their work on the Dockery Commission, accounting practitioners became a vital force in the governmental reform movement. The National Civic Federation and the National Municipal League received the patronage, interest, and participation of accountants.[17] The American Association of Public Accountants (AAPA) received recognition as the national voice of the profession when the Keep Commission (1905) called upon the organization to provide expert advice to those seeking to reorganize the federal bureaucracy.[18]

By 1911, independent accountants had become an integral part of a movement to reform the federal bureaucracy. The President's Commission on Economy and Efficiency (1911), proposed by President Taft to facilitate the introduction of business techniques into the federal government, immediately called upon leading practitioners to serve on a board of consulting accountants. The president's secretary, Charles Norton, wrote that "the subject of administration lies largely in your hands," and suggested that accountants allow the commission the "added privilege of submitting written reports for your criticism while we are formulating and starting our constructive program" (U.S. Executive 1912–14: 1). Four leading practitioners, J. E. Sterrett, E. W. Sells, F. F. White, and W. B. Richards, were appointed to this board.

The commission was composed of three political and three expert appointees. Frederick A. Cleveland, the chairman, and Harvey S. Chase, the municipal accounting expert, had primary responsibility for the papers issued on auditing and reporting problems. The commission issued opinions on topics such as "constructive recommendations with respect to the principles which should govern expenditure accounting and reporting," issued as Treasury Circular No. 34, May 20, 1911. By the conclusion of the investigation, the commission had recommended numerous system reforms, published in either Treasury circulars or commission reports (U.S. Congress 1913: H. Doc. 104).

Uniform Governmental Accounting Systems

Chase's appointment to the commission solidified his position as perhaps the leading expert on municipal accounting systems in the nation. Like many other early practitioners, he traveled extensively within the United States to act as a consultant to municipalities installing new accounting systems. The AAPA recognized that demands for municipal reforms provided a golden opportunity for accountants. Chase chaired many of the AAPA's early committees on uniform municipal accounting and served as the profession's liaison to the National Municipal League.[19]

New York City's fiscal problems in 1906 gained widespread notoriety, and the city undertook sweeping reforms that addressed many of the accounting problems faced by other municipalities.[20] Accountants advocated "uniform" accounting systems for governmental agencies because they shared progressive reformers' conviction that government officials were incompetent. But the AAPA may have done its work too well; uniformity became a panacea for politicians, a solution to all abuses.[21]

While development of uniform governmental accounting systems increased the visibility of independent accountants, uniform systems, once implemented, usually led to displacement of professional accountants by technicians.[22] Governmental officials concluded that since uniform systems did not require professional judgment but rather a knowledge of specified procedures, technicians could be employed to implement the system adequately and more cheaply.[23] The profession's initial advocacy of uniform governmental accounting systems would haunt the profession throughout the Progressive Era; uniformity became the political sector's "simple solution" for all reporting abuses, including perceived abuses in the corporate sector.

Given their experience with uniform financial reporting systems, practitioners welcomed President Taft's call for efficiency, that is, application of business methods through development of cost accounts, in the governmental sector. They vigorously promoted establishment of cost systems for municipalities and state governments, arguing that the function of a governmental entity should be one of business, not politics.[24] Cost accounts and budgets could be used to evaluate efficiency, to control costs, to provide incentives for good work, and to make citizens feel that their tax dollars were well spent.[25] The demand for more effective cost-accounting systems to improve efficiency in the public sector paralleled a similar movement in the private sector.[26]

Efficiency in the Private Sector: The Role of Cost Accounting

As noted earlier, in the industrial sector, demands for efficiency culminated in "scientific management," which made "time" its ruling dimension.[27] Frederick Taylor (1903, 1911B) and his disciples broke down every task in minute detail, making the work unit their focus of attention.[28] Taylor first published his new method in 1903, in a book titled *Shop Management*. "Shop management" did not receive accolades from engineers nor did it receive widespread public attention.[29] Louis Brandeis, whose demands for publicity to protect investors would have a great impact on the development of financial accounting, caught the public imagination when he coined the phrase "scientific management" when referring to Taylor's system.[30] Throughout the Progressive Era, engineers and accountants made substantive advances in the area of cost accounting, and the United States became the clear leader in the field.[31] However, independent public accountants viewed cost accountants as employees and technicians, not as professionals, and the cost-accounting area remained tangential to the movement for professional status throughout the Progressive Era.[32]

The emergence of large multidepartmental industrial firms, combined with overproduction and shrinking profits in the 1890s, gave both large and small businesses incentives to develop cost systems.[33] Cost accountants and engineers initially concentrated on accumulation of product costs; the debate centered on the segregation of direct and indirect costs and whether all indirect costs should be allocated to products (Garner 1954). Engineers generally favored allocation of all costs; accountants believed that general and administrative (noncontrollable) costs should not be allocated to products.[34] Until the turn of the century, containment of material cost remained the focal point of cost accounting.[35] During the first two decades of the twentieth century, control of "time" (labor) costs replaced control of material costs as the major objective of cost systems.

Johnson and Kaplan (1987) attribute this de-emphasis of product costing to the growth of multidivisional firms that needed cost data for coordination and control (i.e., to manage "transaction costs") and for decision-making.[36] They suggest that minimization of transaction costs increased efficiency and benefited both management and labor. However, a review of the literature suggests that labor did not view this change as beneficial, nor did all accountants consider cost accounts as beneficial.[37]

The accounting literature reflects the widespread interest generated by the concept of "scientific management."[38] Established in 1905, the *Journal of Accountancy* carried numerous articles written by proponents of scientific management and several articles by labor leaders opposed to the concept.[39] When one compares the articles written by scientific management theorists with cost-accounting articles in that *Journal,* it becomes clear that the two groups differed with respect to the benefits that could be obtained by the introduction of scientific management procedures. Accountants and engineers clearly focused on different objectives.

Wildman (1911: 424, 428) reflected the cost accountants' view when he lauded scientific management as a way by which the accountant could increase his value to the client by "saving the client money." He noted that labor costs provided the best area in which to decrease cost and that adoption of Taylor's and Gannt's methods could be used to increase productivity and effect cost savings.[40] Taylor (1911B, 118) thought that increased productivity should benefit all and rejected the focus on money, writing that "money is in no sense wealth."[41] Labor leaders clearly felt accountants would prevail and that cost accounts would be used to squeeze more work out of workers to benefit the property owners.[42]

The accounting literature suggests that this perception was true; accountants rarely mentioned labor except in terms of reduction of cost.[43] Cost accountants helped to commodify labor and construct what Miller and O'Leary (1987) have called "the governable person." Labor became a cost to be controlled.[44] While cost accounting made significant advances during this period and provided work for many accounting firms, cost accountants, employed by corporations, continued to be regarded as "mere" technicians. The AAPA, and its successor the American Institute of Accountants (AIA), took care to dissociate the independent professional from the hired cost accountant. The distinction appeared to rest on the employee relationship, rather than the technicality of the discipline; tax accountants, engaged in a highly technical discipline, were accorded professional status within public accounting firms.

Tax Reform: The Impact of the Income Tax

The graduated income tax was one of the few permanent progressive reforms.[45] For accountants, the 1909 corporate excise tax had become a highly profitable nightmare. The law as passed clearly stated that revenues and expenditures must be calculated on a cash, not an accrual basis. Accountants objected vigorously and eventually the Treasury issued a regulation that permitted the use of the accrual method of determining net income.[46]

When the Supreme Court declared the 1909 tax law unconstitutional, progressive reformers pressed for a constitutional amendment to give the federal government the power to tax income. Accountants closely monitored the debate.[47] With the ratification of the Sixteenth Amendment to the Constitution, the income tax became a permanent fixture of American life. The passage of an income tax law in 1913 created another "statistical community" as Americans became members of "tax brackets" and income (rather than wealth) became the measure of the nation's well-being (Boorstin 1973: 211ff.).

Accountants, through the AAPA, worked closely with the federal government throughout the period to assure no more debacles like the 1909 corporate excise tax. In 1913, Robert H. Montgomery, as president of the association, reminded the Ways and Means Committee of the House of Representatives that "the American Association of Public Accountants . . . shall always be ready and glad to render every assistance in our power to further the preparation of efficient legislation" ("Corporation Tax Returns," *Journal of Accountancy*, February 1913: 139).

The income tax law had a mixed impact on the accounting profession.[48] The increased demand for accounting services provided security to many practitioners, but the demand also attracted many unqualified people who called themselves accountants and tax experts. To some established practitioners, tax work seemed to impair their claim to professional status since it might undermine the profession's appearance of independence. Initially, some of the AAPA leadership tried to convince their colleagues that accountants should be impartial in tax work, as concerned with protecting the government's interests as with their client's interests. That message did not have widespread appeal, and most accountants viewed themselves as their clients' advocates in tax matters.

The tax law not only expanded the market for accounting services but also greatly facilitated acceptance of techniques, such as depreciation, that businessmen had long resisted. The accrual procedures that the AAPA had vigorously lobbied for as the basis for determination of taxable income were most beneficial to those who served small businesses. Not wanting to incur the costs of keeping two sets of books, small businesses allowed auditors to determine income for credit reports on a sound basis (Montgomery 1912A: 193ff.). Overall, tax reform must be regarded as having had a salutary effect on a nascent profession, and it had a dramatic impact on acceptance of accrual accounting by business. While progressives' demands for governmental accounting reforms and tax reform provided accountants with work and increased their visibility, demands for corporate reform would confer upon independent accountants the necessary social obligation central to legitimization of their claim to professional status.

The Rise of Financial Capitalism

The rise of financial capitalism had a profound impact on the development of the public accounting profession in the United States. The panic of 1893 had provided the opportunity for investment bankers and other outside promoters to become actively involved in organizing corporate trusts. Prior to the panic, most consolidations occurred through vertical integration and were internally financed. Before 1893, investment bankers rarely served on boards of directors; by the end of the next decade, however, it had become common for financial capitalists not only to occupy directors' chairs, but also to control the trust. The Pujo investigation (1913) found that the "money trust" held 341 directorships in 112 corporations, controlling resources and assets capitalized at around $22 billion (Hacker 1961: 26f.).

Progressive reformers did not assume that corporations had an inalienable right to exist, nor did they assume that corporations had the same freedoms as individuals.[49] The overriding public sentiment in the Progressive Era was that "a business conducted by corporate methods is not a private business. Corporate powers are not natural rights and the general welfare is the only justification for the grant of them. The right of public supervision inheres in them" (E. L. Suffern 1909: 399). Suffern, president of the AAPA, maintained that this sentiment was "popularly held."[50] During the Progressive Era, the right of government to regulate business ceased to be an issue as most people agreed with the idea that corporations were artificial entities created by the state and subject to control of the state.[51]

Financial capitalism highlighted the growing separation of ownership and control and created severe tensions between the legal system, based on ownership and private property rights, and actual economic relationships. Berle (1963: 45) outlined the dilemma this posed for the political sector.[52] "Passive property," he argued, "eroded the moral base [reward for capacity and thrift] and the organizing rationale [the need for individual skill in applying capital]" for an unregulated economy.[53] The separation of ownership and control posed a significant threat to the legitimacy of private property rights.[54]

Since financial capitalists used "other people's money" to form holding companies or trusts, this created a further discrepancy among the justification for private property rights, hard work, and thrift.[55] While promoters usually cited "economies of scale" as the rationale for trusts,[56] reformers rejected this claim. They feared that the priority of financial capitalists was to create monopolies, not to produce the goods and services society desired.[57] Independent audits emerged as a mechanism to provide that the stockholder-owner would have ultimate control over the use of corporate resources.[58]

Demand for Greater Corporate Oversight

The failure of one trust after another in the 1890s renewed the outcry for more direct government supervision of corporations. When the effort to restore competition by passing antitrust legislation proved futile, demands for greater corporate accountability accelerated. Accountants joined in the criticism; there were few more scathing denunciations of the "money trust" than those found in the early editorials of the *Book-Keeper.*

Industrial Commission

On June 19, 1898, Congress created the Industrial Commission to hold hearings on the subject of combinations in restraint of trade and competition. The commission met from 1898 to 1902 to investigate and to report on questions relating to immigration, labor, agriculture, manufacturing, and business. Experts were employed in each field, and it probably was a reflection of the status of accountants in 1898 that none were engaged. The commission had the specific charge of determining whether financial capitalists had used their power to the detriment of the nation's economic well-being.[59] The evidence presented at the hearings lent credibility to those who claimed that many of the promoters of large industrial combinations were more interested in financial gains than in producing goods and services.[60]

Documentation of overt abuses by those who controlled the nation's economic resources severely eroded confidence in the business sector. In 1899, by admission of the promoters, combinations had issued $3.395 million of common stock, of which two-thirds ($2.254 million) was "water" (i.e., goodwill).[61] Documentation of stockwatering and other overt abuses added credibility to those who argued that economic concentration had eroded the moral justification for private property rights (Berle 1963).

One of the conclusions reached in the commission's preliminary report, which appeared in 1900, was that an independent public accounting profession ought to be established if corporate abuses such as stockwatering and overcapitalization were to be curtailed. Many of the people who testified before the Industrial Commission, including most of the businessmen, felt that corporate publicity was the best available alternative. There were some who objected vigorously to any form of corporate control and maintained that the doctrine of *caveat emptor* must apply to the investor as well as the consumer. The best known of those who opposed publicity was Henry O. Havemeyer, who, however, did little to promote the continuation of government laissez-faire.

The exchange between Havemeyer and John North, lawyer for the commission, seemed to reinforce rather than mitigate the demand for published financial statements. Havemeyer, president of the American Sugar Refining Company, was asked, "How do you carry on business at a loss and still declare dividends?" Havemeyer responded: "You can carry on business and lose money, you can meet and declare dividends. One is an executive decision and the other is a business matter." Somewhat bewildered, North asked: "Where do you get the money?" "We may borrow it," said Havemeyer. Puzzled, North asked, "How many years can the American Sugar Refining Company keep up the practice?" "That is a problem to everyone," conceded Havemeyer and explained that "we should either buy or sell (our) stock if we knew that" (U.S. Congress 1900: 132f.).

Some witnesses had opposed publication of financial reports, contending that the information signaled by the payment of dividends was sufficient to permit investors to make informed decisions. Havemeyer's testimony negated that argument, and most businessmen conceded that some form of corporate publicity was needed.[62]

Recommendations of the Commission

In its preliminary report, the commission stated that its prime objective would be "to prevent the organizers of corporations or industrial combinations from deceiving investors and the public, either through suppression of material facts or by making misleading statements." The final report, issued in 1902, concluded that "the larger corporations—the so-called trusts—should be required to publish annually a properly audited report, showing in reasonable detail their assets and liabilities, with profit and loss; such a report and audit under oath to be subject to government regulation" (U.S. Congress 1902: 650).

A minority report, rejected by the commission, advocated that a bureau be established in the Treasury to register all state corporations engaged in interstate commerce and to secure from each an adequate financial report, to make inspections and examinations of corporate accounts, and to collate and to publish information regarding such combinations (U.S. Congress 1902: 649ff.).

The only argument presented in opposition to the reporting of financial data was that no independent group of technically qualified professionals was available to perform the necessary audits. The lack of an organized accounting profession appeared to preclude reliance on the private sector for adequate, accurate, and reliable information. The conclusions of the Industrial Commission established the need for independent public accountants.

Numerous witnesses supported publication of corporate accounts, citing their willingness to disclose financial data as evidence of their nonmonopolistic intent. Klebaner (1964: 165ff.) concludes that acceptance of voluntary disclosure was a victory for the business sector as businessmen were able to convince the commissioners that "under modern conditions a monopoly cannot abuse its power to any great extent without rivals springing up to dispute its supremacy."[63] Voluntary disclosure offered a seemingly viable means of avoiding fundamental structural changes, and political leaders accepted the arguments of the business sector.

In 1903, an amendment to the legislation establishing the Department of Commerce created the Bureau of Corporations. The bureau, authorized to compile and publish information and to investigate and supervise corporations, promoted "efficient publicity" and conducted numerous corporate investigations. Commenting on the new bureau, the *New York Times* wrote: "It will appease the public clamor against trusts and it will do the trusts and combinations no harm" (*New York Times* February 10, 1903, in Leinwand 1962: 80). While the *Times* suggested that the legislation would have minimal impact, the existence of a federal bureau that could assume responsibility for monitoring corporations probably enhanced the appeal of "voluntary" independent audits.

The Bureau of Corporations (1902–14) requested federal licensing legislation that would give it the right "to directly inspect corporate accounts to protect the public interest."[64] The bureau's position reflected a consensus among reformers that the only real reform would come from passage of a federal incorporation law. Such legislation was proposed annually from 1903 to 1914 and sporadically from 1919 to 1930 but never became law.[65] Merino and Neimark (1982) concluded that "voluntary" disclosure may have precluded a more draconian federal government incorporation law.[66]

The Role of the Accountant in the Corporate Reform Movement

Financial capitalism had evoked a storm of protest; making accounts public and conducting independent audits became the primary mechanisms used to reconcile private property rights with an economic system characterized by concentration of industry and separation of ownership and control.

While accountants benefited from progressive reformers' demands for corporate publicity and audits, they did not support the indictment of financial capitalists. Most accountants empathized with the opinion of the famed jurist Oliver Wendell Holmes, who is purported to have said that the "Sherman Anti-Trust Act is based on pure economic ignorance and the Interstate Commerce Commission isn't fit to have rate making powers" (Persons 1958: 273).

Holmes commended Elijah Watt Sells's widely distributed pamphlet,

"Corporate Management Compared with Government Control," which denounced government intervention in the free enterprise system. Sells (1908) contended that "it is an unassailable truth that almost anyone of the men who stand at the heart of our great business institutions is far more competent to run the government, and would run it more economically, more wisely, and more honestly than any of those who are in the business of running government."[67] It seems somewhat ironic that accountants, generally, did not share progressive reformers' distrust of financial capitalists since demands for greater accountability stemmed from that distrust.

The British Influence

In the previous chapter, some mention was made about the influence of the English chartered accountants in gaining recognition for accountancy in the United States. Undoubtedly, increased British investments, which required close scrutiny given the wild, freewheeling business environment in the United States in the 1880s, brought English professional accountants to the United States. But until there was some call for control of business, chartered accountants were not very successful in promoting accounting services. One has only to look at the blatant techniques used by Jay Gould who, when called to account for defrauding English investors of $60,000, simply asked for the return of the stock certificates to verify the amount of investment. When the certificates were returned to him, he promptly shredded them, destroying any evidence against him. There was no strenuous objection voiced in the United States, and it was several years before British investors recovered their losses.

Of course, the initial demands for reform did not evolve to protect British investors but rather because conditions in the United States became unacceptable to many. The arrival of chartered accountants undoubtedly added to the prestige of the discipline, but it seems that the domestic reform movement was more important in gaining recognition for accountancy in the United States. Despite the obvious rhetoric concerning corporate control, no federal corporation law was enacted nor were any statutes similar to the English Companies Acts promulgated.

The progressive movement, accompanied by demands for municipal and corporate accountability and the income tax reform, all had salutary effects on the development of accountancy. Pragmatism gave philosophic justification to political reforms and had a decided impact on the evolution of accounting theory, educational standards, and ethics. Accountants had to provide an institutional framework if the profession was to respond effectively to contemporary demands. Initial efforts concentrated on securing legislation that gave statutory recognition to the profession. The first CPA law was passed in New York in 1896, and for the next twenty-five years efforts to secure similar legislation in the remaining states would preoccupy accountants.

The Institutional Framework

In the United States, under our Constitution, both professional licensing and education are "residual powers" and deemed state prerogatives. Accountants' early organizational efforts, therefore, were oriented to forming viable separate state professional organizations. Thus, after 1896, the American Association of Public Accountants ceased to be an effective institution and became moribund even in New York as state societies addressed the major issues confronting the profession. Hostility surfaced between native-born practitioners and the chartered accountants who had gained effective control of the AAPA, and that rift severely hampered its operations. Rivalries developed among different state organizations; that, too, delayed steps toward professional unity. Three major state societies—New York, Pennsylvania, and Illinois—assumed preeminence in the profession until 1905.

New York State Society of Certified Public Accountants (NYSSCPA)

New York's CPA law limited the granting of certificates to citizens or those who duly intended to become citizens, which effectively barred many resident British chartered accountants from certification in New York. The waiver privilege of the 1896 law, which exempted experienced persons from the exam, was of very short duration, and decisions to seek U.S. citizenship had to be made quickly.

The NYSSCPA revealed the direction it would take when fifteen men met to incorporate the society in 1897. Prominent among the NYSSCPA incorporates was Henry Harney, who had served five terms as president of the Institute of Accounts. The American Association (dominated by the British) was virtually unrepresented. Eleven of the fifteen charter members had never joined that association; three of the remaining four who were association members had joined only for the duration of the effort to secure a CPA law, and all but one were native-born. Conspicuous by their absence were men like W. Sanders Davies and Frank Broaker. Davies was a naturalized citizen; Broaker was native-born, but he studied in Scotland and was closely allied with the British element in the association (Webster 1954: 336, 343).

Charles E. Sprague

Henry Harney. *Source: Financial Record* (October 15, 1897).

New York State practitioners pioneered efforts for cooperation between universities and accountants. Many of the NYSSCPA members had been associated with the abortive New York School of Accounts; most were convinced that a major factor in its failure was its isolation from any established institution.[68] Leaders of the New York State Society had approached several universities, often to be met with condescension and ultimately rejection; accounting was not deemed an appropriate element of a higher education curriculum.

Success, as was so often the case during those formative years, was primarily due to the efforts of a single man. In this case, the man was Charles E. Sprague. He rented a faculty house at Washington Square for the summer, near the home of Henry M. McCracken, president of New York University. Each night, Sprague managed to accompany McCracken on his habitual walk and never failed to mention the value that a school of commerce would afford citizens of New York (Jones 1933: 357–58). In October 1900, New York University agreed to the proposal advanced by the New York Society for a new School of Commerce, Accounts and Finance. Accounting practitioners served as guarantors against any and all financial loss and agreed to furnish a large part of the necessary faculty. This pattern was to be emulated by practitioners in other states who held the strong American faith in the efficacy of formal education.

The Pennsylvania Institute of Public Accountants

Pennsylvania practitioners' experiences roughly paralleled those in New York. There, however, the hostility toward chartered accountants evident in New York did not arise, for from the beginning the profession in Pennsylvania was in the control of native-born accountants (Ross 1940A: 8–12). The Pennsylvania Institute was incorporated in 1897; a CPA law was enacted in 1899. Inspired by the New York Society's example, in 1902, the Pennsylvania Institute inaugurated evening courses in accountancy. The institute continued efforts to affiliate with a university, an effort made more imperative when members who taught the courses began to feel the pressures of practicing and teaching, too. Finally, in 1904, the University of Pennsylvania's Wharton School of Finance agreed to take over the institute's program (Bennett 1922: 60–64).

Pennsylvania accountants added another dimension to the role of state societies when the institute inaugurated the *Public Accountant.* Although short-lived, the publication recognized a real need and reflected early leaders' emphasis on the development of a body of professional literature.

The New York and Pennsylvania experiences are somewhat reflective of all early efforts in industrialized states along the East Coast, with the exception of Massachusetts. The comparative advantage eastern states enjoyed in securing legal recognition meant that after 1902, practitioners there could focus their energies on a national organization. In other sections of the nation, practitioners' efforts necessarily remained focused on local issues.[69]

The Illinois Society of Public Accountants

To reply to an obvious question—Where did the chartered accountants go after New York State passed its carefully drafted CPA laws?—one has only to look west to Illinois to find a powerful British presence. The Illinois legislature, under strong populist influence, resisted early efforts to enact a CPA law. One state senator, whose notion of equality meant free entry of all into any profession, lack of training or ability notwithstanding, distrusted accountants' motives in seeking a CPA law. The senator was alleged to have announced to George Wilkinson: "I would like to know what youse fellows want; if youse want a lead pipe cinch, I am agin you" (Ross 1940A: 16). Given such attitudes, Illinois practitioners had to demonstrate that they meant to exclude no one. The Illinois State Society had earlier opposed incorporated audit companies. In 1903, the society admitted Edward Gore, of the Audit Company of Chicago, and Maurice Kuhns, of the Safeguard Account Company; their influence was needed to lobby for a CPA law. Another result of the political necessity of excluding no one was that chartered accountants, citizens or not, were eligible for membership. In 1903, twenty-one of the society's fifty-three members were from the firm of Price Water-house, practitioners who could not be certified in New York State because they were British subjects, but who could be certified in Illinois under broad waiver provisions (Wilkinson 1904). Even after Illinois accountants finally extracted a CPA law from a hostile legislature, practitioners there had to be constantly alert to petitions to undercut certification standards in the interests of persons who complained of discrimination (Reckitt 1953: 73–74).

The Illinois Society followed the pattern of other states in convincing Northwestern University to inaugurate a school of business and commerce. Practitioners from New York and Pennsylvania joined their Illinois colleagues as guarantors against financial loss to the university. Among the most lasting contribution of the Illinois Society was the publication of the *Auditor,* a professional journal later taken over by the American Association and renamed the *Journal of Accountancy.*

The Illinois experience reflected the hostility faced by leaders of the CPA movement in many midwestern and southern states. Efforts in 1902 to bring about national unity in the profession appeared to have failed largely because regional differences had not been properly appreciated by the national leadership.

The Federation of Societies of Public Accountants in the United States

Practitioners met in 1902 ostensibly to discuss means of forming a national group to promote CPA laws in every state. The fruit of their efforts was the organization of the Federation of Societies of Public Accountants in the United States with the announced intention of promoting uniform CPA laws. But the three major state societies of New York, Pennsylvania, and Illinois were engaged in heated competition. Available evidence suggests that an unnamed objective of the federation had been to mitigate the effects of this legacy of rivalry and bickering that threatened to undercut professional goals (Suffern 1922). George Wilkinson worked diligently to gain the cooperation of those three powerful states and is granted the major credit for the federation's organization. The New York State Society, never enthusiastic about the federation and reluctant to surrender any of its prerogatives, made two demands at the organizational meeting that created dissension and almost at once precluded the federation from ever becoming an effective national body. The New York delegates demanded that federation membership be based exclusively upon affiliation with a state society and be closed to individuals. They also insisted upon an invidious distinction between CPA and non-CPA societies. The first demand was accepted, the second defeated, and it was only after extraordinary efforts by federation supporters among the New York State Society members that it agreed to join the federation (NYSSCPA, *Minutes* 1902: 17).[70]

The reluctance of the New York State Society to participate fully and completely in the federation centered on a fundamental disagreement as to goals. The federation's announced goal was to seek CPA legislation in those states that lacked CPA laws. New York accountants perceived that goal as considerably less important than the development and enforcement of professional standards. In 1904, New York State Society members voted 28 to 18 to withdraw from the federation and suggested the unification of existing organizations (NYSSCPA, *Minutes* 1904: 89). This position formed a principal element of the agenda of the 1904 International Congress of Accountants.

Meeting in Saint Louis—The First International Congress

The Saint Louis meeting in 1904 was a milestone in the development of accountancy in the United States: it marks the coming of political maturity within the profession's leadership. The most difficult task facing the delegates was to convince practitioners that their professional interests could be best promoted by a national organization. The ability to bring together, in a cooperative enterprise, men who, by the nature of the profession, were strong-willed and independent and accustomed to defending personal positions, was critical during those first organizational efforts. Compromise, moderation, discussion, accommodation—perhaps the true politics of any profession—were mandatory. Subsequent to the negotiations at the congress, the federation agreed to merge with the older AAPA organization in 1905. Once again, accountants had a single national voice, but fundamental divisions as to goals and priorities remained unresolved.

The American Association of Public Accountants, 1905–1916

Many of those participating in the International Congress viewed the merger of the two national organizations as the first step in obtaining uniform national standards for the accounting profession. But it soon became apparent that the AAPA simply did not have the authority to enforce meaningful standards. The merger had attempted but failed to heal regional and ethnic rivalries among practitioners.

The association's presidential election of 1906 confirmed that chartered accountants were viewed with hostility in most states and would soon be

Figure 5.1 Cartoon drawing of Arthur
Lowes Dickinson and Elijah Watt Sells.
Source: Program of the 1916 annual meet-
ing of the AAPA, Columbus, Ohio.

systematically excluded from positions of leadership. The nominees for
president that year were Arthur Lowes Dickinson and Elijah Watt Sells
(Fig. 5.1). Meeting just before the annual convention of the AAPA, the New
York State Society threatened to withdraw from the association if Dickinson
were elected. A motion was offered stating that the New York Society's interests would be best served only if the president of the AAPA was a "distinctly
representative American professional accountant . . . familiar with American institutions and customs" (NYSSCPA, *Minutes* 1906: 160–62). Sells
moved that the society simply resolve to support whomever was elected.
Although Sells's motion was overwhelmingly defeated, he managed to have
the original resolution tabled. Webster recalled that this election was especially vitriolic and observed that "those who spoke for or against particular
candidates seemed not to have thought of professional ethics" (Webster
1954: 141). One goal of the New Yorkers was achieved in that before 1916
no chartered accountant ever became president of the association. The
1906 election exacerbated anti-British sentiment. It narrowed effective
control of the AAPA to a small group of practitioners from New York and
Pennsylvania, and the national authority the association sought was never

realized. Accountants faced severe criticism from outside the profession and the AAPA was powerless to respond adequately and effectively.

Inadequate CPA Legislation

One of the major goals of the association was the standardization of CPA laws. The association had adopted the federation's "model bill for CPA legislation," which John A. Cooper had drafted, and endeavored to use it as a yardstick to determine the effectiveness and acceptability of new state legislation.[71] But the association could do little to upgrade inadequate legislation or to gain passage of new CPA laws that conformed to Cooper's ideal. The hardworking Committee on State Legislation conducted voluminous correspondence but to no avail. In 1911, Ohio, Georgia, and Louisiana enacted CPA laws unacceptable to the national leadership (AAPA, *Year Book* 1911: 834). The association refused to recognize CPA certificates from those states and practitioners in them were not eligible for association membership. By 1915, the situation had deteriorated to the point that the AAPA would not accept the CPA certificates issued by nine of the thirty-nine states that had CPA laws.

Criticism, especially from federal authorities, that a CPA certificate often was worthless and afforded little protection to the public began to appear in the press. The association certainly could not argue convincingly that existing legislation could ensure professional competence. The call for more stringent laws became a major factor in reinforcing beliefs that an "Eastern Establishment" allegedly in control of the association did not care about promoting accountancy nationwide. Southerners and Midwesterners argued that, given the strong antipathy among legislators in their states to any CPA law at all, even a bad law was better than none. Insistence upon legislation that conformed to the Cooper model, they argued, meant no CPA law at all.

Disillusioned with the experience of dealing with state legislators, the association attempted to solve the problem by appealing to the federal government. Earlier in 1889, John A. Cooper had formulated a process for federal registration of accountants who met certain qualifications, to be known as registered public accountants.[72] The association's committee on federal legislation, under the leadership of Robert H. Montgomery and Edward L. Suffern, explored that possibility over several years. Practitioners, with few exceptions (among them Cooper), continued to believe that the federal authorities would permit the association to define and control admission standards. Cooper had declared it to be an unrealistic assumption and believed that any federal registration plan would probably have to be administered by the Civil Service Commission or a similar body (Cooper 1913). Nothing appeared to move Washington; suddenly, in 1914, Federal Trade Commission Chairman Edward Hurley announced a plan for the commission to recognize a limited number of accountants as "zone experts." The proposal was a shock, and the association quickly backed off from its earlier enthusiasm for federal recognition (AAPA, *Year Book* 1915: 199–200). Hurley's plan for "audits according to rigidly prescribed procedures . . . under a predetermined fee schedule" made accountants wary of the notion that outside authorities could put the profession's house in order without exacting a price.[73]

By 1916, the national organization and its leadership found itself in a critical situation. Legislation proved inadequate in some states; efforts to seek federal recognition almost resulted in government administration of the profession itself. This dilemma alone probably would have been enough to lead to the fall of the AAPA. However, external critics' charges that established practitioners sought to secure a monopoly ensured its demise.

Professional Exclusion

The charge that in certain states, especially New York and Illinois, established CPAs had restricted entrance into accountancy through unreasonable admission standards was devastating. When James G. Cannon, president of the Fourth National Bank of New York, publicly charged that CPAs were conspiring to create a monopoly, knowledgeable practitioners were dismayed (AAPA, *Year Book* 1908: 120–24). During the 1890s Cannon had been among the first advocates of independent audits for credit purposes and subsequently had been considered a strong ally of the profession. Many accountants, including most of the officers of the association, were especially sensitive to the allegation that the qualifying examination was a tool for monopoly because they had received their certificates through waiver.

Newspapers in New York and Chicago were especially critical of the profession's alleged policy of deliberate exclusion. The *Chicago Herald* revealed that in Illinois, between 1903 and 1908, some 111 persons sat for the CPA examination and only six had passed. Moreover, no less than ninety-eight certificates had been granted by waiver. The situation in New York was, if anything, worse. The New York State annual failure rate had always been above 90 percent; in 1916 even that record was broken when 3 of 156 candidates were issued CPA certificates. W. Sanders Davies, who rejected the monopoly charge publicly, privately considered the situation intolerable. He contended, "a man in my office . . . doesn't dot his I's or cross his T's just where the examiners require them to be dotted or crossed. This may be alright for schoolboys but not for accountants" (AAPA, *Minutes* 1916: 54–55). Had that been Davies's perception alone, reform might not have been necessary. But a New York State examiner corroborated the allegation of picayune grading when he remarked that he allowed "one-fifth for the correctness of an answer and four-fifths for the arrangement" (E. S. Suffern 1909).

The American Institute of Accountants

By 1916, a decade of frustration convinced association leaders that the national body must be reorganized to still criticism of the profession. The charges of professional exclusion and meaningless CPA certificates had to be answered if federal intervention was to be averted.

A critical element of the reorganization scheme of 1916 was to permit the national organization (hereafter called the institute) to admit new members on an individual basis. Among the requirements for membership was five years of practical experience and passage of the institute's examination. One of the reasons for individual memberships was to give residents of such states as New York and Illinois, notorious for apparently arbitrary CPA examination grading, an opportunity to enter the profession. The same reasoning applied to residents of those states whose CPA qualifying procedures were unacceptable; good persons could enter the profession free of the taint of poor standards. A major purpose, overriding others, appeared to be to bring under the control of the institute all practitioners who for one reason or another had formerly belonged to no professional group at all.[74]

The plan for direct, individual admission to the institute of persons who met its qualifications and passed its examination appeared to many to be an abandonment of nearly a quarter-century's effort to gain legislative recognition for the profession.[75] Ironically, the very men who inaugurated the reform of 1916 had also been in the vanguard of the CPA movement in New York, Illinois, and Pennsylvania. They now faced charges of selling out. The 1916 reorganization achieved two major objectives: criticism of a CPA monopoly abated and, for a time, federal intervention was forestalled. But the abandonment of the CPA certificate left the institute open to challenge as the "national" body, and a rival organization, the American Society of CPAs, would soon emerge. Therefore, although the reorganization of the national body was politically effective, control over the profession remained illusory. The institute, like the association, had no recognized, legitimate power by which to enforce professional standards.

The Evolution of Professional Standards

"Legislation for a profession only grants opportunity," observed Joseph Sterrett in 1904. He continued, "Education must be underneath and around all our legislation and organization" (32). His advice reflected native-born practitioners' faith in the efficacy of education, a belief that had a unique influence upon the development of accountancy in the United States.

Early practitioners' view of education's role was influenced by contemporary ideas of the nature of a profession. The most widely accepted definition of a profession at the end of the nineteenth century was "an occupation that involves a liberal education or its equivalent and mental rather than physical labor" (Joplin 1914A). The concept of "liberal education" incorporated the Aristotelean concept of "spiritual condition" and was in its essence ethical. Education imparted not only academic skills but imbued the young person with such values as righteousness, wisdom, and a sense of justice. Experience in the broadest sense completed the education. One must keep that background in mind when discussing and evaluating early practitioners' actions and recommendations on education.

Accountants at the turn of the century lived during a time of endemic change induced by the economic and social adjustments that rapid industrialization had introduced in the United States. Rapid change can precipitate political and social instability, but it may also promote intellectual flexibility and receptiveness to new ideas. American pragmatism advocated the injection of practical skills into education and provided the necessary philosophical justification for the introduction of accounting into university curricula; the progressive movement advocated the kinds of reforms that created a social need for accountancy.

The major constraint to fulfillment of the practitioners' ideal of placing the profession firmly upon an educational base was the hostility of state legislators. Reluctant even to incorporate rudimentary technical prerequisites in CPA laws they were finally induced to enact, state legislators could not be expected to accept formal education requirements (which lawmakers often interpreted as attempts to restrict free entry into the profession). Before World War I, it was rare for most people to complete high school. In 1900, the median number of school years for the general population was between seven and eight years; the practitioners' ideal of at least a high school diploma for accountants therefore faced insurmountable opposition (Counts 1922). Practitioners concluded that under those circumstances no single criterion—formal education, relevant experience, passing the CPA examination—could be sufficient. Some combination of criteria therefore was believed necessary to assure the competence of aspiring accountants.

Educational Qualifications

Practitioners recognized that at the turn of the century they could not realistically demand a high school diploma; the term most commonly incorporated into CPA legislation was "high school degree or its equivalent." Enforcement and interpretation were left to individual states' examining boards, and consequently applicable standards varied. At that time, the completion of high school appears to have signified a level of sophistication significantly higher than present-day expectations.

Most early practitioners held as a model the preliminary examination then administered in Scotland. (It is important to note that the preliminary examination was designed to test general background; it was *not* the CPA qualifying examination.) In Scotland, the candidate was required to write from dictation; compose an essay; display competence in arithmetic and algebra to include quadratic equations and the first four books of Euclid; have knowledge of geography, Latin, and English history; and demonstrate mastery in two fields chosen from Latin, Greek, French, German, Italian, Spanish, higher mathematics, physics, chemistry, physiology, zoology, botany, electricity, light and heat, geology, and stenography. Under Sterrett's influence, Pennsylvania implemented an examination based upon the Scottish model, but in most states the high school equivalency procedure was a sham (Sterrett 1905).

The CPA Qualifying Examination

Early practitioners revealed a decided reluctance to rely upon a single examination to support entry into the profession. They believed that CPA legislation was justified only if it provided some protection for the public. Standards among the states varied widely, and the comprehensiveness of early examinations often left much to be desired. What concerned practitioners most about the situation was that the public risked relying upon certificates that were meaningless. Edward Suffern spoke for the most thoughtful practitioners when he wrote that accountants must seek to safeguard "the interests of the public . . . which should not be misled through supposing . . . protection where none exists" (AAPA, *Year Book* 1911: 99).

The most common criticism of early CPA examinations was their tendency to be narrowly technical; practitioners were naturally reluctant to place reliance upon such a single prerequisite for entry. John Cooper that "one with any practical knowledge of affairs can not argue that a passing of an examination is proof of intellectual superiority, and still less that it is a guarantee of judicial temperament, common sense, logical faculty, and professional instincts" (Cooper 1907C: 85). To understand this attitude one must recall that these practitioners tended to view the awarding of the CPA certificate as a sign of professional competence. Therefore the candidates' preliminary education and experience became vital to the certification process. But the ultimate goal was to combine education and experience, and practitioners began to look to universities to provide the requisite programs.

University Affiliation

State societies from their inception promoted accounting courses in universities. Practitioners faced the task of convincing university administrators, who shared the view that only the arts and sciences were proper subjects for higher education. The business world exhibited a similar skepticism about the value of a college education. Some accountants found it difficult to convince businessmen of the value of education. If anti-intellectualism was not common, there was a definite attitude that long, formal educational preparation was neither necessary nor desirable for business careers.

American practitioners had no precedents and no models when it came to outlining the kinds of courses of study the new business schools might offer. As Charles Waldo Haskins, the first dean of the New York University School of Commerce, Finance and Accounts, pointed out: "The question could not be answered in Great Britain, because of the absence there of any system of commercial education in which to place it, it could not be answered on the Continent, from which has come the present wave of activity in economic education, because bureaucratic bookkeeping is still the continental idea of accuracy" (Haskins 1901A: 10).

The Role of University Education

The original purpose of the first higher educational programs in accounting was to train practitioners' assistants. After securing acceptance for accounting curricula in universities, accountants began to advocate an expansion of university education to realize the goals of broader, more conceptual programs. Most practitioners believed that mastery of the technical procedures of auditing and accounting was most effectively learned through practical experience; education's role was to develop a person's analytic ability. Accounting, they believed, required a wide range of knowledge and minds trained to think analytically and constructively. They supported a broad program emphasizing theory and philosophy and were disappointed when the evidence accumulated that accounting educators tended to emphasize narrow, technical training.

It was the university accounting educators who moved from a theoretical to a procedural orientation. As early as 1907, the association's Committee on Education received repeated requests for practitioner-teachers. Practitioners did respond, and most of the faculties in schools of business were composed of practicing CPAs. Academicians supported their requests for practitioner-teachers on the grounds that "professional subjects must be practically applied[,] [and] theoretically oriented professors could not handle accountancy in a satisfactory manner." It is possible, though not certain, that those first academic accountants might have been influenced by contemporary developments in major university law schools. The law schools were restructuring curricula to accommodate the so-called case method of legal instruction, which was designed as a deliberate departure from traditional emphasis on legal theory and philosophy.

After 1910, one specific issue, the ever-increasing orientation of academic programs toward the CPA examination, aroused the wrath of most of the national leadership (AAPA, *Year Book* 1912: 138). Some academicians joined with the institute in voicing criticism. Duncan (1914) noted that whenever a question on a specific industry—railroads, utilities, breweries— appeared on a CPA examination, accounting departments went searching for an expert to add one more narrowly specialized course to the program. In 1918, W. Sanders Davies, president of the institute, chided educators for proceeding on the "erroneous assumption (that) preparing men for the CPA examination was what was most needed," and said that as a result academicians "placed too little emphasis on accounting theory" (AIA, *Minutes* 1917: 46). The debate continued into the 1920s; but the introduction of practice sets and their growing use in accounting courses were clear evidence that Davies's position had lost ground and that accounting curricula had repudiated conceptual approaches in favor of technique and procedure.

Perhaps this change in emphasis in accounting curricula reflected what one might have called a "generation gap." The "first" accountants, who reached maturity and position by 1900, believed in the concept of broad, general, and liberal education. The accounting educators of the next generation were influenced by John Dewey and his followers, who stressed practicality and relevance. Unfortunately, "progressive" education became interpreted to mean a kind of vocationalism with little sympathy or use for so-called classical subjects. Deeply disappointed with the trends in versity business schools they had done so much to foster, some practi advocated yet another reform similar to the present-day movement for professional accounting schools. Interviewed for the *New York Post* in 1921, a disillusioned Joseph Sterrett recommended that "every young man who wishes to take up accounting (ought to) take up, if possible, a full college course in general subjects, followed by post graduate work in accounting" (Watson 1921).

The apparent inadequacy of the evolution of accounting curricula notwithstanding, early practitioners made a significant and major contribution to American culture. Accountants, in many states, were responsible for introducing business subjects into universities. They had convinced educators of the legitimacy of business subjects; they had either financed directly or guaranteed against loss of first university business schools; and they provided faculty. Nevertheless, they did not believe that education alone was sufficient and retained a deep conviction of the need for practical experience to assure true competence.

The Experience Requirement

A significant development prior to World War I was that, despite the expansion of accounting and applied business courses in institutions of higher education, the recommended practical experience requirement for CPAs was consistently lengthened by both state and national organizations. It is possible that this development was a function of practitioners' efforts to adapt the British apprenticeship system to the American environment.

American practitioners presented what they believed were sound philosophical arguments for the experience requirement. Both the classical tradition of liberal education and the progressive reforms advocated by the Deweyites supported practitioners' advocacy of experience. John Dewey (1939), in "Education and Experience," declared that experience, not formalized education, was the vital factor in developing an educated person. Experience enabled a person to interpret "truth" in different circumstances.

Among accounting practitioners, the principal justification for experience was the need to develop "professional judgment." An actual, functioning, accounting practitioner's office was perceived as an ideal environment within which to inculcate in the aspirant a "proper . . . attitude." Also, although no formal programs may have existed, the necessity to sensitize the young accountant to the ethical norms of the profession was key in defense of the experience requirement.

Ira Schur remembered his early years with S. D. Leidesdorf and recalled that developing an appreciation of ethical standards was fundamental to a "young man's practical experience." Schur could not explain specifically how it occurred. The attitude "was just there, it was just there." He added that "S.D. told me to watch him closely, if he ever did anything I thought was wrong, to tell him because we all wanted to sleep at night" (Schur 1976).

Practical experience had a second purpose, important to practitioners at a time of varied and uncertain entrance standards: it enabled established, reputable CPAs to screen aspirants and prevent incompetent or unethical persons from entering the profession. Experience completed the process of professional preparation (Merino 1977).

Early accountants found no lasting solution to the problem of assuring that all licensed CPAs were competent professionals, but they developed an initial conception of professional "attitude." They accepted the idea that accountants had an obligation to protect the public from unqualified practitioners and concluded that no single instrument could function as a reliable admission standard. They formulated a combination of education, experience, and the CPA qualifying examination as the best possible compromise. They conceived professional attitude as proceeding from recognition of moral responsibility, which required appreciation of professional ethics.

Ethics

Edward Ross (1916: 67) wrote: "The patron of [a] calling which involves the use of highly technical knowledge, since he is not qualified to judge the worth of the services he receives, is in a position of extreme dependence (and requires assurance) of the trustworthiness of the practitioners he engages." The stress that practitioners placed upon the need to protect the public's interest was identifiable throughout the Progressive Era. A clear manifestation of that concern was the reliance early practitioners placed upon ethics to ensure acceptable technical standards were maintained. Among the commonest criticisms of the profession by outsiders was that accountants considered their discipline to be essentially ethical rather than "scientific" (Smith 1912: 169f.).

Finding the means to introduce and impress new members with the ethical norms of the profession was not an easy task. There was little agreement over whether it was more effective to rely on informal systems of internalization through monitored experience in a practitioner's office, or to attempt to enforce compliance by adopting a written code of conduct that provided strict sanctions against improper conduct.

Two practitioners, Joseph Sterrett and John Cooper, became acknowledged spokesmen for the accounting community on the subject of professional ethics. Although in basic agreement that professional standards must be maintained, they differed in their approach to the problem. Sterrett, in his classic 1907 paper, "Professional Ethics," suggested that a written code of conduct was necessary but expressed some serious reservations. First, he warned his colleagues, "let us first divest ourselves of the thought that any system of professional ethics for accountancy . . . can or should supersede or even modify those fundamental principles of right and wrong . . . which from the beginning of time were formulated and given expression in the decalogue" (Sterrett 1907: 409). Second, he noted that ethical standards were not absolute; they were evolutionary, and, therefore, rules incorporated into any formal code of ethics must change over time. His position may be called "pragmatic" because he recognized that what was "fair" or "true" or "just" was dependent upon social norms; what one generation considered ethical might not be appropriate for future generations. Sterrett firmly believed that there were absolute fundamental principles that superseded any written rules. At the same time, he maintained that any standards that were set would be viable only so long as they met the social needs of the day, and therefore he supported limited written rules.

The idea that written rules must inevitably be the result of compromise and therefore would only be minimum standards was accepted by many early accountants. John Forbes perhaps expressed the sentiment against written rules best when he said, "I have an abiding impatience with written rules of conduct. . . . I have a deep contempt for him whose obedience to a natural principle of right must be regulated by a few poorly constructed lines over the meaning of which he would probably quibble" (AAPA, *Year Book* 1915: 83).

Cooper, in his 1907 response to Sterrett, insisted that the association should promulgate an ethics code immediately. He felt that every possible rule of conduct that could be codified, should be. Inflexible, sardonic, and totally unwilling to compromise, Cooper often aroused hostility among his colleagues. He continuously introduced rules proscribing contingent fees, advertising, and audit companies that not only were opposed by many accountants but also would have provoked external criticism from those who thought CPAs were trying to create a monopoly by stifling competition.

Independence and Confidentiality

Henry Rand Hatfield (1913) summed up the prevalent view within the profession on ethics when he reviewed Montgomery's *Auditing Theory and*

Practice (1912). He mentioned the special section on professional ethics but maintained that the importance placed on professional integrity and personal conduct throughout the book was far more significant. Fundamental and pervasive concepts, such as confidentiality and independence, were not codified. Many believed to do so would mean inevitable dilution of intent. Accountants sought, rather, through the national organization and within the practitioners' offices, to internalize those values so that they were completely accepted and respected by everyone who entered the profession of public accountancy. They believed that intellectual independence and confidentiality were absolutes that must apply in all circumstances.

It was assumed that any person permitted into the ranks of accountancy had been conditioned to accept both notions as fundamental norms during this period of practical experience. If that were not the case, then the practitioner-mentor had an ethical and moral responsibility to see that the person who did not measure up was barred from admission into the profession. Practitioners rejected the idea that by promulgating rules—especially rules that by their nature could have dealt only with peripheral matters— either confidentiality or appropriate independence could be assured.

To imply that accountants were independent because they observed certain minor prohibitions was considered dangerous. The public might be misled by assuming that this guaranteed independence, which was not true. The most telling argument appeared to be that if a practitioner was going to be influenced by a relatively minor interest (ownership of stock or a seat on the board of directors of a client company), then he certainly might be equally swayed by the threat of losing the audit fee (Montgomery 1907).

One could also suggest that since the association had no power to enforce compliance with its rules (its strictest sanction was to expel the offending member and to forbid his use of the phrase "member of the American Association of Public Accountants" on business correspondence), any rule was subject to constant violation. In an area such as independence, the benefits of rules that could deal with form only and not substance were considered negligible.

Confidentiality was the second fundamental concept of the early profession. Although there had been at least some discussion of rules to deal with independence, there was no such debate concerning confidentiality. Most practitioners sympathized with this norm and agreed that it was pervasive. Without confidentiality there could be no profession. Practitioners large and small, from all regions, were united in this belief.

In several states, accountants sought statutory recognition of their responsibility to remain silent concerning clients' affairs. Recollections of young men entering the profession are clear on this point. Established practitioners, whether in small or large firms, told their assistants "to keep their mouths shut" about any client's business. There seemed little need for any rule; any assistant violating a client's confidence faced the prospect of losing his job and thereby expulsion from the profession. The implications of third-party responsibility, as discussed below, would later affect issues of confidentiality as well.

Rules of Conduct

As might be expected, because formal rules of conduct were necessarily the result of compromise, they did not really deal with substantive issues. Only eight written rules were promulgated, and they dealt primarily with issues classified today as "other responsibilities and practices." The only agreement the group was able to reach was that a code of ethics that dealt with overt abuses might be beneficial. Minimal standards in some areas were perceived as better than none. But even those rules enacted that dealt with obvious violations of professional conduct were often ignored by state societies.

The most effective means that the national organization had to control practitioners (given its limited power) was not by enforcement of its code of ethics but through a provision incorporated in its bylaws, known as "acts discreditable to the profession," a concept broadly interpreted to deter professional misconduct.

Acts Discreditable

The observation that early practitioners treated accounting as an "ethical" system and resisted demands for the establishment of uniform technical standards is well founded. In the absence of technical standards, the notion of "acts discreditable" became the primary means of ensuring technical proficiency among practitioners.

The concept of acts discreditable was common to most professions but its application within accounting was unique. The medical and legal professions had specific rules that proscribed any action that threatened to dishonor medicine or law, but these standards referred to the personal conduct of the individual practitioner. Accountants' interpretation of the concept of acts discreditable expanded the idea to cover areas of technical competence. The principal reason for the difference lay in the recognition that accountants were potentially responsible to third parties—investors and creditors—whereas doctors and lawyers were primarily responsible to their patients and clients. Accountants noted that the law had not yet evolved to protect the interest of third parties, whereas the client-professional relationship had been clearly delineated by the courts. The lack of a contractual relationship between the accounting practitioner and third parties prohibited the ultimate user from suing for redress in cases of professional incompetence. Despite demands by practitioners as early as 1908 that the situation be remedied by a broader interpretation of accountants' legal liability, the situation was not remedied until the 1930s. Accountants, therefore, attempted to develop their own means of policing the profession and protecting third parties from incompetent practice.

When the AAPA was organized, a general statement was incorporated into its bylaws that permitted the national organization to control the technical quality of accountants' work. The association "on the written complaint of any person aggrieved, whether a member or not," could expel or suspend a member "guilty of an act discreditable to the profession" (AAPA, *Year Book* 1907: 238). This power permitted wide latitude in condemning actions that, though not specifically proscribed by the code of ethics, could be construed as harmful to colleagues, clients, or the general public. After reorganization, the council members of the institute took this duty seriously and were not averse to bringing charges against prominent members of the profession. But the lack of power vested in the national body soon became apparent. When James Anyon was suspended, he was furious and demanded to know what suspension meant. He was told that he could no longer use "member of the AIA" on his letterhead. To which he retorted, "I don't use it anyhow," and quit the institute (AIA, *Minutes* 1918: 25–80; 142–92).

Unfortunately, the only power that the institute might have had—publicity—was unavailable. There has always been a strong tendency among professionals for "guild selfishness" and "group bias." Within the national organization, a very influential group believed that accountants should not censure their colleagues. A concession made to these opponents of self-policing, which many considered unwise but unfortunately necessary, was that the names of persons or firms found guilty of professional misconduct not be published in the *Journal*. Only the facts of the case and its determination would be reported (AIA, *Minutes* 1917: 30ff.).

The foundation of ethical and education standards was laid during this trying period, although the issues were not satisfactorily resolved given the institutional framework of the profession. No one body had the power to mandate compliance with professional standards, a problem that was equally perplexing in early efforts to develop a conceptual framework for the discipline.

Accounting and Auditing Theory

Accountants began to discuss the need for a "science of accounts" before the turn of the century, but it soon became apparent that the use of the term "scientific" was creating widespread misunderstanding among persons outside the profession. When accountants used the term, they meant a systematic approach to accounting problems through which judgment, guided by experience and education, enabled the practitioner to arrive at appropriate solutions in each specific engagement. The goal was to develop informal guidelines that would be acceptable to all accountants, rather than to promulgate absolute rules of procedure applicable in all situations, circumstances notwithstanding. Uniformity bred dogmatic solutions, and this, accountants feared, would compromise their hard-won recognition as professionals.

External Pressure for a "Science" of Accounts

Businessmen and government officials were in the vanguard of the movement for "scientific" accounting theory, by which they often meant development of uniform procedures. Alexander Smith declared that "accounting is, or ought to be, a science, not a system of ethics; amenable to definite axioms and capable, in proper practice, of producing definite and exact results" (Smith 1912: 170). Arthur Lowes Dickinson replied that Smith demanded a "rule book" and that accountants "could never have a rule book, circumstances must rule, you have to use experience, that is why we are professional accountants." Accountants feared that demands such as Smith's were designed to reduce the accountant's function to that of a clerk (AAPA, *Year Book* 1912: 59ff.). They argued that "accountancy never was nor could be an exact science and every profit and loss to which he is asked to certify is in a very substantial measure an expression of opinion and therefore subject to honest divergence of views both as to substance and form" (editorial, *Journal of Accountancy,* May 1912: 360).

Practitioners had excellent reasons to be wary of efforts to enforce so-called scientific accounting (uniformity). Public accountants had been displaced by nonprofessionals whenever standard procedures had been introduced. The Interstate Commerce Commission had required uniform reporting in the railroad industry; almost immediately independent audits were dispensed with and CPAs replaced by technicians. Similar losses of clients and engagements closely followed the introduction of uniform audit procedures for banks, insurance companies, utilities, and other regulated industries (Carey 1969: 60ff.). Accountants, understandably, rejected "scientific" accounting when it was used very narrowly simply to mean the determination of "fundamental axioms" that permitted "uniform procedures" to be established and applied in all circumstances.[76]

Practitioners started a public education campaign whose central message was that, through the uncertainty faced by the accountant, the essence of professional work must be the exercise of judgment to find the appropriate procedures in each individual circumstance (May 1915). They argued that financial statements based on blind acceptance of uniform procedures would be more misleading in most cases than if accountants were permitted to choose among alternative accounting methods. Early practitioners believed that, because of the vastly different circumstances encountered in the business world, accounting practice was best viewed as an art.

Accountancy as an Art

A standard definition of an art is "the power of performing certain actions especially as acquired by experience, study, or observation." The artist does not seek fundamental truths but relies instead upon the independent, informed judgment of the individual in the interpretation of phenomena as they emerge through circumstances. George O. May wrote that "accounting is an art, not a science, but an art of wide and varied usefulness" (May 1943: 189).[77]

Both pragmatism and economic conditions in the United States appeared to support the practitioners' position that accountancy was an art. Pragmatism was suited to the development of concepts and principles within the context of an art. Truth was perceived as phenomenally relative; ideas must be tested for practicality and attainability; experience enabled each individual to judge the validity of ideas according to specific circumstances. Pragmatic epistemology asserted that "knowledge" emerged through experimental, informed observation and testing of ideas within a "social" context. It dismissed "contemplative knowledge" (for which Dewey's term was "spectator theory of knowledge") as inadequate to manage in the context of a dynamic environment (Dewey 1910: 450ff.). Pragmatism rejected traditional conceptions of theory and maintained that theory that rested upon abstract or metaphysical truth was without meaning unless its application resulted in some kind or form of social "good." It could be deemed neither "true" nor "false" unless "tested" in the "laboratory" or social context. This pragmatic concept of "adaptive" theory, which emerged from the crucible of experience, was a foundation of early practitioners' theory. As Seymour Walton explained: "Being based on experience, theory is able to . . .

further illuminate a subject. . . . It does so by applying the law to other activities besides those from which it was formulated. . . . Thus, theory using men's limited experience broadens into a practically unlimited field" (Walton 1917: 277).

The Development of Accounting Theory

Accounting theory, consistent with its pragmatic inspiration, became primarily concerned with the proper interpretation of economic values. Contemporary economic conditions required that practitioners retain flexibility in valuation. Deflation, which persisted from 1865 through 1897, with some respite between 1879 and 1884, was the most pervasive mind-set before the turn of the century. From 1898 to 1919, inflation was general, but accounting practitioners were reluctant to preclude renewed deflation. Faced with duodirectional price level changes, practitioners had begun to hedge their views on valuation procedures. Reluctance to make any general assumption about price level disparities became even more pronounced after the depression of 1919–21, when the nation began again to experience deflationary trends that reopened the whole question of price and value adjustments.

The 1904 International Congress can be identified as the genesis of the profession's classical intellectual phase. Although both practitioners and academicians had begun discussion of the need to provide a theoretical framework for the profession before World War I, it was often difficult to distinguish between accounting and auditing theory. Practitioners and academicians often perceived matters related to accounting as coincident to the auditor's concerns. Typically, public accountants functioned in both roles; as accountants they interpreted accounting information and as auditors they attested to it. This dual role is important, since today, interpretation of information is left largely to the analyst or user (as witnessed by the Cohen Commission recommendation in 1978 that accountants spell out salient facts but leave interpretation to the user). During this early period, clients and users expected if not demanded CPAs to audit, analyze, and interpret financial reports.

The Theoretical Framework

Guided by philosophical pragmatism, early accounting theories attempted to define a conceptual framework based upon logic to replace "rationalization" as used in personification of accounts. The first integrative theory to evolve was labeled "proprietary," and most accounting theorists before World War I may be identified as "proprietary theorists." Pragmatists, institutional economists, and some progressive reformers argued that industrial concentration enabled those who controlled the nation's large corporations (i.e., trusts) to maximize profit by limiting production and administering prices; they thus questioned the relevance of accounting profit (Mitchell 1918).[78]

Pragmatists and institutionalists challenged the relevance of accounting profit calculations in a corporate era.[79] They asked: How does calculation of accounting profit impact the three basic functions of an economy—production of goods and services, improvement of the quality of life, and coordination of reciprocal relationships—when competitive forces are not operable? (Dewey and Tufts 1908). If those who controlled the nation's trusts could administer prices, would accounting profit reflect efficiency or simply the ability to restrict supply and administer prices? Critics contended that association of business success with monetary profit and loss would *not* result in production of goods and services society desired but, rather, would enrich those who controlled the trusts.[80]

Accounting theorists faced a formidable task: they had to reconcile traditional accounting profit measurement, based on individualistic economic theories, with an emerging corporate economy. Proprietary theory was an imaginative response to that challenge.[81] Given the challenges that accounting theorists faced and the issues they had to address, it seems singularly unfortunate that most current accounting theory texts dismiss this theory as irrelevant.[82] This dismissal obscures an interesting power struggle and the partisan role that proprietary theorists played in resolving the ongoing ideological conflict between democratic values and private property in the United States.[83]

Corporate abuses had given accountants a clear mandate from the political sector. Demands for corporate publicity to protect both investors and creditors accelerated throughout the period, and it became clear at the Industrial Commission hearings that secrecy would no longer be tolerated.[84] While proprietary theorists welcomed the call for publicity, they also recognized the potential threat if the stockholder/owner were not kept at center stage.[85]

The Proprietary Model

Proprietary theorists explicitly rejected the concept of retention of earnings and focused on calculation of dividends available for distribution in order to allow the "proprietor" (stockholder/owner) to appear to be firmly in control.[86] Hatfield (1909) noted that retention of earnings would turn a "going concern" into a "permanent" concern, limiting ownership rights.[87] Goodwill, created by watered stock, created a difficult problem for proprietary theorists. "Goodwill" theoretically represented promoters' estimates of "expected future earning power"; practically, for accounting purposes, goodwill equaled the excess of par value of common stock issued over the fair market value of corporate assets.[88] They could not admit that goodwill *typically* accrues to those who have monopoly power without addressing the question of the relevance of accounting profit measurement in a noncompetitive market. They resolved that problem by arguing that any "excess" earnings would only be temporary; therefore, goodwill should be amortized.[89] Proprietary theorists acknowledged that amortization of goodwill, generated by watered stock, resulted in a "fictitious" expense (a charge where no cost had been incurred) and limited dividend distribution. Amortization was justified as a means of correcting past abuses.[90] The procedure had significant benefits. It not only enabled successful corporations to "make good" on watered stock by providing funds for reinvestment; it also reestablished the integrity of capital and reduced income, quieting criticism of "unfair" monopoly profits.[91] Perhaps because of the problem of significant overstatement of assets and capital in corporations that issued watered stock or the desire to ignore harsh external criticisms of accounting profit, proprietary theorists did not stress the income statement.

Profit and Loss

Most proprietarists agreed with Hatfield that the profit and loss account was "a subdivision of the Capital account . . . [that indicated] current changes in net wealth." Income determination was merely another aspect of asset valuation (Hatfield 1909: 197). They ignored the earnings process and concepts such as revenues and expenses. Hatfield defined expense as "negative proprietorship" and did not address the question of what is revenue. He was content to explain the revenue account as a "temporary, collective account, recording the changes in net wealth due to business operations of a stated period" (Hatfield 1909: 72f., 195ff.).

Later accountants would find it difficult to visualize an accounting theory in which income determination was not of primary concern. Accountants' propensity to totally disregard the profit and loss statement had been criticized prior to the turn of the century. In 1899, an editorial in the *Book-Keeper* chastised the profession, claiming that "the profit and loss account is the most absurd in the whole . . . system, it is positively a kind of back door ash heap, where people throw their refuse and nobody clears it away" (Editorial, May 1899: 1). Most early theorists simply viewed profit and loss as a residual of the asset valuation process. Despite references one finds in the 1930s about the return to "orthodoxy" of early theory, it seems clear that there was no single, acceptable procedure for profit determination in this time period.

As late as 1928, Howard Greer noted that accounting textbooks often referred to two nominal accounts, the mixed merchandise and the expense account. He pointed out that the use of only two accounts did not lend itself to accuracy in determination of profits. The mixed merchandise account was debited for purchases (at cost) during the year and credited for sales. At year's end, the closing inventory was debited at sale price, which resulted in some startling annual profit figures. This problem had long been the subject of debate without successful resolution.

In 1917, the institute charged Maurice Kuhns with a violation of its by-laws (committing an act discreditable to the profession) for certifying a misleading statement due to technical incompetence. Robert Montgomery, acting as the institute's "prosecutor" presented the following schedule as evidence.

Gross Sales	$ 16,000
Beginning Inventory	$ 6,000
Purchases	$ 47,000
Ending Inventory	$ 98,000
Profit	$ 50,000

(AIA, *Minutes* 1917: 219–20)

Caustically, Montgomery asked if some doubts did not arise concerning the statement's validity. Consider the following: Gross Sales plus Ending Inventory minus Beginning Inventory minus Purchases equals *gross* profit. Since the expense account was not shown in the minutes one can only assume that, since the mixed merchandise account showed a gross profit of $61,000, there were $11,000 of other expenses in the other nominal accounts, and no "cost of goods sold" could have been calculated. Kuhns replied that the client only wanted a balance sheet audit and besides, he argued, "since it had been held in courts that accountants are not considered detectives . . . [he] had done all that is necessary." Montgomery replied that at least since 1905 accountants knew they should not certify a misleading statement (AIA, *Minutes* 1917: 250f.). The outcome of the hearing appears to have been negligible, since Kuhns's name appears on the 1918 roster of members.

Paton and Stevenson wrote that although it was fallacious to argue that recognition of appreciation in the accounts was to anticipate profits, there could be no question that "to use selling price in taking inventories—in other words to capitalize the services of the firm before those services are performed, is to anticipate profits." The cost of inventory replacement, they argued, only mirrored relevant changes in economic events; they held that accountants should record all changes if they hoped to show "a true financial posture" of the firm (Paton and Stevenson 1918: 462f.). Those who suggested that appreciation be recognized in the accounts were accused of reverting to the dark ages of single-entry bookkeeping (Littleton 1933A: 578f.).

One finds little advanced discussion of the need for income determination; although the concept of realization was addressed, it was not fundamental to the development of most early theory. Implicit in the early debate was the enduring belief that accountants must view either the income statement or the balance sheet as fundamental, and the other residual. It was during this period that the perplexing enigma of double entry was recognized. One had to choose up sides by opting for a proper income statement or a proper balance sheet, the belief being that you could not have relevant values in both.

William Paton (1922) criticized the proprietary focus, arguing that the goal of corporate business should not be simply to maximize the wealth of its owners. He believed that management perceived its purpose to be to increase the return "to all equities" and "not the return to common stockholders" (Paton 1922: 89). Paton used the term "equities" to encompass all sources of financing for the firm, and entity theory would evolve from the assumption that management was not primarily concerned with returns to only one group of claimholders. While it is often suggested that Paton's entity theory was an advance in conceptualization, its underlying assumptions, inconsistent with private property rights, have never been accepted. Accounting theory today continues to adopt a proprietary focus; that is, managers should maximize stockholders' wealth, rather than an entity focus.

Proprietary theorists' discussion of profit measurement indicated an unquestioning acceptance of classical economic theory and reflected a clear naturalistic tendency.[92] They never acknowledged that prices could be administered and sought scientific status by claiming to be "objective" reporters of fact. An editorial in the *Journal of Accountancy* (1908: 238) captured the tenor of the proprietary theorists' discourse, stating that "the science of accountancy makes inquiry into the *laws* determining the money results of business operations."[93] The depiction of prices as "natural"—that is, the result of the *laws* of supply and demand—had two major benefits. First, if prices reflected objective facts, then criticism about monetary profit measurement could be ignored. In competitive markets, accounting profit could be assumed to reflect success in producing goods and services consumers demanded and to result in an efficient allocation of resources.[94]

Depiction of prices as determined by "natural" law had a second and perhaps more important benefit. Accountants could disclaim all responsibility for moral judgments. Cole stated the proprietary position most succinctly, writing that "the accountant has nothing to do with a 'fair profit,' or with measurement of risk, or with social desirability or spiritual progress or social justice" and that accountants were and *should be* impartial observers of economic reality (1911: 128). He concluded that "accountants should not deal with *policy,* but with *fact;* they "tell the truth, the economic truth." Proprietary theorists' failure to recognize the inconsistency between uncritical *assumption* that competitive forces remained operative and their claim to "objectivity" also has been a lasting legacy in the accounting literature.[95]

Concepts of Income

Having rejected criticisms of accounting profit, the central distinction between proprietarists and later entity theorists lay in their different assumptions about the purpose, not the form, of business. Proprietary theorists argued that the purpose of a business, its organization or form notwithstanding, was to increase the wealth of its owners. Specifically with respect to corporations, the owners—those who bore the risk of business operations—were investors. The accounting function did not change with separation of ownership from control but remained as the measure of net wealth accruing to owners (Hatfield 1909: 195f., 358).

Since the purpose of proprietary theory was to measure "the return to the owner," the accounting equation was posited as *assets = liabilities + equities.* Proprietarists made a careful distinction between liabilities and equities since a common accounting equation to this time had been *assets = liabilities.* They felt that viewing the creditor and owner in the same terms had led to abuses because there was no account to ensure that the integrity of original capital be maintained. Sprague caustically noted that the opposite of proprietorship was insolvency, which transformed the accounting equation to *assets + insolvency = liabilities.* He noted that even those who suggested that proprietorship was a liability could not argue "that insolvency is an asset." But, he added, many accountants were willing when capital was impaired "to find some alleged asset . . . goodwill, etc., and water is added" to the accounts. He maintained that clearly distinguishing between capital and liabilities was the mandatory first step for the profession to take (Sprague 1908: 61–62).

Not only did proprietary theorists find proper segregation of capital and liabilities essential, they also sought to keep a strict segregation between capital and income. Proprietary theory was rooted in classical and neoclassical economics and, much in the manner of Adam Smith, income was defined as "the amount that can be consumed without encroaching upon capital." It is important to recognize that both capital and income were viewed as a "stock of wealth," and proprietarists rejected Irving Fisher's assertion that income be viewed as "flow of funds" over time.[96]

Numerous reasons could be given as to why proprietary theorists did not develop a more sophisticated income model, but the focus on "profits available for distribution" is understandable, given the political climate of the period. Pragmatists and the popular press raised disquieting questions about the relevance of accounting profit, maintaining that accounting profit did not measure corporate efficiency; rather, it measured the power of corporations to exact a tribute from the citizenry by administering prices (Dewey and Tufts 1908). By relegating income determination to a secondary status and focusing on income available for distribution, accountants avoided addressing the more disquieting questions raised by external critics. The continued focus on the balance sheet had an additional benefit in that heavily watered (overcapitalized) corporate balance sheets had to be wrung dry to restore the integrity of capital. To do this, proprietary theorists devised techniques such as amortization of goodwill where no cost had been incurred. Such techniques did not generate as much public discussion or criticism as did income measurement (Merino 1993).

Overcapitalization and Segregation of Capital

The demand/response view of our discipline holds that accounting theory does not evolve in isolation but in response to the specific problems of any given age. Several different reasons have been advanced as to why the accretion concept of income became central to proprietary theorists. George O. May attributed this phenomenon to the fact that in the United States, which was experiencing great industrial growth, the quickest way to increase one's wealth was through capital accumulation rather than annual earnings. "Ask an American how much it is worth," wrote May, and "he will say x number of dollars. Ask an Englishman, and if he answers you at all, it will be in terms of so many pounds per year" (May 1936A: 92). May was probably correct in his assessment of the American character, but other circumstances seemed to mandate acceptance of the accretion concept of income, with its focus on asset valuation and segregation of capital and income, given the financial problems of the era.

The major concern of accountants around 1900 was the development of a theory that could adequately cope with the overcapitalization of industry. The Industrial Commission in 1902 specifically demanded that independent accountants develop methods that would protect investors from the grossly misleading financial reports circulated by some promoters.

Two views existed as to what constituted proper capitalization. The most common practice was to issue preferred stock in an amount equal to the market value (not cost) of tangible assets and common stock equal to the "value" (primarily promoters' estimates of the firm's expected earning power over its life) of intangible assets. The minority opinion was "that the amount of capitalization should be limited to the actual value of properties owned" (U.S. Congress, 1901A: ix). Accountants preferred the latter view, although they conceded that the value of a going concern was its expected future earning power. They objected to "going concern" capitalization procedures because earning power could not be objectively measured.

The allegation that dividends paid provided sufficient informational content about the quality of earnings had been proved false by evidence given at the Industrial Commission. Thomas Greene, in *Corporation Finance* (1897), addressed the problem of grossly inflated balance sheets and concluded that even if financial reports were made public, investors, probably, would not discern the source of dividends.[97] This suggested to most proprietarists that the major problem facing the profession was to ensure the integrity of the balance sheet, to wring it dry of "water."

Asset Valuation

Although accountants turned their attention to asset measurement, the most obvious omission of proprietary theory was the failure to adequately define the term *asset*. Assets were defined by most proprietarists as "things owned or for the benefit of the proprietor." Liabilities were "negative assets." Hatfield explained that "in a strict sense, liabilities as well as valuation accounts are a subtrahend from the assets, for debt is merely a negative asset" (Hatfield 1909: 184). The failure to agree on what constituted an asset led to some strange results. The modern reader can only wonder at such items as obsolete machinery, or water, and ice pond listed under the broad classification of "other assets." Early theorists seemed more concerned with overcoming the prevalent notion of the time that anything that had a debit balance must be an asset. All discounts (bonds, common stock, etc.) were listed by many accountants as assets, and early proprietary theorists were greatly concerned about such classifications.[98] Therefore, they devoted much time to developing the concept of contra-accounts while assuming that all CPAs knew a tangible asset when they saw it (an erroneous assumption in many cases). But, although they did discuss proper classification of all accounts, the bulk of their energy was spent trying to find an acceptable measurement base for assets. The different views of capital maintenance that evolved significantly affected the measurement base deemed correct by early theorists.

Capital Maintenance

One of the most persistent problems of historical analysis is that, as terms evolve, usage and meaning may change, and at any given point in time a single term may have different meanings to different persons or groups. To say that capital maintenance was central to all early theorists is true but may be misleading because the expression telescopes three differing concepts into one term.

Most accountants agreed that it was mandatory for investors' and creditors' protection to maintain invested capital intact. This seemed to require that all expenses, including the cost of the expiration of fixed assets, be accounted for periodically. Since businessmen viewed such expenses as discretionary—increasing them in profitable periods, ignoring them in difficult times—most accountants believed their first priority should be to gain acceptance of the idea that such costs were not discretionary. Capital maintenance, used in this context to mean preservation of legal capital, required, first, recognition of all legitimate business costs and, second, acceptance of the "operating" concept of depreciation discussed below.

Dickinson and Cole were among those who expanded the concept of capital maintenance to include not only legal capital but also maintenance of the physical productive capacity of the firm. They argued that, in addition to annual depreciation charges to record expired costs, a depreciation reserve must be established to provide sufficient funds so that the assets might be replaced. They were not advocating adjustments for price level changes but suggesting that, since a common practice of the day was to pay out earnings as dividends, some earnings be deferred in a depreciation reserve to replace existing assets (Dickinson 1904B; Cole 1908: 78f.).

A third concept of capital maintenance surfaced during World War I when accountants began suggesting that "real" capital be preserved. By 1918, Livingston Middleditch, William Paton, and Russell Stevenson began questioning the validity of the assumption of a stable dollar. Middleditch argued that financial statements should be adjusted for general price level changes to accurately reflect changes in the purchasing power of the dollar (Middleditch 1918). Paton and Stevenson went one step further and suggested that specific price level changes must be reflected in the accounts if true corporate profits were to be reported (Paton and Stevenson 1918: 462). These early theorists were attempting to carry the accretion concept of income to its natural conclusion: there could be no increase in wealth unless the stockholder or the firm was "better off," as measured in terms of purchasing power, at the end of the period than at the beginning. This concept of capital maintenance implied that the integrity of "real" capital had to be maintained.

Although it is possible to say that capital maintenance was central to early accountants, it should not be concluded that there was general agreement as to what this term meant. Theorists used the concept to justify various asset valuation measurement bases. Perhaps the greatest contribution this group made to accountancy was gaining acceptance to modify historic cost for fixed assets. It would have been interesting if the weight of theoretical arguments carried the day, but it appears that the income tax law was far more important in convincing businessmen that deviations from cost and the practice of depreciation were acceptable. Tax considerations seemed to preclude any general acceptance of the natural extension of accretion theory to include appreciation, and this concept never fully evolved.

Asset Measurement

Although some theorists (e.g., Esquerre) continued to advocate maintenance of original cost for assets on the balance sheet, many leading accountants agreed that some departure from cost was essential if the balance sheet was to reflect the "true financial condition" of any firm. Both depreciation and appreciation were recognized as valid concepts, but accountants were far more successful in gaining acceptance of the former. This departure was a signal achievement for the group of proprietary theorists.

Depreciation

W. Sanders Davies, who taught theory at the short-lived School of Accounts, had, as president of the American Association in 1898, urged his fellow members to insist that all firms make an adequate provision for depreciation. Most practitioners agreed that this provision was theoretically sound but impossible to implement in practice. William Lybrand reflected the mood of accountants in 1908 when he predicted that it would take another generation before CPAs realized acceptance of such charges to income. Lybrand did not foresee that an income tax would have a profound effect on attitudes and would render the accountant's task of convincing businessmen much less formidable (Lybrand 1908: 255ff.).

Although most theorists acknowledged the need for depreciation, two distinct views emerged as to why such charges were necessary. Henry Rand Hatfield, who made the classic statement that all machinery was on an "irresistible march to the junk heap," led those who took an operating view. Citing unfairness to future consumers if prices did not reflect all expenses incurred at one point in time, he used the benefit/sacrifice approach (Hatfield 1909: 121). The Interstate Commerce Commission (ICC), with its insistence that depreciation be based upon historic, not replacement, cost, concurred with the operating view of depreciation (i.e., an allocation). This concept, however, was inadequate to those who perceived depreciation as a means of maintaining capital in terms of physical capacity (i.e., a valuation).

Dickinson and Elijah Watt Sells were highly critical of the ICC's position. They believed that depreciation charges should be sufficient to ensure asset replacement. They argued that only in this way could one prevent the erosion of capital through payment of dividends in excess of funds required to maintain the firm's productive capacity (Sells 1908).

The idea that depreciation provided a "reserve" for replacement of assets was a concept that plagued accountants for decades. The operating school clearly stated that depreciation, which they defined as the expiration of value in use of fixed assets, prevailed. Those who referred to a "depreciation reserve" implied to some that depreciation provided funds to a firm. This view of depreciation as a "source of funds" greatly irritated Henry Rand Hatfield. He demanded that accountants quash such an illusion. "That depreciation is a 'retention of profits' is simply not true," he wrote. "A Paul may at one time have been a prosecutor of saints; a Lucifer may have at one time held high rank among the heavenly host. But never, no never, could a 'hole in an asset' have been under any circumstances, a constituent part of profits" (Hatfield 1928: 211). This split among the ranks of theorists was not reconciled before World War I, but those who viewed depreciation in terms of maintenance of physical capital (i.e., valuation) had their arguments extended by appreciation theorists to all values on the balance sheet. And the most obvious conservative valuation—lower of cost or market—was almost universally rejected by early theorists.

Lower of Cost or Market

Conservatism is the usual rationalization for acceptance of lower of cost or market.[99] Most proprietary theorists noted the logical inconsistency of recognizing only decreases in market value and suggested it be discarded. The obvious exceptions to this trend were the English-trained (May and Dickinson) or English-influenced like Montgomery (who edited Dicksee's *Auditing* for U.S. publication in 1905). Hatfield, in 1909, was willing to concede the need for "conservatism" in practice, although he noted that this violated the principle of valuation in a going concern (Hatfield 1909: 101f.). But by the twenties, he had concluded that such a departure was void of theoretical merit and should be precluded in favor of "cost or market" (Hatfield 1927: 274). Paul Esquerre agreed with Hatfield's assertion of lack of theoretical merit but concluded that "there is a good reason why market values should not be used at all" and advocated strict adherence to original cost (Esquerre 1920: 171). Roy B. Kester felt that lower of cost or market was not acceptable and favored disclosing market values on the face of the balance sheet while retaining original cost in the accounts (Kester 1921: 77–78). Those who continued to use lower of cost or market noted that "conservatism in valuation of assets, especially in inventory is the safest course since one could otherwise deceive both the banker and the creditor" (Montgomery 1912A: 159ff.).

But Montgomery's assertions that "conservatism" and the needs of bankers and creditors should guide accountancy were being challenged.[100] Many American accountants felt he placed undue emphasis on creditors and criticized his books (see, for example, Freemen 1914: 341–42). By 1918, Paton and Stevenson had clearly condemned conservatism, writing that this concept was often interpreted to mean management could do what it wanted. They believed accountants often failed to make a "clear distinction between conservatism and down-right concealment," concluding that "understatement of assets" is not warranted since it "hurts stockholders and bondholders" (Paton and Stevenson 1918: 467–68). By the second decade of the twentieth century, a clear trend toward valuation theory seemed to be emerging.

Market

Market value, which would incorporate appreciation as well as depreciation in the accounts, became more widely accepted by theorists as this period progressed. Practitioners, especially within the institute, countered with the objection that accounting profit must be "realized," and a major debate centered on the classification of "unrealized gains."

The debate about "unrealized" gains focused primarily on noncurrent assets, and two distinct views emerged. The central issue in the debate became determination of the value of an asset to a "going concern." Those who opposed recognition of appreciated values argued that to a going concern, the only value that had any meaning was value in use.[101] Wildman, who discussed the problem during this early period, most concisely stated his position in the twenties. He contended that the value of any firm was dependent upon its future earning power. Therefore, unless an asset's appreciated value enhanced future earning power—that is, unless it became more valuable in use—appreciation should not be recognized in the accounts. He noted that value in exchange was a meaningless concept to a going concern; certainly, he continued, no one could rationally argue that an increase in the market price of an asset, which would not, and probably could not, be sold, should be recognized in the accounts. Wildman conceded the appreciation of natural resources and certain intangible assets (patents and trademarks) acquired at a nominal cost, which probably did increase future earning power. But he felt it was illogical to argue that a fixed asset, held for use and not for sale, increased earning power while systematically being used up in production (Wildman 1928B). Wildman foreshadowed the direction that debate would take with his clear differentiation between value in use and value in exchange.

At the turn of the century, it would have been inappropriate for accountants to have accepted "value" theory. Overcapitalization was a major problem, and promoters had been overoptimistic in predicting future earnings. One observation, that "promoters were not only discounting the future but the hereafter," seemed appropriate. But by 1918, conditions had changed and so had the direction of accounting theory.

Appreciation theory was gaining widespread acceptance and would become the focal point of heated debate in the following decade.[102] The most significant conceptual arguments occurred after World War I, and extended discussion of the question is left for the following chapter. But it is important to reiterate that "value accounting" was acceptable to many early theorists, that appreciated values were considered relevant, and that conservatism did not justify procedures totally devoid of theoretical merit. The balance sheet orientation facilitated discussion of asset valuation; as long as income was viewed as a stock of wealth and not as a flow concept, there was little need to emphasize periodic operating results.

The Seeds of Entity Theory

Unfortunately for any historians facing the inherent limitation of a chronological order, accounting theories do not readily emerge to accommodate specific time periods. Most theories have antecedents that predate their formulation and acceptance by years and that have a lasting residual effect on succeeding generations. A comprehensive statement of entity theory did not appear until the publication of Paton's *Accounting Theory* (1922), but the effects of the separation of ownership and control had been examined in earlier periods. The business entity concept (the fact that the legal entity existed apart from its ownership) was not questioned, only ignored, by proprietarists. Entity theory, as presented by Paton, never achieved primacy in accounting; indeed, his basic assumption that the purpose of management was to increase the wealth of all sources of financing has yet to be fully appreciated.

Littleton traced entity theory back to the sixteenth century in connection with agency accounting but acknowledged that it did not affect the direction of accounting thought until the twentieth century. William Morse Cole was among the earliest American accountants to ask whether in a corporate era accountants could ignore the need to report on management's effectiveness in the use of assets entrusted to them. He suggested that the profit and loss account could no longer be viewed as residual. He also attempted to provide information as to the sources and uses of funds in his "Where Got—Where Gone" statement (Cole 1908: 101, 178ff.).[103] Cole approached entity theory, but he never fully developed the concept. H. C. Bentley (1911A) viewed the capital of the corporation as its capital, not the capital of the owners, and drew fire from home and abroad for his error. An editorial in the *Accountant* chastised Bentley, stating that "no one ever suggested that they (properties owned) were the capital of the business itself" (September 14, 1914).

Practitioners often implicitly acted on Bentley's assumption when need seemed to dictate abandonment of proprietary theory. W. J. Filbert, controller of U.S. Steel, developed consolidation theory based on the entity premise (*Journal of Accountancy* February 1906: 90–91). The methodology of consolidations has changed over the years, and today, many would say it reflects the assumptions of proprietary, not entity, theory. But in this early period, the methodology was significantly different. Entity theory maintains that the source of financing (debt, stock, minority interest) is immaterial to the corporation and all returns to every supplier of capital are distributions of profits and not "expenses" to the corporation. Since the primary purpose of most early consolidations appears to have been to eliminate intercompany transfers, there was no attempt made to show a minority interest in either income or surplus (see figures 5.2A and 5.2B). The lack of concern about greater reporting sophistication may be due to the fact that financial capitalists, not accountants, led the drive for consolidated statements. Mumford (1989)[104] reports that Filbert was responding to the demands of J. P. Morgan and E. Gary to provide a vehicle they could use to market the stock of the large trusts that they promoted. Since money trusts were "watered," the objective of consolidations may have been to obscure rather than to inform (Merino and Neimark, 1982: 56–57).

Accountants agreed that the overriding consideration in financial reporting was that financial statements not be misleading.[105] If it became necessary to abandon any particular theory to report the financial condition of any enterprise more accurately, they did so without hesitation. The idea advanced by early accountants that no single theory or set of procedures could be evolved to handle all situations equally well has remained a fundamental conviction of many accountants.

Although a complete discussion of entity theory is left for the next chapter, it is important to note that at this early stage the fundamental difference between proprietary and entity theorists lay in their views of corporate income. Proprietarists held that the effectiveness of any business, whether controlled by its owners or managers, was measured in terms of the increase of wealth accruing to the stockholders. Paton contended that in a corporate age, income must measure the "total return" to all suppliers of funds. Therefore, he argued, "net operating revenue is then the excess of values received over purchased assets utilized in connection with product sold, and represents the increase in capital to be apportioned or distributed among all individuals or interests who have committed cash funds or other property to the undertaking" (1922: 259). But, Paton, at this time, did not exclude appreciation from earnings calculations, nor did he view accounting purely as a cost allocation process. The revenue-expense orientation that became familiar to accountants of the thirties was not simply an extension of entity theory, but an adaptation of only selected elements of that theory. Proprietary concepts, such as earnings per share, became firmly rooted in the subsequent development of accounting. Finally, the rejection of institutional theory casts doubts on two popular interpretations of proprietary theory of this period: (1) a lack of concern for investors and (2) acceptance of "conservatism" as the guiding light for the profession.

Institutional Theory

Francis Pixley introduced institutional theory to American accountants at the 1904 International Congress. In a paper delivered before the congress, Pixley argued that "the duties of an auditor of a company were to the company as an institution, not to the individual stockholder." He argued that accountants should permit the accumulation of secret reserves to assure the continuance of business in times of distress (Pixley 1904: 34). Pixley had legal precedent on his side; case law suggested that accountants had no liability for understatement of assets.

Newton v. Birmingham Small Arms (1906) granted accountants absolute immunity from prosecution in cases where the value of assets was understated. The judge ruled that "assets are often by reason of prudence,

CONDENSED GENERAL BALANCE SHEET, DECEMBER 31, 1902.

ASSETS.

PROPERTY ACCOUNT:

Properties owned and operated by the several companies....................		$1,453,635,551.37
Less Surplus of Subsidiary Companies at date of ac-		
quirement of their Stocks by U. S. Steel Cor-		
poration, April 1, 1901..................... $116,356,111.41		
Charged off to Depreciation and Extinguish-		
ment Funds............................... 12,011,856.53		
	128,367,967.94	
		$1,325,267,583.43

DEFERRED CHARGES TO OPERATIONS:

Expenditures for Improvements, Explorations, Stripping and Development at Mines, and for
Advanced Mining Royalties, chargeable to future operations of the properties.............   **3,178,759.67**

TRUSTEES OF SINKING FUNDS:

Cash held by Trustees on account of Bond Sinking Funds....................................   **459,246.14**
($4,022,000 par value of Redeemed bonds held by Trustees not treated as an asset.)

INVESTMENTS:

Outside Real Estate and Other Property...................................	$1,874,872.39	
Insurance Fund Assets...	929,615.84	
		2,804,488.23

CURRENT ASSETS:

Inventories	$104,390,844.74	
Accounts Receivable..	48,944,189.68	
Bills Receivable...	4,153,291.13	
Agents' Balances...	1,091,318.99	
Sundry Marketable Stocks and Bonds....................................	6,091,340.16	
Cash	50,163,172.48	
		214,834,157.18

$1,546,544,234.65

Audited and found correct.
      PRICE, WATERHOUSE & CO.,
                                  Auditors.
New York, March 12, 1903.

Figure 5.2 Condensed general balance sheet of U.S. Steel Corporation, 1902.
(A) Assets.

LIABILITIES.

CAPITAL STOCK OF U. S. STEEL CORPORATION:
Common	$508,302,500.00	
Preferred	510,281,100.00	**$1,018,583,600.00**

CAPITAL STOCKS OF SUBSIDIARY COMPANIES NOT HELD BY U. S.
STEEL CORPORATION (*Par Value*):
Common Stocks	$44,400.00	
Preferred Stocks	72,800.00	
Lake Superior Consolidated Iron Mines, Subsidiary Companies	98,714.38	**215,914.38**

BONDED AND DEBENTURE DEBT:
United States Steel Corporation Bonds	$303,757,000.00	
Less, Redeemed and held by Trustee of Sinking Fund	2,698,000.00	
Balance held by the Public	$301,059,000.00	
Subsidiary Companies' Bonds	$60,978,900.75	
Less, Redeemed and held by Trustees of Sinking Funds	1,324,000.00	
Balance held by the Public	59,654,900.75	
Debenture Scrip, Illinois Steel Company	40,426.02	**360,754,326.77**

MORTGAGES AND PURCHASE MONEY OBLIGATIONS OF SUBSIDIARY
COMPANIES:
Mortgages	$2,901,132.07	
Purchase Money Obligations	6,689,418.53	**9,590,550.60**

CURRENT LIABILITIES:
Current Accounts Payable and Pay Rolls	$18,675,080.13	
Bills and Loans Payable	6,202,502.44	
Special Deposits due Employés and others	4,485,546.58	
Accrued Taxes not yet due	1,051,605.42	
Accrued Interest and Unpresented Coupons	5,398,572.96	
Preferred Stock Dividend No. 7, payable February 16, 1903	8,929,919.25	
Common Stock Dividend No. 7, payable March 30, 1903	5,083,025.00	**49,826,251.78**
Total Capital and Current Liabilities		**$1,438,970,643.53**

SINKING AND RESERVE FUNDS:
Sinking Fund on U. S. Steel Corporation Bonds	$1,773,333.33	
Sinking Funds on Bonds of Subsidiary Companies	217,344.36	
Depreciation and Extinguishment Funds	1,707,610.59	
Improvement and Replacement Funds	16,566,190.90	
Contingent and Miscellaneous Operating Funds	3,413,783.50	
Insurance Fund	1,539,485.25	**25,217,747.93**

BOND SINKING FUNDS WITH ACCRETIONS **4,481,246.14**
Represented by Cash, and by redeemed bonds not treated as assets (see contra).

UNDIVIDED SURPLUS OF U. S. STEEL CORPORATION AND SUB-
SIDIARY COMPANIES:
Capital Surplus provided in organization of U. S. Steel Corporation	$25,000,000.00	
Surplus accumulated by all companies since organization of U. S. Steel Corporation	52,874,597.05	**77,874,597.05***
		$1,546,544,234.65

* NOTE.—In preliminary Report submitted to stockholders at the First Annual Meeting, February 17, 1902, the accumulated surplus of all subsidiary companies to November 30, 1901, was shown as $174,344,229.32. This total, however, included the surplus of the subsidiary companies at time of the original acquisition of their stocks by United States Steel Corporation in 1901, which surplus in this balance sheet is stated in diminution of Property Account.

Figure 5.2 *Continued.* (B) Liabilities and undivided surplus.

CONDENSED STATEMENT OF THE CONDITION

OF

General Motors Company

September 30, 1909

ASSETS

Cash and Cash Items	. . .	$1,365,235.24
Stocks Owned	. . .	16,288,048.59

(Valuations Based on
Inventories Sept. 30, 1909)

Other Investments	. . .	690,571.96
Other Assets	. . .	37,512.07
	Total,	$18,381,367.86

LIABILITIES

Companies and Individuals	.	$11,593.14
Dividend (Due Oct. 1, 1909)		237,173.79

Capital Stock	Common,	$4,211,630.00	
	Preferred,	6,782,493.89	10,994,123.89

*Surplus	. . .	7,138,477.04
	Total,	$18,381,367.86

* After charging off $1,040,000.00 for Depreciation, Patents
and Questionable Accounts.

Figure 5.3 General Motors annual report, 1909

GENERAL INFORMATION

Volume of Business	. . .	$34,000,000.00
Number of Motor Cars Produced During Fiscal Year	.	28,550
Number of Employees	. . .	14,250

OFFICERS

President	.	W. M. Eaton
Vice-President	.	W. C. Durant
Vice-President	.	W. J. Mead
Secretary	.	Curtis R. Hatheway
Treasurer	.	Curtis R. Hatheway

BOARD OF DIRECTORS

W. M. Eaton	Curtis R. Hatheway
W. C. Durant	H. G. Hamilton
W. J. Mead	John T. Smith

Henry Henderson

estimated and stated to be estimated, at less than their probably realizable value. The purpose of the Balance Sheet is primarily to show that the financial condition of the company is as least as good as there stated—not to show that it is or may not be better" (*Journal of Accountancy* 1913: 335). Although settled in an English court, the opinion was widely known in the United States, and English law was regarded as providing precedent. (There is little to be said about American legal precedent at this time; despite practitioners' urgent requests for clarified legal liability, American courts had not acted.)

American accountants could not so completely disregard investors (Pixley was British), and they rejected institutional theory. J. Porter Joplin, president of the American Association from 1914 to 1916, provided the clearest exposition of contemporary views on the subject. Joplin held that no convention, not even conservatism, could justify understatement of assets to create secret reserves. Accountants, he believed, must "stand firm for principle—no understatement or overstatement of assets." Like many early practitioners, he argued that the most obvious danger in the United States was excess optimism and overstatement of assets. In most cases, conservatism was beneficial to prevent abuses. But, consistent with the attitudes of early practitioners, Joplin was most concerned that reports should not mislead any user. To that end, he suggested that "increased values in assets must be shown on the Balance Sheet (parenthetically) or in another schedule" to provide the reader with all relevant information (Joplin 1914B: 407–8).

That is not to say that all accountants objected to establishment of such reserves. Seymour Walton probably typified the views of most CPAs when he wrote of the merits of the "objective to provide out of prosperous years, a fund which can be drawn upon to increase profits of less prosperous ones, a sort of governor to make the machinery at least appear to be running at a nearly uniform rate. *No one can dispute this is good policy.*" Walton continued that the real question is not a matter of policy, but whether or not such reserves should be kept secret. He concluded that they should not; the present owner of stock could be harmed if he wished to sell his stock and had no knowledge of the accumulated reserve strength (Walton 1909: 465). Dickinson hedged on this issue, perhaps in an attempt to reconcile British and American views. For corporations, he recommended publicity of any such reserves. For banks, which were subject to sudden unexpected losses, secret reserves should be tolerated so that "losses can be met without any apparent disturbance of normal conditions, so investors would not panic" (Dickinson: 1914: 113–14). Full disclosure became an accepted concept among American accountants, and they generally rejected contentions that management had the right to conceal assets. Paton and Stevenson were adamant on this point; there was no justification for understatement of assets to create secret reserves since stockholders would be misled (Paton and Stevenson 1918: 468).

But it is perhaps equally important to note that although management's right to create secret reserves was challenged, there was acceptance of the contention that earnings should be regularized by increasing or decreasing discretionary reserves. There was little if any discussion about the propriety of making income appear to be relatively stable when it was not. The idea that accountants should encourage such stabilization was accepted and would have a definite impact on the later development of accounting theory. That it did not become the subject of debate at this time is perhaps a reflection of the minor status of the profit and loss account.

A significant discussion of income was generated by cost accountants, led by Clinton Scovell of Scovell and Wellington, who insisted that profits accrued only after all factors of production received payment for their factor shares, including payment for the use of capital. Thus, Scovell argued that imputed interest on equity should be a cost of production (AIA, *Minutes* 1917: 156ff.).

The *Minutes* of the institute (1912–19) and issues of the *Journal of Accountancy* during those same years show that the debate was indeed heated. Cost accountants (who took an entity view) claimed that it was immaterial to management whether investors or creditors provided funds. There was a cost for use of such funds, and all costs should be included in production. Had the debate continued it might have been effective in raising some pertinent questions in the twenties, but it was rendered moot by the appearance of *Uniform Accounting* (1917), which specifically precluded interest on capital as a cost of production, choosing to follow the classical economic model, and showing interest as an "other" cost after income. Scovell, addressing Robert Montgomery, who had been one of his steadfast opponents, asked what this meant. Montgomery told him that as a member of the AIA, he was prohibited from including such charges in audited financial statements. Scovell indicated he just might ignore such a prohibition, which, in fact, many practitioners did.[106]

Developing Technical Standards

Although Scovell's reaction was understandable, the institute welcomed the chance to gain some authority within the profession with the issuance of *Uniform Accounting*. Prior to 1917, each practitioner determined his own procedures, and there were no authoritative pronouncements save an early dictate of the AAPA that had directed the American form of balance sheet order (current assets first) be used.

An Accounting Court

Seymour Walton (1909: 469) supported a "supreme tribunal which can pass on questions about which there is honest difference of opinion," as one means of establishing authority, adding, "lawyers have their Supreme Court, why should not CPAs?" A decade later, a similar idea surfaced when Vannais (AIA, *Minutes* 1919: 258) complained at a meeting of the institute that because so many contradictory opinions existed as to proper treatment of accounts, the practitioner had no direction.

He cited Montgomery's statement that treasury stock was an asset and Paton's contrary opinion that it was not. Why, he asked, could not the institute establish a court of appeals (AIA, *Minutes* 1919: 258). Unable to resolve such problems, the American Institute of Accountants readily acceded to a request that it cooperate with governmental officials to establish technical standards.

Uniformity—The Simple Solution

Uniform Accounting marked the culmination of a trend that began around the turn of the century, namely, the propensity to look upon uniformity as the panacea for accounting problems. Accountants themselves had contributed to the growing "faith" that politicians placed in uniformity. In an attempt to respond to progressive reformers' demands for greater accountability by elected officials, public accountants helped to design municipal accounting systems that won the profession widespread praise and recognition in the financial press. They also were instrumental in developing more sophisticated accounting systems for rate-regulated industries.

In 1904, Robert Montgomery delivered a paper, "The Importance of Uniform Practice in Determining Profits of Public Service Corporations Where Municipalities Have the Power to Regulate Rates," at the International Congress in Saint Louis (Montgomery 1904: 34–38). The association immediately appointed a committee to study the recommendations made in the paper and to report to Congress any suggestions that would facilitate rate regulation. The AAPA continually advocated uniformity when statements were to be used for a specific purpose in homogeneous, regulated industries.

By 1906, the AAPA became an active participant in the movement to establish uniform systems for municipal accounts. At the conference on uniform municipal accounting (called by the U.S. Census Bureau, February 13–14, 1906), a tentative schedule of uniform accounts was presented. The association responded to this event by appointing a committee "to consider the practical application of true accounting principles in connection with standard schedules for uniform reports on municipal industries and public service corporations" (AAPA, *Year Book* 1906: 2).

Harvey Chase, chairman of the committee and widely acknowledged as a leading authority on the subject of municipal accounting, conducted an extensive campaign to secure adoption of the association's system (see Fig. 5.4). The National Municipal League had long advocated such a system, and the new schedule did improve the quality of municipal reporting and was adopted by several major cities. Reformers claimed that the "one great advantage of a uniform standard system of accounts is that by the means of the same it becomes possible to compare" revenues and costs and the efficiency of public officials in handling public funds (*Chronicle* November 18, 1905: 1463). Accountants readily acknowledged the merit of such arguments, but they were not prepared to have them extended to the private sector without considering the different circumstances involved—primarily multiple users and the multiple objectives of financial reporting. But uniformity had struck the fancy of federal officials as the solution to all reporting and accounting problems. The next extension of "uniform" systems came in the area of cost accounting. Edward Hurley, chairman of the Federal Trade Commission, was convinced that the lack of knowledge of costs caused most businessmen to underprice their products, which led to disastrous competition.[107] Certainly, in firms with no cost systems, there were definite advantages to be obtained in introducing any cost system that permitted the manager to more effectively determine an adequate selling price. But Hurley's main objective seemed to be to introduce uniform cost standards for every industry to prevent "cutthroat" competition. Once again, the AAPA willingly promoted uniformity, working with the FTC to develop uniform cost systems. Accountants did not find the FTC's system threatening because it did not limit choice of accounting principles. It only required uniform classification of the various charts of accounts.[108]

However, Hurley became enamored of the concept of uniformity, and he missed the subtle distinction between uniformity in classification and uniformity of accounting rules. Next, he suggested that "uniform" accounting would be beneficial to creditors who used audited financial reports. He proposed that the AAPA work with the FTC to develop "standard financial statements for all purposes, a set of rules and regulations for the valuation of assets and liabilities" and, as discussed previously, verification of such

Schedule for Standard and Uniform Reports
For Municipal Industries and Public Service Corporations

Suggested Form for Standard Schedule

Revenue from Operating

Gross Earnings from Public Services	$
Gross Earnings from Private Consumers	$
Gross Earnings from By-Products, etc.	$
Total	$
Deduct Rebates, Refunds, Discounts, etc.	$
Total Revenue from Operating	$

Expense of Operating

1.	Expense of Manufacture	$	
	Operation	$	
	Maintenance	$	
	Product Purchased	$	
2.	Expense of Distribution		
	Operating	$	
	Maintenance	$	
3.	General Expense (Salaries, Office Supplies and Expenses)	$	
	Total (1, 2 and 3)	$	
4.	Taxes (Real Estate and Other)	$	
5.	Franchise Taxes (paid or accrued annually or otherwise)	$	
6.	Rentals (Leaseholds, etc.)	$	
7.	Insurance (Fire, Accident & Fiduciary)	$	
8.	Damages (including Extraordinary Legal & Other Expenses and Losses)	$	
9.	Guaranty (Bad Debts Written Off and Reserve for Doubtful Accounts)	$	
10.	Depreciation (Deterioration Written Off & Reserve for Depr'n.)	$	
	Total Expense of operating		$
a.	Net Revenue from Operating (or Deficiency)		$
b.	Other Revenue, or Income, net (from Sources other than Operating)		$
c.	Appropriations for Operating, Provided by the Municipality from General Funds		$
	Total Available Income		$

DISPOSITION OF AVAILABLE INCOME

11.	Interest on Funded and Floating Debts		
	$		
	Remainder of Available Income		
12.	Reserve for Sinking Funds	$	
13.	Reserved for Amortization Funds	$	
14.	Reserve for Other Funds	$	
	Total Reserves	$	
15.	Dividends (Private Plants)	$	
16.	Appropriation to Gen'l City Funds (Public Plants)	$	
	Total Disposition of Available Income		
	$		
	Credit (or Debit) Balance Transferable to Surplus		
	$		

Figure 5.4 Schedule for standard and uniform reports for municipal industries and public service corporations. *Source:* Report of the Committee upon Standard Schedules for Uniform Reports on Municipal Industries and Public Service Corporations. 1906 Annual Meeting Papers. AICPA, New York.

statements by accountants registered by the Federal Reserve Board or by federal banks (AIA, *Minutes* 1916: 175).

The AAPA reacted negatively to Hurley's suggestion of federal registration but tried to placate his demand for a uniform accounting system. Hurley decided that creditors could use "uniform" information and transferred

UNIFORM ACCOUNTING
Form for Profit and Loss Account

Gross sales	$ _____
Less outward freight, allowances, and returns	
Net Sales	$ _____
Inventory beginning of year	_____
Purchases, net	
Less inventory end of year	_____
Cost of sales	_____
Gross profit on sales	_____
Selling expenses (itemized to correspond with ledger accounts kept)	_____
Total selling expenses	_____
General expenses (itemized to correspond with ledger accounts kept)	_____
Total general expense	_____
Administrative expenses (itemized to correspond with ledger accounts kept)	_____
Total administrative expense	_____
Total expenses	_____
Net profit on sales	_____
Other income:	
Income from investments	
Interest on notes receivable, etc.	_____
Gross income	_____
Deductions from income:	
Interest on bonded debt	
Interest on notes payable	_____
Total deductions	_____
Net income--profit and loss	_____
Add special credits to profit and loss	_____
Deduct special charges to profit and loss	_____
Profit and loss for period	_____
Surplus beginning of period	_____
Dividends paid	_____
Surplus ending of period	_____

Figure 5.5 Form for profit and loss account. *Source:* Federal Reserve Board, *Uniform Accounting* (Washington: Government Printing Office, 1917).

the "uniformity" project to the Federal Reserve Board (FRB) in 1917. The institute responded to the FRB with a version of an internal memorandum written by J. Scobie for Price Waterhouse.[109] The FRB adopted the document as *Uniform Accounting* in 1917, and the FRB's publication of an AIA document certainly enhanced that body's claim to being the profession's national organization. But acceptance of a document based on the practice of one firm that had large clients with good internal controls had an invidious effect on practitioners in small- and medium-sized audit firms.[110]

Uniform Accounting suggested that verification of receivables and observation of inventories be considered optional and recommended use of a standard certificate that did not indicate the scope of work done. Clients now had a source document to prevent auditors from conducting "optional" procedures; unfortunately, the document did not stress that these procedures were "optional" only if businesses had good internal controls.

Bankers were concerned by the position taken on inventories and receivables; the standard certificate compounded the problem. Bankers claimed that the short-form opinion, introduced in *Uniform Accounting,* was useless for their purposes.[111] They could not rely on the opinion unless the audit firm was well known or the banker had worked with the firm directly. The institute's leadership did not contest this statement; they agreed that many practitioners abused the procedures in *Uniform Accounting* and issued worthless short-form certificates. Their solution: select a reputable audit firm.[112]

Thus, a document purporting to develop uniform accounting standards left almost all accounting choices to the professional judgment of the practitioner. Furthermore, it eroded auditing standards; as Maurice Peloubet observed prior to the issuance of this document, most firms routinely confirmed accounts receivable and physically inspected inventory. Management now had an "authoritative" source to prohibit such procedures as too costly, and they fell into disuse in the 1920s.[113]

Whereas *Uniform Accounting* provided wide discretion to the practitioner in choice of audit procedures, the institute attempted to dictate some accounting procedures that did not have widespread support. Most academics were alienated by the arbitrary announcement that only "lower of cost or market" could be used for inventories, a proposition they had specifically rejected as void of any theoretical merit, and cost accountants were upset by the prohibition of capitalization of interest as a cost of production. The document failed to deal with many of the significant problems of the day, most notably, the proper classification of surplus. Although the issuance of *Uniform Accounting* successfully forestalled federal intervention, the profession paid a heavy price. By issuing a document that did not have widespread support, the illusion that there was an established and accepted accounting and auditing theory had been created.

Whether intentional or not, the document served to undermine rather than strengthen the credibility of certificates issued by practitioners in new or small audit firms. The well-known firms appeared to be the "winners," greatly exacerbating the tensions between the "Eastern Elite" who controlled the AIA and the other practitioners throughout the country. Many practitioners ignored *Uniform Accounting* as they felt it was simply the opinion of a few accountants. *Uniform Accounting* provides a classic illustration of the almost impossible task that accountants face when they attempt to settle questions of principle by acting defensively; it provided little protection to the public or direction for the profession, while alienating many practitioners and reinforcing the belief held outside the profession that "uniformity" was *the* solution to all accounting problems.[114]

The Significance of the Formative Period

If accounting theory evolves in response to the major problems that exist in any given era, then prior to World War I, the most pressing problem in the United States was to restore credibility to balance sheet valuations. Preclassical/proprietary theorists made a significant contribution to accounting theory by developing the concept of modified historical cost. There is evidence that CPAs were concerned with both stockholders and creditors, and inroads were being made to find a comprehensive basis for asset valuation.

A very small number of accountants had helped to achieve extraordinary progress in gaining recognition for the profession. CPA legislation had been secured in key states, business courses had been introduced into university curricula, and the question of professional standards had been seriously addressed. Most of the efforts in these early years were designed to promote the public aspects of the profession; this is not to say that accountants were inactive in the cost or not-for-profit area, but simply a recognition that the major efforts were concentrated in the auditing area.

The major social demands of the day—greater corporate accountability and publicity, implementation of a progressive income tax, and better control of municipal finances—placed accountants firmly in the vanguard of progressive reforms. It was an era of significant accomplishment for the profession. In the next decade, there would be a significant shift in the demands made on professionals that would cloud their social obligation to the public.

Chapter 6 *1919–1945*

Accountancy Comes of Age:
The Interwar Period

> The business of America is business.
> —Calvin Coolidge

> The only thing we have to fear is fear itself.
> —Franklin Delano Roosevelt, 1933

The period from World War I to the end of World War II was as volatile as any in the nation's history. Major socioeconomic changes and a global war reshaped the social fabric of the nation. The 1920 census alerted Americans to the urbanization of the nation. Some time after 1915, the rural majority had become a minority (Mowry 1965). The self-reliant yeoman farmer, the backbone of democracy, had been replaced by a multitude of industrial, urban workers, many raising questions about the viability of the political system and laissez-faire economic policies.

Antitrust policy, an effort to restore competition as the guiding force in the economy, had proved ineffective (Galambos and Pratt, 1988). Technological innovations in manufacturing, transportation, and communications made large corporations not only feasible, but desirable. Throughout the twenties, the political sector sought to reinforce the traditional American Creed: an abiding belief that private property rights were the most fundamental rights in a democratic society, despite the increasing evidence that corporate growth had undermined the concept of "ownership" expressed in individualistic economic tradition.

The crash of 1929 was an epochal event, testing the nation's faith in its dominant public philosophy. Means described the "Roosevelt revolution" as a revolution in point of view, rejecting the assumption of classical theory that "the modern free enterprise system would automatically tend to maintain full employment . . . or that the unemployed were responsible for their own unemployment . . . or that incomes reached through the market system tended to reflect the individual's contribution to production" (1962: 30). The crash led finally to mandated governmental action, but government intervention was aimed at restoring the moral legitimacy of private property rights, not at radical change. Accountants played a critical role in resolving these contradictions throughout the interwar period.

The decade of the twenties presented an interesting challenge to accountants. While the public rhetoric reaffirmed the "traditional American Creed," public policy that promoted "cooperative capitalism" stripped the profession of its third-party obligation. The belief that business had reached a new plateau and would operate to preserve "social justice" significantly reduced the importance of external monitoring devices, such as independent audits. Accountants had based their claim to professional status on their independence and obligation to third parties; but in the 1920s, the political sector asked CPAs to serve as advisers to, not monitors of, corporate clients. The rapid increase in work in the tax and cost areas, combined with the growth of advisory services, forced the profession to walk a fine line in maintaining its claim to professional status.

The crash of 1929 resulted in a public outcry against the business sector for violation of the public trust and had a significant impact on the direction of accounting practice. The rejection of laissez-faire policies signaled an era of "federal capitalism" that mandated external oversight of the corporate sector. Since politicians and corporate managers preferred independent audits to direct government control, the new public philosophy reestablished accountants' claim to professional status by reinforcing the profession's obligation to those who owned the businesses: the stockholders. But again, accountants had to tread carefully. Regulators demanded that accounting data be perceived as sufficient to allow investors (owners) and regulators to curb managerial excesses, but they wanted requirements to be sufficiently flexible to restore confidence in the economy.[1]

The two world wars each served to end debate about the viability of the "traditional American Creed." The victories quieted public criticism of the business sector and significantly reduced demands for stringent oversight. Politically the United States became a legitimate world power and then a dominant force, capable of realigning colonial systems and cartel practices rooted in Europe and advocating its own model of market-based enterprise. Accountants also benefited by their increased visibility during these national emergencies, gaining public trust through their efforts in each war. The accounting profession, like other institutions of these times, was usually limited to traditional sources of entrants. The first black CPA, John W. Cromwell Jr., who would become a mentor to many aspiring minority candidates, passed the CPA examination in New Hampshire in 1921 (Levy 1971: 21). Seventy-five years later, Bert Mitchell of New York would become the first black CPA to be honored as the recipient of the American Institute

John W. Cromwell Jr., first black CPA

of CPAs' Gold Medal for Meritorious Service. Accountants' successful responses to the diverse challenges of the interwar period display an interesting mosaic of the drive to achieve professional recognition.

World War I: The Beginnings of Cooperative Capitalism

World War I had an unsettling effect on those who advocated laissez-faire economic policies. The war effort, enormously successful, showed that government, labor, and business, working together, could increase the nation's productivity significantly. Cooperation, not competition, had enabled the nation to marshal its economic resources to meet the stringent demands of the war effort.[2] Accountants played an important role in the coordinated war effort; volunteer services of such groups as the Dollar-a-Year Men brought the profession much favorable publicity.[3]

Pragmatists and other reformers hailed the "social possibilities of the war," arguing that the war effort had shown that coordinated economic planning, not laissez-faire policies, would be of greatest benefit to the nation.[4] John Dewey (1918) asked that the government intervene to ensure that corporate resources were used to produce the goods society needed, rather than to limit production to maximize profits. He warned that those who predicted massive social change after World War I should be aware of the forces that would be unleashed to prevent change. Financial interests, he predicted, would fight to keep the control of the nation's wealth. As long as public opinion appeared to be indifferent to the "guerrilla warfare" between employer and employees, the "propertied class" would fight fiercely to maintain the primacy of ownership rights (Dewey 1918: 292). Despite widespread support among industrialists and technocrats for subordination of the profit motive to the production motive, the Industrial Democracy movement failed.[5]

The Twenties: The Golden Age of Business

The decade of the 1920s has received extensive examination by historians in all fields, yet in many respects, the analysis and interpretation are inadequate. Perhaps this is due to the contradictions inherent in periods when major social changes occur. The cooperation between labor, business, and government did not survive long after the war effort was completed. The Allied victory in World War I dramatically changed public opinion toward business; the hostility toward business, evident in the Progressive Era, dissipated as businessmen received credit for winning the war.[6] President Harding's (1920) call for a return to "normalcy" inaugurated a "New Era," the so-called Golden Age of Business. Business required no monitors; the war had proven that business was "moral." A new faith echoed through the streets; "capitalism had transcended its individualism and materialism, becoming social and spiritual," fueled by social justice and guided by the profit motive (Schlesinger 1956: 71). The return to "normalcy" reflected a reaffirmation of the primacy of private property rights. President Coolidge perhaps best expressed this sentiment when he said that the right to accumulate property is "founded on the constitution of the universe," concluding that business had been the "greatest contributing factor to the spiritual advancement of the race." However, business efforts to restrict competition were in inherent contradiction to the public philosophy.

Politicians, supported by legal theorists, tolerated no social legislation that infringed on a corporation's private property rights. Competitive market forces would protect the individual. Yet they viewed the same competitive forces as destructive and actively supported government paternalism for corporations. One historian concluded that politicians "were keenly for maintaining the individualistic, social ideas and values among the masses. But, for themselves and their fellow businessmen, especially in economic matters, they had to a startling degree become collectivists who depended upon a restricted kind of governmental paternalism" (Mowry 1965: 62–63). The war had shown that cooperative economic planning efforts worked; politicians including Herbert Hoover urged business leaders to continue efforts to cooperate via trade associations and to avoid the unnecessary ravages of "cutthroat competition."

In this environment, the independent audit function became less important; CPAs were asked to work with businesses and federal regulatory agencies to collect and disseminate data so that business could earn a "fair return" on their investments.[7] Philosophically, most accountants identified with the probusiness attitude of the New Era. The call for cooperative capitalism (i.e., use of government agencies to maximize corporate profits) had a dramatic impact on the function of regulatory agencies.

The Changing Direction of Federal Regulation

The FTC did not abandon its mission immediately after the war and continued to try to restrain companies engaging in unfair methods of price competition. But the Supreme Court in a series of cases continuously narrowed the FTC's authority to act against companies that tried to "substantially lessen competition" under the Clayton Action of 1914, making it almost impossible for the FTC to enforce its mandate.[8] When the 1920 Republican platform included a plank censuring the FTC for its intrusion in business affairs, it became clear that the FTC would not be encouraged to investigate business abuses, such as price fixing.[9]

The agency instead became an adviser to businesses, gathering and disseminating cost information so that "fair prices" could be maintained. By the time that William Humphreys became FTC chairman in 1925, the agency had completed its transformation. Senator George Norris expressed the disillusionment of reformers when he lamented the passing of FTC authority to Humphreys, whom he called "one of the greatest reactionaries of all times" (Davis 1962: 439).

Other regulatory agencies also worked to foster cooperation. The Department of Commerce, under Herbert Hoover, worked with businesses to standardize products, to establish uniform pricing policies, and to form trade associations. Regulatory agencies had little concern with corporate control; they asked CPAs to aid in the cooperative effort by helping clients to gather data on costs that could be forwarded to the FTC and Commerce Department for dissemination so businesses could set "fair prices." Government's paternalistic policies did not go unchallenged, but those challenges were muted by the business sector's apparent willingness to behave responsibly and share its increased profits with others in society.

Corporate Social Responsibility

It has often been overlooked, or perhaps dismissed as mere rhetoric given October 1929, but the 1920s marked the beginning of the debate over business's social responsibility. Many industrialists believed that in a mass-production, mass-consumption society, a more equitable distribution of income made good business sense. They supported paternalistic policies, such as pensions, health insurance, and profit sharing, and protective legislation, such as minimum wage and child labor laws, as good business policy (Mitchell 1989). The law, however, had not adapted; the Supreme Court consistently found state protective legislation unconstitutional because it infringed on an individual's (usually a corporation's) right to contract.[10]

Industrialists as different as Walter Gillette and Henry Ford actively promoted different forms of industrial democracy.[11] Both men believed that the wage motive must supersede the profit motive in order for society to receive the full benefits of technological advances.[12] Ford's speeches were as radical as those of Thorstein Veblen (1918); he, like Veblen, disliked financial capitalists, particularly those on Wall Street (Ford 1926). Ford directly challenged the relevance of the concept of ownership in an industrial age, writing that "a machine belongs neither to the man who purchased it nor to the worker who operated it but to the public. . . . [I]t advantages the worker and the proprietor only as they use it to the advantage of the public" (Mowry 1965: 8–9). Ford could not be ignored; he was the nation's most successful industrialist.[13] His efforts to maximize production, however, reduced payouts to shareholders, and the judiciary viewed this as an infringement of ownership rights.[14]

Technocrats joined in the criticisms of focusing on money (accounting) profit. H. A. Scott organized the Technical Alliance in order to ally management, labor, and consumers in a common effort to direct production for the common good. Scott argued that the alliance should "collect data, design or co-ordinate systems, [in order] to give progressive bodies the data of the present mechanism with no sympathy toward any ideal" (Dorfman 1946: 98–99). Scott, with his call for "neutral" data, did not present a direct challenge to accountants, but Stuart Chase, a third-generation CPA and one of the initial organizers of the alliance, did. Chase had technical expertise viewed as "very dangerous" by members of the profession.[15]

Chase led a minority group within the alliance that adopted a pragmatic perspective, objecting to depiction of any data as "neutral." He warned that traditional accounting data was not neutral; it faced in one direction— toward the owner.[16] Chase (1921A: 284–85) also warned that if left to accountants, waste would be defined narrowly, only in terms of financial profitability. He argued that technocrats must develop broader measurements to "include the greater waste of undesirable goods, unemployment, and even war, when evaluating corporate performance." [17] Most accountants had little sympathy with Chase's message and simply ignored such criticism since the legal system continued to support traditional accounting profit measurement.

The Legal Environment: The Dominance of Private Property Rights

Legal theory had failed to adapt to changing social conditions, as the courts continued to protect property rights and the privity of contract. As already mentioned, a conservative, activist Supreme Court consistently interpreted the Constitution to prohibit social legislation as infringements of an individual's (primarily the corporate individual) right to contract (Conant 1974).

A series of Supreme Court decisions also rendered the FTC powerless to continue to pursue its original mission of preventing corporations from colluding to fix prices. While the shift from the prewar concern with the preservation of competitive market forces to the postwar desire to prevent cutthroat competition can be regarded as a shift in emphasis, the shift was fundamental.[18] Competition, once regarded as the automatic mechanism that protected society from undue use of power by those in control of the nation's economic resources, became undesirable. The rationale for antitrust legislation disappeared. The Northern Securities antitrust case demonstrated that the courts did not construe bigness per se as unfair or illegal.

This change in legal attitude helped fuel the merger mania of the twenties.[19] Louis Brandeis, the most liberal voice remaining on the Supreme Court, stood alone when he disagreed with the concept expressed in Northern Securities. He argued that "the proposition that mere bigness cannot be an offense is false, because . . . our society, which rests upon democracy cannot endure under such conditions. Something approaching equality is essential" (Dorfman 1959: 153). The other progressive jurist on the Court, Oliver Wendell Holmes, disagreed. Holmes believed in economic realism. Therefore, he argued, preserving a competitive economic system was not only unnecessary but also inefficient. "What difference does it make," he asked, "whether Rockefeller or the United States owned all the wheat so long as the people consumed it?" (Persons 1958: 273). This argument rested on the assumptions that those who controlled the nation's largest businesses would either be constrained by market forces or that their social consciousness would prevent them from administering profits and exacting a tribute from society. The lengthy depression after the crash of 1929 sorely tested both assumptions.

The failure of the legal system to recognize or adapt to the changing character of American industry left not only the public but also security holders at risk (Berle 1926). The legal system afforded little protection to passive property interests (i.e., stockholders) throughout the decade.[20] Instruments such as nonvoting common stock or two-class common stock became more common and surrendered ownership of control.[21] Ripley claimed that the disenfranchisement of shareholders undermined the "foundation of our civilization built as it is on the bedrock of private property" (1927: 128). Reformers' demands for greater investor protection fell on deaf ears. Until the 1929 crash, the legal system's focus on the right to contract left corporate managers in firm control.

Accountants found themselves in what now may seem a strange position; many of the leaders of the profession advocated passage of laws that would increase the profession's legal liability. The objective was to drive out incompetent practitioners so that the profession's image would not be tarnished while simultaneously strengthening accountants' claim to professional status by reinforcing their obligations to third parties. Stricter legal liability may have been perceived as a necessary step to counter the growth of nonaudit work in most CPA firms.[22] The decreased importance of audit work led to extreme tensions within the profession; many practitioners felt that the American Institute of Accountants (AIA) sought to restrict entry by imposing rules that were not appropriate for firms not engaged in audit work. Sectional rivalries and ethnic tensions created hostility within the profession, leaving accountants with no single recognized national voice throughout the 1920s.

A Profession Divided

The 1916 reorganization of the AIA accomplished the immediate goals of allaying external criticisms of the profession and stopping the drive for federal licensing of accountants.[23] The new organizational structure restricted entry into the AIA, as even holders of CPA certificates had to pass the institute's uniform CPA examination. The AIA's leadership tried to depict its new admission process as egalitarian, allowing people in nine states whose certificates the AIA did not recognize a chance for admission. It also allowed people in states, such as New York and Illinois, whose examinations were thought to be unfair, a chance to become members of the institute.[24] Many CPAs did not find the institute's explanation convincing; they believed that the AIA was out to undermine state control and the credibility of the CPA certificate. But the institute's abandonment of the CPA certificate as an absolute requisite for membership created what John Carey (1969) called the "Great Schism."[25] Practitioners in all regions of the country, except the East Coast, still had to struggle to gain or maintain restrictive CPA legislation.[26] They did not appreciate the institute's apparent disregard of their CPA credential.

The AIA's slow response to the National Association of Certified Public Accountants (NACPA), an organization accused of "selling" CPA certificates, confirmed this opinion.[27] Sale of CPA certificates threatened the livelihoods and reputations of CPAs in less urbanized states. William Dolge, in an attempt to discredit the NACPA, submitted an application in the name of I. A. Duarf. After paying $25, he received a CPA certificate, with no questions asked. Dolge pointed out that Duarf was "fraud" spelled backwards (Herrick 1969).

The institute's failure to act quickly against the NACPA opened the door for other organizations to sell worthless certificates. Members of state societies, like those in Texas and Michigan that had memberships of 20 and 47, respectively, in 1920, saw the value of their CPA certificates rapidly diminished. Struggling state societies in the Midwest and the South simply could not tolerate the proliferation of CPAs, given the lack of sophistication among their clients. The financially hard-pressed state societies had to fight the legal battle alone, increasing distrust of the national organization (Tinsley 1962).

The AIA's actions at its 1921 council meeting fueled further suspicion. The council instructed one of its committees to introduce a bill in Congress to provide for the incorporation of the Institute of American Chartered Accountants (Scovill 1924). Many practitioners viewed this as an effort to establish a new "professional" elite of chartered accountants. When the AIA finally secured an injunction against the NACPA, in August 1922, its actions were too little and too late. In a little more than a year of existence, the NACPA had sold more than two thousand bogus certificates, which in turn polarized opposition to the AIA. The institute's delayed response contributed significantly to the formation of a rival organization that laid claim to national status.

A group of practitioners, primarily from the Midwest, established the American Society of Certified Public Accountants (ASCPA) in December 1921. The ASCPA's two basic objectives were to prevent the sale of CPA credentials and to protect the CPA title as the designation for professional accountants (Scovill 1924). The two organizations engaged in a bitter rivalry until the threat of external intervention in the thirties forced unification. CPAs who experienced the rift refer to the animosity that existed between the leadership of the two groups. But the autobiographies or memoirs of members of each organization show that important philosophical differences probably made the split inevitable.

One of the clearest and most dispassionate expositions of the differences between the two groups appeared in an editorial in the *Certified Public Accountant*, written by Frank Wilbur Main, the society's president. He wrote that the institute embraced national control of the profession, uniform CPA examinations and grading procedures, regional associations, strict rules of conduct, a decided emphasis on auditing, and national publicity of the profession. He contrasted this with the society's perspective, which included state-promulgated and self-administered examinations that reflected state standards; no formal rules of conduct; an emphasis on broader accounting services, and state publicity of the profession (Main 1923). The institute and the society can be described as federalist and states' rights, respectively.

Institute membership tended to be concentrated in urbanized states, and its leaders were often connected with large, well-established, and prosperous firms. The institute represented, to use a modern phrase, an Eastern Establishment. Homer Dunn (1923: 261ff.) believed that the institute did not try to understand regional differences. "Why," Dunn had asked, "do you need uniform standards for commercial ventures in agricultural and mining states?" He alleged that the institute simply sought to establish "a professional body above the regulatory laws of any state" to gain personal satisfaction for its leadership clique.

The institute's continued emphasis on independent audit work also divorced it from many new entrants and CPAs practicing in rural states. In an age where many practitioners had to struggle to survive, the AIA's emphasis on independence seemed unrealistic. Leo Levanthal and Ira Kirkstein, both Wharton graduates, vividly recalled the difficulty that young men had in obtaining employment.[28] They, like most others starting out, were totally dependent on bookkeeping and tax work for small clients. Auditing simply would not support most small CPA firms; accountants provided a variety of services, including serving as secretaries to the clients' boards of directors. Independence from such involvement in a client's business was a luxury that not many could afford. While the AIA's reorganization and its emphasis on auditing may have created the rationale for a schism, the strong personalities of the leaders of both organizations contributed to the hostility that made unification highly improbable, if not impossible.

The enmity between Eric Kohler, prominent in the ASCPA, and George O. May, a leader of the institute, outlived the Great Schism. Kohler (1975), who was inclined to attribute all major contributions to the ASCPA, often ignoring specific documentary evidence to the contrary, reflects the lasting impact of this bitter rivalry. Kohler believed that May represented the "embodiment of the Eastern establishment" and detested what he perceived as May's arrogance.[29] Kohler's perception was probably accurate. May, brilliant and undoubtedly one of the leading spokesmen for the profession through the institute, did not accept criticism kindly. Even those who admired his

Eric Kohler, Northwestern University

Durand Springer, Secretary of the
American Society of Certified Public
Accountants

R. H. Montgomery, President
(1935–1937), American Institute
of Accountants

abilities admitted that May was opinionated and often raised the hackles of
contemporaries by his abrupt dismissal of them.[30]

Similar resentment existed between A. P. Richardson, secretary of the
AIA and editor of the *Journal of Accountancy,* and Durand Springer, secretary
of the ASCPA. Many agreed with one Midwest practitioner's complaint that

Richardson, who was neither an accountant nor American-born, had far too much influence in professional matters.[31] Springer and Richardson were constantly at odds and some of their confrontations became legend. Carey concluded that each secretary "personified his organization in the eyes of the CPAs. . . . The conflict [was] between aristocracy, an exclusive organization, the elite [Richardson] and a democracy [Springer], a grass roots organization devoted to the common man" (Carey 1975A). John Forbes felt that both May's and Richardson's demeanors lent credence to the belief held by many California practitioners that the reorganization was merely a ploy to keep the "bahstads" (pronounced with a broad English accent) out (Carey 1975B). From 1921 through the next decade when it became imperative for the profession to present a united front to counter the threat of federal intervention, the profession had no authoritative national voice.

Professional Standards

The AAPA had provided effective leadership in the development of both ethical and educational standards. The institute faced a significantly different environment; regulators, who viewed cutthroat competition as inefficient, now demanded rules to limit competition. While the AIA's leadership appears to have been reacting to external pressure to pass rules that limited competition, many CPAs perceived these rules to be simply another way for the institute to benefit established practitioners. The passage of rules that limited contingent fees and advertising further eroded the AIA's support.

The ASCPA had a very democratic (perhaps anarchic) position toward ethical standards: Each practitioner would be guided by his own conscience. No rules would be enacted (Main 1923). The AIA did not share that attitude. The institute focused on promulgating rules to stop "unseemly" competition during the twenties, although rules did not proliferate. From 1918 until the next decade, the institute passed only two major rules, dealing with contingent fees and advertising. But the severe restrictions placed on advertising and the absolute ban on contingent fees raised the ire of many practitioners.

Contingent Fees

The AAPA had tried to ban contingent fees but had been unsuccessful.[32] The environment of the twenties made the passage of such a rule not only possible but mandatory. The wartime excess profits taxes proved to be a mixed blessing. While they created an enormous amount of work for accountants, they also attracted many unqualified people into the profession.

The proliferation of self-styled "tax experts," working on a contingency, attracted the attention of the Treasury Department, which demanded that the AIA pass rules prohibiting contingent fees and "unseemly" advertising.

In 1919, the institute's council responded, banning contingent fees after a heated debate. The rule read as follows: "No members shall render professional services, the anticipated fee for which shall be contingent upon his findings and results thereof. (This rule shall be construed as inhibiting only services in which the accountant's findings or expert opinion might be influenced by consideration of personal financial interest)" (AIA, *Year Book* 1920: 72). The sentence in parentheses was deleted in 1920 because some practitioners contended that it permitted tax work by accountants on a contingent fee.[33] This new rule proved ineffective and was widely ignored. In 1923, the AIA passed a yet more stringent rule, banning contingent fees absolutely: "Members and associates should neither render nor offer to render services for which the fees are contingent" (AIA, *Year Book* 1924: 95, 145–146). Practitioners could accept no contingent fees for any type of service.

Even institute members rebelled against the ban. Robert H. Montgomery, a past president of the AAPA and one of the most influential members of the AIA, and Walter Staub mentioned the rule in their 1923 edition of *Auditing Principles* but concluded it was too strict to be enforceable. The authors suggested that tax practitioners might ignore the rule and accept work on a contingent fee basis (Montgomery and Staub 1924: 9–10). Normally, influential members of an organization are expected to comply with its norms; when they do not it becomes clear that the organization does not have the authority to enforce its sanctions. The ASCPA condemned the ban on contingent fees; these restrictions provided support for the society's claims that the institute sought to protect the elite in the profession. The institute's efforts to restrict advertising simply added more fuel to the fire.

Advertising

The institute's effort to limit advertising effectively undermined any claim the AIA may have had to being the national voice of the profession. The institute actively encouraged institutional publicity to promote the profession and to educate the public about the value of accounting services. Institutional publicity gave large, established firms a free hand to promote their services. Small firms did not have the funds to afford this luxury. When the AIA moved to ban all personal advertising, it appeared to many to be another effort to limit competition to benefit large firms.

CPAs in small firms, struggling to establish or maintain their practices, pointed out that the opponents of advertising tended to have well-established practices. They viewed any ban on advertising as an unnecessary barrier to entry. That perception may have been correct, but the institute's leadership may have had little choice in the matter, given the external pressure for such a rule. The rapid growth of people using the self-granted title of "Income Tax Expert" on business cards and in newspapers irritated the Treasury Department.[34] In 1919, Fred R. Angevine, assistant solicitor for the Bureau of Internal Revenue, who spoke for the commissioner, told the AIA that if its members and officers did nothing to curb misleading advertising, the federal government would (AIA, *Minutes* 1919). The institute recognized that any rule would be controversial and tried to compromise. The council asked W. Sanders Davies to chair a Committee on Ethical Publicity, established to enforce a new rule that all "proposed circulars or instruments of publicity" be forwarded to the AIA for evaluation and approval.[35] The compromise did not work; institute members were unhappy. Some, when asked to submit promotional material for evaluation, refused, resigning from the organization. The rule also did not satisfy Treasury officials; they threatened to promulgate a rule that clearly banned advertising if the AIA did not act.[36] Davies concluded that "the only thing worthwhile to say is that the Institute will not allow its members to advertise" (AIA, *Year Book* 1920: 88–89).

In 1921, the AIA's Committee on Professional Advancement (Davies, chairman; J. E. Sterrett; Arthur Teele) responded with the following rule: "Accounting is a profession. Self-praise is unprofessional. All advertising must be characterized by a certain amount of self-praise, therefore all advertising is unprofessional and accountants should abstain from it" (AIA, *Year Book* 1922: 74–75). The debate over the rule was heated and it might have been defeated had not Angevine been present at the annual meeting. He warned if the institute did not act, the Treasury was prepared to enact its own rule, proscribing advertising not only with respect to tax matters but to all accounting services. The recommendation passed, 150 to 68, and the following year, a rather long and tedious rule was incorporated into the code of ethics (AIA, *Year Book* 1922: 71ff.). The rule, limiting advertising, created havoc for the institute; practitioners found it picayune and ridiculed the leadership of the AIA. Some prominent practitioners, including A. C. Ernst, simply withdrew from the AIA. Even those who accepted the rule expressed sardonic reservations concerning its fairness and effectiveness. Thus, while the rule met the demands of the Treasury, it precipitated cynicism among practitioners and rendered cooperative efforts in the profession more difficult than ever.

The AIA's effort to limit competition, through passage of restrictive rules, reflects one of the anomalies of the twenties. While the public philosophy lauded individual freedom in the abstract, public policy ran counter to that philosophy. Rules to limit competition, severely restricting an individual's freedom, had broad political and business support. Restrictive codes of conduct were common in all fields. Flynn (1939) examined the proliferation of codes of conduct during the decade, concluding that most codes were a sham to create an advantage, an opportunity to create little monopolies (guilds) that protected established practitioners.[37] While Flynn's analysis lends credence to the ASCPA's claims, the Treasury Department played a significant role in enactment of the AIA's restrictive rules. The AIA's rules became more prescriptive and more specific throughout the decade. The institute passed rules forbidding CPAs to deal in securities and prohibiting its members from associating with schools practicing discreditable methods of operation (AIA, *Year Book* 1929).

The broad conceptual issues that had been heatedly debated before the war received little attention during the twenties. Debates over independence, a major concern of early accountants, virtually ceased. The growth of nonaudit services, combined with political demands that CPAs view themselves as advisers to their clients, probably made debates over independence less urgent.

Accounting Practice in the Twenties

Investment bankers and politicians had been among the earliest proponents of independent audits in the United States.[38] Accountants lost the strong support of both groups during the 1920s. Despite the marked increase in share ownership and the emergence of the small investor, politicians voiced little concern about protection of investors. If capitalism had overcome its materialism and if managers, guided by profit, could be relied upon to protect the public interest, as the dominant view held, then inves ors needed no other safeguards. CPAs would fulfill their obligation to investors by working with corporate managers to ensure that every firm received a fair return on its investment.[39]

A dramatic change in corporate financing made creditors less interested in independent audits. After the war, corporate managers adopted a new strategy that helped to free their firms from bankers' control (Sobel 1968). Corporations began to pay regular dividends, akin to interest, in order to attract people who had invested in Liberty Bonds during the war into the equity market. The strategy worked brilliantly. Small investors purchased equities in unprecedented numbers. Corporate managers found themselves awash with cash, and the corporate sector went from a net cash surplus of $3 billion in 1921 to $9 billion in 1929 (Sobel 1968).

Corporate demand for bank loans plummeted, and bankers had to find other outlets for their funds. Banks became direct participants in equity markets, increasing their portfolios of corporate stocks and through their affiliated holding companies floating $19 billion in equity issues (Brooks 1969). Given the apotheosis of business in the period, the mass influx of investors did not translate into increased demand for audits.[40] The handful of reformers who called for greater protection of investors were ignored. Nor were investors, who did not rebel when stripped of their voting rights through issuance of nonvoting common stock, likely to demand independent audits to protect their interests.[41] The New York Stock Exchange, faced with demands by New York State legislators for reform in the Progressive Era, had imposed reporting requirements on companies listed after 1913. As accountants became more familiar with the listing requirements, probably making it cost-beneficial for listed companies to employ auditors, the number of audited companies on the NYSE did go up. But the Exchange, a strong ally of the AIA, refused to require independent audits. Nor does the historical evidence suggest that these early audits necessarily improved the perceived quality of financial reports.[42]

The AIA had contributed to creditors' dissatisfaction with the quality of financial reports when it had provided the Federal Reserve Board (FRB) with an internal control memorandum that was issued as *Uniform Accounting* (1917) and reissued under the title of *Approved Methods for a Balance Sheet Audit* a year later.[43] Knowledgeable bankers were unhappy with the effect that this document had on the quality of audits. They claimed that they could no longer rely on any audit certificate; they could rely only on those of audit firms that they knew and deemed reputable.[44] Thus, they argued that the issuance of *Uniform Accounting* eroded standards and made it more difficult for small firms and new entrants to compete successfully in the audit area.

The AIA concurred with the assessment that many audit certificates were worthless; editorials in the *Journal of Accountancy* as well as letters to the editor continuously denounced the proliferation of worthless certificates, "weasel worded" qualifications, and the growing number of misleading financial reports.[45] Since the institute was perceived as the voice for established firms, the tirades against "shyster accountants" seemed self-serving by many practitioners. The institute's focus on the independent audit function further undermined its authority as other types of services became more important to most CPA firms. Until after the crash of 1929, when public concern rekindled political interest in corporate accountability, most small CPA firms and practitioners in nonindustrial areas survived by providing a wide range of advisory services to their clients.

Advisory Services

In a decade when many businessmen had little understanding of accounting, CPAs often became active advisers in the decision-making process of their client's business. Emerging firms, such as the one founded by Arthur Andersen, challenged the status quo of services provided to audit clients. Many businesses had no accounting staff, and the CPA firm furnished the staff for internal management control. Smaller firms also turned to CPAs to interpret financial statements, suggest operational improvements, and design new control systems. S. D. Leidesdorf, a leader in the field of management services, believed that it was during this period that the image of the CPA as a nearly infallible adviser to the client became widely accepted (Kent 1975). The ASCPA actively promoted advisory services throughout the twenties (McGladrey 1933). Implementation of cost systems for private businesses and for state and local governments became the mainstay for many small accounting firms.

Implementation of Cost Systems

Prior to World War I, engineers, not accountants, had dominated cost accounting.[46] The AIA voluntarily abdicated leadership in the cost-accounting area. Many of its leaders were disdainful of cost accounting, characterizing it as a "mere technical discipline" (Montgomery 1919). The National Association of Cost Accountants (NACA) provided national leadership in the cost area. The NACA opened its membership to nearly all interested in cost accounting and the organization grew quickly. The NACA through its bulletins brought cost accounting to the attention of many business organizations who had to be sold on the need for more sophisticated systems.[47]

The NACA's timing was fortuitous. The FTC's and the Department of Commerce's desire to gather cost information so that businesses could earn "fair returns" on their investments, generated a great deal of interest in design and implementation of cost systems.[48] The "fair return" concept provided an opportunity for the growth as "measurement remained the prerogative of the accountant" (Prickett 1931).

Simultaneous with the demand for "fair returns" to business, the Commerce Department, under Secretary Hoover's leadership, began an all-out attack on waste and inefficiency. Boorstin (1973) points out that at the end of the nineteenth century, the nation developed a fetish with speed and clock time: efficiency meant not quality, but the speed with which each task was accomplished. Hoover demanded measurement tools to eliminate waste to force "lazy workers" to be efficient, that is, to do each task as quickly as possible.[49]

Miller and O'Leary (1987) suggest that the efficiency movement resulted in demands for measures that made each individual visible, thus making him or her easier to control. Cost accountants focused on measurements that facilitated control—control of material, labor, and overhead.[50] The benefits that Frederick Taylor thought would accrue to workers when he introduced the concept of scientific management did not receive much attention in the cost-accounting literature. The "fair return" concept was oriented to the owner and the cost-accounting literature did not reflect the influence of the Industrial Democracy movement or the paternalism of Henry Ford. It focused on elimination of "waste" by isolating inefficiencies in use of materials, labor, and overhead.[51]

Chase's (1921A) warnings that if the definition of waste were left to accountants, the term would be defined narrowly in terms of financial profitability, proved true. Those articles that cite Hoover's call for elimination of waste as a rationale for a company to install budgeting and standard cost systems focus almost exclusively on benefits to the firm in terms of financial profitability. Benefits to be derived by workers or the consumers were usually ignored.[52]

The crash of 1929 did not significantly change the direction of cost accounting, as it did financial accounting. The Depression made cost control more imperative, and with a surplus of workers, more stringent controls became possible. Time and motion studies that resulted in minute divisions of labor that served as the basis for scientific wage schemes became the order of the day.[53] Cost analysis also became more finite and the types of costs subject to analysis expanded. Distribution costs became a major concern (Castenholz 1930; Greer 1931: 136–39), and costs became disaggregated into more finite categories, such as controllable and noncontrollable classifications (Dean 1937: 55ff.). Flexible budgets and relevant costs attracted attention during this period.

During the thirties, the increased demand for cost systems activated the AIA's interest in cost accounting; in 1932, the AIA accepted Camman's book on *Basic Standard Costs* for publication, the first work that it published on cost accounting. Thomas Sanders (1933: 175) noted that the preface said "only a small amount of discussion [of standard cost] has taken place" and suggests that this must have been the case only at the AIA since "for twelve years . . . the topic has been regarded as perpetual."

DR Scott (1937B) prematurely predicted that we had entered a new era and that the dominance of the individualistic social theories that assumed business existed simply to make a profit would end. He thought that managerial accounting would be redirected from the chief administrative officer to the policy executive, recognizing that "the current trend toward social control of business is not an invention of either radical reformers or meddlesome politicians but is rather a byproduct of the failure of the traditional system of private ownership to afford a vital and effective control" (Scott 1937B: 130ff.).

The full cost and cost-plus contracts, used during World War II, made cost accounting an integral part of the independent auditors' portfolio. Cost accounting would capture the institute's full attention in the postwar years and, perhaps, contribute to what Johnson and Kaplan (1987: 195–204) conclude was the end of the relevance of cost accounting because it was held captive by financial accounting objectives. Kaplan and Johnson also recognized that, as early as 1914, it was an engineering-trained financial executive, Donaldson Brown, whose ideas about financial planning and control were the start of a profound internal recognition of ROI (Return on Investment), first at Du Pont, then at General Motors (1987: 87). Perhaps this "cost control" innovation, in turn, drove financial accounting?[54]

Governmental Accounting Systems

During the twenties, governmental accounting had begun to receive some attention from accountants, but it was still in an embryonic state. Accountants simply did not take a leadership role in this area (Previts and Brown 1993: 119). The National Municipal League and the Municipal Finance Officers Association provided much of the technical expertise. These organizations designed uniform accounting systems and established technical standards for municipalities, which had taken the lead in implementation of governmental accounting systems (Chatters 1935).

James McKinsey (1923) warned accountants that they would lose the opportunity provided by demands for municipal budgeting if they did not take the time to understand the administrative systems of cities. Accountants, he contended, focused too much on the bookkeeping, limiting their contributions.[55] Despite the efforts of a handful of people like McKinsey and Lloyd Morey, the accounting profession did not make a major contribution to developments in the governmental area.[56] While the Depression made any type of work attractive to many practitioners, the practice of awarding governmental work on the basis of competitive bids limited the participation of CPAs.[57]

During the thirties, universities, hospitals, and other not-for-profit industries also began to design uniform accounting systems. Industry associations, like the American Hospital Association, produced new systems that paid scant attention to accounting measurements used in the private sector.[58] While some accounting academics advocated tying not-for-profit accounting to traditional income measures (Frisbee 1936), these efforts met with a cool reception. Others reflected the predominant view in the governmental sector: that you cannot measure effectiveness in the traditional manner because government revenues are not affected by efforts expended by administrators nor is there a necessary relationship between revenues and the cost of government operations.

In the audit area, the National Committee on Municipal Accounting worked diligently to establish uniform standards for municipal audits. Many states passed laws requiring municipal audits, but most laws did not require that the audits be conducted by CPAs.[59] By the end of the decade, Hurdman (1939) noted that while governmental entities had become increasingly complex "during the last fifteen years," the "area had lacked expert advisors" owing to the failure to utilize CPAs. The Budget and Accounting Act of 1921, which established the Office of Managment and Budget (OMB) as well as the General Accounting Office (GAO) at the federal level, foretold the shift in emphasis that would soon occur in national government activity.

Roosevelt's New Deal and World War II greatly increased accounting practitioners' interest in governmental accounting. New Deal programs required states to develop better reporting systems. Programs like the National Recovery Administration also accelerated interest in governmental accounting.[60] The complexities of fixed fee and cost-plus contracts during World War II brought significant interaction between CPAs and the federal government; after the war, this area of practice would expand dramatically. The expertise of leaders such as Paul Grady and P. K. Seidman in the navy's cost inspection system program during World War II set a level of expertise later useful in defense contract accounting standards work.[61]

Tax Practice

The passage of the 1913 income tax law significantly changed the image of the profession.[62] Early practitioners had perceived independence as the cornerstone of accountants' claim to professional status. During the long debate over the constitutionality of a corporate income tax, Edward L. Suffern (1912), AAPA president, reminded his colleagues that as independent accountants they had a duty to see that all parties, including government, shared equitably in corporate profits. The passage of the 1913 income tax, followed by wartime excess profits taxes, greatly increased demand for accountants' tax services, and Suffern's position eroded. Advocacy, not independence, became an accepted norm for tax practice.

The wartime excess profits taxes created an enormous amount of work for accountants. The American Association of University Instructors in Accounting (AAUIA)—forerunner of the American Accounting Association—devoted a good portion of their 1919 annual meeting to the topic.[63] The major concern for accountants was the definition of invested capital in the 1918 law. The law stated that the "corporation's books were presumed to show the facts"; while restoration of excessive depreciation, and so forth, from prior years was permitted, the burden of proof was on the corporation to show that those charges had been excessive (Paton 1920B: 48). The 1918 excess profits tax not only had a direct impact on tax practice; it also had a significant impact on financial reporting.

Accounting practitioners benefited from the tax laws, but they did not view taxes positively. Most accountants appeared to share the philosophy of Andrew Mellon, secretary of the treasury from 1921 to 1930, who regarded all taxes as government usurpation of private property. An opponent described Mellon as the only secretary "under whom three Presidents served." Mellon foreshadowed supply-side economics and "trickle down" tax policy.[64] He believed that taxes on the rich should be minimized, arguing that the wealthy are better able to manage economic resources than the poor. The more the rich controlled, the better off the country would be. The poor would benefit residually as the enhanced national wealth flowed downward. Although some reformers questioned Mellon's synergistic approach, which assumed that the wealth of the rich would eventually filter down to the poor, the message of no taxes had great appeal to the public.[65]

The tax law of 1924, which created the Board of Tax Appeals, gave both lawyers and CPAs the right to represent clients. This recognition solidified the profession's advocacy role with respect to tax work since CPAs, like lawyers, could claim professional status in such tax matters. Even after 1929, when economic conditions and social attitudes no longer supported Mellon's "trickle down" theory, accountants did not reopen the question of advocacy in tax practice. Nor did academicians question practitioners about the propriety of maintaining an advocate's role. Tax planning and preparing tax returns became the accountant's chief functions, a much narrower role than that perceived by the earliest practitioners.

The wartime excess profits taxes not only benefited tax accountants but also increased demands for cost accounting and systems development. The rapid growth of the scope of services offered by CPAs attracted many people to the study of accountancy (McKinsey 1924). As demand grew and the profession became more specialized, the number of schools offering accounting courses expanded and the accounting curricula became more specialized and more technical.

Educational Standards

If one looks at the rapid growth of accounting programs in universities and colleges, the early practitioners' efforts to place accounting on a higher educational foundation was an overwhelming success. In 1900, there were no institutions of higher education offering a B.A. in accounting. By 1930, more than three hundred schools awarded degrees in accountancy, at both the undergraduate and graduate levels (Allen 1927). But these statistics mask the variety of accounting programs.[66]

By the mid-1920s, 36 percent of all native-born practitioners had college degrees (as opposed to only 9 percent of foreign-born accountants), but the quality of education varied widely (Higgins 1965). Only two schools, New York University and Harvard University, ever graduated more than ten prospective CPAs in any given year during this period. Twelve other schools produced professional accountants at the rate of four to seven a year, but more than 50 percent of new entrants graduated from schools with very small programs.

During the twenties, accounting curricula became increasingly specialized. By the mid-1920s more than ninety different accounting courses were being offered in universities, often reflecting specific questions that had appeared on prior CPA examinations. Many academics in other disciplines came to view accounting as a "mere" technical skill, requiring little more than rote memorization of rules, and accounting academics came to be perceived as less scholarly than their colleagues in other disciplines (Marshall 1926).

Although one might understand the need in certain regions of the country for courses in mine, farm, and forestry accounting, more than forty such courses in the area of financial accounting seem to indicate that little thought was given to basic principles of accounting (Allen 1927). Ironically, while most practitioners and academics agreed that accountants needed a broad conceptual base, the increased demand for accounting programs appeared to outstrip efforts to place accounting education on a broad conceptual foundation.

As early as 1917, Seymour Walton expressed the practitioner's disillusionment with the direction of accounting education. He charged that accounting educators taught the "how" not the "why" of accountancy.[67] Facts per se, he noted, are meaningless unless one can systematically order those facts. Education, Walton suggested, "should ground a young man in fundamental scientific principles" so that he could combine his experience and education to adapt his responses when circumstances warranted. He concluded that students exposed only to factual cases would not be adequately prepared to cope with unanticipated events or novel situations.

Walton's statement partially reflects the pragmatic perspective that had provided the initial justification for inclusion of accounting in university curricula. His thought that education should develop a person's critical intelligence and ability to deliberate (i.e., to use technical expertise to assess the impact of what one was doing by its outcomes) is pragmatic. However, he did not complete the pragmatic message and urge that accountants should gauge those outcomes by their impact on society or use their expertise to ameliorate social ills (Dewey 1922).

Academics and practitioners called for a more conceptual orientation in accounting education throughout the twenties.[68] Reynold Blight (1925: 604) noted that there existed a "popular fallacy that an accountant should have what is known as a mathematical mind—that is he must be an expert with figures, be able to perform prodigious feats in addition and multiplication, have a deep knowledge of the esoteric meaning of professional mathematical formulas and be a prestidigitator of numbers."[69] "This," he concluded "is a grave error," adding that specific knowledge would not produce professionals, only technicians.

The Role of the American Accounting Association

Organized in 1916 as the American Association of University Instructors in Accounting (AAUIA), the first national body of accounting academicians addressed the educator's most immediate problem: development of curricula. The rapid proliferation of schools offering accounting courses and the lack of uniform educational standards made reform necessary. The AAUIA limited admission to university instructors specifically to ban teachers in "fly-by-night" business schools. Many of the organizers of the AAUIA felt that the organization should develop a standardized curriculum. Fayette H. Elwell (1917: 17) presented a paper at the AAUIA's first annual meeting, calling for such standardization since "the business world . . . has the right to expect that courses given in different institutions under the same name cover approximately the same ground." The *Proceedings* of the AAUIA from 1917 through 1922 show that pedagogical reform was the organization's first concern.[70]

Accounting educators usually came from practice and as long as the AAUIA focused primarily on education, relations between the practitioners and academics remained cordial. But when academics seemed to challenge practitioners' leadership, as they appeared to do when Paton suggested the AAUIA change its name to the American Accounting Association (AAA) in 1921, or when practitioners attempted to direct curriculum development, as the AIA did in 1924, differences flared. Montgomery, in order to preempt the change of the name of the AAUIA so that another organization would not be perceived as a national organization that might challenge the AIA's leadership, took out incorporation papers in several states to prevent the use of the proposed name (AAA 1966A). The AAUIA also protected its turf when practitioners announced that they were going to establish educational standards. Both the AIA and ASCPA Committees on Education were chaired by past presidents of the AAUIA, John Wildman and John Madden, respectively. Wildman (1924: 34) reported that his AIA committee had been instructed to develop "standards whereby institutions giving instruction in accounting may be judged and rated." The AAUIA reacted negatively until the AIA softened resistance to its program by agreeing to admit academics as associate members if they had five years' teaching experience and a CPA certificate (AAA 1966A: 8f., 36f.).

John R. Wildman, New York University

Committees of the AAUIA, reorganized as the American Accounting Association (AAA) in 1935, worked with the AIA, the ASCPA, and the NACA throughout the period to develop educational programs. While some academics argued for graduate programs, efforts to increase entrance standards to require a college degree met with stiff resistance from populist state legislators who viewed accounting as a business of no great importance to the public.[71] They argued that competition would eliminate incompetence and viewed efforts to restrict entry as unnecessary. While academics made some improvements in pedagogy in the 1920s, their major contribution came in development of accounting theory.[72] Not until the late 1920s did the State of New York initiate legislation establishing a bachelor's degree as an entry-level requirement. Other states were slow to follow, and it would not be until 1963 that states like Ohio required the bachelor's degree to sit for the CPA examination.

Accounting Theory

In the 1920s, the acceptance of management's right to retain earnings seemed to undermine the basic assumptions of proprietary theorists. Stephen Gilman (1939) evaluated accounting theory in the post–World War I period and found it inexplicable that income determination had not become the focal point of financial reporting. He concluded that the maturity of large corporations, the income tax laws, and rapid advances in cost accounting ought to have led to the primacy of the income statement. But the emphasis on the balance sheet was understandable, given demands that accounting data be used to ensure that business earned a "fair return" and, perhaps more important, the provisions of the wartime excess profits taxes. Both made measurement of capital of primary importance.

The excess profits tax also led to a reexamination of the relevance of historic cost and made conservatism (understatement of income) less desirable. Companies that had followed "ultra conservative" practices fared badly under the provisions of the excess profits tax of 1918. The law allowed adjustments to capital for excessive depreciation, depletion, and so forth, but it stated that a company's books were presumed to be correct.[73] Thus, companies had the burden of proof of showing that prior charges were excessive. Bankers, who had provided support for conservative accounting practices, became less interested in "sound values" due to the new corporate policy of retention of earnings and to the fact that they became active participants in the equity markets. Dampening investor enthusiasm by understating income had little appeal.

During World War I, most companies capitalized almost all expenditures, and many abandoned historic cost measurement to avoid paying additional taxes under the excess profits tax.[74] The deflationary pressures of the postwar depression in 1921 raised further questions about how conservative historic cost really was. These events, combined with the call for a "fair return" on capital, placed the conservative historic cost measurement model under siege throughout the twenties.

The Challenge to Historic Cost Measurement

In the 1920s, the call for a fair return to business (a return based not on the cost incurred but on the current value of assets employed) contributed to the belief that "capital growth" was as important, if not more important, than operating results. The emphasis on capital led to calls for new measurement procedures so that the balance sheet would reflect both economic (operating) and financial (holding) gains. With the emphasis on measurement of capital, the balance sheet continued to be the focal point of financial reporting. The first comprehensive statement of entity theory did not mandate abandonment of the balance sheet (Paton 1922). Paton wrote that "in the study of the theory of accounts, the income statement is of little importance, showing as it does the elaboration of an element already incorporated in the balance sheet" (Paton 1922: 20). While Paton criticized proprietary theorists for implying that the "earnings" process was not real, he could not abandon the balance sheet as long as he accepted the accretion concept of income.

Paton's entity theory attempted to represent more realistically corporate relationships between managers and absentee owners (stockholders). His theory never received widespread acceptance because he suggested that management no longer sought to "maximize stockholder's wealth" but, rather, the return to all equity holders (including creditors). Entity theory presents a clear threat to a moral justification for private property rights since it abandons the view that corporations operate for the benefit of their "owners."[75] Most accountants rejected Paton's argument that both interest and dividends should be treated as distributions of profit (Paton 1922: 84ff., 259). Given the income tax laws, few practitioners favored the suggestion that interest was not an expense. Perhaps more important, Paton's entity theory and concept of corporate income are incompatible with economic theories based on private property rights and existing theories of finance. Despite Paton's criticism of proprietary theory or, as he called it, "residual equity" theory, accountants continued to emphasize ownership and such *proprietary concepts* as earnings per share, book value per share, and net book value as methods of analysis throughout the 1920s.[76] While accountants rejected entity theory and measurement of enterprise income, Paton's work had a significant impact because it introduced the idea that income could be used to measure managerial efficiency (Paton 1922). This idea would later serve Paton well.

The Nature of Income

Early proprietary theorists were not naive: they recognized the contradictions between traditional profit measurement and the emergence of corporations, characterized by passive ownership. They responded brilliantly by developing a model that kept the owner (whether in control or not) at center stage. The model reinforced the idea that (1) corporate efficiency should be measured by wealth that accrued to the owners (shareholders) and (2) the owners retained ultimate control over corporate assets (Merino 1993).

Paton (1922) recognized the relevance of dual income measures to report corporate wealth and operating profits. Total income (wealth) accrued to the entity, not to its stockholders. To determine corporate wealth, accountants had to determine the value of resources entrusted to management and the annual increment in that value. Paton advocated recognition of specific price level changes (holding gains and losses) as well as operating profits in calculation of total income. But wealth change (total income), he asserted, was irrelevant to the stockholders.

Stockholders wanted an income number that would serve as (1) a measure of managerial effectiveness in the use of assets entrusted to them and (2) an indicator of expected future earnings (Paton 1922). Paton assumed that the revenue associated with a particular set of enterprise operations (realized revenue) was most important to stockholders. He implied that earned (realized) income was not only a good indicator of future earnings but also of future distributions to stockholders.

The recognition of the need for segregation of income into two distinct flows (financial and operating) by accounting theorists in the twenties seems to have been the result of the increasing sophistication of the economics literature dealing with income determination, not, as some have suggested, a natural result of the adoption of entity theory. The influence of Irving Fisher (1906) can be seen in the work of both Paton and John Canning, a proprietary theorist.

The most perplexing problem for both Canning and Paton was development of a model that defined revenue independently of asset valuation. Canning simply defined gross income (revenue) as "the summation of gross operating income (the fruition in money, or the equivalent of money, effected within a period, of all those elementary services which are components of enterprise operations) plus the amount of gross financial income (the higher earnings, effected within the period arising from the grants of monied funds made by one person, or persons, to another)" (Canning 1929: 100). Paton defined revenue as "benefits accruing to the firm" and expenses as "sacrifices made in the generation of benefits." But, since "benefits accrued" throughout the production process, the above definition was unsatisfactory for determination of earned (realized) income. Paton never resolved the issue of what is revenue; instead he focused on realization of revenue by developing a "matching" model that associated revenues and expenses to determine operating income. Canning outlined the realization process more explicitly:

1. The future receipts of money within one year have become highly probable.
2. The amount to be received can be estimated with a high degree of reliability.
3. The expenses incurred or to be incurred in the cycle can be estimated with a high degree of reliability. (Canning 1929: 103)

Canning, like Paton, never resolved the question of benefits accruing that increased asset values but were not realized. By the end of the decade, academic theorists appeared to agree on how to measure operating profits; the key question, still unresolved, was how, given the constraints of double entry, could the accountant adequately report both an increase in corporate wealth and earned income.

As Alexander pointed out three decades later, the idea that operating income could be measured to facilitate predictions of future receipts to shareholders required definitions of revenues and expenses that were antithetical to wealth measurement (Alexander 1950: 57ff.). The debate between the balance sheet versus the income statement schools, and, more recently, the "asset/liability" versus "revenue/expense" views, indicates the difficulty the profession has had in resolving the issue. During the twenties, theorists explored various measurement models and reporting schemes that would enable them to report a relevant income number to stockholders and to present an adequate statement of corporate wealth.

Accounting theorists concerned with the issue of the adequacy of their measurement base reflected the influence of Fisher's definition of wealth. Paton and Stevenson (1918) suggested that the accountants' assumption of a stable dollar was unsound. They contended that accountants could not hope to show the "true financial condition" of a firm if they persisted in using an inappropriate measurement assumption.

Measurement of corporate wealth required acknowledgment of price-level changes. Paton and Stevenson (1918) concluded that the accounts must reflect "specific, not general, price-level changes." They advocated specific price-level adjustments because they believed that "the most important function of accounting is to provide data to management . . . [and therefore] accounts should reflect the most relevant values, present values." Accountants had a duty to ensure capital maintenance (in terms of "real capital," defined by Fisher in terms of productive capacity) (Paton and Stevenson 1918: 462ff.).

Accountants debated the capital maintenance issue throughout the 1920s. A. C. Littleton rejected the idea that accountants should concern themselves with the "preservation of capital," which was and should be the responsibility of management. He contended that accountants should be content to do what they could do, namely, measure the flow of earnings to the stockholders (Littleton 1928). Henry W. Sweeney, whose work did not appear until the thirties but who had worked on his dissertation in the twenties, differed sharply with Littleton. Sweeney maintained that capital maintenance should be a major concern of the profession; the call for a "fair return" to business had made this position acceptable in the 1920s.[77]

The Problems in Accounting Practice

As noted, Gilman (1939) found it strange that income determination had not become a matter of central concern during the 1920s. But external factors, such as the excess profits taxes and the development of no-par stock, probably best explain the continued focus on the balance sheet. The emergence of no-par stock created serious problems for accounting practitioners. Initially no-par reform was welcomed by accountants as a means of halting previous abuses in the manipulation of par stock (Hurdman 1919). Accountants were faced with a curious dilemma with par value stock. The law required that capital be stated at par value; if stock was sold at a discount, accounting theory was inadequate to handle the debit balance. Paton in "Theory of the Double Entry System" (1917) attempted to explain the accounting in terms of assets (properties) = equities (rights in properties). But he conceded that "to the extent the stock is overstated" (par is greater than property received), "the amount of discount [appears] among the property items" (Paton 1917: 10). It was through this method that "water" was usually introduced into the balance sheet, and many investors did not recognize this.

However, no-par stock was not exempt from manipulation directly affecting surplus. Accountants generally agreed on the means of classifying surplus. This posed no theoretical problem: they argued that paid-in capital, capital surplus (gains from disposal of capital assets), surplus from appreciation, and earned surplus should be segregated. Legal statutes complicated the issue. Charles Couchman warned that it was "held by some that surplus attaching to no-par might be created to the capital account on the theory that the very purpose of no-par stock is to show unit ownership *only*, without differentiation as to contributed value and earned value." He said accountants must say an absolute no to such procedures (Couchman 1921: 273). The problem was that the law said yes.

Robert Montgomery (1927) explained this dilemma of accountants in the proper treatment of surplus. First, there had been the problem of appreciation. He noted that when accountants first began writing up fixed assets, there was "almost unanimous agreement" that unrealized appreciation should be credited to a separate account. Then "came no-par value stock, stated capital, paid-in capital, initial and capital surplus complications coupled with formidable legal opinions that accountants should mind their own business and *not* use such terms as earned surplus." He concluded that legal pressure had forced accountants to use a single surplus account, an unwise and dangerous procedure (Montgomery 1927). The debate on this complicated issue continued throughout the 1920s.[78]

John Wildman and Weldon Powell, recognized authorities on the subject of no-par stock, comprehensively examined this problem in their book *Capital Stock Without Par Value* (1928). They defined three basic principles: (1) capital must reflect consideration received, (2) dividends cannot be paid out of capital, and (3) cash dividends must come out of earned surplus. Although accountants may have agreed on these principles, examination of financial reports during the 1920s would lead to the conclusion that they were either not applied or could not be applied. One of the most striking examples of the failure in this area can be found in the financial reports of Dodge Brothers, Inc.

When Dodge Brothers was reorganized in 1925, the corporation paid $246 million for assets with a fair market value of $85 million.[79] One question rarely asked in subsequent decades but that might be asked is how historical cost would have aided accountants in this kind of transaction. The assumption underlying acceptance of cost as an original valuation is that exchange price is a "reasonably prudent act" (Canning 1929: 231). Accountants would have had verifiable, objective evidence of $246 million being paid for the assets of the firm; they probably could not have coerced management into showing a loss under the lower-of-cost-or-market-valuation concept. When examining the financial chicanery of the 1920s, one must remember that accountants were operating in an economic arena where conduct that would be regarded as unethical today was condoned by the markets and government. Insider trading, preferred stock lists (which included most of the important government officials), and a pernicious bonus system were all accepted. It is also well to remember that the following maneuvers of Dodge Brothers were legal at the time.

After the initial sale of the assets by the Dodge family to the corporation, the firm went public. The corporation received $90 million for 2 million shares of common stock and 850,000 shares of preferred stock. The preferred shares sold for $10 per share ($8.5 million) but were reported at the nominal figure of $1 per share ($850,000) on the balance sheet; $7.65 million had simply disappeared. Similarly, the two classes of common stock (no-par) sold for approximately $81.5 million were capitalized at $.10 per share ($200,000), and $81.3 million disappeared from the books. Some juggling of the surplus account, combined with the understatement of $89 million of invested capital, permitted the corporation to list its assets at $85 million, or approximate market value. Obviously, the accountants did not follow Wildman's principles, and the question remains whether it would have been better to overstate assets at their original cost or to understate capital. Such transactions were legal, and accountants were in no position to force management to comply with theoretical principles by properly classifying the surplus account.[80]

In many states during the 1920s, a corporation could include only a portion of the proceeds received from stock in the capital account. Having only one surplus account, corporations would issue dividends from surplus as they saw fit, regardless of the origin of the funds. One interesting, if unresolved, issue was linked to both no-par stock and the popular management policy of retention of earnings. It was not clear that society desired or expected managers to exercise such economic control. Accountants questioned the propriety of this policy. Charles B. Couchman mirrored the feeling of the day when he wrote that "profits retained by a corporation above the amounts necessary for preserving its commercial and financial arrangements are the equivalent of reinvestment of capital by the stockholders without his individual consent" (Couchman 1935). Accountants were unsure of their role. Could the profession exclude from surplus those amounts legally available for dividend distribution?

Wildman felt that accountants must be guided by economic principles, not law. But, he conceded, there was little an auditor could do to enforce any principle with a client, except to use moral suasion, which was not notably successful in the 1920s (Wildman 1928B). Modern accountants can perhaps empathize with the position of these early practitioners. It was not clear what the auditor's position should be when a client acted legally (law is commonly supposed to reflect social values) but with questionable ethics.

The most perplexing question for practitioners was whether or not the accounting profession had the right or the mandate to insist that clients do more than comply with the law. Ripley obviously believed they should. But with no support from the federal government, it is unlikely that the profession would have been able to enforce proper accounting principles. It would be many years before the notion of "economic substance over legal form" would migrate from other literature to serve as a guide in theory.

The irony of historical analysis is that those practitioners who warned investors that income and surplus accounts, although legally correct, were misleading often faced the severest criticism. Ripley condemned one "auditing house" for issuing an audit certificate that said "the profit and loss account, read in conjunction with the statement of no-par value stock attached to the balance sheet, sets forth the results of operations for the year." The company reported a profit (by refusing to recognize certain discretionary expenses, such as depreciation, and by deferring operating expenses to future years), increased surplus through refinancing, and then wrote off those "discretionary expenses" directly to surplus. The auditors were not able to follow an "accepted accounting theory." But by referring the reader to the increase in surplus owing to the no-par issue, it became apparent to Ripley and presumably to other readers, that a substantial operating loss had been incurred (Ripley 1927: 197f.). If the auditors had not qualified their certificate, they would not have received any criticism. The reader probably would not have been aware of the refinancing transaction. Certainly by today's standards, the auditors' actions were not sufficient, although one could argue that the requirements of full disclosure had been met. Finally, it should be mentioned that during this decade businessmen continued to advocate secrecy on the grounds that dividends provided sufficient information to investors.[81] Although this argument had been rejected during the Progressive Era, it became acceptable again in the 1920s. Ivar Krueger, the "Match King," avoided accountability by his refusal to provide any financial information.

Krueger attributed his success to "secrecy, more secrecy, and even more secrecy." While he refused to tell anyone anything, he was fawned over by bankers.[82] Joseph J. Klein, whose accounting firm was called in to consult with brokers and the Krueger empire, recalled in his memoirs that Krueger would not answer any questions. If any banker had the audacity to question him, Krueger would simply threaten to withdraw his proposed new issue from that bank. Even after the stock market crash, International Match stock and bond sales were strong. It was among the few companies that never suspended dividend or interest payments, which, as Klein notes, is understandable as dividends never had been based on operating profits.

The Depression had no effect. Krueger had simply rolled over his financing, paying dividends and interest from the proceeds of each new issue. Surplus was not stratified (it included operating profits as well as additional paid-in capital and premiums on bonds), and the investor had no way of penetrating this financial thicket (Klein 1969: 76).

The Krueger pyramid was bound to topple, as finally it did, but not before thousands were victimized by the scheme and their own blind speculation. Why did bankers fight to promote Krueger's bond issues? Why did they accede to his demands for continued secrecy? Krueger, Samuel Insull (the utility wizard), and other promoters had no fear that independent auditors would be called in. The reaction of the stock exchange was disinterest when the AIA attempted to devise a plan for audits of all corporations; no one wanted to tamper with the "prosperity of the times." Subsequent criticism of the accounting profession has often suggested that accountants could have done more. But, given the massive indifference to investor protection in both the governmental and financial sectors, that criticism would appear to be unfair. Accountants could do little with respect to abuses perpetrated by those who relied on "secrecy." The advent of no-par stock had presented a new mechanism for financial manipulation that had to be addressed, and it helps to explain why the balance sheet and capital valuation, not income determination, remained a central concern throughout the decade.

Given the importance of capital, one finds surprisingly little debate over definitions of capital. Most theorists accepted the idea that capital was "the present advantage of a right to receive future benefits" (Sweeney 1933A). There was even a consensus that capital value must be measured in terms of productivity. Accountants, however, could not agree on two basic issues. First, which type of productivity—past, present, or future—should capital valuation reflect? Second, did capital maintenance mean maintaining actual physical productive capacity or simply that the firm continue to be in a position to provide a stock of services, irrespective of the type of physical capital employed in the future? Given these basic divisions, we find advocates of a variety of measurement bases in the literature. Proponents of historical cost, replacement cost, and price-level accounting sought and found economic theories to support their measurement preferences.

Measurement and Capital Valuation Theory

Those who advocated historical cost bolstered their arguments by referring to Kemper Simpson's *Economics for the Accountant* published in 1921.[83]

Simpson believed that "the value of capital goods arises only from their productivity" and that capital investment should not be measured in terms of economic sacrifice but "in relation to postponement of claims on consumption goods." He cautioned accountants to beware lest they confuse the value of capital goods with the value of capital. He argued that if you recognized a gain owing to appreciation, you simultaneously must infer that capital investment had increased. This was wrong, Simpson wrote, because "the rate of interest on capital is fixed at the time of investment, and no additional sacrifice was required." He would permit only one valuation—the original cost (Simpson 1921: 121–22.).

Littleton cited Simpson to support his argument that appreciation did not lead to increased capital values. But he relied on classical economic theory to justify deviations from original cost, that is, depreciation. Accountants, according to Littleton, should be content to measure the "value in use" of capital assets. At the date of purchase, cost reflected expectations about "future productivity." Littleton (1929: 148–49) suggested that while economists might say that the value of assets is determined by supply (cost of production) and demand (for both consumer and productive goods), accountants need not worry about demand.[84] They should concern themselves only with the measurement of the supply side. Historical cost theorists used this rationale to reject all suggestions that accountants measure replacement or reproduction cost, which required a focus on present or future estimates of productivity based on demand.

The Replacement Cost Debate

Canning denounced suggestions that accountants should measure replacement cost. He thought that some accountants failed to differentiate clearly between the cost of replacement of capital goods with other capital goods of like kind and quality (maintaining physical capacity) and replacing a stock of services (maintaining productive capacity). The latter, not the former, should be the primary concern of the accountant (Canning 1929). He warned that "the consequential difficulties and losses from substituting one instrument for another, whether they are like or unlike in physical characteristics, are in general so great, that the actual cost of the unused stock of services is nearly always more appropriate" (Canning 1929: 242). He branded efforts to approximate replacement cost as misleading, writing that any attempt "to smuggle in, consciously or unconsciously, a preconceived value of the capital instrument and then capitalize the service series is worse than guesswork." He concluded that "confessed guesswork misleads no one, but to express a valuation process in the form of a capital valuation process when the essential data are fictitious, or derived from the value to be found, is statistically vicious" (Canning 1929: 243ff.). Since it was rare, according to Canning, to have an establishment reproduced in kind, the only value that a measure such as "cost of reproduction less depreciation" might have was as a working rule for a damage suit. But it was invalid as the sole rule for a going concern whose primary objective was to reproduce a stream of services, not actual physical capital in any specific form (Canning 1929). The Depression effectively aborted an interesting measurement debate; the rapid decline in prices pointed out the downside of replacement cost, and while a few academic treatises, prepared in the twenties, would continue to appear in the literature, those arguments sounded hollow in the midst of a severe depression.[85]

There are references to the post–World War I period, providing the "hard historical evidence" that deviations form historical cost-based, conservative accounting led to the crash of 1929. Many accountants empathized with George O. May's statement that "in the 1920's accountants fell from grace and took to adjusting capital values on the books . . . to an extent never before attempted. . . . In extenuation they might plead unsound laws, unpractical economics and a widespread if unfounded belief in the new order of things combined to recommend such a course, but . . . the wiser course is to admit the error and not be misled again" (May 1936A). During the early 1930s, there would be an effort to divorce accounting from economic theory on "practical" grounds. Topics such as the accountant's function in a regulated society, the need for multiple valuations, and the problems of articulation introduced in the 1920s were subsequently ignored as the work of "valuation theorists." The crash of 1929 changed the agenda for accountants; the profession spent most of the next decade responding to critics and reaffirming its independence from management. Auditing and financial reporting captured the profession's attention. Both accounting academics and practitioners addressed more immediate problems, such as development of accounting and auditing standards in order to preserve the autonomy of the profession, in the 1930s.

Criticisms that, during the twenties, CPAs had catered to management and lost their independence had merit, but as noted, those criticisms must be evaluated in light of the environment of that decade. Perhaps the atmosphere of the decade was most succinctly captured by Sobel as he traced the Piggly Wiggly Corner in 1923 and concluded that "it is fitting that the first major corner of the bull market began with a Livermore-Bliss victory, the wreck of a businessman, avoidance of responsibility on the part of the Exchange, all this in connection with a stock named after a pig" (Sobel 1968: 264).

The Decade of the Thirties

It is a formidable task to assess the impact of the 1929 stock market crash. Historical evidence suggests that contemporary observers did not foresee the lasting impact that this crisis would have.[86] But politicians could no longer argue that Americans would prosper under a business system managed—or unmanaged—as it had been in the 1920s. The ideological debates of the past began to give way to a new agreement on the practicalities of managing a modern economy. There developed a new consensus that gave hope of harnessing government, business, and labor in a rational partnership for a steadily expanding American economy (Schlesinger 1959).

The Great Depression of the 1930s and its aftermath was, in terms of its impact on American society, second in importance only to the years 1776–89 (from the War of Independence to the inauguration of George Washington as president). Before 1936 and the so-called Keynesian revolution, the most common attitude toward business was that, apart from some obvious ameliorative legislation (child labor laws, and so forth), the overall performance of the nation's economy was best left to the private sector. In the absence of calls for a positive government policy with respect to the economy, the accountant's role had primarily been one of "information processor" for the business sector. The New Deal was perceived by many contemporaries as profoundly altering demands being made upon the profession. Yet it is questionable whether or not New Deal policies significantly altered the traditional financial reporting process.[87]

From the crash until the end of World War II, political reformers were attempting to integrate capitalism and administrative theory. At first it was assumed that regulation could not be reconciled with capitalism because regulation rejected the fundamental belief in the efficacy of competition in the marketplace. But it soon became apparent that administrative theory did not negate the need for a self-regulating mechanism; it simply shifted the focal point from the individual to groups—from self-regulation through economics to self-regulation through politics (Lowi 1969: 29f.). Political leaders did not look to accountants initially to implement reforms; the profession had to convince politicians, and later regulators, that independent audits could provide protection for investors. Accountants found support from businessmen and the leaders of the stock exchanges, who preferred private sector audits to direct government oversight.

The thirties reflect the contradictions often found in periods of economic instability. Franklin Delano Roosevelt's election in 1932 signaled the end of more than a decade of "managerial capitalism" and ushered in what

has been called the era of federal "collective capitalism." New Deal reformers suggested that concentration of industry had made laissez-faire
economic policies obsolete. Richberg (1937), an active participant in the
Roosevelt administration, depicted the New Deal as an adaptation to the
realities of a corporate age, an acknowledgment that collective competition, not individual competition, dominated the economy. As noted by
Chandler (1977), the "visible hand" of professional corporate managers,
not markets, coordinated economic activities; they had the power to administer prices and override market controls.[88] In their seminal work, Adolph
Berle and Gardiner Means (1932) claimed that separation of ownership
and control had undercut the role of profits to "owners" as an efficient
means of allocating economic resources.[89] The concept of "managerial
capitalism" raised serious questions about the relevance of traditional accounting data. Accountants responded creatively and effectively to this new
challenge. By the end of the decade, accounting theorists had developed a
historic cost allocation model that effectively silenced questions about the
relevance of accounting profit and reaffirmed the primacy of ownership
rights.

The passage of securities legislation should have changed relationships
between accountants and management.[90] It did not because the stated
objectives of the legislation—to curb managerial power, to promulgate
uniform reporting rules, and to provide information that was useful to investors for decision-making—were not implemented. By the end of the
decade, management continued to have great flexibility in selection of accounting principles; acceptance of the concepts of consistency and conservatism did not increase the usefulness of financial reports to the "average"
small investor. In many respects, securities legislation appeared to be symbolic, its primary purpose being to mollify public concern.[91] A paradoxical
relationship existed between CPAs and the political sector throughout the
thirties. Accountants spent most of the decade refusing greater responsibility for the content of financial statements, while stressing the limitations
of audits and the subjectivity of financial reports. Regulators, while periodically chiding the profession for its affinity to management, accepted most
of the profession's disclaimers while simultaneously promoting independent audits to protect investors. The McKesson-Robbins scandal in 1939
(discussed later in this chapter) reopened questions about the adequacy of
the monitoring process, but the war diverted attention from the profession.
After World War II, the relationship between the SEC and the accounting
profession would change significantly, but accountants had withstood the
threat of loss of professional autonomy.[92]

The Legal Environment

During the twenties, Berle lamented the fact that the law seemed to offer no protection to third parties, adding that the courts viewed accounting techniques as neutral and would not question accounting practices (1927: 428). He contended that management gained their power "through control of accounting." Given this legal attitude and the increased number of new entrants into the profession, who survived through providing consulting and tax services to their clients, the profession's obligation to third parties had been obscured. A series of court decisions in the 1930s forcefully reminded CPAs of this obligation.

In 1930, a federal court upheld an injunction brought by stockholders opposed to the Bethlehem Steel–Youngstown Steel merger, who claimed that they had been presented with a mass of contradictory accounting facts. The judge warned accountants that financial reports should be prepared for laymen, not for skilled accountants, and called for greater uniformity. While the merger failed due to a decline in stock prices and a subsequent court held the initial suit to be frivolous, this case captured the profession's attention.[93] Later that year, perhaps unintentionally, Justice Cardozo of the New York Supreme Court greatly extended the profession's legal liability in the Ultramares case. Cardozo concluded that accountants could be held liable for gross negligence tantamount to fraud. According to reports of a conversation between S. D. Leidesdorf and Cardozo (who was related to Leidesdorf's wife), the judge thought his decision would benefit accountants by clarifying their position. Leidesdorf was horrified; he felt the decision would be devastating since few juries would be able to make the subtle distinction between simple and gross negligence (Schur 1976).

The passage of the Securities Acts in 1933 and 1934 changed the independent auditors' legal environment dramatically. Accountants objected strenuously to the liability provisions of the legislation, arguing that the recision provisions of the 1933 act had gone much too far.[94] While some have compared securities legislation to the British Companies Acts, the legal liability provisions certainly were much more onerous and, in the minds of most accountants, fatally flawed.[95] George O. May vigorously attacked the provisions of the 1933 law. He noted that the act not only abandoned the old rule that "the burden of proof is on the plaintiff"; it also rejected the "doctrine of contributory negligence and the seemingly sound theory that there should be some relation between the injury caused and the sum to be recovered" (May 1934: 9–11). But May and the other AIA leaders were not paralyzed by fear; they believed, correctly, that this section would be repealed.[96]

The uncertain legal environment may have contributed to the AIA's reluctance to accept greater responsibility for financial reports, a position that it maintained throughout the 1930s. Prior to 1929, accountants legitimately claimed they did not have the power to dictate to clients; but during the thirties they made few coordinated attempts to increase responsibility or power. When the New York Stock Exchange (NYSE) and, later, the Securities and Exchange Commission (SEC), offered their support to increase the authority of the profession, the profession's leaders temporized. It can be pointed out that these leaders were likely distracted by intraprofessional quarrels.

The Impact of Securities Legislation

When it became clear after Roosevelt's election that securities legislation would be forthcoming, the AIA's leadership, especially George O. May, lobbied behind the scene for audits.[97] The NYSE sent its correspondence with the AIA Committee on Cooperation with the Stock Exchange to Congress to show that reforms had been enacted. Arthur Carter, president of the New York State Society of CPAs, took a public initiative, testifying before the Congressional Committee on Banking and Currency. His testimony is credited with convincing the committee that the failure to require audits was a major omission in the suggested reforms (Carey 1969).

Given the tenor of Carter's and May's arguments, acceptance of independent audits as a viable alternative to direct federal oversight suggests that the congressional panel wanted to avoid a direct confrontation with the business community. Carter and May did not engage in a "hard sell"; both men stressed the limitations of independent audits and the limited protection that financial reports would afford to investors.[98]

Passage of securities legislation, while increasing demands for audit services, also had the potential to limit severely the autonomy of the accounting profession with respect to accounting standards. The Securities Act of 1933 gave the FTC the authority to "prescribe the methods to be followed in preparation of accounts, in the appraisal or valuation of assets and liabilities, in the determination of depreciation and depletion, in the differentiation of recurring and nonrecurring income, in the differentiation of investment and operating income and in the preparation of income accounts."[99] The 1934 act established a new agency, the SEC, to regulate the financial reporting process for publicly traded companies.

Only if one views securities legislation as a conservative reform, designed to restore public confidence in the economic system, do regulators' subsequent actions make sense.[100] Roosevelt (1933) sought to reaffirm the primacy of private property rights and to promote economic democracy through widespread stock ownership. To do so, the perceived inequities among market participants in the pre-SEC market had to be redressed.[101] Regulators promoted audited financial statements as the means by which stockholders could exercise their ownership rights. But attitudes toward investors remained Brandeisian; the average investor did not have the capability to understand financial reports.[102] Thus, while audited financial statements fulfilled the political objective of restoring investor confidence, negative attitudes about investors' abilities rendered implementation of the legislation less important. Regulators had little reason to engage in divisive struggles with accountants and managers about reporting methods if they did not believe that small investors could or would employ financial reports.

The establishment of the SEC in 1934 had initially sent tremors through the financial community, but the concern of the business sector diminished significantly when Roosevelt named Joseph P. Kennedy as the first chairman of the SEC. Kennedy's appointment was considered acceptable to the financial community because he was "one of their own." Reformers lamented the choice, so typical of Roosevelt, who sponsored reform and then modified its impact by making conciliatory appointments. Compromise also became evident in implementation of the law; faced with serious opposition from both accountants and businesspeople to the concept of "uniformity," the SEC opted for the far less controversial concept of full disclosure.[103]

Passage increased demand for accounting services and had two more immediate benefits. The legislation conferred upon CPAs a legally defined social obligation: to assist in creating and sustaining investor confidence in the public capital markets. Accountants now had an acknowledged social obligation that justified their claim to professional status. The threat of governmental intervention also provided the impetus for the profession to unite; talks for a merger of the AIA and ASCPA began in 1934, and the merger took place in 1937.[104]

The SEC and Full Disclosure

Securities legislation is referred to as "disclosure" legislation, but the type of disclosure that most reformers advocated did not focus on traditional accounting data. Roosevelt did not think that investors would benefit greatly by financial reports nor did he think that any legislation could prevent people from making errors in judgment about a firm's prospects (1933: 226, 234). But legislation could force corporations to tell investors how their money was being used by disclosing managerial "bonuses and commissions" and by preventing presentation of "malicious misinforma-tion" to stockholders. Legislation also could ban practices, such as insider trading and preferred stock lists, that New Deal reformers believed had cre-ated gross inequities in the capital markets.

Accountants were more likely than New Deal reformers to suggest that investors had been misled by inadequate financial statement disclosure (May 1932).[105] Accountants probably shared reformers' attitudes toward in-vestors' abilities, but they had to offer some alternative to uniformity. The idea that investors had been hurt by inadequate financial reports enabled the profession to advocate full disclosure, rather than uniformity, as an ef-fective remedy for prior abuses.[106]

The fear that the call for "uniformity" (i.e., a rulebook approach) in-stilled in many of the leaders of the profession would be difficult to over-state. Rules did not require judgment, and implementation of uniform systems would result in displacement of CPAs by technicians.[107] Robert Montgomery captured the dominant view within the profession when he wrote that "our most precious asset is our independence in thought and action." Judgment, he warned, is our means of using that asset, concluding that "slavish adherence to definitions or precedents would reduce our use-fulness to a vanishing point" (Montgomery 1927). Full disclosure, unlike uniform rules, made judgment an essential part of the reporting process.[108]

The call for "uniform accounting principles" provided sufficient incen-tive for the AIA and the ASCPA to form a joint committee to respond to regulators' demands.[109] The committee argued that uniform accounting was unrealistic and ineffective, its primary virtue being simplicity. "Unifor-mity has been greatly overemphasized," the report contended, adding "it may be more misleading than informative." The report advocated that uni-formity be limited "to a few general principles so broadly stated that they will permit wide variation in application to meet different circumstances" (AIA and ASCPA 1934: 5–8). This report marked the beginning of a long debate over the merits of "flexibility" versus "uniformity," a debate that Robert Trueblood felt significantly retarded progress since it focused on "extreme" positions, not on the middle ground of "making like things look alike, and unlike things look different" (Lawler 1969: 3). The ASCPA/AIA joint committee also advocated two other reporting concepts: consistency and conservatism.

Consistency had an important practical benefit for accountants: it lim-ited the profession's responsibilities. The accountant did not have to de-termine if a technique was preferable, only that it had been accepted in practice and had been consistently applied.[110] Financial analysts and man-agers also preferred consistency to uniformity. Financial analysis could be reduced to routine adjustments, once an analyst determined the policies that a company used. Since disclosure of accounting policies was not required in annual reports until 1963, consistency probably gave analysts a competitive advantage over the "average" investor.[111] Managers found consistency appealing because it did not reduce their flexibility in selection of accounting practices. No one argued that consistency would result in more informative financial reports.

Most accountants also advocated conservatism. The SEC's acceptance of this concept suggests that the regulatory agency may have been more concerned with restoring confidence in the economic system than in providing useful information to investors. Conservatism justified procedures, such as the write-down of fixed assets to nominal amounts, that relieved future years of significant charges to income, enabling some firms to experience a "speedy" accounting, if not an economic, recovery.[112] Gilman (1939: 235) correctly noted that conservatism gave management a "virtual free hand" to tell stockholders "untruths" about their own companies, a practice antithetical to the underlying premises of securities legislation. The SEC's acceptance of consistency and conservatism, combined with its advocacy of full disclosure, resulted in very little change in pre/post-SEC reporting relationships.

The AIA/NYSE Correspondence

The New York Stock Exchange, anticipating some form of regulation after the 1929 crash, asked the American Institute of Accountants to join with the Exchange and enact reforms.[113] The institute agreed to cooperate, but the AIA committee's responses to the NYSE's requests that the profession assume greater responsibility for the content of financial statements left no doubt that in an age of legal uncertainty, the profession would not do so voluntarily.[114]

J. M. B. Hoxsey asked the institute committee to delineate the degree of responsibility that accountants would be willing to take for (1) determining the propriety of the accounting principles management selected (i.e., preferability decisions), (2) mandating disclosure of income data, and (3) curbing use of reserves to artificially smooth income. The institute's answer was that accountants could not take responsibility for any of the above.[115] The statements were management's responsibility.

Preferability Decisions

With respect to preferability decisions, the AIA committee argued that "the primary responsibility for selection of principles and scope of disclosure must remain that of directors and officers of the corporation" (AIA 1931A: 2–3). They concluded that if the auditor has "no reason to doubt their [corporate officers] competence or good faith," then "he may properly certify accounts without qualification even though his own preference would be for a different treatment."[116] Carter (1933), when testifying before the congressional committee, reiterated this position. He stressed that accountants could not substitute their preferences for those of management and explicitly rejected the suggestion that officers of corporations be required to verify under oath that "the statements . . . are correct." Neither management nor the accountant could provide such assurances.[117]

The passage of securities legislation did not change the profession's position. In 1935, Hoxsey again requested that auditors assume responsibility for determining the appropriateness of various accounting practices.[118] A group of eleven large accounting firms formulated the institute's response; they advised the NYSE that accountants "would not care to place themselves on record with definite replies" because accounting principles were not "inflexible."[119]

During the thirties, the profession developed an argument that could be called the "accounting impossibility theorem." Conflicting user interests made it impossible to be "fair" to all users when preparing general purpose financial statements.[120] There simply was no "right" answer to accounting questions; the appropriateness of any method was determined by the intended use of the financial report. The committee concluded that "for the present" various methods must be tolerated, a position the AIA reiterated to the SEC a year later.

The SEC acknowledged that conflicting user interests made it difficult to set standards, but they had a solution. Financial reporting rules should be designed to meet the needs of only one group, investors in publicly traded companies. The AIA's Committee on Cooperation with the SEC replied that this was impractical; most businesses did not issue financial statements to provide information to investors. They also noted that this class of users, investors in publicly traded corporations, was relatively small. Therefore, they concluded that they would "hesitate to ask the Institute to lay down principles for universal application upon a consideration of the problem from the standpoint of the listed corporations alone" (AIA, 1935: 2–3). George O. May (1936B) dismissed the SEC's suggestion that accountants could make preferability decisions if they focused on one user group as "naive." Current and potential investors, he noted, also had conflicting interests.

The SEC's delegation of its authority to set accounting standards to the AIA and the Committee on Accounting Procedure (CAP) in 1938 did not make auditors any more willing to make preferability decisions. CAP emphasized that financial reports were necessarily a "matter of opinion" and that management, not auditors, determined the content of reports. The legal environment certainly colored the profession's responses, but the close allegiance between most practitioners and their managerial clients also made an adversarial relationship unattractive.

Income Determination

By the end of the 1930s, the NYSE, the SEC, and CPAs had come to the view that investors were primarily interested in "future income" and the income statement must be the focal point of accounting. In 1931, Hoxsey asked the AIA whether or not full and fair disclosure mandated disclosure of income statement data. The AIA committee responded no.[121] While the committee acknowledged that the income account was of "cardinal importance to investors," they concluded that the nascent state of audit practice made it impractical for CPAs to insist on disclosure of income data (AIA, 1931B: 3).

Hoxsey (1931: 8–9) also asked the AIA committee if accountants were willing to condemn deliberate understatement of assets or artificial leveling of income. The committee again responded negatively, stating that neither practice was antithetical to the concept of disclosure, since management had the prerogative of choosing what was disclosed. They agreed that incomplete disclosure of "artificial" leveling of income (i.e., use of reserves to increase or decrease annual income) could be viewed as impairing "the value of accounts as indicative of earning capacity." But they added that smoothing was not necessarily bad since "measurement of profits as between years is necessarily in large measure conventional" and soundness of conventions must be based on "broad considerations." Stabilization of income (income smoothing) was from a broad perspective sound; it modified rather than accentuated the effects of changing economic conditions (AIA, 1931B: 8–9).

Accountants continuously stressed the "conventionality" of accounting income measurement. Fearful of those who viewed accounting income as a "fact" and suggested that accountants could provide a "true" income number that investors could multiply by 10 or 20 to determine the current value of a firm, practitioners pointed out the arbitrariness of accounting allocations (May 1932: 337). Given the subjective nature of accounting income determination, these disclaimers made a good deal of sense. But arguments that accountants should not insist on disclosure of any income data are less understandable.

The AIA's Committee on Cooperation with the Securities and Exchange Commission, chaired by C. Oliver Wellington, clearly showed the animosity that some practitioners had toward New Deal reforms.[122] The committee chided the SEC for granting too few confidentiality exceptions, that is, management claims that disclosure of income statement data would put them at a competitive disadvantage. Many accountants viewed disclosure of income data as beneficial only to speculators, not to long-term investors. The AIA's SEC committee reflected this view, objecting to disclosure of sales, gross profit, and salaries of officers and employees, because it "might be damaging to the company and therefore of injury to the stockholders" (AIA, *Minutes* 1936: 53). The committee apparently reflected a broad consensus within the AIA; the institute issued an official pronouncement, "Disclosure of Sales, Cost of Sales and Gross Profit" that mirrored the committee's views. Morrison (1935) states that auditors lobbied for clients (management) to convince the SEC that income data should be considered confidential. Accountants' motives for lobbying remain unclear; however, the lobbying reinforced the perception that CPAs felt a close allegiance to their clients.[123]

The AIA's disclaimers and practitioners' apparent allegiance to the clients (managers) upset the more proactive SEC commissioners. James Landis expressed the frustration of some SEC commissioners when he stated that "the impact of almost daily tilts with accountants, some of them called leaders of their profession, often leaves little doubt that their loyalties to management are stronger than their sense of responsibility to the investor. . . . Such an experience does not lead readily to acquiescence in the plea recently made by one of the leaders of the accounting profession that the form of statement can be less rigidly controlled and left more largely to professional responsibility alone" (1936: 4).[124]

While the SEC commissioners supported Accounting Series Release No. 4 (1938), which would recognize standards used by private sector accountants, the outcome did not end debate; some commissioners continued to threaten that the SEC might withdraw this acknowledgement of such standards.[125] In 1938, Robert Healy shocked the practicing community when he suggested to accounting academicians that they, as "disinterested parties," might be better able to establish accounting principles. Healy categorized practitioners "as special pleaders for their most lucrative clients" and claimed that they waffled whenever asked to take a definite stand on any issue. He contended that the SEC should force CPAs to state clearly whether accounting procedures used by their clients were appropriate. "Not," he warned, "in ciphers that would stump Francis Bacon himself."

While the AIA was able to parry these attacks successfully and retain private sector standards, the American Accounting Association's (AAA) efforts to develop a conceptual framework created significant tensions among academicians and practitioners. These tensions heightened whenever the AAA issued a publication that recommended departures from accepted practice; the publications also created dissension within academia due to the perceived conservatism of the AAA position.

The AAA's Tentative Statement of Accounting Concepts

The AAA, through the work of various committees and its sponsorship of research monographs, sought to provide a conceptual framework for financial accounting theory. The AAA issued a series of statements between 1936 and 1948 that developed the historical cost allocation model.[126] The 1936 statement, titled "A Tentative Statement of Accounting Principles Affecting Corporate Reports," marked the beginning of what many academics believed was a retreat to "conservatism." [127]

The "Tentative Statement" had three sections: cost and values, measurement of income, and capital and surplus. Academic critics focused on the first two sections. Scott (1937A) felt that the AAA had completely failed to recognize changing economic relationships; that is, the committee had claimed a "neutrality" for accounting data that did not exist.[128] Husband (1937) concurred; he noted that the historic cost allocation model was based on one view: "a select group of owners, the original owners." May (1952) reached a similar conclusion; he believed as financial accounting became dominated by the historical cost allocation model, it might have been more accurately called "investor-ownership accounting." Academic critics also chastised the committee report for calling a section "measurement of income" when the report ignored the measurement problem, focusing solely on classification of income (Husband 1937; Rorem 1937).

Practitioners generally applauded the committee's conservatism and its advocacy of historic costs, but they were unhappy with the committee's absolute ban on any charges to surplus and with the "wrong headedness" of the concept of all-inclusive income (Montgomery 1937). The concept of all-inclusive income was the most significant departure from practice, and the profession would spend the better part of two decades debating the merits of the "all-inclusive" versus the "current operating" concepts of income.[129] However, the AAA reports, combined with the publication of the Paton and Littleton monograph in 1940, virtually ended debate over attribute measurement. The latter work claimed that historic cost was the "natural" measurement base in a corporate economy.

William A. Paton, University of Michigan   A. C. Littleton, University of Illinois

The Paton and Littleton Monograph

In 1940, the AAA released *An Introduction to Corporate Accounting Standards,* by W. A. Paton and A. C. Littleton, a seminal work in the accounting literature. The authors developed a model that creatively responded to the challenge posed by Berle and Means (1932), who argued that separation of ownership and control had rendered traditional accounting profit measurement useless as a means of allocating economic resources. They also suggested that with the acceptance of entity theory, historic cost measurement was "natural." [130] Entity theory contained a critical assumption, namely that managers sought to maximize returns to the firm, not to any particular user group, such as stockholders. That assumption never received widespread acceptance.

After nearly a century of development, Paton and Littleton (1940) presented "entity" theory as the first integrative theory of accounting (figure 6.1). They outlined a "matching" model for income determination that would enable all external users to assess managerial performance. If accountants could accurately measure revenues, which represented managerial accomplishments, and expenses, which represented managerial efforts, then the resultant income could be used by investors to allocate economic resources. The matching model created an aura of certitude that masked the arbitrariness of the allocation process. [131] Although historical cost allocation dominated accounting textbooks after World War II, the texts

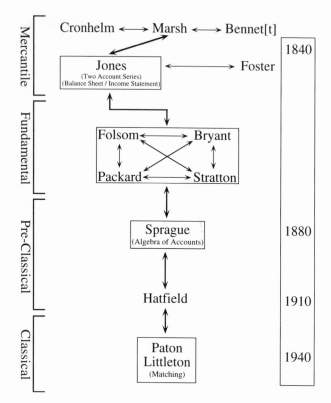

Figure 6.1 The continuity of American accounting thought,
1840–1940

ignored the "entity" aspect of Paton and Littleton's model and continued
to assume that managers sought to maximize returns to stockholders. Paton
and Littleton's efforts to make the historic cost model appear to be a "natural" result of entity theory may have obscured their broader message. The
subsequent debate ignored the questions that entity theory raised about the
role of accounting data in a corporate society. By the end of World War II,
the historic cost "matching" model had become the dominant accounting
model. The focus on "invested cost" turned accounting back toward the
"owner" (i.e., stockholder), while the "matching" model presented a "true
income" number that seemed to enable the owner/stockholder to monitor management, rendering questions of separation of ownership and control moot.

Despite the widespread acceptance of the Paton and Littleton monograph, accounting procedures—that is, computation of book value, treat-

ment of a holding company's investment in a subsidiary, and the accounting for stock dividends—continued to be viewed in terms of proprietary, or residual equity, theory (Husband 1938). The acceptance of "entity" theory to support the historic cost allocation model, combined with rejection of its basic premise that managers sought to maximize returns to the firm, effectively resulted in a reaffirmation of proprietary theory with a change in focus from the balance sheet to the income statement.[132]

The Positive Reply: The Sanders, Hatfield, and Moore Study

Arthur Carter of Haskins & Sells decided to respond to the 1936 AAA committee report by commissioning three academics, Thomas Sanders, Henry Rand Hatfield, and William O. Douglas, to review accounting practice and prepare a monograph. Douglas resigned from the study when Roosevelt appointed him as an SEC commissioner in 1937 and recommended his colleague Underhill Moore as his replacement.[133] Douglas's initial appointment proved fortuitous for practitioners because his association with this project convinced him that practice should be the basis for standard setting.[134] Sanders's reply to the 1936 AAA report foreshadowed the content of the Sanders, Hatfield, and Moore study; he harshly criticized that report for departing from the "best" practice by advocating the "all-inclusive" income concept and banning any charges to surplus.

The publication of the Sanders, Hatfield, and Moore study evoked harsh criticism from the academic community. Paton (1938) expressed the sentiment of many when he wrote: "In view of the distinguished authorship of this statement, I was expecting a report which would be outstanding in scholarly approach, in clarity of expression, and in sound and constructive formulation." But he found the work "has little or nothing to offer . . . by way of substantive recommendations" and concluded that what the authors "seem to be saying to business management is, 'Give the problem careful consideration and then do as you think best, subject to legal limitation.' " Andrew Barr (1938) concurred with Paton's sentiment, suggesting that "a better title for their statement would have been *A Statement of Accounting Practices,* with a footnote referring to Professor Hatfield's book for a statement of principles."

The criticism, while just, is interesting in that Carter had told the Haskins & Sells Foundation to commission "three eminent academicians to survey existing practice and write *a definitive statement of the best practice,*" which the authors had done (Carter 1937). When the manuscript was complete, Carter (1937) asked the institute to consider publishing the statement "without necessarily committing the Institute to the adoption of principles stated." The Executive Committee, perhaps motivated by the desire to counter the effect of the 1936 AAA statement, agreed.

One of the reasons for the reaction against the *Statement of Accounting Principles* in academia may have been because it bore the imprimatur of Henry Rand Hatfield, whom most considered an eminent accounting scholar. Hatfield, after publication of the work, tried to make it clear that he disapproved of any effort to "tabulate the practice of many corporations and swear by the results." This procedure for establishing accounting principles, he said, rests on the dictum "spite of pride, in erring reasons spite / One truth is clear; What ever is, is right." He clearly rejected this positive approach. The problem, Hatfield implied, was that the profession did not know what a principle was. "The search goes on," he lamented, "for the still undiscovered accounting principle," suggesting that "perhaps some day an AIA President will come upon it, extend his hand, and say 'Ah, Major Accounting Principle, I presume'" (Hatfield 1939). But despite Hatfield's protestations, the appearance of the original statement, combined with the appointment of Thomas Sanders as the research director of the Committee on Accounting Procedure (CAP), convinced some that accounting principles need be no more than reflections of existing practice. The Sanders, Hatfield, and Moore study provided an authoritative source for many practitioners who served on the CAP.[135]

Establishing a Standard-Setting Process

After the SEC decision in 1938, the AIA began the process of establishing a formal standard-setting body, and by 1939, the Committee on Accounting Procedure began to issue accounting research bulletins (ARBs). May, vice chair of CAP, urged his fellow committee members to adopt a practical approach, adding to the perception that CAP only gave lip service to theory. Thomas Sanders, research director, and William Paton, Roy Kester, and A. C. Littleton, members of CAP, ensured that academics had a voice, if not a significant influence, on the committee.

Because it is impossible in a general history to examine and evaluate all the opinions and related issues promulgated by the AIA's Committee on Accounting Procedure, we focus on one issue, the debate over proper treatment of unamortized discounts on refunded bond issues (ARB No. 2). This was one of the earliest issues referred to the AIA Committee on Cooperation with the SEC (1937). The SEC outlined three alternative treatments— (1) amortization over the life of the old bond issue, (2) amortization over the life of the new bond issue, and (3) direct write-off to surplus—for the committee to consider.[136] The committee, acting without any real authority, decided that legitimate differences of opinion existed and found support for all three methods, concluding that "full disclosure of the particular method used, the justification for its use, and consistency in application are primarily the important features" (Starkey 1938: 82).

Since the SEC's objective of "limiting" alternatives had not been met, CAP decided to address the bond discount problem as its first procedural problem. May believed it would provide the committee with a good start because it would not be an issue that generated great controversy. That assessment proved to be wrong. Committee members submitted position papers to May or Sanders, and those papers showed that members held widely varying opinions as to the nature of and preferred treatments for bond discounts.

Littleton felt that the committee must address two major questions: "Will the balance sheet contain an item that cannot be called an asset and will the income statement fail to report an item now, which if it had been known when the bond was issued, would have been amortized during past periods?" (CAP 1939: Littleton file). Most committee members did not care to debate these issues; they sought to meet the SEC's objective, that is, to limit existing alternatives. The CAP would not waste its time engaging in "conceptual" debates.

Committee members, who felt that the refunding completed an accounting transaction, supported a direct write-off of the discount. May explained that he favored a direct write-off because "I feel it would be most unfortunate for the Institute to initiate this service by putting forward as a preferable procedure the carrying forward of a non-existent asset" (May 1939). May argued that the charge to surplus could be justified as the refunding losses were unusual and nonrecurring. The direct write-off to surplus posed no theoretical problem to advocates of the concept of current operating income.

Paton, an advocate of the all-inclusive income concept, was put in an untenable position by the three alternatives. He agreed that refunding represented a completed transaction and that no asset existed, but he could not accept a write-off to surplus. He tried to convince the members of the committee that the loss was "real" and that the loss should be written off to income immediately (Paton 1939B). Direct write-offs to income did not generate widespread support among practitioners.

Proponents of amortization argued that refunding did not reflect a completed transaction and that an asset existed; therefore, they argued, any write-off would "distort" income. George Bailey contended that, although it was a basic concept in accounting that "losses should not be carried forward after they are determined, . . . premature retirements are not losses. . . .They are deliberate investments made for future benefits" (Bailey 1939). Some of those favoring amortization cited the Sanders, Hatfield, and Moore study (1938) that stated, "It is reasonable to defer abnormal losses which are not convenient to write off" to support their position (114). Since direct write-offs could impair a firm's ability to pay dividends, it might be decidedly inconvenient to write off the total discount.

The argument that refunding did not result in a completed transaction offered theoretical support for deferral of the losses, but proponents were hard-pressed to justify CAP's preferred solution: amortization over the life of the old bond issue. Paton and Henry Horne joined forces on this issue, although Horne, unlike Paton, supported amortization. Horne argued that no immediate loss occurred because "a normal refund was constructive . . . not a lamenting over borrowing badly done." But how, he asked, could you contend that the future benefits accrued to a nonexistent bond issue? (Horne 1940). Paton said he could conceivably support amortization on the basis that a transaction had not been completed. But how, he asked, could anyone contend that the transaction ended with the expiration of the retired issue? (Paton 1939B). The answer was you could not, but conservatism dictated use of the shorter period.[137] Since "the settled practice" was to classify discounts as "assets," most practitioners preferred the shorter amortization period as it would reduce the risk of constant refunding that might lead to overstatement of assets.

The decision to allow direct write-off to surplus as the acceptable alternative concerned several CAP members. Frederick Andrews, who favored a direct write-off to income, was concerned that the write-off was not to income. "How," he asked, "can an income statement be distorted if it truly reflects what happened during a period?" He challenged anyone to show him the wisdom of trying "to approximate uniformity of successive income accounts if they lack conformity with reality." He rejected amortization because he felt that "no good can come from a procedure which would result in surplus where there will not be assets," concluding that "this is real distortion" (Andrews 1939: 1). Andrews's refusal to accept surplus adjustments did not make him popular with his fellow practitioners, and he did not last long on the committee.[138]

Paton and Kester found ARB No. 2 so theoretically unacceptable that they formally dissented. The negative vote of two academicians did not go unnoticed; Kohler suggested that perhaps practitioners did not want theoretical solutions but justification for what they did. He asked why the dissents were not printed, implying that the CAP probably silenced the two academicians because they were right (Kohler 1939: 445). May, in his usual style, responded in a letter to the editor of the *Review*, that the only thing jaded was Kohler's "critical faculty." May wrote that Kester dissented because he advocated amortization over the life of the new issue, while Paton objected to direct write-offs to surplus. The debate over this issue foreshadowed the difficulty that CAP would have whenever it discussed principles that affected income determination.

If one examines this issue, or the many others discussed by CAP, purely with respect to theoretical considerations, then CAP is found wanting. The only alternative that everyone agreed had theoretical merit in this case—amortization over the life of the new bond issue—was the only alternative prohibited. But one must ask, What would have been the reaction in the political sector to direct write-offs to income? This approach was preferred by many academicians.[139] Roosevelt's messages constantly reiterated the need to overcome the Depression mentality and what he believed to be the pervasive but unwarranted economic pessimism of the day.

Regulatory agencies usually required direct write-offs, but to surplus where they could be hidden. Even with "uniform" procedures, these agencies were not hesitant to permit any of the alternatives suggested by CAP, if it was inconvenient for a company to absorb the loss currently.[140] Amortization was the more attractive alternative for those who hoped that investors could be persuaded to return to the capital markets. Surplus would be only nominally impaired, income would not be greatly affected, and in most cases, net assets would increase. May (1952) prophetically warned that accounting principles could not be developed without regard to their practical consequences because *accounting income was on its way to becoming a political, not an economic concept.*

The Distortion Argument: An Invitation to Stabilize Income

Roosevelt's desire to stimulate investment and restore investor confidence was clear. In 1939, Undersecretary of Commerce Edward Noble addressed the annual meeting of the AIA and told the assembled practitioners that the government felt that the basic problem of the age was "finding ways and means of stimulating the flow of new investment." He added that new investment "depends entirely upon the prospects of return on that investment" (Noble 1939). There was an implicit message in Noble's speech, apparently not lost upon accountants. Risk deterred investment, fluctuating income patterns increased perceived (if not actual) risk, and such uneven income streams could be detrimental to economic recovery. Acceptance of these ideas, with the related acknowledgment that the government viewed the financial reporting process as a means of stimulating investment, appeared to dampen enthusiasm for the all-inclusive income concept and curb efforts to clean up "dirty" surpluses.

This prewar attitude provided support for the current operating concept rather than the all-inclusive concept of income. The debate over these two concepts of income had been characterized as an academic-practitioner schism, and although there are obvious exceptions to such a generalization, it is basically valid. The debate, which divided the profession for several decades, did not focus on fundamental issues. Everyone agreed that current operating income provided the best surrogate for future earnings, but they disagreed about whether users were "fixated" on the bottom line. Academics thought users could be taught to raise their eyes to current operating income, which would be shown, but not as the last figure on the income statements.

Practitioners argued that investors were not that sophisticated and that the financial press had conditioned people to look at the bottom line. Accountants, they contended, could not effectively educate users of financial statements to do otherwise (AIA, 1939B). The debate quickly disintegrated (failing to focus on such basic questions as what is income or what effects reporting "all-inclusive" versus "current operating" income had on investors' perceptions of future earnings) into a series of accusations about the motives of practitioners.

Paton, one of the leading proponents of the all-inclusive concept, told his fellow CAP committee members that the "income sheet should be from 'Genesis to Revelation'—start with sales and end with surplus." He warned that if the profession did not adopt this position, practitioners would face extreme pressure from management to "tuck away, through the back door of the surplus account, charges or credits which management finds it inconvenient to disclose explicitly" (Paton 1939A).

At least one practitioner, Warren Nissley, felt that Paton's assessment was correct. Nissley (1940) criticized the Sanders, Hatfield, and Moore study for stating that "some charges could be made directly to surplus to facilitate prediction of current earnings." He predicted that this assertion would cause "many grey hairs for auditors" because management certainly would prefer a "private burial in surplus which was much less noticeable than a public funeral in the income account." The SEC had tipped the balance in favor of current operating income when it accepted direct write-offs to surplus if write-offs to income would "distort" income; however, postwar SEC attitudes would change on this subject.[141]

By the end of World War II, companies had been permitted to write off large, unusual losses, bond discounts, foreign exchange losses, goodwill, renegotiation agreements, and any other special items to surplus if management determined that a charge to income would be distortive. Management also had the discretion to determine that only part of a charge was "unusual" and, therefore, "distortive"; they could allocate that portion of the charge to surplus and the balance to income. Given this discretion, management of reported income could be raised to a high art form. Eric Kohler's (1945: 633) cryptic comments about the lack of definition of what "distortion" meant appear to have been on target.

Acceptance of the "distortion" argument created some fundamental contradictions in the accounting literature. Accountants, acting as standard setters, justified charging unusual items to surplus because charges to income would "seriously impair the income statement as an indicator of earning capacity, [past and future]." Accountants, acting as auditors, claimed that a one-period income statement was necessarily arbitrary; the resultant income number could not be considered an adequate indicator of future earning power or even a complete picture of the operations of one period.[142] If, as auditors suggested, income determination was "conventional" and arbitrary, then the question became, What was being "distorted?" CAP never resolved the question.

Moonitz, in his survey of the various CAP and later Accounting Principles Board (APB) opinions, concluded that opinions dealing with the form of presentation, the extent of disclosure, or the amount of detail were accepted readily. But "those opinions which bear on valuation of assets or liabilities, and, therefore, recognition of revenue and expenses" failed (Moonitz 1974: 23). Because prior to World War II the political sector gave clear indications that it did not want accountants to dampen investor enthusiasm by insisting on draconian procedures for measurement of income, Moonitz's conclusions with respect to CAP are not surprising. CAP clearly showed that determining accounting principles was more a political than a theoretical process, and its responses, although of a "brush fire" variety, enabled accountants to retain the right to set accounting standards.[143]

Recent commentators have suggested that the SEC should have assumed control of the standard-setting process in the 1930s, the presumption being that there would have been a more consistent and equitable resolution of issues. The historical evidence does not support this conclusion; the SEC did not encourage conceptual debate nor did the agency seem intent on restricting management's reporting options unduly. The SEC's acceptance of the distortion argument clearly was inconsistent with its stated objective of limiting management's power to "manipulate" financial statements, but it met the more general political objective of restoring investor confidence. If politicians and regulators wanted flexibility in reporting practices to avoid "fluctuating income," which might dampen investors' enthusiasm, accounting practitioners would not object. Since the SEC did not pursue its mandate to limit reporting alternatives vigorously during the thirties, that agency had to rely upon the audit process to ensure the integrity of financial reports. Yet, the legal liability provisions of the Securities Acts made accountants decidedly reluctant to assume greater responsibility. Audit procedures did not change significantly during the twenties and thirties until the McKesson-Robbins case in 1939 led to reform.

Defining the Independent Audit Function

The issuance of *Uniform Accounting* (1917) generated a great deal of hostility toward the AIA, since many believed that its issuance created a competitive advantage for well-known accounting firms.[144] Bankers contended that since *Uniform Accounting* debased audit standards, they could only rely on audit certificates of well-known, reputable accounting firms. Queenan (1977) recalled that audit procedures had been so eroded and criticisms so heated that pressure to publish a new bulletin mounted two to three years before the crash. The institute once again called upon the FRB for support, and "Verification of Financial Statements" was published in 1929.

Verification of Financial Statements

"Verification" contained some minor improvements in audit procedures, but it did not address the major concerns of critics nor did it greatly extend auditors' responsibilities.[145] The document's general instructions mentioned that "the scope of the work includes . . . an examination of the accounting system for the purpose of ascertaining the effectiveness of internal check," but the bulletin did not make it clear that the procedures outlined were appropriate *only* if the auditor had determined that a firm's internal controls were satisfactory. This continued what many felt had been a critical omission in *Uniform Accounting*, for the short-form certificate gave no indication of the scope of an audit.

"Verification," issued partially in response to bankers' criticisms, did not address bankers' primary concern: observation of inventories.[146] Auditors thought they had clearly disclaimed this responsibility by stating they were not insurers and that audits involved testing procedures, but even sophisticated users missed this connection. Many external users erroneously believed that since auditors assumed responsibility for overstatement of assets that the profession had satisfactory procedures for validating receivables and inventories. Again, the McKesson-Robbins case in 1939 demonstrated that this assumption was wrong.

Audits of Corporate Accounts

The 1932–34 correspondence between the AIA and the New York Stock Exchange perpetuated the misunderstanding about the responsibilities of the profession. Hoxsey (1931: 2) asked the AIA Committee for "its conception of the character and extent of the responsibility assumed by accountants in connection with such audits." Accountants replied that the auditor was responsible for expressing "an informed and independent judgment on the question of whether the accounts which he approves are a full and fair presentation" insofar as it is possible to ascertain the "facts . . . by the exercise of professional skill and due diligence." The reply then contained a list of specific limitations with respect to detection of fraud, understatement of assets, and evaluation of internal check.[147] While the final committee reply stressed that reliance is "commonly and rightly placed on an adequate system of internal check," the committee rejected Hoxsey's request that they recommend that auditors explicitly state the relationship between evaluation of internal controls and audit scope. Instead, the accountants suggested that the public be educated to the limitation of audits by including a phrase that "we did not make a detailed test of transactions" in the audit certificate. Users would then be put on notice that audits were based on testing procedures rather than on a comprehensive examination. Privately, auditors agreed that inclusion of this statement might not enlighten the user as to audit limitations, but they felt that it might be "extremely useful" in limiting auditors' potential liability (AIA, 1933B).

The uncertain legal environment after passage of securities legislation seemed to strengthen the profession's resolve to limit its responsibilities. AIA members spent what appears to have been an inordinate amount of time debating terminology; for example, would the use of the term "examination" rather than "audit" or "report" rather than "certificate" be helpful in limiting the profession's legal liability?[148] The initial title of the correspondence, "Value and Limitations of Corporate Accounts and General Principles for Preparation of Reports to Stockholders," more accurately depicts the tenor of the correspondence, than does the final title *Audits of Corporate Accounts*. The carefully worded certificate that appeared in *Audits of Corporate Accounts* (1934) resulted in criticisms similar to those that followed issuance of *Uniform Accounting*.

ERNST & ERNST
AUDITS AND SYSTEMS
TAX SERVICE

February 16, 1932.

We Hereby Certify,

That we have audited the books of account and record of THE COCA-COLA COMPANY, ATLANTA, GEORGIA, AND ITS SUBSIDIARIES, as at December 31, 1931, and, based upon our examination and information obtained, it is our opinion that the annexed Consolidated Condensed Balance Sheet is drawn so as to correctly reflect the financial condition of the Companies at the date named, and that the relative Consolidated Statements of Operations and Profit and Loss-Surplus are correct.

ERNST & ERNST,
Public Accountants and Auditors.

Figure 6.2 Depression-era audit report, Ernst & Ernst

Bankers expressed concern. Robert Morris Associates (RMA) condemned the new certificate, asking, "What purpose does the new report serve?" Answering its own question, RMA concluded that "the certificate said nothing," it simply "protected the auditor" (qtd. in AIA, *Year Book* 1935: 8). Couchman (1935: 1–2) noted that the RMA had concluded that the limitations in the first paragraph served to render the opinion in the second paragraph meaningless.[149]

SEC commissioners, who had not been directly delegated authority to establish audit standards, reserved their harshest criticism for the audit process. Landis, Mathews, and Healy continuously chided the profession for refusing to accept its responsibilities.[150] The familiar threat of a federal audit bureau resurfaced in proposed congressional legislation. Federal incorporation laws, like the proposed Borah-O'Mahoney Act, which called for audits by "certified corporate representatives" to be licensed by the federal government after passing a civil service examination, periodically resurfaced in Congress.[151] To forestall these external threats, the AIA decided to issue a new audit bulletin, "Examination of Financial Statements" (1936B).

Examination of Financial Statements

The minutes of the AIA show that the institute's major objective was to establish the autonomy of the accounting profession over audit standards. "Examination" (1936B) accomplished that objective.[152] The AIA committee made a conscious decision "not to ask for the sponsorship of the Federal Reserve Board or to ask for the approval of the SEC." They also did not discuss "this with the Robert Morris Associates or other people with whom we might have discussed it" (AIA, *Minutes* 1936: 82).

Samuel Broad, chairman of the committee, tried to ease practitioners' fears that the institute was trying to impose uniform procedures. He explained that some auditors felt that the major problem with the previous bulletin was "that it was not elastic enough"; therefore, he continued, "we attempted to make this more elastic, to provide for room for the individual judgment of the accountant." Broad explained that the suggested audit program was simply a "guide," and he pointed out that the committee had been careful not to use the word "must" at all; they used "should" with respect to recommended disclosures. The final determination as to the adequacy of disclosure continued to rest with the company, with the auditor qualifying his certificate if disclosures were not adequate. He concluded that the document "only set forward as procedures or disclosures those which we felt were pretty generally recognized. . . . We did not," he finished, "try to break new ground" (AIA, *Minutes* 1936: 83ff.).

The emphasis on increased elasticity did not strengthen the audit process. Managers, not auditors, gained power from the issuance of the new audit bulletin. Given the political climate of the 1930s, one can understand the desire of the profession to limit its responsibilities. But the stress on limitations seems to have had unfortunate ramifications. In subsequent years, the emphasis continued to be not on what auditors can do, but on what they cannot do. This negative orientation raised serious questions about the willingness of the profession to meet its social expectations effectively. The SEC's acceptance of this document probably reflected the limited power of that agency in its formative years. Regulators might chide auditors for pandering to clients, but they did not want to cast aspersions on the audit process. Independent audits provided the primary mechanism for monitoring management; if the process did not work, then it would be difficult to restore public confidence in the economic system or to propose a cost-effective alternative. The McKesson-Robbins case would contribute substantially to the defensive posture that the institute seemed to adopt.[153]

The McKesson-Robbins Case

The McKesson-Robbins case brought to light the ineffectiveness of audits in detecting fraud involving collusion. Early in the century, the profession had conceded that audits could not be designed to specifically detect fraud; the costs would be too high (Sells 1906). But this message was not fully understood. The AIA leadership, although greatly concerned about McKesson-Robbins, did not act precipitously. Most accountants believed that this was a most unusual case of collusive fraud and that it did not require a wholesale restatement of auditing procedures (*Journal of Accountancy* 1939: 65–69).

The press treated the case in a sensational manner, and New York Attorney General John Bennett conducted a series of hearings at which both the New York State Society and the AIA were represented. Bennett called accountants to task, citing the *"Whitney* case, *Interstate Hosiery, McCaffrey and Co., and Coster-Musica* (McKesson-Robbins)" as reflections of certain fundamental weaknesses in the preparation of financial statements by large corporations (Bennett 1939). The CPAs responded that "in most, if not in all, of the cases cited by the attorney general . . . in which questions of auditing have been involved, it has been human behavior which has failed rather than the procedures commonly followed" (Bennett 1939: 14). Despite the unfavorable publicity, the AIA decided not to revise the 1936 statement but, instead, to extend accepted auditing procedures.

"Extensions of Auditing Procedures" (AIA, 1939A) acknowledged the need for confirmation of receivables and verification of inventory. More important, it recognized the relationship among internal control, risk, and evidence. The document stated that "it is the duty of the independent auditor to review the system of internal check and accounting control so as to determine the extent to which he considers that he can rely upon it." [154] A contribution of the postwar years was clarification of the relationship between internal control and the scope of the auditor's work.

The McKesson-Robbins scandal strained the strong ties between the NYSE and the AIA. John Hoxsey (1939A: 1–3) wrote to George May that "what bothers me is whether the Stock Exchange and the Institute did not both fall down in our consideration of the auditor's certificate" in 1932–34.[155] Quoting from the letter of nine auditing firms sent to Whitney (February 24, 1933), he pointed out that the firms stated, "the essential point is to guard against any overstatement of income," which the auditors pointed out could be best accomplished by "the auditor satisfying himself of the correctness of the balance sheets at the beginning and end of the period covered."

Hoxsey wrote he simply could not "reconcile this [statement] with the absence of procedures to validate both inventories and receivables." He concluded that "I think I am excusable for not having grasped the fact that it was not regarded as necessary to make those checks." While he empathized with the cost/benefit argument, he concluded that presentation of an income account, absent this check of inventories and receivables, "is likely to be . . . harmful . . . for it creates an appearance of care greater than that which really exists.[156] Hoxsey offered to write a public letter of apology, but May (1939) convinced him that such an action would simply undermine investor confidence even more.

Thus, the decade of the thirties ended as the decade of the twenties had begun, with shrill criticisms of audit certificates. At the 1939 AIA Spring Council meeting, J. Chester Crandell shared with his colleagues what he characterized as an absurd audit certificate, which stated that "having made an examination, the balance sheet represents a true financial condition of the affairs of such corporation as disclosed by its books, subject to the same qualifications as made by the directors above their signatures to the certificate." A host of limitations followed and the report concluded, "We the undersigned officers and directors, in signing this certificate, make and intend to make no representation whatsoever as to the value of the assets or any of them, or that the amounts set against them represent either accurately or approximately the value thereof, and make and intend to make no representation whatsoever that there are no liabilities or obligations, contingent or otherwise, which are not shown in the books of the company and therefore not included in the foregoing balance sheet, or that any reserves which are set up upon the books of the company and reflected in the foregoing balance sheet are adequate for the purpose for which they were set up" (Crandell 1939: 143–44). Overall, the criticisms sparked by the McKesson-Robbins case had a significantly different impact than did the earlier criticisms. In the prior decade, bankers and others believed that they could rely on certificates signed by "reputable" audit houses. The testimony of expert witnesses at the SEC's investigation of McKesson-Robbins shattered that illusion (SEC 1939).[157]

William Morse Cole, a venerable member of the accounting profession, perhaps best expressed the frustration of those who recognized that passage of legislation may have masked the continued unreliability of financial reports. Cole (1936: 9) lamented that "the longer I live, and I have been dealing with accounts for almost half a century, the less faith I have that I can read a corporation statement, or a private internal report, and from it determine what is the financial situation behind it, *unless* from some outside source [such as my knowledge of the accounting practices of the people responsible for it] I know what accounting theories it embodies." After World War II, the relationship between the SEC and the accounting profession would change markedly; but the war provided a respite for the profession from criticisms as accountants played a vital role in the administration of wartime controls and gained much favorable publicity for the profession.

The Significance of the Interwar Period

As the national effort involved in World War II concluded, the profession of accounting was firmly established. Accountants had retained the right to set audit standards, and the SEC had assigned the authority to set accounting standards to the private sector. The profession had retained its autonomy despite the fact that an uncertain legal environment and an empathy with business had led accountants to respond negatively to demands that the profession expand its responsibilities. Although criticisms of the audit and financial reporting process continued, these remained the primary mechanisms for protecting stockholders' rights.

Figure 6.3 AIA Speakers at a wartime accounting conference, 1944

While independent audits played an important role by providing an acceptable corporate monitoring device, accounting theorists played an even more critical role in restoring investor confidence in the economic system by developing a model that reestablished the primacy of private property (ownership) rights. By the end of World War II, questions about the relevance of accounting profit were rarely heard; the income statement had become, to parapharse Paton's words, "the golden text." The historical cost allocation model seemed to provide an income number that was acceptable as a relatively precise measure of managerial efficiency, enabling investors to channel economic resources to their most effective use, the traditional function of accounting profit posited by individualistic economic theories. Accountants had played a vital role in achieving Roosevelt's objective of restoring "the sacredness" of private property rights.

While accountants' contributions to the war effort have not yet gained much historical attention, Carey (1970) dedicated a chapter to this period. In the fall of 1945, AIA President Samuel Broad stated, "The accounting profession has had an important part to play in the war effort and will continue to play an important part in dealing with the economic problems which constitute a major part of the aftermath" (Carey 1970: 53). This role and the related expansion and controversy surrounding accountancy is the subject of the next chapter.

Expansion and Controversy:
Accountants in an Age of Uncertainty

> Accountants must supply the reasoning underlying the applications of accounting principles and be able to explain why they produce fairness in financial statements.
> **—Leonard Spacek, AICPA 73rd Annual Meeting, 1960**

The postwar period (1945–72), before the oil embargo episode, was, once again, one of rapid and dynamic changes in the social, political, and economic structures. The cold war would unify the nation against an external enemy, but technological changes made the great disparities among various interest groups more visible. Three instruments of modern culture—television, bank charge cards, and the jet airplane—had a profound effect on people's expectations about quality of life as individuals and as a society. During this period, the nation came full circle, from a feeling of unbridled optimism, reflected in the Employment Act of 1946, that government and business, working together, could ensure economic prosperity for all Americans, to the experience of Vietnam and the reemergence of global economic competition that ended illusions about the nation's economic invincibility.

The Employment Act of 1946

The successful cooperative war effort resulted in a fundamental change in economic and political relationships. Big business and big government became a fact of American life. The remarkably successful wartime effort left many convinced that a government/business coalition could permanently stabilize the economy. The Employment Act of 1946 reflected that belief, and the law identified the responsibility of the federal government to "promote maximum employment, production and purchasing power." The act created a Council of Economic Advisers, composed of the CEOs of the nation's largest corporations, who were charged with developing and recommending to the president national economic policies to foster and promote free competitive enterprise, to avoid economic fluctuations or to diminish the effect thereof, and to maintain employment, production, and purchasing power.[1]

Americans wanted to believe that a permanent government/business coalition could direct economic growth and prevent the cyclical disruptions that had undermined the economic security of the nation's workers. The plan seemed feasible since the war had swept away the productive capacity of most of the industrial countries of the world, leaving the United States alone and dominant as a global economic power. The war-ravaged countries had to be rebuilt, and through financing of the European Recovery Program (Marshall Plan), the U.S. government made what many believed was the "downpayment on the American century."[2] Corporate executives headed the Economic Cooperation Administration and directed $23 billion of new investment abroad during the seven years following the war. Thus, during the 1950s, despite several recessions, it seemed plausible to most Americans that the economy could be stabilized and security assured.

In prior decades, concentration of economic power had generated public protest as concentration had been perceived as a threat to democratic values and to the free market system.[3] But the cold war that united the American people against a common enemy, communism, also toned down criticisms of the big business/big government alliance. This alliance was viewed as essential to maintaining the nation's freedom. Defense spending accelerated and the government became a major source of funding for basic research and new technology. By the end of the 1950s, what Eisenhower labeled the "military industrial complex" (big business and big government) had emerged and exercised enormous influence over all aspects of the nation's life.

The economy had undergone a permanent and fundamental structural change. Some theorists, like Herbert Simon (1947), argued that it would be best to abandon free market rhetoric and acknowledge that the United States now had an organizational economy. His message: Adam Smith's invisible hand was not operative. Corporations could administer prices; corporate managers, not the market, controlled allocation of societal resources.[4] Most Americans, including accountants, were not ready to accept a message that appeared to undermine the fundamental tenets of the private property rights paradigm.[5] The government eased fears of private power by conducting frequent investigations to ensure that corporate cartels did not overtly abuse their power.[6]

Throughout the 1950s, Congress conducted a series of extensive investigations of the various industries accused of administering "unfair" prices.[7]

The threat of antitrust legislation, while implausible given the need for large capital accumulations, always loomed in the background.[8] In 1960, the publicity surrounding the huge fines levied in the Eisenhower administration's successful prosecution of General Electric, Westinghouse, and other companies in the electrical industry for price fixing reawakened the public to the enormous power that had been ceded to the nation's corporations.[9] While the immediate escalation of the cold war muted public concerns, the seeds had been sown for the radical shift in public opinion about corporate America that would occur in the mid-1960s.

The decade of the 1950s, generally, is depicted as a quiet decade, where most Americans prospered, but that picture clearly is incomplete. The prosperity usually did not extend beyond white American male workers. Even among that group, automation introduced insecurity in the workplace, creating alienation in the midst of plenty (Burns 1989). This decade also has been described as an "age of rules"; workers became the subjects of frequent testing, as industrial psychology and human engineering became common in the workplace. While designed to achieve harmony of interests between workers and management, unions resented these tools of control, and conflict between labor and management occurred with some frequency throughout the decade.

The decade of the 1960s also would be a decade of contrasts; a youthful president, John Kennedy, would energize the nation's youth. His call to reestablish American preeminence in science by placing a man on the moon and his challenge: "Ask not what your country can do for you; ask what you can do for your country," could be viewed as an appeal to traditional American values. Television brought the Cuban missile crisis, the building of the Berlin Wall, and the Berlin airlift into the nation's living rooms and served to silence temporarily criticism of the power elite.[10]

Kennedy's assassination, coming in the wake of escalation of military assistance to Vietnam, ended the nation's apparent unity and optimism. Vietnam would divide the nation and open floodgates of protest. Advocates for civil rights, affirmative action, environmental protection, consumerism, and nuclear control would also arise to demand reform.

In a divided country, calls for corporate social responsibility did not go unheeded. Corporate executives responded, acknowledging that those who controlled the nation's largest corporations had an obligation that transcended their obligation to stockholders (Bradshaw and Vogel 1981). While domestic turmoil led to reexamination of the corporate power structure, the resurgence of the Japanese and German economies in the late sixties reopened questions about the effectiveness of American management. The conglomerate merger movement led to harsh criticisms of accountants for their failure to curb managerial reporting abuses.[11] The Mideast oil embargo of 1973 ended the perception that a government/business coalition, working together, could ensure economic stability and prosperity for all.

The nation had come full circle. The same concerns that politicians raised at the turn of the century about the enormous power of financial capitalists reemerged. Once again, accountants would be under scrutiny. The profession's right to establish practice accounting standards was in jeopardy, and criticisms of the audit process accelerated. By 1973, the profession faced an identity crisis: Would it "one day be noted for something other than that which they now seek to provide?" (*Wall Street Journal,* October 30, 1973: 18).

The crisis came, in part, from the profession's strong commitment to the private property rights paradigm. Throughout the period, accountants continued to depict their primary function as providing data to direct corporate constituencies (i.e., creditors and investors and management) to facilitate regulation via the marketplace (economic control). The profession strongly resisted the idea that a primary function of accounting was to provide data for self-regulation by the administrative process (political control).[12]

Challenges to the Property Rights Paradigm

Joseph Schumpeter (1946), the conservative Harvard economist, expressed serious reservations about the ability of the free market system to survive in the face of increasing concentration of industry. He feared that the emergence of an independent managerial class would condemn capitalism to failure. He predicted that managers, "private bureaucrats," simply would not have the entrepreneurial spirit critical to capitalism. Managers, he argued, sought a steady income; they would not take the risks needed to maintain the capitalistic system. But Schumpeter did not allow for the fact that government after the Sputnik episode would provide the needed entrepreneurial spark by funding basic research and new technologies that resulted in a steady flow of new products into the private sector.[13]

Throughout the period, the growing disparity between the assumptions underlying neoclassical economic theory and the new economic order raised questions about why managers should be expected to focus primarily on maximization of stockholders' wealth (Galbraith 1956). Edith Penrose (1959) asked why we should assume that managers care more about stockholders than any other group if those firms, freed of price competition, controlled the allocation of capital? Schumpeter (1946) and Penrose

(1959) did not object to "bigness" per se; they both concluded that trying to turn back the clock so that the "invisible hand" was operative was unwise and undesirable. Constant innovation required that corporations command large amounts of resources and have sufficient market power to recoup large investments. But, they noted, that same market power could be used to erect barriers to entry and to stifle innovation. Penrose explained the dilemma simply, "Competition was at once god and the devil." An examination of financial accounting and reporting shows that throughout the period, most accounting academics and practitioners paid fealty to the god but refused to acknowledge the devil (1959: 265). [14]

Financial Reporting and Standard Setting

DR Scott (1933) had predicted that in an administered economy, accounting income would become the primary mechanism for distribution of societal wealth. The debate over replacement cost accounting after World War II led George O. May (1952) to reach a similar conclusion, writing that if accounting income had not already become a political phenomenon, it was well on its way to becoming one. May's statement reflected acknowledgment of the fact that an "organizational" economy required accounting data for administrative (political) control. Edith Penrose asked a more pointed question, "What does profit represent if corporations administer prices?" Clearly, she responded, not the efficiency of management.[15] What is interesting about the postwar accounting measurement debate is that while a rich body of literature developed related to the impact of inflation on traditional profit measurement, the literature was virtually silent on the more interesting question, What did accounting profit reflect if corporations could administer prices?

The postwar income determination debate centered on which market-based attribute (historical cost, current cost, or current exit value) accountants should measure. The perseverance of the historical cost allocation model was not due to its theoretical superiority. The persistence of the model can be attributed, in part, to conflicting user interests. In a period of rising prices, historical costs would be the least detrimental to consumer and labor interests. Economists and political scientists introduced the concept of interest group pluralism (bargaining) as the mechanism to replace Adam Smith's invisible hand. Galbraith stated this thesis explicitly, writing that "private economic power is held in check by the countervailing power of those who are subject to it" and that "the first begets the second" (1956: 111).[16]

George Oliver May

Arthur Andersen

A. C. Ernst

Accounting data would play a pivotal role in facilitating the bargaining (contracting) process; as such, it would become too important to be left solely to the discretion of accountants. The replacement of two standard-setting bodies, the Committee on Accounting Procedure (CAP) and the Accounting Principles Board (APB), during this period, can be attributed, in part, to the failure of the profession to appreciate the extent to which both income determination and standard setting had become politicized.

The Committee on Accounting Procedure

Immediately after World War II, the SEC gave notice that although the authority to set standards had been delegated to CAP, it intended to exercise more direct influence on the financial reporting process. In 1944, the American Institute engaged Carman Blough as their first research director. Blough, who had been the SEC's first chief accountant, would enhance the effectiveness of these early efforts. Previously, a fledgling SEC focused on improving disclosure in its filings and paid little attention to the content of annual reports.[17] In 1946, the SEC conducted an investigation of annual reports of over the counter (OTC) companies and indicted the accounting profession for failing to curb the use of misleading accounting techniques. The AIA leadership was disturbed by the accusation. Probably correctly, they viewed the SEC's investigation as a self-serving play designed to broaden the agency's authority to include OTC companies. The AIA did not deny the allegations that some financial reports were misleading. Instead the AIA issued a rejoinder, stating that the SEC would find equally unacceptable practices used in audited annual reports of companies under the SEC's jurisdiction ("SEC Seeks Control," 1946; 93–95).

The SEC's criticisms should not have surprised accountants although they may have come as a surprise to the public. Accountants understood that the historical cost allocation model allowed management great latitude in determining income.[18] CAP had done little to promote uniformity before the war. Wartime wage/price controls and postwar inflation led to increasing criticism from corporate managers that historical cost measurement overstated profits. CAP adopted a simple solution to placate corporate critics: reserve accounting. Managers could establish reserves for contingencies, inventory, war terminations, and so forth, and thus manage reported income.[19] The SEC lost all patience when CAP issued a standard that allowed companies to set aside "reserves for future losses." Earle King (1948), the chief accountant at the SEC, called for a "definitive statement of principles" that would leave no doubt as to what constituted "accepted accounting principles." He suggested that the AIA might join with the American Accounting Association (AAA) to derive a comprehensive statement, warning that if the AIA did not act, then the SEC might turn to academics to establish accounting principles.[20] While practitioners were not ready to cede the setting of accounting standards to academics, the SEC's threat was probably hollow. Subsequent events, beginning with the replacement cost debate, demonstrated that regulators and politicians viewed accounting standard setting as too important to be left solely to accountants.

Inflation Accounting: The Political Debate

The members of CAP understood that inflation had eroded the usefulness of accounting numbers; they struggled with the issue throughout the war. CAP's refusal to abandon historical cost frustrated many, but the committee did not appear to have a choice. The SEC had sent a clear message in 1945, issuing ASR No. 53, which stated that the proper function of income was to present "an accurate historical record." [21] After the war, U.S. Steel decided to test CAP's and the SEC's resolve.

U.S. Steel interpreted a statement in ARB No. 33 that "plants that have less than normal life can properly be depreciated on a systematic basis related to economic usefulness" to justify use of replacement cost depreciation. The SEC said no and CAP concurred. But the SEC also understood that inflation eroded corporate purchasing power. It did not object to Chrysler's using accelerated depreciation, which Chrysler's financial report said approximated replacement cost. George O. May became upset.[22] He believed that George Bailey, chairman of CAP and a partner in Touche, Niven, and Bailey, Chrysler's auditors, had undermined accountants' efforts to gain acceptance for replacement cost. May (1949) concluded that Bailey had been successful because he argued that Chrysler's three-year depreciation period fell within ARB No. 33 while U.S. Steel's one-year accelerated depreciation period did not. It seems more likely Bailey's method was accepted because "invested" cost remained the basis for allocation.

The SEC's intransigence on this issue must be viewed in political context. After the war, the government held a fire sale, disposing of its surplus productive properties for as little as 2 cents on the dollar. Two-thirds of the wartime property and equipment with a cost of approximately $68 billion and a current market value of more than twice its cost was sold, primarily to the nation's 85 largest corporations. U.S. Steel had received 71 percent of the total value of all government-built integrated steel plants at fire sale prices (McQuaid 1994: 33–34). The same company had battled the Truman administration over wartime profiteering and had been embroiled in bitter wage negotiations with its workers.[23]

In addition, the FTC had just finished an investigation of the "monopoly power" of the iron and steel industry, concluding that U.S. Steel, the leader of the cartel, set prices for the industry to the detriment of consumers.[24] Since the company had received a huge capital inflow from the government at virtually no cost, it would have raised the wrath of politicians and labor negotiators had the SEC allowed U.S. Steel to reduce its reported income by using replacement cost depreciation.[25]

The SEC could accept Chrysler's accelerated depreciation because charges to income would be limited to the actual (invested) cost. The issue transcended one company as taxpayers had, in effect, donated more than $130 billion in new productive facilities to the nation's corporate sector. Corporate managers left little doubt that their ultimate goal was to gain acceptance of replacement cost accounting for tax purposes. There was little political or public support to reduce the corporate tax burden by allowing corporations to charge a hypothetical cost for taxpayer funded assets.[26]

The accounting debate about "correct" income measurement would continue for a decade, but accountants lost the support of corporate managers when Congress accepted accelerated depreciation for tax purposes in 1954. Most companies quickly reverted to straight line depreciation for financial reporting purposes. Even U.S. Steel used accelerated depreciation for financial reporting only during the Korean War period when wage/price controls were in effect. Later, the correctness of financial reporting became less of a concern and the company switched to straight line depreciation for financial reporting purposes (Reed 1989). The replacement cost debate became primarily one of academic interest after 1954 but would surface during the high inflationary period of the late 1970s.

The Conceptual Debate

William Blackie (1948), an eloquent spokesman for current cost, advocated "economic accounting" (recognition of current values) so that accountants could fulfill their major function: stewardship. The separation of ownership and control, he argued, had been completed; society had a right to demand greater accountability from management. Accountants now must provide information for social as well as economic control. Blackie (1948: 1377) believed that current value accounting would "preserve the integrity of the balance sheet while making the income statement also serve its purpose effectively." Recognition of current cost levels would not only enhance stewardship; it would also move "toward an increasingly desirable coordination of financial accounting, economics, national statistics . . . and, not least, valuation."

Most accountants listened sympathetically to arguments that historical cost income resulted in "illusory profits" and excessive taxation. Blackie's (1948) message that accountants produce data for social control was not well received. Part of the resistance to abandoning the historical cost income model may have come from the profession's desire to continue to portray accountants as objective reporters of fact.[27] Howard Greer (1948: 131) offered the profession's traditional defense, arguing that "the correct solution to this problem lies in the *education* of the public to the limitations of financial statements." He concluded that "this requires not a revision of accounting statements but a thorough exposition of their significance as stated."

Blackie (1948: 1351) remained skeptical, writing that the "unchanging continuance of present accounting practice would seem to call for a change in people," which, he argued, would be a bit more difficult for accountants to achieve than resolving their own reporting problems. But Greer's solution—educate the public—while notably unsuccessful throughout this century, has been the profession's preferred response.[28]

The Study Group on Business Income

The Study Group on Business Income was composed of economists, labor leaders, academics, and practitioners who raised important questions about the adequacy of accounting income measurement. Although the study group's work did not have an impact on the CAP, it did open the door for a floodgate of criticism of accounting income measurement procedures and ushered in what Mouck (1988) has called the "golden age" of academic normative theorizing. In a classic study prepared for the study group, Sidney Alexander, an economist, surveyed existing accounting and economic concepts of income and concluded that much of the accounting debate was useless as accountants had not reached agreement on the nature of income.[29] He outlined three basic income concepts:

- Economic income—change over the period in capitalized value of dividends of this and future periods.
- Tangible income—economic income—change in value of goodwill over the period, total change in value of tangible equity.
- Accountant's income—tangible income—change in value of tangible assets not realized in the period + change of value of tangible assets accrued in other periods and realized in this period = proceeds of all assets—costs assigned to those assets.

Alexander criticized accountants for their rigid adherence to claims of objectivity and for their conservatism. He outlined three major issues that he believed should (and did) become the focus of debate among academic theorists. He suggested that the principal differences among concepts of income were (1) real versus money measure, (2) inclusion versus exclusion of capital gains, and (3) accrual versus realization as the criterion for timing of a gain or loss. Alexander challenged accountants' traditional realization concept—point of sale—arguing that realization was dependent on a "critical" event and for a large corporation point of sale was not the critical event. More important, Alexander's study concluded that "accountants present a false and misleading picture and misleading results when they ignore" changes in the value of the dollar (1950: 93).

The study group unleashed a spate of literature critical of financial reports, and while we cannot do justice to the rich debate that ensued, the exchange between Raymond Dein and George Husband, discussed below, provides a brief glimpse of the tenor of the subsequent debate. Dein (1955) surveyed the postwar accounting literature and noted that he found it curious that accountants consistently criticized their basic product by characterizing financial reports as "incorrect and misleading" because of the failure to recognize the changing value of the dollar. Dein suggested that even Alexander, an economist, was not that critical.

Husband (1955) disagreed. He pointed out that while Alexander had agreed that accounting income could be depicted as reliable if accountants assumed a stable dollar, he also warned that "to ignore the world of uncertainties does not get rid of them." As mentioned, the debate continued but was confined mostly to academic circles after 1955.

Academic Contributions to the Inflation Debate

From 1936, the American Accounting Association (AAA) began its ongoing effort to derive a conceptual framework for financial reporting. The SEC's call for a comprehensive framework gave added impetus to the AAA's efforts in the postwar period.[30] In 1951, the Committee on Accounting Concepts and Standards issued Supplementary Statement No. 2, which called for experimentation with price level adjustments as supplementary data in financial reports. The AAA published three monographs, Jones's *Case Studies of Four Companies* (1955) and *Effects of Price Level Changes on Business Income, Capital and Taxes* (1956) and Mason's *Basic Concepts and Methods* (1956), all of which contributed to the ongoing and important debate among academics.

A. C. Littleton, who remained the champion of historical cost, would part company with his co-author of the classic 1940 AAA monograph, William Paton, on this issue. Littleton continued to defend the historical cost model, arguing that "the central purpose of accounting is to measure

the periodic matching of costs (efforts) and revenues (accomplishments)"
(1953: 30). He described the matching concept as the "benchmark" that
affords a fixed point of reference for accounting theory. Paton (1963) forcefully disagreed; he contended that the Paton and Littleton monograph had
emphasized the "cardinal importance of earning power," that is, the ratio
of income to assets. The matching model required accurate asset valuation,
but inflation made historical cost asset valuation useless, making assessment
of earning power impossible. Paton's (1972) rhetoric became increasingly
strident as he claimed that historical cost advocates were unwilling dupes
of those with socialistic predispositions. This type of rhetoric certainly
buttressed the opinions of those who perceived accounting current value
theorists as pleaders for business interests.[31]

The replacement cost debate would continue into the 1960s, as academic theorists developed more comprehensive models. Edgar Edwards
and Philip Bell's (1961) classic work provided a comprehensive economic
analysis of business income that justified use of current (replacement cost)
entry values. Raymond Chambers (1966) and Robert Sterling (1967A)
made powerful cases for use of current exit values, while Arthur Thomas
(1965) made the case for exit values by highlighting the subjectivity of the
historical cost allocation model. But as Zeff (1962) noted, the heated theoretical debate had little impact upon accounting practice. Chambers (1966)
suggested that the debate floundered not only because inflation abated, but
also because those who argued for the new paradigm were perceived as
pleaders for business interests. The tenor of some of the debate, as noted
above, certainly reinforced the latter perception. Academic theorists tried
to divorce themselves from such criticisms by calling for a more scientific
research agenda.

A "Scientific" Research Agenda

A. C. Littleton's *Structure of Accounting Theory* (1953) would become the
focal point of criticism from those accountants who adopted a deductive
(scientific) approach to accounting theory. Criticism of Littleton's work was
widespread, not only for his alleged failure to fully understand the scientific
and deductive process but also for his narrow conception of accounting's
role. Chambers contended that Littleton described the center of accounting as it then existed. The important question, he suggested, was not how
but why income is calculated. Accountants had to be concerned with "all
fields of human action" if they hoped to be able to communicate relevant information to various user groups. People needed information for
decision-making, and the accountant's job was to convey information

concerning both income and financial condition. Chambers (1957: 206) noted that if other "practical" disciplines, such as medicine, used a "series of methods known as scientific methods," then accounting also should be able to develop a general theory applicable to all entities, not *an* accounting theory, applicable only to a particular set of circumstances.

Littleton (1958) would continue to fight a rearguard action to develop accounting theory from observing practice, but he lost the immediate battle. Decision usefulness became a clarion call as the deductive approach gained widespread acceptance. In Littleton's view, the *Accounting Review* had become an outlet for controversial material (April 1958). Mattessich (1956), Yu (1957), McCredie (1957), and Chambers (1957) introduced general theories without regard to existing practice. This body of research clearly increased the rigor of the academic theoretical debate, but it also enabled researchers to ignore the more disquieting questions that could have been asked about the relevance of the raw data of accounting (market prices) in an administrative economy.[32]

Carl Devine (1960), who supported the adoption of scientific methods, issued a pragmatic caution. He warned that "scientific method alone cannot solve all the problems of society" and suggested that the "most urgent field for accounting research may not be related to problems concerned with efficient measurement of transaction flows unless efficiency is itself defined in terms of the accomplishment of socially worthy objectives" (399). His caution went unheeded. The claim to scientific status not only had great appeal to academics but also suggested a possible solution to practitioners' standard-setting dilemma. Robert Mautz (1978) recalled that the sudden surge of research led the profession to hope that accounting standard setting would be less contentious if placed on a firm theoretical foundation.

The Development of a New Standard-Setting Process

Criticisms of the CAP's "brush fire" approach accelerated throughout the early 1950s. Much of the criticism came from accounting academics, who argued that the accounting standard-setting process would be inadequate as long as the profession continued to focus on existing practice.[33] The replacement cost debate escalated criticisms. A flurry of articles appeared in the popular press, chastising accountants for issuing "misleading" financial reports. Practitioners could and did ignore academic criticisms, but when a leading practitioner, Leonard Spacek, joined the attack on CAP and financial reporting, practitioners took notice. Spacek (1956) termed CAP pronouncements as "generally accepted and antiquated accounting principles." Headlines that read "Accounting Has Failed to Prevent Major Misrepresentations" did not endear him to the profession. He dismayed many reputable practitioners when he asserted that if CPAs had bothered to follow the objective standards that already existed, 95 percent of the abuses would not have occurred (Spacek: 1958B). In an era when advertising was prohibited, many of his fellow practitioners felt that Spacek's criticisms stemmed from his desire to promote his firm. While many questioned his motives, his voice could not be ignored.[34]

Marquis Eaton, president of the institute in 1956, established a committee on long-range objectives for the profession to counter external criticisms. Louis Penney compared the pressures to "those in '33 and '34," concluding that "if these pressures reach the explosive stage as they did in 1933 and 1934, we CPAs may not have the opportunity the next time to continue" to control our destiny (1960: 2, 3). It was left to Alvin Jennings, who succeeded Eaton, to outline the new plan. Jennings, who has been described as one of the few CPAs who could bridge the gap between academicians and practitioners, seemed ideally suited for that task (Schur 1976).

At the 1957 annual meeting of the institute, Jennings explained that CAP provided little, if any, opportunity for sound experimentation. Accounting principles, he said, should be regarded as arising from pure research. He suggested establishing a formal research organization within the institute that would seek the active cooperation of the academic community (Jennings 1957). The function of this research body would be to conduct a continuous examination and reexamination of accounting assumptions in order to develop authoritative principles. After some delay, Jennings's proposal was accepted and formed the basis for the organization of the Accounting Principles Board (APB), which came into existence in the fall of 1959.[35] The by-laws of the APB endorsed the idea that research studies precede official pronouncements, whenever possible, to provide guidance to the board. But these studies, although informative, were to be considered "tentative only," and the board was to issue "a clear statement" with each study indicating whether "it has been approved or disapproved by the Institute" (AICPA 1959: 20). The conditional endorsement of normative research foreshadowed the strong resistance that would occur whenever a research study deviated from existing practice.

The Accounting Principles Board

George O. May (1957A) was somewhat skeptical about the call for reform. He said that forty years in the profession convinced him that every proposal for material change met with one of two objections: "Either, the proposal is inadequate and nothing should be done in the matter until the subject is dealt with comprehensively (e.g., ARB No. 33) or that the proposal is too sweeping so that the subject should be dealt with piece by piece" (36). May's reservations proved to be well founded. Jennings, while urging normative research, qualified his endorsement by noting that practicality was a vital element of "good" accounting theory (1958A). He issued what could be deemed a pragmatic restatement of the relationship between theory and practice, writing that "where science looks within the fact to discover the principle, accounting looks, or should look, to the desired end result" (34).

Weldon Powell, the first chairman of the APB, clearly rejected the notion that accounting principles could or should be regarded as a matter of "pure" research. He emphasized that "research in accounting is more in the nature of applied research than of pure research, an important criterion [being] the usefulness of its results" (Powell 1961: 29). Since the APB had placed great emphasis on examining four levels of broad problems of financial accounting (postulates, principles, rules, or other guides for applying principles in specific situations and research), Powell's suggestion that the first step in any research program should be a study of prevailing practice seemed inconsistent. The reaction to Accounting Research Studies (ARS) No. 1 and No. 3 showed that deviations from existing practices would not be acceptable to most APB members and practicing members of the community.

Postulates and Principles

In 1958 an Institute Special Committee on Research recommended that early research be directed toward identifying postulates and principles of accounting given: "Postulates are few in number and are the basic assumptions on which principles rest." The committee recommended that "a fairly broad set of coordinated principles should be formulated on the basis of the postulates." The report concluded that "the principles, together with the postulates, should serve as a framework of reference for the solution of detailed problems" (AICPA, "Special Committee on Research" 1958: 62). Maurice Moonitz agreed to undertake a study of accounting postulates and then joined with Robert Sprouse to define accounting principles. Accounting Research Study No. 1, *The Basic Postulates of Accounting* (1961), met with a very subdued response.[36] An editorial in the *Journal of Accountancy* noted that "few accountants should find any difficulty in agreeing with these and other postulates; . . . most are self-evident" (September 1961: 36). It was precisely this point that led William Vatter to question whether the study served any useful purpose. He argued that most of the so-called postulates were not basic assumptions of accounting but, rather, "general descriptions, rationalization of double entry, and/or statements of existing conditions" (Vatter 1963: 183). But since postulates did not directly have an impact on income measurement, most accountants appeared to be reserving judgment until the principles study was completed.

ARS No. 3, *Tentative Set of Broad Accounting Principles for Business Enterprises* (1962), probably signaled the demise of any attempts to adopt a normative research orientation for the APB. The board issued the following statement with respect to the research studies on principles and postulates. "We are treating these two studies as conscientious attempts by the accounting research staff to resolve major accounting issues, which, however, contain inferences and recommendations in part of a speculative and tentative nature. . . . [W]hile these studies are a valuable contribution to accounting thinking, they are too radically different from presently generally accepted accounting principles for acceptance at this time."[37] Members of the APB were widely divided on the advisability of releasing the study. Nine comments by board members were attached to the monograph, only one being completely favorable. The dissents covered a broad range of views, from Leonard Spacek's assertion that there need only be one concern for accountants: "fairness," to Paul Grady's contention that one must begin the search for principles by summarizing generally accepted accounting practices.

William Shenkir's (1974: 10) analysis of ARS No. 3 concludes that "the study's focus on the measurement of assets and liabilities shattered tradition and differed from the cost and revenue allocation model that the APB had inherited from CAP." Raymond Marple (1963: 479) deplored the willingness of the authors to abandon historic limitations on concepts of profits, that is, profits "available for dividends" and "subject to taxation." He predicted that if practitioners failed to address themselves to such specific needs, two events would occur. First, management would be convinced that accounting data were useless; and second, financial analysts would simply begin focusing on cash flow rather than accounting profit. Marple suggested a very narrow role for the accountant: "If accounting is to serve the business and financial community—and it has *no other use*—its practitioners must never forget that the only test of good practice is its usefulness in developing information for the purpose for which the information is to be used." But the greatest antagonism was generated by the suggestion that historical cost was not the bedrock of accounting measurement.[38]

John Queenan (1962: 31), president of the AICPA, hoped that his fellow practitioners would offer "constructive criticism" of the research studies.

John W. Queenan

Alvin R. Jennings and Carman Blough
Source: AICPA, New York.

But his pleas seemed to go unheeded as most of the dissent could not be labeled "constructive." Jennings (1964: 31–32) indicated that the lack of enthusiasm for these studies "was largely responsible for a definite, if subtle shift, in the direction of the Board's efforts." The APB decided to take a less "risky" approach and place "greater stress on solutions of particular problems." Paul Grady was commissioned to do an inventory, identifying principles that appeared to have achieved general acceptance. Grady's (1965) study, although comprehensive, was not unlike the Sanders, Hatfield, and Moore work that had surveyed practice in the 1930s.[39] Despite the AIA's initial optimism that normative research might resolve the more contentious disagreements among standard setters, practice once again became the focal point for standard setters.

After disclaiming the two research studies, the APB faced the daunting task of gaining consensus to limit alternative accounting procedures in the absence of a consensus as to what constituted the "best" or even preferable practices. The board had limited authority and could not force compliance with its pronouncements (Powell 1961). The APB assumed that the SEC, which had indicated over a long number of years that it sought to reduce the alternatives in accounting practice, would support all of the board's efforts to limit alternatives. The threat that the SEC might take over the standard-setting process if accountants could not reach consensus gave the board its only real leverage. The SEC's actions with respect to the investment tax credit undermined even that limited authority and effectively signaled the demise of the APB at its outset.

Investment Tax Credit

The investment tax credit was a politically conceived economic incentive designed by President Kennedy's administration to stimulate capital investment. The APB, forced to respond quickly, could not gain consensus among its members on the proper treatment of the credit. The board acted, perhaps precipitously, employing a "matching" rationale that prohibited the "flow through" method. This action diluted the immediate economic (and political) benefit of the credit. Many corporate managers expressed their displeasure at not being allowed to show the immediate impact of the credit in income. They took their complaints to their audit firms and to the halls of Congress. Since the motivation for passage of the tax credit was to improve the economic outlook, policy leaders in Washington were sympathetic to the complaints. When three of the Big Eight firms announced they would not follow APB No. 2, the SEC became involved in the controversy.[40] Commissioner Manuel Cohen explained that the SEC, consistent with its administrative policy, found substantial authoritative support for using alternative treatments to the board's preference for the "deferred" method. Thus, the SEC decided it would not bind registrants to APB No. 2 (Cohen 1964).

The political sector had delivered a strong message; accountants' theoretical and/or technical preferences would not be allowed to undermine political objectives. Nor would the SEC respond favorably to efforts that "unduly" constrained management. Accountants must have been surprised to read SEC Commissioner Bryon D. Woodside's statement that "I believe . . . it is better to have some looseness—the creaking of a joint, if you will—some sacrifice of the ultimate in consistency and uniformity and acceptability under such a system than to seek a rule." He admonished the APB that the "task you set for yourselves to force conformity on matters of accounting principle where there is not in fact acceptability of conformity, I think, is an impossible one." Woodside made it clear that the APB must rely on education and persuasion, not on the SEC. "Those who wish to compel conformity, or rather seek to have us compel conformity, for only we have the tools," he wrote, "are no doubt less than happy with the approach" (Woodside 1964: 67–68).

In retrospect, even those associated with the SEC would acknowledge that the strength of the APB had been undermined by the SEC's actions. John C. Burton (1974) characterized the association of the SEC and the

AICPA as a "partnership" designed to provide federal support for accounting principles established by the profession. Accountants were not so sanguine; as one practitioner stated, "There are *partners* and there are *Partners.*" Burton considered the investment credit episode as a conspicuous exception to the rule. He explained that the SEC "concluded that it would not support an opinion when representatives of leading accounting firms had not only voted against it but said that they would not require their clients to abide by it."

Burton argued that the "commission was not enforcing a view contrary to the Board but rather refusing to enter a dispute among major firms on the side which the Board favored. In retrospect," Burton concluded, "it is the judgment of most parties involved that the Commission made an error in declining to support the Board," adding, "it is certainly clear that neither the profession nor the Board benefited from the episode which ultimately culminated ten years later in an act of Congress which enshrined the diverse practices which had been used" (Burton 1974: 269). While legislation mandating flexibility in accounting standards was unique to the tax credit, this episode made it more difficult for the APB to respond satisfactorily to subsequent controversial issues.

Subsequently, the AICPA attempted to strengthen the rules of professional conduct to enforce compliance with APB opinions. In 1965, a resolution was passed making it a "requirement to disclose deviations from generally accepted accounting principles in an auditor's certificate." But the AICPA had no effective sanctions to impose upon any accountant who failed to disclose departures from the generally accepted accounting principles (GAAP).[41] The AICPA's actions were too little and too late. The APB would continue, but the failure of the board to curb perceived abusive reporting practices in the merger wave of the late 1960s would once again lead to denunciation of financial reports in the popular press and then to a review that could create a new standard-setting process.

Subjugation of Shareholders

Adolf Berle and Gardiner Means's (1932) classic study that documented separation of ownership and control initiated a provocative debate about the role of stockholders in a corporate economy. In the 1950s, numerous economists suggested that significant changes in the economic structure and changing corporate relationships had rendered traditional accounting profit irrelevant. Edith Penrose (1959) argued that managers viewed stockholders as "quasi creditors," who must be paid enough to keep silent and content. The aim was to control corporate assets without interference. She concluded that hired managers did not care any more about stockholders than they did about creditors or any other supplier of funds, a thesis not new to accounting, having been developed by Paton in his *Accounting Theory* (1922) and further refined in Paton and Littleton's (1940) monograph. Organizational theorists, like Peter Drucker (1948), echoed this message. Oswald Knauth (1957) concisely outlined the interaction between various group interests and management in the new "quasi-permanent" public corporations.

Paton and Littleton's (1940) entity theory, which attempted to reconcile neoclassical economic theory with separation of ownership and control, foreshadowed a rich but short debate that occurred in the accounting literature during this period. Paton and Littleton's entity theory assumed that managers sought to "balance the interests of all parties"; therefore, managers should be assessed on entity income, not on income to stockholders. While the matching model they outlined gained widespread acceptance, the entity aspect of that model—namely that dividends, interest, and taxes must all have the same relationship (either distributions of income or expenses)—never gained widespread acceptance.[42] William Vatter's (1947) fund theory also represented a major departure from the traditional stockholder orientation and was similarly ignored. Not only did Vatter challenge the idea that corporate management sought to maximize stockholders' wealth; he also questioned the relevance of market prices and suggested that a different income number could and should be calculated for each user group.[43] George Husband (1954) used an agency framework to develop a residual equity theory that justified continued focus on calculation of income to stockholders. But he did so by raising the disquieting suggestion that accountants admit that accounting income was simply what accountants decided to measure.[44] Accountants, he suggested, should simply state that they provide "a measure of realized or extractable [or approximately extractable] income" to stockholders (Husband 1955: 393).

Waino Suojanen's (1954) "enterprise theory" sought to reflect corporate relationships more realistically by measuring the distributions (value added) made to *all* corporate constituencies. The idea that corporate management should be assessed by measuring value added did not win favor.[45] Nor did Louis Goldberg's (1965) "commander theory," which more realistically depicted corporate management's position. This interesting and provocative body of literature, which challenged the stockholder orientation, was phased out in the late 1960s as a new body of empirical research that assumed away any orientation problem became dominant in the academic community.

It should be noted that while accounting theorists were willing to examine what Zeff (1962) termed the orientation postulate, only Vatter (1947) earlier had questioned the relevance of market prices. If corporations could administer prices, as a series of FTC and congressional investigations concluded, then accounting profit, based on market transactions, could not be assumed to measure corporate efficiency or effectiveness. Galbraith (1956) contended that in an age of "managed demand and engineered consent," accounting profit merely reflected the power of corporate management. Even in the fervor of the late 1960s, most accountants did not raise this issue.

Corporate Social Responsibility

Although accountants have attempted to respond positively to government demands for disclosure for investor protection, they have been reluctant to extend their activities to become societal watchdogs. In the early 1940s, accountants contended that "if the social aspects of accounting had not been recognized in the past, the fault, in a measure, at least, lay in the fact that accountants did not occupy a sufficiently independent position" (Dohr 1941). But after World War II, when accountants could have pressed to extend their responsibilities, they did not. Most accountants viewed their role as enhancing social welfare by facilitating the accumulation of capital within a manufacturing-oriented society, the traditional neoclassical economic view. Accountants dealt with the supply side of the economic equation. If one assumes market competition ensures an equitable distribution of income, then all corporations can be viewed as price takers. But not all corporations produce goods or services at the same cost. The accountant's role is to determine the most efficient, lowest cost producer, so as to facilitate allocation of capital.

This accounting framework left social measurement to economists. This is not an indictment of the practitioners; there is little to suggest that politicians or the public expected more. The Temporary National Economic Committee turned to economists, not accountants, to stimulate interest in social statistics. Accountants, viewing their work as practical, considered the notions in the committee's Monograph No. 7 ("Measurement of Social Performance of Business") with disbelief. Social analysis of corporate performance was not considered to be within the traditional scope of the profession's responsibilities, and it seemed that many practitioners hoped that this would continue to be the case. These social demands attracted the attention of some accounting academics during the decade of the 1960s.

Social Accounting and Social Audits

The question of whether or not CPAs should be making implicit value judgments or simply reporting economic events for use by others in society continued to receive attention (Hylton 1962). There was increasing recognition among accounting academics and some practitioners that accounting could not be divorced from broad social considerations. Carl Devine (1960) suggested that while accountants could not be expected to alter the ethical standards of society significantly, the profession must consider its social responsibilities and develop a practical structure to help fulfill social goals.

Accountants could not totally ignore the phenomenon of consumerism, which led many corporate managers to acknowledge that they had an obligation to operate their corporations in a socially responsible manner. David Linowes (1968), Ralph Estes (1970), and Sybil Mobley (1970) were among the earliest accountants to recognize the importance of social accounting and their pioneering work captured the attention of academics and practitioners. While the concept of "corporate social responsibility" never was widely accepted, practitioners did begin to acknowledge that when specific standards existed (e.g., war on poverty, city planning, environmental reporting) to implement specific social goals, the profession had an obligation to respond.[46] In 1972, the AICPA's response to calls for social performance measures was the monograph *Corporate Social Measurement,* which proposed a type of social audit.

However, while many accountants supported social accounting and social audits in theory, efforts to make operational social measurements met significant resistance. Critics claimed that advocates of social accounting and auditing presented vague proposals with little thought to implementation. David Linowes (1973) sought to counter those critics, specifying measurement procedures and mechanisms to conduct a social audit. The invited responses to his article reflect the resistance to implementation. John C. Burton, then SEC chief accountant, who one year earlier had urged the profession to add a new dimension to practice that might be called "social needs" practice, suggested that Linowes's proposal was both theoretically and practically deficient (1973A: 43). He argued that the inherent subjectivity of social data made it unauditable and that traditional matching of "bad things [costs] with good things [revenue]" was inappropriate when social costs and benefits did not accrue to the corporation. This brief interlude, where private property rights were no longer deemed sacrosanct, ended abruptly with the 1970s oil embargo; economic concerns once

again became paramount and interest in social accounting and social audits waned.

Human Resource Accounting

Galbraith (1956) and Penrose (1959) pointed out that in an oligopolistic
economy, characterized by rapid technological change, knowledge (human
resources) became a key determinant of corporate success. By the late sixties, concerns about the adequacy of conventional accounting systems to
reflect the resources employed by corporations or to hold managers ac-
countable for development of their workforces led to a brief period of interest among accounting academics in human resource accounting.

Lee Brummett, Eric Flamholtz, and William Pyle (1968) outlined the arguments for human resource accounting, noting that measurement would
be a significant problem. One company, R. G. Barry, responded to the challenge to place people on their balance sheet by capitalizing training costs
for its employees.[47] While human resource accountants acknowledged that
capitalization of training costs, as R. G. Barry had done, was inadequate to
measure the "value" of employees, it was still seen as a step in the right
direction (Brummett 1970). The popular press often did not take such a
positive view. When the R. G. Barry financial statements appeared, an editorial in the Louisville *Courier Journal* lambasted accountants: there go the
accountants again, trying to reduce people to numbers and dehumanize
the workplace. But it was not public misunderstanding, but rather the issue
of how to measure human resource "value" that signaled the demise of
human resource accounting. Two decades later, Elliott (1994) would reas-
sert the need for accounting to incorporate human resources into corporate performance measurement; knowledge workers had become critical to
corporate success.

Reaffirmation of Stockholders' Rights

While entity, fund, enterprise, and commander theories had attempted
to depict corporate relationships more realistically and social and human
resource accounting sought to extend the boundaries of financial accounting, there remained strong resistance to depiction of the corporation as a
social entity, and none of the above efforts had a lasting impact on the discipline. By 1973, empirical research would render questions about corporate relationships moot; in the early 1960s, a shift to decision usefulness
served to silence the exchanges about attribute measurement.

The resistance to abandoning the private property rights paradigm is clearly highlighted in the debate among the members of the AAA's 1957 Committee on Concepts and Standards Underlying Financial Reporting. The report acknowledged that significant changes had occurred in the nation's economic structure, but the committee made it clear that they did not believe that this called into question the underlying tenets of the private property rights paradigm. The report concluded that the "corporation is the dominant medium for pooling and utilizing economic resources contributed by investors." The AAA committee split over what constituted corporate income and compromised by adopting two definitions of income—enterprise net income and net income to shareholders—based on the proprietary or residual equity view. The compromise satisfied few, but by recognizing that two income numbers could be relevant, the AAA committee avoided reexamination of the orientation of financial statements.

The Relevance Debate

George Sorter and Charles Horngren (1962) challenged conventional theory and suggested that "relevance" should be the primary determinant of whether or not an asset existed. They argued that Paton and Littleton's dictum that "costs attach" had been widely misinterpreted and that their subsequent statement that "accounting is concerned with economic attributes and [concern over] measurements" had been largely overlooked. They wrote that if one is concerned primarily with economic attributes, then the asset-expense measurement problem becomes dependent on two factors: future expectations and relevance. The authors concluded that, if this were so, then only one rule was necessary for asset determination; namely, that "a cost is carried forward, if, and only if, it has a favorable economic effect on total future costs or total future revenues" (Sorter and Horngren 1962: 392–93). This idea did not go unchallenged, but it did foreshadow the direction that the next definitive works, the AAA's *Statement of Basic Accounting Theory (ASOBAT)* (1966), and the AICPA's *Objectives of Financial Statements* (1973) would take.

A Statement of Basic Accounting Theory

ASOBAT marked the culmination of more than a decade of normative research, designed to develop accounting theory without regard to existing practice. The document defined four basic standards (relevance, verifiability, freedom from bias, and quantifiability) for evaluating accounting information. The statement contained several significant departures from prior AAA statements. First, it adopted a user orientation. Instead of defining accounting in terms of what accountants did, *ASOBAT* suggested that accounting should be defined in terms of the information needs of users (AAA 1966: v). *ASOBAT* also reflected the influence of the debate over attribute measurement that occurred in the postwar period. The statement suggested that financial reports might contain multiple valuations, mirroring earlier recommendations.

The argument that accounting theory must be "useful" had been the subject of debate for many years. Critics, like Hylton (1962), claimed that substituting the accountant's judgment for that of users was not a satisfactory solution. Accountants had not resolved the issue of what users' needs were or how to meet the needs of users with conflicting interests. Robert Sterling (1967: 98), while applauding the AAA's efforts to divorce theory from existing practice, found the AAA statement wanting precisely because it did not specify what information accountants "ought" to provide nor did it divorce itself completely from the cost allocation "matching" model. He warned that it would take a "master weaver to weave accounting as a matching and attaching model" together with "accounting as a measurement and communication system" and expressed doubt as to whether such a weaver could be found.

Sterling's reservations seemed to be well founded, and *ASOBAT*'s focus on multiple measurements was not well received by the practice community. A new body of empirical research would render the questions raised in *ASOBAT* unimportant by assuming the primacy of stockholder interests.

The emergence of a rigorous and rich body of capital markets research in the late 1960s created a profound shift in the type of questions that academic researchers addressed. Ball and Brown's (1968) influential study shifted attention from attribute measurement to the impact of accounting information on stock market prices. Subsequent studies, based on the efficient market hypothesis (EMH), not only laid to rest questions about whom accounting information should be directed toward but also suggested that accountants need not be overconcerned with income determination, since investors, on average, could not be fooled by accounting data.[48] This research not only increased the prestige of accounting academics within the academic community but also rendered most financial reporting problems trivial. Beaver (1973) offered six prescriptions to the newly established Financial Accounting Standards Board that, if the board had been free to follow, would have greatly simplified the task of standard setting.[49] From a historical perspective, the most intriguing prescription was that accounting standard setters need not be concerned with limiting accounting alternatives; management was free to choose any acceptable method as long as the method was disclosed. While standard setters may have welcomed that message, it seems to have been perilous advice.

Managerial Accounting: Revolution or Suppression?

Carl Devine (1964) noted that the war effort during World War II had a significant impact on the tools used to make decisions in corporate America. The war had required quick solutions to problems, so problems had to be structured in terms of choices. The focus on decision-making, combined with the use of simulation models, computer technology, and analytic models, would have a noticeable impact on the subsequent development of cost accounting. After the war, academic accountants developed quantitative models to facilitate decision-making and began to question the relevance of the traditional cost allocation procedures.[50] Since quality was of utmost importance in wartime production, the standard practice of tolerating some defects in order to maximize production was not acceptable.[51] Walter Shewhart, a statistician, developed the concept of a Statistical Quality Control Circle to maximize the quality of all wartime products and to prevent defects before they occurred.

W. Edwards Deming, who worked under Shewhart during the war, brought that message to corporate America.[52] In the new era quality would be of primary concern; thus, Deming suggested that corporations should spend money to train workers rather than focus on minimization of labor costs.[53] Increasing productivity by reducing labor costs, a focal point of scientific management, would not increase a firm's organizational capability. Deming recalled that when he brought this message—improve quality by spending money to train all workers—to American managers, he received a frigid reception. The idea was alien to American corporate culture. The reception may have been due, in part, to the fact that American managers faced little competition in the immediate postwar period, lessening concerns with the need for constant innovation. Or the reaction could have been due to the American propensity for viewing expertise as an intellectual property right to be jealously guarded and not shared with the workers. Deming pointed out that American managers did not ignore quality; rather than make quality the concern of everyone, they relied on "experts" whom they segregated in quality control divisions. Functional separation of expertise also was consistent with scientific management techniques that continued to be dominant in the United States.

The Direct Cost Debate

In 1936, Jonathan Harris published in an *NACA Bulletin* what appears to be the first technical paper on direct costing; the method quickly grew in popularity. Direct costing was not controversial until cost accountants suggested that it might be relevant for financial reporting.[54] Dixon (1940) and other cost accountants had suggested that "contribution margin income statements" would be more useful than absorption costing for both internal and external users.[55] After the war, the battle was joined. David Green accurately summarized the intensity of feelings when he concluded that the decade of the fifties might ultimately become known as the "Ten Years War on Direct Costing" (1960: 218).

Given the increased sophistication of cost systems and the advance in computer technology, many corporations kept two sets of books. Thus, it may be difficult for contemporary readers to understand why direct costers felt it necessary to sell direct costing for both financial, as well as managerial, accounting. Some companies simply did not want to keep two sets of books, but, more important, new governmental regulations, beginning with the New Deal and in place for subsequent government contracts, created pressure for all companies to reconcile financial and managerial accounting. Post–World War II inflation, combined with a permanent change in income tax structure and pressure by labor unions for increased wages, made direct costing very appealing to most managers.[56]

Academic advocates of direct cost cited "objectivity" as its primary theoretical advantage, but they also noted it had practical advantages for corporate management. If accepted for external financial reports, it could help companies avoid the price/cost squeeze by reducing reported income. Not only would this mitigate pressure for wage increases, the government might accept the reported income for tax purposes. In 1957, Vatter and Henry Hill, strong supporters of direct costing, dissented from the 1957 revision of the AAA statement on financial reporting standards because they believed that "direct costing is at least as acceptable in accounting theory as is the full cost concept" (AAA 1957: 545).

But as with replacement cost, strong political deterrents existed that prevented the SEC or accounting standard-setting bodies from accepting direct costing. Labor perceived that its negotiating position would be adversely affected as would governmental revenues. Acceptance of direct costing also would have an adverse impact on the government with respect to cost-plus defense contracts and collection of the excess profits tax. In addition, direct costing could undermine the wage/price controls as used effectively during the Korean War. Direct costing proponents had strong theoretical arguments against allocation of costs, but other considerations precluded acceptance of the method for financial reporting that had been the heart of the heated debate.[57]

Data for Motivation and Control

In the early 1950s, various American Accounting Association committees responded to demands for greater uniformity in cost accounting by trying to develop "principles" of cost accounting. These early committees defined cost concepts and also examined the possibility of using cost accounting concepts, such as standard costs, in financial reports (Benninger 1950). By 1953, the AAA committee's emphasis changed to identification of data useful to decision-makers and "managerial" replaced "cost" in the name of AAA committees. The change in name was more than cosmetic; it reflected the impact of a growing body of work in organizational theory and economics. Herbert Simon's (1947) classic book increased awareness of management's need for more sophisticated accounting data to fulfill its administrative function of allocation of economic resources within the firm, while Chris Argyris's (1953) work spawned a spate of articles that directed accountants' attention to the impact of budgets on behavior and performance.

Andrew Stedry's *Budget Control and Cost Behavior* (1960) would usher in a decade of research on motivation and control, while David Solomons's (1965) book on divisional performance measurement would provide new guidelines for allocation of capital within the firm as would the spate of literature related to capital budgeting.[58] While all of this work increased the sophistication of cost accounting, it should be noted that the focus remained on techniques that would reward managers who maximized production by minimization of labor costs. The central theme was to motivate workers to work harder.[59]

Myron Gordon (1963) suggested that accountants switch their emphasis from product costing to the activities over which a person has control. He had two basic objectives: minimization of cost and better evaluation of subordinates' performances. William Ferrara (1963) and R. Golembiewski (1964) examined the concepts of responsibility accounting as a more equitable mechanism for assessing managerial performance. By the late 1960s, managerial accounting had assumed a clear and separate identity from financial accounting. By the early seventies, American cost accountants had won a world reputation as having a dynamic and aggressive approach to the subject. The Organization for European Economic Cooperation looked to the United States to attempt to improve cost-accounting methodology and for methods of reducing operating costs.

Given this apparent success, American managers were as unwilling to listen to a dissenting voice as they had been to listen to Deming's (1986) warnings after World War II. Thus, when George Staubus's (1971) book, *Activity Costing and Input-Output Accounting,* noted that cost accounting had lost its relevance, it received little attention. Staubus challenged a number of "myths" such as "matching" and the variable/fixed costs dichotomy, suggesting that cost accountants provide data that focused managers' attention on activities, such as acquiring assets or holding assets. While Staubus's book foreshadowed Johnson and Kaplan's (1987) influential book, his message simply appeared to be too early. Success bred complacency and managerial accounting textbooks continued to reflect the basic message that cost accountants should continue to focus on providing data that allowed managers to improve productivity by reducing costs. Until 1973, the only serious challenge to continued reliance on traditional cost allocation methods came from the governmental sector.

The Cost Accounting Standards Board

During World War II, government regulations created a new cost category (allowable/nonallowable) costs (Peloubet 1943). Those regulations remained in effect, and cost accountants had to "prove" costs for government contracts. Throughout the next two decades, defense spending spiraled and cost accountants continued to refine their techniques. Despite sporadic criticism of cost overruns and profiteering, the cold war diverted criticisms. The war in Vietnam dramatically changed public opinion. As had been the case in World War II, any suggestion that corporations might be engaged in "profiteering" while young people died, ignited the media and the public. Although periodic calls for uniform cost-accounting procedures had occurred throughout the period, it was not until Admiral Rickover, testifying before Congress in 1968, championed standardization that accountants faced the real possibility of loss of autonomy over cost-accounting standards. Rickover, a popular and charismatic person, suggested that the Defense Department was being ripped off by defense contractors and that the losses amounted to more than $2 billion per year. He argued that the lack of uniform and/or consistent accounting methods, combined with the subjectivity of allocating costs, had facilitated cost overruns and profiteering. His recommendation: the government take control of the process by establishing uniform cost standards that would prevent corporate abuses.[60]

The political sector, responsive to public cynicism about the "military industrial complex," joined in the chorus for active governmental oversight. Cost accountants countered that governmental personnel seemed to have developed an aversion to any profit (Heuser 1969: 2). Despite accountants' protests, Congress responded by ordering the General Accounting Office (GAO) to conduct a feasibility study on applying uniform cost-accounting standards to negotiated defense contracts (Rayburn 1991). The GAO study concluded that uniform standards were feasible, and congressional hearings began.

Accountants responded as they had to demands for uniformity in financial accounting; they agreed that standards should be set but suggested that the work must be preceded by development of a conceptual framework for managerial accounting. In the words of I. Wayne Keller (1970), testifying for the NAA, the government must go slowly, starting with careful research on cost concepts, then issuance of a tentative statement of those concepts followed by a tentative statement (like a discussion memorandum) on proposed standards, with standards to be issued when consensus had been reached.

The nation was not in the mood to move slowly; the hearings resulted in the establishment of the Cost Accounting Standards Board (CASB), under the chairmanship of Comptroller General Elmer Staats. Congress authorized the CASB to set standards for defense contracts. The CASB gradually and successfully began to expand its authority to include other governmental agencies. By 1973, the CASB added to the proliferation of official pronouncements that threatened to overwhelm accountants. The CASB reflected the preferred political solution, uniformity, which had been periodically resurrected whenever accountants appeared to be unable or unwilling to constrain perceived corporate abuses. The reaction of managerial accountants to the CASB was predictable; they did not appreciate the government intrusion.

Johnson and Kaplan (1987) examined this period and concluded that cost accounting had ceased to be relevant for cost management; they attribute that loss of relevance, at least in part, to academic accountants and to the dominance of inventory valuation for financial reporting. While corporate management may have briefly appreciated the message that this success had been limited because they had not received appropriate cost data, that answer was too convenient, or too simple.[61] There were other factors (e.g., desire to reconcile managerial and stockholder interests, which led to use of incentives, such as bonuses and stock options) that may have created pressure to increase short-term profitability.[62] Taken together these factors may have made managers less willing to listen to Deming's message to increase investment in the workforce to ensure the quality of the product. Perhaps it might be more reasonable to say that cost accountants mirrored other groups within the profession; they focused on developing rigorous quantitative models and used psychological theories to develop more sophisticated techniques to motivate employees and evaluate performance, but they did not examine the broader implications that the new economic structure might have had for the discipline.

Taxation: The New Growth Area

The war had a profound impact on federal tax policy. Unlike previous war periods, when the wartime income taxes would be rolled back, no rollback occurred after World War II.[63] The income tax became the primary federal revenue source, enabling the federal government to become an active participant in the private sector. Tax policy also became one of the primary mechanisms for managing and stimulating the economy; tax laws reflected interest group bargaining and became increasingly complex throughout the period. Witte (1985) describes the period as one of going from elite to mass taxation as the government assumed responsibility for new social welfare programs and for funding a massive defense program. The number of individuals subject to federal income tax expanded dramatically. Before the war, fewer than 5 million people filed tax returns; by 1973, more than 70 million returns were filed. In 1996, a June 12 *Wall Street Journal* "Tax Report" column would disclose that total individual returns filed for 1994 were 116.1 million. The tremendous growth in returns filed, combined with the increased complexity of the tax laws, resulted in a significant increase in demand for tax accountants throughout this period.

The war also introduced an excess profits tax, based on a rate of return on invested capital, which created challenges for both financial and tax accountants. With surtax rates of 82 percent and a total marginal rate of 93 percent, tax planning received significant attention from corporate management. After the war, President Truman vetoed several efforts to roll back taxes, citing the need to control inflation and the promise Roosevelt had made to expand social programs after the war as the reasons for his vetoes (Truman 1956). The latter argument became less persuasive as the federal surplus grew, as in 1948 when it was $6.8 billion. Congress overrode Truman's veto, and marginal rates decreased, but the rates were still 4 to 6 times higher than prewar rates. The excess profits tax of 1950, justified by the escalation of the cold war and the Korean War, once again stimulated demand for tax practitioners (Witte 1985).

The codification of the Internal Revenue Regulations in 1954 reflected interest group pluralism at its best; Congress handed out benefits to a wide group of people. Accountants who testified before the House Ways and Means committee before the codification were ardent advocates for reduction of corporate taxes.[64] Paton (1953) gave Congress a tongue-lashing for confiscating corporate capital and suggested that socialism was just around the corner. Congress muted business critics by granting a broad spectrum of benefits to corporate America, allowing accelerated depreciation, extending depletion allowances, and extending net operating loss provisions.

In the 1960s, the government used tax policy to stimulate the economy or to promote certain social objectives. Witte describes the Revenue Act of 1962 as a resurrection of Mellon's (trickle down) tax policy; the act included an investment tax credit (ITC), which, as discussed earlier, mortally wounded the APB (1985: 164).[65] The 1964 tax code revision contained even more economic stimuli, further increasing the complexity of the tax code and providing more work for accountants. Most accountants, including AICPA's representatives, who testified at all major tax hearings argued for simplicity in the tax law, but since they also supported all corporate tax benefits, such as capital gains exclusions, foreign tax credits, and so forth, the pleas for simplicity lacked consistency.[66]

In 1968, tax policy changed dramatically; the focus shifted from offering economic incentives to business to using the tax law to promote social objectives. The Tax Reform Act of 1968 created incentives, such as generous amortization of pollution equipment, to encourage corporations to act in a socially responsible manner. This type of incentive was not well received by accountants. While legislators were responding to popular demand for social reform and greater corporate accountability, accountants warned Congress about the detrimental impact such incentives would have on corporate stockholders.[67]

In the late sixties, the IRS created a bonanza for tax preparers and a nightmare for reputable accountants when Form 1040A was discontinued. The IRS estimated that in 1969, 70 percent of all taxpayers filing returns had required help in filing their returns. The increasing complexity of the tax law, combined with the IRS decision to eliminate the simplified tax form, created a burgeoning new industry of tax preparers. Many of the self-styled tax preparers did not have the requisite technical knowledge. They offered to work at bargain basement prices and engaged in advertising practices that threatened the reputation of all tax preparers, especially those CPAs with small practices whose primary livelihood came from individual tax practice.[68]

The explosive growth of an unregulated tax industry created monitoring problems similar to those faced by auditors at the turn of the century. Various committees of the AICPA and of state societies spent considerable effort trying to promote regulations that would eliminate unqualified persons from tax practice. Those efforts succeeded to a degree when the IRS promulgated rules that required non-CPAs to practice as "enrolled agent[s]." One of the more contentious episodes with the bar was addressed in 1956 as well. Under the leadership of Arthur Foye, the institute was able to resolve, at least for a period, the claims by the bar that tax services were an encroachment on the practice of law. The AICPA also took a more proactive role in establishing ethical standards for its tax practitioner members when its Division of Federal Taxation began to issue Statements on Responsibilities in Tax Practice. As with auditing, the AICPA had no effective sanctions against CPAs who were not institute members, but the issuance of standards did serve as a reminder of the important role that a code of conduct played in legitimizing claims to professional status.

Throughout the period, the profession also had to address external demands that the same methods be used to calculate income for financial reporting and for tax reporting. In most other nations of the world, tax reporting was required, thereby making tax benefits, designed to stimulate the economy, more effective policy tools. By 1972, the profession once again must have felt under siege as proposals for tax/financial reporting compliance surfaced with each new tax law.[69]

Edelman (1964) notes that politicians often respond to public unrest with symbolic regulation (regulation that does not affect wealth transfers); he concludes that the concept of progressive taxation has been the most effective symbolic regulation ever promulgated. Financial accounting standards require companies to match tax expense with current revenues, creating the appearance that most corporations pay their fair share of taxes even if they owe no taxes for the current year or will receive a refund. If tax compliance had been required in financial reporting, then the relatively low tax rate that many of the nation's largest corporations paid throughout the decade of the sixties would have been highlighted, raising questions about the progressivity (fairness) of the tax code. Neither politicians nor accountants seemed eager to address such questions, and with the exception of LIFO, compliance was not required.

Governmental and Not-for-Profit Accounting

The demands of the cold war, combined with a belief that the federal government could work with business to ensure social fairness and the nation's prosperity, led to a dramatic increase in the federal bureaucracy that also created opportunities for accountants. Congress passed the George Bill (1945), which established a new division of the General Accounting Office (GAO), the Division of Corporate Audits, which required that all government corporations be subject to audit. While the AIA did not convince Congress that these audits should be done by independent auditors, the bill did require the GAO to conduct audits in accordance with generally accepted auditing standards (GAAS). The profession applauded the appointment of T. Coleman Andrews, a CPA, as the first director of corporation audits.[70] Two years later, the AIA appointed a committee to make recommendations to the Hoover Commission (the Committee on Reorganization of the Executive Branch) as to how best to improve the financial reporting system of the executive branch. Hoover also appointed three CPAs, Andrews, Arthur Carter, and Paul Grady, to serve on different task forces for the commission.

The AIA suggested that an office of accountant general be created, but that idea was not implemented. The comptroller general retained the right to establish accounting principles.[71] The new laws dramatically increased the GAO's case load, but the refusal of the federal government to grant CPAs the same professional status as given to doctors and lawyers limited the attractiveness of federal employment to most CPAs. The burgeoning federal sector provided opportunities for people with accounting training and contributed to the exponential growth in the number of accountants during this period.

The AIA also recognized that state and municipal government service afforded a potentially lucrative field for accountants. A 1950 survey reported that only ten states had audit requirements, and only six of those required independent audits ("Audits of Governmental Units," 1950: 464). The AIA, however, did not establish audit standards or accounting procedures; the Municipal Finance Association (MFA) had assumed that responsibility, and accountants had to work with the MFA to advance municipal accounting practices. The same situation existed in other not-for-profit areas; the American Council of Education established accounting standards for colleges and universities, and the American Hospital Association did so for hospitals.[72] The need for hospital accountants exploded with the passage of Medicare on July 30, 1965, and neither hospitals nor accountants were prepared for the challenge (Freitag 1969). In its first year of implementation, Medicare resulted in 5,000,000 subsidized hospital admissions. Medicare regulations required complex cost allocations that hospital accounting systems could not provide and that created a market and opportunity for trained accountants (Toussaint 1970).

By the 1970s, the number of federal grant programs had skyrocketed; most required the services of accountants for audits and for complex cost calculation. But traditional accounting measurements were not adequate to assess the effectiveness and efficiency of government programs. The comptroller general of the United States, Elmer Staats, became an active proponent of "operational audits." Staats (1972) explained the concept of accountability from his perspective as the integration of data and systems analysis. He explained that while "accountants strive for right numbers, systems analysts strive to estimate degree of uncertainty in numbers available." The governmental accountant's role was threefold; one had to determine (1) fiscal accountability (fiscal integrity, disclosure, and compliance with law), then (2) managerial accountability (efficient use of personnel and resources), and (3) program accountability (attainment of program objectives). The comptroller general's office issued *The Standards for Audit of Governmental Organizations, Programs, Activities, and Functions* (U.S. General

Accounting Office 1972), which outlined procedures for operational audits. This so-called Yellow Book became the government accountant's Bible.

While the accounting profession contributed to advancement in the area
of not-for-profit and governmental accounting, often in cooperation with
other groups, the not-for-profit area did not receive so much attention as
other areas of specialization. While new areas of specialization dramatically
increased the number of accountants, external auditing, which had provided the justification for claiming professional status and for CPA legislation, remained the core activity.

External Auditing

The period after World War II was one of dynamic and rapid growth for
audit firms. The leadership of the AIA, which became AICPA in 1957, faced
a formidable task in preserving the profession's right to self-regulation as its
membership virtually exploded from 9,500 in 1945 to almost 104,000 in
1973 and its scope of services offered changed dramatically.[73]

The audit environment also changed dramatically during this period;
corporate growth mandated more sophisticated audit techniques while accounting applications using computer technology increased the complexity
of audits. Auditors' responsibilities and legal liability seemed to increase
exponentially. By 1973, the inability to curb the excesses associated with
the merger mania of the late 1960s led to a crisis in public confidence and
demands for significant reform of the monitoring process. From a historical perspective, the profession appeared to have come full circle—from
McKesson-Robbins to equity funding—and audit practice, once again, came
under close political and public scrutiny.

Criticisms and Responses

In 1939, the Richard Whitney scandal and the McKesson-Robbins fraud
had raised doubts about the leadership of the New York Stock Exchange in
the former case and the adequacy of the independent audit process in the
latter. The AIA had reacted by promulgating GAAS to guide practitioners.
The war temporarily halted an extensive investigation of public company
practices that the SEC had planned to conduct, but by the end of the war,
that investigation was completed. The report presented a list of reporting
deficiencies found in the annual reports of OTC companies and noted that
most of the statements had been audited by the most prestigious audit firms
in the country.[74] Auditors questioned the SEC's motives and accused the

agency of duplicity in order to expand its own jurisdiction. But despite the profession's protests, significant damage had been done.[75] In 1947, a survey by Opinion Research found that 45 percent of the public believed that companies' financial statements were untruthful and 40 percent believed that reported earnings were falsified. As it had in the 1930s, the AIA's immediate reaction was to reformulate the audit report to educate the public about the limitations of the audit process.

A New Short-Form Audit Report

The AIA leadership concluded that two major deficiencies existed that must be immediately corrected. First, the public did not understand that a report, signed by a CPA, but issued without an opinion, was not an audit. To remedy this situation, the AIA issued Statement on Auditing Procedure (SAP) No. 23 (1948), requiring the auditor to issue a disclaimer of opinion and indicate why the disclaimer was being made.

Second, the AIA concluded that the short-form certificate misled the public and had to be reworded. The Committee on Auditing Procedure issued SAP No. 24 in 1948 to eliminate several objectionable phrases in the short-form reform.[76] The new standard omitted any reference (1) to examination of internal control and (2) to the statement that a detailed audit of transactions had been conducted. In addition, the new short form report did not include what the committee called "the inconsistent expression" that auditing standards applicable in the circumstance had employed ("Audits of Governmental Units," 1950: 389). These new standards were perceived as affording protection to both the public and the auditor by giving the public the right to hold accountants liable for reports they signed if they did not issue a disclaimer, while providing the accountant with a measure of protection by rewording the short-form certificate (Cannon 1950).

Implementation was not effective; many auditors simply began to issue long-form reports to avoid the new restrictions.[77] Nor is it clear that the 1948 revision was beneficial to the public. The exclusion of all reference to internal control seemed singularly unfortunate in that the public and many auditors seemed to recognize the critical importance that evaluation of internal control played in the audit process.[78] Despite its shortcomings, the 1948 revision remained in place until 1973 when public criticism mandated reform.

Internal Control

Somewhat ironically, after recommending deletion of any reference to internal control in the short-form report in 1948, the Committee on Auditing

Procedure adopted the second standard of field work, which required auditors to make a proper study and evaluation of internal control as a basis for reliance thereon and for the determination of the extent to which auditing procedures are to be structured. The second standard proved to be too general to result in a significant improvement in the audit process. One practitioner pointed out that the standard never had the desired effect on audit practice because auditors generally did not document the relationship between use of specific audit procedures and specific internal controls (Harlan 1974).

SEC regulators would continuously cite the lack of evaluation of internal control as a significant weakness of the certification process, but the profession did not readdress the issue until the late 1960s, when public criticism of the audit process left the AIA little choice. The failure to specify guidelines for evaluation of internal control or to sufficiently emphasize the relationship between internal controls and audit objectives probably contributed to the perception of audit failures that undermined public confidence in the profession.

Auditing in the 1960s

Robert Reich (1989) suggests that America has seen cyclical shifts in attitudes toward business; the consumerism of the 1960s marked one of those major shifts when social values became dominant. Consumers' rights, civil rights, environmental protection, and equal opportunity laws all generated hostility toward business. No longer did the public believe that what was good for G.M. was good for America. Corporate power had become a matter of grave concern. As with prior eras, such as the Progressive Era, auditors were asked to assume greater responsibilities for monitoring management and to extend the scope of their work. The expectations gap between auditors and the public continued to grow throughout the decade as bankers, investors, consumer advocates, and accounting academics became increasingly critical of the audit process.

One survey showed that the general public, bankers, and investors delineated a broad role for CPAs, while corporate executives viewed auditors as "nonquestioning reporters" working within the confines of GAAP. The SEC may unwittingly have fostered this latter view by insisting that independent accountants state that financial statements were in accordance with GAAP. Although accountants have never been absolved from assessing risk and determining that a particular practice, permissible under GAAP, was appropriate in a given circumstance, there seems to have been, during the 1950s, a general impression among managers that auditors could not reject the use of an "accepted" principle (Trueblood 1963). This tension between appropriate versus acceptable would surface again in the 1990s when the Kirk Panel on the Public Oversight Board would consider broad criticisms made by the SEC.

By the end of the decade, external auditors must have felt under siege. Not only had their legal liability increased substantially, they were being asked to address areas previously deemed beyond the scope of the profession. Auditors faced demands to extend the attest function to include interim data, reports on internal control, management audits, and forecast data.[79] As Hill (1973) noted, auditors also were increasingly being asked to report on uncertainties, such as going concern qualifications, changes in estimates, and subsequent events. The profession responded, albeit reluctantly, to these demands, but auditors successfully resisted calls for managerial audits that could have resulted in direct confrontation with their clients. Wallace Olson recalled that it took a series of legal liability cases in the 1960s to remind the profession of its "third party" obligation; the SEC would reinforce that message (1982: 3). But above all the marketplace would again begin its relentless pursuit of reckoning with the auditors when at 5:35 P.M. on Saturday, June 20, 1970, Federal Judge C. William Kraft Jr. signed the bankruptcy order for the Penn Central. The largest bankruptcy (in terms of assets) in history, the $4.6 billion transportation empire's failure called into question not only regulators', but also auditors' effectiveness (Loving 1970).

The Legal Liability Revolution

In the late 1950s, the SEC and the courts began to remind auditors of their "third party" responsibilities. A brief examination of the SEC's Accounting Series Releases (ASRs) shows that the agency, while always concerned with independence issues, became increasingly more proactive in matters of audit procedure and presentation.[80] The SEC called the profession's attention to its third-party responsibility in ASR No. 78 (1957), writing that "the responsibility of the public accountant is not only to the client who pays his fee but to investors, creditors and others who may rely on the financial statements which he certifies."[81] Seaboard (1957), Yale Express (1965), and Westec (1967), among others, would remind the profession of its responsibility for ensuring that financial statement presentations were not misleading. The courts shocked practitioners by holding that an auditor was not protected simply by following GAAS or GAAP. Court decisions extended the profession's responsibilities to examination of subsequent events and for preparation of "unaudited" financial statements.[82] On

November 15, 1966, the *Wall Street Journal* reported accountants faced more than one hundred lawsuits; the number would continue to grow.

Expanding the Audit Function

As corporations became larger and electronic data processing systems came into widespread use, evaluation of internal controls to limit detailed audit work became increasingly important. Statistical sampling and compliance testing became more common, while guidelines for evaluation of internal control continued to be embryonic.[83] Perhaps because of the profession's growing legal liability, auditors appeared reluctant to expand their responsibilities, but faced with growing external criticisms, the AIA issued SAP No. 49 that required auditors to issue reports on internal control, and SAP No. 52, two years later in 1972, that provided explicit guidelines for evaluation of internal control. SAP No. 52 identified two distinct types of audit tests, compliance and substantive tests, which while widely used had not been recognized explicitly in professional pronouncements to that time (Harlan 1974).

The renewed interest in internal control evaluation and the growing use of quantitative techniques created an opportunity for academic researchers, who, with the exception of Mautz and Sharaf's (1961) classic monograph, *Philosophy of Auditing* (1961), had not played a critical role in the development of audit standards. Carmichael's (1970A) study of the behavioral hypothesis of internal control foreshadowed a decade of an increasingly rigorous body of experimental behavioral research.[84] Academic research in auditing was augmented by accounting firm programs to support projects with direct funding. Academics also would contribute by developing models, such as Yu and Neter's (1973) stochastic model of an internal control system and Ijiri and Kaplan's (1971) model of integrating sampling objectives into auditing. While auditors successfully addressed the need to develop more sophisticated audit techniques, adequate financial reports continued to be perceived by many as inadequate.

The Merger Mania

The merger wave of the late 1960s, as had previous merger waves, led to calls for more stringent monitoring. The failure of the APB to effectively restrict earnings manipulation with respect to mergers led to criticisms of the financial reporting process in the popular press. Abraham Briloff, an insightful and trenchant academic critic, captured the attention of the public with a series of articles in *Barron's*, with titles such as "Dirty Pooling—

How to Succeed in Business without Really Trying."[85] The press depicted auditors as lacking the will to check their corporate clients' most overt reporting abuses. Homer Kripke (1970: 794), a lawyer, characterized auditors "as professional men with the backbones of overcooked spaghetti," expressing his complaints not only in law journals but directly to the SEC. He joined the chorus of those echoing a familiar strain: accounting had simply become too important to be left to the technical vagaries of accountants. The criticisms were not unfounded. Accounting for consolidations was a controversial topic at the APB's inception; the board commissioned two research studies to look at business combinations and goodwill, but the APB could not reach consensus. GAAP for consolidations continued to provide managers enormous flexibility in determining earnings.[86]

Some bankers also joined the chorus, complaining that GAAP had become almost a cliché and demanding reform. They argued that accounting practices, while they may have been appropriate to previous generations, failed to recognize the changing needs of creditors. In the early decades of the century, most loans were short-term and, therefore, working capital analysis and conservative valuations of accounts receivable and inventories were applauded by bankers. But by the 1960s most major banks were engaged in long-term or "cash-flow lending." Bankers wanted to predict future cash flows and maintained that this was impossible given the inconsistencies in GAAP. Moreover, they noted that the flexibility of GAAP made it impossible to compare company reports even within the same industry (Laeri 1966).

Accounting for consolidations highlighted fundamental contradictions that had existed for decades. Auditors continued to reject vigorously implementation of uniform accounting methods, arguing that in a dynamic economy, they must use their professional judgment to determine what accounting method was appropriate in a given circumstance (Trueblood 1969). But practitioners also refused to take direct responsibility for "preferability" decisions (i.e., making an assessment that procedures used were "appropriate" in a given circumstance) despite repeated external demands that they make such judgments. The profession continued to maintain that financial statements were management's representations; hence the decisions were management's.

The emphasis on judgment and flexibility is understandable, as it served as the basis for accountants' claims to professional status; technicians could apply uniform standards adequately and more cheaply. But somewhat inexplicably, many auditors seemed to believe that codification of GAAP relieved them of the need to exercise judgment and that management had the right to chose any method permitted by GAAP. Some seemed to believe that a fundamental concept of the profession—that financial statements not be misleading—had been changed to the concept that all statements, prepared in accordance with GAAP, were presumed *not* to be misleading. Auditors who testified in *U.S. v. Simon* (Continental Vending) expressed this belief; Judge Friendly forcefully disabused the profession of this notion. He stated that "fair" means "fair," and accountants did not have legal protection by modifying the term "present fairly" with a nebulous term like GAAP.[87] Judge Friendly's decision reverberated throughout the profession as it forcefully reminded auditors of their responsibility to "third parties" and lent some urgency to restatement of the standard audit opinion, recodification of ethical standards, and a reexamination of the standard-setting process.

A New Short-Form Report

The number of lawsuits that accountants faced convinced most auditors of the need to change the short-form audit report. William Roth (1968), chairman of the AICPA Committee on Auditing Procedure, issued an indictment of the "old opinion." He suggested that it was too terse to be understandable, that it did not tie the opinion to scope, that it used the term examination (which, he suggested, was less clear than audit), that the term "present fairly" was widely misunderstood, and that the term GAAP was meaningless. While most auditors agreed that the old opinion was inadequate, it was difficult to get consensus on the wording of a new opinion. It took more than four years; a new opinion was issued in 1973. The new opinion was not a model of clarity. Roth's "meaningless term" GAAP survived, and his "widely misunderstood" present fairly remained. Nor did the opinion clearly specify the auditor's obligation to evaluate internal control. But it did specify more clearly the scope of an audit and the nature of the testing process.

Another suggestion, that auditors conduct management audits and issue a report on management's effectiveness to investors, was ignored. Many thought the profession was at a crossroads; the "merger mania" of the late sixties had led to a plethora of negative publicity about the traditional financial-reporting process, and restoring public confidence became the profession's first priority.

Ethics

Despite the rapid growth in scope of services to include tax and management services, which created serious questions about the independence of audit firms, accounting practitioners probably would welcome a return to conditions of this period.[88] Subsequent FTC-induced price competition would not be viewed as salutary, and while the profession's enforcement mechanisms remained weak, most of the enforcement activity related to colleague violations.[89] Since competition was deemed "unseemly," prohibitions against encroachment (solicitation of clients of other audit firms), offers of employment to auditors working for other firms, bans on contingent fees and commissions, and restrictions of advertising remained part of the 1973 code of ethics. Accountants, like all professionals, walked a fine line. No one welcomed the adverse publicity associated with imposition of sanctions, but as Marshall Armstrong (1971) noted, most audit practitioners understood that if the profession did not appear to be able to enforce its code of ethics, it might lose the privilege of self-regulation.

Since the enlarged scope of services offered by audit firms created significant concern about auditors' independence, the 1973 revision focused primarily on promulgating rules that addressed the appearance of independence. Thomas Higgins and Wallace Olson (1972: 33), two members of the AICPA's committee charged with restructuring the code of ethics, viewed a code of ethics as integral to all professions. They suggested that "agreement on ethical concepts and adherence to them by an overwhelming majority of practitioners . . . transform a vocation into a profession."[90] Accountants had long recognized the importance of maintaining independence in appearance as well as in fact; the 1962 code had included a rule to that effect. The 1973 restatement attempted to provide more specific criteria to make this ethical construct operational. The code also included specific prohibitions. Auditors should not knowingly countenance misrepresentation of facts, and they should not subordinate their judgment to that of others. The code contained a bailout provision for tax practitioners who were allowed to take a client's position if that position was reasonable.

From a historical perspective, the 1973 code does not appear to have entailed a revolutionary departure from prior codes. But many practitioners viewed the code as dramatically different; Willis Smith (1973) concluded that the new code reflected the "advent of consumerism where the profit motive must take second place to the public good." He noted that it emphasized responsibility to the public and downplayed responsibility to the client. However, the code was not as forceful as it could have been. While clearly stating that it was critical to assess the integrity of management and to maintain the appearance of independence, the revision qualified both by stating integrity was difficult to assess and it was difficult for the CPA to appear always to be completely independent. With a few exceptions, such as the academic work of Stephen Loeb, development of ethical standards and enforcement of codes of ethics had not attracted research attention, but the 1973 revision would renew interest in this area.

The Challenge to Accounting Education

The war years had the effect of suspending debate over the quality of accounting education, but the passage of the G.I. Bill, combined with the increasing number of white-collar jobs, would change the entrance requirements into the profession and lead to a reexamination of accounting curricula. But, prior to 1957, when the launching of Sputnik by the USSR sent shock waves through government and the educational establishment and led to several comprehensive studies of university curricula, the debate in accounting focused primarily on increasing educational requirements for entrance into the profession. The debate, while spirited, met with limited success. Several reasons could be cited for the profession's resistance to increasing entrance standards (including the resistance of state legislators to promulgating higher standards), but a major factor seems to have been the pride many accountants had in being considered the most "open" of the professions. Arthur Cannon (1956) reflected that view; he felt that a B.A. should be the normal prerequisite for entry, but he called for an "escape clause." "I'm still enough of a believer in the Abraham Lincoln or American Boy concept," he explained, "to want to leave some way for the occasional underprivileged or handicapped but otherwise qualified individual who may gain a[n] education by less common means."

The expressed belief in self-education reflected the profession's early heritage when most practitioners had been self-taught and practical experience, not education, was deemed to be the critical factor in preparing someone for the profession (Merino and Coe 1978). However, the "openness" argument became less convincing, given the democratization of higher education through the G.I. Bill that occurred during this period.

The Perry Report (1956)

Identification as members of a profession had united accounting academics with accounting practitioners throughout the century and AIA committees took an active role in developing educational standards. In 1956, the Commission on Standards of Education and Experience for CPAs issued its report (commonly referred to as the Perry Report after its chairman, Donald Perry). The commission recommended five criteria—college graduation, a qualifying entrance examination, a professional academic program, an internship, and completion of the uniform CPA examination—for admission to the profession. The educational requirements did not provoke great controversy because the commission suggested that accreditation of accounting programs be left to the joint efforts of the American Assembly of Collegiate Schools of Business and the Standards Rating Committee of the AAA.

Practitioners, however, voiced strong opposition to the abandonment of a formal experience requirement. The Association of Certified Public Accountant Examiners had debated this issue the previous year and concluded that there was little support for such a measure. The examiners had formulated a compromise measure, a two-tier system, whereby a person would receive a certificate as a public accountant upon completion of the CPA examination and a CPA license after completion of three years' practical experience. The Perry commission concluded, however, that the CPA certificate signified no more than entry-level competence, not attainment of professional competence. Henry Hill (1956) countered that if one expected other professionals (doctors and lawyers) to have practical experience, then certainly one "should support the idea that the newest and most recently made certified public accountant must have experience."

Most of the commission members who dissented from the Perry Report accepted Hill's argument and cited what they believed was a basic inconsistency in recommending an internship program when also arguing that practical experience had little benefit. The internship program could be viewed as a necessary political compromise although it did not have widespread support from accounting academics.[91] By placing an experience requirement with education, criticisms that the experience requirement had been used to limit entry of minorities and women and to create a professional monopoly could be defused (Moonitz 1973). Internship programs, however, did not address the major criticism of proponents of the experience requirement, namely, that practitioners could not rely solely on educational criteria because accounting educators had failed to provide criteria for measurement of the "quality" of accounting programs.

The director of research of the AIA had a simple solution. He conducted a survey and concluded that in "good" schools, the percentage of people passing the CPA examination was eight times higher than in "bad" schools (Pedelahore 1956: 6). This suggestion was in direct conflict with the Perry Report's conclusion that the CPA examination measured no more than minimal competence and accounting education should not focus on preparing students to pass the CPA examination but to prepare them to become professionals.[92] Since the debate about how to assess quality of programs related to entrance to the profession, accountants had the luxury of leaving the issue of quality assessment unresolved. But in the aftermath of Sputnik, the Pierson (1959) and Gordon and Howell (1959) reports that severely criticized business education, including accounting, for being too technical and narrow raised a host of new challenges for the profession.

External Pressure to Improve Business Education

Educators in all business disciplines were affected by the Pierson and the Gordon and Howell reports. Both studies concluded that mediocrity and vocationalism permeated business education, that students were not as bright or motivated as their liberal arts counterparts, and that business faculties did not have appropriate academic credentials. Accountants could take some comfort from the fact that accounting students were generally considered superior to other business students, but both academicians and practitioners viewed with dismay the reports' suggestion that the study of accounting should be perceived primarily as an instrument to aid management in their day-to-day decisions. Accountants countered that both reports failed to understand that as professionals, accountants had a broad social obligation that transcended their obligation to management.

Raymond Dein (1961) felt that the reports were not "aware that accounting is the only discipline that supplies such vitally useful (if somewhat imprecise) information on the net income of business enterprises" to facilitate social control. Accountants' criticism of the two reports for their failure to recognize the profession's social obligation or the important use of accounting information for social control is curious in that if one examines accounting textbooks of the period, they do not emphasize these social aspects, either. Robert Trueblood (1963) noted that accounting curricula had not changed since the 1930s and that most accounting educators continued to focus on the technical aspects of the discipline. The call for curriculum reform did not result in substantive changes in accounting education, but by the late 1960s, the business accreditation process established criteria for accounting faculty that were the equivalent of a requirement to hold an earned doctorate as the terminal degree. This had been the previous requirement for all other academic business disciplines, whereas accounting had recognized a master's degree with a CPA. This "investment" in the academic process would prove to be a significant event (Bricker and Previts 1990).

The Issue of Academic Credentials

In 1958, an AAA committee had surveyed twenty-nine universities that offered doctoral programs and asked if accounting faculty should have a degree above the master's degree. Twenty-four of the schools responded no. The negative response may have reflected the close relationship that existed then between accounting education and practice, but the Pierson (1959) and Gordon and Howell (1959) reports' criticisms, combined with the desire to gain academic legitimacy for accounting faculty, gave added impetus to academic leaders' efforts to upgrade credentials. By 1965, an AAA committee concluded that a doctorate should be the terminal degree for future accounting academics. The AAA report considered a CPA certificate beneficial but not essential and recommended that doctoral programs have a broad, theoretical base with the emphasis on research (AAA 1965C: 415–16). The AAA recognized that future educators should have professional or technical training but concluded that professional work should be completed prior to admission to a doctoral program.

The requirement that accounting faculty have a doctoral degree did not have an immediate impact on the close relationship between academia and practice, but it did have a significant impact on the direction of accounting research. Academic legitimacy was enhanced through basic, not applied, research, and the gulf between accounting academics and practitioners widened throughout the period. In 1973, Maurice Moonitz observed "that academics and practitioners can't talk" because academics were out of touch with the profession. He suggested that those who would like to work on "stock market behavior, employee motivation, and economic issues, should find a home in other academic departments." [93]

Interestingly, the academic/practitioner schism did not appear to affect accounting curricula. Robert Sterling (1973) correctly noted that if one examined accounting textbooks, education and practice remained in harmony.[94] Accounting educators continued to teach practice even when practice was inconsistent with their own research. He concluded that research had little impact on practice or education because it was isolated.[95] Perhaps the reluctance of accounting educators to respond substantively to demands for curriculum change can be attributed, in part, to the desire to retain the close affiliation between academia and practice.

Curriculum Changes

Accounting curricula have been exceedingly slow to change despite the constant demands for reform. Academics ignored the Gordon and Howell (1959) and Pierson (1959) reports' suggestion that the accounting undergraduate curriculum abandon its emphasis on financial accounting and auditing in favor of a broader, managerial orientation. The AICPA held a conference to respond to a report and passed a resolution stating that the university must remain "the principal seat of CPA training" in the United

States. The conference also called upon the AICPA to issue a statement of educational objectives, which the institute released in 1961. The report concluded that university education should be designed to prepare a student "to learn to be" and not "to be" a CPA. The statement also recognized that social, economic, and business theories were important and that accounting education must be oriented to "broad problem solving" and not to "specialized competence." The student should be able to intelligently address managerial problems, but the report concluded, not unexpectedly, that accounting curricula must be based on a "hard core of accounting, tax and auditing principles" (Bach, Davidson, and Trueblood 1961: 18ff.).

The AICPA then sought external support to define educational objectives. Working with the Carnegie Mellon Foundation, the institute sponsored a research study to determine a "common body of knowledge" for accountants. Robert Roy, an engineer, and James MacNeill, an accountant, undertook a comprehensive survey to determine the components of this body of knowledge (Roy 1964). In 1967, the institute published *Horizons for a Profession* by Roy and MacNeill as a definitive statement on the educational requirements for prospective accountants.

The authors outlined a broad academic program and endorsed a five-year educational requirement and professional schools of accountancy.[96] The latter recommendation, while not new, was given added impetus by the "new" look in business school curricula that appeared to threaten the traditional CPA orientation of accounting programs. The emphasis in business curricula was on management, planning, and quantitative analysis. Accountants did not react with favor to curricula that de-emphasized accounting and viewed accounting primarily as a "tool" of management. If accounting was not to be marginalized, then accounting curricula must be reoriented. Charles Horngren (1971) warned that if accounting academics did not meet the challenge, they could expect "a takeover of the internal accounting function by mega-information specialists." He predicted that financial accounting would disappear "as a legitimate subject worthy of study" if accountants did not adopt a more conceptual, interdisciplinary approach to their subject. Not all agreed that the recommendations of the Roy and MacNeill (1967) study could or should be implemented.[97] Some eminent practitioners, like Leonard Spacek (1964B), criticized the common body of knowledge study because he believed that it was useless to "glibly address ourselves to such a fundamental task (as defining a common body of knowledge) while failing to recognize that the very premise of such an objective prevents its realization." Until accountants could define the objectives of accounting, Spacek contended, they could not define the knowledge and intellectual habits or technical skills needed to apply them. While *Horizons* did result in some curriculum changes, many curriculum changes during this period occurred also in response to the American Assembly of Collegiate Schools of Business's (AACSB) accreditation standards.

Professional Schools

Professional schools of accountancy afforded one means of divorcing accountants from the criticisms of business education and of maintaining student identification with the profession (Ashburne 1958). In response to charges of vocationalism, the AACSB's accreditation standards for business school curricula had been changed to the 50 percent/25 percent/25 percent model with 50 percent of a student's course work being in liberal arts. Recommendations for professional schools of accountancy were not new, but accounting educators could now cite the broadened liberal arts requirements, combined with the increasing complexity of the accounting environment, to justify five-year programs and professional schools of accountancy. The breadth of knowledge, documented in *Horizons for a Profession* (1967), further supported calls for professional schools.

The failure of accountants to gain early acceptance for five-year programs, despite the increased complexity of the accounting environment and increased demand for accounting programs after 1957, can be attributed to several factors. First, state legislators did not appear to be convinced that additional education was needed; they looked skeptically at increased educational requirements as one means of restricting entry into the profession. Second, many practicing accountants, especially those working in small firms, agreed with state legislators that professional schools were not needed. Third, leaders probably underestimated the time needed to convince academics and practitioners that change was indeed needed. It was "summertime" and the living was "easy." The pressures of competition were still many years away from being felt on campuses. Despite a decade of calls for reform, little changed during the 1960s, leading the AICPA to conduct another study to reinforce its prior calls for change.

The Beamer Committee

The period would end as it had begun: an AICPA committee reexamined the issue of accounting education and its recommendations mirrored those found in the Perry Report, more than a decade earlier. AACSB accreditation standards had defused (to a degree) the "quality" issue and provided strong support for a broadened educational base. But despite continuous recommendations that the CPA exam be de-emphasized, many schools and faculty regarded passage rates on the exam as a measure of quality. Maurice Moonitz (1973) interpreted the Beamer Committee (1969) as a "golden opportunity" because it forcefully rejected focusing on the examination and recommended a broad conceptual base for accounting. Moonitz attributed the failure of accounting curricula to change to educators having been constrained by overemphasis on the CPA examination and the relatively low level of entrance and experience requirements. A new day, he asserted, was at hand. Accounting academics had the opportunity to make significant changes to curricula to overcome the narrow, technical basis that permeated accounting education. Moonitz's assessment appears to have been optimistic as subsequent criticisms would parallel those in the Beamer Committee; the educational establishment proved to be extremely resistant to change.

The Significance of Accounting in an Uncertain Age

The Mideast oil embargo marked the end of an era where American companies could succeed without trying. The "downpayment" on the American century had promoted prosperity for fewer than three decades, and the emergence of global competition demonstrated the vulnerability of the American economy. Neither cost nor financial accounting provided adequate signals for the demise that would occur. But many accountants would benefit from the return to this type of competition as the renewal of debates about economic performance (profit measurement) again took center stage. Few could have predicted the radical changes that would occur within the profession with the onset of deregulation in the next decade, but accountants (both academic and practitioner) appeared to welcome a return to the mythical setting where global competition would place the private property rights paradigm and the nation's largest corporations in harmony, operating for the benefit of shareholders.

Soon the profession would be embarked on a new era: the Wheat Committee's (1972) recommendation for a broader-based, autonomous standard-setting body had been implemented with the establishment of the Financial Accounting Standards Board (FASB) in 1973. In addition, in 1973, the AICPA issued its "Objectives of Financial Statements," commonly referred to as the Trueblood Report after the committee chair, Robert Trueblood. The report specified "objectives" that clearly emphasized the profession's obligation to direct a broader stream of financial *reports* (not only statements) to corporate constituencies (investors and creditors). The

SEC, under a new chief accountant, John Burton, gave some indication that it would become more active; its proposals seemed to be a simple extension of the trend to provide more information to investors and creditors.

The increasing dominance of academic empirical research also provided a welcome respite to practitioners weary of academic criticism. The shift from normative theorizing about the attributes of accounting to capital markets research that examined the effects of accounting data on the stock market seemed distant, if not entirely disconnected, from practice concerns and unlikely to generate open persistent clashes over the authority for leadership of the profession. Further, the new research suggested that many of the past heated debates about accounting had been trivial; efficient market theorists showed that the market "saw through" the manipulation of accounting data. William Beaver (1973) synthesized six prescriptions that efficient market research could offer to the newly formed FASB. One prescription, that standard setters need not spend undue time worrying about limiting choices of accounting methods but allow management to choose freely as long as they disclose the method used, must have been welcome to practitioners, who had been so severely criticized for permitting "earnings manipulation" during the merger mania of the late 1960s. However, as Mautz (1978: 178) would note, investors do not sue on average and the courts had not absolved accountants from responsibility if financial statements misled a single investor. The debate, therefore, would continue—albeit at new levels and with new participants and in new settings.

Accountancy and the Global Capital Market:

From the Trueblood Report to the Jenkins Committee

I firmly believe that accounting improvement in the U.S. has not come about merely as a matter of nature taking its course. Improvement has occurred as a result of sustained, committed, cooperative effort. Every step of accounting evolution has been helped along by a good firm push. Improving international accounting standards will require the same kind of commitment, the same kind of effort, the same kind of push.

—Dennis R. Beresford, FASB chairman, 1989

The Changing Profession and Markets

Sidney Jones, a contemporary economic demographer and recently an assistant secretary of the U.S. Treasury, uses numbers, population numbers, to gauge the pulse of economic trends (Jones 1989). When confronted by a particularly difficult analysis, he observes, "You can bet on demographics." Using this as a guide, we introduce the considerations of this most recent period of historical episodes of accountancy in the United States in basic demographic terms both from a long-term and a short-term perspective (figure 8.3., see below).[1] The baseline demography comes from the population data on the oldest U.S. professional accounting institution, the AICPA. Keeping in mind that the initial CPA certificates were awarded after passage of the New York law of 1896, by 1945, following the unification of the national CPA bodies (the American Society and the American Institute), there were but 9500 members overall in the institute.

By 1973, AICPA membership had increased tenfold from the 1945 figure, to 95,000. This phenomenal growth and the consequent development of the profession's infrastructure taxed the leadership and practice community of the profession in countless ways. By 1973, this infrastructure was beginning to be outmoded thanks to additional growth in services and expansion of markets and shifts of membership from public to corporate practice. By 1995, the AICPA membership would exceed 320,000.

With such major demographic change, some would argue that all bets were off in terms of looking to the past for clear precedents in managing the growing institutional arrangements necessary for the accounting professional to serve businesses, clients, and other entities in society. This era, from 1973 to 1995, also defies full historical consideration because several key institutional initiatives of the period, such as the Treadway Commission, the AICPA Excellence program, the Jenkins Report, and the Elliot Committee, are recent. To attempt to develop a perspective on matters so inchoate is risky—and some would say inappropriate—but these episodes are too important to omit in drawing a complete sketch of the development of accountancy in the United States.

During the 1970s and 1980s, the U.S. accountancy profession underwent an identity change instigated by a rapidly expanding practice base and the Federal Trade Commission (FTC) as well as a change in the range and scope of service. The singular essential role of attest engagements as the trademark of the public accounting profession was being supplanted as the market made competing demands upon accountants' skills and abilities and public practitioners pressed to expand the market for their services. The age of "auditing as king" was passing, as other attest, tax, and advisory services were offered to assist businesses facing an increasingly complex legal, international, and technological environment. Accountants in corporate practice found that their traditional cost management techniques were to be challenged by a new orthodoxy, that of activity-based costing. Governmental accounting at the federal level was to be affected by legislative initiatives such as the Single Audit Act and the Chief Accounting Officer Act and at the local level by the structuring of the Governmental Accounting Standards Board (GASB).

By the 1990s, the profession of accountancy had grown to include hundreds of thousands of college-educated individuals in public practice, corporate practice, the public sector, and education. Journalists in the business press, newspapers, dedicated newsletters, and other forms of media would specialize in publicizing accountants' activities. Accountants were, at first, uncomfortable and unfamiliar with the ways to accommodate such scrutiny but were to become adept at relating to the press, while perhaps preserving a preference for anonymity. The concepts of accounting underlying the financial reporting and auditing implications for managerial and investor decisions at the dawn of the mutual fund–driven capital market of the 1990s were debated by a generation of accounting academics characteristically uninterested in the applied or practical aspects of such issues.

By the 1990s, CPAs had advanced to levels of national visibility and pre-eminence. For example, the S&L crisis and management of the "bailout" procedures became a principal focus for accountancy overall and for two accountants in particular. Former CPA firm partners William Seidman, chairman of the Federal Deposit Insurance Corporation and also the Resolution Trust Corporation, and Charles Bowsher, comptroller general of the General Accounting Office, were commonly seen on television, being quoted almost daily in the financial and popular press (Friedrich 1991). They were viewed as knowledgeable, honest brokers in the political maze that had grown out of the reorganizing frenzy of the banking system and the recapitalizing of U.S. businesses during the 1980s.[2]

What do so many professional accountants have in common? What is their view of the role of the professional accountant? Aside from their education and their professional examination, what are the common points of their identity as professionals? What has been their role in society? A consideration of some of the more significant events, institutions, and personalities responding to these questions and the practice of accounting at this stage of accounting's development are the subject of this chapter.

The Mask Is Lifted

It was a chilly but bright January morning in 1987 when the small group of AICPA members climbed up the grandstand steps toward their bench row of seats in Pasadena to view the Rose Bowl Parade (figure 8.1). The contingent, led by AICPA President Phil Chenok, had been on hand for several days to view the construction of the AICPA's entry into the parade. Now they would watch and cheer as AICPA Chairman J. Michael Cook and his family, dressed in frontier period costumes, rode down the parade route aboard the living work of art that represented the AICPA's debut into an arena spotlight, celebrating the institute's centennial year. This high-profile, controversial media investment, lampooned by some and thoughtfully supported by others, was a first tentative step into a new era of institutional recognition of the CPA profession in the information age. A decade and a half earlier, in 1973, the formation of the Financial Accounting Standards Board (FASB) had hardly been noticed even though it had been included in the February 5, 1973, issue of *Newsweek*. At that moment, the world had focused its attention elsewhere. In this case the magazine's three top stories were the announcement by President Nixon on January 23 that "we today have concluded an agreement to end the war and bring peace with honor in Vietnam and Southeast Asia"; the death of Lyndon Baines John-

Figure 8.1 AICPA's award-winning float at the 1987 Rose Bowl

son, the nation's thirty-sixth president at age 64; and the details of a 7 to 2 vote of the U.S. Supreme Court to legalize abortion (*Roe v. Wade*).

In 1977, *U.S. News & World Report* noted that accounting was "America's Mystery Profession." Accountants were about to be called upon to explain the pervasive impact of their practice upon the American economic system and culture (Mayer 1977). The Mideast oil embargo, followed by rampant inflation, had dissolved public confidence in postwar capitalism's role in an increasingly managed economy. Markets, global in scope, regulated by competition and fueled by nationalism, again became the mechanism to achieve economic allocation.

The well-being of societies, nationally and globally, would become increasingly dependent upon competition and market-based capital formation. This increased political and public curiosity and the need to know about the individuals whose character formed the basis of confidence that one could get a "fair shake" about corporate information, public capital markets, and investing. This issue would create an attractive agenda for politicians at the national level to "socialize" (remove control from the private sector) the responsibility of accountants as well as the determination of

TABLE 8.1
Number of U.S. Workers per Professional

	1900	1910	1920	1930	1940	1950	1960	1970	1980	1990
Accountants	2,104	1,563	599	441	406	283	294	197	163	132
AICPA	526,120	61,280	51,858	17,595	17,791	6,771	3,215	1,865	1,121	644
Engineers	1,274	792	527	390	326	204	141	116	119	102
Lawyers	448	530	575	526	531	601	577	541	327	261
Physicians	369	401	484	540	576	552	561	549	400	328

Source: U.S. Department of Commerce, Bureau of the Census of the Population.

Note: For U.S. population over 16 years of age.

what services professional accountants should perform (*Wall Street Journal* October 30, 1973: 18).

A cause of this notoriety can be attributed, in part, to the unprecedented growth and change in the scope of services of practicing accounting professionals during the late post–World War II period. Evidence about the comparative population statistics for several disciplines in the United States for part of that period is provided in table 8.1. A separate additional column shows the increase, from 1900 through 1990, of membership in the AICPA.

Upward Mobility in Accounting

"Common knowledge" of the 1970s asserted that accountancy was a middle-class profession, one that provided opportunities for persons to move up the ladder of success, both personal and financial. It would be a popular profession in the "yuppie" 1980s. Increasing numbers of college-educated women entered and ascended the ranks of the accounting profession, raising important new issues about managing the talent available to the profession (see figure 8.2). The same issues, but to a lesser degree, related to adapting to the entrance of multinational, Hispanic, and minority students.[3] As the "up or out" (make steady progress toward partner or leave

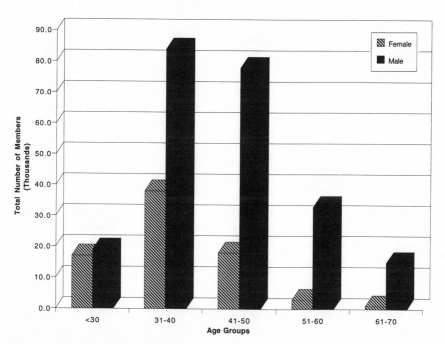

Figure 8.2 Demographics of AICPA members, 1994

the firm) attitude of major public firms changed in the face of competitive pressures and efforts to fashion a team of professionals at various levels of competency, the acceptance of permanent paraprofessional staff increased, changing the traditional "up or out" view of careers.

The Environment: Society En Masse and Global Change

Demographics

The U.S. resident population was estimated by the Census Bureau to have reached the quarter-billion mark in March 1990. Urban society in the United States had become characterized by mass production, mass consumption, mass transit, mass marketing, and mass media. One characteristic is the virtual completion of the massive 43,000-mile interstate highway system, which knit together the population centers of the country. The 1970s and 1980s confirmed one other dimension, *mass investment,* via individual 401(K) plan contributions, pension funds, and related institutional investment vehicles such as mutual funds. Portfolio investment theory dominated this process—which heretofore had been considered the domain of the individual investor selecting individual stocks—sustaining at least the plausible role of individual involvement in investment as a property right exercise.

The disenchantments of Watergate and the outcome of the Vietnam conflict in the 1970s would be offset by the Bicentennial celebration, by the "borrowed" prosperity of the 1980s, and the decline of communist bloc countries and the USSR. New challenges and realities were manifested in the form of the evolving European Economic Community and the continuing tensions throughout the oil-rich Mideast. Increasing friction developed between federal and state systems in matters of resource allocations, civil rights, states' rights, and fiscal responsibility.

America's urban lifestyle emphasized that it was no longer a land of immigrants and farmers but, rather, one that had become a capital-intensive business civilization, with an economic policy tainted by fear of inflation and geared to almost endless consumption. Americans walked on the moon, sought ways to offset inflationary prices, searched for new energy sources, and worried about what their health and finances would be when they were older. There were shock waves from instant access communications, via fax machines and the World Wide Web. Airlines and interstate roadways made travel and commercial transport relatively inexpensive, rapid, and accessible to almost all. The markets grew because changes in transport and communication had made more markets more accessible to more people.

The End of History?

"Applying conventional wisdom to perestroika is unproductive. . . . Nothing and no one, no pressure, either from the right or the left, will make me abandon the positions of perestroika. . . . To me, it is self-evident that if perestroika succeeds, there will be a real chance of building a new world order." So spoke Soviet President Mikhail Gorbachev in his Nobel Prize speech in Oslo in June 1991. His comments established that in the wake of the changes in Eastern Europe and the Persian Gulf War, a new era of world politics would emerge. The essential political character of this era would be "democratic," and the economic ingredient would be market-based. To some intellectuals, the triumph of a democratic markets–based system of government was so apparent as to be final. Others were less convinced. By 1996 the outlook had become more sanguine.

Was the end of the cold war a triumph of capitalism? In *Centesimus Annus,* Pope John Paul II (1991) inquires: "Can it perhaps be said that, after the failure of Communism, capitalism is the victorious social system, and that capitalism should be the goal of the countries now making efforts to rebuild their economy and society?" He answers his own inquiry by pointing out that if by capitalism is meant the "primitive" and often "ruthless" system criticized by the church a century ago, "the reply is certainly negative." But "if by capitalism is meant an economic system which recognizes the fundamental and positive role of business, the market, private property, and the resulting responsibility for the means of production, as well as free human creativity in the economic sector, then the answer is certainly in the affirmative" (*Wall Street Journal* May 2, 1991: A18). In short, capitalism is to be commended for encouraging initiative and creativity, but "its practitioners [must] give their system a liberal dose of ethics and compassion" (*Universe Bulletin,* May 10, 1991: 1).

Perhaps this "new capitalism" will develop the capacity to serve developing and developed nations alike. No one would dare to guarantee it, but the accounting discipline may be one important element in addressing it by means of developing a consonant theory of disclosure that evolves from proprietary and entity approaches toward a broader "community" view.[4]

The "New Capitalism" and Property Rights

The standard of living and the way of life in the United States are looked upon by many as an enviable accomplishment. Others are critical of the contrast between the extremes of wealth and poverty and the extent to which waste and pollution are prevalent. Is there too much concern about the standard of living and less about the quality of life? Is there too much "wealth" and too little "commonwealth"? What promise can such a system hold when there is poverty in the midst of plenty? Others are concerned that the ability of future generations to maintain and improve such an energy-rich standard of living is limited.

Why, to quote Alexis de Tocqueville's words of more than a century ago, is there so much "Anxiety in the midst of Prosperity" (*Wall Street Journal* May 16, 1996: A20)? Because, critics argue, the cradle of incentives represented by individual ownership of private productive property may not have the systemic capacity for a global age where information and community property rights must be equitably addressed on a broader scale. Physical property rights and intellectual property rights may differ (Manne 1975). The present prosperity is based on the former; the future is based on the latter. Can a system of private property rights, fundamental to the achievement of improvements in both the quality and standard of living be equitably implemented in an intellectual property rights age with a global population of five billion? Is the manner of passive investing identified with mutual funds served by a disclosure system that responds to a different order of agency issues—separation of owners and managers of operating companies?

Technology

Several devices were popularized in the 1970s and 1980s: the personal computer (PC), and communication inventions, such as the FAX machine, compact disc data storage, and the cellular telephone. Consumer electronics products and services introduced cable TV, the videocassette recorder, and more recently satellite dish reception. All have had a profound effect on lifestyles and standards of living as well as the location of the population; again today there is a promise of the increasing capacity of technology announced by Texas Instruments to have "the power of 20 PCs in a thumbnail-sized chip."

The central appliances of this space age, atomic, and electronic culture are the television, a sort of modern "hearthstone," and the computer, a device used by many but understood by few. As computer technology passed through successive generations of increased capability, it has created new opportunities for the sharing of knowledge and abetted decision-making ability by providing instant access to vast quantities of data and information. As this facilitated the standard of living, it caused increased need to coordinate interdependencies between the sectors of the economy, thereby creating a need for increasing reliability and sophistication in preparing and using information provided by the accountant. At the same time, the computer's complexity has challenged the auditor's ability to employ "electronic" logic and become adept at assessing the proper use of technology in accounting and auditing applications. The computer's dependence on electronic messages erases the paper audit trail that had conventionally served as a basis for evidence. Ease of access to the computer in the business world has created the need for new accounting skills and for team auditing. It foretold the means to create a paperless society based on the electronic transfer of funds between financial institutions. Hardware alone, however, was not the trigger to the information revolution. "User-friendly software" was. It served as the key to unlocking information technology, permitting it to flow through "windows" into homes and offices. PCs are now as common as the typewriter was a generation ago, creating the expectation of database accounting and continuous auditing.

One of the first products to afford accountants with this entree was spreadsheet software such as *Lotus 1-2-3,* introduced in 1983. The longer-term prospect of reporting via electronic media, skipping intermediate reporting vehicles and agents and obtaining direct access to corporate databases was entering a stage of serious consideration (Beaver and Rappaport 1984). The Securities and Exchange Commission, about this time, under the direction of then Chairman John Shad, contracted for the development of direct electronic filing of financial reports to the SEC, at first on a voluntary basis, using the EDGAR (Electronic Data Gathering, Analysis and Retrieval) system, with a plan for its becoming mandatory by 1996. In addition, the SEC also approved in 1991 the creation of an electronic library for municipal bond documents.

Market Characteristics

One might have felt a slight difference on Monday, June 23, 1980, in picking up the *Wall Street Journal,* which heretofore had been printed in a single section. Now it was to be published in two sections, representative of the burgeoning information (and advertising) market the *Journal* commanded. A few years later, it would again expand into a third section. In similar fashion, the Dow Jones Industrial Average, the pulse of the American capital market since 1896, would rise above the 2,000 level for the first time on Thursday, January 8, 1987. The Dow would trade over the 3,000 mark in 1990, and on April 17, 1991, it would "close" at that level; by the early months of 1996 it was regularly recorded well above 5,000. During the first twenty-three trading days of 1991 alone, 24 initial public offerings (IPOs) would be brought to the market for $1.3 billion; by April, 64 IPOs totaling $6 billion had been registered with the SEC. A similar IPO surge through March 1983 had required 128 issues to reach that dollar level. The five-trillion-dollar-a-year U.S. economy was achieving milestones that, at the trough of the October 1987 market, would have been but a faint hope. This run of the 1990s bull market defied clear explanation, even granting that the opening of world-class competition and the development of expeditious technologies fueled optimism about prospects for a new round of business expansion.

Pension Funds, Portfolios, and Capital Formation

"Socialism came to America," writes Peter Drucker, "neither through the ballot box nor through class struggle . . . nor through a 'crisis' brought on by the 'contradictions of capitalism.' Indeed, it was brought about by the most unlikely revolutionary of them all—in April 1950 when Charles Wilson, then GM's president, proposed the establishment of a pension fund for workers" (Drucker 1976: 5). Defining socialism as "ownership of the means of production by the workers," Drucker proceeds to argue that the United States is the first truly "socialist" country, given that by 1976, "employees of American business . . . own[ed] at least 25 percent of its equity capital, which is more than enough for control." Furthermore, he guessed that by 1985, employees would probably own at least 50 percent of equity capital (Drucker 1976: 1). In fact, using only the New York Stock Exchange data available through 1988, the 1976 equity holdings of pension funds as a percentage of total share listed value were not quite so extensive as Drucker asserted, having reached about 30 percent of listed shares by 1988. (In 1960, *all* institutional investors owned only 17 percent; in 1950, they had owned 1 percent.) However, both the trend and the evidence support his contention (Lazonick 1988: 123). Viewing this from the investor perspective, by the end of 1986, 38 percent of all pension fund portfolios were invested in equities, compared with 32 percent in 1981. By the end of 1986, the assets of all pension funds had risen to more than $1.7 trillion, roughly double the value of such assets in 1981. (This phenomenon had, of course, triggered the "defeasance" issue for accountants when major companies arranged to substitute contracted annuities financed by portfolio gains in lieu of continuing pension fund contribution payments, leaving unaffected the actuarial soundness of the pension funds (Melloan 1987).)

Commenting on the pension fund phenomenon in 1991, the *Economist* observed: "Once the GM's union agreed to the plan, a bandwagon rolled: within a year 8,000 new plans had been written along the same lines" (April 27, 1991: S8). The GM plan differed from funds previously in operation in that it did not operate as an ESOP (employee stock ownership plan), which principally invests in the company's own stock. It sought instead broad, diversified investment in the American economy. The phenomenon of such a diversified and funded scheme now applies in Britain and is becoming recognized in Japan but not yet in Germany where such plans operate principally as ESOPs.[5]

The advent of *pension fund socialism,* as termed by Drucker, has escaped wide popular notice and avoided notoriety, political and otherwise. Yet the power of pension funds and related 401(K) tax plan contributions to mutual fund investment institutions is such that pensioners' funds "own" "practically every single one of the largest industrial corporations in America . . . [and] also control the fifty largest companies in each of the 'nonindustrial' groups, that is, in banking, insurance, retail, communications, and transportation." "These are," Drucker reminds us, "what socialist theory calls the 'command positions' of the economy; whoever controls them is in command of the rest" (Drucker 1976: 2). Even considering Drucker's views, there are other substantial complex institutional forces, including bank creditors and small, individual investors, at play in the marketplace. Can a market economy of such a multilevel dynamic construction—representing hundreds of millions of personal value judgments embodied as the bases of resource decisions—be fully represented by any single theory or system? Does pension plan investment in operating and service companies truly translate to "control" of those entities? If not, are the professional managers the true sovereigns of this new economic order?

Two ingredients thought to facilitate such a market economy's process are the timely availability of reliable and relevant information and confidence that the system affords a fair opportunity to invest. To the extent that the confidence of responsible individual investors is enhanced by reliable financial information and other disclosures provided by the activities of the responsible accounting professional, any capital market structure of society is strengthened.

A relevant question thus becomes, If pension funds are in command, who is in command of the pension funds? And further, Are the businesses that pension funds control under the managerial influence of the funds? Plausible answers to these questions provide candidates for first principles about the role of investment information needed by capital market participants as supplied by accountants, corporate financial reporting management, and public auditors.

So, again, who is in control? Surely not the individuals who constitute the beneficiaries of the fund (i.e., laborers or knowledge workers). But if they are not in control, who is? The investment fund managers? Perhaps, but their role is to invest, achieve a target return and, as fiduciaries, to "divest" if the rate of return and/or corresponding risk become unsuitable. Thus, in matters of control over the company they "own," it is far from clear that investors exercise control over the investee! For as fiduciaries, investment managers are bound to regard the management of the pension fund to be their role, and not the management or the investee's business per se. So investment fund managers are more likely to "vote with their feet," or to become "punters" and not "players" in the ultimate sense of controlling the assets of investee companies. Despite notable activism policies by large institutional investors of pension funds, the issues remain.

If the individual pensioners and the fund managers are not in control, then who is? Who controls the assets of corporate America, which the pension funds own? Pension fund socialism fails to resolve this question; therefore, it falls short of providing guidance for proper public policy as to the timing and content of financial decision information, reporting, and disclosure. As a single explanation it is lacking.

Writing in 1977, Chandler observed that the rise of the professional management class nearly a century ago in large, publicly held companies established the "visible hand" of managerial capitalism. This view asserts that the "*invisible* hand," or marketplace formed by the action of individuals acting in their own self-interest as portrayed by Adam Smith, had been supplanted by the "visible hand" of professional managers whose control over the resources of major enterprises constitutes the means of the modern marketplace. Taken together, Drucker's pension fund socialism and Chandler's managerial capitalism afford useful, if not powerful, ideas with which to attempt an understanding of debt and equity, capital, markets, control, and the information needed to inform managers and investors in today's setting. Together they suggest that institutional fund managers and corporate managers have the capacity and incentive to control both pension fund assets and the corporate investee assets in both domestic and global markets. Providing the information necessary to achieve allocational efficiency in asset investment and in utilization therefore becomes a principal goal of information professionals in managerial and financial accounting roles. And providing information to pension fund and mutual fund investees as to the performance of their fund managers also becomes a concern as fundamental as providing information to shareholders about corporate performance.

An International Dimension: Geoaccountancy

In April 1991, the California Public Employee Retirement System (CALPERS), whose pension assets are currently valued at upwards of $70 billion—the largest public pension fund in the nation—threw out applications from ninety-one international money managers, saying a majority failed to comply with the state's 1989 affirmative action law.[6] This type of social activism on the part of pension fund management seems somewhat atypical. Nevertheless, given CALPERS's formidable size, its move into international investment on such terms provides an important preview to what may become part of the method of selecting international investing contracts (*Wall Street Journal* April 16, 1991). The burgeoning internationalism of U.S. pension and investment funds, as has been noted, is one of the forms of change having increasing influence on the capital market. FASB standards, which address such issues as foreign currency translation and financial instruments involving international rate swaps, have served to highlight the difficulty of resolving differences of a fundamental nature among diversified multinational corporations. Today corporations work in the legal form of a single entity but operate in economic substance as multiple individual operations in various foreign and domestic locations.

"Accounting and Auditing in One World," the theme of the Eleventh World Congress of Accountants (Munich, October 1977), suggested the importance that accountants place on achieving harmony in accounting practices in industrial countries throughout the world. This importance has been accentuated by the subsequent movement of former Soviet bloc countries into some stages of a capital market system.

The formation of the International Accounting Standards Committee (IASC) in 1973 provided the vehicle for national professional institutions to work together toward harmonized reports. The subsequent formation of the International Federation of Accountants (IFAC) provided a vehicle to address auditing issues that exist between countries with different economic systems and accounting customs.[7] By the 1990s, the International Organization of Securities Commissions (IOSCO) had begun to identify and discuss authoritative arrangements for disclosure standards with professional groups. Among the basic issues to be resolved are the blend of the host nation's accounting principles and the guest company's accounting principles to be followed when there are differences and the degree to which the individual accountant's and auditor's judgment based upon general principles will prevail over a rules-driven standards approach. If there is a need for comparable financial information to be made available for an internationally integrated capital market system, there will be a corresponding need for some internationally recognized principles and/or standards to harmonize such global financial disclosures throughout the global capital market process. Although it would appear to be an almost impossible task to cut through the cultural, language, monetary, and legal differences among multinational industrial societies, the necessity for cooperation and a spirit of accounting professionalism on a national and international scale affords an excellent opportunity to make progress with these difficult matters. Furthermore, since systems of accounting are based on the double-entry method, there is, at the heart of all commercial accounting systems, that common element of procedure from which an internationally responsive and comparable system of accounting can be developed. During the 1980s, several accounting directives, approved and implemented in the European Economic Community's member countries, provided a prototype of the process and options that provide initial solutions to multinational standards for measurement and reporting. Addressing international investment and disclosure issues and understanding the historical context of their origin should assist in a more effective strategic deployment of our national accounting education and practice resources in the future.

International Investees

Our economic world is no longer directed chiefly by geographically defined nations, but by twin transgeographic entities: the multinational corporation and its companion, the institutional portfolio investment fund. Their combined appetite to consume and capacity to provide capital have sped the integration of financial markets from London to Tokyo and created incentives for instruments, such as interest rate swaps, to expedite the flow of capital while avoiding costs peculiar to purely national market structures. By 1992, the planned financial unification of the European Economic Community reduced transaction barriers to capital flows within the boundaries of its twelve member countries.

In order to facilitate broad and rapid capital flows among countries, the Dow Jones World Index, a comprehensive measure of world stock market performance, was placed into development in 1988. This step toward a monolithic bellwether for the world capital market shows the evolution of "stock-around-the-clock" trading plans that are being tested by major exchanges.

A polarization of investors toward stocks with large stock-market values that trade on major world exchanges has become apparent. These stocks, referred to in the press as "haves" because they have access to large liquid global markets, include companies such as IBM of the United States, BP of Great Britain, Sony of Japan, and Siemens AG of Germany (see table 8.2). The "have nots," which include a vast majority of stocks of smaller companies, tend to be passed up by international investors who dominate global trading (*Wall Street Journal* May 8, 1991).

These companies represent target investees for major investors world-

TABLE 8.2

The Global "Haves" Corporations with Access to World Capital

Base	Index	No. of Firms
U.S.	Standard and Poor's 500	500
Japan	Nikkei	225
U.K.	Financial Times–Stock Exchange	100
EEC	Eurotrack	100
Total corporations		925

wide (and also represent the major clientele sought and serviced by public accounting firms). NYSE's consideration of 24-hour trading, said to be years away, is a response to "off-hours trading systems," such as Globex, operated by Reuters, and the Chicago Mercantile Exchange, which are pressing the timetable of the Big Board (Torres 1991). The NYSE system in 1990 was said to have the capacity "on average" to handle all the trading capacity of all the stock exchanges of the world. NYSE officials questioned the need for the substantial duplication of trading systems caused by off-hours operators, noting that when sufficient investor demand exists for 24-hour trading, the Big Board would act. To assess this demand, the NYSE began a two-year test in June 1991 of an extended trading session after the regular 4:00 P.M. closing hour. The Board returned to normal trading hours shortly after and began instead to monitor trades at other global locations by member firms.

The Market's Black Monday: October 1987

In a dinner speech to professors attending a symposium at the St. Charles Center of Arthur Andersen & Co. in October 1988, David Ruder, chairman of the SEC at the time of the October 19, 1987, stock market plunge (the Dow fell 508 points), characterized it as "a rush for the exits by a large number of institutions—the system was not structured to handle that level of demand." In Ruder's view, the key player in the episode was the institutional investor. The policy issue that Ruder raised in his remarks was, Are institutional investors justified in getting out of the market on their own? This implies the question, To whom are funds responsible? Little attention is paid in the routine education of accountants, or in their later training, to such contextual issues related to the evolving role of institutional investors and the derived demand this places on accounting information and services.

Technically, Ruder said, the likelihood of a repeat of such a problem could be alleviated by improvements in the system, by creating "smarter" systems and circuit breakers, and reducing systematic problems.

But another issue remained: What is there about the institutional investor, the individual investor, and the publicly held company that collectively specifies the market's information needs, and what accounting services are appropriate to provide the investing public the assurance that investments are properly overseen? In short, what role does the accounting profession assume to ensure that the public will be disposed to trust the global investment marketplace? The consequences of a shortfall of public confidence and the reduction in the supply of capital are of such consequence as to warrant consideration of the question with continuing care.

Technical analysts, reviewing the relationship between the market's plunge in 1987 and capital asset pricing model investment theory, have asserted that potential congressional action under consideration the week prior to the market decline was rumored to affect the tax-deductible status of interest on corporate bonds, which had been vital in financing the corporate consolidations of the 1980s. In turn, the loss or limitation of such deductible status would affect the cost of capital, earning power, and dividend policy of corporations, perhaps especially those with high levels of debt (*Economist* April 27, 1991). Regardless of the proximate causes of the plunge—tax interest policy, institutional trading practices, overcapitalization, or ignorance—this episode and the related concerns over the savings and loan (S&L) banking and insurance company investment practices have led to an examination of the relevance of basic federal statutes related to capital markets.

By mid-1991, reforms in banking and securities legislation were being debated in the light of investment theory, global stock trading, tax policy, and the Federal Reserve, Treasury, SEC, and the myriad of other federal establishments (Commodity Futures Trading Commission; Office of the Comptroller of the Currency; Office of Management and Budget, and so forth) that interrelate to capital and commodity market institutions and practices. Disputes over allowing banks into areas such as insurance or stock brokerage, previously prohibited by the Glass-Steagall Act, seemed to be nearing resolution, but debate continued about permitting nonbank entities to own commercial banks. So-called industrial banks, including one owned by Ford Motor Co., had been formed but were not authorized to accept consumer deposits. The support of a system of money-center banks was a sign of moving away from the community hometown institutions that had characterized America's Main Street image. This change, and the reality of the two-tiered nature of the securities market, one level involving sophisticated investors managing large portfolios and the other involving small individual investors picking individual stocks, identified capital market events at the close of the 1980s and the beginning of the 1990s.

Private Sector Reform

Financial Reporting: The Wheat and Trueblood Studies

All these changes were occurring during the period in which Jacques Barzun, a noted professor at Columbia University, observed that the learned professions, most notably medicine and law, were under siege. In 1978, Barzun noted:

> This comprehensive resentment against the visible professions does not spring wholly from experience, though facts at second hand or in print are not lacking. Part of the animus comes from the general unrest and impatience with authority in the Western world, coupled with the belief that anything long established is probably corrupt.

> A profession is an institution, and as such it cuts a figure in public that may or may not match the prevailing habits of the practitioners. The insiders genuinely believe in that figure; they live by it in more ways than one, and they can hardly help thinking of The Profession as going on forever.

> Modern professions have enjoyed their monopoly for so long they have forgotten that it is a privilege given in exchange for a public benefit.

> The upshot is that a profession is by nature a vulnerable institution. It makes claims; it demands unique privileges; and it has to perform. (Barzun 1978: 63)

In an attempt to manage their own affairs better, CPAs established two major fact-finding committees in the early 1970s and subsequently formed a commission to study the change in public expectations with regard to auditors' responsibilities.

The initiative of the AAA's Commission to Establish Accounting Principles by then President James Don Edwards and the subsequent formation of the Wheat Committee of the AICPA in 1971 signaled the start of a series of efforts by academics and practitioners to reevaluate the process for establishing accounting standards. The APB's failure to capture the confidence of professionals and gain the support of the SEC, beginning with the investment credit issue, foretold that the APB lacked the necessary stature to influence the outcome of debates over accounting principles. The deliberations of the Wheat Committee led to the establishment of the Financial Accounting Standards Board (FASB), consisting of seven full-time members, which began operations in 1973 (Seidler 1973).[8] The recommendation for such a board confirmed the preference for an autonomous, appointive, due-process approach to private sector standard setting versus a legalistic court system approach, as had been suggested by Seymour Walton as early as 1909 and revitalized in the speeches of Leonard Spacek in the late 1950s.

The formation of the FASB was the profession's response to the many criticisms directed toward the APB. Lobbying and political pressure on Congress at the time of the reinstitution of the investment tax credit in 1971 resulted in the enactment of a law specifying either the flow-through or the deferral technique for financial accounting of the credit as appropriate. This excursion by Congress into the realm of financial accounting standard setting awakened accounting professionals to the prospect that further political legislation in other matters related to financial measurement and reporting was possible. The political message was clear: The APB had ignored or misinterpreted the intention of Congress as to the investment tax credit. The political and economic consequences of modern accounting rules were closely monitored by corporate and government officials. The standard-setting process could not be effective without regard for all constituents' concerns, including those of the business community, which was becoming a more vocal constituency.

The Wheat Committee (1971), the Trueblood Committee (1971), and the Cohen Commission (1974) represented the profession's major attempts to address the need to govern and direct its own standard-setting activities, to identify the reporting population to which it holds a prime responsibility, and to report to society in view of the expectations of the latter. In forming these groups and addressing these issues, the accounting profession began to acknowledge its diverse constituency and the "political" implications thereof. It would also become necessary to take steps to increase the AICPA's enforcement support of private sector standards by establishing a new rule in the code (Rule 203, instituted in 1973) that would require AICPA members to employ FASB-promulgated standards, unless to do so would result in a material misstatement. Wally Olson, serving as the chief staff officer of the AICPA during this period, identifies the years between 1969 and 1980 as the institute's "years of trial" in his book-length record of these episodes (Olson 1982).

The Trueblood Committee maintained that the primary purpose of published financial reports was to provide information useful for making economic decisions by those who were primarily dependent on annual reports and who had limited resources, authority, and ability to obtain such information. The contribution of Robert Trueblood and his committee was to target as a constituency the broad nonprofessional group of financial statement users and to seek to expand the disclosure horizon from financial statements to financial reports.

The Cohen Commission: Auditing

The Cohen Commission, established in October 1974, addressed the matter that through custom had long been represented in the maxim "The auditor is a watchdog and not a bloodhound"; that is, if the auditor takes reasonable care, he is justified in believing that the management of the company in whom he has placed confidence is in fact honest, and that he, as an auditor, may rely upon management's representations.[9] However, in the wake of the massive computer fraud underlying the collapse of Equity Funding and the creative accounting manipulations in the National Student Marketing case, questioning became common: "Do auditors know how to perform EDP audits?" and "Where were the auditors?" (AICPA 1975A). In each case, prominent auditing firms were directly or indirectly involved in the filing of the financial statements of these publicly held companies. These concerns, accented by the post-Watergate revelations of questionable political and business payments, have made it important to reconsider whether the auditor is expected to accept a responsibility to be both watchdog and bloodhound. With a view toward establishing and identifying the role of the auditor in today's society, the Cohen Commission considered several key issues. Are society's expectations of auditors realistic? Are all auditors' views about their role somewhat identical? Do they differ from society's? The tone of the Cohen Commission's report was sobering. If auditors were to address the needs of society, it observed, they must begin by amending their own deficiencies, by reexamining the process by which auditing standards are established, and by seeking to improve the fundamental education and continuing education processes applicable to auditor training.

Financial Fraud: The Limitations of Auditing

A contemporary advertising slogan in the financial community framed this topic well. "How can you trust your judgment," it asked rhetorically, "if you can't trust the numbers?" One might ask, "Whose numbers are they, anyway?" The answer is not simple, particularly if one views the role of the professional accountant within the firm and the external auditor in the

Architects of Modern Practice

Francis Wheat

Robert Trueblood

George Anderson

Edmund Jenkins

Source: AICPA, New York.

larger frame of being part of the social policy and process of socializing credit and investment risk. That is, professional persons in positions of responsibility are part of a broad safety net to diversify the risk and cost of investment. Consider the following known examples. "A 52-year-old accountant was convicted yesterday of helping cover up a massive securities fraud at the carpet cleaning company founded by former whiz-kid entrepreneur Barry Minkow" (*Plain Dealer*, December 20, 1988). So read the press report by Reuter news service. Another black eye for accountants, be they CPAs or other practicing professionals? To the public in general, to whom accountants and CPAs seem to be interchangeable, it was more evidence of a breach of faith. Perhaps it was not so disturbing as the conviction of José Gomez, a former CPA firm partner and auditor convicted in 1986 of fraud for accepting a bribe of $225,000 to falsify financial statements of ESM Government Securities Inc., a firm that defrauded state-insured Home State Bank in Ohio, resulting in losses in excess of $150 million (Maggin 1990). Gomez received a twelve-year prison sentence, and his firm's insurance company paid an $80 million settlement. This entire regrettable episode was made more memorable by an anecdote carried in the media quoting Marvin Warner, the Home State owner, and broadcast on March 21, 1985. "I never made a dishonest dollar in my life," said Warner. "It's all the accountant's fault."

In the case of ZZZZ Best, not only was the internal accountant, Norman Rothberg, convicted, but the company's auditors were also accused of failing to detect the fraudulent fire and water damage restoration business of ZZZZ Best. In the case of Brookside Savings and Loan of Los Angeles, Peter Cartmell, president of Brookside and formerly the chief financial officer of Westwood Savings & Loan of Los Angeles, was convicted of constructing a complex set of real estate and securities transactions on Brookside's books, designed to create a phony $3 million profit (*Wall Street Journal* 1991). Other episodes include the settlement between Coopers & Lybrand and the FDIC in which the firm, in order to preclude a lawsuit, agreed to pay $20 million to the FDIC to settle possible malpractice claims arising from its audits of the failed Silverado S&L (*Wall Street Journal* 1991).

Perhaps the most useful summary about the crisis in financial institutions that erupted in the late 1980s was provided by an observer who noted that among potential parties to fault, including the Congress, the federal government, executives, regulators, auditors, and real estate promoters, there was enough blame to go around for everyone. And so it seemed. But that did not prevent some from attempting to shift the blame for what was coming to them onto others. Even in cases where no factual impropriety had been proven, appearances caused persons to become suspicious about accountants and financial institution clients. For instance, there was the case of a former audit partner in the firm that issued favorable reports on Charles H. Keating's Lincoln Savings's operations who was later hired by Lincoln's parent, American Continental Corporation in 1988 at a reported salary of more than $500,000.

Accountants seemed particularly vulnerable. Disclosures about mortgage and business loan arrangements between financial institutions and individual partners of their audit firms, while addressed by remedial standards, raised issues about independence in appearance (AICPA 1991B). Furthermore, other outcomes implied some auditor responsibility, as in the $1.5 million settlement between Ernst & Young on behalf of its predecessor, Arthur Young & Co., to settle charges of professional negligence in the audit of Lincoln Savings and Loan (*Wall Street Journal* April 29, 1991).

Critics of capital market economies often denounce the system for its greed and lack of principle. This is pretty standard stuff for critics, sort of like a "dog bites man" story in the newspaper. But when patriarchs of the system are critical of capital markets, it is a "man bites dog" story. Consider, for example, centenarian Frederick C. Crawford, chairman emeritus of the aerospace-defense contracting giant TRW, who, while acknowledging that running the business in his day was easier than it is now, observed: "Wall Street has become a gambling joint" (Yerak 1990). Or consider investment banker Felix Rohatyn's 1986 speech to the Urban League of Greater New York: "I have been in business for almost forty years and I cannot recall a period in which greed and corruption appeared as prevalent as they are today." Rohatyn continues: "As a result of the ongoing revelations of scandals, the securities industry will have to accept new legislation and regulation to curb the speculative abuses of the past several years. This is long overdue" (*Wall Street Journal* December 5, 1986).

It was not until several years later, following the 1987 market plunge, that Harry Markowitz, a high priest of modern portfolio theory, characteristically observed, in what can be seen as a rebuttal to Rohatyn, that "I know of no *study* that shows financial industries of the '80s had more lawbreakers than other industries or other times (Markowitz 1991; emphasis added). Even if true, the retort does not excuse the lapses. The issue is that markets must be perceived to be fair if they are to be seen as an efficient world resource allocation vehicle.

Business Decision Information in a Dynamic Global Competitive Financial Market

Consider as well the implications of aggressive marketing strategies implemented by banks in the 1980s to compete with insurance companies such as Prudential, who entered the home mortgage market. Dime Bank of New York, for example, a conservative institution that shunned commercial real estate and junk bonds (the bane of S&L portfolios) was not known as was Wells Fargo Bank for involvement in HLTs (highly leveraged transactions, such as in the management buy-outs of RJR Nabisco or Time Warner) but instead invested in so-called low-doc mortgages. In 1987, for instance, Dime issued new low-doc mortgages worth about $3.4 billion. Low-doc or no-doc loans are mortgage loans made without "documentation" (i.e., "doc") or traditional investigation as to the credit worthiness of the applicant. The view given was that as it was nearly impossible to lose money on home mortgages, it was appropriate to reduce or eliminate costly processing such as confirmation of salaries or similar applicant information. Such business decisions, while perhaps involving the purview of accountants acting as chief financial officers, clearly go beyond the realm of an accounting matter and represent management strategic policy and risk assessment. In these circumstances, how does the role of the auditor affect such matters after the fact, several years later, when the strategy fails and mortgage foreclosures begin to threaten a bank's solvency? If such situations are to be reduced, ongoing involvement by auditors in risk decisions and options may be needed.

The Treadway Commission

Earlier, in 1985, at the instigation of then AICPA Chairman Ray Groves, a private sector commission chaired by former SEC Commissioner James Treadway, after whom the group's name has been taken, worked to provide recommendations for both the private and public sector to improve financial management and deter financial fraud. Its final report, issued in 1987, contained recommendations for the publicly held company, the independent public accountant, the SEC, law enforcement agencies, and for the educational community.

Some Treadway recommendations have not been implemented. Some recommendations, to increase the SEC's ability to invoke nonjudicial punishment, have been. These include increased powers to fine and to suspend corporate officials who violate the securities law by barring them from working in publicly held companies or in the securities business. The independent auditors' responses have been directed at the commission's recommendations about the expectation gap; that is, the difference between what the general public thinks the auditor does and what in fact an audit does undertake to do. A series of expectation gap auditing standards were approved and have been implemented; they include amending the form and content of the auditor's report and redefining the auditor's responsibility to detect and report errors, irregularities, and illegal acts by clients. In 1996, the AICPA also released an exposure draft for auditors to meet their fraud detection responsibilities.

In order to attempt to make corporate internal control systems more effective, the commission had recommended external auditor review of management reports on corporate internal controls. This recommendation reflected the new "mega risk" facing PC-based control systems whether mainframe or LAN (local area network). This proposal has been opposed by corporate financial officers who argue the cost exceeds the benefit and that it duplicates the work of internal audit staffs.

CPAs in public practice have also sought the SEC's support for a Treadway recommendation for mandatory quality review of public company auditors. As with all such private sector commissions that lack authority to implement change, many of Treadway's recommended reforms will not come to pass, despite the efforts of an implementation follow-up group, the Committee of Sponsoring Organizations of the Treadway Commission. However, Treadway has been effective and, perhaps more important, has left as a legacy the message that there is a compelling need to set the proper ethical "tone at the top" of the organization (*Report of the National Commission on Fraudulent Financial Reporting* 1987).

Institutional Maturity

With estimates that its members constitute about 85 percent of those licensed to practice, the AICPA is important, even granting that it is not alone on the institutional scene, sharing the role with the Institute of Management Accountants, the Financial Executives Institute, the Institute of Internal Auditors, the Association of Government Accountants, the American Accounting Association, state CPA societies, and many other associations or groups. The AICPA has emerged, however, as the leading professional organization, in part because of its ability to serve the greatest number of professionals at the national level (see figure 8.3). This has oc-

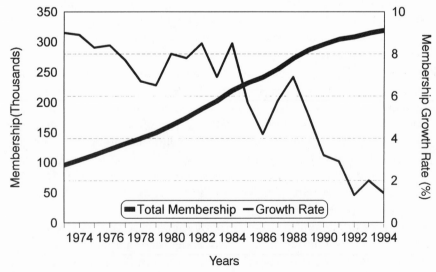

Figure 8.3 AICPA membership and membership growth rates, 1973–1994

AICPA Presidents, 1972–1995

Wallace E. Olson (1972–1980)   Philip B. Chenok (1980–1995)
Source: AICPA, New York.

curred even though CPA licenses are awarded by a particular state or territory and are not a national or federal certificate. As a practical matter, the profession's basic or "franchise" service remains the audit/attest engagement, which is commonly performed in an interstate setting, so that a national professional organization is essential to communicate information and to assure consistent and comparable quality of practice.

Professional accounting in the U.S. has long departed its "pioneering" phase of pastlessness. It now has more than a century of experience upon which to draw and dwell. Newspaper stories about centenarian accountants still "practicing," while novel, provide evidence of the longevity that underlies the profession's maturity and successfulness ("Centenarian takes Account," 1989).

A price of this new maturity and success is an added responsibility to become proactive in addressing the seemingly endless pressures found in practice and technology that require change in any number of technical practices and institutional arrangements. The AICPA, for example, has revised its Mission Statement since 1986 to specify the responsibilities involved in serving both its members and the public. The transition to a broader view of its role was evidenced in the manner the AICPA celebrated its centennial in 1987. In a keynote essay, published in the centennial celebration issue of the *Journal of Accountancy*, James Don Edwards and

Paul Miranti conclude that the profession's role "has flourished because practitioners have rightly believed their expertise is valuable in protecting the public interest (1987: 38).

The 1987 Excellence Campaign of the AICPA offered six proposals reflecting the commitment to this role, all of which were overwhelmingly approved by the membership.[10] The proposals, including mandatory quality review of public reporting services, required continuing professional education for all members, increased entry-level formal education to an equivalent of postgraduate work, restructured the trial board process, and promoted a reformed Code of Professional Conduct, establishing broad ideals as positive goals for all members in corporate and public practice.

From Financial to "Business Reporting"

The Jenkins Committee concluded its work in fall 1994. The committee, which included as vice chairman Michael Sutton, who would be appointed SEC chief accountant in May 1995, directed its research toward learning about "user's needs" in financial reporting. It advanced a view that "business reporting" (i.e., information that a company provides to help users with capital allocation decisions about the company) was the cornerstone of good reporting (AICPA, 1994).

Accountants of the future as professional preparers and auditors would thus provide a broader element set of "business reporting" information of which financial statements were but a modest part. In 1994 as the Jenkins Committee was winding up its efforts, another one of its committee members, Robert Elliott, was selected to lead yet another special committee to address CPA "assurance services," a term developed to suggest a broader scope of service than audit or attest work. The term "assurance" was defined to include those independent professional services that improve the quality of information, or its context, for decision-making. This committee's work would continue through 1996.

Regulation, Litigation, and Oversight

Public Agencies, Public Control: RAP or GAAP?

SEC, FTC, CASB, OSHA, IRS, ICC, FCC, DOE, DOD. What do all of these acronyms have in common? They represent the variety of federal government agencies that directly interact or influence financial and management accounting practice and policy, thereby shaping the economy and accounting's environment.[11] The fact that those agencies establish special information measures—referred to as Regulatory Accounting Principles or RAP—adds more complexity to the process of accounting, to the determining of authoritative standards, and to providing the public with a comparable basis from which to evaluate the spectrum of companies and activities affected by such agencies. Is it GAAP or is it RAP?

The increased tendency to establish standards in the public sector that affect financial reporting via peculiar specifications established by each of these agencies led some, including then Commerce Secretary Juanita Kreps, to propose that agency requirements demonstrate effectiveness by means of a cost-benefit test (Kreps 1978).

Beginning with the move to deregulate the airlines and to de-emphasize government regulation throughout the economy during the Reagan presidential terms, the actions of regulatory agencies, while less aggressive themselves, did not conform to a specific pattern. The FTC, for example, continued to pursue the alleged anticompetitive practices of professional groups, leaving mostly uncontested the consolidation of manufacturing industries such as steel making. Savings and loans were "deregulated" in the early 1980s; the Cost Accounting Standards Board, which was permitted to lapse from existence in the early 1980s was reconstituted and made its reappearance in the late 1980s, keeping in place its previously issued federal contracting cost-accounting standards. Meanwhile, the ICC announced a decision to maintain its accounting regulations in accordance with GAAP while federal regulators of financial institutions furthered their efforts to enforce RAP for purposes of capital requirements for financial institutions.

Deep Pocket Liability

The 1970s, 1980s, and 1990s witnessed an increasing number of complex litigations involving accountants. To the extent that each of these cases evidenced a particular social expectation, the courts via case law redrew the dimensions of accountants' responsibilities. Practitioners cynical about the ability of the courts to resolve the matter on the basis of legal principles indicate that case law is nothing more than a rationalization of the judge's preconception. That is, the courts will look for available resources to redress the grievance and then produce a legal precedent to support the economic outcome of the preconception. A "deep pocket" liability theory, as applied to accountants, reflected the view that accountants' earnings and assets are sufficient to provide a source of social relief. A 1978 disclosure in the financial press noted that partners in most major public accounting firms earn between $90,000 and $100,000 per year. A figure double those amounts would constitute a conservative approximation for 1990. However, very little specific information is available and often such general or average numbers are misleading.[12]

Securities and Litigation Reform

The 1136 Tenants decision implied that the courts expect the public accountant to warrant at least to a limited extent that accounting reports are "sound" in the absence of an engagement agreement specifying a nonattest service. This case was decided in favor of the owners of a cooperative apartment complex against a small practitioner who had not, in the court's view, clarified the scope and responsibility of the engagement that he had agreed to undertake.[13] The decision also highlighted a technical deficiency; that is, the need to describe, in the form of an engagement memorandum, the nature of accounting services to be provided. Both small and large practitioners have therefore been made aware of the need to educate specific clients about the variety of services that they provide other than the audit. The 1136 Tenants decision was important, because it established in case law the public's expectation that when a CPA was involved in an engagement, absent some other explanation, an investigation of basic discrepancies was expected. Whether or not such a view is justified is arguable, particularly in light of the distinct traditional difference between private company services offered by public practitioners (financial statement compilation or review services) as contrasted with the audit of financial statements. If private company CPA practitioners' services, such as compilations, were indistinguishable from audits, would it then be expected that private companies also conform to the disclosure standards followed by major public company–SEC accounting firms? This would ignore important differences of levels of credit market disclosure requirements, in that not every entity requires an audit. There have evolved over time essential unaudited financial statement preparation services to privately held and developing companies, offered by small and major public practitioners. This decision contrasted the fundamental differences in CPA practice between private and public companies. Another aspect of this difference is the "information overload" criticism, which holds that not all disclosures made at the level of publicly held companies should be considered mandatory or useful at the private company level. In recognition of this, the FASB has acknowledged that certain earnings-per-share data (APB No. 15) and certain segment disclosures (FASB No. 14) should not be required of small privately held companies.

A set of decisions by the Supreme Court of the United States in 1976 also established important precedents for publicly held corporations, their accountants, and their auditors. In a June 1976 decision (*TSC Industries, Inc.*

et al. v. Northway, Inc.), Justice Thurgood Marshall defined the notion of a "material fact" for the purpose of complying with disclosure requirements of federal securities law proxy filings (Rule 14a-9, 1934 act). Since the adequacy of disclosure in SEC terms tends to be based on this notion, the Supreme Court definition is important. The Court noted: "An omitted fact is material if there is a substantial likelihood that a reasonable shareholder would consider it important" in deciding how to cast a proxy vote. It should be observed that the definition of materiality might differ if proxy voting is not involved.

Accountants' liability under federal securities law is specified under Section 10b-5 of the 1934 Act, which governs the annual reporting requirements of registrants. In 1976, a Supreme Court decision (*Ernst & Ernst v. Hochfelder*) led to a reconsideration of the extent of the auditor's liability in cases when there is a contention that false and misleading financial statements have been filed with the SEC. In this case, the Supreme Court ruled that there must be proof that the auditor *knowingly intended to deceive* if there is to be remedy under the law. Negligence alone does not provide a basis for relief under Section 10b-5.

Because of the difficulty of proving intent to deceive, accountants believe that this interpretation has eliminated one route to secure judgments against them in matters involving SEC disclosures.[14] The significance of the Hochfelder decision as a precedent in federal securities law, however, remains in doubt. Other courts might infer *scienter* (i.e., knowing intent) as an element of deception if, in fact, the accountant is adjudged as having been grossly negligent. Furthermore, the Hochfelder decision does not reduce the vulnerability of public accountants to suit under state laws, which are not necessarily influenced by federal court decisions.

Since the 1970s, there have been increasing attempts by third parties to establish their right to recover damages from professional accountants when a question about the adequacy of financial disclosures arises. Case law precedents indicate that small and large practitioners are equally vulnerable in such an environment.

The tide of auditor litigation continued to roll in the 1980s as public firms' practices grew and the complexity of the market system seemed to outpace the ability of internal controls and external reviews to stem fraud. During the period 1980–85, for example, Arthur Andersen alone paid out more than $137 million in court settlements, according to SEC reports, with the most notable being the Fund of Funds settlement (Abramowitz 1985). Accountants are popular targets of the plaintiff's bar, sometimes because of the notion that firms have the resources (deep pockets) to reward the litigants. Federal legislation (H.R. 1058) to modify the legal doctrine of joint and several liability in some civil actions and limit the liability to a degree proportionate to the fault passed both houses of Congress, and Congress subsequently was successful in overriding President Clinton's veto on December 22, 1995. The price paid by the CPA profession? Only agreeing that auditors notify the SEC directly of illegal acts not properly addressed by management. Accounting leaders argue the current provisions and decisions of the law placed the accountant in the position of being society's insurer—a kind of social underwriter of investments held accountable for investors' poor risk choices, or management's poor practices, and the aggressive tactics of the trial bar (Hoagland 1991). Accountants point out that no level of disclosure can eliminate investment risk. Further, they argue that the role of the professional accountant and auditor in society is not to be the ultimate resource for lawsuits. Who then will get the "full" bill? Investment banker Theodore Forstmann, speaking at the Manhattan Institute dinner, observed this: "I would submit that since the day of [J. P.] Morgan, credit has been increasingly socialized by the federal government. It has introduced all manner of insurance toward this end. Parenthetically, many feel that this process sped up dramatically during President Reagan's term in office, a curious result given his political beliefs. Obviously the insured deposits in the S&Ls created the perfect context for the debacle which has ensued. This insurance created a no-lose situation that many people of dubious character could not wait to take advantage of. In fact, the final bill to the American people of $500 billion will exceed the entire amount the country needed to finance all of World War II" (Forstmann 1990).

Confidentiality

Litigation has also addressed other aspects of an accountant's work product, such as confidentiality, as in the 1984 Supreme Court decision *United States v. Arthur Young & Co. et al.* The accountant's assertion of a client confidentiality privilege as the basis for auditors to withhold tax accrual workpapers from authorities was not upheld. In the decision, Chief Justice Burger offered the rationale for the particular decision:

> Corporate financial statements are one of the primary sources of information available to guide the decisions of the investing public.

> By certifying the public reports that collectively depict a corporation's financial status, the independent auditor assumes a responsibility transcending any employment relationship with the client. The independent public accountant

performing this special function owes ultimate allegiance to the corporation's creditors and stockholders, as well as to the investing public.

The SEC requires the filing of audited financial statements in order to obviate the fear of loss from reliance on inaccurate information, thereby encouraging public investment in the nation's industries. It is not therefore enough that financial statements be accurate; the public must also perceive them as being accurate. (All citations from United States Supreme Court Case No. 82–687, March 21, 1984)

Granted these quoted statements do not constitute law, they are the "dicta" of the decision. Granted too these statements are taken selectively from an extensive document. Nevertheless, they portray an important statement of society's expectations of the auditor as seen in the early 1980s.

Not all court decisions were unfavorable from the viewpoint of the profession. A 1991 jury decision in Jefferson, Texas, rejected claims alleging millions in damages and that KPMG Peat Marwick had committed commercial fraud and negligence in a 1982 audit of a local bank. The case involved allegations that the firm allowed a bank officer to approve loans in violation of an established procedure. The firm argued that the approval policy had been changed prior to the alleged acts (Miller and Lambert 1991).

In the case of *DiLeo v. Ernst & Young,* U.S. District Court of Appeals Judge Marovich ruled that "although accountants must exercise care in giving opinions on . . . firms' financial statements, they owe no broader duty to search and sing." The decision stressed that if the client does not supply information, the auditing firm is not legally required to dig it up. In the view of the court: "Securities laws do not guarantee sound business practices and do not protect investors from reverses" (*Public Accounting Report* June 15, 1990: 6).

In the *Credit Alliance* case decided in 1985, an appeals court threw out an $8.8 million judgment against Arthur Andersen, saying the firm was not liable to a party other than its client because it hadn't developed a direct relationship with the third party. Overall, however, it seemed that society and trial bar advocates were more demanding of public accountants and had become adept at filing suits to gain or induce settlement.

While court decisions at the federal level were affecting national and regional firms' practices, other court decisions reflecting changes in business practices of CPAs and CPA competitors caused a flurry of litigation that continued to focus attention on the fundamental state-based structure of the CPA certificate and the license to practice (Mednick 1996). For example, a Florida attorney, Silvia Ibáñez, asserting her right to free "commercial speech" identified herself as a CPA as well and included that credential on her business card. She received a reprimand from the Florida State Board of Accounting and sued. The case was heard by the U.S. Supreme Court and decided in June 1994 in favor of Ibáñez. In 1995, the Florida CPA profession took action against American Express Tax and Business Services (AETBS), alleging an employee, Steven M. Miller, was illegally "holding himself out to be a CPA," when in fact he was in the employ of a nonlicensed accounting firm (AETBS). In a narrowly worded decision, the court upheld Miller's right to identify himself as a CPA, although it appeared that in doing so it might be necessary for him to make explicit that employment circumstances limited him from performing some CPA services as an employee of AETBS.

In 1996, a Texas district court held AETBS in violation of Texas law for issuing "reports" accompanying financial statements. AETBS as an entity indicated it would agree not to issue such accompanying "reports."

The outcome of such competitive and professional cases (as in a series of episodes a decade earlier involving H. D. Vest Investment Services) seems designed to employ the cachet of the CPA as a trademark to increase the volume of various services that tie in ultimately to providing investment management services.

However, to the extent that court rulings revise the state licensure structure of the CPA profession, reform on a national scale may be warranted. To that end, proposals to establish a national CPA certificate that would be recognized by state licensure boards are being considered. An AICPA Special Committee and joint efforts with the National Association of State Boards of Accountancy (NASBA) are also under way.

The Accounting Establishment and the Politics of Disclosure

In a capital market society highly leveraged on the skills of professionals to ensure the fair and proper functioning of the investment process, it is not unexpected that professional accountants, whom Lee Berton of the *Wall Street Journal* called a "private priesthood," would be subject to increasingly frequent oversight (Berton and Schiff 1990).

Beginning in the mid-1970s, Congress demonstrated increasing interest in the role of the accounting profession as evidenced in the hearings conducted by Congressman John Moss and Senator Lee Metcalf during the sessions of the 94th Congress. These hearings provided the profession with an opportunity to respond to criticism and to address the issues raised in a staff study entitled *The Accounting Establishment* (U.S. Congress 1976). Moss and other colleagues later filed a bill in the House, the Public Accountancy

Regulatory Act, to establish a National Organization of Securities and Exchange Commission Accountancy with which independent public accounting firms would be required to register in order to furnish audit reports with the SEC. The bill was not successful. In the meantime, the AICPA established within its organization a Division of Firms and the Public Oversight Board designed to respond to concerns raised in the Moss bill (*Congressional Record* 1978).

Thereafter, the intensity of congressional interest in the accountancy profession increased. For example, during the period from 1985 to 1988, accountancy was the subject of more than twenty oversight hearings conducted by Rep. John Dingell (Dem., 16th Dist., Michigan), chairman of the Subcommittee on Oversight and Investigations of the House Energy and Commerce Committee. The 1985 hearings began in February and extended through the fall of that year. The hearings addressed scope of service issues related to the independence of CPA firms and the SEC's delegation of rule making to the private sector FASB.

As part of the 1985 hearings, Dingell requested in an August 15 letter that the major public accounting firms respond to a questionnaire structured along the lines of a Form 10-K (which public corporations are required to file with the SEC). The firms' filings, including those of Price Waterhouse and Deloitte Haskins & Sells, dated September 1985, revealed levels of individual compensation for senior partners and other structural information not available before about the firms. The firms noted that these responses were "voluntarily" given, in that no legal requirement existed for such unprecedented disclosure (Connor 1985).

The hearings and proposals of the 1990s reflected what the popular press characterized as the "S&L backlash against accountants." Another member of Congress, Rep. Ron Wyden (Dem., 3d Dist., Oregon), proposed legislation amending an earlier version of his 1986 bill to provide for "early warning bells . . . from auditors . . . to prevent this kind of debacle from happening again." "One can't say," observed Wyden, "that accountants caused the S&L mess, [b]ut they certainly should have picked up on these financial practices" (Cowan 1990).

Overall, the lengthy series of hearings addressed the role of independent accountants auditing publicly held companies under the provisions of the Securities Acts. The franchise of public auditing under these federal laws provides political access to accountancy issues at the national level, and broader social leverage was applied. Responding to public and political concerns and in an attempt to "open" the public accounting profession and to stimulate competition and contact between firms and potential clients, for example, the AICPA in 1987 reconstituted its Mission Statement and for the first time explicitly included an expressed commitment to serve the public interest. Bans on advertising of services were amended, opening the way for more competitive pricing of services. The National Association of Accountants, in an effort to open its identity toward the needs of managerial accounting, voted in 1991 to rename itself the Institute of Management Accountants. Earlier, the AICPA board of directors was expanded in representation to include three "public" members. Acting upon recommendations of a committee of the Financial Accounting Foundation (FAF) chaired by Russell Palmer in early 1977, there was an end to the required majority representation on the FASB by public accounting–based CPAs and for the adoption of a simple majority approval rule for passage of a proposed standard. This voting rule was again changed in 1991 back to a supermajority requirement (five of seven votes required for passage). This latest voting change, recommended by a FAF committee chaired by Ray Groves, then of Ernst & Whinney, was a possible way to slow down the pace (more than one hundred standards issued) of the FASB. The original change in the 1970s from supermajority to simple majority was alleged to be a response to the concern that the board was not producing a sufficient flow of standards (Berton 1989). In response to a further concern that the board's due process was too slow to provide timely guidance on developing issues, a task force of the FASB was created in late 1982 that recommended the formation of the Emerging Issues Task Force (EITF) as a FASB unit to act on such matters that might be resolved by a less formal process based upon consensus. Since it began operations in 1984, the EITF has addressed dozens of issues via this consensus approach.

The tensions about the FASB peaked again in late 1995 in the wake of the board's standards for stock option compensation disclosures. Bitterly opposed by the Financial Executives Institute (FEI), there was initially strong support for disclosure from the public practice community, but this support waned as both the technical complexities and business considerations of the expense-measurement proposal were deliberated. By early 1996 leaders of the corporate community, using the FEI as their spearpoint, proposed that the FASB be reduced in size and that the agenda for its work be done by others. SEC Chairman Arthur Levitt, sensing that the perception was now being created that the FASB was "in play" (i.e., up for "grabs"), wrote Financial Accounting Foundation Chairman J. Michael Cook on April 22, 1996, suggesting that Cook advise Levitt "of the steps the FAF is prepared to take to assure that a majority of its Board of Trustees consists of individuals of strong public service backgrounds who are able to represent the public interest, free of conflict." He continued, "In addition appointments to the Board should be subject to approval by the Commission" (Arthur Levitt to J. Michael Cook April 22, 1996). Levitt's proposal was perceived as a de facto federal takeover of the financial standards process, without benefit of hearings, due process, funding review, and so forth.

Cook wrote to Chairman Levitt on May 20, assuring Levitt that concerns about the public interest were being addressed as a result of a recently initiated strategic planning process. "Finally," Cook noted, "we could not accept any arrangement which would have the effect of permitting the SEC to approve . . . nominations" (J. Michael Cook to Arthur Levitt, May 20, 1996).

The political equilibrium and composition of the FAF board toward a more noticeable "public interest" profile was the outcome of this episode. The implications for the profession worldwide, while yet unclear, suggest an ever greater public role in the "politics of disclosure" as global capital reporting for business decisions begins to gravitate toward sources of authoritative standards. The political importance of the U.S. role in standard setting is now being defined in the wake of this latest "rite of spring"; it would appear that those who call for a policy favoring more disclosure and the emerging American model—as identified with the Jenkins Report— will be in a position to advance their ideas.

As suggested above, the response of the profession to its critics has not been limited to changes in the number and makeup of the AICPA board of directors, the composition of the FAF, or name changes or revised procedures at the FASB. In September 1977, the membership at the institute's annual meeting authorized a reorganization plan that would permit practicing firms to identify and enroll as members of either or both the SEC and the private firms divisions of the AICPA. At the same time, the institute took steps to establish a senior technical committee to deliberate on matters relating to accounting principles for privately held companies.

The profession has also responded to the criticisms and concerns of politicians about specific areas of accounting responsibility for quality control over the reporting and attest services. Following upon a vote in late 1987, AICPA members, for example, in cooperation with state societies and state accountancy boards, continued implementing programs of peer review and quality review for all individuals whose firms offer services related to public reporting or attest functions. These multi-endorsed review programs, fashioned with a self-regulatory and remedial emphasis, provide a vehicle for regular constructive interpractice inspection and critique as a basis to ensure the proper conduct of services important to the structure of a capital market economy (Fogarty 1996).

In Search of Orthodoxy

Re-Solving the Accounting Equation

The orthodoxy characterized by Paton and Littleton's (P&L) 1940 monograph had become increasingly challenged by the mid-1970s. The FASB too had decided to attempt to change the emphasis in financial reporting from the income statement/matching concept toward the balance sheet, which was perceived as more relevant to investors and which lent itself to value-based accounting.

The "'matching and attaching' concepts of Paton and Littleton did not prove capable of resolving cost deferral and cost anticipation controversies of the past two decades," observed FASB Chairman Kirk in 1981. The FASB would, Kirk said, "undertake to frame a 'decision' usefulness model, requiring that each standard be based on its assessed cost and benefits to users of financial information" (Kirk 1981: 84). The controversy over the primacy of the income statement (historical cost, transaction-based model) versus the balance sheet (value, market-based model) reflects history. During the late 1930s, the institute inaugurated its *Accounting Research Bulletins* about which Paton observed: "As you know, the research department is approaching its study of principles from the point of view of corporate reports, particularly those issued to stockholders. Moreover, in one of the early meetings it was proposed and agreed that *we take as a 'golden text' the proposition that the most important purpose of corporate reporting is the periodic income statement rather than the balance sheet, something of a departure from accounting tradition"* (Paton 1939A: 231–32, emphasis added).

In 1961, David Solomons, later to be a principal force in the drafting of the report of the committee chaired by Francis Wheat, said "my own guess is that . . . the next twenty five years may . . . be seen to have been the twilight of income measurement" (Solomons 1961: 383). In 1969, Howard Ross's *Financial Statements: A Crusade for Current Values* joined the chorus of valuation theorists proposing value-based accounting (Ross 1969). But in 1984, Gene Flegm, a leading member of the financial executive community, reaffirmed the basis for the income statement–historical cost model in his book, *Accounting: How to Meet the Challenges of Relevance and Regulation*. The lines were again drawn between income statement–historical cost theorists and balance sheet–current value proponents. Persistent post–World War II inflation effects (figure 8.4) were by the late 1970s acting as a "driver" to support current values.

Net income, opponents argued, lacks an empirical referent. It is unabashedly judgmental and thereby, critics note, subject to earnings management since no single verifiable interpretation of an income number exists

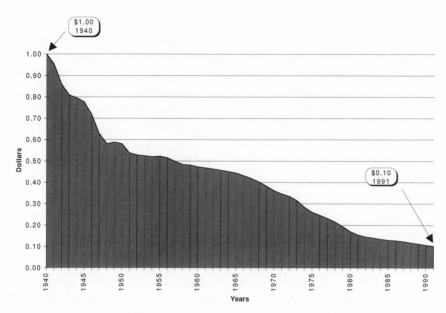

Figure 8.4 Plunge in purchasing power of the dollar, 1940–1990. *Source:* U.S. Department of Labor, Bureau of Labor Statistics, table 738 in *Statistical Abstract of the U.S., Consumer Price Index: Urban Consumer Annual Average* (Washington: Government Printing Office, 1992).

in a set of circumstances. Earnings per share, a distillation of profit and loss orthodoxy, "confuses investment decisions with financing policies," critics charged (Stern 1972). They noted further that the discretion to manage earnings that preparers attempted to preserve was not useful since efficient capital markets were not "fooled" by selections of accounting principles to manage income that otherwise had no real or economic effects. The income model therefore was a waste of managerial talent and accounting effort.

Income–historical cost proponents countered that income measurement while judgmental is based on objective transaction-based historical cost and does not require continuing subjective balance sheet valuations as in the case of value-driven models. As Flegm argues: "The fundamental use of accounting is control in the broadest sense which would include budgeting and forecasting so that management can plan intelligently. I have no use for short-term speculators and do not believe we should attempt to serve their 'needs.' I believe that the goals of management and the long term investor are the same and are best served by reliable data rather than someone's estimate of 'values'" (Flegm 1991).

The focus of income determination to afford measures of earnings and

return on investment, thereby to assess the efficiency of allocation of resources, was flawed, critics argued, because of the broad judgmental discretion permitted. Market efficiency, on the other hand, held that all publicly
available information was "impounded" in the price of a security. It did not,
however, establish that this "price" was necessarily a resource "allocation
guide"; rather, that the price was the "investment value" of a security in a
market efficient with respect to its use of information. In fact there are two
markets at work: (1) a market for information about securities and (2) a
market for the securities themselves. Equilibrium in the information market determines pricing in the securities market. Persons who are most effective in the information market make the most in securities. Thus, income
determination was useful, albeit approximate, because it served as a guide
to resource allocation; market efficiency was focused upon objective measurement of the reported information used in the capital markets and established a trading or investment value.

This schism between traditional P&L accountants and those influenced
by finance and capital markets views affected academic research and reporting practice. For example, in the early to mid-1980s, as the SEC revised
its registration processes, it acknowledged that publicly held companies
that were widely traded should have less costly access to capital and need
provide only a modest amount of information to accompany initial regis-
trations. First-time registrants, however, were required to continue to file
voluminous material on the pretext that little public information was available and the market's opportunity to assess information on the registrant
had not previously occurred. SEC Commissioner Grundfest also noted
that other aspects of the finance literature, in addition to efficient market
theory, related to regulatory considerations, including reallocating risk via
securitizing forms of debt via new securities instruments; portfolio theory,
namely, that picking stocks in isolation is less desirable than doing so in a
coordinated manner involving a whole set of stocks with a desired set of
risk and return characteristics; and specialization, or the tendency of investment bankers to follow certain entities and securities and to make
themselves expert in these aspects of the market (Grundfest 1987). Taken
altogether, with pension fund socialism and managerial capitalism in context, modern finance and market efficient techniques have affected the
marketplace for information and corporate control as have few other contemporary phenomena.

The market plunge and 500-point drop in the Dow Jones Industrial Average in October 1987 raised serious doubts and fueled new debate about
the efficient market hypothesis (EMH). How, critics ask, can a 500-point
drop be explained if the market is efficient? True, fluctuations around mar-

ket values are to be expected even in the form of a perfectly efficient market, but a 500-point free fall tests even the most faithful and leaves others more skeptical than ever (Lee 1988: 20). "The fact that the discrepancy existed for days 'is a clear gap in the theory,'" said Professor Lawrence Summers of Harvard. For years, "every finance professor in America has taught that can't happen" (qtd. in Donnelly 1987: 8). EMH research has not, critics argued, proved anything conclusive about market behavior. The focus in the majority of its literature has been on equity securities on the New York Exchange. Over the counter and other major markets, including long- and short-term credit markets, have been less than adequately tested (Davidson, Stickney, and Weil 1984). And what of mass-psychology factors at play in the market? What bearing do they have on efficient market information treatment and pricing? (Schaefer 1988).

David Solomons, writing in 1987, twenty-five years after his first speculation about the decline of income theory, observed: "Earnings seem to be as important to financial analysts and to academic researchers as they ever were" (Solomons 1987: 1). But to those who demur and ask, "Does anyone care about a company's reported earnings anymore?" the response, by those leading large-market value-driven mergers is more likely to be, "Cash flow, not earnings, is the name of the stock valuation business these days." Yet, according to a survey of sixty securities analysts by Ketchum Communications, 52 percent of the analysts polled considered profitability measures like earnings and return on investment more important than cash flow in their evaluations of companies. Only 27 percent thought that cash flow was more important than earnings (Wechsler 1989).

The FASB: Products and Controversy

In recent years, the FASB has addressed any number of challenging technical issues, from inflation accounting to deferred taxes, to pension benefits, stock compensation, and derivative securities. From its inception in 1973 through 1995, the board had pronounced 124 standards. FAS 106, *Employers' Accounting for Postretirement Benefits Other than Pensions,* is among its most carefully studied and most significant standards. Its effect, for example, was reported in the financial press as resulting in a $2.3 billion one-time implementation charge to IBM's shareholders' equity in 1991 (Hooper and Berton 1991).

In 1979, the domestic U.S. annual inflation rate was 13 percent. In September 1979, the FASB issued Statement No. 33, *Financial Reporting and Changing Prices.* It required major companies to make a supplemental price level–adjusted and current cost disclosure, replacing the earlier SEC's 1976 replacement cost approach.

For example, in 1979, General Motors reported earnings of $2.9 billion, or $10.04 a share, and showed an investment return of 15.1 percent. In supplemental 1967 CPI (consumer price index) common dollar terms, upon which GM chose to base their supplemental inflation disclosures, results showed that GM's return on equity was only 6.7 percent, equal to net earnings of $817 million or earnings per share of $2.83 (Kelly 1980). Considering that a company's taxable income was also likely to display an inflated outcome, thereby making corporations pay taxes in cash on illusory earnings, the inflation issue was particularly sensitive.

By 1986, the CPI's annual increase had continued to slow, dropping to the 3 percent to 4 percent annual range. The issue of inflation accounting lost significance and was crowded out by other off–balance sheet accounting subjects, such as financial instruments, deferred taxes, and postemployment benefits. FAS 33, the standard requiring supplemental disclosure, was rescinded, because, in the view of the board, it was not cost justified and was not being used by investors.[15]

The treatment of accounting for income taxes continued to vex the board and its constituents from the time of its initial consideration in January 1982, through the issuance of FAS 96, *Accounting for Income Taxes*, in December 1987 (Rayburn 1986). FAS 96 was to have become effective for fiscal years beginning after December 15, 1988, replacing APB Opinion No. 11. Although several major companies adopted the standard early, the board, responding to other criticisms, issued FAS 100 deferring the implementation one year. FAS 103 deferred the implementation date two additional years, to take effect with fiscal years beginning after December 15, 1991. In 1991, the board, issuing a new exposure draft on income taxes potentially to supersede FAS 96, proposed to delay implementation another year (FASB 1991B). In early 1992, the board produced its final standard, FAS 109. From beginning to end, the decade-long gestation of the standard would be singled out as an example of why the process was unsatisfactory.

Process and Politics

Controversy about the board has existed from the start. Herbert Miller, long respected as a professor, text author, and practitioner, observed: "Recent developments suggest that accounting is a series of political decisions which we now call accounting principles" (Previts and Merino 1979: 304). The politics of the process, however defined, remain centered in the private sector, directed by capital market forces, with government involving itself frequently in an oversight capacity. And while standard setters and the framers of the process argue that standards should be "neutral" (i.e., devoid of economic consequences), others, particularly those charged with implementing the standard, are more convinced about costs, as they bear them. Often, they argue, the benefit is to others, such as investors, and even then it may not be justifiable.

Given the schism in the financial accounting community, one that some characterize as management (preparers) versus analysts and professional (sophisticated) investors or P&L versus EMH, it could be expected that the FASB's issues agenda would become bogged down if either faction felt poorly served by the product (Previts 1991). Furthermore, these two groups, while powerful constituents, are not the only major groups to be considered. Government through congressional and SEC inquiries has expressed its interest and concern as to the board's activities. The professional accounting community through institutional groups, including the AICPA, FEI, NAA, IIA, AAA, and others, have also become heavily involved in the actions of the board. And major accounting firms, whose task it is to "enforce" the standards of reporting by means of audits of major companies, also are principal actors, whose representation on the FASB has been telling. For example, the FASB chairmen to date have come from public accounting firms. And major corporations, who are the users of the board's product, are major contributors to the financing of the board. This mix of constituents causes constant tensions as described above.

Transaction-Based versus Market-Based Accounting

Each traditional orthodoxy, P&L and EMH, has a faithful following. Neither group falters in the face of criticism of its credo. Each view seems to serve a set of constituent needs in the information marketplace. Preparers identify with the traditional P&L orthodoxy; analysts and sophisticated users with the EMH. The contest of these orthodoxies also portends the shift from a classical, transaction-based accounting model to a market-based accounting model. The former is woven deeply into the fabric of disclosure issues and continues to dictate much of what is controversial or resolvable between these two approaches. In modest ways, a mixed approach using market values in inventory areas (lower of cost or market) has always been recognized with traditional transaction accounting–based costs. The likelihood in the future is that the arguments for market-based values will be made in those areas where transaction-based values' usefulness is not appropriately current or relevant. Market value is likely to be addressed first among financial institutions. Terming historical cost accounting as "once

Chairmen of the FASB, 1973–1997

Marshall Armstrong (1973–1977)

Donald J. Kirk (1978–1986)   Dennis R. Beresford (1987–1997)

upon a time accounting," advocates of market-based accounting, including SEC Chairman Breeden, argued as follows in 1990:

> [W]e should consider a fundamental shift in the goal we set for the accounting standards for financial institutions. Financial institutions are in the busi-

ness of buying and selling financial instruments, all of which have a value measured in terms of current market conditions. Determining the current value of an institution's assets, not recording their original cost, should increasingly be the goal toward which we must work.

In this regard, at the SEC we have raised the issue of whether we can improve the current accounting conventions that permit financial institutions' holdings of marketable securities to be valued on the basis of yesterday's costs, even if actual market values are readily available and reliably quoted. (Breeden 1990: 29)

In June 1991, the FASB put on its agenda a project to study whether to require holders of debt securities to mark such holdings to market value in order to provide better guidance in those areas where trading versus investment status of debt securities provides potential for selectively trading only for gains, while retaining at book value those securities whose market has dropped (Berton 1991B). The discipline of such a rule would reduce "pressure from bankers and politicians [for] bank regulators to [loosen] some important accounting and reporting rules which [w]ith a pen stroke [could make] shaky banks . . . magically appear healthier" (White 1991: A10). By May 1993, the FASB had promulgated FAS 114 and 115 in response to general concerns.

Re-engineering Financial Reporting

In late 1990, the AICPA sponsored a conference on the FASB's process and addressed such issues as the international role of the board, its relationship with constituencies, and the need for changes, including the use of "field testing" of major reporting standards (Ihlandfeldt 1991). Ultimately, as education, technology, and methodology provide the capacity to apply it, a multidata-level approach to reporting could accommodate database *reporting* of either or both market-based and transaction-based *accounting*. Thereafter, the current double-entry equation (Assets = Liabilities + Equities), reflecting Sprague's 1880 quantifications of property rights, would serve as an initial enumeration but be only one dimension of accounting.[16] Financial reporting, the application of accounting data, would be multifaceted. A potential illustration of this is depicted in figure 8.5. This elliptical conception of a core reporting model initially envisioned by Shaun O'Malley was one product of the AICPA conference in 1990 at which AICPA President Chenok noted that "financial reporting should be 're-engineered'" as we move from an industrial to an information era (Chenok 1991: 11). Chenok's observation was shared by others including R. J. Chambers, who

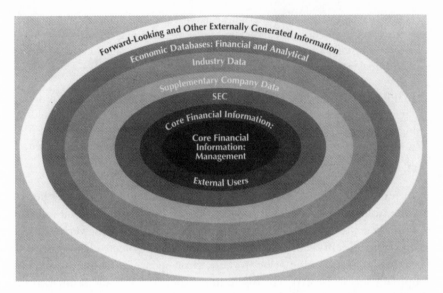

Figure 8.5 A core reporting model, as envisioned at a 1990 AICPA Wharton School conference

commented that boards and committees around the world concerned with accounting standards should consider as a "simple and elegant" conceptual framework for a new era of corporate reporting those features that would make reports *valuable* by observing such key factors as "realism, additivity and intelligibility" (Chambers 1989: 26).

In 1991, the special AICPA Committee on Financial Reporting chaired by Edmund L. Jenkins of Arthur Andersen initiated its major review of financial reporting. In 1997, Jenkins would become chairman of the FASB.

The SEC and the Profession

Among the multitude of federal regulatory agencies, the SEC has significant capacity to alter the strategic role of accountancy in our society. By means of its reporting releases, its enforcement rulings, and significantly, its role in determining the parameters of auditor "independence," it possesses substantial powers. Through the presence of its chief accountant in oversight of FASB deliberations, the SEC's influence is continually felt. By means of exercising its authority over the contents and dimensions of reports and documents filed by publicly held companies, it sets the tone for what is proper disclosure. Beginning in 1972, the five permanent chief accountant appointments were filled by John C. (Sandy) Burton (1972–

76), Clarence Sampson (1976–87), Edmund Coulson (1988–90), Walter Schuetze (1992–95), and Michael Sutton (1995 to date).

Burton was an activist in the sense of directing disciplinary sanctions against public accounting firms as in Accounting Series Release (ASR) 173 in 1975, which related to Peat Marwick's auditing of National Student Marketing and other enterprises. He instituted peer review and suspended firms from accepting new SEC clients until practice reforms were satisfactory (Previts 1978). His efforts to enhance auditor oversight of client accounting by requiring an auditor's letter assenting to the "preferability" of a client's choice for a changed accounting principle were among the more controversial policies he established. He set up a process for the issuance of Staff Accounting Bulletins (SABs) as a means of capturing the informal decisions of SEC staff in an attempt to minimize inconsistency on key decisions. Burton's term coincided with the initial surge of congressional interest in the CPA profession as evidenced in the 1976 staff report *The Accounting Establishment*. Also in 1976, Burton, during the SEC chairmanship of Roderick Hills, addressed the subject of inflation accounting, issuing ASR 190 mandating "replacement cost information" as a supplemental disclosure for major firms. Burton's successor, Clarence Sampson, had no lesser agenda, including the thorny issue of oil and gas accounting, which was resolved, after years of countermoves, by the issuance of FAS 69, which recognized both full cost and successful efforts methods while requiring substantial supplemental disclosure. Sampson's tenure in office also saw the resolution of inflation accounting via FAS 33 on supplemental price level and current cost disclosure requirements for major companies. Other innovations came about as well, including "shelf registration," the codification and update of accounting series releases into a reporting and an auditing and enforcement series, and the "integration" of the annual report and 10-K annual financial reporting contents in a basic financial disclosure package. Coulson's tenure, although brief, was actively engaged in continuing the follow-up on the recommendations of the Treadway Commission, including increased auditor involvement in quarterly reports and in reports of internal controls, as well as the issue of mandatory quality or peer review of auditors. Coulson also addressed what he called the two "I"s, *independence* of auditors and *international* accounting (Coulson 1989). Schuetze, who was outspoken in his criticism of perceived weaknesses of public auditor "fortitude" with regard to clients' wishes, instigated a special review by the Public Oversight Board, published in 1994, which found that concerns rested not only on one area but were traceable to weaknesses in corporate governance—the fortitude of the board of directors in particular. Schuetze and his successor Sutton both seem disposed to support the direction of change toward "business reporting" that the AICPA Special Committee recommended in 1994.

The SEC's activities during these years reflect the agenda of several chairmen including Ray Garrett (1973–75), Roderick M. Hills (1975–77), Harold M. Williams (1977–81), John S. R. Shad (1981–87), David Ruder (1987–89), Richard C. Breeden (1989–93), and Arthur Levitt (1993 to date). Each chairman brought an emphasis with implications for accounting. For example, Williams's focus on the need for current cost information in an inflation reporting standard shaped FAS 33's requirements. Williams sought an "Accountability of Power" and espoused a belief in corporate stewardship (Williams 1979). Shad came from "the Street," having served as a principal executive in a major brokerage firm. His focus was on addressing enforcement and trading excesses and abuses. A principal reporting initiative he supported was the pilot and subsequent mandatory adoption of the EDGAR (Electronic Data Gathering Analysis and Retrieval) filing system. EDGAR has moved the SEC's filing processes from being paper-based to an electronic medium to enhance rapid and easy access to complex and voluminous reports. In 1990, for example, it was estimated that the commission processed some 80,000 documents, including 12,000 10-K annual reports. EDGAR is seen as a possible first step toward corporate database reporting.

Chairman Ruder's brief term was marked by the October 1987 market plunge and the need to investigate and propose actions to address concerns about market stability. In addition, his reporting agenda included following up on several initiatives of the Treadway Commission, such as a required separate report by public company management as to their role in providing reliable financial information and maintaining adequate systems of internal control.

When Chairman Breeden took the oath of office on October 11, 1989, he had recently, as a member of the White House staff, concluded involvement in the design of the savings and loan reform. The *New York Times* characterized his agenda as "changing the rules" (that is, addressing the Glass-Steagall Act [1933], which restricts commercial banks from engaging in brokerage activities) and "changing the tools" (e.g., making it easier for private placements of securities to occur in Rule 144a of the 1933 act and loosening restrictions under Section 14d of the 1934 act on foreign companies so that American shareholders can access tender offers) (Labaton 1991). Breeden has acted on both of these "tools" issues. The "rule" matters, such as revisions in banking laws, were part of a broader legislative initiative in Congress assessing the entire capital market structure, including the trading of commodities, stock futures, branch banking, the regulation of insurance companies, pension and mutual funds, as well as commercial and savings banks. Levitt's term has been marked by tort and securities reform initiatives and the 1996 FAF structure debate.

Regulating in a "Two-Market" System

At the time of its formation the SEC was conceived as an investor protection agency, to serve as a powerful advocate for fair play in the marketplace. As a regulatory agency, it has had to contend with those whose beliefs are that the market provides sufficient discipline and that the "dead weight" of disclosure is neither necessary nor cost beneficial. For those investors with sufficient sophistication to protect their self-interest, usually large portfolio investors, this argument has particular appeal. But as to the small, unsophisticated investor, the SEC has assumed, at least in the public's mind, a necessary role as an advocate.

But doesn't this "create" two markets? Speaking in 1988, then SEC Chairman Ruder dismissed concerns over the "creation" of two distinct markets, one for institutions, the other for individuals. "Creation," said Ruder, "isn't the right word. It is a *recognition*, I think, that these two markets exist" (Nash 1988: D2; emphasis added). Given this "two tiered market," and the SEC's role as protector of the smaller investor, it appears that calls for the "death of securities regulation" are premature (Cohen 1991: A12) (figures 8.6 and 8.7). What remains to be debated and resolved is the role that accounting,

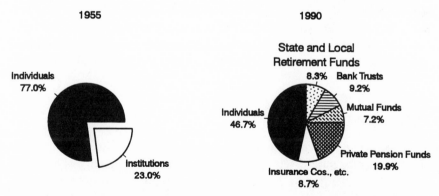

Figure 8.6 Distribution of corporate equity ownership, individuals vs. institutions. *Note:* While the number of individual shareholders has shown strong growth, their share of total equity has fallen. Total assets of pension plans have risen from $17.5 billion in 1950 to nearly $2.5 trillion in 1990. *Source:* Testimony of Richard C. Breeden before U.S. Senate Banking Subcommittee, 1991, *Deloite & Touche Review* (November 4, 1991: 4–5).

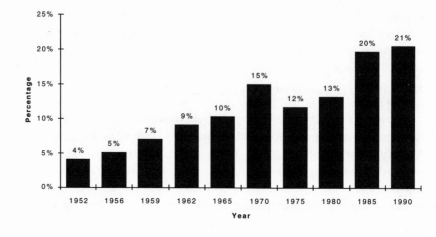

Year	1952	1956	1959	1962	1965	1970	1975	1980	1985	1990
Total Shareholders	6.5	8.6	12.5	17.0	20.1	30.9	25.3	30.2	47.0	51.4
Total Population (In Millions)	158	169	178	187	194	205	216	228	238	250

Figure 8.7 New York Stock Exchange shareowners as percentage of U.S. population, 1952–1990

corporate reporting, and auditing serve, given these circumstances. Senior SEC staffers espouse that "[t]he best way to help and protect investors is to make sure they can make informed investment decisions" (McGrath 1990: 64). Others are seeking to understand the role that modern corporation finance theory plays in such disclosures (Zecher 1986).[17] The questions relate not only to the proper amount and frequency of public corporation reporting but also to the proper disclosure by investment fund managers about matters that involve the information rights of individual fund investors and pensioners.

Political Reality and Self-Regulation

While academics continue to argue the propriety of the SEC's de facto delegation of standard setting to the private sector via ASR No. 4 (1938) and No. 150 (1973), the process has been long accepted but continually challenged. The trade-offs that have become institutional arrangements over seven decades reflect a balance between a search for uniformity and a practical level of "disclosure" insurance in a dynamic capital market (Merino and Coe 1978). Modifications can be expected as laws and needs change, but the fundamental involvement of professionals performing a review of public company reporting while under a form of self-regulation will likely continue. In 1995, one observer expressed concern about this as a manifestation of "the drive to transfer national power from the State to the counting house" (Schlesinger 1995: 33).

A consideration of the public policy of these arrangements set in place during the dark days of the 1930s depression provides perspective on the purposes served by this balance: "Central to the regulatory strategy these leaders chose was the use of the accounting profession as a neutral third party to assure the accuracy of financial information needed from business. By using independent accountants, the SEC avoided the need for a large public bureaucracy. In trading some part of its traditional standing as the employee of business for the status of a detached third party, the accounting profession enhanced its prestige and also created new jobs for its members. The investing public was the big winner. It gained more reliable data about potential investments and could compare opportunities more accurately" (Galambos and Pratt 1988: 104).

Scope of Services

Legislative and administrative actions during the post-Vietnam era contributed to a reshaped market for professional accountants' services. Examples of important legislation include the Foreign Corrupt Practices Act (FCPA) (1977), the Federal Managers' Financial Integrity Act (1982), the Single Audit Act (1984), and a series of federal tax laws with acronyms such as ERTA (the Economic Recovery Tax Act of 1981) and TEFRA (the Tax Equity and Fiscal Responsibility Act of 1982) plus the Tax Reform Acts of 1984 and 1986, followed by the Revenue Act of 1987. The government sector was also affected by the Office of the Federal Procurement Policy Act of 1988, the Financial Institutions Reform, Recovery and Enforcement Act of 1989, and the Chief Financial Officers Act (1990).

At the same time these federal laws were coming into effect, the Federal Trade Commission, as noted above, was seeking to remove what it considered barriers to advertising and competition. The FTC's actions would result in "price" competition among major firms over a maturing market for audit services and the perception that audits were a "commodity" to be used to gain access to the client base. Also, auditing services of firms became subject to forms of solicitation and price competition unknown in previous decades. Audit services were put up for bid and awarded commonly to the lowest bid, driving down the margin from this stream of service while lawsuits and public expectations for auditor performance continued to rise. The attempts to make up margin by increasing the volume of auditing services led to the consolidation of auditing practices; fewer than ten major public firms now account for more than 90 percent of the auditing services offered to publicly held companies. At the same time, as a result of the FCPA law, many industrial companies shifted their resources to hiring internal auditors and establishing control functions, further eroding the need for external auditing services. This shift is confirmed by the increased interest in the CPA examination and the increased level of such certificates awarded after 1977.

And, as revealed in table 8.3, the relative percentage of income of accounting and auditing services declined to less than 55 percent of the firm's revenue in the case of almost all of the Big Six firms and to less than 60 percent among others, by 1994.

In the midst of this change, firms shifted their efforts from the "franchise" audit business to marketing tax services. Advice was needed more than ever in the wake of the multitude of 1980s tax laws. The "franchise" business and the tax business both were perceived as being an "annuity" in character, subject to be continued barring a catastrophic service failure of the public firm or economic failure of the client. And while lawyers provided a form of competition for the tax services, the audit services were legislatively unique to CPAs and therefore offered a comparative advantage from which to market a broader range of services. The attractiveness to the firm of promoting one-stop shopping included the ability to extract a potential premium for other services offered from a single source. Advisory services, for example, could be offered in such a fashion as to be attractive to the CPA firm and still be less expensive than what might be required if the client chose to staff the project internally. The economics of this "rent versus buy" strategy provided a means of leverage into clients. However, advisory services were not "annuities." These services were subject to short-term and project-based revenues. Once a job was complete new projects had to be found; that is, advisory services had to be "marketed" on a non-renewing basis. Furthermore, in the event of an economic downturn, such services were subject to being canceled as companies sought means of cost savings. And nonattest services were subject to competition from non-CPA consulting firms, who were quick to complain that such "one-stop shopping" arrangements created problems, at least in appearance, about the independent role of the CPA firm in the auditor capacity, which was at the root of the service package being offered. In response the CPA firms argued that these services were another means of learning more about the client, enhancing the efficiency of the audit and reducing the "learning curve" costs of providing such services. This "scope of services" controversy tended to appear whenever CPAs were called to legislative account for their activities as independent auditors or whenever the technology or changes in the mix of production factors provided an entrée for firms to aggressively expand the market for services.

These changes in the marketplace for CPA firm services were not the only economic event of the period. Each of the other branches of the profession, those involving preparers of statements, internal auditors, management accountants, financial analysts, planners, and governmental accountants, were also demonstrating their abilities to provide the types of services on an internal basis to business investment or governmental entities that heretofore were offered by external CPA firms. That is, as businesses and government internalized personnel for accounting, tax, and reporting, they "rented" fewer accounting firm services. The "profession" working in the U.S. economic community, and in the growing world of practice, had become truly multifaceted and pluralistic. The CPA retained a legislative distinction as the supplier of assurance services but was under continuing pressure to find new and more effective services to provide to the client base it had dominated in the past. Now the corporate client had the option of putting the audit engagement out for bid on a more frequent basis or using the threat of this to keep audit fees and other charges more in concert with its desires. The power within this client-auditor relationship and negotiation had shifted. Professional firms were not in a position to form a cartel, as was done by oil suppliers, to combat this shift and therefore chose to compete using price competition. All of this was perceived as happening at the very time that auditor independence and credibility were being subjected to question and financial institution failures reached epidemic levels.

Through legislation and administrative actions, society and government had restructured the economics of auditing, introducing price competition into the market for a judgment-based professional service critical to the information operations of the capital markets. Case law and pre-1996 legislation similarly served to provide additional means to force upon auditors new levels of accountability to a wider range of "stakeholders." As one observer remarked: "Society is asking the CPA profession to do a $500 paint job for $300 and then to indemnify the job!" The market for auditing services, at least, seemed to reflect this sentiment.

Lest we consider this interpretation an apology for CPA firms, we should keep in mind that other changes occurring in the economy and society overall were no less rending. One example is the television broadcast market. Before 1975, the three major networks, NBC, CBS, and ABC, enjoyed a virtual monopoly over both advertising revenues and what entered the program stream, including the national agenda-setting vehicle of the "nightly news program." By 1990, however, these networks were subsidiaries of other multinational companies and were seeking ways to repackage their programming and profiles to address the potentially dominating ability of cable TV and satellite-dish and Internet-based systems. A series of legislative and regulatory actions involving communications companies, including the Bell system, during the 1970s and 1980s, leveraged the technology and growing leisure markets and resulted in an entirely different medium by 1990. Changes in these TV institutions, which are perhaps more obvious to consumers, suggest a parallel to the magnitude of change that was occurring in the commercial auditing/information/reporting practice of professional accountants.

Public Practice: And Then There Were Six . . .

By the mid-1980s, professional accountants, including CPAs entering positions in corporate practice, began to outnumber CPAs in public practice by greater margins. Yet public practice remained the preferred, if not common, entry-level experience forum; for CPAs, public practice, and the experience it represented, was a "rite of passage." By the end of the 1980s, four major public practice units consolidated into two, and the Big Eight firms were recast as the Big Six. Table 8.3 shows the U.S. revenues of the Big Six firms, as of 1994, following the mergers of Ernst & Young and Deloitte & Touche. U.S. firm revenues were commonly less than half the total firm revenue, suggesting that the world market for firm services represented the targets for potential growth. Some asserted that the competition among

TABLE 8.3
Revenues and Sources of the Big Six Accounting Firms in the United States, 1994

Firm	Year End 1994	U.S. Revenue (millions)	Percent from		
			A&A	Tax	MAS
Arthur Andersen	Aug. 31	$2,922	35	19	46
Ernst & Young	Sept. 30	2,351	51	22	27
Deloitte & Touche	May 30	2,055	54	23	23
KPMG Peat Marwick	June 30	1,907	n/a	n/a	26
Coopers & Lybrand	Sept. 30	1,640	56	19	25
Price Waterhouse	June 30	1,430	44	26	30

Source: Public Accounting Report, August 31, 1994.

Note: A&A = accounting and auditing; MAS = Management advisory consulting services.

These firms reported worldwide revenues in 1994 as follows: Arthur Andersen, $6.73 billion; Ernst & Young, $6.01 billion; Deloitte & Touche, $5.20 billion; KPMG Peat Marwick, $6.10 billion; Coopers & Lybrand, $5.50 billion; Price Waterhouse, $3.98 billion (*Accountancy,* May 1995).

major firms to position themselves to serve a clientele of the major global companies (called "the haves," as opposed to the nonglobal "have nots") reflected a strategy of managing the firms by the "top line" (revenue growth) rather than the "bottom line" (partner-shared net income). Mergers of the major firms announced in 1989 and 1990 caused adjustments in firm operations and dislocations throughout this tier as duplications of duties following mergers resulted in reductions in personnel and changes in the base of support and administrative operations. Popular authors, hopping on the bandwagon to criticize the firms in the wake of the savings and loan failures, cited fee-cutting practices and competition for audit clients as leading to the downfall of the "once-cushy status" of partnership in the major firms (Berton 1991A: A3).

The consolidation of the Big Eight had been anticipated by a merger of Peat Marwick and Klynveld Main Goerdeler of Amsterdam in 1987. The mergers of the late 1980s had been preceded by other international federations of practice between U.S., Canadian, and United Kingdom firms: Ernst & Ernst with Whinney Murray; Haskins & Sells with Deloitte; and Lybrand, Ross Bros. & Montgomery with Coopers. Only two firms, Arthur Andersen and Price Waterhouse, remained unchanged in name among the original eight firms. Andersen's consulting practice, however, was separately constituted shortly after the 1980s mergers, but as "Andersen Consulting" it retained a broader identity as part of a Swiss international cooperative society management form.

Major firms also recognized that it was going to be very difficult to serve large multinational clients from a small base of operations. In addition, there were financial pressures upon firms from price competition and settlements following upon legal challenges from market shakeouts. All of these and the changing cost of rendering services, from using labor intensively to moving to capital–computer-based skilled labor, compelled firms to seek efficiencies via leveraging key partner functions to meet global service opportunities. What continued to evidence itself was that at the international level of practice, the ability to provide a massive array of specialized functional (accounting, auditing, tax, advisory) services developed by a line of business emphasis (telecommunications, transportation, banking, manufacturing, mining, oil and gas) was necessary to compete efficiently. Both internally and externally, CPAs' scope of services had become increasingly diversified along the client's specialized functional and industry/line of business needs. Major international companies had become "nationlike" in their complexity, becoming in a sense, almost private economic and market systems (Lerner 1957: 287). They employed the most skilled financial executives to perform functions much like those of a secretary of the treasury in government, but who hold less formidable titles, such as controller or financial vice president. In addition, such firms doing business around the world need access to a global network of reliable, high-quality external reporting and information professionals connected through a single firm, people who can "hit the ground running," with services geared to meet their particular line of business needs. As this international market *demand* defined itself, the accounting firm's service realignment *response* was necessary if not predictable.

In November 1990, the efforts of one of the major "second tier" firms, Laventhol and Horwath, to keep up with the pace resulted in the firm's declaring bankruptcy, an unprecedented event in modern public practice (Pae 1990). Some commentators, however, expressed the view that overall, the mergers and dislocations among the firms would create significant opportunities for second-tier and larger local firms while big firms were distracted by matters of realigning and were focused internally. By 1990–91, national firms found that maintaining profitability in the face of an economic downturn was more challenging because the mix of revenues was now "softer." That is, as nonattest fees constituted more of the fee structure, the fact that such fees are for discrete services, not renewable ones, as in tax or audit services, made overall revenues more volatile in a recession.

Public Practice

Accounting, Assurance, and Business Reporting Services

By the mid-1980s, the AICPA had promulgated standards for attest services, as distinguished from auditing services. The AICPA effort, then under the leadership of Robert Mednick, a partner of Arthur Andersen and future chair of the AICPA board, was a step to identifying the prospective market for attestation services as differentiated from traditional auditing of financial reports (Mednick 1984). By the mid-1990s, this approach would be exploited by the AICPA Special Committee led by R. K. Elliott.

The issuance of several new auditing standards by the Auditing Standards Board (ASB) during the 1980s, including Standard No. 54, *Illegal Acts by Clients,* were direct attempts to reduce the so-called expectations gap addressed in recommendations of the Treadway Commission. Under the direction of AICPA senior staff, including Tom Kelley and Dan Guy, and during the chairmanship of Jerry Sullivan of Coopers & Lybrand, Donald Neebes of Ernst & Young, and David Landsittel of Arthur Andersen, the ASB sought to reshape the auditing function to be responsible and responsive in a demanding and competitive environment.

Some of the most constructive criticism of public company auditors was rendered by the General Accounting Office and the comptroller general of the United States, Charles A. Bowsher. In 1989, in a post-Treadway assessment of CPA auditors, for example, the GAO noted that although the profession had made substantial progress, some audit guides for specialized accounting and auditing practices of particular industries had not kept up to date with changes (General Accounting Office 1989).

In another area of auditing, the potential jurisdictional overlap between the FASB and the GASB, both subject to the oversight of the Financial Accounting Foundation (FAF), has resulted in a reexamination by the ASB of the hierarchy of GAAP, so that "an entity subject to the jurisdiction of one board does not become required to change its reporting principles as a result of a standard issued by another board" (Auditing Standards Board 1991). This proposal along with the significant revisions to the auditor's standard report (Statement on Auditing Standards No. 58), which became effective in the late 1980s, are significant examples of how the auditing process and product are changing. SAS 58 provided for the auditor's report to be expanded from two to three paragraphs, requiring a reference to consistency by inclusion of a separate paragraph following the opinion paragraph only when accounting principles have not been applied consistently. SAS 58 also changed the manner in which uncertainties are reported upon by eliminating the "subject to" qualification and replacing it with a paragraph following the opinion paragraph describing the matter in question.

In other audit-related initiatives, the AICPA has amendments to the 1934 Securities Exchange Act that would require auditor reports on internal control structure of public companies. Also, the CPA Institute studied the administration of the independence requirements for auditors under the Securities Acts with a view toward increasing the self-regulatory role in the process and streamlining the body of accumulated independence rules, emphasizing instead individual behavior norms.

Management Advisory Services

American public accountants have been offering advisory services since the inception of the profession before the turn of the century (Previts 1985A). Attention of the national and regional firms to management advisory services (MAS) as a "specialty" dates from the post–World War II era. Furthermore, separate general and technical standards for management advisory services work are enforceable under the AICPA rules of professional conduct.[18] In 1982, the SEC, recognizing the ability of informed management to decide the question about MAS providers, rescinded its ASR 250, which, since its adoption in 1978, had required disclosure in proxy statements of public companies nonaudit services performed by their independent public accountants.

Those supportive of the expanded MAS role point out that there is a difference between audit and MAS services that makes the latter inherently different than auditing services; namely, that since a third-party relationship (creditor, investor) is not directly involved, there is very limited risk to independence in fact since the contractual arrangement involves the firm and the client only (AICPA 1991A).

A fundamental question remains, however. Can certified public accountants provide advisory services and remain independent with regard to audit relationships with a client? Although MAS activities for major publicly held companies may be performed by nonauditing staff under conditions of different responsibilities, there may be an appearance of loss of independence and a question about the willingness of the firm to point out its own faults should the auditing team discover subsequent weaknesses in the performance by their MAS team. These situations risk the impression that the public accounting firm may be incapable of objectively evaluating a system they recommended.

From one point of view, the comparative advantage maintained by accounting firms that enables them to provide advice to their clients is a social asset. In the process of conducting an effective audit, the public accountant is likely to become more familiar with the strengths and weaknesses of a client system and, therefore, is in a position to make recommendations that the client may acknowledge and implement to improve the service or product of the firm and thus pass the cost savings of new efficiency on to the consumer. By eliminating the CPA firm as a source of technical advice, society loses the potential beneficial efficiency effect that would come from the auditor's talent as an adviser. The risk of sacrificing audit independence because of MAS involvement must be balanced against the loss of this advisory resource. Can accounting firms offer both advisory services and audit services to the same client and not suborn independence? Can society afford not to have the advice of the expert accountant available in nonaudit matters? Some argue that short of the adviser's becoming a surrogate for management (i.e., assuming the duties for management in decision making and ultimate responsibility), no true conflict exists even in publicly held companies where advisory services can be argued to be at least indirectly provided for the benefit of third-party stakeholders.

Even so, as advisory services extend into areas including litigation support and investment counseling, it becomes challenging to provide points that differentiate advisers from managers (Ashton and Bayliss 1989). Therefore, the need to increase self-regulatory oversight of CPA activities in this area seems warranted. A first step would be to include a consideration of suitable controls over MAS service as part of a progressive application of peer review to MAS activities per se. This action would provide evidence of the CPA profession's commitment to provide self-regulation across its entire scope of services, even to include a consideration of the international practice aspects, which by all appearances, have long been diversified along similar lines of service.

Taxation

Taxes come in a variety of types and amounts. For instance, there are taxes on real estate, on income at the federal, state, and local levels, on retail sales, on gasoline for automobiles, on estates and gifts at certain levels, on "sinful" commodities such as alcohol and cigarettes, and on wages as a means of transfer funding to what are considered social security "benefits." Hotel guests pay a "bed" tax in convention cities, and employers pay an "unemployment tax" to fund benefits for qualified jobless. And, recently, a tax has been levied on luxury automobiles.

Accounting for the tax revenue transactions affords professional accountants nearly endless opportunities to display and develop their expertise.

On the eve of World War II, the federal income tax affected fewer than five million people. By 1988, the seventy-fifth anniversary of the Internal Revenue Code, nearly twenty times that number of returns were filed. The twin, and oft-elusive, objectives of equity and simplicity continue to provide fertile ground for controversy (and some say, contributions) for politicians who exercise power over the tax legislation process not only on Capitol Hill but in statehouses around the nation. And, of course, tax compliance and planning are among the largest sources of professional service fees for accountants and for competing groups, including attorneys and other tax preparers. Internal corporate tax services, which facilitate similar compliance and planning purposes, are also a principal source of corporate employment for accountants and attorneys.

The recent series of federal tax laws noted above reduced to mid–30 percent range the personal marginal tax rates of the 1970s, which had gone as high as 70 percent. The change reflected a policy of "supply side economics" and the expectation that funds not taxed away would be spent and/or invested by individuals, with a beneficial market-multiplying effect.

These laws, as those that preceded them, were attempts to reduce the financial burden on low-income taxpayers and to simplify filing and reduce loophole advantages that had developed as a result of the provisions of complex tax regulations and court decisions. Tax reforms sought to accomplish various social objectives, including redistributing income, addressing perceived tax inequities, and providing stimulation for acquisition of capital goods and the formation of capital. It may never be clear that such policy goals in both personal and corporate taxes have been economically successful, but it is likely that the political intention to use tax policy as a means of achieving social objectives will persist (Rosenbaum 1990; Kibbe 1991).

Tax rules, as with all regulation, are subject to interpretation, reinterpretation, litigation, and appeal. With the establishment of the AICPA membership taxation division, CPAs further enhanced their ability to participate in the national agenda over particular issues. In January 1987, the AICPA further increased its commitment in the taxation area by appointing a vice president with responsibilities for tax matters, assigned to the Washington, D.C., offices. Furthermore, by means of the series of "Statements of Responsibilities in Tax Practice," guidance was provided for tax practitioners.

Expert tax preparation and advice, with the accountant serving all classes of personal and corporate taxpayers, have become increasingly important and necessary functions. In fact, it is precisely this quasi-advocacy role that creates an ethical issue for CPAs. Lacking the recognized privileged-communications immunity of an attorney, CPAs are limited in the advocacy role they can play. As noted by Chief Justice Burger in 1984, the CPA's role is to serve the public interest—and yet the CPA community's collective tax expertise is a valuable resource to society in tax matters (Jackson and Milliron 1989). Balancing this ethical issue presents an important challenge to CPA tax accountants. The AICPA has explored legislation that would establish a type of tax preparer's privilege to address these concerns (AICPA 1991A).

Differentiating and designing a fee structure for tax compliance and tax planning services also presented a controversy, given the August 1990 FTC agreement with the AICPA. The agreement's implications for tax fees involved the interpretation of which services constitute compliance services subject to usual fees, and which constitute planning or consulting services (which may permit fees contingent upon outcomes). The AICPA's resolution of this Rule 203 Code of Conduct issue for taxes would be complex, but by the mid-1990s, a balance was found that permitted court-determined fees to be accepted while banning outright contingency fees for preparing or amending a return or filing a claim.

Technology has also taken hold in tax compliance, with estimates that during the 1991 filing season seven million of the 68 million taxpayers who got a refund filed electronically (Barnes, Wendling, Cook & O'Connor, Inc. 1991).

The direction of CPA firm tax practice in the 1970s and 1980s was growth-oriented because, many argue, the frequency of tax law changes fostered an opportunity for fee services as tax strategies and plans needed to be overhauled to respond. Vermont Royster, editor emeritus of the *Wall Street Journal,* has noted: "But if the tax law is to be constantly changing in directions no man knows whither, then everything is at sixes and sevens. He can't plan for tomorrow today. To all the other uncertainties of life there is now added the uncertainty of the tax collector" (Royster 1987).

Tax accountants (and attorneys), as "beneficiaries" of this uncertainty, have not relied on an endless boon. However, when one considers the "big picture" there is reason to expect that as demand for federal tax services decreases, there will be an increasing market for services relating to state and local taxation (*Wall Street Journal* 1989).

Government and Nonprofit Practice

The tax revenues raised, as the source of government income, represent one-half of the equation of government accounting. Expenditures for government and nonprofit entities make up the other half. Prior to the 1970s, governmental accounting professionals recognized the need to develop a coherent body of ideas applicable to not-for-profit and governmental agencies. They undertook a research study sponsored by the AICPA in the early 1960s, but it was terminated before being published. However, the Municipal Finance Officers Association (MFOA) did assert practitioner influence through a document entitled *Governmental Accounting, Auditing and Financial Reporting.* In the late 1960s, the AAA sponsored a series of committees to study the need for developments related to reporting and disclosure in this area. In 1974, the National Council on Governmental Accounting (NCGA), with twenty-one representatives, was formed to replace the ad hoc National Committee on Governmental Accounting, which had operated in a fashion similar to the APB. Thereafter, the AICPA again turned its attention to not-for-profit matters, issuing a number of audit guides that acknowledged the importance of the MFOA document. With the amount of resources committed to public sector governmental and not-for-profit agencies increasing, the need for the involvement of CPAs in their traditional role as attestors to reports of public sector management has increased. Because of the situation of major city governments and the need for a more complete accounting of the resources at their disposal, increasing public pressure was brought for revision or replacement of the traditional fund approach to governmental and not-for-profit agencies' accounting. In 1978, the FASB released a research report, *Financial Accounting in Nonbusiness Organizations* by Robert N. Anthony, in an attempt to explore the conceptual issues related to the controversy over proper approaches to public sector and nonbusiness accounting.

In 1984, the Governmental Accounting Standards Board (GASB) was formed to succeed the NCGA, and the Financial Accounting Foundation, which oversees the FASB, also undertook this role for the GASB. The GASB, with a full-time chairman, James Antonius, was composed of four other part-time members from practice, government, and academia. It operates from the same Norwalk, Connecticut, location as does the FASB. The mission of the board is "to establish and improve standards of State and local government accounting and financial reporting that will result in useful information for users of financial reports and guide and educate the public, including issuers, auditors, and users of those financial reports" (GASB 1991).

Since the formation of the GASB there have been instances of overlapping authority, as in the case of public versus private university accounting, which relate to whether the FASB or GASB has jurisdiction over these institutions. For example, private colleges and universities are in the same category as nonprofit institutions such as museums, which come under the jurisdiction of the FASB. The controversy began in 1987 when the FASB ruled that colleges (private institutions) were to include depreciation on their buildings and equipment in their financial reports. The GASB had no such rule and therefore state schools were not obligated to report such practices (*Chronicle* 1989). More recently, the GASB has turned its energies toward the development of a concepts statement on the elements of financial statements. This in turn is related to a reporting model project, with governmental and business activity aspects being addressed.

Single Audit Act of 1984

Audited information requirements that are included in the provisions for federal grants have also created an increased demand for professional accounting services. These federal requirements, coupled with the increased needs of security analysts for information to compare the quality of municipal investments, have resulted in a market pressure for reporting reforms in the governmental accounting area. The technical bankruptcy of both Cleveland and New York City in the 1970s and continuing difficulties in communities such as Hartford and Orange County during the 1990s have crystallized the concerns of many for more information about municipalities and other governmental institutions. In this regard, the SEC has recently approved the creation of an electronic library for municipal bond documents as a central repository for all original documents filed by issuers of municipal bonds in an attempt to increase information availability. Noting that the size of the municipal bond market is roughly equivalent to the corporate bond market, SEC Commissioner Richard Roberts noted, "The municipal market has operated in an environment that largely has been free from the same specific disclosure and reporting requirements that apply to corporate issuers" (Salwen 1991: C1). Past attempts at federal legislation that would place the reporting and accounting rule-making authority for governmental agencies seeking funds through public capital markets in the hands of the SEC have been unsuccessful. This approach is not likely to succeed because of the issue of conflict between the roles of state and federal governments with regard to the Tenth Amendment (a constitutional question about the federal government's limiting or governing the ability of other governmental units to raise money and maintain their own financial integrity).[19] Does the federal government's power over national capital markets include the right to "regulate" disclosures by other political entities attempting to raise capital? This issue remains open.

Through other legislative efforts, however, such as the Single Audit Act (1984), state and local government entities receiving federal grants have been induced to a greater level of accountability. The 1984 law requires comprehensive single audits for state and local governments that receive federal assistance. Circular A-133 of the Office of Management and Budget extends this requirement to colleges and nonprofit grantees. This and comparable legislation in statehouses around the country has increased the use of CAFR (Comprehensive Annual Financial Report) documents at local levels. This reporting and the related auditing are the start of a process from a commonly based system that observes GASB standards. Once the hierarchy of GASB and FASB authority is clarified in these areas, a significant step will have been taken toward establishing accountability and reporting in government and nonprofit institutions (Auditing Standards Board 1991).

Federal Accounting and Financial Management

Recent attempts toward more meaningful accountability at the federal operating level can be traced to the Federal Managers' Financial Integrity Act (1982) and to the appointment of inspectors general in cabinet-level agencies.

Guesses that paperwork and internal reporting processes cost the federal government well in excess of $2 billion a year are but a gesture toward grasping the significance of federal operations. Management audit and review responsibilities for this process have been the task of the U.S. General Accounting Office (GAO) and its leader, the comptroller general, since 1921. "Accountability" investigations by the GAO, based on *Standards for Audits of Governmental Organizations, Programs, Activities and Functions* (June 1972), have gained favor as providing useful "watchdog" information to Congress and society. The incumbent comptroller general, Charles Bowsher, has maintained a high profile in Washington and earned both praise and criticism. (The comptroller general is an appointed post, for a single fifteen-year term. This process was designed for continuity and to insulate the comptroller general from political pressures.) A November 22, 1988, *Wall Street Journal* editorial complained that Bowsher aimed to please his congressional patrons and ignored the message from voters: "Washington is known for audacious politicians, but Charles Bowsher, head of the General Accounting Office, may be one of the first to qualify in a job that pretends to be apolitical. Mr. Bowsher's latest political exercise is an unsolicited 16-page lecture on 'The Budget Deficit.' The nation's Number One accountant exhorts us all to read his green eye shade" ("Creature of Congress," 1988: A20).

Bowsher's authority also extends into other politically sensitive areas: for example, when Oliver North was sentenced to probation and fined for his involvement in the Iran-Contra scandal, the Navy said it was suspending North's pension earned during twenty years of service. However, the Navy later "recommended that it be restored by Comptroller General Charles Bowsher, who has the final say" (Rosenthal 1989). The GAO also reviewed controversial areas of CPA activity such as auditor involvement in failed Savings and Loan (S&L) units. The GAO criticized several large and local firms for providing insufficient workpaper evidence and concluded that for six of the eleven audits of twenty-nine failed S&Ls in the Dallas district "the independent auditors did not adequately audit and/or report the S&Ls financial or internal control problems in accordance with professional standards" (Grant Thornton 1989). In 1991, Bowsher also was reported to be supporting a proposal to require rotation of bank external auditors on a periodic basis and prohibit auditors from providing nonattest services, but the proposal was not further developed (Berton 1991C).

The burgeoning federal budget and the proliferation of government programs have, however, called into question whether any single agency can hope to properly oversee and review the vast array of financial activity represented by an annual multitrillion dollar federal budget.[20] A step toward further accountability was achieved with passage of the Chief Financial Officers Act (1990). This legislation, sponsored by several of the professional accounting and financial management associations, called for estab-

TABLE 8.4
1993 U.S. Federal Government, a Macro Income
Account

	Amount (in billions)	%
Income/receipts		
Taxes	1,266	84.01
Borrowings	241	15.99
Total	1,507	100.00
Expenditures		
Foreign aid	16	1.06
State and local governments	186	12.34
Interest expense	184	12.21
Subsidies	36	2.39
National defense	166	11.02
Other suppliers	73	4.84
Armed forces	136	9.02
Payments to American people	710	47.11
Total	1,507	100.00

lishing a role for twenty-three chief financial officers in federal agencies who would fall under the jurisdiction of the OMB. Opponents, concerned that these CFOs would be subject to an administration's influence and would impede congressional appropriation prerogatives, sought to deny the $105 million to fund the positions in 1991 but were unsuccessful. The act also established a deputy director of management and an Office of Federal Financial Management at OMB (Priest 1991).

Cost Accounting Standards Board

Procurement waste and fraud in government contracting reached a point of high political sensitivity in the late years of the Vietnam War and was first addressed by a federal agency, the Cost Accounting Standards Board (CASB). The board, established in 1970, was decommissioned in 1980 when Congress decided not to provide further funding. The twenty standards promulgated by the CASB "dealt with the topics of consistency, allocating costs to objectives, employee compensation, fixed assets and specific . . . problems such as the cost of . . . research and development" (Parker 1989). By 1988, however, concerns about weaknesses and fraud in procurement led to the reestablishment of the CASB, this time as an independent board within the Office of Federal Procurement Policy. The former standards then became part of federal acquisitions regulations. The prospect for the CASB to be a major influence in establishing government sector cost allocation rules is again at hand. The CASB, under the auspices of the law, has the capacity to dominate government cost allocation policy and procedures. Furthermore, it could gain de facto control of procurement cost standards at other levels, particularly state government, and thereby establish a cost-accounting domain by the mere fact of its existence. Small state governments and contractors, in particular, it has been argued, when faced with choosing required CASB or other costing options will likely select the former for expedience, conformity, uniformity, and thus cost savings (Rayburn 1991: 108).

When one views the legislation of the last decade, which has attempted to place systems of accountability in place at federal, state, and local accounting operations, and when one also considers the formation and agenda of the GASB, one would grant to legislators a sense of accomplishment. But conclusive proof of the value of this legislation and of the GASB remains to be provided. The principle of accountability, never uppermost in American political culture, has all but vaporized, say some journalists. And others observe, "Small wonder that accountability has become unpopular; there is little reward in it" (Borger 1992: 8).

Corporate Practice

Financial Management and Public Accountability

Federal disclosure legislation and professionals have promoted the issue of corporate accountants' responsibility and professionalism over many decades. In 1950, Vatter in his text *Managerial Accounting* observed: "The major function served by *both* public and managerial accountants is to use their independent judgment with complete freedom; thus they may observe and evaluate objectively the fortunes and the results of enterprise operations" (Vatter 1950: 8; emphasis added). Vatter's view foretold what is now perceived as an increasing need for professionalism by accountants in corporate practice (Campfield 1988). It has established the basis for the position that a "detached and independent viewpoint" be part of the standard of performance for the internal professional (Kapnick 1977).

The expanding role of professional accountants in the financial operations, management, reporting, and analysis of publicly held and privately owned business has been, since the early 1970s, a substantial and notable area of practice growth. An uncritical and simplistic view of this area, lumped together under the old rubric of "cost accounting," is a commonplace misreading of this development. In fact, the practice of corporate accountants has become increasingly substantial, more complex and sophisticated. Corporate practice is specialized by control aspects, such as internal auditing and budgeting; it involves cost transaction and activity-based accounting, information systems, and financial reporting and analysis for internal and external parties. Each of these may in turn be delegated through a sophisticated international structure involving a chief financial officer (CFO), a chief information officer (CIO) and/or a chief reporting officer (CRO), and countless subordinates. Or, in smaller entities, these duties may be the summary responsibility of an "only financial officer" (OFO), the sole accounting professional within the enterprise.

This growth, particularly of the corporate-practicing CPA, is a phenomenon that recently drew the following editorial comment in the July 22, 1991, *Accounting Today:* "In efforts to raise revenues . . . the AICPA and the Institute of Management Accountants have put themselves on a collision course with state societies. . . . The AICPA and the IMA should . . . let state CPA societies and local IMA chapters take the lead with management accountants."

Since the inception (1972) of the Certificate of Management Accounting (CMA), and more recently with the announced award by the IMA of a CFM (Certified in Financial Management) designation, professional accountants working in corporate environments now have alternatives to the CPA certificate as a means of gaining credential identity. The Certified Internal Auditor (CIA) designation was also established in the early 1970s. Under a program sanctioned by the Institute of Internal Auditors (IIA), it has gained a following. Internal auditors' increasing stature reflects the demand for internal control aspects of corporate operations, as emphasized in the Treadway Commission report (1986), and added responsibilities for operational auditing within large corporations following the Foreign Corrupt Practices Act (1977). SEC officials too have noted that the approval of the IIA's "Standards for the Practice of Internal Auditing" increases the prospects that internal auditors will be asked to perform tasks relating to public reports on internal controls and to assume the growing responsibilities of the corporate audit committee of the board of directors.

The CMA reflects an increase in the stature and maturity of management accounting. Moreover, research conducted on the issues of importance to financial executives and management accountants continues to increase, supported by the IMA, the Financial Executives Research Foundation (FERF), and the IIA Research Foundation.

As noted above, a number of professional associations, including the IMA, the IIA, the FEI, and the AICPA, have a membership identified with the corporate practice of professional accountants. The two largest of these groups, the IMA (93,000) and the AICPA (320,000 members)—and therefore also by proxy, state CPA societies—are seen to be in a contest for dominion over the corporate accounting practitioner (Berton 1991D). The encounter among these rivals may be overstated, since the organizations in this field have coexisted for several years and have already defined, self-selected constituencies.

The stake of CPA organizations in serving the CPA corporate practice community is based upon the premise that "just as physicians and attorneys retain their identity as doctors and lawyers irrespective of whether they work in public practice or corporate practice . . . a doctor is still a doctor and a lawyer is still a lawyer. So also the CPA possesses a 'monolithic identity.' A CPA is CPA whether in public practice or corporate practice. The recently adopted AICPA membership and ethical requirements place the corporate reporting CPA under the same expectations as the public practice CPA" (Magill and Previts 1991: 27).

Public Expectations

The Treadway Commission's 1986 report contained nearly two dozen suggestions for public companies. These addressed numerous areas of corporate accountability, including the role of top management, internal auditors, control systems, the corporate board, its audit committee, and the content of financial reports.

The report signaled a commencement of formal recognition of financial managers and their broader social role and responsibility. Several Treadway recommendations directed to external auditors also affected the corporation. One of the most contested Treadway recommendations involved mandatory external auditor involvement in quarterly reports and in the assessment of internal accounting control. Legislation addressing these points was introduced in 1990 and 1991. It was opposed by the FEI, while being supported by the AICPA, indicating the quarrelsome policy implications related to the self-regulatory reform movement (Financial Executives Institute 1990, 1991).

Financial Reporting

As noted earlier in this chapter, controversy has also continued over the "appropriate role" of financial management and preparers of financial reports in the FASB standard-setting process. The Business Roundtable, for example, published the results of a survey of its active members in 1988 which revealed that 91 percent felt that the FASB was too conceptual and that 73 percent believed that the FASB did not give enough weight to the views of financial statement preparers (Financial Executives Institute 1988).

This controversy and subsequent episodes reflected a watershed of developments relating to the implementation of several FASB standards, the most "annoying" being those related to stock options and the accounting for deferred income taxes. Another contemporary FASB agenda issue, accounting for other postemployment benefits, heightened and further polarized the preparer and auditor communities engaged in seeking a resolution to "standard-setting" tensions. The preparer community also expressed concerns over "process" issues, including the lack of required field testing of major proposed rule changes (Ihlanfeldt 1991).

Management Accounting: Controversy Renewed!

With the decline in the impact of direct labor costs during the 1970s and 1980s—they constituted only about 10 percent of operating expenses of most industrial companies by 1991—there was revived interest in the conceptual basis of cost accounting (Rutledge 1991). The discord grew up between those employing techniques of traditional "cost management" (CM) and those identified with "activity based costing" (ABC) (Kaplan 1983).

Attempts to outline the subject were to be found in the writings of Staubus, Kaplan, and others (Staubus 1987). The issues were structured in a historical exposition, Johnson and Kaplan's *Relevance Lost: The Rise and Fall of Management Accounting* (1987). Central among commentators' concerns were that cost accounting had forgotten its "identity" and had become driven by external financial-reporting considerations. In short, it had lost "relevance" to internal management uses. Staubus contended that the theoretical development of cost accounting had been at a standstill for decades because of misguided efforts in the literature that failed to distinguish "different costs for different purposes" (1987). These items, while perhaps not original to the specialty, were considered timely, especially given the ongoing debate over financial accounting and decision information.

In a standard text, *Cost Accounting: A Managerial Emphasis* (Horngren and Foster 1991: 92), for example, the authors develop the argument by noting that "product costs reported as inventoriable costs to shareholders may differ from those reported to tax authorities and may further differ from those reported to managers for guiding pricing and product mix decisions." The authors, assimilating the applications of ABC into the entire spectrum of CM, also note that ABC helps "cost control by focusing attention on cost drivers; it can also yield more accurate product cost data by using multiple cost drivers (including non-volume-based as well as volume-based drivers) that more accurately reflect the *causes* of cost" (Horngren and Foster 1991: 150).

Cost accounting, by renewing the debate over the origin and meaning of the costs, has invigorated academic interest in the subject. The shift of cost-accounting theory to respond to the various applications in industrial and service businesses indicates the form of "demand/response" adjustment that historians have identified in previous eras of accountancy's history.

Academic Accountancy

Education Reform

While practitioners and politicians have been debating the social and political consequences of auditing and accounting, the academic branch of accountancy has been assessing its identity in relationship to society and the practicing professional (Bricker and Previts 1990). The sociology of the structure of the profession, which identifies an educational treatment effect to act with integrity, objectivity, and technical competence, addresses the relational ties between academics and practitioners and each group's views. The establishment of more than three dozen professional schools since the early 1970s also evidences the extent to which universities have begun to accept the need to amend curricula to be in concert with the scope of professional services. The educational views and objectives of professional schools and programs have become more focused with the efforts of organizations such as the Federation of Schools of Accountancy, formed in the mid-1970s.

Accounting accreditation, first awarded in 1982, now recognizes the distinctive attributes of more than one hundred professional schools and customary business school–based programs (American Assembly of Collegiate Schools of Business 1989–90). Each of these two educational approaches will continue into the future, but the trend toward professionalized and functionally specialized accountancy programs, given the acceptance of a graduate-equivalent entry-level education for CPA status, can be expected to be increasingly influential (AICPA 1988). The deficiencies, real and imagined, of contemporary accountancy education have been the object of a variety of studies and recommendations during this period. Each major professional organization and several special groups have produced documents on accounting education, including the Commission on Professional Accounting Education (1983), the Treadway Commission (see chapter 5), the IMA's 1994 Education Goals Statement, the AAA Bedford Committee (1986), Coe and Merino's *Future Accounting Education* (1987), the chief executives of public accounting firms' "Perspective" study, the AAA's "Reorienting Accounting Education" monograph, edited by J. J. Schultz (1989), and the 1990 FERF survey by Keating and Jablonsky, *Changing Roles of Financial Management.*

However, not until the formation of the Accounting Education Change Commission (AECC) in a joint arrangement proposed by the academic community and funded by professional firms was a vehicle established to coordinate and find reform. Led by AAA presidents Gerhardt Mueller, John K. Simmons, and Doyle Z. Williams, the AECC funded innovative curriculum proposals and sought to create a "dynamic" attitude. The AAA has also exhibited increased activism following its executive committee's decision to represent the AAA on "academically relevant matters." In an August 1988 policy statement, the executive committee also reaffirmed the postbaccalaureate education concept as guided by the Bedford Committee report (Mueller 1989). The association, which at the start of this period included a membership of approximately 70 percent practitioners out of 11,500-plus members, reported a membership of 9,300 (70 percent academic) by mid-1990. The AAA's development during the 1970s and 1980s, following along the lines of becoming an increasingly international and academically oriented specialized organization, operated in eight regions with more than a dozen special interest sections. The scheduled publications of the association, based in Sarasota, grew from a single quarterly journal, the *Accounting Review,* to nearly two dozen newsletters and journals (Flesher 1991).

Other propriety publications serving the needs of the academic community also increased. By 1996, Zeff noted the existence of forty-two academic journals in the United States alone (Zeff 1996), up from seventeen in 1980. An accounting faculty directory produced annually by Jim Hasselback of Florida State University was begun in 1974 and became an invaluable source of information linking the academic community.

Throughout the period, the CPA examination served in the role of a content target or "driver" of the undergraduate accounting curriculum. The examination itself became a focus of study to reflect the changing needs of practice. In 1989, the AICPA Board of Examiners, in conjunction with the National Association of State Boards of Accountancy, approved several changes in the content of the examination to take effect in May 1994; in 1996 the examination was changed to a "nondisclosed" basis. The content changes included restructuring the exam from five to four sections and refashioning the business law section into coverage of "business law and professional responsibilities." This was the first content adjustment of a decades-old format. This adjustment, accreditation efforts, the activities of the AECC, and the adoption of the 150-hour education requirement were all part of a series of initiatives to reshape the educational process.

Academic Influence

Despite what might be termed a "popular misconception" as to their lack of "clout" in practice matters, several individual accounting academics have in fact been influential in bridging the perceived gap between the two communities. For example, Wharton's David Solomons was a member of the Wheat Committee, which recommended the formation of the FASB; he also played an influential role as draftsman of that report. George Sorter of New York University was a member of the Trueblood Committee on the objectives of financial statements; and Robert Sprouse and Robert Swieringa, as members of the FASB, influenced accounting standards. Herbert Miller, a professor, then a partner of Arthur Andersen & Co., influenced changes in professional education. Robert Mautz, an academic and then a partner of Ernst & Young, was a charter member of the Cost Accounting Standards Board and later a member of the Public Oversight Board of the AICPA division of firms. John C. Burton, as chief accountant of the SEC, and deputy mayor of New York during that city's financial crisis in the late 1970s, significantly influenced accounting practice and the public through his public service and leadership. More recently Arthur Wyatt, now again a professor, but then a policy partner of Arthur Andersen & Co., served as a member of the FASB and subsequently as chairman of the International Accounting Standards Committee (IASC); concurrently he was selected to serve as president of the American Accounting Association. Other academics, including James Don Edwards and Doyle Williams, served as presidents of the AAA and were active as board of directors members of the AICPA. They were also involved in important activities such as George Anderson's AICPA committee, which reformed the code of professional conduct, or the Accounting Education Change Commission. Accounting Hall of Fame members Sidney Davidson and Charles T. Horngren, while remaining identified with their academic careers as teachers and writers, were also influential and responsible participants in AICPA, APB, and Treadway implementation activities. These are but some of the prominent examples of academics who have served the practice community.[21]

Accounting Thought

Today, as compared with the periods before, academics are more apt to learn of problem situations by observing the practitioner than from firsthand experience. An academic's role to propose ideas and to test them has gradually extended itself to field testing of propositions as well, but this role does not ordinarily extend to implementation. Practitioners are primarily involved in implementation such that the problem-solving process, from beginning to end, is one of communication and of working in areas of comparative advantage. The comparative advantage of the academic is in the realm of research and modeling of "ideas," that is, the "R" part of "R & D" (research and development). The practice and standards community does the "D." Therefore, multiple alternatives offered by contemporary accounting theorists should not be criticized but commended. It is to the existence of alternatives that the profession owes progress. Alternatives create the opportunities to select the most suitable approach for dealing with the changing and particular needs of a vast array of clients. The mania that seeks to eliminate alternatives in the search for accounting "truth" is popular, but it is based on the misconception that there is such a thing as a "precise" answer or a single interpretation of "value" or "income" measurement. Other theorists have argued that it is relatively impossible to develop a meaningful normative standard given the myriad expectations that the population of investors develop from their individual social value judgments. The primary resource for learning the appropriate reporting requirements, in an environment concerned with the efficient market and information economics, they assert, is "positive" in nature: tabulating the reporting activities of information producers and assessing the influence of changes in informational content upon the trading price of securities. Accounting theory should respond to the needs of an efficient market and provide predictive information useful to sophisticated portfolio investors. This contrasts with the traditional view of supplying information based on historical cost for purposes of manager stewardship and "scorekeeping" useful to individual stock and bond investors.

Also prominent among contemporary approaches to accounting thought formulation is Chambers's view that accounting measurements reflect a "continuously contemporaneous" approach. Supporters of so-called positive theory reflected, perhaps unwittingly, the preceding literature tracing back to the 1938 work of Sanders, Hatfield, and Moore, and Grady's Accounting Research Study No. 7 (1965) (Watts and Zimmerman 1986). Sterling, on the other hand, has argued that accounting should be more "science-like." He asserted that so long as accountants accept accounting as led by convention, they will seek to address issues as if accounting were an art and not a science. Advocates of accounting science see the need to redefine the nature of accounting and the process by which accounting problems are solved; they suggest adhering to a scientific approach (Sterling 1976). Advocates of accounting science argue that the scientific method thus far has failed accountants because their problems are not developed in scientific terms.

Commentators like Eddie Stamp remained unconvinced that the nature of accounting can be altered simply by changing the way in which the discipline views itself (1981). There was recognition that accounting problems cannot be overcome by the use of science routines alone. A corresponding appreciation for behavioral research was only of late sufficiently established to encompass accounting problems. Others critical of the accounting science approach pointed out that accounting was more like medicine or engineering (i.e., an applied science) than it was like physics or chemistry (so-called pure science) (Mattessich 1984). They asserted that to consider accounting as a hard science was improper. Those evaluating the claims of "scientists" responded by noting that the history of hard science suggests that "soft" stages of theory agreement are a part of the evolution of a discipline toward the state of "hardness" (Wells 1976). Accounting, they argued, has just begun to take on the properties necessary to supply it with this "firmness." Therefore, it is now appropriate to address problems "scientifically" and remove from accounting prior solutions biased by old thought habits and social convention. Those of a more pragmatic view asserted that P. W. Bridgman's 1945 *Yale Review* essay "The Prospect for Intelligence" had shattered the illusion of the simple duality of art versus science rhetoric; what mattered according to Bridgman was doing "one's damnedest with one's mind—no holds barred" (1945: 450).

Perhaps the traditional view of accounting, as a past-oriented, stewardship function, remains at the heart of the schism between academics and practitioners, with the latter group continuing to recognize the value-in-use and scorekeeping role of accounting. To the extent that all accounting theories represent a rationalization of the limitations of a conventional double-entry system of reporting, they all afford a basis for conceptual comparability. Beyond the point of this rationalization, arguments for the preference of one accounting theory over another often are reduced to the mere desire to institutionalize subjective preferences under the guise of "rational and systematic" approaches. If, over time, accountants' functions transcend the system of accounting based on the double-entry model and accountants begin to take on reporting responsibilities not primarily limited to financial measurement, then there will be an expanded social theory of our reporting obligation. To the extent that theorists have defined broader accounting goals under such headings as "social accounting" or "human resource accounting," there is an indication of the potential for theory that transcends conventional financial measurement (Nelson 1967).

The AAA's 1977 *A Statement on Accounting Theory and Theory Acceptance* was an attempt to assess the developments and theories of the financial area relative to the AAA's 1966 study *A Statement of Basic Accounting Theory*. The 1977 document attempted to chart a course for progress in theory development by identifying the main streams of thought and assessing their differences without judging the merit of one approach over another.[22] The statement of this posture of nonpreference followed upon a debate and resolution at the AAA 1973 annual meeting in Quebec. The debate concerned whether the AAA should take positions on such matters or serve to support and develop individual work. The outcome of the Quebec debate reaffirmed the importance of the individual academic's view and limited the association's endorsement of general statements on accounting principles. As such, it provided increased impetus to theoretical experimentation by individual researchers; if the association were precluded from taking a definitive position, then alternative individual positions would merit equal opportunity for exposure, recognition, and acknowledgment, based on the ability of the individual to convince the community as a whole of the merit of the proposition. This opening up of the discovery process fostered new approaches, including a nascent literature in critical inquiry and more attention to historical and contextual research (Mattessich 1991: 4).

Of course, the development of accounting thought in the 1970s, 1980s, and 1990s warrants more than this brief outline; indeed, the discipline continues to need a "history of thought" literature as found in other fields such as economics. Recent books by Chambers (1995), J. R. Edwards (1994), and Chatfield and Vangermeersch (1996) are strong contributions to this area. Many of the theoretical propositions advanced in this time period have been tested but remain contested although they have been widely discussed and debated in academic journals, at conferences, and in workshops. If there has been increasing academic concern over the drift toward legal formalism in a codification of accounting via the regulatory and quasi-legislative posture of practicing accountants' boards and government agencies, accounting academics and theoreticians have not acknowledged this concern by relenting in the development of proposals for positive/descriptive or normative systems to improve the content of accounting information and reports. The importance of these different views and the continuing fresh input of ideas seem to have benefited the thoughtful practitioner and the standard-setting process. Perhaps the frequent quibbling among academics is viewed by practitioners as a sign that academics simply can't agree on anything. Such a view is lamentable and unsophisticated (Van Wyhe 1993).

Research Reform

In light of the diversity of academic opinion about the conceptual structure of accountancy, it is not a surprise that the impact of academic research
on accounting practice may be seen to be limited (Burton and Sack 1991;
Dopuch and Ronen 1991). But increasingly there is a view that practice
does take note of research and, as one experienced practitioner notes,
"does catch up—eventually" (Hall 1987: 34). Contracting academics to undertake research seems to be increasing, aided by programs at major public
accounting firms and by increasing consultation of academics by the FASB,
as well as academic involvement in studies at the AICPA, FEI, IMA, and IIA.
And catalogues of research and more convenient modes of Internet technology for accessing abstracts promise to facilitate awareness and utilization
of research findings (Klemstine and Maher 1984).

As pluralistic influences, behavioral, contextual, critical, historical, technical, and empirical, affect the range and agenda of researchers, it may be
time to recognize the richness that has come from the investment in accounting academia's restructure since the early 1970s (Frecka 1989). Previously, the career academic was poorly trained in research skills and less able
to relate research results to practice. The first major numbers of doctorates
to enter the accounting classroom during the 1970s were rewarded more
for their research and not their contributions to practice. Beginning in the
1960s and 1970s, "finance theorists invaded the field of accounting" (Putnam and Stevens 1991: B2). Out of this orthodoxy developed a cult of a
sort, akin to the "political correctness" criticized in the broader academic
community (Zuckerman 1991). But as this new academic community matured, it began to address more relevant and applied issues (Previts 1985A).
Today academics seem to be heeding the advice, paraphrased for accountants, given by Merton Miller in his Nobel Prize lecture: "Now that our field
has officially come of age, as it were, perhaps my colleagues in [account-
ancy] can be persuaded to take their noses out of their data bases . . . and
bring the insights of our field . . . to the attention of a wider audience"
(Miller 1991: 488).

Accounting's Heritage and Its Future

How much of the past as prologue remains relevant now? Can we be too
mindful of our past? If there is any conclusion to be drawn, it would be that,
while accountancy has achieved a position of unquestioned importance in

the U.S. economic and social order, it continues to face growing responsibility to mutual fund business investors, management, traditional shareholders, clients, employees, and society as a whole, but in a worldwide capital market context. The challenges facing accountants today are both reflective of the issues of the past and driven by society's present demands, formed by the legislative and institutional character of the capital market and the related market for information-based services. As each generation finds for itself a path through this network of conflicting obligations and expectations, history, as fact and as interpretation, provides by analogy the only catalogue of experience to guide us. Some would argue that history is less valuable today because the character of future expectations and institutions is unparalleled in the past. We would respond that historical study can provide the thoughtful reader evidence that there are parallels between the past and the present, between what *was,* what *is,* and what *ought to be.* Many issues recurred in slightly altered fashion in the 1970s, 1980s, and 1990s. Other issues are so long-term, or obstinate in their tenure that they must be faced by each generation. Some might infer, for example, that the recent scandal involving the Bank of Credit & Commerce International and First American Bank is a parallel to the McKesson-Robbins fraud of the 1930s but in the context of a global capital market (Beaty and Gwynne 1991). In this sense, there are historical generalizations that foretell the continuing need for assurance services in such a broader setting.

The Limitations of Accounting

In 1931, DR Scott published his *Cultural Significance of Accounts,* bearing witness to a perception that accounts had become an important thread of the nation's fabric. Today accountancy, as an academic discipline and a profession, has become a fundamental element of the American way of life (*Novus Ordo Seclorum*) and the evolving world system of capital market development.[23] Nevertheless, accountancy has its limitations, the most important being that while it can assist many groups—lenders, preparers, sophisticated and individual investors, and the government, for example—it does not and cannot eliminate the risk of investing. Put another way: "The bottom line is that lenders . . . will continue to lose money until they stop making dumb . . . loans" (Eskey 1991: 4E). This is important to recall, given that legislation, at both the state and federal levels, furnished the profession with its mandate as part of the process of socialization of the risk of credit. Accountancy is then a means to an end and not an end in itself. But it is not merely a technique. As Skinner has observed:

Since roughly 1850, accounting has increasingly been used to provide information for decisions rather than merely to provide a record of property owned and transactions in property. Two branches of accounting have emerged in this period, distinguishable by the type of decision made. *Management accounting* is concerned with the production and interpretation of information that will be useful for an entity's internal decisions about investment, production, pricing, marketing and so on. *Financial reporting*, on the other hand, is concerned with the production and interpretation of information for use by persons outside the entity. One very important purpose of financial reporting is to facilitate decisions by outside parties whether to invest in the entity or provide credit to it. (Skinner 1987: 2)

To this, one must add that those who "invest in the entity" vary widely in their sophistication and in the type of information they require; that is, there are substantial differences among individuals and institutions as investors. In determining the level and content of reports and disclosures to satisfy this spectrum, the need for academia to prepare accounting professionals who are even more highly qualified and educated seems clear.

The Challenge of a Global Vision

The 1990s brought a realization that the end of the cold war was as telling in economic impact as the two previously denominated world wars concluded in this century. The nation's dividends from this post–cold war period were less apparent perhaps because these returns were belied by the effect of reallocations of production from and to locations not limited to the United States. Outsourcing was not limited to local communities in any one country. One of the costs of winning global peace was a global economic reordering. This new arrangement was perilous to narrow national economic identities because technology collapsed status quo economic barriers to time and distance at unprecedented rates. For accountants whose role affected capital allocation and cost decisions, this meant that despite nationality or location the value they provided through timely and relevant decision information was a source of newfound economic identity, political influence, and cultural significance.

Paul F. Grady, a parent of our profession's auditing standards, observed the following about his CPA peers: "Most of us are so occupied in serving our clients and our profession that we seldom consciously evaluate our programs in philosophical terms" (Zimmerman 1978: 383). And yet it is in this philosophical dimension that accountants must succeed if they are to justify their role and serve society. In some areas, particularly academic preparation, accountants are now trained only slightly differently than a generation ago. The advent of graduate-equivalent entry-level education for CPAs holds tremendous promise and potential to replace the traditional, solely technical emphasis toward an education based upon a commitment to life-long learning and the ideals of integrity, objectivity, competence, and serving the well-being of others.

"This is a whitewater time, and the staid old profession is right in the middle of the wild currents. . . . It's a lot more exciting than it was twenty-five years ago," observes Edward Kangas (Weinstein 1987: 4). A successful transit of these exhilarating "rapids" may lead to accountancy reaching its full potential. This true potential of accountancy lies in its cultural significance and its importance as a social strategic resource to aid in improving the quality of life in a global capital market system through its capacity as a profession to supply the data from which decision information essential to choices about economic and social investments is shaped.

Accountancy should enable the processes of all capital market societies, existing and evolving, so as to achieve an effective allocation of resources that is likely to improve the standard of living and the quality of life overall. We find this challenge noble and daunting. As Barry Melancon, newly selected AICPA president, noted in July 1995, his job was to work to reposition the accountancy profession for the twenty-first century.

The term *bottom line* is a U.S. idiom, representing our discipline's signature on our culture. It is in origin an accounting term, not a medical term, not a legal term, not an engineering term. It has become a pervasive expression that compactly identifies our way of life, our competitive values and goals. The "bottom line" is as much a part of identifying the U.S. way of life as is baseball or blue jeans. As its usage becomes adapted to a global capital market order, the term will continue to signify that the role of accountants is one that is determining and results-oriented.

Notes

Chapter 1

1. Charles Snell, in his folio pamphlet, "Accompts for Landed Men" (London: 1711), makes it very clear, in a full-page advertisement at the end, that

> Such Persons as desire, may have their children taught by the *Author*, a most Noble and Generous Way of *Writing all Hands*, and *How to Command their Pen*.

> The *Practical Manner* (of *Arithmetick*) used by Merchants in *Calculating*, and *Examining* their Accompts.

> *Foreign Exchanges*, their *Calculations*, *Negotiations*, and *Arbitrations*.

> The True Manner of Keeping *Merchants Accompts* (the *Waste-Book* having been Real Business) stated in the *Italian* Method of *Book-keeping* by *Double Entry*."

He added, of himself:

> He also Fits Persons for *Publick Offices;* and *Boards* at his House such as desire it.

Snell was an excellent example of the writing-master/accountant genre, which flourished particularly in the 1750–1830 period. Another work of his is a much smaller pamphlet, "A Short and Easy Method. After which Shop-keepers may State, Post, and Balance their Books of Accompts," in which he styles himself "Writing-Master and Accomptant . . . With whom Young Gentlemen may Board" (London: 1714). This little book opens with a catechism, the answers to which were presumably to be learned by heart. "*Q*. What is the first Thing I must do, who design to keep my Books of Accompts after this Method? *A*. You must make an Inventory; an Example of which is at the End of these Instructions." These are superb examples of the writing-master's art (Dunlop 1968).

2. Pure barter was supplemented in the seventeenth century by the use of wampum. Wampum was made of clam and whelk shells and accepted as a form of currency, usually bound in the form of a belt. When wampum factories were set up and counterfeit beads flooded the markets around 1800, the shells were outlawed as legal tender.

3. John Chamberlain, a business historian, suggests that Obadiah Brown may have been initially responsible for bringing a knowledge of double entry to the colonies. In light of the other evidence and the implications of this chapter, it seems unlikely that Chamberlain's contention is merited.

4. This calls to mind the auditor's epitaph, which we have seen cited more frequently, found at Saint Mary's Church, Chesham, England: "Here lyeth part of

Richard Bowle, who faithfully served divers great lordes as auditor on earth, but above all he prepared himself to give up his account to the Lord Heaven. He was a lover of God's ministers, a father of God's poor, a help to all God's people. He died on the 16th December, 1626 and of his age 77."

Chapter 2

1. Accountants of the early nineteenth century learned to "reduce Federal money to Old Lawful" and "Old Lawful to Federal Money." Daniel Adams's book, *Scholars' Arithmetic or the Federal Accountant,* which supplied countless examples of these conversions, was widely used throughout the first three decades of the 1800s.

2. Statements on an annual basis would have been rare before 1752, for it was not until then that an act of Parliament promulgated that the first day of January would be considered the beginning of the year for all purposes.

3. For a lighthearted but thorough "investigation" into the "padding" of expenses by Washington, read *George Washington's Expense Account,* by Marvin Kitman (Simon & Schuster, 1970), or consult the review which appears in *Management Accounting* (December 1970: 60). A quotation on the significance of the military audit, attributed to George Washington, was found in 1990 in the U.S. Naval Audit Service manual by Professor L. Kreiser. His attempts to establish the authenticity of the remarks were not successful. However, the remarks add to the folklore of the times, and to that of Washington as well.

To the Continental Congress:

I am truly sensible that time of Congress is much taken up with a variety of important matters, but. . the establishing of some office for auditing accounts is a matter of exceeding importance to the public interest.

Two motives induce me to urge the matter: first, a conviction of the utility of the measure; second, that I may stand exculpated if hereafter it should appear that money has been improperly expended. . . .

For me, whose time is employed from the hour of my rising till I retire to bed again, to go into an examination of the accounts . . . with any degree of precision and exactness, without neglecting other matters of equal importance, is utterly impracticable. . . .

It is the minutia that must be gone into; the propriety of each charge examined, the vouchers looked into . . . and . . . [if] a person . . . was inclined to be knavish, [he] might purchase large quantities with publick money, and sell one-half of it again for private emolument, and yet his accounts on paper will appear fair, and be supported with vouchers for every charge. . . .

I do not urge this matter from a suspicion of any unfair practices. . . . But there should nevertheless be some control, as well as upon their discretion as honesty; to which may be added, that accounts become perplexed and confused by long standing, and the errors therein not so discoverable as if they underwent an early revision and examination . . .

George Washington
14 July 1776

(Source: *U.S. Naval Audit Service Manual,* c. 1975, Prologue, p. iii)

4. Bennett's twelfth edition appeared in 1829, but the illustrations of his later editions remained largely unchanged. Note that in the balance chart illustration in this chapter, the accounts are dated 1817. Forty-one editions of his work are known to have been printed through 1862.

5. Littleton states that "Accountancy" denotes a field of knowledge, while "accounting" means the processes active in that field (1933A: 165).

6. The debate over identifying the era of the origins of professional public practice in America is not likely to be resolved by the materials provided in this work. However, it seems warranted to propose as unfounded the position previously held by James Anyon and Richard Brown that it was not until 1880 that America witnessed the birth of a public accounting profession. Neither Anyon nor Brown were native Americans, the former having come to the United States from England in 1886 and the latter having written in Edinburgh.

7. The rare book room at the Washington Square School of Business of New York University contains several bound volumes of very early railroad reports. The existence of these reports suggests that some distribution, formal or informal, of basic financial information was taking place before 1850.

Chapter 3

1. Williard Stone tells us that *Hunt's Merchants' Magazine and Commercial Review* (hereafter *Hunt's*) was published from 1839 to 1849; it used the title *Hunts Merchants Magazine* from 1850 to 1860 (Vols. 23 to 43) but returned to the former title in 1861. After Hunt's death, the same company, which had begun the *Commercial and Financial Chronicle* (hereafter *Chronicle*) in 1865 merged *Hunt's* into its pages in 1870. Substantial archival research was conducted by G. J. Previts during 1989 and 1990, utilizing the Gorgas Library at the University of Alabama, with the assistance of M. J. Previts, and the Case Western Reserve Library, with the assistance of Sameer Shahani, reviewing these periodicals for the period 1839–1900.

2. Early authors who contributed to the antebellum school of American accounting writers include:

J. A. Bennet[t]	1788–1863
Peter Duff	1802–69, born in Canada
B. F. Foster	1803?–59
Thomas Jones	1804–89, born in United Kingdom
C. C. Marsh	1806–84
R. M. Bartlett	1807–91
John C. Colt	1810–42?
E. G. Folsom	1821–97
H. B. Bryant	1824–92
H. D. Stratton	1824–67
S. S. Packard	1826–98

3. John Caldwell Colt was born in Connecticut in 1810, the oldest son of eight children. He left home at seventeen, having had to abandon his education and aspiration for military school. He roamed about the country holding various positions.

By 1834, at age twenty-four, he had drifted south, first to New Orleans and then, seeking cooler weather, to Louisville, teaching the craft of bookkeeping in order to defray expenses. He wrote his first text, which went into eight editions in three years. Moving back east to New York in 1839, Colt sought to sell (along the seaboard) the copies of another ill-starred publication venture. It was during this period that his work, *The Science of Double Entry Book-Keeping* appeared. The fourth edition, published by the New York firm of William Jackson, Robinson & Franklin, was the subject of the review in *Hunt's*.

Colt's new authorship success notwithstanding, he found, by the summer of 1841, that there would be need for a new version of his materials. The printer, Samuel Adams, and Colt were, however, having a disagreement about failure of the printer to deliver on schedule and the fees to be paid for printing. Adams called at Colt's office in midafternoon Friday, September 17, 1841, apparently to settle the dispute. Adams was not seen alive afterward.

The trial and fate of Colt are an interesting subject. Howard Ross relates the tale as follows:

> The disagreements between the two men resulted in a bitter argument, blows were struck and a violent struggle ensued. Colt stated that he was being choked when he grabbed a hatchet from the table and struck Adams twice on the head. Adams fell to the floor and died immediately. Colt washed up the blood that was spattered about and remained in the office until evening, trying to decide what to do, then he went out and walked the streets and made one attempt to communicate with his brother, Samuel. Finally, he resolved to conceal the killing and returned to his office. His plan was to force the body into the large packing box and dispatch it by ship, via New Orleans, to an address in St. Louis. Part of this plan was carried out that evening, then he went home very late and returned to the office early the next morning. He then accompanied a drayman to the steamer Kalamazoo, saw the box placed in the hold, and obtained a bill of lading which he promptly destroyed.
>
> A public notice, reporting Adams' disappearance, was published on Tuesday the twenty-first, and the authorities began an investigation. Adams' employees told of his intention of going to Colt's office, suspicious noises in Colt's office were reported by other tenants, and the janitor told of the box being taken down the stairs on the following morning. On the strength of these and other affidavits, the Major, Robert H. Morris and other officials went to Colt's office on September 24th and arrested him. He was charged with suspicion of murder and confined in the City Prison known as The Egyptian Tombs or simply The Tombs. On the following day the box with Adams' body was located in the ship which was still in the harbor. (Reprinted from *Dividend,* the magazine of the Graduate School of Business Administration, University of Michigan)

The result of the murder of Adams was not only a sensational trial but a touch of scandal as well, for shortly after Colt's incarceration, a son was born to Colt and Caroline Henshaw, a young woman he had met in Philadelphia, and who had moved to New York to live with Colt. Marriage was considered, but Colt's lawyers suggested delay, for her appearance as a defense witness was not deemed advisable if she were his wife.

Colt was found guilty of willful murder by the jury even though there was no evidence of premeditation and the judge had instructed the jury on that point, namely, that premeditation had not been shown in the evidence. On the day scheduled for his execution Colt and Caroline Henshaw were married in the presence of friends and his brother Samuel. Caroline left early and later was followed by the others, his brother Samuel being the last to leave. Shortly before four o'clock the sheriff's party arrived to conduct Colt to the gallows. They found him dead, having been stabbed in the heart, an apparent self-inflicted act. No one was able to say how he had obtained the knife (Ross 1974). This somewhat chilling mystery elicited widespread news coverage in papers and even resulted in a book about Colt's life, *Authentic Life of John C. Colt* (1842).

One can speculate whether it is important that a well-known American accounting writer of the first half of the nineteenth century earned that distinction not solely because of his contributions to accounting but because he was convicted of murdering his publisher and then himself met a mysterious death!

4. Texts during this period were not as scarce as some historical writers would have us believe. For an interesting analysis of an accounting primer published in Boston in 1831, refer to Kistler and Jennings (1969). The article examines the 116-page book *The Young Accountants Guide* and its approach to accounting instruction.

5. Jones referred to the balance sheet and income statement result as follows: "A merchants position is defined by reference to his accounts, each of which shows by its result some item of his Resources, Liabilities, Gains or Losses."

6. The single-entry ledger, according to this treatise, consisted entirely of personal (individual) accounts. No impersonal accounts were kept, not even for cash. At the end of the year an inventory of assets would be taken, which included "cost and other effects." This, together with personal accounts receivable, minus accounts payable, constituted the proprietor's "net worth."

7. In considering, from the view of the development of accounting instruction, the importance of Jones and Foster, it is not difficult to regard Jones as deserving credit for distinguishing between "real" and "nominal" accounts and for a pathbreaking effort among American writers. His regard for the "merchants position" and the role of financial statements is significant. Foster too had the shrewdness to recognize an important idea when he saw it and, notwithstanding his copycat ways, deserves just credit for his missionary efforts on behalf of the concept as well as for his important efforts to provide a brief history of accounting in the midst of an active career.

8. *Hunt's* in December 1848 (p. 670) recalls that we are "a people who were denominated by Napoleon as a nation of shopkeepers."

9. Although it is not clear that financial statements were widely used as they are today for purposes of evaluating prospective acquisitions or obtaining credit, the "ledger focus" of mercantile account systems seems to suggest that merchants preferred to limit the "account books" information and its contents to a means of controlling an enterprise. Chamberlain tells us also that when Rockefeller was sent on business in the 1850s: "He came as the agent for Cleveland businessmen who had been impressed with . . . his ability to judge a balance sheet" (Chamberlain 1974: 149).

Chapter 4

1. By 1880, Standard Oil of Ohio noted that approximately 90 percent of the oil refining business was under its control.

2. It is important to consider the Gilded Age as distinct from the years of the Civil War. Too often there is a tendency to equate the origins of the Gilded Age solely as an aftermath of the Civil War. In fact, the industrial propensity of America was established before the Civil War and may even have been retarded by the Civil War.

3. There is no convincing evidence that the cattle business responded any differently to the peaks and depressions of market conditions, investment enthusiasm, and overall national economic conditions, than did any other phase of the economy. What has been largely overlooked in economic, business, and accounting history is the existence per se of mine, railroad, and cattle investment and the part it played in the development of a central capital market.

4. For the last two decades of the nineteenth century, the total number of incorporated cattle companies in the west numbered as follows: Montana, 181; Wyoming, 188; Colorado, 324; and New Mexico, 186. The aggregate capitalization for these respective states came to $27 million for Montana, $94 million for Wyoming, $102 million for Colorado, and $61 million for New Mexico (Gressley 1971: 105).

5. Several studies by Richard Brief and other sources describe the aspects of the controversy over fixed asset accounting in this period.

6. The prevalent method of rate setting during the 1890s provided for a fixed return on railroad investment, predominantly on capital assets. It is significant that the increased use of this criterion approximately coincides with the increased use of the retirement method for asset valuation, the demise of the use of appreciation reserves among railroads, and a trend toward capitalizing rather than expensing new assets. One concludes, therefore, that railroads found it expedient to use accounting practices for asset valuation that maximized their base for rate-setting calculations regardless of the validity of underlying valuation. Some historians suggest that the Interstate Commerce Commission Act and the potential implications for regulation of the railroads may have been a significant factor in creating financial uncertainties and panics in 1893. Others note that the classification of operating expenses requirements of the ICC went into effect in 1894, in response to the financial panics of 1893, so as to begin to supply some vestige of uniformity to financial reports of railroads.

7. Deficiencies in railroad reports also pointed toward a value basis of assets, as another writer in the *Railroad Gazette* noted: "It's not what a railroad has cost that the stock and bond holders want to know; it is the value in gold, and this will not be given except by legal compulsion." These sentiments were perhaps fanned by the panic of 1893 and may have influenced the Interstate Commerce Commission's first excursion into regulation with its July 1, 1894, implementation of the classification of operating expense format. This action established a precedent for what was to become a system of uniform accounts and standardized reports for railroads under its jurisdiction (Boockholdt 1977).

8. One of the difficulties of research about women arises from the fact that names are not always a suitable clue. Florence, for example, though predominantly

a feminine name, is occasionally bestowed upon male offspring as well. So when we find Florence Crowley listed as an accountant in the New York Directory in 1797 at 237 Water Street, in 1798 at 59 Cherry Street, and in 1802 at 16 Banker Street, and Florence Crowdy similarly listed in 1801 at 9 Frankford Street, we cannot be sure whether Florence Crowley, or Florence Crowdy, was a man or a woman.

9. Joseph Sterrett of Pennsylvania, writing in 1898, is somewhat "cool" about the importance of the AAPA: "The association has done some excellent work as a pioneer, but as each State has charge of its own internal affairs [the AAPA was incorporated in New York] it has been found that better results can be accomplished by separate state organizations, and these have been effected in several states."

10. Ohio University established a commercial college coincident with the University of California in 1898.

11. High schools in the post–Civil War period were few in number in relationship to the total population (there were as few as 108 high schools in 1859 and that number had increased to only 536 by 1873, with a total estimated student enrollment of only 40,000). Their curriculum was directed largely at college preparation, not commercial education. The high school had usurped the character of the academies. During the early years of the development of the high school, very little was accomplished toward placing commercial course offerings; these were not deemed sufficiently rigorous, and the training and the status of such a curriculum were deemed inferior by other high school faculty.

12. S. W. Crittenden's 1877 text on bookkeeping and accounting, however, was not substantially changed from earlier editions that date back to the pre–Civil War period.

13. Paton also considers the works of Hatfield to have been as influential as those of Sprague in determining his career choice.

14. In 1890, E. D. Moore's *Principles of the Science of Accounts* was published.

15. It should be remembered that, prior to the turn of the century, for the most part cash-basis public agency systems were in use. There was, however, a stirring of interest in uniform accounting in the large cities as a reaction to public concern over the lack of effective accountability on the part of politicians. Within twenty years of passage of the county administration practices acts in Minnesota and Massachusetts, fiscal controls were applied to duties involving public funds at the municipal level. States also began to take an interest in the supervision of municipal accounts by providing examiners with review guidelines.

Chapter 5

1. See Veblen's (1904) denunciation of the consolidation of industry; see Moody (1904) for view that such concentration is salutary for the nation as the "best" men should have control and profit from the nation's economic resources.

2. John Dewey (1928: 1) suggested that George belonged alongside Plato in respect to the influence each had on his society.

3. See Alfred Chandler, "The Origins of Progressive Leadership," in *The Letters of Theodore Roosevelt,* ed. by E. E. Morrison (Cambridge: Harvard University Press, 1954). Chandler prepared a profile of progressives and concluded that reformers

were primarily middle-class, native-born Americans living in urban areas and having a distinct business orientation.

4. See McNaught (1966) for discussion of why socialism, which gained adherents in Europe, never became a strong political alternative in the United States.

5. Starting in the 1880s, we find a rich body of literature criticizing continued laissez-faire policies and traditional profit measurement. Bellamy's utopian book, *Looking Backward 2000–1887* (1888), blamed the profit motive for the increase in poverty that accompanied the increase in wealth. See also Bellamy (1902) and novels such as Sinclair's *The Jungle* (1906) for criticism of the inequities generated by concentration of wealth. In addition, magazines such as *Harper's Weekly, Century Magazine, Forum,* and the *New Republic* provided outlet for muckrakers' exposés that were widely read.

6. See Cochran (1967), 5–18, for discussion of the pervasiveness of business values in the United States. See Galambos and Pratt (1988) for an overview of the emergence of the modern corporation.

7. For economic criticism, see George (1879), Veblen (1897, 1904), and Mitchell (1918); for pragmatic criticism, see James (1907), Dewey (1910, 1918), Dewey and Tufts (1908); for political criticism, see Roosevelt (1904) and Brandeis (1914).

8. The debate over the intent of those who organized trusts continues; Chandler (1982) continues to view the emergence of large corporations as salutary, necessary to achieve economies of scale and efficiency. See Lamoreaux (1985) and Fligstein (1990) for recent studies that support the monopolistic intent theory.

9. Prior to 1889, some holding companies existed; but it required a separate legislative act for each company; therefore, the device had limited use. Meade (1903: 34) concluded that the New Jersey law had "momentous consequences" and that New Jersey "by the simple act of amending its corporation law nullified the antitrust laws of every state that had passed them." See Moody (1904) for a listing of the greater and lesser trusts; see also Industrial Commission (U.S. Congress 1902, House) for discussion of Morgan trusts such as steel and shipbuilding.

10. The Sherman Act marked the federal government's first attempt at general business regulation, but regulation, aimed at specific industries such as railroads, had been passed in the prior decade. See Edwards (1939) and Kirkland (1967) for discussion of earlier regulation; see Lowi (1969) for discussion of gradual erosion of regulatory standards throughout the twentieth century.

11. The legislation proved initially ineffective due to a conservative judiciary that continuously eroded the law beginning in 1895 with the Knights Sugar Decision and concluding with the U.S. Steel case (1920) in which the Supreme Court concluded that mere "bigness" did not constitute monopolistic intent. See Miller (1969: 295) for discussion of how the meaning of "restraint of trade" narrowed over time. See Pinchot (1958), who credits J. P. Morgan for making a subtle distinction between "good" and "bad" trusts that supported the notion that "bigness" per se was not bad. The 1911 "rule of reason" decision that broke up Standard Oil and American Tobacco was the central event of the early years of the law.

12. See Edelman (1964), who discusses the conditions under which the public is likely to accept symbolic reassurance and when politicians are likely to promulgate

symbolic regulation. Moody (1904: 498–99) characterized the Sherman as "foolish," noting that while the legislation "pretends to aim at the 'regulation' of monopoly, it never really touches the monopoly, and simply frustrates the natural growth of modern economical means of production and distribution," an opinion shared by many politicians.

13. Parrington (1930) concludes that the lasting contribution of Progressive Era scholars (the three he cites as most prominent are Charles Beard, Thorstein Veblen, and John Dewey) was to show the people that economics controlled the political state. He considers Beard's widely read *The Economic Interpretation of the Constitution* the most influential. See also Merino and Neimark (1982) and Galambos and Pratt (1988) for discussion of fear of private power.

14. See Hofstadter (1963) for writings by progressive reformers who exhort the public to action. See Dewey (1900) who demanded changes in education so that the citizenry could demand required reforms.

15. It should be noted that Dewey (1922) felt that society should not allocate its resources based on accounting pecuniary profit; he believed that accounting should serve as a "statistic," an input measure, not as an output measure of corporate performance.

16. See Sells (1908), who reflects the prevalent view of the most visible accounting practitioners; while condemning inefficiency in the public sector, he rejects progressive reformers' suggestion that regulation was needed to eliminate similar inefficiencies in the private sector.

17. The early presidents of the AAPA who lived in New York—Sells, Sterret, Suffern, and Montgomery—became active members of the National Civic Federation. See Merino (1975: 275).

18. For a contemporary discussion of the Keep Commission, see C. H. Forbes Lindsay (1908). For accountants' reactions to the Keep Commission, see AAPA *Year Book* (1907: 31ff.). All correspondence related to the Committee on Economy and Efficiency and referred to in this chapter can be found in the National Archives, RG 51, Sec. 31, Washington D.C.

19. Chase (1902) began his work in his home town of Boston; he presented a paper titled "Uniform Municipal Accounting Applied to Boston, Baltimore, and Other Municipalities" to the annual meeting of the National Municipal League in 1902; see Chase (1903, 1904, 1906, 1908) for papers presented at other annual meetings of the league, describing the development of uniform accounting systems in other parts of the country.

20. For discussion of New York's reporting and accounting problems, see Cleveland (1906); see Force's (1909) series of articles about New York City's reform.

21. See *Minutes* 1907–10 of the AAPA for discussion of the association's work with various state governments to pass laws to promote uniform accounting systems.

22. See Carey (1969), who discusses displacement of accountants by technicians in regulated industries, such as railroads, insurance, and banking, once uniform systems were developed. See also AAPA *Year Book* (1906) for discussion of the Interstate Commerce Commission's rejection of the organization's request that only properly qualified accountants be permitted to audit railroads; the AAPA justified the request

on the basis that the testimony at the Armstrong Hearings (1905) had shown that
state-appointed insurance examiners were ineffective because they had no accounting training.

23. Accountants had raised congressional hackles with the amount of their bill-
ings for work as consultants to the Commission of Economy and Efficiency; see
correspondence, RG 51, National Archives. In March 1914, Congress passed an
"urgent efficiency" bill that virtually eliminated employment of CPAs; for the profession's reaction see "Government Out of Place," *Journal of Accountancy* (1916).
However, the demands of World War I ended the government's boycott.

24. See Hamman (1914) for discussion of work in the area of municipal and
state cost accounting.

25. For benefits of cost accounts, see Eggleston (1911), Staub (1912); for benefits of municipal budgets, see Herrick (1911).

26. For bibliography of books available in the cost area, see NACA (1921); for a
concise history of flexible budgeting, see Raymond (1966); for the contributions of
engineers, see Wells (1978B). See Nicholson (1913) for example of coverage found
in textbooks during this period.

27. Boorstin (1974: 360) defines efficiency as an "American gospel" that viewed
speed, not quality, as a measure of efficiency, concluding that "time became a series
of homogenous—precisely measured and precise repeatable—units." Miller and
O'Leary (1987) use a Foucaultian approach to examine the efficiency craze and discuss accounting's role in creating the governable person. While the use of cost accounting as a control tool to discipline the new "community" can be documented,
cost accounting may not have been the precipitator, but rather the facilitator, of
control. See Armstrong (1991), who suggests that Foucaultians may overstate cost
accounting's role by ignoring other structural factors that enabled cost accounting
to be used as a control device.

28. Taylor (1911B: 118ff.) explains that scientific management requires that
managers reduce "workman's traditional knowledge" to "rules and laws" to create
a science, then scientifically select the best workmen, and bring the two together.
He provides examples of how tasks such as shoveling, bricklaying, and bicycle manufacturing had been reduced to the number of movements required (Taylor, 1911B:
181ff.).

29. George (1968) discusses the lukewarm reception Taylor's method received
at a 1903 meeting of the American Society of Mechanical Engineers and the difficulty that Taylor had in gaining acceptance of his method.

30. Brandeis, testifying before the Interstate Commerce Commission in 1910,
argued that rate increases should not be granted since railroads were poorly run
and profits could be increased by "scientific management" as outlined in Taylor's
1903 book (Boorstin 1974).

31. Many excellent histories of the early development of cost accounting exist;
we do not attempt to present a comprehensive treatment of the emergence of various cost techniques. For detailed descriptions and comprehensive overviews of the
development of cost-accounting techniques, see Garner (1954), Solomons (1968),

and Wells (1978A); for a comprehensive description of standard costing, see Sowell (1973); and see Epstein (1978) for influence of scientific management.

32. See AIA *Minutes* (1918) for comments by Montgomery, who dismissed the establishment of the National Association of Cost Accountants (NACA) as a body of technicians who posed no threat to true professional accountants. Montgomery's position is interesting in that his senior partner, William Lybrand, was one of the organizers of the NACA.

33. See Solomons (1968) for discussion of why small producers need to know costs for pricing and other decisions; see Tyson (1988) for a case study of how a small company used cost information to change its business strategy; see Chandler (1977) and Johnson and Kaplan (1987) for explanation of why multidepartmental firms needed cost data for coordination and control.

34. See Church (1914) for an engineering view that all cost should be allocated and Vangermeersch's (1986) excellent biography of Church that details his contributions to the overhead allocation debate; see Wildman (1911) and Nicholson (1913) for the accountant's position on segregation of costs.

35. More recent work by Hoskin and Macve (1988) details use of time and motion studies at the Springfield Armory to control labor, but the Springfield experience does not appear to be typical even at military installations; see Smith (1977), who shows that efforts to introduce the same type of discipline at Harpers Ferry failed.

36. See Chandler (1977), who suggests that when corporations engaged in more than one economic activity (i.e., manufacturing, marketing, transportation, financing), data to coordinate internal transactions became a necessity; see Williamson (1981) for extension of Chandler's thesis to transaction cost minimization. Johnson and Kaplan (1987) adapt Chandler's and Williamson's views to explain the emergence of cost accounting.

37. See Loft (1991) and Ezzamel, Hoskin, and Maeve (1990) for contemporary criticisms of Johnson and Kaplan's position; see also Miller and O'Leary (1987), who argue that cost accounting became a mechanism for making each person visible, thus creating "the governable person."

38. See Hofstadter (1955) for discussion of the hold that anything "scientific" had on the American population; pragmatism offered philosophic support for use of scientific methods to ameliorate the harsh economic conditions that accompanied consolidation of industry for much of the populace; see, for example, Dewey and Tufts, 1908.

39. From May through July, the *Journal* provided readers with articles or speeches by some of the leading proponents of scientific management; see for example, Emerson (May 1911), Brandeis (1911: 35–43), Taylor (June, July 1911B: 117–24; 181–88), Gilbreath (July 1911: 195–201). The *Journal* also published two articles by labor leaders, opposing the new movement; see Duncan (May 1911: 26–34); Golden (July 1911: 189–94).

40. Wildman prepared a series of articles titled "Cost Accounting," designed as a text to implement cost procedures. The articles ran monthly from November 1910 through April 1911.

41. Wildman (1911: 424) implied that all the benefits of "scientific" methods should accrue to the company; he rejected "piece rates" because the benefits accrue "primarily [to] the workman."

42. Duncan (1911: 32) viewed scientific management as a way to harass the worker; Golden (1911: 192–93) noted that during the years when the productivity of textile workers had increased more than 100 percent, wages had decreased from $10 to $8 per week; he suggested that managers should aspire to a higher ideal than "standing over a man with a stopwatch." Dickinson's (1911) interesting application of economic concepts to cost accounting, in which he suggested anything above subsistence wages were not costs and should be paid out of capital, seems to support the labor leader's contention that scientific management would benefit only a select few. Dickinson concluded that capitalists had not been willing to absorb such costs unless they could pass them on to consumers.

43. During the Progressive Era, resistance to commodification of labor still existed; labor leaders continued their protests with support from institutional economists, like Veblen (1918A, 1918B, 1918C), and popular writers like Upton Sinclair (1911). In 1918, Charter Harrison answered Taylor's (1911B) call for laws to be reduced to mathematical formulas by developing such formulas for variance analysis.

44. Miller and O'Leary's (1987) Foucaultian analysis is consistent with the conclusions of traditional historians. See, for example, Boorstin (1974: 369), who concluded that scientific management, which turned "the worker into a labor unit and judged his effectiveness by his ability to keep the technology flowing, had made the worker himself into an interchangeable part."

45. King (1915) provided data that supported progressive taxation. King's statistics showed an increasing concentration of wealth: in 1890 the richest 1.6 percent of Americans received 10.8 percent of the national income; by 1910 they received 19 percent. Boorstin (1974) points out that the tax law created a new "statistical" community as Americans became part of a "tax bracket." See Edelman (1964) for view that the concept of "progressive taxation" has been one of the most effective symbolic reforms ever enacted; i.e., a reform that stills public outrage without affecting significant changes in distribution of wealth. "Loopholes" (or tax incentives) made progressivity a myth, but the public remained quiet, satisfied with the concept and not mandating implementation.

46. See correspondence between accountants and George W. Wickersham (Deloitte and Touche Archival Collection, New York). For the most comprehensive statement of the problems created by the 1909 law, see A. M. Sakolski. Treasury Regulation No. 31, December 1910, permitted the use of accrual accounting, but the law was not changed. See also Kingwill (1909: 248ff.) for discussion of AAPA's efforts and "The Proposed Corporation Tax Bill" (1909: 237–39), which discusses a letter to Congress, signed by twelve large accounting firms outlining the accounting deficiencies in the 1909 proposed legislation.

47. See the May 1910 issue of the *Journal of Accountancy* for debate about the wisdom of a constitutional amendment. Borah, a leading congressional advocate of the amendment, suggested passage was simply a matter of time.

48. While the income tax increased demand for accounting services, its impact in 1913 should not be overstated; only 4 percent of the people paid personal taxes in 1913. Initially, the law achieved its objectives of taxing the wealthy, but the percentage of people subject to the income tax has increased dramatically over time. Boorstin (1974: 209) provides more statistics with respect to the percentages of people paying personal income taxes: 4 percent in 1913; 7 percent in 1920; 11 percent in 1940; 37 percent in 1945; and 60 percent in 1979; corporate tax returns grew from 300,000 in 1913 to 1.5 million in 1968.

49. See Conant (1974: 137ff.) for discussion of the cultural lag between popular/political views and judicial views. He concludes that the Supreme Court precluded enactment of effective legislation until 1937, when the Court reinterpreted "substantive due process." Until that time, corporations were presumed to be imbued with "individual freedoms" that limited the government's power to regulate them.

50. Suffern was quoting from a speech by F. L. Lehman, president of the American Bankers' Association. An examination of both the business and nonbusiness literature of the period indicates that Suffern was correct. For example, if one examines *Commerce, Accounts and Finance* (1901–3) or the *Public Accountant* (absorbed *by Business, Office and the Public Accountant,* 1903) it is clear that editors of business journals shared this sentiment.

51. See McConnell (1966) for a discussion of fear of power in the abstract that has been characteristic of the United States since its founding; see Mintz and Cohen (1976: 5f. and 31f.) for discussion of the threat that economic concentration posed to politicians.

52. Bowles and Gintes (1983: 225ff.) highlight the fundamental discrepancy between democratic values and economic concentration. The "just" society must ensure (1) individual liberty and (2) popular sovereignty. It is difficult to reconcile a corporate autocracy and market regulation by dollar voting with the fundamental democratic tenets. See also Pateman (1970), who explains why Locke and Rousseau felt that democracy could not survive if income inequalities became extreme. Bell (1960: 246ff.) had an alternate view, arguing that the emergence of passive property would enhance democracy, and that widespread stock ownership would lead to "economic" democracy, which would result in the "break up of the middle class." For an alternate view, see Mills (1959).

53. See Veblen (1904), Berle (1926), Ripley (1927), and Laidler (1932) for early views of how separation of ownership and control undermined the strength of private property rights.

54. Ripley (1927: 127) reflected the popular view, writing that the disenfranchisement of stockholders could "undermine" the foundation of our civilization.

55. While men like John D. Rockefeller (Standard Oil) had been the targets of muckrakers' attacks, they had managed the companies that they owned; financial capitalists did not use their own money and did not manage the companies they controlled. See Edwards (1939) and Berle (1963) for discussion of the dissonance this created.

56. See Chandler (1977) for historical interpretation that focuses on these bene-

fits; see Johnson and Kaplan (1987) for adaptation of Chandler's perspective to the development of accounting. For recent criticisms of the transaction cost and efficiency theses, see Fligstein (1990) and Lamoreaux (1985), who conclude that the desire for monopolistic profits seems to have been the primary motivation for formation of trusts at the turn of the century.

57. Morgan would not have disagreed with the assessment. Morgan's stated goal was combination and control; he thought one of the major benefits of trusts was that they would not be subject to "destructive" forces (Galambos and Pratt 1988). However, Morgan would not agree he sought to exploit; he claimed all would be better off if he were in control (Merino and Neimark 1982). See also Garraty (1957) and Sinclair (1981).

58. See Benston (1969), Phillips and Zecher (1981), Wallace (1980), and De-Angelo (1981) for views that economic incentives (i.e., the need to raise capital and the need to monitor an autonomous management class) created the demand for audits during this period. See Merino, Mayper, and Sriram (1994) for discussion of actual relationships in the trusts and why the economic thesis appears to be inapplicable to the trusts. However, creditors did appear to create demand for audits of small businesses and the need to raise borrowed capital would appear to be relevant in this case.

59. Criticism of trusts was not limited to radical reformers. President McKinley, a Republican conservative, lambasted the trusts for trying "to control the conditions of trade among our citizens, to stifle competition, limit production and determine the prices of products used and consumed by our people" (*Business,* December 1899: 749). The accounting literature also reflected these criticisms; see the *Book-Keeper* (1899) for editorials denouncing unfair practices of trusts.

60. See U.S. Congress, House, 1900, 1901A, 1901B, 1902 for documentation of abuses. Simpson (1921: 152–53) concluded that the evidence gathered at the turn of the century had made all of the assumptions of "traditional" economic theory—that competitive markets determine prices, all factors of production have equal bargaining power (mobility of capital, land and labor), and that no collusion occurs—suspect.

61. See U.S. Congress (1900: 13ff.) for preliminary report of the Industrial Commission Hearings, and Moody (1904) for losses accrued by investors. The most common way of watering stock was to issue preferred stock for the fair market value of assets received in a consolidation and to issue common stock as a bonus, based on promoters' expectations of the future earning power of the firm.

62. See U. S. Congress, House (1901B) for testimony of business leaders; A. S. White, president of National Salt Company, and Charles Schwab, president of U.S. Steel, acknowledged that management could mislead investors through dividend policies. They advocated publication of annual reports and suggested that either independent audits or direct government supervision could be used to protect investors.

63. This is reflected in the Industrial Commission's (U. S. Congress, House, 1902: 650) recommendation that "the larger corporations, the so-called trusts should be required to publish annually a properly audited report, showing in reasonable detail

their assets and liabilities, with profit or loss; such report and audit under oath to be subject to Government inspection. The purpose of such publicity is to encourage competition when profit becomes excessive, thus protecting consumers against too high prices and to guard the interests of employees by a knowledge of the financial condition of the business in which they are employed."

64. The concept of "efficient publicity" with respect to shareholders is expanded in the following section. For an example of the bureau's position, see "First Annual Report. 1904," Bureau of Corporations. Annual reports are available at the National Archives, RG 122.

65. Nearly all proposed legislation from 1903 to 1914 required the filing of annual statements with some government agency. The Temporary National Economic Committee (1937) compiled a list of laws introduced between 1903 and 1930. Thirty-four bills were introduced between 1903 and 1914: ten between 1919 and 1930. The list is available from the authors or from the National Archives, RG 144. For reference to presidential messages calling for publicity or federal franchising between 1901 and 1910, see Congressional Record, 35:83f.; 36:7ff.; 38:2ff.; 39:12; 40:91–93; 41:27f., 42:70, 1352, 3854f.; 43:17ff., 45:31, 381–83; and 46:24.

66. The opinion expressed by the editor of *Business* (Editorial, 1900: 201–2) reflected skepticism about the efficacy of publicity since it was considered a "superficial" reform. The writer chided that its "superficiality lays itself open to the charges of insincerity and demagoguery," noting that it was akin to "rendering the octopus harmless by taking away his ink bag by which he clouds his movements rather than [removing] his tentacles by which he seizes his victims."

67. See "Scrapbook—Elijah Watt Sells" (Deloitte and Touche Archival Collection, New York). In a letter dated February 2, 1908, Herbert G. Stockwell criticized Sells's position, but most of the voluminous correspondence is laudatory. The scrapbook includes a letter from Oliver Wendell Holmes who commends the author for publication of the pamphlet.

68. A letter from Charles Waldo Haskins to Dr. Henry McCracken of New York University, December 11, 1898, states: "We recall with regret the attempts that have heretofore been made to establish independent schools of accounts. We believe the failure of these attempts has been due to the absence of this very university foundation which we honor to suggest to you." See New York State Society of Certified Public Accountants (NYSSCPA), *Ten Year Book* (New York: NYSSCPA, 1907: 24).

69. See, for example, Battelle (1954) for a description of difficulties accounting practitioners in midwestern states (like Ohio, where populist sentiment was strong) faced when attempting to develop standards for the practice of accounting.

70. All subsequent references to NYSSCPA are to the Minute Books of Meetings of the Members and of the Board of Directors—1897–1910; bound handwritten manuscripts; 1911–20, bound typescripts; the minute books were located at the NYSSCPA office in New York City.

71. See AAPA *Year Book* (1907: 215–18) for Cooper's "Draft of a Model CPA Law to Regulate the Profession." This resembles an earlier model that he presented to the federation in 1902 as a guide for uniform legislation.

72. See "Public Accountants in the United States," the *Accountant* (October 17,

1903: 1251–53), which contains excerpts from Cooper's address "National Legislation for the Public Accountant" presented at a meeting of the Illinois State Society in 1899.

73. See AIA *Minutes* (1916: 115ff.) and (1917: 30ff.) for discussion of Hurley's suggestion. Robert Montgomery, who stated that he was acting as the "Devil's advocate," labeled Hurley as an "unknown quantity" in 1916. By 1917, when federal regulation was no longer a threat, Montgomery lamented the loss of "our boy in Washington" when Hurley resigned. Discussion of the "zone expert" scheme also can be found in an editorial in the *Journal of Accountancy* (August 1915: 129–34).

74. J. E. Sterrett and E. W. Sells devised this plan; see AAPA *Minutes* (1916: 50ff.) and the 1916 *Year Book* of the Institute of Accountants in the United States for details. Three months later, the organization's name was shortened to the American Institute of Accountants, hereafter cited as AIA.

75. The AIA modeled its examination on New York State's content. One of the AIA's stated objectives was to gain acceptance for a uniform CPA examination in all states. Initially, the AIA's exam covered five fields: practice, theory, auditing, business law, and actuarial science. Since many states objected to the inclusion of actuarial science, the AIA dropped that field after two years, in 1919. Despite this compromise, the AIA would not obtain completely its objective of uniform adoption of its exam for more than three decades.

76. See "Public Accountants' Audit vs. the Interstate Commerce Commission," *Commercial & Financial Chronicle* (January 1914).

77. See Green (1966: 52–64) for discussion of the constant debate over "art vs. science." Green concludes that this debate provided little direction; he suggests it would have been better had the debate focused on the question of human knowledge and accounting's contribution to that knowledge. While it seems clear that the art/science debate has not been useful, it clearly has permeated the literature.

78. For economic criticism, see George (1879), Veblen (1897, 1904), and Mitchell (1918); for pragmatic criticism, see James (1907), Dewey (1910, 1918), Dewey and Tufts (1908); for political criticism, see Roosevelt (1904) and Brandeis (1914).

79. See Dewey (1922), Mitchell (1918), and Veblen (1904) for denunciations of traditional accounting measurement in an oligopolistic society.

80. See Dewey and Tufts (1908: 455), who cite iron, coal, and clothing as examples of which producers found "it more profitable to combine and produce a limited amount." See also Veblen (1918C), Chase (1926B), and Scott (1933) for the technocrats' view of why those with oligopolistic power would not maximize production.

81. Names, such as proprietary theory, often mask significant differences in evolution of accounting theory. This study examines proprietary theory, as it developed in the post-1880 period. The restatement of the accounting equation from Assets = Liabilities to Assets = Liabilities + Proprietorship (Sprague 1880: 1901) initiated a significant change in direction in accounting thought.

82. See, for example, Schroeder, McQullers, and Clark (1987), who write that "proprietary theory is applicable where the owner is the decision maker." They con-

clude that "when the form of enterprise becomes more complex and the ownership and management become separated, this theory becomes less acceptable." See Belkaoui (1985), Hendricksen (1982), and Wolk, Francis, and Tearney (1984) for similar criticism of proprietary theory.

83. See Parrington (1930: xxxiii) for description of the ideological compromise and conflict that has existed between the Declaration of Independence, based on the philosophy of the French Enlightenment, which posited human perfectibility and postulated an egalitarian democracy "in which the political state should function as the servant of the common well being" and the Constitution, based on English laissez-faire economics that posited the universality of the acquisitive self-interested instinct in which the political state functioned to preserve the rights of private property interests, since the birth of the nation.

84. Proponents of corporate secrecy who testified before the Industrial Commission contended that dividends paid provided all the information investors required about corporate operations. Since many corporations that never suspended dividends had, nonetheless, declared bankruptcy (a good number having done so while the commission was collecting its evidence), it was not a notably successful apology. The commission's final report specifically charged accountants with the duty of protecting investors from the erosion of capital as a result of dividends being paid in excess of earnings (U.S. Congress 1902: 650ff.).

85. See Berle (1963), who points out that separation of ownership threatened to undermine the legitimacy of private property rights if the owners could not be kept firmly in control. He argues that while there is a moral justification for those who own property to benefit from its use, there is no moral justification for allowing the "power" holder (i.e., those who control corporations) to appropriate resources to their own benefit.

86. See Hatfield (1909: 215–16) and Montgomery (1912A), and Couchman (1924) for the tenor of the debate with respect to "retained earnings" as a policy for corporate capital sourcing. See Veblen (1918C: 409), who concluded that Adam Smith would have rejected the new industrial order, which Veblen labeled "the going concern of production."

87. Hatfield (1909) felt so strongly about the right of owners to control investment that he suggested that depletion and depreciation might rightfully be regarded as a return of capital so that owners would have absolute control over reinvestment.

88. See Hatfield (1909) and Simpson (1921) for a full discussion of the extent to which "future earning power" had been capitalized by the trusts.

89. Hatfield (1909: 110ff.) acknowledged that "if any business is protected by a monopoly, whether a legal monopoly of a patent right or a partial business monopoly resting on the combination of all present competition in a trust, there is a possibility of maintaining prices at a level which will yield profits in excess of the normal rate." But prudence required that goodwill be assumed to be temporary and expensed.

90. Hatfield (1909: 110) suggested that accountants use a more direct method: write off goodwill against invested capital, which then would be reported below par

to highlight that a corporation had issued watered stock (which would have been consistent with reporting "facts"). This suggestion received little support from his fellow accountants.

91. See May (1916), who argued that since stock watering had led to criticism of corporate profits the public perceived profits on watered stock as unfair returns.

92. Parrington (1930: 323–24) lists four characteristics of naturalism: (1) objectivity—give the truth in the spirit of the scientist; (2) an amoral attitude—no brief for moral standards; (3) a philosophy of determinism; and (4) a bias toward pessimism. These characteristics seem applicable to the discourse of proprietary theorists. Some late twentieth-century accounting research, based on positive economics (see Jensen and Meckling [1976]), has a similar naturalistic tenor.

93. This discussion of proprietary theory is limited to those who recognized that large corporations presented a significant challenge to legitimacy of accounting measurement. This does not mean that most practicing accountants entered into this debate. An editorial in the *Journal of Accountancy* (1909: 239) probably reflected the views of the majority of accounting practitioners, concluding that the accountant "has in mind solely the needs of the business man who employs him."

94. Sterrett (1916) reflects this view, writing that accountants provided the "first class of knowledge of cost" which is essential in the fixing of prices, the maximum of which is regulated by the "inexorable law of competition." See Berle (1963) for a brief description of assumptions of classical theory; that is, a free, competitive market with no barriers to entry or monopoly, where one could presume that individuals' pursuit of profit would result in optimal allocation of resources.

95. It is probably an accurate reflection of our heritage that two accountants, Chase (1920) and DR Scott (1931A), who questioned the relevance of accounting profit in a corporate society, receive little space in contemporary accounting theory texts.

96. This concept can be traced from Adam Smith to John Stuart Mill to Alfred Marshall. See, for example, Marshall (1964) for discussion of profits as the difference in the value of the owner's stock at the beginning and the end of a year. Sprague (1908: 61) explicitly rejected Fisher's (1906) contention that a business entity is "a fictitious person holding certain assets and owing them all out again to real persons." Sprague concluded that "even admitting there is a fictitious entity, it owes nothing to its owners."

97. Greene, president of the Audit Company of New York, was called to testify before the Industrial Commission as a railroad expert, not as an accountant. He took the opportunity to advocate publication of corporate reports (U.S. Congress 1901A: 476ff.).

98. See, for example, Sprague (1906) and May (1906) for discussions of treatment of premiums and discounts.

99. Littleton (1941) and Parker (1965) trace the antecedents of "lower of cost or market" to prior centuries.

100. Montgomery accepted "conservatism" in this period and again in the thirties; however, in the twenties he joined with those who rejected conservatism as a basic concept. See Montgomery (1927: 251), where he writes that fear led to con-

servatism, adding that the "so called conservatism of the accountant hides understated value which can never harm anyone to know or hides overstated values which it would be useful to know." He concluded that accountants did not have a "moral right" to conceal information.

101. The going concern concept has had an interesting evolution. Dicksee, in his classic *Auditing* (1905), wrote that "the basis of valuation will be a going concern." But he acknowledged that the term had no definite meaning, adding that "the term is an elastic one." He first used the going concern concept to support depreciation, but the concept seemed to imply that current assets should be carried at market (increase or decrease) while fixed assets, held for use, could be maintained on a modified (depreciated) historic cost basis. Thus, although the going concern concept supported conservative valuation for fixed assets, it did not justify practitioners' desires for conservative valuation methods for most current assets. See Storey (1959) for discussion of how theorists and practitioners "overcame" this problem.

102. See Paton and Stevenson (1918) for one of the most explicit statements on this topic; see also Walton (1915), who argued that cost should always be maintained for fixed assets, then the institute's definitive position.

103. See Rosen and DeCoster (1969) for a historical overview of the development of the funds statement.

104. Personal correspondence from Michael J. Mumford, University of Lancaster, U.K., 1989.

105. See AIA *Minutes* (1917: 16ff.) for discussion of the Park-Potter case. The members, hearing the case, concluded that suppression of a contingent liability that was material, was misleading and a violation of the code of ethics under the concept of "acts discreditable to the profession."

106. Montgomery's attitude toward cost accounting upset cost accountants. He told Scovill, "I not only will say I know nothing about cost accounting, I claim it." He contended that there are "certain broad principles we can adhere to . . . and I don't think that in industrial cost accounting, we are obliged to depart from them for the sake of expedience" (AIA, *Minutes* 1917: 158–9). In 1919, when the National Association of Cost Accountants was being promoted, Montgomery dismissed this group, telling the AIA Council that "I think that the Institute, as an Institute for professional accountants, need fear no specialized, technical organization, no matter how large and powerful it may be" (AIA, *Minutes* 1919: 178).

107. See Hurley (1916A) for a comprehensive statement of his position. For discussion of Hurley, as a champion of business, see Kolko (1963). Although Kolko's work has been challenged, see McQuaid (1986); it seems clear that Hurley and other FTC commissioners were sympathetic to business interests.

108. See, for example, Federal Trade Commission (1916, 1918); see also Merino and Coe (1978) for overview of this topic.

109. See Demond (1951: 125) for discussion of this response. We examined J. Scobie's memorandum: with the exception of one page on procedures for verifying internal check and omissions of examples of various types of fraud and how they might be perpetrated, *Uniform Accounting* appears to have been taken verbatim from the Scobie memorandum, which in turn can be traced to Dickinson (1904B).

110. The original document that appeared in the Federal Reserve Bulletin (1917) was entitled "Uniform Accounts"; the title changed when the GPO reprinted the article in pamphlet form. Since our references relate to the pamphlet, we use the title *Uniform Accounting* throughout the section. The FRB reissued the document with the more appropriate title "Approved Methods for the Preparation of Balance Sheet Audits" in 1918 and a set of future announcements attest to this lineage of early "authoritative" literature.

111. Robert Morris Associates (RMA) collected examples of useless certificates and presented them to the AIA, asking what the profession intended to do about the situation. The major criticisms were that there was no standard of verification and no indication of scope; see Campbell (1928: 1ff.). The AIA did very little, except agree that some auditors should have said "I believe *X* Company is in good condition but I have not made an attempt to do the things an auditor should do" (Editorial, *Journal of Accountancy* 1926: 286–87).

112. Richardson, editor of the *Journal of Accountancy*, concurred with these criticisms. The AIA waged a war against "weasel words" throughout the twenties. Richardson concluded auditors were not dishonest: they did not mean to deceive; they had simply developed a "Uriah Heep" mentality, making them incapable of issuing any type of "positive" statement ("Editorial," *Journal of Accountancy* 1926: 33–40; 441–44).

113. A series of editorials in the *Journal of Accountancy* supported this idea. See "Responsibilities for Inventories" (April 1927: 286–88); the editor quotes George O. May who said, "I do not believe the verification of physical inventories is within the competence of auditors." Montgomery (1927) and Nichols (1927) dissented, but subsequent editorials reflected May's position.

114. See Merino and Coe (1978) for further discussion; Hurley, and later Frank Delano of the Federal Reserve Board, implied that a "scientific" methodology could be used to develop an "accounting rule book."

Chapter 6

1. See Merino and Neimark (1982) for discussion of disclosure regulation as a mechanism to preserve the status quo by restoring faith in the market system.

2. See Soulé (1967) for critical assessment of the new era and the return to normalcy; see Dewey (1918) and Carver (1925) for discussion of the effectiveness of the cooperative war effort.

3. The most obvious example was Joseph Sterrett, who served as the transfer agent of the Dawes Commission for reparations. Sterrett was decorated by several foreign countries for his work. See also AIA *Year Book* (1917: 84ff.), for a discussion of the work of the Dollar-a-Year Men.

4. See Rorty (1982) and West (1989) for comprehensive analyses of the development and influence of pragmatism in the United States; see Dewey (1918) and Veblen (1918C) for pragmatist' and institutionalist' responses to the war.

5. While the Industrial Democracy movement did not have a direct impact on accounting in the twenties, the questions raised remain relevant today. During the

1980s, accounting researchers began to examine the role of accounting from various critical perspectives, raising questions similar to those asked by reformers after World War I and throughout the twenties; see Hines (1988), Hopper, Storey, and Wilmott (1987), Arrington and Puxty (1991), Cooper and Sherer (1984), Lehman and Tinker (1987), and Merino (1993).

6. In the 1979 edition of this book, we stated that "present day readers may find it hard to visualize a period when 'business' enjoyed near apotheosis from almost all elements of society." Given the 1980s, we no longer consider this a problem for readers.

7. See Hurley (1916B) for an early uniform cost system that the FTC distributed to retail merchants; see Kolko (1963) and Blaidsell (1932) for different interpretations of the role of the FTC.

8. See FTC (1939), "Discussion of Court Decisions," for comprehensive overview of FTC enforcement actions under sections 7 and 8 of the Clayton Act (1914). Section 7 allowed the FTC to take action to prevent a corporation from purchasing stock in another corporation if the purchase would "substantially lessen competition." But court decisions left the FTC with virtually no enforcement power; if a company that acquired stock took action to purchase the assets of the acquired company prior to an FTC complaint, the Supreme Court ruled that the FTC "was without authority." See discussion of Swift & Company/Moultrie Packing in Federal Trade Commission, 1939; also, see testimony of William Kelley (1939) for summary of FTC enforcement actions and reversals by the judiciary.

9. See O'Dell (1921: 36), who examines political reaction to the FTC in the postwar period; he focuses on pressure brought to bear by politicians on the FTC to stop the meat-packing investigation. He also points out that the Republican platform of 1920 contained a clause "censuring the FTC for . . . attacks on legitimate business."

10. In the area of social legislation, the dichotomy between liberal-conservative jurists becomes pronounced. Conservatives viewed the corporation as a federal citizen, a doctrine first accepted in 1882 and finalized with the *Smith v. Ames* case in 1898. The Supreme Court overturned child labor laws, protective legislation for women, and mandatory pension and other social welfare plans, as infringements of the right to contract, a rationale that seemed strange to some since women and children did not have the legal right to contract for further discussion; see Conant (1974). Dewey and Tufts (1908) noted that the right to contract was not worth much if the alternative was to starve to death. Contemporary agency theorists continue to depict contracting (bargaining) as the mechanism by which pursuit of individual self-interest translates into societal well-being in a postindustrial society (see Williamson 1983; Watts and Zimmerman 1986); for critical rebuttal of modern contracting theory, see Dugger (1983, 1989), Tinker (1988), and Hunt and Hogler (1990).

11. See Mitchell (1989) and McQuaid (1986) for excellent overviews of the Industrial Democracy movement and the fundamental philosophic difference between Ford and Gillette. Gillette outlined his plan to reorganize society in *The People's Corporation;* he claimed that the world was "out of gear" since production occurred not when it is best for all but profitable for a select few (Soulé 1924: 5). In his book *Today*

and Tomorrow, Ford (1926) reached a similar conclusion, but unlike Gillette, he did not advocate that the people control corporations.

12. For advocacy of Ford's plan to make labor a major beneficiary of the technological advances by increasing wages, reducing the workweek, and payment of wage dividends, see Chase (1926A), Foster and Catchings (1927), and Stidger (1923); for opposition to labor participation, see Merritt (1922) and Hooper (1923) "Is Industrial Democracy a Misnomer?" For an overview of accountants' reaction to Ford's call for a wage dividend, which appeared to erode ownership claims, see Merino (1993).

13. Ford viewed a decrease in the workweek as efficient; he believed the time had come to recognize the "economic value of leisure." See Crowther (1926: 13–16).

14. See *Dodge v. Ford;* the Dodge brothers owned part of Ford Motors and sued Ford for dividends and won; see Collier and Horowitz (1987) for Ford's reaction and why he took his company private.

15. See May Papers (1933) where May states he wishes that the accounting profession had the power to have Chase deported as a Bolshevik and calls him one of the "most dangerous" men in the United States.

16. See Chase (1920: 416–34). In the only article that Chase wrote for the journal, he made the point that the question of "what constitutes a reasonable profit" would not be of concern if free competition existed, but it did not. He challenges the relevance of traditional profit in an industrial age but writes that for the purposes of this article he would view the corporation from the investor's perspective. He justified use of the investor's definition because if an economic definition were to be followed "it would necessitate a considerable modification in current bookkeeping methods."

17. See Robinson (1925), who discusses the social impact of scientific management; Robinson, like Chase (1925A), considered Taylor's system socially desirable as long as the productive gains were shared by labor through higher wage brackets for productive workers; but, he noted, if "increased productivity" comes from "greater relative human costs" then it is not within the social goal of the economist. Chase (1925A) thought the "profit" motive was contrary to Taylor's goals in that monetary profits could be maximized by restriction of output, which he viewed as one of the major forms of waste that went undetected in traditional accounting measurement systems.

18. See Rublee (1926).

19. See testimony of Frank Fetter (1939) for discussion of how the courts aided the merger movement; see Allen (1931) and Brooks (1969) for a historical overview of the extent of the movement.

20. See Berle (1963) and Ripley (1927) for discussion of the failure of the law to provide adequate protection for intangible property rights, like stock issues; see Ackerman (1975), Alchian and Demsetz (1973), Bowles and Gintes (1983), and Conant (1974) for different interpretations of the relationship between economics and law.

21. See Stevens (1926) and Berle (1926) for discussion of the types of financial instruments used to disenfranchise shareholders; Stevens suggests that the 1917

excess profits tax provided the incentive for development of these new financial instruments.

22. As noted in chapter 5, independence had been a crucial issue for the leadership of the AAPA, but not in the roaring twenties. In 1931, the AIA defeated a rule requiring independence, but external pressure forced passage of the rule at the next meeting.

23. See Merino and Coe (1978) for discussion of the institute's success in countering efforts by the FTC and the FRB to establish a federal registry of accountants, titled zone experts, and a Federal Audit Bureau. By 1921, the AIA apparently felt it could begin to lobby for mandatory independent audits in federal legislation; see "Report of the Committee on Federal Legislation" (New York: AIA, *Year Book* May 15, 1921), which outlined the Kenyon bill requiring corporations with new issues to file with the postmaster general and the FTC particulars regarding the issue; the committee recommended to the senator that independent audits be required.

24. See AIA *Minutes* (1916: 105ff.) for the rationale for abandoning the CPA certificate as the requirement for membership in the AIA.

25. John L. Carey, secretary of the AIA for many years, played an important role in healing the schism. His many works about accounting history and, especially, his definitive study of the institute provide a contemporary view of the problems of administering a "national" organization. The term "Great Schism" refers to the split between the AIA and the American Society of Certified Public Accountants.

26. See "Constitutionality of C.P.A. Legislation," *Journal of Accountancy* (1923) for examples of the hostile environment that practitioners faced in retaining restrictive legislation in many populist states.

27. See Scovill (1924: 49ff.) for an excellent overview of the competing accounting associations that emerged after the war; the National Association of Certified Public Accountants, organized on June 4, 1921, by 200 state-certified public accountants working for the government in Washington, quickly had 5,000 members; its stated objectives were "to protect the designation C.P.A., to create a standard uniform balance sheet and statement for the purpose of a uniform tax accounting system, and for the purpose of making accounting a profession." Scovill points out that within six months it had issued 2,100 certificates of membership, for $10 each, and had an official publication, the *C.P.A. Bulletin*.

28. At this time, accounting remained a profession for men, with firms divided by religion. An editorial in the *Journal of Accountancy* (December 1923: 443–44) reflected the attitudes of most practitioners, the editor writing that women are not wanted on staff by public accountants; heterogeneous personnel would "hamper progress and lead to infinite embarrassment." The editor blamed clients' attitudes, but he acknowledged that since firms would not employ women, they could not meet the experience requirement. He concluded that the prospects for women "are not brilliant."

29. The May (1934) papers at Price Waterhouse indicate the strength of the feud; Kohler, editor of the *Accounting Review,* raised May's wrath with his criticism of the AIA throughout the early 1930s.

30. See Carey (1975A: 6), one of May's contemporaries at the institute and

an admirer of his intelligence, who acknowledged that "his [May's] greatest weakness . . . was an egoism which made him impatient of any disagreement . . . he offended people by brushing aside their ideas brusquely."

31. While May never became president of the institute, he appears to have written many of the editorials that Richardson published; see the May Papers at Price Waterhouse Library, New York City.

32. As early as 1907, John A. Cooper introduced a rule at the annual meeting of the AAPA that stated "no member shall perform accounting services payment for which is by arrangement upon the contingency of the result of litigation or other form of adjustment." Views polarized, and Robert Montgomery and Cooper were continuously at loggerheads. Cooper contended that "a client could persuade an accountant to sign a dishonest certificate in a case where the latter is interested in the results." "If he'd sign one on a contingent basis," reported Montgomery, "he would just as likely sign one on a fixed fee" (AAPA, *Year Book* 1907: 60ff.). The FTC's insistence on opening competition in the pre–World War I period probably would have doomed any efforts by the AIA to enforce such a rule.

33. See AIA *Year Book* (1920: 70, 118–19). The rule adopted in 1919 was expected to permit management services (e.g., installation of cost systems) on a contingent basis. But it also was interpreted by many to permit tax work on a contingency basis. The Committee on Ethical Publicity said abuses were "so flagrant that they bid to bring scandal upon this Institute and the entire body of the profession."

34. See the editorial in *Journal of Accountancy* (February 1919: 134–36), and AIA *Minutes* (1917: 35ff.) for discussions about the problem of self-styled income tax experts.

35. Davies had long been a champion of a total ban on advertising; in 1893, he had introduced a resolution in the AAPA banning advertising. Through continual attendance at monthly meetings, he succeeded in getting the resolution passed in 1894 when only a few members were in attendance. But Davies's position had no widespread support; two weeks later, a special meeting was called and members voted overwhelmingly to repeal the advertising ban (Webster 1954: 121–25).

36. See "Report of the Special Committee on Professional Advancement" (New York: AIA, 1921). The report contains examples of unprofessional advertising, most of which are for tax work.

37. See Flynn (1939: 224–25) for discussion of the prevalence of codes of ethics; he reiterated Untermeyer's warning that the Lockwood hearings in New York had uncovered a "maze of monopolies," including the "little monopolies [guilds]" that should be of greatest concern; Flynn considered the wave of code-making a sham to gain an advantage; he cites a ministers' code, providing a two-week vacation, guarantee of territory, no proselytizing in the congregation of a minister who was a member of the association, as an example of use of ethical codes to gain an advantage.

38. See McKinsey (1924) for discussion of early demands for accounting services from investment bankers; see Merino and Neimark (1982) for political demands for independent audits, starting with the *Final Report of the Industrial Commission* (1902).

39. See Stuart Chase (1923: 95) who fervently disagreed with the "fair return" concept, maintaining that it justified gouging labor and consumers. He did agree

that it would benefit stockholders, writing "that every public utility has trained seals in the form of engineers and accountants ready to take the stand and swear to the high gods that the cost of duplication, market values, capitalized earning power, or any other device which will increase the claims of the private investors as against the public, is the only correct, ordained, scientific and equitable basis" of calculation of a fair return.

40. See Wallace (1980) and DeAngelo (1981), who suggest that market incentives created demands for audits in the twenties in the absence of regulation; see Merino and Neimark (1982) and Seligman (1982) for an alternative explanation of the use of audits in the twenties.

41. Adolph Berle consistently pointed out the dangers of this trend; see Berle (1926) where he advocated disclosure to arouse public opinion since the law was unable to provide adequate protection to investors. See also Berle (1927: 424), where he contended that "private property was passing out of existence . . . power of corporate managers becoming practically absolute while social controls remain embryonic" and lamented the fact that the courts wouldn't question accounting practice since management gains power through "control of accounting."

42. Most contemporary accountants concluded that auditors could not insist on reporting standards that they deemed appropriate, supporting Ripley's (1927) contention that audits simply masked the continued unreliability of financial reports; see Kohler (1926), Hatfield (1927), Couchman (1928), Wildman (1928B), Robbins (1929), and Farr (1933). Recent empirical studies have reached a different conclusion, finding that financial reporting did improve in the twenties; see Benston (1969) and Dillon (1978). See Merino and Neimark (1982) for historical analysis that concludes that audits did not significantly improve the quality of financial reports.

43. *Uniform Accounting*, written for clients with good internal controls, made confirmation of receivables and observation of inventories optional, contained a standard report, and gave clients an "official pronouncement" to refuse to pay for "optional" procedures. Even established small firms, like S. D. Leidesdorf & Co., did not have the authority to insist on such procedures when internal controls were weak. The option of resigning from the engagement did not appeal to most practitioners (Schur 1976).

44. See editorial "Accountants and Bankers," *Journal of Accountancy* (November 1923: 346–49) which quotes from *RMA Bulletin*, where bankers concluded after the issuance of *Uniform Accounting* they could only accept certificates issued by "recognized and reputable firms"; see also Crandell (1939: 141–44).

45. The lack of power made even certificates issued by "reputable" audit firms suspect, and client misuse of certificates was an area of constant concern; see, for example, editorials such as "Misuse of Accountants' Certificates," *Journal of Accountancy* (August 1920: 138–39) and "Misuse of Accountants' Reports" (April 1920: 299–300).

46. See Garner (1954), Solomons (1968), Johnson and Kaplan (1987) for historical analysis of cost accounting in this period; for historical analysis of standard costs, see Epstein (1978) and Sowell (1973); for an overview of the development of budgeting, see Theiss (1935).

47. See Hubbard (1925), Bass (1927), and Howard (1930) for examples of articles appearing in the *NACA Bulletin* that appear to be designed to sell cost accounting to businesses.

48. See Schlesinger (1956) for discussion of men, like George Perkins of Morgan & Co., who deplored the "evils" of competition and lauded the benefits of cartel systems, akin to the German system, and affected political attitudes. See Merino and Coe (1978) for discussion of accountants' role in gathering information to be disseminated by the FTC and Prickett (1931) for response to that demand.

49. Dewey (1922) pointed out that Bentham's utilitarian calculus that equated work with pain justified the assumption that people would avoid work and led to widespread acceptance of the belief that people were intrinsically lazy. He maintained that the conditions of the workplace were designed to make work as painful as possible so that workers would act in the way that the economic theory predicted.

50. For use of budgets and cost analysis for control purposes, see Sanders (1929); for use of budgets to control overhead, see Frazer (1923) and Hatch (1923); for use of cost data to control labor, see Prickett (1931).

51. See Johnson and Kaplan (1987), who conclude that by 1950, cost accounting had become irrelevant due to the domination of financial accounting; see Ezzamel, Hoskin, and Maeve (1990) and Loft (1991) for critical interpretations of Johnson and Kaplan; see Vollmers (1993) for comprehensive analysis of the cost-accounting literature from 1925 to 1950.

52. See Holden and Ford (1928) for direct reaction to Hoover's call for efficiency through elimination of waste; see also Owen (1926), Tobey (1925), and Kilduff (1927).

53. See Blocker (1936), who discusses budgeting in relation to standard costs; he notes that determination of efficiency standards had progressed to a higher degree for direct labor than for material and overhead because of the availability of time and motion studies that allowed minute division of labor and implementation of scientific wage systems. See Holmes (1938) for discussion of use of calorie expended per labor hour for minute weekly wage adjustments, discussion of therbligs, standard time for a large number of basic body movements and nervous system reaction, such as turning one's head 15 percent to the right or 30 percent to the left, that were measured in ten one-thousandths of a minute.

54. See Dohr (1932) for discussion of flexible budgeting; Clark's *Economics of Overhead* (1923) provided the economic foundation for accountants who focused on relevant costs and accumulation of different costs for different uses; accounting academics at the University of Chicago built on Clark's work to introduce the concept of differential costs in accounting. Rorem (1928B) and Vatter (1945) reflect adaptation of Clark's concept to cost accounting; see Vatter (1947) for extension of the concept to financial reporting. See T. C. Davis (1950). Davis points out the applications of *ROI*.

55. Numerous states and cities enacted budget reforms during this period; in 1928, the National Municipal League published a "Uniform Municipal Budget Law" for cities.

56. See Chatters (1939), who noted the dearth of textbooks in the governmental

accounting area, indicating that only two were then in print: Morey's *Introduction to Governmental Accounting* and Walton's *Municipal Accounting*. See Morey (1948) for a historical overview of the development of governmental accounting.

57. See "Competitive Bidding for Municipal Audits," *Journal of Accountancy* (February 1935: 88–89), and "Increasing Interests in Municipal Accounts," *Journal of Accountancy* (November 1932: 323–27), for the AIA's objections to competitive bidding.

58. For an excellent overview of hospital accounting, see Rorem (1932). Rorem left the University of Chicago faculty to serve as an economist and accountant on the Committee on the Costs of Medical Care and then continued in a variety of positions in the health care field including an important role in the "Blue Cross" movement. The introduction to his *A Quest for Certainty: Essays on Health Care Economics, 1930– 1970* contains a list of his writings; Rorem (1981) explains his philosophy that "health care should be businesslike, but I am disturbed when hospital spokesmen and physicians describe their activities as a 'industry,'" concluding that "in my opinion, health care is a broad public service not private property to be traded over the counter and withheld from those unable to or unwilling to pay."

59. See "Municipal Audits and Municipal Reports," *Journal of Accountancy* (May 1941: 388–89), for discussion of use of state auditors and CPAs in Maine, reaction to the proposed Maryland law that did require CPAs, and a pamphlet issued by the Illinois Society stressing the need for CPAs.

60. The National Recovery Act attracted a great deal of attention from the ASCPA; see Boyd (1934, 1935) and Taggart (1934).

61. See the editorial "Federal Government Accounting," *Journal of Accountancy* (January 1944: 4–5), for discussion of a conference sponsored by AIA, General Accounting Office, and the United States Treasury Department. The article called this an event of "historic significance" as the discussion indicated that outside accountants might play a role in monitoring the federal accounting system.

62. For an excellent history of the federal income tax, see Witte (1985).

63. Haig, Adams, Holmes, Friday, and Andersen presented papers, addressing the topic "Should the Excess Profits Tax Be Retained as a Permanent Part of Our System?" while Kohler and Castenholtz gave papers addressing the primary concern to accountants, "Invested Capital as Defined in the Revenue Act."

64. See Mellon (1924). Montgomery (1927: 252) wrote that Mellon's conservative tax estimates (revenues were grossly underestimated throughout Mellon's tenure) were the secretary's way of dealing with an "extravagant" Congress. In effect, Mellon curbed the power of the legislative branch by saying, "Boys, that's all you have to spend."

65. See Stuart Chase (1925B: 728–29) for a technocratic view. Chase notes that "we have mastered the Coolidge-Mellon ideas that the best way to help the poor is to lighten the tax on millionaires, and that heavy levies on the dead discourage thrift and industry." See also Schlesinger (1956), who discusses Mellon's synergistic taxes and his secret rebates to friends of the Republican Party and to his own bank when he felt that the Congress had not been sufficiently accommodating.

66. The three volumes of the *Proceedings of the American Association of University*

Instructors in Accounting that contain papers presented at the organization's annual meetings held from December 1917 through December 1925 contain numerous articles that express members' reservations about the proliferation of accounting programs and concerns about the quality of instruction; see the reports of the various committees on standardization. Until 1922, the committee considered developing a standard curriculum, but the 1922 committee concluded that imposing a standard program would not be desirable as it would stifle innovation and creativity (AAUIA, 1923: 141).

67. See also Lyon (1924), who reaches a similar conclusion; Lyon contended that university curricula placed too much emphasis on bookkeeping in most accounting curricula.

68. See *Proceedings of the American Association of University Instructors in Accounting* (1921) statements by Andersen, Cornell, Reitell, Wildman, Jackson, and Bacas for discussion of the need for a broader conceptual foundation for people entering the public accounting profession.

69. See Belser (1927) for a contrary view; he contended that although "it was all right to learn theory in school," practice and application were as important as theory. He suggested that educators "duplicate practice" because the role of education should be to provide technically competent men who had been exposed to various factual situations.

70. One day of the two-day meeting each of these years was devoted to pedagogical issues; see Round Table Discussion (1918), six papers included in the topic "The Future Trend of Accounting Instruction" (1919); see three papers presented related to "Development of Accounting Courses" and "Round Table on Teaching Methods" (1920); and "The Correlation of Accountancy Instruction in Universities with the Needs of Public Accountants" and "Round Table Conferences" (1921). Starting in 1921, more papers dealing with specific courses began to appear, such as Sanders's (1921) discussion of the content of a graduate course in industrial accounting and Rittenhouse's (1921) and Rosenkampff's (1921) papers describing the scope and content of courses in accounting systems.

71. See "Constitutionality of CPA Legislation," *Journal of Accountancy* (April 1923: 278–79). The Court held restrictive legislation was acceptable, but the editorial lambasted the Court's statement that "it is true that neither morals, health nor safety of any one is jeopardized by the practicing of this profession," concluding that there is "real and great jeopardy in incompetence."

72. See Paton (1924) for a review of the literature and immediate impact of the AAUIA; he noted the dearth of literature prior to 1917 but concluded, somewhat plaintively, that recent output had "assumed the proportions of a flood."

73. See Paton (1920B: 48) for discussion of how the excess profits tax highlighted the "viciousness of ultra conservatism."

74. See Castenholtz (1919), Kohler (1919), and Paton (1920B) for discussion of the importance of measurement of capital. The Special Bulletins of the AIA, issued throughout the twenties, indicate that accounting practitioners found measurement of capital, not income, the primary technical problem.

75. See Berle (1963) and Berle and Means (1932) for discussion of the struggle

to maintain the primacy of private property rights in the face of separation of ownership and control; see also Scott (1933, 1937A).

76. At the same time, some accountants advocated that more emphasis be placed on earnings per share to overcome what they felt was undue reliance on dividends paid as an indicator of corporate performance. See Leo Greendlinger (1923). It should also be noted that discussions of the concept of "cost of capital" tended to reinforce the proprietary view.

77. Sweeney did not begin to publish his work until 1930, but it continued to have an impact on academic theorists, who would debate the relevance of historical cost until the late thirties when the historic cost allocation model reoriented accounting to ownership interests.

78. The institute published a prize essay on this topic in 1924. See S. Gundelfinger (1924). See also the Special Bulletins No. 10, No. 11, No. 13, No. 15, No. 17, No. 25, and No. 28 that the AIA issued dealing with the problems of capital valuation and/or no-par stock.

79. See Ripley (1927: 195ff.) for details of the Dodge manipulations. Ripley, a Harvard economist, was widely known through his articles in the *Atlantic Monthly* in 1926.

80. Although the details presented by Ripley appear to be correct, see May (1927) for considerations of Ripley's motives. May accurately states that one of Ripley's main theses is that "disclosure, itself, is the vital thing; the form of disclosure is of little importance" (an argument that the SEC was to accept). May agrees; he asks, Why condemn the Dodge report?—although it may have been technically unsatisfactory, the concept of full disclosure was followed. In fact, the disclosure may have totally confused the reader.

81. For a more passionate view of corporate abuses of the period, see Wormser (1931).

82. See *Time,* October 23, 1929. Krueger was on the cover as an example of the successful financier. J. J. Klein, in his memoirs, said that all one could say about investors and bankers was "that they were honest but damnably dumb" (Klein 1969: 119).

83. Most theorists accepted only parts of Simpson's thesis and rejected original cost in favor of some modified system of historical cost; that is, they would recognize the decline in value due to depreciation. An exception was Paul Joseph Esquerre (1920, 1928), who remained a staunch original cost advocate.

84. See Littleton (1929) for discussion of cost and value, which he states are not related; he believed that value was a psychological concept, associated with demand, and varying with individuals whereas cost was an "ascertained fact."

85. For example, Henry Sweeney's timing was unfortunate; his book *Stabilized Accounting* (1933) and a series of articles that appeared in the *Accounting Review* in the thirties advocating general price level changes to handle inflationary pressures had little impact.

86. See Fisher (1930: 257–69), who argued that the 1929 crash was just a technical correction; he attributed the panic almost exclusively to margin accounts and saw no reason to be pessimistic.

87. See DeBedts (1964), Degler (1970), McCraw (1981), Parrish (1970),

Sargeant (1981), and Schlesinger (1959) for historical interpretations of the New Deal and securities legislation.

88. See Means (1962) for discussion of administered prices and evidence that corporations continued the policy of administering high prices even during the Depression; Means argued that corporate control of prices had rendered supply and demand and traditional economic concepts obsolete.

89. See Best (1982), who cites the policies of General Motors, Standard Oil, and Firestone Tire to dismantle the extensive electric rail network in the United States in the 1920s to increase sales of the more profitable gas-driven vehicles as an example of why traditional economic theories, based on supply and demand, fail; he argues that it is not rational to say that consumers chose cars over public transit; producers dictated consumers' choices and producer, not consumer, sovereignty determined the allocation of resources.

90. Accounting historians and economic-based interpretations of the securities acts make different assumptions about the impact of the legislation and thus reach different conclusions. Historians do not view an event as warranting periodization, unless it can be shown that the event changed existing relationships (see Carr 1961; Porter 1981; and Breisach 1983). Economic interpretations assume that passage of legislation warrants periodization, that is, a pre/post SEC dichotomy; see Benston (1969), Wallace (1980), and Phillips and Zecher (1981). Historical analyses do not; see Merino and Neimark (1982) and Seligman (1982). See Ball and Foster (1982) for discussion of the importance of periodization in empirical research.

91. See Edelman (1964: 13ff.) for discussion of conditions needed for symbolic regulation; that is, Congress's objective is not to produce substantive changes, but simply to provide symbolic reassurance to the public. Symbolic legislation need not be implemented to be effective. See also Lowi (1969) for discussion of the abstract nature of securities legislation. See Rayburn (1933); for an overview of Rayburn's legislative agenda, see Shanks (1964), since his view of the legislation was as a conservative reform.

92. See also Pines (1965), who depicts World War II as the dividing line in SEC/AIA relationships but has a different interpretation than presented here; see also Veblen (1918B) for discussion of why wars create attitudes that favor the autonomy of business.

93. See editorial in *Journal of Accountancy* (February 1931: 84–89) for discussion of this case and the accounting profession's reaction. See May's (May Papers 1936) letter to Bonbright in which he explains that this labels this case "comic error" and that the reasoning had not been tested because stock prices fell and the merger could not be consummated; May provided Bonbright with a copy of the appellate order that deemed the initial suit frivolous.

94. See May (1933B, 1934) for the profession's reaction to the legal liability provisions of the securities legislation; see also Seligman (1934A) for vitriolic denunciation of the 1933 act and Douglas (1934) for rejection of Seligman's arguments; see Seligman (1934A, 1934B) for proposed amendments.

95. Carey (1969) suggests that the British Companies Act provided the model

for securities legislation, and it is true that the AAPA and the AIA had advocated adoption of legislation along the lines of the British model for several decades. But a letter from Berle to Douglas, December 30, 1933, suggests that New Dealers may not have been greatly influenced by the British law; Berle wrote "that it is a strange thing that no one working on the Securities Act had studied the history of the British Companies Act." It is also important that one law registered "securities," the other registered "companies."

96. See *Securities Exchange Act of 1934* (Washington, D.C.: GPO, 1934), pp. 5–44, which amended the original act so that plaintiffs had to at least prove that they had sustained a loss as a result of reliance on an audited statement. CPAs also could defend themselves by proving they had "acted in good faith and had no knowledge that statements were false or misleading."

97. See Douglas (1936B), who noted that May had sent him a memorandum that May had submitted to Sam Rayburn in 1933. Carey (1969) suggests that the legislation caught the profession unaware, but that seems unlikely given the tenor of the correspondence between the NYSE and the AIA; see Merino, Koch, and MacRitchie (1987). The AIA's leaders, especially May and Montgomery, had experience in responding to numerous securities bills and federal incorporation legislation introduced in prior decades. See Edelman (1942) and Wiesen (1978) for discussions of earlier legislative proposals.

98. Carter explicitly warned that "investors are too prone to regard balance sheets and income accounts as positive and indisputable statements of fact," while accountants knew that they were simply a matter of opinion (U.S. Congress 1933: 62). See U.S. Congress, Senate Committee on Banking and Currency Hearings on Senate Bill 875, April 1, 1933 (p. 58) (15 USC Section 78D-1). The following exchange between Senator Alben Barkley of the committee and Colonel Carter (Elijah Watt Sells's son-in-law) provides a key insight.

Senator Barkley: "You audit the controller?"
Mr. Carter: "Yes, the public accountant audits the controller's account!"
Senator Barkley: "Who audits you?"
Mr. Carter: "Our conscience."

99. See Securities Act, 1933, Sec. 19. For historical overviews of the SEC, see DeBedts (1964), Parrish (1970), Seligman (1982); for legislative history of the 1933 act, see Landis (1958); for discussion of framers of the legislation, see McCraw (1984); for analysis of enforcement proceedings under the 1933 law, see MacRitchie (1983).

100. While many accountants viewed the legislation as revolutionary, the leading proponents of regulation characterized the securities acts as conservative reforms; see, for example, Frankfurter (1933), Roosevelt (1933), and Rayburn (1933); some of the framers of the legislation viewed it as a first step, not an ultimate solution; see letter from Berle to Douglas (1933), which laments that Frankfurter, whom Berle characterized as knowing "next to nothing about the subject except on paper," felt that he had reached the definitive conclusion" with the 1933 act. Both Berle and

Douglas supported federal incorporation to get at the "really fundamental problem of the increment of power and profit inherent in our present form of organization" (Douglas 1934).

101. Securities legislation when examined from a contrast between "fairness vs. efficiency" perspectives leads to different conclusions about the need for regulation. Those who believe that securities regulation must be assessed from an efficiency basis usually conclude the legislation was not needed; see Benston (1969) and Ross (1979); while those who adopt a fairness perspective conclude that the legislation was needed; Friend and Herman (1964).

102. Contemporary writers suggest that passage of securities legislation reflected a change in attitude toward investors; see, for example, Phillips and Zecher (1982: 9), who write that "it was believed that disclosure . . . would provide sufficient information to investors so that they could make informed decisions that would serve to regulate the allocation of capital," but they do not tell us who believed this. Roosevelt (1933) and other New Deal reformers, like Douglas (1934), clearly did not believe financial statements would be of direct benefit to investors. A later-era SEC commissioner, Jack Whitney (1963), concluded that "providing information to the average investor" was not considered a viable objective by regulators either at the time of passage of the legislation or thirty years later.

103. See Pines (1965) for discussion of the Northern States Power case where the commission voted 3 to 2 to accept a registration statement that contained unacceptable write-ups, but the commission decided that full disclosure was sufficient.

104. See AIA *Year Book* (1936: 373ff., 410ff.) for discussion of the details and rationale for the merger of the AIA and the ASCPA.

105. See Merino and Neimark (1982), who argue that there is little evidence to show that investors could have or did use financial reports to make investment decisions in the 1920s, concluding, therefore, that it is unlikely that investors had been misled by "inadequate" disclosure. See also Edwards (1939: 312ff.), who surveyed prospectuses related to bond issues in the 1920s, concluding that managers were not afraid to disclose even negative information as they had an abiding faith in the "stupidity of the investor."

106. Wellington (1936: 48ff.) told his AIA colleagues that the disclosure approach had one important benefit: it could reduce the profession's legal liability. He said a lawyer told him that you could put in "one of the numerous footnotes the fact that the president of the company has abstracted $1,000,000 a year for each of the last five years" and the issue could be sold. The public might not understand the footnote, but the auditor had no liability; the information was disclosed.

107. As noted earlier, industries that had implemented uniform systems, such as railroads, insurance, and banks, had replaced CPAs with technicians, the rationale being that if you had a rule book, you did not need to pay for professional expertise (Carey 1969).

108. Mattesich (1978: 55) offers an interesting hypothesis that full disclosure is a doctrine of financial concealment; he contends that a "theory of disclosure" should be a "disquieting notion" for accountants as the term implies that "account-

ants possess a general pool of data from which management permits disclosure of a minimal number." Accordingly, accountants need a set of rules or guidelines telling them which data they are "allowed" to reveal and which they are obliged to conceal. Whether or not one agrees with this hypothesis, disclosure makes judgment central to the financial reporting process.

109. See "Financial Statements Under the Securities Acts and the Securities Exchange Act," a report submitted by a Joint Committee of the AIA and the ASCPA, August 8, 1934.

110. See "Memorandum of Luncheon Meeting at the Broad Street Club, May 28, 1935" (1935); at this meeting a group of practitioners, representing nine large firms, agreed that the primary benefit of consistency would be that it might absolve the auditor from making preferability decisions.

111. While the "average" investor, like the analyst, could have obtained this information in the SEC's 8K, the investor's access to SEC data was probably more limited. A 1946 SEC report contained criticisms of audited annual reports, claiming that they were totally inadequate for investors. Annual reports still did not have to have a statement of accounting policies.

112. See Fabricant (1936), who concludes that write-offs in the early thirties far exceeded the write-ups of the twenties and were not justified from an economic perspective.

113. Hoxsey (1931), secretary of the NYSE, left doubt as to the Exchange's motivation, writing that "if we act now . . . we may retard unwarranted intrusions" in his initial communication with the AIA. While some have characterized the NYSE reforms of the early 1930s as voluntary and as evidence that regulation was not needed—see Wallace (1980) and DeAngelo (1981)—the term "voluntary" is questionable if the reforms were enacted to minimize external intervention.

114. This correspondence foreshadowed the emphasis that the profession would place on the limitations of financial reports; see Commission on Auditors' Responsibilities (1976), known as the Cohen Commission, for discussion of the debilitating impact that this attitude had on the development of the profession.

115. The text citations refer to the letters sent between the AIA's committee and the NYSE, but the ideas appear to be more a reflection of the ideas of George O. May, chairman of the committee, than a consensus of the committee. See the May Papers, Price Waterhouse Library, for correspondence between May and other committee members and May and Hoxsey. May forwarded letters throughout the thirties to be signed by the president or the secretary of the AIA; often they only added their signature to May's letter. This clearly creates some problems for historical analysis since the letters sent from the institute do not indicate May's role and he did not limit himself to sending letters solely related to committees that he chaired.

116. The committee report contained a subtle, but important, shift with respect to auditors' responsibility for assessing the integrity of management. Earlier practitioners argued that accountants should enter an engagement with "judicious skepticism" (i.e., actively look for evidence that would raise questions about

management's motives); see, for example, Suffern (1911). In the 1930s, the institute posited a more passive role for accountants; they could assume the integrity of management unless something came to their attention to suggest otherwise.

117. We find the same message throughout the correspondence between the NYSE and the AIA Committee (1932–33), which the NYSE forwarded to the congressional committee, and in "Memorandum Regarding Securities Bill—HR 4313" that May had sent to Sam Rayburn.

118. See Hoxsey to G. Armistead, April 17, 1935. Hoxsey requested that the institute furnish an opinion about accounting for fixed assets, asking questions about the degree to which property should be written off; for example, Should serviceable plants be written down to nominal amounts? And how should such write-offs be accounted for? The institute's response was not only delayed for a considerable period, but also the AIA decided that auditors could not take responsibility for the items Hoxsey mentioned; see also Carey to Hoxsey, February 11, 1936, in "Correspondence File, 1936" (AICPA Library, New York).

119. See "Memorandum of Luncheon Meeting," p. 3.

120. Currently the FASB has not resolved this problem; SFAC No. 1 may abrogate debate by positing common interests, but the fundamental dilemma inherent in measurement bias can not be assumed away. Recently the work of the AICPA Special Committee on Financial Reporting (1994) again addressed "User's Needs" with studies including the information uses made by analysts.

121. Hoxsey (1931: 2, 7) also asked if accountants could require (1) segregation of operating and nonoperating income and (2) separate disclosure of sources of income, that is, extraordinary items and a clear statement of creation and disposition of reserves. The AIA's answer was that auditors could not and should not be expected to compel clients to classify income in this manner (AIA Special Committee, August 1931).

122. See AIA *Minutes* (1936–39) for work of this committee. If Wellington reflected the attitude of most of the AIA's leaders, then they certainly were antagonistic to securities regulation; he denounced New Dealers for promulgating legislation designed to "set the classes against the masses and vice versa" (*Minutes* 1936: 52f.). The *Minutes* from this period show that most members did not believe that voluminous registration statements would be beneficial to investors; they would merely impose unnecessary costs on corporations.

123. Wellington highlighted the differences between the two regulatory bodies, explaining that the Exchange is "not so much interested in disclosure, although that is important, as they are in disclosure of the income statement in a way that will convey to the average stockholder as nearly as possible a correct picture as to what the corporation actually has done." He added that the Exchange did not like the SEC idea "that it doesn't make much difference how it is put out as long as the facts are disclosed" (AIA, *Minutes* 1936: 51–52).

124. See also Mathews (1938), who presents a case-by-case analysis of deficiencies in registration statements and for discussion of the questions that the SEC forwarded to the AIA's Committee on Cooperation with the SEC and that committee's

responses to those questions. See AIA *Year Book* (1937) for reports and discussion of the work of the AIA Committee on Cooperation with the SEC.

125. See Douglas (1974) for a description of the division within the commission. The chief accountant Carman Blough was instrumental in maintaining the balance for standard setting in the private sector, according to some reports.

126. The AAA issued two statements prior to World War II: *A Tentative Statement of Accounting Principles Underlying Corporate Financial Statements* (1936) and *An Introduction to Corporate Accounting Standards* (1940).

127. See, for example, Lorig (1937: 401), who concluded that the committee tried to force accountants back to conservatism, "a god so domineering that the objective of accounting—providing useful information for intelligent guidance—is somewhat forgotten." See also Husband (1937) and Rorem (1937) for similar criticisms. For an analysis of the cost allocation doctrine as developed by the AAA studies, see Deinzer (1965).

128. Scott (1937A) contended that accounting had become an instrument of economic adjustment and social control.

129. Practitioners also objected to the AAA statement's treatment of bond discount and treasury stock, as contra-accounts, rather than assets, because they went against "settled practice." The debate often became heated as reflected in Paton's (1937) reply to Montgomery's (1937) criticism of the AAA's treatment of bond discount. Paton (1937: 290) traced the treatment of the discount back to Sprague (1880) to show support and somewhat sarcastically concluded that while the issue was "not of great importance, straight thinking was." Charles Sweeney (1937: 403) accused Paton of lack of temperance, asking: "Is the New Deal method of meeting criticism so pervasive that dislodging an opponent by indirection and assumptions, rather than logic, is an accepted method?"

130. Paton and Littleton's (1940) claim that cost was "natural" did not go unchallenged, but they had to make that claim to justify their assertion that "costs attach" and could be traced by the accounting process. The matching model required that costs attach if accountants were to trace costs to realized revenues so that income would reflect management's efforts and accomplishments. The model offered managers considerable latitude to stabilize income since they could determine the timing of expense recognition. Paton and Littleton explicitly rejected smoothing of income, but their definition of an asset as an "unamortized cost" certainly went a long way to help managers achieve that objective.

131. Paton and Littleton's (1940) advocacy of one method to handle items, such as first in first out for inventory valuation and straight line depreciation, added to the appearance of certitude in the model; both academics and practitioners appeared to ignore these recommendations.

132. Articulated financial statements require that accountants focus on either the income statement or the balance sheet for "precision"; one statement is primary, the other residual. The primary statement will be "accurate"; the residual statement becomes the receptacle for the resolution of uncertainties. The perceived needs to "balance" and for statements to "articulate" do not stem from theoretical

considerations. See Montgomery (1927), Vatter (1947), and May (1952) for the retarding effect this mentality has had on the development of accounting theory. The recent heated debate over the "revenue/expense" view versus asset/liability view reflects the strong hold that articulation has on the profession.

133. See Correspondence between Douglas and Sanders, and Douglas and Carter, Manuscript Division, Library of Congress, William O. Douglas Papers, Box 2, for discussion of Douglas's association with the study, his resignation with regret, and his recommendation of his colleague, Underhill Moore, as his replacement (Douglas to Sanders, February 24, 1936). Douglas felt that the work would be of great importance in that "its recommendations will go far toward standardizing accounting principles to the end that the interests of both investors and accountants may be better served." Douglas invited the committee to call upon him at any time (Douglas to Carter, March 2, 1936).

134. Douglas provided a critical vote in 1938 when SEC commissioners voted 3 to 2 to allow accountants to set standards. The record at the commission indicates a 5 to 0 approval vote. However, this reported solidarity is not reflective of the positions held.

135. Moonitz (1974) concludes that the Sanders, Hatfield, and Moore study was largely ignored, and that was probably true of academics. But it is not equally clear that practitioners ignored the work.

136. See "Report of Special Committee on Cooperation with Securities and Exchange Commission," Council Minutes (April 12, 1937), submitted by Rodney F. Starkey, chairman of the committee. In response to SEC criticisms, the council had asked the SEC to submit specific cases to its SEC committee for adjudication; the SEC had agreed.

137. See CAP Correspondence File (1939) for responses to initial draft of unamortized bond discount issue. Littleton sent a memorandum to G. O. May (May 1935) reflecting the conservative position. He suggested that the "amortization period should be over the old or new issue, whichever is shorter." See also Bailey to G. O. May (April 25, 1935), who wrote that "I am not quite prepared to accept the shorter period as theoretically preferable," but he concluded that "the difference can hardly be material" and, therefore he would not object.

138. See CAP Correspondence File (1939) for letters in G. O. May/F. W. Andrews conflict. When asked to continue on the committee in 1939, Andrews expressed interest, but he had made George O. May, vice chair of the CAP, angry because he objected to issuance of ARB No. 1 as a "committee statement" when most of the committee had not had an opportunity to see it and because he insisted that minority opinions be expressed. See Andrews to Carey (October 25, 1939) and Andrews to Mathieson (November 7, 1939). May did not appreciate disloyalty. May took charge, writing to Carey (November 2, 1939) that he had concluded that since Andrews seemed not to be convinced "of either the integrity or competence" of CAP that "I should not feel warranted in urging" that he should continue on the committee. Mathieson (November 7, 1939) informed Andrews that he regretted he could no longer continue, and Carey (November 8, 1939) notified May that the

president (Mathieson) had written Andrews saying that he had reluctantly accepted Mr. Andrews's refusal of reappointment (CAP, 1939).

139. Although practitioners could be accused of yielding to clients in this case, it should be mentioned that after the economic downturn in 1938, political leaders would not have looked favorably on any method that might cause a decrease in reported corporate earnings.

140. See Freeman (1939) for discussion of the question of unamortized bond discount as handled by California regulatory agencies with a "uniform" system. Accounting convenience justified departure from direct write-offs to surplus in the minds of public utility commissioners, who permitted, within a three-year period, all three methods discussed by CAP.

141. The AIA pronouncements adopted the current operating concept of income while the AAA 1936, 1941, and 1948 statements advocated the all-inclusive concept of income. Nonetheless, SEC's chief accountant Earle King notified the AIA that it would recognize only the all-inclusive approach, even following the issuance of ARB 32 (1948).

142. See AIA and NYSE (1934), AIA (1936), and AIA (1939). These pronouncements reflect May's (1934: 10) sentiment that "arbitrary allocation of costs to artificial time periods to report income would be indefensible if it were not indispensable."

143. See AIA *Minutes* (1939) for debate about whether the AIA should publish CAP standards; the answer was no since if it appeared that CAP opinions had the authoritative support of the institute, many practitioners would rebel.

144. *Uniform Accounting* had been reissued with the more appropriate title *Approved Methods for Preparation of Balance Sheet Statements* in 1918 but the title was the only change.

145. "Verification" made some changes; for example, verification of receivables was no longer optional; that procedure becomes "best" although still not required. The bulletin also mentioned contingent liabilities (taxes, damages, real estate bonds, and so forth) for the first time.

146. Bankers cited the large number of credit losses related to overstated inventory as the most pernicious problem in the 1920s. The AIA's Special Committee on Cooperation with Bankers addressed the issue several times in that decade but refused to expand audit responsibilities in this area (AIA, *Minutes* 1921–23).

147. See "Letter from J. M. B. Hoxsey to the Governing Committee: New York Stock Exchange," October 24, 1933.

148. See, for example, letter from Couchman to G. O. May, January 21, 1935. Practitioners from nine major firms were involved in this correspondence; all the letters reflect similar concerns.

149. See AIA *Yearbook* (1935: 36–39) for report of committee on cooperation with bankers that Couchman chaired for criticism of Robert Morris Associates (RMA). See also letters from Couchman to G. O. May (May Papers [AIA File], January 1935) outlining RMA concerns. RMA contended that acceptance of the certificate would open a "Pandora's box"; without any indication of audit scope, standard

certificates would continue to be useless from a creditor's perspective. Once again bankers demanded reform, a return to long-form reports. The AIA rejected this possibility, arguing that long-form reports would be subject to more abuse.

150. See letter from Rodney Starkey to G. O. May (June 28, 1935) in May Papers, 1935 (AIA File), for SEC criticisms; Starkey discusses conversation between representatives of the AIA and the SEC concerning the inadequacies of audit certificates.

151. Federal incorporation was not an idle threat; correspondence between Adolph Berle and William Douglas suggests that both men, influential in formulating securities regulation, saw that as an initial first step, not a final outcome. In late 1933, Berle (1933) had begun to work on a federal incorporation law to present to Congress, and he wrote to ask for Douglas's support. Douglas (1934) responded "you can count on me to pull an oar on federal incorporation." Both men thought that securities legislation would place the United States government into the investment banking business and thought that if that occurred it would be something that they could look to with pride. The Borah-O'Mahoney Bill (Federal Corporation Act of 1937) was not unlike Hurley's zone experts proposals; see AIA *Minutes* (1937) for discussion of this latter threat.

152. Norman J. Lenhart (1939: 224), testifying in the SEC inquiry into the McKesson-Robbins case, was asked by William Werntz, chief accountant, about the 1936 restatement; Lenhart indicated that he had brought the issue to the Executive Committee in 1934 and served on the committee until the restatement was completed. When asked what the primary purpose of the restatement was, he replied that "in my opinion the primary purpose of preparing and publishing this bulletin was to forestall publication of a similar bulletin by some body, governmental or otherwise."

153. See, for example, Victor Stempf (1944A: 1–8). For details of the case and accountants' views of McKesson-Robbins, see "Testimony of Expert Witnesses at SEC Hearings," *Journal of Accountancy* (April–May 1939: 199–203, 279–97).

154. "Extensions" (1939) also omitted the phrase "but, we did not make a detailed test of transactions," which auditors had suggested would be sufficient to place the public on notice that they did not observe inventory.

155. See Correspondence, J. M. B. Hoxsey to G. O. May, February 22, 1939; G. O. May to J. M. B. Hoxsey, February 28, 1939; and J. M. B. Hoxsey to G. O. May, March 8, 1939. G. O. May Papers, Price Waterhouse Library, New York, File McKesson Robbins.

156. A Special Subcommittee on Independent Audits and Audit Procedure of the Committee on Stock List of the New York Stock Exchange (1939) reached the same conclusion after the McKesson-Robbins debacle. See also *United States of America Before the Securities and Exchange Commission in the Matter of McKesson and Robbins, Inc. (Report of Investigation)*, Washington, D.C.: GPO, 1940; reprinted 1982 as *Accounting in Transition*, ed. R. P. Brief (New York: Garland, 1982).

157. Empirical researchers, who assume that the audited/unaudited dichotomy is a meaningful division prior to 1939, may confound analysis by use of that classification; see Chow (1982), for example.

Chapter 7

1. See Vatter (1963) for discussion of the 1946 employment act; see McQuaid (1994) for detailed description of the involvement of corporate executives in the political sector, through the activities of the Business Council, as advisers to the Commerce Department, and on the Committee for Economic Development.

2. See McQuaid (1994), who describes the Marshall Plan as a way to subsidize the largest U.S. corporations without generating public protest; see Manchester (1975: 438) for an alternative view; he concurs with Churchill's sentiment that this plan was "the most unsordid act in history."

3. See McConnell (1966) for a historical overview of the fear of growth of large corporations generated in the United States; see Merino and Neimark (1982) for discussion of concerns about how private power has made an impact on the accounting profession.

4. Simon's (1947) message was not new; Coase (1937) had reached a similar conclusion before the war, acknowledging that economic activity could be coordinated either by the market or by the market price mechanism or by authority relationships within large firms. He concluded that market coordination was no longer synonymous with efficiency and that large firms had assumed the entrepreneurial and coordination functions. For more critical assessments, see Galbraith (1956) and Penrose (1959).

5. See Berle (1954, 1963) for discussion of the deep roots that private property rights had in American culture and the fierce resistance to suggestions that the moral justification for those property rights had eroded; see also Means (1962), who discusses strategies (limiting supply) that corporations used throughout the 1930s to administer prices.

6. See Means (1962) for discussion of how large corporations administered prices during this period; the federal government did not abandon its regulatory functions, conducting a series of hearings on price fixing in the early 1950s, but the government did not actively enforce antitrust policy to restore competition. That policy now appears to have been naive.

7. See Federal Trade Commission (1947A, 1948B, and 1950A) for investigations of the sulphur cartel, the copper cartel, the steel cartel, and the alkali industry, four of the investigations held on administered prices.

8. The Cellar-Kefauver Bill of 1950 did make it more difficult for vertical and horizontal corporate mergers to occur; part of the preference for conglomerates, characteristic of the 1960s merger wave, can be attributed to this law. Ironically, as Chandler (1990) points out, the change to the conglomerate form of merger did not necessarily reduce transaction costs (the traditional defenses for mergers) and often resulted in inefficiency.

9. It should be noted that the McCarthy hearings, which appeared to many to be a witch hunt in the name of patriotism, raised questions about the cost of suppression of criticisms to promote the common objective of protecting the nation from the Communist threat. See Manchester (1975) for discussion of the McCarthy hearings and reaction when McCarthy came too close to corporate members of the CED;

while McCarthy was sanctioned, the House Committee on Un-American Activities continued to be active into the 1960s.

10. Academics, like C. Wright Mills (1959), had continued to issue warnings about the "power elite" and the control that they had assumed of American life. But, until Rachel Carson's *Silent Spring* (1962) captured public attention, demands for social reform had languished.

11. See "Conglomerate Earning: Credibility Gap," *Wall Street Journal* (July 24, 1969) and "Cooking the Books to Fatten Profits," *Time* (April 11, 1969) for examples of the types of articles that appeared in the business and popular press during this time. See also Briloff (1967 and 1968A) for similar criticisms.

12. See May (1952), who warned at the outset of the period that accounting had become more a "political" than an "economic" phenomenon, and Gerboth (1972), who delivered the same message. See also Chambers's (1973) response to Gerboth and Gerboth's (1973) reply.

13. See McQuaid (1994) and Manchester (1975) for discussion of the symbiotic relationship that existed between business and government after Sputnik as the government assumed an ever-increasing burden for funding basic research in the United States. Manchester (1975) concludes that by the 1960s, the government spent approximately $15 billion a year on research and development while the private sector spent about $6 billion per year. He asks, what risk did IBM incur when it invested $5 billion in integrated circuits for its third-generation computers when the Pentagon provided all the funding? The privatization of publicly funded technological advances blurred the risk/return relationship normally associated with private property rights, but the imperatives of the cold war seemed to justify the new symbiotic relationship between government and business.

14. See Bond (1946) for a passionate defense of the "free market" model; see also Kelley (1951). The ideas expressed by the two authors appear to have been shared by most, if not all, accountants. See Tinker, Merino, and Neimark (1982) for a critical assessment of how this orientation influenced development of accounting theory.

15. See Best (1990) for discussion of the implications of Schumpeter's and Penrose's works for economic theorists. Penrose viewed profit as a "quasi rent" for organizational capability.

16. See Berle (1954), who concluded that ideological commitments remained strong and that many economists simply refused to acknowledge that the market was not infallible; it was simply an instrument that facilitated flow of capital in secondary markets. See also Knauth (1957) for an insightful article on why bargaining, a legal concept based on the assumption of operative competitive markets for all groups, was totally incongruous with relationships in the new managerial enterprises.

17. See Kaplan and Reaugh (1939), which documents the continued unreliability of annual reports after passage of securities legislation. See Merino and Neimark (1982) for discussion of the political sector's negative attitudes toward investors' abilities to understand financial reports, which may explain the SEC's apparent lack of concern prior to 1946.

18. As Vatter (1947) correctly noted, the definitions of an asset as an "unamor-

tized cost" or "revenue charge in suspense" in Paton and Littleton (1940) had operational content, but lacked homogeneity of substance. The definition provided maximum flexibility to management as they decided when a cost should be amortized; this resulted in the balance sheet's becoming a repository for dangling debits and to the ARB No. 43's definition of an asset "as something represented by a debit balance that is or would be carried forward upon the closing of the books of accounts according to the rules of principles of accounting (provided such a debit balance is not in effect a negative balance applied to a liability) on the basis that it represents either a property right or value acquired, or an expenditure made which has created property rights or is properly applied to the future."

19. See, for example, ARB No. 26 (1946) for use of special war reserves, ARB No. 28 (1947) contingency reserves, and ARB No. 33 (1947) inventory reserves.

20. The AAA did issue a comprehensive restatement of its conceptual framework in 1948, *Accounting Concepts and Standards Underlying Corporate Financial Reports,* but the AIA continued to invite individual academics to sit on CAP, rather than to work directly with the AAA.

21. The SEC's advocacy of accurate historical records is understandable, given the "donated" wartime facilities provided to the private sector (McQuaid 1994), the excess profits tax provisions (Witte 1985), and the beginning of congressional hearings to determine if corporations administered prices (Federal Trade Commission 1948B).

22. See introduction to AIA report of the *Study Group on Business Income* for more denunciation: see May Papers, Study Group, 1947–50, Price Waterhouse Library, New York. May's anger can be partly attributed to the fact that he had asked one of his partners, Percival Brundage, to step down and allow Bailey to become chair of CAP; thus, he felt betrayed by Bailey. Earle King, the chief accountant at the SEC, also incurred May's wrath.

23. See Federal Trade Commission, "Monopoly and Competition in the Steel Industry," submitted by the FTC to the Temporary National Economic Commission, March 7, 1939, National Archives, RG 144, Box 259. See also Federal Trade Commission, "Report on the International Steel Cartels," Washington D.C.: GPO, 1948. See also Truman's (1955, 1956) memoirs for discussion of the battle that occurred when U.S. Steel resisted efforts to increase steel production to meet defense needs during the Korean War; see Manchester (1975) for discussion of U.S. Steel/Kennedy conflict in 1960.

24. See U.S. Congress, House of Representatives, "Report of the Subcommittee on Monopoly Power of the Committee of the Judiciary—Iron and Steel Industry," 81st Congress, December 12, 1950. The subcommittee also investigated a number of other industries such as electrical equipment, copper, sulphur, and alkali. See also U.S. Congress, Senate, Committee on Judiciary (1957, 1958).

25. See Barkin (1951). Barkin replied to the suggestion that accounting principles should result in a fair presentation from all points of view, saying that he would love to join the movement but that "the [accounting] profession [is] not ready for this undertaking; accountants make no effort to provide information needed by labor."

26. See Paton's (1953) testimony before the House Committee on Ways and

Means, which probably reflected a consensus within the profession that taxes had become "extortionate" and that the government was killing the private sector. This argument loses some of its force, given that the government had just provided more than $130 billion of new capital to the private sector and after a war effort that funded more than 90 percent of the basic research and about 50 percent of all R & D in the United States.

27. See Littleton (1953) and Kohler (1963), who seem to share this view.

28. The response has been remarkably persistent; see, for example, AIA (1932) for a classic example of this strategy. See the Commission on Auditors' Responsibilities (1978) for an example of the constancy of this strategy over time.

29. Alexander's (1950) conclusion was reasonable, given the difficulty that accounting theorists were having in reconciling the traditional orientation (stockholder focus) postulate with separation of ownership and control.

30. See American Accounting Association (1957) and preceding statements and supplements for work done by its committees.

31. Paton's (1963, 1973) attack became increasingly sharp; by 1973, he accused the *Wall Street Journal* and *U.S. News & World Report,* as well as historical cost advocates, of being unwitting stooges for those of the socialist persuasion. His concern was that headlines that touted "record" corporate profits would attract the attention of "agitators, reckless union officials and irresponsible politicians" (1973: 16).

32. See Schumpeter (1946), Galbraith (1956), and Penrose (1959) for interesting questions about the meaning of accounting profit in an organizational economy.

33. See Briloff (1964), who called for a revolution; and Chambers (1973), who synthesized normative theorists' disenchantment with the Board's piecemeal approach; see Gerboth (1973) for an interesting reply to Chamber's article.

34. See May Papers 1961 (AIA File) for letter from G. O. May to J. B. Inglis (April 4, 1961). May wrote that he would like to write an article called "The Charlatan and the Profession," but that he could not do so without further injuring the profession's reputation; May's disdain was reciprocated by Spacek, who indicated that the arrogance of Price Waterhouse partners had made him resolve to head the largest public accounting firm in the nation. (Spacek was the subject of a series of taped interviews during the 1980s. These tapes are in the collection at the School of Accountancy, the University of Mississippi.)

35. See AICPA (1959) and AICPA *Minutes* (1959: 50ff.), AICPA Library, for a discussion of the basic organization and approach of the APB. The APB's first meeting was held on September 11, 1959.

36. Only Leonard Spacek of the advisory board felt strongly enough about the issue to have a formal comment published in the research study. See "Comments of Leonard Spacek," ARS No. 1, pp. 56–57.

37. See "News Report," *Journal of Accountancy,* April 1962, pp. 9–10. A "Statement by the Accounting Principles Board," April 13, 1962, was attached to each copy of the research study issued publicly and contained the above disclaimer.

38. This antagonism toward the proposal to abandon historical cost and stabilized earnings was understandable in the light of the phenomenon of "going public" in the 1960s. Numerous small corporations chose that course under the SEC's

Regulation A; many managers had an interest in maintaining stable earnings; see Ronen, Sadan, and Snow (1976) for discussion of incentives for income smoothing.

39. See Grady (1965). Grady had apparently begun lobbying for such an approach with the issuance of ARS No. 2. See also Grady (1962). Its acceptance, evidenced by prolonged sales at high volume, suggest it was found useful in practice, especially in Europe.

40. The largest eight public accounting firms in the United States were "dubbed" the "Big Eight" in a 1960s article in *Fortune.* Alphabetically, they were Arthur Andersen; Arthur Young; Ernst & Ernst; Haskins and Sells; Lybrand, Ross Bros., & Montgomery; Peat, Marwick, Mitchell; Price Waterhouse; and Touche Ross.

41. See "News Report," *Journal of Accountancy,* January 1970, p. 29, which discussed the defeat of a proposal to make failure to disclose departures from GAAP a violation of the code of ethics of the institute. Woodside expressed the view of most of the opponents when he said that the opinions must stand on their own merit; if they could not, they deserved to be ignored, without penalty, by any practitioner. The provision, however, subsequently was accepted.

42. Paton and Littleton's (1940) insistence on one method for all allocations (i.e., straight line depreciation, FIFO inventory valuation) to constrain managers, also did not gain acceptance. The tax deductibility of corporate interest expense favored creditors and affected perceptions of the singularity of capital sources.

43. It would be wrong to suggest that Vatter's work had a great influence; it did not, although it did impact the subsequent direct cost/relevant cost debate. Vatter's (1947) work could be perceived as consistent with Coase's (1937) transaction cost analysis.

44. While this point of Husband's (1954) theory did not receive widespread attention, the idea that accounting income has no external surrogate has become an important part of the recent critical literature; see Hines (1988, 1989). In modern terms, income has no "empirical referent."

45. In the 1980s, critical accounting researchers picked up this theme (see Hopwood 1983) and began to examine the role of financial accounting in a political economy (see Cooper and Sherer 1984).

46. See Linowes (1968) for an example of the calls for expansion of auditors' role.

47. See R. G. Barry 1969, *Annual Report;* see also Hyatt (1970) for discussion in the popular press of that report.

48. See Bernstein (1975) for a rebuttal to EMH theorists and Mautz (1978), who suggested that practicing accountants would have to be concerned as long as investors sued in "particular," not "on average."

49. The prescriptions included do not be overconcerned with reducing reporting alternatives; do not direct financial reports at naive investors; remember that accountants are not the sole suppliers of information; focus on the costs/benefits of information to be provided; and conduct research to examine the economic consequences of proposed standards.

50. See Devine (1964) for discussion of wartime influence; see also Charnes, Cooper, and Ijiri (1963) for application of quantitative techniques to cost accounting.

51. See Boorstin (1974) for an interesting discussion of prior mode of production, producing products "no better than they had to be."

52. See Deming (1986B) for discussion of quality control circles; Deming (1986A) in a discussion with one of the authors attributed the short-sightedness of American managers to their "misguided fealty" to bottom line income.

53. Schumpeter (1946), Simon (1947), Drucker (1947), and Galbraith (1956) also pointed out that in the new era human resources (knowledge) would be the critical resources as corporations had to be able to respond quickly to technological changes.

54. See Benninger (1950A, 1950B), who called for introduction of standard costs into financial reports; he, like other members of the AAA's committees on cost and management accounting, argued that cost data would be most useful to readers of financial reports. See also Davidson (1963A), who suggests introduction of managerial analysis into financial reporting to resolve the apparent conflict between the two.

55. The Robinson Patman Act and the NRA had introduced strong pressure for uniform cost procedures; these regulations made it desirable for companies to reconcile cost and financial accounting. See Dixon (1943) and Vollmers (1993) for more detailed discussion of the impact of The Robinson Patman Act and NRA on the development of cost accounting.

56. See Marple (1965) for a compilation of selected papers on direct costing that had been published by the NAA.

57. See Brush (1943) for introduction of break-even analysis of cost in the academic literature; see Rice (1944) for discussion of need for a "user orientation"; see Vatter (1945) for discussion of various objectives of cost accounting and an excellent review of the joint cost allocation problem; see Benninger (1949) for distinction between financial and cost-accounting concepts of cost.

58. See Bierman (1960) and Klammer (1973) for discussion of capital budgeting during this time period.

59. Even when accountants borrowed from psychologists, like Abraham Maslow (1965), who was highly critical of the profit motive, they ignored the criticism of accounting data and focused on the hierarchy of needs that could be reconciled with traditional accounting measurements.

60. For an excellent historical discussion of the CASB, see Rayburn (1991).

61. See Johnson and Kaplan (1987: 145ff.) for discussion of this issue; for the widespread impact the Johnson and Kaplan book had, see Wells (1991); for criticisms, see Ezzamel, Hoskin, and Maeve (1990) and Loft (1991).

62. See Galbraith (1987) and Reich (1989), who attribute the decline in American competitiveness to these factors; the decline also may reflect Schumpeter's (1946) process of "creative destruction" delayed by the fact that in the postwar period where the government funded most of the nation's basic research, managers succeeded without taking competitive risks.

63. See Witte (1985) for an excellent discussion of this permanent shift to the income tax as the primary revenue source for the federal government and policy implications.

64. The American Institute established its own lobbying arm and the AICPA increased its tax staff to respond to all tax bills. See also the testimony of L. Spacek (1953) and of W. Paton (1953), who argued against taxation based on traditional (historical cost) accounting income, U.S. Congress, House, Committee on Ways and Means.

65. The AICPA's Tax Division responded to all new tax laws. Summaries of the AICPA's responses are available in the *Journal of Accountancy*'s Tax Clinic or Taxation sections.

66. The *Journal of Accountancy* included a section on taxation each month beginning in the early 1960s that contained all testimony offered by the AICPA before Congress on each tax bill.

67. See AICPA Tax Division (1969) for a summary of the 144-page response that the AICPA submitted to Congress during the hearings related to the 1968 Act. W. Barnes, chairman of the institute's Federal Tax Division, testified.

68. Accounting tax practitioners faced two major problems: first, the profession feared that the entry of unqualified persons who called themselves tax specialists would hurt the profession. The state societies also had to fight efforts by lawyers to bar accountants from tax practice; see, for example, Shelton (1961) and Wisconsin State Bar (1961).

69. For an overview of the profession's stance on this issue, see Barrett and Holtz (1972). As to accountant-attorney professional disputes, see Jameson (1956).

70. See *Audits of Governmental Corporations* (1945A, 1945B) for discussion of the George Bill and appointment of T. Coleman Andrews.

71. See Andrews (1949) for discussion of how the Hoover Commission bill differed from recommendations of the Accounting Policy Committee of the AIA that had been assigned the task of making recommendations, as in "Reform of Federal Government Accounting" (1948).

72. See, for example, the American Council on Education (1968), the American Hospital Association (1968), and the National Committee on Governmental Accounting (1968) for standards. See also Dahlberg (1966) for the history of the New York Bureau of Municipal Research, which played an influential role in establishing municipal accounting standards.

73. See Mednick and Previts (1987) for discussion of the dramatic shift in the scope of services offered by CPA firms after World War II.

74. In 1946, the SEC staff concluded that 55 percent of the companies were deemed to have balance sheets that were materially deficient; 13 percent of the companies did not present income statements at all, of those presenting an income statement, 33 percent did not disclose sales or cost of goods sold. No company presented adequate footnotes and many companies followed policies that were, in the commission's opinion, unsound.

75. An editorial in the *Journal of Accountancy* (1946) indicated that the AIA felt that the SEC's purpose was to justify extension of its jurisdiction. The SEC had proposed an amendment to Section 12 of the 1934 Securities Exchange Act, which would require that all companies with $3,000,000 or more in assets and 300 or more stockholders be subject to that act.

76. See AIA Committee on Auditing Procedure's *Codification of Statements on Procedure,* a condensation of the twenty-four statements issued between 1939 and 1950; see AIA (1953B).

77. See editorials in the *Journal of Accountancy* throughout the 1950s with respect to abuse of long-form certificates; the AIA conducted several studies and found a surprising degree of variation in long-form reports and concluded that many long-form reports might lead investors to infer that the auditor was taking more responsibility than actually intended. SAP No. 27, "Clarification of the Auditor's Opinion" (1957), addressed that issue.

78. Starting in 1917, when the AIA provided J. Scobie's internal control memorandum, which was issued as *Uniform Accounting,* a case can be made that the profession suffered when it failed to specify its responsibilities. Scobie's memorandum was written for companies with good internal control, and failure to emphasize the importance of good internal control undermined the quality of some audits. Recently, critical researchers have begun to raise similar questions about the profession and its objectives and responsibilities; see, for example, Humphrey and Mozer (1990) and Willmott (1991).

79. For an excellent discussion of the extension of auditors' responsibilities, see Norgaard (1972); for extension into areas of internal control, see Carmichael (1970B); for extension into other areas, see Belda (1970) and Neumann (1968); for management and operational audits, see Burton (1968) and Norgaard (1969).

80. For discussion of the way in which the SEC sought to expand Rule 10B to apply to accountants and for a discussion of the ASRs and the relationship to auditors' changing legal liability, see Breberm (1967).

81. Quoted in Breberm (1967: 1459); the SEC reaffirmed this point in ASR No. 105 (1966).

82. See Carmichael (1968), Saxe (1971), and Whalen (1958, 1965) for discussion of auditors' increased liability with respect to subsequent events and unaudited financial statements.

83. See Tucker (1994) for discussion of the contributions made by Kenneth Stringer.

84. Behavioral research in auditing became increasingly important throughout the 1970s; Ashton's (1974) experimental study of the internal control judgments foreshadowed the direction much of the behavioral research would take.

85. See Briloff (1967, 1968A, 1968B, 1969A, 1969B) for tenor of the criticisms and how accounting standards lent themselves to managerial manipulation and led to misleading financial reports. For examples of criticisms in the popular press, see also Fogarty, "Figuring Out the Bookkeeping," *The Exchange* (October 1969); Lyons, "Earnings, Can Anyone Believe the Numbers?" and May, "The Earnings Per Share Trap," *Financial Analysts Journal* (May/June 1968).

86. See Wyatt (1963) for ARS No. 5, *A Critical Study of Business Combinations* and Catlett and Olson (1968) for ARS No. 10, *Accounting for Goodwill.*

87. See Commerce Clearing House, *Federal Securities Law Reporter,* paragraph 92,511 (2d Circuit, November 12, 1969) for the Continental Vending decision.

88. See Casler (1964) for discussion of the evolution of a code of ethics; see Higgins and Olsen (1972) for a brief overview of how the code of ethics changed during this time period; see Armstrong (1971) for discussion of weaknesses of the code and why change was needed to preserve the profession's autonomy.

89. See, for example, Loeb (1972), who conducted a case study of enforcement proceedings in one state; since state boards, not the AICPA, controlled the licensing process, the national organization had limited enforcement power. Carey (1965) concluded that the record of enforcement of the ethics code is not one in which the profession can take pride.

90. Critical accounting researchers have challenged this functionalist view of the role of a code of ethics, mirroring Flynn (1939), who viewed the proliferation of codes of ethics being promulgated by all vocations as "a sham to gain advantage" for a particular select few. See, for example, Neu (1991); for a nonfunctionalist perspective, see Ophir (1989–90).

91. Kell (1958) surveyed accounting department chairmen and noted that while they approved of most of the Perry committee report, they did not support internship programs. This reluctance can be attributed partially to the ongoing struggle to gain academic acceptance for accounting; see Paton (1963), who laments that accounting has been trapped in schools of business, where it was viewed as merely a technical (vocational) discipline. Paton, in his later years, claimed to be a supporter of the school of accountancy concept.

92. See Trueblood (1963) for further discussion of why practitioners felt that passing the CPA examination should not be used to assess the quality of accounting programs; however, despite constant protestation by both practitioners and AICPA committees that the CPA examination should not be used to assess programs, the continued publication of passage rates by schools seems to be counterproductive to de-emphasizing the examination as state legislators often use those statistics to assess the quality of accounting education.

93. See Moonitz (1973) for an unfavorable assessment of the impact of the desire for academic legitimacy.

94. See Moonitz (1973) for similar views; see also Aslaman and Duff (1973), who attribute the schism to the academic reward system. See Bricker and Previts (1990) on the sociology of accountancy.

95. See Sterling (1973) for discussion of the anomalies that result with respect to specific issues; he uses marketable securities as an example of where accounting educators teach practice as a norm despite obvious inconsistencies in practice and conflict with research. Thus, he concludes, students become indoctrinated to accept practice and do not develop the critical faculties needed.

96. See Kester (1936); the Perry (1955) report's recommendation for five-year programs and professional schools may have been premature. Accounting enrollments, which had declined throughout the postwar period until 1957, began to increase after a decade of decline; see Kerrigan (1959).

97. See Zald (1968) for the view that Roy and MacNeill's (1967) study portrayed the wrong concept of a profession and that Roy and MacNeill's study had been

aimed at the needs of the "elite" accounting firms; for rebuttals, see Roy (1968) and MacNeill (1968).

Chapter 8

1. The signal events of American accounting history that have occurred in the period since 1973 are less subject to satisfactory historical analysis than episodes in the periods preceding it, if only because several of the principal issues continue to be even in more complex transition and debate. Our work on drafting the book revision ended in June 1996, after Previts's trip to Tuscaloosa and a meeting involving the Academy of Accounting Historians' Research Center personnel, including A. Roberts, D. Flesher, E. Slocum, W. Samson, T. Lee, F. Graves, R. Sriram, and K. Sivakumar.

2. Both Seidman and Bowsher appeared on the CNN (Cable News Network) television program *Moneyline* on June 11, 1991, to be interviewed by Lou Dobbs, the show's host. The program had been prompted by the media coverage attending the difficulties anticipated in the proposed General Accounting Office audit of the Resolution Trust Corporation. In August 1991, Seidman announced his plans to retire in October 1991. As a true footnote to the history of these turbulent times, it could be added that press reports stated that Ivan Boesky, convicted on charges of stock law violations, was once a member of the consulting staff of Touche Ross in Detroit.

3. John Cromwell, believed to be the first black CPA, passed the CPA examination in New Hampshire in 1932. For discussion of experiences of minorities in accounting, see Hammond (1990) and Hammond and Streeter (1994).

4. Kohler (1970) defines accountancy as "the theory and practice of accounting; its responsibilities, standards, conventions and activities." Accounting is defined as "the recording and reporting of transactions" (pp. 6–7). Also see A. C. Littleton (1933A) for a related discussion wherein his analogy is that accountancy is to accounting as finance is to financing. The first element is the field of knowledge; the second, the processes active in the field (p. 165).

5. Page S8 of the April 27, 1991, *Economist* indicates that in 1965 pension fund shareholdings as a percent of the total value of shares listed on the New York Stock Exchange was 7.5 percent; by 1988 the percentage was just under 30 percent. A host of added perplexities require consideration: Is it proper to assume that an institutional investor/fund manager can obtain sufficient publicly available information to evaluate corporate performance without traditional forms of published reports? Which corporate financial structure will maximize wealth given these views? How does global investment of capital influence these issues? Is separation of ownership and management, as posited by Berle and Means in the 1930s, a central issue useful in guiding public disclosure policy (i.e., mandatory audits of public companies) given that the employees, via pension plans "own" the businesses, but do not "control" them? How should a "publicly held" company be defined today? What are the tradeoffs between managing for short-term goals (as in managerial capitalism) and investing for long-term returns (as in pension fund socialism)? Is this long-term/short-term dichotomy inherently dysfunctional in a capital market system? What

should be the guide to public policy as to "public company" disclosure, particularly to noninstitutional investors?

6. The *Wall Street Journal* of April 16, 1991 (C-1) reports that the California Public Employees Retirement System (CALPERS), whose pension assets, valued at $63 billion, make it the largest public fund, rejected applications from 91 international money managers, saying a majority failed to comply with the state's 1989 affirmative action law. Such actions suggest the seriousness with which large pension funds can pursue social consciousness. Its move into foreign stocks promises to be the biggest international investing contract of the year. The College Retirement Equities Fund, another large stock fund, valued its portfolio of investment assets at $37 billion on December 31, 1990, when the market was at the pre-3000 level. CREF has a companion fund (TIAA) that is separately invested in bonds and is not included in this valuation. TIAA-CREF would likely represent a larger fund than CALPERS. Approximately 13 percent of CREF is invested in equities outside of the United States.

7. IASC has issued a number of standards to date that are recognized by the professional accounting bodies in over forty countries. In addition, the Accounting International Studies Group has sponsored and published a series of comparative studies on accounting thought and practice in Canada, Great Britain, Ireland, and the United States.

The differences that exist between countries can be many. For example, in the treatment of research and development costs, FASB Statement 2 mandates that such expenditures should be charged to expense. Other industrial nations account for research and development costs on a deferral basis when benefits are expected to be derived. The American accounting standard requiring expensing is so singularly opposite that of other nations, it creates a basis for questioning the validity of the American approach. Similar instances in other accounting treatment exist between nations; however, the contrast in the case of research and development accounting is striking.

8. Rule 203 of the AICPA *Code of Professional Conduct* provides that it is acceptable for members to depart from the accounting principles promulgated by the body designated by the Council of the AICPA if failure to do so would result in materially misleading financial statements.

9. This statement paraphrases the wording of the decision handed down by Lord Justice Lopes involving the decision in the *Kingston Cotton Mills* (1896) case in the United Kingdom.

10. The outcome of the Excellence vote was contested by a group of conservative AICPA members, whose sympathies reflect the policies of a group of practicing CPAs identified as the National Conference of CPA Practitioners (NCCPAP). They contended that the procedure used in the vote reflected unfair balloting practices because the check-off arrangement of the ballot permitted a person to check off a single box to vote in favor of all items, but required an individual to check off six individual issue ballots, each in the negative, if one chose to vote against all issues. A settlement provided for the AICPA to fund a series of educational seminars on ethical topics, but the result was not changed.

11. Abbreviations as follows: SEC, Securities and Exchange Commission; FTC, Federal Trade Commission; GAO, General Accounting Office; CASB, Cost Accounting Standards Board; OSHA, Occupational Safety and Health Act; IRS, Internal Revenue Service; ICC, Interstate Commerce Commission; FCC, Federal Communications Commission; FPC, Federal Power Commission; HUD, Department of Housing and Urban Development; ERISA, Employee's Retirement Income Security Act; DOD, Department of Defense. Although it might be inappropriate to single out any one of these agencies as being more or less influential than another, practitioners have been heavily influenced by the policies prescribed by the IRS, SEC, and CASB. The potential for an "exponential explosion" of regulatory accounting policy, given the influence of and tradition for prescribed accounting in regulated industries, is a matter of increasing concern to the profession, despite policy changes in the Congress following the 1994 elections.

12. For instance, partner "take home" versus "earnings" are not the same. Partners have several items that must be covered from earnings, including capital contributions, personal insurance, and tax payments. The latter often necessitate filing state tax returns and paying taxes in several jurisdictions where an individual does not live, but in which the partnership practice has business. Average partnership earnings are also deceptive in that distributions are in correspondence with the number of partnership capital units held. The units are offered to partners and acquired over time in concert with the firm's plans and with the structure of the firm's governing structure. Senior and managing partners would tend, therefore, to accumulate more units and receive more earnings. This does not begin to factor in the additional complications that may derive from international fee income, if any. An "average partner earnings" number, therefore, is a not meaningful statistic except for purposes of the most general citation. Such an average also is not particularly meaningful absent the range of individual partner distributions; that is, what is the lowest and the highest annual distribution in the firm and how that compares with the "average" over time. In part, owing to the secrecy surrounding such compensation which these partnerships seem to prefer, one can only deplore the lack of information and make careful, but inconclusive estimates—barring a "leak" that occurs from time to time, as in the situation involving the merger proposals of two Big Eight firms in the late 1980s.

13. *1136 Tenants' Corporation v. Rothenberg & Co.* (36 A.D. 2d 804, 319 N.Y.S. 2d 1007 1st Dept. 1971). The outcome of this suit has caused a review of the procedures employed for unaudited statements and focused the attention of the profession on the need to provide engagement letters.

14. Corporations of sufficient public consequence to capital market activity must file financial reports with the SEC. Generally speaking, privately held corporations are exempt from SEC filing requirements.

15. A study of financial analysts' use of FAS 33 data by Tondkar (1983) found that as between inflation-adjusted and historical cost data supplied to test groups of analysts, the two groups were different at statistically significant levels, indicating that analysts evaluated such things as earning power and investment requirements differ-

ently. This study supported the view that the information was useful. The board, however, in withdrawing the standard, claimed that the information was not, in fact, being used.

16. Ijiri (1989) is a rare example of an exposition to modify double-entry transaction accounting to include an analysis of factors that contribute to the dynamic "momenta" of the firm, building upon the 1975 study, AAA Monograph No. 10. Another example is Koshimura's *Accounting Matrix* (1988). Mepham (1988C) and Leech (1986) also discuss the historical development of the matrix model. Cushing (1989), who evaluates the double-entry model in "A Kuhnian Interpretation of the Historical Evolution of Accounting," is less than optimistic about the model as an acceptable vehicle for the future.

17. Lee (1988) argues that in a perfectly efficient market (it has not been established that major markets such as the New York Stock Exchange are perfectly efficient), the price of every security equals its investment value. Or, the market price of a stock, for example, equals the present value of its future prospects. As she notes: "In short a perfectly efficient market is one where an amazing amount of information is fully and immediately reflected in prices."

18. *Statements on Management Advisory Services,* AICPA, Management Advisory Services Executive Committee, January 1975. E. Summers, "Academic Opportunities Related to MAS in the CPA Profession," in *Emerging Issues,* ed. G. J. Previts, Proceedings of the 1976 Alabama Accounting Research Convocation, pp. 91–111.

19. The Tenth Amendment was enacted to take effect on December 15, 1791. It states: "The powers not delegated to the United States by the Constitution, nor prohibited by it to the States, are reserved to the States respectively, or to the people."

20. Estimates of federal budget expenditures vary. A broad compendium of sources would likely result in the following breakdown during the 1980s before the events in Berlin and the former USSR: entitlement/benefits 47 percent, military 26 percent, interest on debt 14 percent, operations 5 percent, and transfers to states 6 percent.

21. The list of such influential academics is more extensive. Other notable individuals include Thomas J. Burns, Ohio State University; Paul Garner, University of Alabama; Norton Bedford, University of Illinois; Wilton T. Anderson, Oklahoma State University; Charles Zlatkovich and Glenn Welsch, University of Texas at Austin; and Maurice Moonitz, University of California at Berkeley. Several academics have also held staff or resident posts at the FASB and the SEC. For example, J. T. Ball and Reed K. Storey are senior staff at the FASB.

22. See R. S. Kaplan, "The Information Content of Financial Accounting Numbers: A Survey of Empirical Evidence," *Symposium on the Impact of Research in Financial Accounting and Disclosure on Accounting Practice,* Duke University (December 1975); and R. K. Mautz, "Some Thoughts on Applied Research," in *Bridging the Gap,* Proceedings of the 1975 Alabama Accounting Research Convocation, ed. G. J. Previts, pp. 1–14.

23. The Cohen Commission's recommendations cover the following areas: (1) role of the independent auditor in society; (2) forming an opinion on financial

presentations; (3) reporting on significant uncertainties; (4) clarifying responsibility for the detection of fraud; (5) corporate accountability and the law; (6) boundaries of the auditor's role and its extension; (7) the auditor's communication with users; (8) the education, training, and development of auditors; (9) maintaining the independence of auditors; (10) the process of establishing auditing standards; (11) regulating the profession to maintain the quality of audit practice.

Bibliography

Abdel-Khalik, A. and T. Keller, eds. 1978. *The Impact of Accounting Research on Practice and Disclosure.* Durham: Duke University Press.

Abramowitz, M. 1985. "Accountant Firms Face Tangle of Lawsuits over Negligence." *Cleveland Plain Dealer,* August 11, p. 5-D.

"Accountancy and Economics." 1909. *Journal of Accountancy,* January, p. 239.

"Accounting: A Crisis over Fuller Disclosure." 1972. *Business Week,* April 22, pp. 55–60.

"Accounting Board Is Proposed for Public Colleges." 1989. *Chronicle of Higher Education,* November 15, p. A40.

"Accounting Firms' Merger Talks Said to Be Advancing." 1989. *Wall Street Journal,* July 6, p. A12.

Ackerman, Bruce. 1975. *Economic Foundation of Property Law.* Boston: Little, Brown.

Adams, Daniel. 1817. *The Scholars Arithmetic or Federal Accountant.* Keene, NH: John Prentiss.

Aitken, J. N., Jr. 1938. "The Future Relationship of the Certified Public Accountant and the Public." In AIA, *Accounting Principle and Procedure,* pp. 200–206.

Alchian, A., and H. Demsetz. 1973. "Property Rights Paradigm." *Journal of Economic History,* Proceedings Volume, March, pp. 16–27.

Alexander, Sidney S. 1950. "Income Measurement in a Dynamic Economy." American Institute of Accountants, *Five Monographs on Business Income,* pp. 1–96.

Allen, C. E. 1927. "The Growth of Accounting Instruction since 1900." *Accounting Review,* June, pp. 150–66.

Allen, Frederick Lewis. 1931. *Only Yesterday,* New York: Harper.

American Accounting Association (AAA). 1936A. "A Statement of Objectives of the American Accounting Association." *Accounting Review,* March, pp. 1–4.

———. 1936B. "A Tentative Statement of Accounting Principles Affecting Corporate Reports." *Accounting Review,* June, pp. 187–92.

———. 1944. "Accounting Principles Underlying Financial Statements." *Accounting Review,* June, pp. 51–58.

———. 1948. "Accounting Concepts and Standards Underlying Corporate Financial Statements; 1948 Revision." *Accounting Review,* October, pp. 339–44.

———. 1957A. *Accounting and Reporting Standards for Corporate Financial Statements and Proceeding Statements and Supplements.* Madison, WI.

———. 1957B. "Dissents to the 1957 Revision." *Accounting Review,* October, pp. 544–46.

———. 1965A. Concepts and Standards Research Study Committee. 1964. "The Matching Concept." *Accounting Review,* April, pp. 368–72.

———. 1965B. Concepts and Standards Research Study Committee. 1964. "The Realization Concept." *Accounting Review,* April, pp. 312–22.

———. 1965C. "Doctoral Programs in Accounting." *Accounting Review,* April, pp. 414–21.

———. 1966A. *The American Accounting Association: Its First 50 Years.* Edited by S. A. Zeff. Evanston, IL: AAA.

———. 1966B. *A Statement of Basic Accounting Theory.* Evanston, IL: AAA.

———. 1977. *A Statement on Accounting Theory and Theory Acceptance.* Sarasota, FL: AAA.

———. 1986. *Future Accounting Education: Preparing for the Expanding Profession.* Committee on the Future Structure, Content, and Scope of Accounting Education (Special Report), *Issues in Accounting Education,* pp. 168–95.

———. 1989. *Education Monograph,* No. 10. Edited by J. J. Schultz. AAA.

American Assembly of Collegiate Schools of Business (1989–90). *Accreditation Council Policies Procedures and Standards.* St. Louis, MO.

American Association of Public Accountants (AAPA). 1906. "Collected Papers, 1906 Annual Meeting." Manuscript File. AICPA, New York.

———. 1906–15. *Year Books of Annual Meetings,* 10 vols., various publishers.

American Association of University Instructors in Accounting (AAUIA). 1917–26. *Proceedings of the American Association of University Instructors in Accounting.* New York: Arno, 1980.

American Council on Education. 1968. *College and University Business Administration.* New York: National Committee to Revise Volumes 1 & 2.

American Hospital Association. 1968. *Cost Finding and Rate Setting for Hospitals.* Chicago: American Hospital Association.

American Institute of Accountants (AIA). n.d. *Papers on Auditing Procedures,* pp. 242–44.

American Institute of Accountants. 1916–56. *Minutes of the Annual Meetings and Meetings of the Council.* Bound annually. New York: AICPA.

———. 1916–56. *Year Books of Annual Meetings.* New York: AIA.

———. 1921. "Confidential Communication–National Association of CPAs." Manuscript File. AICPA, New York.

———. 1931A. "Resume of Special Report of the Accounting Procedures Committee of the American Institute of Accountants." Manuscript File. AICPA, New York.

———. 1931B. Special Committee on Cooperation with New York Stock Exchange. "Letter to J. M. B. Hoxey." May 19. Manuscript File. AICPA, New York.

———. 1932. "Value and Limitations of Corporate Accounts and General Principles for Preparation of Reports to Stockholders." New York: AICPA. (Released subsequently as *Audits of Corporate Accounts.*)

———. 1933A. "Special Report to the Membership of the American Institute of Accountants." April 20. Manuscript File. AICPA, New York.

———. 1933B. "Statement of Certain Accounting Principles Recommended by Committee of American Institute of Accountants on Cooperation with Stock Exchanges." January, 9pp. Manuscript File. AICPA, New York.

———. 1934. *Audits of Corporate Accounts.* "Correspondence between the Special Committee on Cooperation with the Stock Exchanges, American Institute of Accountants and the Committee on Stock List of the New York Stock Exchange, 1932–4." New York: AIA.

———. ca. 1935. "How to Read a Financial Statement." Manuscript File. AICPA, New York.

———. 1936B. *Examination of Financial Statements by Independent Public Accountants.* New York: AIA.

———. 1936B. "Proceedings of the Advisory Council of State Society Presidents, January 6." New York: AICPA.

———. 1937. "Correspondence File: Sanders, Hatfield and Moore Study." New York: AICPA.

———. 1938. Papers on Accounting Principles and Procedures. New York: AIA.

———. 1939A. "Extensions of Auditing Procedure." *Journal of Accountancy,* June 1939, pp. 342–49.

———. 1939B. Papers on Auditing Procedure and Other Accounting Subjects. New York: AIA.

———. 1940. *Experiences with Extensions of Auditing Procedure and Papers on Other Accounting Subjects.* New York: AIA.

———. 1941. *Accounting, Auditing and Taxes.* New York: AIA.

———. 1943. *Accounting Problem in War Contrast Termination, Taxes and Postwar Planning.* New York: AIA.

———. 1944. *Termination and Taxes and Papers on Other Current Accounting Problems.* New York: AIA.

———. 1946. *Professional Ethics of Public Accounting.* New York: AIA.

———. 1947. *Tentative Statement of Auditing Standards—Their Generally Accepted Significance and Scope.* New York: AIA.

———. 1948. *New Responsibilities of the Accounting Profession.* New York: AIA.

———. 1949. *Accounting and Tax Problem in the Fifties.* New York: AIA.

———. 1950. *Five Monographs on Business Income.* New York: AIA.

———. 1953. *Accounting Research Bulletin,* no. 43 ("Restatement and Revision of Accounting Research Bulletins"). New York: AIA.

———. 1954. *Generally Accepted Auditing Standards: Their Significance and Scope.* New York: AIA.

American Institute of Accountants, and American Society of Certified Public Accountants. 1934. "Financial Statements Under the Securities Act and the Securities Exchange Act—Report Submitted by a Joint Committee of the American Institute of Accountants and American Society of Certified Public Accountants." August 8. Manuscript File. AICPA, New York.

American Institute of Certified Public Accountants (AICPA). 1957–66. *Minutes of the Annual Meetings.* Bound annually. New York: AICPA.

————. 1958. "Report for the Special Committee on Research." Manuscript File. AICPA, New York.

————. 1959. "Organization and Operation of Accounting Research Program and Related Activities." October. Manuscript File. AICPA, New York.

————. 1969. Tax Division. "Tax Division Views on Tax." *Journal of Accountancy*, May, pp. 79–91.

————. 1971. *The Auditor's Reporting Obligation.* Audit Research Monograph No. 1. New York: AICPA.

————. 1973. *Objectives of Financial Statements.* New York: AICPA.

————. 1974. Statement on Auditing Standards No. 4. *Quality Control Considerations for a Firm of Independent Auditors.* New York: AICPA.

————. 1975A. "Report of the Special Committee on Equity Funding." New York: AICPA.

————. 1975B. "Statements on Management Advisory Services." New York: AICPA.

————. 1976. *Standards for Professional Accounting Programs and Schools.* New York: AICPA.

————. 1977A. Annual Report of the American Institute of Certified Public Accountants. New York: AICPA.

————. 1977B. "A Response by the AICPA to the Study of the Subcommittee on Reports, Accounting and Management, U.S. Senate Committee on Government Affairs, entitled *The Accounting Establishment,*" April. New York: AICPA.

————. 1977C. Social Measurement Committee. *Measurement of Corporate Social Performance.* New York: AICPA.

————. 1978. *Education Requirements for Entry into the Accounting Profession: A Statement of AICPA Policies.* New York: AICPA.

————. 1988. *Education Requirements for Entry Into the Accounting Profession: A Statement of AICPA Policies.* 2d ed. rev. February, 33 pp.

————. 1991A. "Proposed Statement on Standards for Consulting Services." April 1. AICPA MAS Division, New York, 8pp.

————. 1991B. "Regarding Loans to and from Clients for Whom Services Are Performed Requiring Independence." Exposure Draft, July 9.

————. 1994. Report of the Special Committee on Financial Reporting. New York: AICPA.

Andersen, Arthur A. 1926. "Accountant's Function as a Business Advisor." *Journal of Accountancy*, January, pp. 17–21.

Anderson, E. H. 1962. "The Evolution of Management." *Industrial Management*, June, pp. 1–4.

Anderson, J. A. 1928. "The Historical Development of Bookkeeping in the First Half of the Nineteenth Century." Master's thesis, University of Illinois.

Anderson, William. 1881. "The Scope and Value of Accountants' Work." *The Bookkeeper*, June 7, pp. 114–16.

Andreano, R. 1962. *The Economic Impact of the American Civil War.* Cambridge: Schenkeman.

Andrews, F. B. 1939. Letter to G. O. May. July 1, 1939. CAP Correspondence File. AICPA, New York.

Andrews, T. Coleman. 1949. "Hoover Commission Disagrees on Charges in Government Accounting." *Journal of Accountancy*, March, pp. 192–99.

Andrews, Wayne. 1941. *The Vanderbilt Legend: The Story of the Vanderbilt Family, 1794–1940*. New York: Harcourt, Brace.

"The Annual Audit." 1925. *LRB & M Journal*, April, pp. 15–18.

Anthony, Robert. 1963. "Showdown on Accounting Principles." *Harvard Business Review*, May–June, pp. 99–106.

Antoni, Tito. 1977. "The Pisan Document of Philadelphia." *Accounting Historians Journal*, Spring, pp. 17–24.

Anyon, James T. 1909. "Sinking Funds and Reserve Accounts." *Journal of Accountancy*, November, pp. 185–91.

———. 1925. "Early Days in American Accountancy." *Journal of Accountancy*, January, February, and March.

"Architects of the U.S. Balance Sheet." 1932. *Fortune*, June, pp. 64–66, 101–2.

Argyris, C. 1953. *The Impacts of Budgets on People*. New York: Controllers Institute.

Armstrong, Marshall. 1971. "Organizing the Profession's Disciplinary Effort." *CPA Journal*, February, pp. 1–2, 8.

Armstrong, Peter. 1991. "The Influence of Michael Foucault on Historical Research in Accounting." *Proceedings of Third Interdisciplinary Perspectives on Accounting Conference*, University of Manchester, pp. 1–24.

Arrington, C. E., and A. G. Puxty. 1991. "Accounting Interests, and Rationality: A Communicative Relation." *Critical Perspectives on Accounting*, March, pp. 31–58.

Arthur Andersen et al. 1933. "Letter from Nine Accounting Firms to Richard Whitney." February 24, p. 4. Manuscript File. 221N. AICPA, New York.

———. 1989. "Perspectives on Education: Capabilities for Success in the Accounting Profession." Education position statement, April, 15 pp.

Arthur Andersen & Co., S.C. 1991. "Committee of Sponsoring Organizations of the Treadway Commission." *Accounting News Briefs*, May, p. 1.

"Arthur Young and Ernst Firm Plan to Merge." 1989. *Wall Street Journal*, May 19, p. A3.

Asebrook, R., and D. Carmichael. 1973. "Reporting on Forecasts: A Survey of Attitudes." *Journal of Accountancy*, August, pp. 38–48.

Ashburne, Jim G. 1958. "Five Year Professional Accounting Program." *Accounting Review*, January, pp. 106–11.

Ashton, D., and M. Bayliss. 1989. "Quantum Mechanics: The Accountant's Role in Litigation." *International Financial Law Review*, April, pp. 17–19.

Ashton, D., Trevor Hopper, and Robert Scapens. 1991. *Issues in Management Accounting*. Englewood Cliffs, NJ: Prentice Hall.

Ashton, Robert. 1974. "An Experimental Study of Internal Control Judgments." *Journal of Accounting Research*, Spring, pp. 143–57.

Aslaman, Paul, and John Duff. 1973. "Why Are Accounting Teachers So Academic?" *Journal of Accountancy*, October, pp. 47–53.

"The Atchison Disclosures." 1894. *Commercial & Financial Chronicle*, July 28, p. 135.

Auditing Standards Board. 1991. "The Meaning of 'Present Fairly in Conformity with Generally Accepted Accounting Principles' in the Independent Auditor's Report." Exposure Draft, May 31. New York: AICPA.

"Audits of Government Corporations." 1945. *Journal of Accountancy,* August, pp. 81–82.

"Audits of Government Corporations." 1945. Official Decisions and Releases. *Journal of Accountancy,* p. 152.

"Audits of Governmental Units." 1950. *Journal of Accountancy,* June, p. 464.

Babcock, Robert. 1988. *The Spinelli Family: Florence in the Renaissance, 1430–1535.* New Haven: Yale University, Beinecke Library.

Bach, G. Leland, H. J. Davidson, and R. M. Trueblood. 1961. *The Future of Accounting Education.* Pittsburgh: Carnegie Institute.

Backer, Morton, ed. 1955. *Handbook of Modern Accounting Theory.* New York: Prentice Hall.

Badger, Ralph E. 1923. "Interpreting Financial Statements." *Administration,* May, pp. 595–604.

Baggs, George E. 1928. "The Historical Development of American Bookkeeping in the Last Half of the Nineteenth Century." Master's thesis, University of Illinois.

Bailey, George. 1939. "Discussion." In AIA, *Minutes of Council Meeting,* May 5–8, 1939, pp. 17–30; 114–88.

Bailyn, Bernard, ed. 1964. *The Apologia of Robert Keayne, 1653: The Self Portrait of a Puritan Merchant.* New York: Harper & Row.

Baladouni, Vahe. 1981. "The Accounting Records of the East India Company." *Accounting Historians Journal,* Spring, pp. 67–69.

Ball, R., and P. Brown. 1968. "An Empirical Evaluation of Accounting Numbers." *Journal of Accounting Research,* Autumn, pp. 159–78.

Ball, R., and G. Foster. 1982. "Corporate Financial Reporting: A Methodological Review of Empirical Research." *Journal of Accounting Research* (Supplement), pp. 161–234.

Barden, Horace G. 1957. "What Do We Mean by Auditing Standards?" Collected Papers of the Annual Meeting. Manuscript File. AICPA, New York.

Barfour, D. M. 1853. "Operations of the Railways of Massachusetts, 1852." *Hunt's Merchants' Magazine,* May, p. 638.

Barkin, S. 1951. "Letter to the Editor." *Journal of Accountancy,* October, pp. 405–6.

Barnes, W. T. 1968. "CPAs Responsibility in Tax Practice." *Journal of Accountancy,* March, pp. 27–33.

Barnes, Wendling, Cook & O'Connor, Inc. 1991. "Washington Alert." *Tax Outlook,* Cleveland: Issue 2, p. 4.

Barr, Andrew. 1938. "Comments on 'A Statement of Accounting Principles.'" *Journal of Accountancy,* April, pp. 318–23.

———. 1959. "Disclosure in Theory and Practice." *New York Certified Public Accountant,* September, pp. 633–43.

———. 1968. "Accounting Yesterday, Today and Tomorrow." *California CPA Quarterly,* June, pp. 38–39, 41.

Barrett, E. M., and G. J. Holtz. 1972. "The Case Against One Set of Books for Financial and Tax Accounting." *Financial Executive*, September, pp. 36–42.

Barry, W. D. 1982. *A Vignetted History of Portland Business, 1632–1982*. Philadelphia: Newcomen Society.

Barzman, Sol. 1975. *Credit in Early America*. New York: National Association of Credit Management.

Baskin, J. B. 1988. "The Development of Corporate Financial Markets in Britain and the United States, 1600–1914: Overcoming Asymmetric Information." *Business History Review*, Summer, pp. 199–237.

Bass, A. W. 1927. "Cost Accounting as a Basis for Shaping Operating Policy." *NACA Bulletin*, March 1, pp. 477–92.

Battelle, L. G. 1954. *Story of Ohio Accountancy*. Columbus: Ohio Society of Certified Public Accountants.

Baxter, W. T. 1945. *The House of Hancock*. Cambridge: Harvard University Press.

———. 1946. "Credit, Bills and Bookkeeping in a Simple Economy." *Accounting Review*, April, pp. 154–66.

———. 1951. "A Colonial Bankrupt: Ebeneezer Hancock." *Bulletin of the Business Historical Society*, June, pp. 115–24.

Beard, Charles. 1913. *The Economic Interpretation of the Constitution*. New York: Macmillan.

Beaty, J., and S. C. Gwynne. 1991. "The Dirtiest Bank of All." *Time*, July 29, pp. 42–47.

Beaver, William H. 1973. "What Should Be the FASB's Objectives?" *Journal of Accountancy*, August, pp. 49–56.

Beaver, William H., and A. Rappaport. 1984. "Financial Reporting Needs More Than the Computer." *Business Week*, August 13.

Beck, Herbert C. 1903. "The Value of Auditing to the Business Man." *Annals of the American Academy of Political and Social Science*, November, pp. 433–44.

Bedford, Norton, ed. 1977. *Accountancy in the 1980's—Some Issues*. Urbana: University of Illinois.

Belda, B. J. 1970. "Reporting on Forecasts of Future Developments." *Journal of Accountancy*, June, pp. 54–58.

Belkaoui, A. 1985. *Accounting Theory*. New York: Harcourt, Brace Jovanovich.

Bell, Daniel. 1960. *The End of Ideology*. Glencoe, IL: Free Press.

Bell, Hermon F. 1959. *Reminiscences of a Certified Public Accountant*. New York: privately printed.

Bell, William H. 1923. "Audit Reports—A Tool for the Executive." *Administration*, June, pp. 727–34.

Bellamy, E. 1887. *Looking Backward, 2000–1887*. Reprint, 1926; New York: Vanguard Press.

———. 1902. *Equality*. London: William Heinemann.

Belser, F. C. 1927. "How the Universities Can Aid the Accounting Profession." *Accounting Review*, March, pp. 37–42.

Bennett, James. 1842. *The American System of Practical Book-keeping*. New York: Collins & Hannay.

Bennett, John. 1939. "Transcript of Conference with John Bennett, Attorney General of New York State, the American Institute of Accountants and the New York State Society of CPAs, January 6." New York: AICPA.

Bennett, R. J. 1922. "A Brief History of the Pennsylvania Institute of Certified Public Accountants" (PICPA). *Biographical Sketches,* pp. 41–77.

Bennett's Business College. 1889. *The Countinghouse Arithmetic.* Baltimore: W. H. Sadler.

Benninger, L. J. 1949. "The Traditional vs. the Cost Accounting Concept of Cost." *Accounting Review,* October, pp. 387–91.

———. 1950A. "A Proposed Reconciliation of Standard and Current Cost." *Accounting Review,* April, pp. 156–60.

———. 1950B. "Standard Costs for Income Determination, Control, and Special Studies." *Accounting Review,* October, pp. 378–83.

———. 1954. "Development of Cost Accounting Concepts and Principles." *Accounting Review,* January, pp. 27–37.

Benston, George. 1969. "The Effectiveness and Effects of the SEC's Accounting Disclosure Requirements." In *Economic Policies and the Regulation of Corporate Securities,* edited by Henry G. Manne. Washington, D.C.: American Enterprise Institute.

Bentley, Harry C. 1911A. *Corporate Finance and Accounting.* New York: Ronald Press.

———. 1911B. *Science of Accounts.* New York: Ronald Press.

———. 1929. *A Brief Treatise on the Origin and Development of Accounting.* New York: privately printed.

Bentley, Harry C., and R. S. Leonard. 1934–35. *Bibliography of Works on Accounting by American Authors.* Vol. 1, *1796–1900;* Vol. 2, *1900–1934.* Boston: H. C. Bentley.

Bergstrom, Kenneth. 1974. "Looking Back." *Management Accounting,* March, pp. 47–50.

Berle, A. A. 1926. "Protection of Non-voting Stock." *Harvard Business Review,* April, pp. 252–65.

———. 1927. "Management Power and Stockholders Property." *Harvard Business Review,* vol. 5, pp. 424–32.

———. 1933. "Letter to William O. Douglas." December 30. Manuscript Division, Library of Congress, William O. Douglas Papers, Box 2.

———. 1938. "Accounting and the Law." *Journal of Accountancy,* May, pp. 368–78.

———. 1954. *The Twentieth Century Capitalist Revolution.* New York: Harcourt, Brace.

———. 1963. *The American Economic Republic.* New York: Harcourt, Brace and World.

Berle, A. A., and G. Means. 1932. *The Modern Corporation and Private Property.* New York: Macmillan.

Berle, Beatrice, and Travis Jacobs, eds. 1973. *Navigating the Rapids, 1918–1971—From the Papers of Adolph A. Berle.* New York: Harcourt Brace Jovanovich.

Bernstein, Leopold. 1975. "In Defense of Fundamental Analysis." *Financial Analysts Journal,* January/February, pp. 57–61.

Bernstein, Peter L. 1992. *Capital Ideas.* New York: Free Press.

Berton, L. 1989. "FASB Group, Stung by Firms' Criticism, To Keep Tighter Rein on Rule-Making." *Wall Street Journal,* June 13, p. A6.

———. 1991A. "GAO Weighs Auditing Plan for Big Banks." *Wall Street Journal,* March 27, pp. A3, 16.

———. 1991B. "Malleable Money Men." *Wall Street Journal.* Review of *The Big Six: The Selling Out of America's Top Accounting Firms* by Mark Stevens. May 15, p. A12.

———. 1991C. "Rule Makers Confront Accounting Issue of How Institutions Value Debt Securities." *Wall Street Journal,* June 27, p. A2.

———. 1991D. "Two Associations Compete to Dominate Growth Sector: Management Accounting." *Wall Street Journal,* July 9, p. A12.

———. 1995. "All Accountants Soon May Speak the Same Language." *Wall Street Journal,* August 25, p. A15.

Berton, L., and J. B. Schiff. 1990. *The Wall Street Journal on Accounting.* Homewood, IL: Dow Jones-Irwin.

Best, Michael. 1982. "The Political Economy of Socially Irrational Products." *Cambridge Journal of Economics,* vol. 6, pp. 53–64.

———. 1990. *The New Competition: Institutions of Industrial Restructuring.* Cambridge: Harvard University Press.

Bevis, Donald. 1958. "Professional Education for Public Accounting." *Accounting Review,* July, pp. 445–59.

Bevis, Herman W. 1961. "Riding Herd on Accounting Standards." *Accounting Review,* January, pp. 9–16.

———. 1965. *Corporate Financial Reporting in a Competitive Economy.* New York: Macmillan.

Bierman, Harold. 1960. *The Capital Budgeting Decision.* New York: Macmillan.

Bird, Caroline. 1966. *The Invisible Scar.* New York: David McKay.

Blackburn, J. 1975. *George Wythe of Williamsburg.* New York: Harper & Row.

Blackie, William. 1948. "What Is Accounting For—Now?" *NACA Bulletin,* July 1, pp. 1349–78.

Blaidsell, Thomas C. 1932. *The Federal Trade Commission: An Experiment in the Control of Business.* New York: Columbia University Press.

Blight, Raymond E. 1925. "Cultural Value of Accountancy Studies." *Journal of Accountancy,* May, pp. 385–92.

Bill, George. 1945. "Audits of Government Corporations." *Journal of Accountancy,* April, pp. 336–37.

Blocker, J. G. 1936. "Budgeting in Relation to Standard Costs." *Accounting Review,* June, pp. 117–24.

Bloodworth, A. J. 1941. "Case Study in Auditing of Internal Check." In AIA 1941, pp. 10–13.

Blough, Carman G. 1937A. "The Relationship of the Securities and Exchange Commission to the Accountant." *Journal of Accountancy,* January, pp. 23–39.

———. 1937B. "Some Accounting Problems of the Securities and Exchange Commission." *New York Certified Public Accountant,* April, pp. 3–14.

————. 1939. "Accounting Reports and Their Meaning to the Public." *Journal of Accountancy*, September, pp. 162–68.

————. 1941. "The Work of the Committee on Accounting Procedure." In AIA 1941, pp. 125–36.

Boer, Germain. 1966. "Replacement Cost: A Historic Look." *Accounting Review*, January, pp. 92–97.

Bonbright, James C. 1924. "The Dangers of Shares Without Par Value." *Columbia Law Review*, May, pp. 449–68.

Bond, Frederick. 1946. "Economic Abracadabra." *Accounting Review*, April, pp. 181–98.

Boockholdt, James L. 1977. "Influence of Nineteenth and Early Twentieth Century Railroad Accounting on the Development of Modern Accounting Theory." Working Paper No. 31, July. Academy of Accounting Historians.

————. 1978. "Influence of Nineteenth and Early Twentieth Century Railroad Accounting on the Development of Modern Accounting Theory." *Accounting Historians Journal*, Spring, pp. 9–28.

————. 1983. "A Historical Perspective on the Auditor's Role: The Early Experience of the American Railroads." *Accounting Historians Journal*, Spring, pp. 69–86.

Book-Keeper. 1881. "Editorial." July 19.

Boorstin, Daniel J. 1973. *The Americans: The Democratic Experience.* New York: Vintage Books.

Booth, Benjamin. 1789. *A Complete System of Bookkeeping, by an improved mode of double entry.* London: Couchman and Fry.

Borger, Gloria. 1991. "Passing the Buck with a Smile and a Shrug." *US News & World Report*, April 1, p. 8.

Bowles, S., and H. Gintes. 1983. "The Power of Capital: On the Inadequacy of the Conception of the Capitalist Economy as Private." *Philosophical Forum*, Spring–Summer, pp. 225–45.

Boyd, Orton W. 1934. "Uniform Cost Accounting Systems Under the NRA." *Certified Public Accountant*, February, pp. 69–77.

————. 1935. "NRA and Destructive Price Cutting." *Certified Public Accountant*, November, pp. 671–76.

Bradshaw, T., and D. Vogel. 1981. *Corporations and Their Critics: Issues and Answers to the Problem of Corporate Social Responsibility.* New York: McGraw-Hill.

Brandeis, Louis. 1911. "The New Conception of Industrial Efficiency." *Journal of Accountancy*, May, pp. 35–43.

————. 1914. *Business: A Profession.* Boston: Small, Maynard.

Breberm, Robert L., Jr. 1967. "Accountants' Liability for False and Misleading Financial Statements." *Columbia Law Review*, December, pp. 1439–69.

Breeden, Richard. 1990. "Concerning Issue Involving Financial Institutions and Accounting Principles." Statement of Richard C. Breeden, Chairman of the U.S. Securities and Exchange Commission before the Committee on Banking, Housing, and Urban Affairs, United States Senate, September 10, pp. 29–30.

————. 1991. "Accounting in a Rapidly Changing World." Remarks of R. C. Breeden,

Chairman of the U.S. Securities and Exchange Commission at the 18th Annual Conference on SEC Developments, Washington, D.C., January 8, 9 pp.

Breisach, E. 1983. *Historiography*. Chicago: University of Chicago Press.

Brewer, H. Peers. 1976. "Eastern Money and Western Mortgages in the 1870s." *Business History Review*, Autumn, pp. 356–80.

Bridgman, P. W. 1945. "The Prospect for Intelligence." *Yale Review*, March, pp. 444–61.

Bricker, R. J., and G. J. Previts. 1990. "The Sociology of Accountancy: A Study of Academic and Practice Community Schisms." *Accounting Horizons*, March, pp. 1–14.

Bridenbaugh, Carl. 1966. *Cities in the Wilderness*. New York: Knopf.

Brief, Richard P. 1964. "Nineteenth Century Capital Accounting and Business Investment." Ph.D. diss., Columbia University.

———. 1966. "The Origin and Evolution of Nineteenth Century Asset Accounting." *Business History Review*, Spring, pp. 1–23.

———. 1967. "A Late Nineteenth Century Contribution to the Theory of Depreciation." *Journal of Accounting Research*, Spring, pp. 27–38.

———. 1970. "Depreciation Theory in Historical Perspective." *The Accountant*, November 26, pp. 737–39.

———. 1977. "Assets, Valuation and Matching." Proceedings of the Charles Waldo Haskins History Seminar. New York: Ross Institute, New York University.

Briloff, Abraham J. 1964. "Needed: A Revolution in the Determination and Application of Accounting Principles." *Accounting Review*, January, pp. 12–14.

———. 1967. "Dirty Pooling." *Accounting Review*, July, pp. 489–96.

———. 1968A. "Distortions Arising From Pooling of Interests Accounting." *Financial Analysts Journal*, March–April, pp. 71–80.

———. 1968B. "How to Succeed in Business Without Really Trying." *Barrons*, August 15, p. 1.

———. 1969A. "Funny Money Game." *Financial Analysts Journal*, May–June, pp. 73–79.

———. 1969B. "Much Abused Goodwill." *Barrons*, April 28, pp. 1, 3.

Broad, Samuel. 1936. "Comments." AIA, *Minutes*, pp. 79–86.

———. 1939. "Extensions of Auditing Procedure to Meet New Demands." In AIA 1939B, pp. 41–47.

———. 1941. "Auditing Standards." In AIA 1941, pp. 3–10.

Broaker, Frank, and Richard Chapman. 1897. *The American Accountants' Manual*. New York: Broaker.

Brooks, John. 1969. *Once in Golconda: A True Drama of Wall Street, 1920–1938*. New York: Harper & Row.

Brown, Isadore. 1955. "The Historical Development of the Use of Ratios in Financial Statement Analysis to 1933." Ph.D. diss., Catholic University of America.

Brown, R. Donaldson. 1958. *Some Reminiscences of an Industrialist*. Privately printed. National Automobile Collection, Detroit Public Library.

Bruchey, Stuart. 1958. "Success and Failure Factors: American Merchants in Foreign

Trade in the Eighteenth and Nineteenth Centuries." *Business History Review,* vol. 32, pp. 272–92.

———. 1965. *The Roots of American Economic Growth, 1607–1861: An Essay in Social Causation.* New York: Harper & Row.

———. 1976. *Robert Oliver and Mercantile Bookkeeping in the Early Nineteenth Century.* New York: Arno.

Brummet, R. Lee. 1970. "Accounting for Human Resources." *New York Certified Public Accountant,* July, pp. 12–15.

Brummet, R. Lee, E. Flamholtz, and W. Pyle. 1968. "Human Resource Measurement: A Challenge for Accountants." *Accounting Review,* April, pp. 217–24.

Brundage, Percival F. 1926. "Treatment of No Par Stock in New York, New Jersey and Massachusetts." *Journal of Accountancy,* April, pp. 241–56.

———. 1950. "Influence of Government Regulation on Development of Today's Accounting Practices." *Journal of Accountancy,* November, pp. 384–91.

Brush, Lauren F. 1943. "Graphic Analysis of Expense." *Accounting Review,* October, pp. 331–38.

Bryan, Lyman. 1960. "The New I.R.S. Examination." *Journal of Accountancy,* June, p. 20.

Bryant, H. S., H. D. Stratton, and S. S. Packard. 1863. *Bryant & Stratton's Counting House Bookkeeping.* New York: Ivison, Blakeman, Taylor.

Burchell, S., C. Clubb, and Anthony Hopwood. 1985. "Accounting in Its Social Context: Towards a History of Value Added in the United Kingdom." *Accounting, Organizations and Society,* vol. 10, no. 4, pp. 381–413.

Burke, Mimi. 1973. "Reporting on Consistency and Accounting Changes." *CPA Journal,* June, pp. 475–80.

Burns, James MacGregor. 1989. *The Crosswinds of Freedom.* New York: Knopf.

Burns, Thomas J., and Edward N. Coffman. 1976. *The Accounting Hall of Fame: Profiles of Thirty-Six Members.* Columbus: Ohio State University, College of Administrative Sciences.

Burton, John C. 1968. "Management Auditing." *Journal of Accountancy,* May, pp. 41–46.

———. 1971. "Criticism with Love: An Educator Views the Public Accounting Profession." *Arthur Young Journal,* Winter–Spring, pp. 77–82.

———. 1972. "Symposium on Ethics in Corporate Financial Reporting." *Journal of Accountancy,* January, pp. 46–50.

———. 1973A. "Response to 'Let's Get on with the Social Audit.'" *Business and History Society Review,* 1972–73, pp. 42–43.

———. 1973B. "Some General and Specific Thoughts on the Accounting Environment." *Journal of Accounting,* October, pp. 40–46.

———. 1974. "The SEC and the Accounting Profession: Responsibility, Authority and Progress." *Institutional Issues in Public Accounting,* edited by Robert Sterling. Arthur Young Professors' Roundtable.

———. 1975. "The Auditor of Record." Published lecture, October, University of Massachusetts, Amherst.

Burton, John C., and R. J. Sack. 1991. "Time for Some Lateral Thinking." Editorial, *Accounting Horizons,* June, pp. 118–22.

Byrne, Gilbert R. 1939. "Accounting for Depreciation on Appreciation." CAP Correspondence File. AICPA, New York.

Cadwalader, Mary H. 1975. "Charles Carroll of Carrollton: A Signer's Story." *Smithsonian,* December, pp. 64–70.

"California Fund Trips in Overseas Investment Bid." 1991. *Wall Street Journal,* April 16, p. C1.

Callender, G. S. 1902. "The Early Transportation and Banking Enterprises of the State in Relation to the Growth of Corporations." *Quarterly Journal of Economics,* November, pp. 112–62.

"CALPERS' Control Problem." 1991. *Wall Street Journal,* June 10, p. A14.

Campbell, E. G. 1941. Review of *The Vanderbilt Legend: The Story of the Vanderbilt Family, 1794–1940,* by Wayne Andrews, *Journal of Economic History,* May, pp. 111–12.

Campbell, W. B. 1928. "Cooperation between Accountants and Bankers." *Journal of Accountancy,* January, pp. 1–13.

Campfield, W. L. 1988. "When the CPA Works for a Non-CPA Organization: Reconciling Role Conflicts." Working Paper 88–1, School of Accounting, Florida International University.

Canning, John. 1929. *Economics of Accountancy.* New York: Ronald Press.

Canning, R. J. 1958. "Training for an Accounting Career." *Accounting Review,* July, pp. 359–67.

Cannon, Arthur M. 1950. "Significance of Auditing Statement 23 in Relation to Accountants' Liability." *Journal of Accountancy,* November, pp. 373–78.

———. 1956. "Challenges to Education in the Report of the Commission on Standards of Education and Experience for CPAs." Manuscript File. AICPA, New York.

Cannon, James G. 1908. "Relation of the Banker to the Public Accountant." AAPA, *Year Book,* 1908, pp. 120–26. See also *Journal of Accountancy,* November, pp. 1–6.

Caplan, Edgar. 1966. "Behavioral Assumption of the Firm." *Accounting Review,* July, pp. 496–509.

Carey, John C. 1965. *The CPA Plans for the Future.* New York: AICPA.

———. 1969. *The Rise of the Accounting Profession.* Vol. 1. New York: AICPA.

———. 1970. *The Rise of the Accounting Profession.* Vol. 2. New York: AICPA.

———. 1975A. "The CPAs Professional Heritage." Working Paper No. 1, Academy of Accounting Historians.

———. 1975B. "The CPAs Professional Heritage, Part II." Working Paper No. 5, Academy of Accounting Historians.

Carmichael, D. R. 1968. "The Bar Chris Case: A Landmark Decision on Auditor's Statutory Liability to Third Parties." *New York Certified Public Accountant,* November, pp. 780–88.

———. 1970A. "Behavioral Hypothesis of Internal Control." *Accounting Review,* April, pp. 235–45.

————. 1970B. "Opinions on Internal Control." *Journal of Accountancy*, December, pp. 34–43.

————. 1972. *The Auditor's Reporting Obligation.* New York: AICPA.

Carnegie, Andrew. 1962. *The Gospel of Wealth and Other Essays.* Edited by Edward C. Kirkland. Cambridge: Harvard University Press.

Carosso, Vincent. 1987. *The Morgans: Private Investment Bankers, 1854–1913.* Cambridge: Harvard University Press.

Carr, E. 1961. *What Is History?* New York: Vintage Books.

Carter, Arthur H. 1933. "Statement of Col. A. H. Carter, New York City Certified Public Accountant, President of the New York Society of Certified Public Accountants," in U.S. Congress, Senate, Committee on Banking and Currency, Friday, March 31, pp. 55–67.

————. 1937. "Correspondence with Committee on Accounting Procedure." CAP Correspondence File. AICPA, New York.

Carter, L. H. 1986. "U.S. Taxation: An Historical Perspective." *Florida CPA Today*, May, pp. 25–28.

Carver, Thomas Nixon. 1925. *The Present Economic Revolution in the United States.* Boston: Little, Brown.

Casler, Darwin J. 1964. "The Evolution of CPA Ethics: A Profile of Professionalization." Occasional Paper No. 12, Michigan State University, Bureau of Business and Economic Research.

Castenholtz, William B. 1919. "Invested Capital as Defined in the Federal Revenue Act and the Effect Thereof on the Accumulation of Surplus." *Proceedings of American Association of University Instructors in Accounting*, pp. 41–46.

————. 1930. *The Control of Distribution Cost and Sales.* New York: Harper & Bros.

————. 1931. "The Accountant and Changing Monetary Values." *Accounting Review*, December, pp. 282–88.

Catholic News Service. 1991. "Pope Issues Major Encyclical." *Universe Bulletin*, Cleveland, Ohio, May 10.

Catlett, G. R., and N. O. Olson. 1968. *Accounting for Goodwill.* ARS No. 10. New York: AICPA.

Cauley, W. W. 1949. "A Study of the Accounting Records of the Shelby Iron Company." Master's thesis, University of Alabama.

"Centenarian Takes an Account of His Life." 1989. *The State*, Columbia, SC, March 13.

"A Certificate of Industrial Solvency." 1915. *Survey*, March 13, p. 655.

"Certified Public Accountants." 1932. *Fortune*, June, pp. 63, 95–98.

Chamberlin, Henry T. 1940. "Recent Accounting Research." In AIA 1940, pp. 54–59.

Chamberlain, John. 1974. *A Business History of the United States.* New York: Harper & Row.

Chambers, Raymond. 1955. "Blueprint for a Theory of Accounting." *Accounting Research*, January, pp. 17–25.

————. 1956. "Some Observations on Structure of Accounting Theory." *Accounting Review*, October, pp. 584–92.

————. 1957. "Detail for a Blueprint." *Accounting Review*, April, pp. 206–15.

————. 1963. "Why Bother with Postulates?" *Journal of Accounting Research*, Spring, pp. 3–15.

————. 1966. *Accounting, Evaluation, and Economic Behavior.* Englewood Cliffs, NJ: Prentice Hall.

————. 1973. "Accounting Principles or Accounting Politics?" *Journal of Accountancy*, May, pp. 48–52.

————. 1989. "A New Era in Corporate Reporting?" *Accountants Magazine*, February, pp. 26–28.

————. 1995. *An Accounting Thesaurus: 500 Years of Accounting.* Oxford: Pergamon.

Chandler, Alfred. 1954. "The Origins of Progressive Leadership." In *The Letters of Theodore Roosevelt,* edited by E. E. Morrison. Cambridge: Harvard University Press.

————. 1977. *The Visible Hand: The Managerial Revolution in American Business.* Cambridge: Belknap.

————. 1982. "Evolution of the Large Industrial Corporation: An Evolution of the Transaction Cost Approach." *Business and Economic History*, April, pp. 116–33.

————. 1990. *Scale and Scope: The Dynamics of Industrial Capitalism.* Cambridge: Belknap Press.

————. 1992. "Organizational Capabilities and the Economic History of Industrial Enterprise." *Journal of Economic Perspectives*, Summer, pp. 79–100.

Chandler, Alfred, and Richard Tedlow. 1985. *The Coming of Managerial Capitalism: A Casebook.* Homewood, IL: Richard D. Irwin.

Chapman, S. D. 1979. "British Marketing Enterprise: The Changing Roles of Merchants, Manufacturers, and Financiers, 1700–1860." *Business History Review*, Summer, pp. 206–34.

Charles Waldo Haskins. 1923. New York: Prentice Hall.

Charnes, A. C., W. W. Cooper, and Yuji Ijiri. 1963. "Breakeven Budgeting and Programming to Goals." *Journal of Accounting Research*, Spring, pp. 16–43.

Chase, Harvey. 1902. "Uniform Municipal Accounting Applied to Boston, Baltimore, and Other Municipalities." *Proceedings*, Annual Meeting, National Municipal League, Boston.

————. 1903. "Progress of Uniform Municipal Accounting in Ohio." *Proceedings*, Annual Meeting, National Municipal League, Detroit.

————. 1904. "Practical Application of the Schedules for Uniform Municipal Reports and Accounts." *Proceedings*, Annual Meeting, National Municipal League, Chicago.

————. 1906. "Standard and Uniform Reports from Public Utilities Both Municipally and Privately Operated." *Proceedings*, Annual Meeting, National Municipal League, Atlantic City.

————. 1908. "Municipal Accounting as the Basis for Publicity of Municipal Affairs." *Proceedings*, Annual Meeting, National Municipal League, Pittsburgh.

————. 1914. "Financial Plan or Budget for the National Government." *Journal of Accountancy*, July, pp. 13–29.

Chase, Stuart. 1920. "What Is a Reasonable Profit." *Journal of Accountancy,* June, pp. 416–34.

———. 1921A. "The Challenge of Waste to Existing Industrial Creeds." *The Nation,* February 28, pp. 284–87.

———. 1921B. "Waste and Labor." *The Nation,* July 10, pp. 67–72.

———. 1923. "The Miners Present a Plan." *New Republic,* June 20, pp. 93–95.

———. 1925A. "The Waste of Production: The Tragedy of Waste." *New Republic,* August 3, pp. 282–86.

———. 1925B. "Soup, Soap, and Shoes." *The Nation,* December 23, pp. 728–29.

———. 1926A. "The Dogma of 'Business First.'" *Harpers Monthly Magazine,* September, pp. 481–89.

———. 1926B. "Henry Ford's Utopia." *New Republic,* July 21, pp. 53–55.

———. 1929. "Men and Machines: The Balance Sheet." *New Republic,* April 3, pp. 191–96.

Chatfield, Michael. 1974. *A History of Accounting Thought.* Hinsdale, IL: Dryden.

Chatfield, Michael, and R. Vangermeersch. 1996. *The History of Accounting: An International Encyclopedia.* New York: Garland.

Chatters, C. H. 1935. "How Accountants Can Serve Municipalities." *Journal of Accountancy,* January, pp. 42–53.

———. 1939. "Present and Future of Governmental Accounting." *Accounting Review,* March, pp. 48–51.

Chatov, Robert. 1975. *Corporate Financial Reporting.* New York: Free Press.

Chenok, P. B. 1991. "The FASB—Its Mission and Agenda." In *Financial Reporting and Standard Setting,* edited by G. J. Previts. pp. 10–12. New York: AICPA.

Chiba, Junichi. 1987. *British Company Accounting, 1844–1885, and Its Influence on the Modernization of Japanese Financial Accounting.* Tokyo: Moriyama Bookstore.

Chow, Chee. 1982. "The Demand for External Auditing: Size, Debt, and Ownership Influences." *Accounting Review,* April, pp. 272–91.

Church, A. Hamilton. 1913. "On the Introduction of Interest in Manufacturing Cost." *Journal of Accountancy,* April, pp. 236–40.

———. 1914. *The Science and Practice of Management.* New York: Engineering Magazine.

Clark, J. Maurice. 1923. *Studies in the Economics of Overhead Cost.* Chicago: University of Chicago Press.

Clark, John B. 1900. "Trusts." *Political Science Quarterly,* June, pp. 181–95.

Cleveland, Frederick G. 1905. "The Relation of Auditing to Public Control." *Annals of the American Academy of Political and Social Science,* November, pp. 53–68.

———. 1906. "Municipal Credit and Accounting Reform." *Journal of Accountancy,* June, pp. 109–17.

Clews, Henry. 1887. *Twenty-Eight Years in Wall Street.* New York: Irving.

———. 1900. *The Wall Street Point of View.* New York: Silver, Burdett & Co.

———. 1906. "Publicity and Reform in Business." *Annals of the American Academy of Political and Social Science,* July, pp. 143–54.

———. 1908. *Fifty Years in Wall Street.* New York: Irving.

Cloyd, H. 1979. "George Washington as an Accountant." *Accounting Historians Journal,* Spring, pp. 85–89.

Coase, R. 1937. "The Nature of the Firm." *Econometrica,* November, pp. 386–405.

"The Cochran Thesis: A Critique in Statistical Analysis." 1964. *Journal of American History,* June, pp. 77–89.

Cochran, Thomas C. 1959. *Basic History of American Business.* Princeton: Van Nostrand.

———. 1961. "Did the Civil War Retard Industrialization?" *Mississippi Valley Historical Review,* September, pp. 197–210.

———. 1967. "The History of a Business Society." *Journal of American History,* June, pp. 5–18.

Cochran, Thomas, and William Miller. 1942. *The Age of Enterprise.* New York: Macmillan.

Coe, T. L., and B. D. Merino. 1987. *Future of Accounting Education.* Denton: University of North Texas.

Coenenberg, A. C., and Hanns-Martin Schoenfeld. 1990. "The Development of Managerial Accounting in Germany." *Accounting Historians Journal,* December, pp. 95–112.

Cohen, Manuel. 1964. "Current Developments at the SEC." Address at the Annual Meeting of the American Accounting Association, September 1. New York: AICPA.

Cohen, S. S. 1991. "The Death of Securities Regulation." *Wall Street Journal,* January 17, p. A12.

Cohen, Sol. 1968. "The Industrial Education Movement, 1906–1917." *American Quarterly,* Spring, pp. 95–110.

Cole, William M. 1908. *Accounts: Their Construction and Interpretation.* Boston: Houghton Mifflin.

———. 1909. "The Rise of Accountancy." *Journal of Accountancy,* February, pp. 295–96.

———. 1911. "Accounting Methods for Determining Costs and Prices." *Bulletin of the American Economic Association,* pp. 124–35.

———. 1936. "Theories of Cost." *Accounting Review,* March, pp. 4–9.

Coleman, A. R., W. G. Shenkir, and W. E. Stone. 1974. "Accounting in Colonial Virginia: A Case Study." *Journal of Accountancy,* July, pp. 32–43.

Colinson, R. 1683. *Idea Rationaria or The Perfect Accomptant.* Edinburgh: Lindsay, Kniblo, van Solingen and Colmar.

Collier, P., and D. Horowitz. 1987. *The Fords: An American Epic.* New York: Summit Books.

Collier, William M. 1900. *The Trusts: What Can We Do with Them? What Can They Do for Us?* New York: Baker and Taylor.

Collins, Clem. 1938. "Address to the Mountain States Accounting Conference, May 31." Manuscript File. AICPA. New York.

———. 1939. "Accounting in the Public Interest." May 1. Manuscript File. AICPA, New York.

Commager, Henry S. 1950. *The American Mind.* New Haven: Yale University Press.

Commission on Auditors' Responsibilities (CAR). 1978. *Final Report of the Commission on Auditors' Responsibilities.* New York: AICPA.

Commission on Professional Accounting Education. 1983. *A Postbaccalaureate Education Requirement for the CPA Profession.* July, p. 66. New York: AICPA.

Committe, B. E. 1990. "The Delegation and Privatization of Financial Accounting Rulemaking Authority in the United States of America." *Critical Perspectives on Accounting,* no. 1, pp. 145–66.

Committee on Accounting Procedure (CAP). 1939. CAP Correspondence File 1939. AICPA, New York.

Committee on History. 1949A. "Early Development of Accounting in New York State." *New York Certified Public Accountant,* March, pp. 157–62.

———. 1949B. "The New York State Society of Certified Public Accountants." *New York Certified Public Accountant,* May, pp. 327–29.

———. 1953A. "The Incorporators of the New York State Society of Certified Public Accountants." *New York Certified Public Accountant,* March, pp. 217–21, 232.

———. 1953B. "The School of Commerce, Accounts and Finance of New York University." *New York Certified Public Accountant,* April, pp. 260–62.

———. 1954. "Is Accounting History Important?" *New York Certified Public Accountant,* August, pp. 511–13, 518.

———. 1956. "The City College of New York, a History of Its Beginnings." *New York Certified Public Accountant,* November, pp. 663–70.

"Committee Recommends Change in Short Form Certificate." 1948. *Journal of Accountancy,* November, pp. 389–91.

Commons, J. R. 1924. *Legal Foundations of Capitalism.* New York: Macmillan.

———. 1959. *Institutional Economics.* Madison: University of Wisconsin Press.

———. 1963. *Myself.* Madison: University of Wisconsin Press.

"Competition Comes to Accounting." 1978. *Fortune,* July 17, pp. 88–94, 96.

"Compulsory Book-Keeping." 1881. *The Book-Keeper,* October 26, p. 120.

Conant, M. 1974. *The Constitution and Capitalism.* St. Paul, MN: West.

Condon, Thomas J. 1968. *New York Beginnings: The Commercial Origins of New Netherlands.* New York: New York University Press.

Congressional Record 1978. "The Public Accounting Regulatory Act." House of Representatives, Friday, June 16, vol. 124, p. 93.

Connor, Jos. E. 1985. "Accounting Firm Questionnaire." Letter and information, 55 pp., Exhibits A to F. October 7.

Conrad, J. L. 1984. "Entrepreneurial Objectives, Organizational Design, Technology, and the Cotton Manufactory of Almy and Brown, 1789–1797." *Business and Economic History,* pp. 7–19.

Cook, E. M. 1984. Review of *Labor in a New Land: Economy and Society in Seventeenth-Century Springfield,* by Stephen Innes. In *Business History Review,* Autumn, pp. 433–35.

Cook, J. Michael. 1996. Correspondence with Arthur Levitt, May 20, Norwalk, CT.

Cooke, Alistair. 1973. *America.* New York: Knopf.

Cooper, David J., and Michael J. Sherer. 1984. "The Value of Corporate Accounting

Reports: Arguments for a Political Economy of Accounting." *Accounting, Organizations and Society,* vol. 13, no. 3, pp. 251–61.

Cooper, Ernest. 1888. "What is Profit of A Company?" *The Accountant.* November 10, pp. 740–46. Reprinted in *The Late Nineteenth Century Debate over Depreciation, Capital and Income,* edited by R. Brief. New York: Arno, 1976.

Cooper, J. B. 1945. "Accounting by Causes vs. Accounting by Accounts." *NACA Bulletin,* December 15, pp. 315–34.

Cooper, John A. 1907A. "Draft of a Model CPA Act to Create a State Board of Accountancy and to Prescribe Its Powers and Duties to Provide for the Examination of and Issuance of Certificates to Qualified Accountants and to Provide a Penalty for Violation of This Act." AAPA, *Year Book,* 1907, pp. 218–20.

———. 1907B. "Draft of a Model CPA Law to Regulate the Profession." AAPA, *Year Book,* 1907, pp. 215–18.

———. 1907C. "Professional Ethics." *Journal of Accountancy,* December, pp. 81–94; See also AAPA, *Year Book,* 1907, pp. 133–145.

———. 1913. "Federal Relations: Advancement and Regulation of the Profession." *Journal of Accountancy,* January, pp. 1–9.

———. 1914. "Should Accountants Advertise?" *Journal of Accountancy,* August, pp. 85–94.

"Coopers & Lybrand to Pay $20 Million in FDIC Settlement." 1991. *Wall Street Journal,* July 5, p. B6.

Corfias, John. 1973. *125 Years of Education for Business: The History of Dyke College, 1848–1973.* Cleveland: privately printed.

Couchman, Charles B. 1921. "Classification of Surplus." *Journal of Accountancy,* October, pp. 265–78.

———. 1924. "Principles Governing the Amounts Available for Distribution of Dividends." *Journal of Accountancy,* August, pp. 81–97.

———. 1928. "Limitations of the Present Balance Sheet." *Journal of Accountancy,* October, pp. 253–69.

———. 1935. Letter to G. O. May re RMA, January 21. May Papers, AIA File 35. Price Waterhouse Library, New York.

———. 1939A. "The Haunted Balance Sheet—Address at the Third Annual Accounting Conference of the Edison Electric Institute." November 15, Manuscript File. AICPA, New York.

———. 1939B. "Memorandum Depreciation on Appreciation." CAP Correspondence File. AICPA, New York.

Coulson, E. 1989. "Perspective after One Year." *Research in Accounting Regulation,* pp. 185–90.

Counts, George S. 1922. *The Selective Character of American Secondary Education.* Chicago: University of Chicago Press.

Cousins, Norman. 1991. "A Single Voice; The Writer as Leader." *Phi Kappa Phi Journal,* Winter, pp. 10.

"CPAs and Their Legal Affairs." 1985. *Public Accounting Report,* August, p. 7.

Cowan, A. L. 1990. "S&L Backlash Against Accountants." *New York Times,* July 31, pp. C1–C5.

Crandell, J. Chester. 1938. "Principles Related to Inventory Valuation." In AIA, 1938, pp. 21–25.

———. 1939. "Statement." AIA, *Minutes of Council Meeting*, 1939, pp. 142–44.

"Creature of Congress." 1988. Editorial. *Wall Street Journal*, November 22, p. A20.

Crittenden, S. W. 1877. *An Elementary Treatise on Book-keeping by Single and Double Entry*. Philadelphia: W. S. Fortescue.

Cronhelm, F. W. 1818. *Double Entry by Single: A New Method of Book-Keeping*. London: Bensley and Sons–Longman.

Crowther, Samuel. 1926. "Henry Ford: Why I Favor Five Days' Work for Six Days' Pay." *World's Work*, October, pp. 13–16.

Crum, R. P. 1982. "Value-Added Taxation: The Roots Run Deep into Colonial and Early America." *Accounting Historians Journal*, Fall, pp. 28–42.

Cushing, Barry. 1989. "A Kuhnian Interpretation of the Historical Evolution of Accounting." *Accounting Historians Journal*, December, pp. 1–41.

Cyert, R. M., and J. G. March. 1963. *A Behavioral Theory of the Firm*. Englewood Cliffs, NJ: Prentice Hall.

Dahlberg, Jane S. 1966. *The New York Bureau of Municipal Research*. New York: New York University Press.

Daily, R. A. 1971. "The Feasibility of Reporting Forecasted Information." *Accounting Review*, October, pp. 686–92.

Daines, H. C. 1929. "The Changing Objectives of Accounting." *Accounting Review*, June, pp. 94–110.

Davidson, H. Justin. 1970. "Accreditation of CPA Specialists." *New York Certified Public Accountant*, June, pp. 455–61.

Davidson, Sidney. 1963A. "The Day of Reckoning—Management Analysis and Accounting Theory." *Journal of Accounting Research*, Autumn, pp. 117–26.

———. 1963B. "Old Wine into New Bottles." *Accounting Review*, April, pp. 278–84.

Davidson, Sidney, C. P. Stickney, and R. Weil. 1984. *The Language of Business*. 6th ed. Englewood Cliffs, NJ: Prentice Hall.

Davies, W. Sanders. 1898. "Professional Accountants Not Detectives." *Business*, January, pp. 33–34.

———. 1926. "Genesis, Growth and Aims of the Institute." *Journal of Accountancy*, August, pp. 105–11.

Davis, G. C. 1962. "The Transformation of the Federal Trade Commission." *Mississippi Valley Historical Review*, December, pp. 437–55.

Davis, Lance E. 1958. "Stock Ownership in the Early New England Textile Industry." *Business History Review*, Spring, pp. 204–22.

———. 1960. "The New England Textile Mills and the Capital Markets: A Study of Industrial Borrowing, 1840–1860." *Journal of Economic History*, March, pp. 1–28.

Davis, T. C. 1950. "How the DuPont Organization Appraises Its Performance." *Financial Management Series*, American Management Association, pp. 3–7.

Day, J. 1829. "Original Papers in Relation to a Course in Liberal Education (The Yale Report of 1828)." *American Journal of Science and the Arts*, January, pp. 299–320.

Dean, Joel. 1937. "Correlation Analysis of Cost Variation." *Accounting Review,* March, pp. 55–60.

DeAngelo, Linda. 1981. *The Auditor Client Contractual Relationship.* Ann Arbor, MI: UMI Research Press.

"Dear Woman." 1857. *Harper's Weekly,* January 3, p. 2.

DeBedts, J. 1964. *The New Deal's SEC: The Formative Years.* New York: Columbia University Press.

"Debt Statement June 30." 1894. *Commercial & Financial Chronicle.* July 7, pp. 14–15.

Degler, Carl N. 1964. "American Political Parties and the Rise of the City: An Interpretation." *Journal of American History,* June, pp. 41–59.

———. 1970. *The New Deal.* Chicago: Quadrangle Books.

Dein, Raymond C. 1955. "Price Level Adjustments: Fetish in Accounting." *Accounting Review,* January, pp. 3–24.

———. 1956. "Rejoinder to Professor Husband." *Accounting Review,* January, pp. 58–63.

———. 1961. "A Glance Backward at Research in Accounting." *Accounting Review,* January, pp. 1–8.

Deinzer, Harvey T. 1965. *Development of Accounting Thought.* New York: Holt, Rinehart and Winston.

Deloitte, Haskins & Sells. 1985. "A Report for Congress and the Public." 35 pp. September.

"Demand for Compulsory Book-Keeping." 1881. *The Book-Keeper,* November 22, pp. 120–21.

Deming, W. Edwards. 1986A. *Out of the Crisis.* Cambridge: MIT Press.

———. ed. 1986B. *Statistical Method from the Viewpoint of Quality Control.* By W. A. Shewhart. New York: Dover.

"Depreciation and the Price Level." 1948. *Accounting Review,* April, pp. 115–36. Remarks of J. Dohr, H. C. Greer, E. L. Kohler, W. A. Paton, and M. Peloubet.

Demond, C. W. 1951. *Price Waterhouse and Company in America.* New York: Price Waterhouse.

Devine, Carl. 1960. "Research Methodology and Accounting Theory Formation." *Accounting Review,* July, pp. 387–99.

———. 1964. Reviewer's Corner: *A Behavioral Theory of the Firm. Journal of Accounting Research,* Autumn, pp. 197–220.

Dewey, John. 1900. *The School and Society.* Chicago: University of Chicago Press.

———. 1910. *How We Think.* New York: Heath.

———. 1918. "A New Social Science." *New Republic,* April 6, pp. 292–94.

———. 1922. *Human Nature and Conduct.* New York: Modern Library.

———. 1929. "Philosophy." In *Research in the Social Sciences,* edited by W. Gee. New York: Macmillan.

———. 1939. *Intelligence in the Modern World: John Dewey's Philosophy.* Edited by Joseph Ratner. New York: Modern Press.

Dewey, John. 1978. *The Middle Works, 1899–1924.* Edited by Jo Ann Boydston. Carbondale: Southern Illinois University Press.

Dewey, John, and James H. Tufts. 1908. *Ethics.* In Dewey 1978, vol. 5.

Dickinson, Arthur L. 1902. "The Duties and Responsibilities of the Public Accountant." *Commerce, Finance and Accounts,* April, pp. 23–27.

———, ed. 1904A. *Official Record of the Congress of Accountants at St. Louis.* New York: Federation of Societies of Public Accountants.

———. 1904B. "Profits of a Corporation." *Financial Record, Lawyers' and Accountants' Manual,* November 2, pp. 38–43.

———. 1905. "Some Special Points in Accounting Practice." *Business World,* April, pp. 157–61, and May, pp. 233–36.

———. 1911. "The Fallacy of Including Interest and Rent as Part of Manufacturing Cost." *Journal of Accountancy,* December, pp. 588–93.

———. 1914. *Accounting Practice and Procedure.* New York: Ronald Press.

Dicksee, Lawrence R. 1905. *Auditing: A Practical Manual for Auditors.* Edited by R. H. Montgomery. New York: Ronald Press.

Dillon, Gadis J. 1978. "Corporate Asset Revaluations: 1925–34." *Accounting Historians Journal,* Spring, pp. 1–17.

"Discussion of the Report of the Committee on Federal Legislation and FTC and FRB Proposals for Accounting Registration." 1916. AIA, *Minutes,* pp. 106–31.

"Dispraise of Appreciation." 1932. *Accounting Review,* December, pp. 307–9.

Dixon, Arthur J. 1977. "Commentary on the Metcalf Committee Report." *CPA Journal,* June, pp. 11–18.

Dixon, Robert L. 1940. "Fixed and Variable Costs. *Accounting Review,* June 1940, pp. 218–22.

———. 1943. "The Need for a Statement of the Principles Underlying Cost Accounting," *Accounting Review,* July, pp. 256–58.

Dodd, Donald, and W. S. Dodd. 1976. *Historical Statistics of the United States, 1790–1970.* Vol. 2, *Midwest.* Tuscaloosa: University of Alabama Press.

Dodge v. Ford Motor Company. 1919. 204 Mich. 170 N.W., 668, *Corporations,* pt. 7, pp. 782–85

Dohr, James L. 1932. "Budgetary Control and Standard Costs in Industrial Accounting." *Accounting Review,* March, pp. 31–33.

———. 1941. "The Use of Accounting Data By Economists." In AIA 1941, pp. 88–95.

———. 1948. "Depreciation and Price Level." *Accounting Review,* April, pp. 115–18.

Donnelly, B. 1987. "Efficient-Market Theorists Are Puzzled by Recent Gyrations in Stock Market." *Wall Street Journal,* October 23, p. 8.

Dopuch, N., and Ronen, J. 1991. Group Statement of J. Demski, N. Dopuch, B. Lev, J. Ronen, G. Searfoss, and S. Sunder entitled "Statement on the State of Academic Accounting." 6 pp. unpublished. Cover letter dated April 22.

Dorfman, Joseph. 1946. *The Economic Mind in American Civilization, 1865–1918.* New York: Viking.

———. 1959. *History of Economic Thought.* Vol. 3, *The Economic Mind in American Civilization, 1918–1933.* New York: Viking.

Douglas, William O. 1933. Draft Letter to *Atlantic Monthly,* Manuscript Division, Library of Congress, William O. Douglas Papers, Box 31, Washington, D.C.

———. 1934. Letter to A. A. Berle, January 3. Manuscript Division, Library of Congress, William O. Douglas Papers, Box 2, Washington, D.C.

———. 1936A. Address Before the Bond Club, January 7. 8 pp. . Manuscript File. *721U, AICPA, New York.

———. 1936B. Handwritten Note Regarding Memorandum on HR 4314 Submitted by G. O. May to Samuel Rayburn. Manuscript Division, Library of Congress, William O. Douglas Papers. Washington, D.C.

———. 1974. *Go East Young Man.* New York: Random House.

Dreiser, H. n.d. *A Brief History of the University of Chicago Graduate School of Business.* Chicago: University of Chicago Press.

Drucker, Peter F. 1947. *Political Problems of American Capitalism.* Toronto: Heinemann.

———. 1948. *The New Society.* New York: Harper & Row.

———. 1976. *The Unseen Revolution: How Pension Fund Socialism Came to America.* New York: Harper & Row.

DuBoff, R. B. 1980. "Business Demand and the Development of the Telegraph in the United States, 1844–1860." *Business History Review,* Winter, pp. 459–79.

DuBoff, R. B., and E. S. Herman. 1989. "The Promotional Financial Dynamic of Merger Movements: A Historical Perspective." *Journal of Economic Issues,* March, pp. 107–33.

Dugger, William M. 1983. "The Transaction Cost Analysis of Oliver E. Williamson: A New Synthesis?" *Journal of Economic Issues,* March, pp. 95–114.

———. 1989. *Radical Institutionalism: Contemporary Voices.* New York: Greenwood Press.

Duggan, E. P. 1979. Review of *Before the Industrial Revolution: European Society and Economy, 1000–1700,* by Carlo M. Cipolla. *Business History Review,* Spring, pp. 140–41.

Duncan, James. 1911. "Efficiency." *Journal of Accountancy,* May, pp. 26–34.

Duncan, John C. 1914. "Some Scientific and Educational Problems of the Accountancy Profession." AAPA, *Year Book,* 1913–14, pp. 134–49. See also *Journal of Accountancy,* October, pp. 260–75.

Dunlop, Anna B. 1968. "New Old Books." *Accountant's Magazine,* July, pp. 358–61.

Dunn, Homer A. 1923. "Reorganizing the Institute." *Certified Public Accountant,* October, pp. 261–80.

Durkee, Rodney S. 1939. "What Management Expects of the Auditor." In AIA 1939B, pp. 31–34.

Dykema, Frank E. 1976. "American Business and Businessmen's Problems in 1776." Western Economic and Business Historians Meeting, April 30, Tempe, Arizona.

"The Ebb Tide: A Survey of International Finance." 1991. Supplement Section, *The Economist,* April 27, 46pp.

"Economists and Costs." 1934. *Accounting Review,* September, pp. 258–61.

Edelman, Jacob. 1942. *Securities Regulation in the 48 States.* Chicago: Council on Government.

———. 1964. *The Symbolic Use of Politics.* Urbana: University of Illinois Press.

Eden, R. H., ed. 1989. *The New Deal and Its Legacy.* New York: Greenwood.

Edey, H. C. 1956. "British Company Accounting and the Law, 1844–1900." In *Studies in the History of Accounting,* edited by A. C. Littleton and B. S. Yamey. Homewood, IL: Richard D. Irwin.

"Editorial." 1900. *Business,* May, pp. 201–2.

Edwards, Edgar, and Philip Bell. 1961. *The Theory and Measurement of Business Income.* Berkeley and Los Angeles: University of California Press.

Edwards, Franklin, ed. 1979. *Issues in Financial Regulation.* New York: McGraw-Hill.

Edwards, George W. 1939. *The Evolution of Finance Capitalism.* New York: Macmillan. Reprint, New York: Augustus M. Kelley, 1967.

Edwards, James Don. 1960. *History of Public Accounting in the United States.* East Lansing: Bureau of Business and Economic Research, Michigan State University.

Edwards, James Don, and P. J. Mirtanti. 1987. "The AICPA: A Professional Institution in a Dynamic Society." *Journal of Accountancy,* May, p. 38.

Edwards, J. R., ed. 1980. *British Company Legislation and Company Accounts, 1844– 1976.* 2 vols. New York: Arno.

———. 1991. "The Process of Accounting Innovation: The Publication of Consolidated Accounts in Britain in 1910." *Accounting Historians Journal,* December, pp. 113–32.

———. 1992. "Industrial Organization and Accounting Information: Charcoal Iron Making in England, 1690–1783." *Management Accounting Research,* June, pp. 151–69.

———, ed. 1994. *Twentieth-Century Accounting Thinkers.* London: Routledge.

Edwards, J. R., T. Boyns, and M. Anderson. 1995. "British Cost Accounting Development: Continuity and Change." *Accounting Historians Journal,* December, pp. 1–41.

Eggleston, D. C. 1911. "A Municipal Cost System." *Journal of Accountancy,* December, pp. 573–87.

Eichner, A. S. 1978. Review of *The Visible Hand: The Managerial Revolution in American Business,* by Alfred Chandler. *Business History Review.* Spring, pp. 98–101.

Eldridge, H. J. 1954. *The Evolution of the Science of Bookkeeping.* 2d ed. Reprint, Osaka: Nihon Shoseki, 1975.

Elliot, Robert K. 1992. "The Third Wave Breaks on the Shores of Accounting." *Accounting Horizons,* June, pp. 61–85.

———. 1994. "Confronting the Future Choices for the Attest Function." *Accounting Horizons,* September, pp. 106–24.

Elliott, Robert K., and J. R. Rogers. 1972. "Relating Statistical Sampling to Audit Objectives." *Journal of Accountancy,* July, pp. 46–55.

Elwell, F. H. 1917. "Report of the Committee on Standardization." *Proceedings of the American Association of University Instructors in Accounting,* pp. 48–52.

Emerson, Harrison. 1911. "The Fundamental Truth of Scientific Management." *Journal of Accountancy,* May, pp. 17–25.

Engelbourg, Saul. 1980. *Power and Morality: American Business Ethics, 1840–1914.* Westport, CT: Greenwood.

Engstrom, J. H., and R. A. Shockley. 1985. "Financial Reporting for the Georgia Colony." *Accounting Historians Journal,* Fall, pp. 43–58.

Epstein, M. J. 1978. *The Effect of Scientific Management on the Development of the Standard Cost System.* New York: Arno.

Ernst & Ernst. 1976. *Accounting under Inflationary Conditions.* Cleveland, OH: Ernst & Ernst.

———. 1977A. *FASB Conceptual Framework: Issues and Implications.* Cleveland, OH: Ernst & Ernst.

———. 1977B. *Social Responsibility Disclosure: 1977 Survey of Fortune Five Hundred Annual Reports.* Cleveland, OH: Ernst & Ernst.

"Ernst & Young Will Pay $1.5 Million to Settle Case." 1991. *Wall Street Journal,* April 29, p. B2.

Eskey, K. 1991. "No Regulations Will Remedy Bad Judgments of Lenders." Commentary. *Cleveland Plain Dealer,* August 4, p. 4E.

Esquerre, Paul J. 1920. *Applied Theory of Accounts.* 2d ed. New York: Ronald Press.

———. 1921. "Some Aspects of Professional Accounting." *Administration,* July, pp. 102–7.

———. 1925. "Resources and Their Application." *Journal of Accountancy,* May, pp. 424–30.

———. 1928. "Philosopher-Accountant Takes Inventory of Soul of the Profession." *American Accountant,* July, pp. 19–22.

Estes, Ralph. 1970. "Accountants' Social Responsibility." *Journal of Accountancy,* January, pp. 40–43.

———. 1972. "Socioeconomic Accounting." *Accounting Review,* April, pp. 284–90.

Etor, J. R. 1973. "Some Problems in Accounting History, 1830–1900." *Business Archives,* June, pp. 38–46.

Eversole, H. B. 1942. "Concerning the Perpetuation of Accounting Fallacies in the Classroom." *Journal of Accountancy,* February, pp. 143–45.

Ezzamel, M., K. Hoskin, and R. Macve. 1990. "Managing It All By Numbers: A Review of Johnson and Kaplan's *Relevance Lost.*" *Accounting and Business Research,* pp. 153–66.

F. W. Lafrentz & Co. 1949. *A Half Century of Accounting.* New York: F. W. Lafrentz.

Fabricant, Solomon. 1936. "Revaluation of Fixed Assets, 1925–1934." Bulletin No. 62. National Bureau of Economic Research, December 7, 11 pp. Reprinted in Solomon Fabricant, *Studies in Social and Private Accounting.* New York: Garland, 1982.

Faircloth, A. 1988. "The Importance of Accounting to the Shakers." *Accounting Historians Journal,* Fall, pp. 99–129.

Farr, Anderson F. 1933. "Give the Stockholder the Truth: How American Finance Can Restore Confidence." *Scribners Magazine,* vol. 93, pp. 228–34.

Faulkner, Harold U. 1951. *The Economic History of the United States—The Decline of Laissez Faire.* New York: Rinehart.

Federal Reserve Board. 1917. *Uniform Accounting.* Washington, D.C.: GPO. Reprinted from *Federal Reserve Board Bulletin,* April. Reprinted in *Approved Methods for the Preparation of Balance Sheet Statements.* Washington, D.C.: GPO, 1918.

————. 1929. *Verification of Financial Statements.* Washington, D.C.: GPO.

Federal Trade Commission. 1916. *Fundamentals of a Cost System for Manufacturers.* Washington, D.C.: GPO.

————. 1918. "A System of Accounts for Retail Merchants." Washington, D.C.: GPO.

————. 1933. *Federal Securities Act Registration—Statement Form.* Washington, D.C.: GPO.

————. 1939. "Discussion of Court Decisions and a Summary of Formal Actions Taken by the Federal Trade Commission Under Sections 7 and 8 of the Clayton Act," in *TNEC,* Verbatim Record, March 30, pp. 30–43.

————. 1974A. *Report on the Copper Industry.* Washington, D.C.: GPO.

————. 1947B. *Report on the Sulphur Industry and International Cartels.* Washington, D.C.: GPO.

————. 1948A. *Report on the International Equipment Cartel.* Washington, D.C.: GPO.

————. 1948B. *Report on the International Steel Cartels.* Washington, D.C.: GPO.

————. 1950A. *Report on the Fertilizer Cartel.* Washington, D.C.: GPO.

————. 1950B. *Report on the International Cartels in the Alkai Industry.* Washington, D.C.: GPO.

"Federation of Associations of Public Accountants." 1903. *Commerce, Accounts and Finance,* January, p. 8.

Fels, Rendig. 1951. "American Business Cycles, 1865–79." *American Economic Review,* June, pp. 325–49.

Ferrara, William L. 1963. " 'Relevant Costing': Two Points of View." *Accounting Review,* October, pp. 719–22.

Fertig, Paul E. 1960. "Organization of an Accounting Program." *Accounting Review,* April, pp. 190–96.

Fetter, Frank A. 1939. "Testimony of Frank A. Fetter of Princeton University." Temporary National Economic Committee, *Verbatim Record,* February 28, pp. 205–14.

Financial Accounting Foundation. 1977. "The Structure of Establishing Financial Accounting Standards: Report of the Structure Committee." Russell E. Palmer, Chairman.

Financial Accounting Standards Board. 1976. "An Analysis of Income Related to the Conceptual Framework for Financial Accounting and Reporting: Elements of Financial Statements and Their Measurement." *Discussion Memorandum.* Stamford, CT: FASB.

————. 1991A. *Accounting for Income Taxes.* Exposure Draft, No 104-A, June 5.

————. 1991B. *Accounting for Income Taxes—Deferral of the Effective Date of FASB Statement No. 96.* Exposure Draft, No 104-C, June 17.

Financial Executives Institute. 1988. "Business Roundtable Publishes Survey on FASB Standard Setting Process." *FEI Briefing,* November, p. 4.

————. 1990. "Legislation Passes House, Expand Auditor Responsibility to Report on Internal Controls and on Illegal Activities." *FEI Alert,* September 28.

————. 1991. "Public Interest in Internal Control Issues Escalate." *FEI Alert,* March 25.

Firmin, Peter A. 1957. "Educating Tomorrow's Accountant Today." *Accounting Review*, October, pp. 569–75.

Fisher, F. J. 1976. Review of *The Ledger of John Smythe, 1538–1550*, edited by Jean Vanes. In *Economic History Review*, February, p. 151.

Fisher, F. S. 1933. "Legal Regulation of Accounting." *Journal of Accountancy*, January, pp. 9–29.

Fisher, Irving. 1906. *The Nature of Capital and Income*. New York: Macmillan.

———. 1930. *The Stock Market Crash—and After*. New York: Macmillan.

Fitch, John A. 1914. "Ford of Detroit and His Ten Million Dollar Profit Sharing Plan." *Survey*, February 7, pp. 545–50.

———. 1915. "Absentee Ownership of Industry on the Stand in New York." Vol. 18, "Probing the Causes." *Survey*, January 30, pp. 467–69.

Flamhotz, Eric G. 1972. "A Field Study Assess the Validity of Human Resource Accounting." *Empirical Research in Accounting*, pp. 241–60.

Flegm, Eugene H. 1984. *Accounting: How to Meet the Challenges of Relevance and Regulation*. New York: John Wiley and Sons.

———. 1991. Correspondence with Oscar S. Gellein, dated June 19.

Fleischman, R. K., and L. D. Parker. ca. 1990. "British Entrepreneurs and Industrial Revolution Cost Management: A Study of Innovation." Unpublished manuscript.

———. 1991. "British Entrepreneurs and Pre-Industrial Revolution Evidence of Cost Management." *Accounting Review*, April, pp. 361–75.

Fleischman, R. K., L. D. Parker, and W. Vanplew. 1991. "New Cost Accounting Perspectives on Technological Change in the British Industrial Revolution." In *The Costing Heritage*, edited by F. Graves. Harrisonburg, VA: Academy of Accounting Historians.

Fleming, John. 1854. *Bookkeeping by Double Entry*. Pittsburgh: W. S. Haven.

Fleming, Thomas. 1974. "The Cable That Crossed the Atlantic." *Readers Digest*, October, pp. 200–204.

Flesher, D. L. 1991. *The Third-Quarter Century of the American Accounting Association, 1966–1991*. Sarasota, FL: AAA.

Flesher, D. L., and T. K. Flesher. 1979. "Managerial Accounting in an Early 19th Century German-American Religious Commune." *Accounting, Organizations and Society*, no. 4, pp. 297–304.

———. 1980. "Human Resource Accounting in Mississippi before 1865." *Accounting and Business Research*, Special Accounting History Issue, pp. 124–29.

Flesher, D. L., J. Soroosh, and H. Givens. 1986. "Riverboat Stewardship Accounting: The Betsey Ann." Working Paper 67, Academy of Accounting Historians.

Fligstein, N. 1990. *The Transformation of Corporate Control*. Cambridge: Harvard University Press.

Flynn, John T. 1939. "Testimony of John T. Flynn, Economist, New York City." Temporary National Economic Committee, *Verbatim Record*, February 28, pp. 214–30.

Folsom, E. G. 1873. *The Logic of Accounts*. New York: A. S. Barnes.

Fogarty, Frank. 1969. "Figuring Out the Bookkeeping." *Exchange*, October, pp. 1–5.

Fogarty, Timothy J. 1996. "The Imagery and Reality of Peer Review in the U.S.: Insights from Institutional Theory." *Accounting, Organizations and Society*, vol. 21, nos. 2–3, pp. 243–67.

Force, Harold D. 1909. "New York City's Revision of Accounts and Methods." *Journal of Accountancy*, May/June/July/August, pp. 1–7; 106–23; 182–89; 270–86.

Ford, Henry. 1915. "Paying $5 a Day: A Year's Experience." *Survey*, March 20, pp. 673–74.

———. 1926. *Today and Tomorrow.* New York: Doubleday, Page.

Foster, W. T., and W. Catchings. 1927. "How Far Can Ford Go?" *World's Work*, February, pp. 437–44.

Foucault, M. 1980. *Power and Knowledge.* Edited by Colin Gordon. New York: Pantheon Books.

Forstmann, Theodore. 1990. "Notable and Quotable." Editorial. *Wall Street Journal*, August 1.

Frank, Jerome H. 1939. "Accounting for Investors: The Fundamental Importance of Earning Power." *Journal of Accountancy*, November, pp. 295–304.

———. 1940. "The Sin of Perfectionism." AIA 1940, pp. 97–113.

Frankfurter, Felix. 1933. "The Federal Securities Acts." *Fortune*, August, pp. 53–55, 106–11.

Frantz, Joe B. 1950. "The Annual Report as a Public Relations Tool in Three Industries." *Bulletin of the Business Historical Society*, March, pp. 23–42.

Frazer, George E. 1923. "Budgetary Control of Manufacturing Burden—How Should It Be Done?" *Official Publications*, April, pp. 31–38.

Frecka, T. J., ed. 1989. *The State of Accounting Research as We Enter the 1990's.* Urbana: University of Illinois, Department of Accountancy.

Freeman, Herbert C. 1914. Review of *Auditing Theory and Practice*, by Robert H. Montgomery. *Journal of Accountancy*, October, pp. 341–42.

———. 1939. "Unamortized Discount and Premium on Bonds Refunded." *Journal of Accountancy*, December, pp. 397–99.

Freitag, William. 1969. "Medicare and the Hospital Revolution." *Journal of Accountancy*, January, pp. 39–43.

Friedrich, Otto. 1991. "The Trail Boss of the Bailout." *Time*, January 21.

Friend, Irwin. 1976. "Economic Foundations of Stock Market Regulation." *Journal of Contemporary Business*, Summer, pp. 1–27.

Friend, Irwin, and E. Herman. 1964. "The SEC through a Glass Darkly." *Journal of Business*, October, pp. 382–405.

Frisbee, Ira N. 1936. "Accounting for 'Income' Municipalities." *Accounting Review*, June, pp. 164–70.

Fuller, Edmund. 1977. "Our Least Affluent Treasury Secretary." *Wall Street Journal*, January 13, p. 14.

Funk, Roland. 1950. "Recent Developments in Accounting Practice and Theory." *Accounting Review*, July, pp. 292–301.

Gabriel, Ralph. 1956. *The Course of American Democratic Thought.* New York: Ronald Press.

Galambos, Louis. 1983. "Technology, Political Economy, and Professionalization: Central Themes of the Organizational Synthesis." *Business History Review,* Winter, pp. 472–93.

Galambos, Louis, and Joseph Pratt. 1988. *The Rise of the Corporate Commonwealth.* New York: Basic Books.

Galbraith, John K. 1956. *American Capitalism: The Concept of Countervailing Power.* Boston: Houghton Mifflin.

———. 1987. *Economics in Perspective.* Boston: Houghton Mifflin.

Gallatin, Albert. 1796. *A Sketch of the Finances of the United States.* New York: William A. Davis.

Gambino, Anthony, and John R. Palmer. 1976. *Management Accounting in Colonial America.* New York: National Association of Accountants.

"GAO Finds Uniform Accounting Standards Feasible." 1970. News Report, *Journal of Accountancy,* March, pp. 10, 12.

Garcke, Emile, and J. M. Fells. 1893. *Factory Accounts—Their Principles and Practice.* London: Crosby Lockwood & Son.

Garner, S. Paul. 1954. *Evolution of Cost Accounting to 1925.* Tuscaloosa: University of Alabama Press.

———. 1996. *Evolution of Cost Accounting to 1925.* [http://weatherhead.cwru.edu/Accounting/pub/garner/scroll/index.html].

Garraty, John A. 1957. *Right Hand Man: The Life of George W. Perkins.* New York: Harper & Bros.

Gee, Walter. 1977. "President's Perspective." *Management Accounting,* March, pp. 1, 61.

Geer, George P. 1887. *Geer's Analysis of the Science of Accounts.* 4th ed. Springfield, MA. Reprint, Tokyo: Yushodo Booksellers, 1982.

Geijsbeck, John B. 1914. *Ancient Double-Entry Bookkeeping,* Denver: published by author. Reprint, Osaka: Nihon Shoseki, 1975.

"General Electric Company, Eighth Annual Report for the Year Ended January 31, 1900." *Commercial & Financial Chronicle,* April 21, pp. 795–98.

George, C. S. 1968. *The History of Management Thought.* Englewood Cliffs, NJ: Prentice Hall.

George, H. 1879. *Progress and Poverty: An Inquiry into the Cause of Industrial Depression and of Increase of Want with an Increase of Wealth.* New York: W. M. Hinton.

Gerboth, Dale. 1972. "Muddling through with the APB." *Journal of Accountancy,* May, pp. 42–49.

———. 1973. "Accounting Techniques or Policy Making." *Journal of Accountancy,* May, pp. 81–82.

Gilbert, G. 1967. *The Growth of the Seaport Cities, 1790–1825.* Charlottesville: University Press of Virginia.

———. 1984. "Maritime Enterprise in the New Republic: Investment in Baltimore Shipping, 1789–1793." *Business History Review,* Spring, pp. 14–29.

Gilbreath, Frank B. 1911. "The Theory of Work." *Journal of Accountancy*, July, pp. 195–200.

Gilchrist, D. T., and W. D. Lewis. 1965. *Economic Change in the Civil War Era*. Greenville, DE: Eleutherian Mills-Hagley Foundation.

Gilman, Stephen. 1937. "Is College the Only Way?" *Accounting Review*, June, pp. 105–11.

———. 1939. *Accounting Concepts of Profit*. New York: Ronald Press.

Givens, H. 1980. "Peter Duff: Accountant and Educator." *Accounting Historians Journal*, Spring, pp. 37–42.

Glad, Paul W. 1966. "Progressives and the Business Culture." *Journal of American History*, June, pp. 75–89.

Glover, P. W. R. 1926. "Regulation of Accountancy by Law." *Journal of Accountancy*, October, pp. 244–53.

———. 1939A. "Basic Questions of Auditing Procedure." *Journal of Accountancy*, August, pp. 92–100.

———. 1939B. "Introduction." In AIA 1939B, pp. 1–4.

"The God of Supply and Demand." 1921. *New Republic*, May 21, pp. 344–46.

Goldberg, Louis. 1965. *The Commander Theory: An Inquiry into the Nature of Accounting*. Sarasota, FL: AAA.

Goldberg, Louis, and W. E. Stone. 1985. "John Caldwell Colt: A Notorious Accountant." *Accounting Historians Journal*, Spring, pp. 121–30.

Golden, John. 1911. "The Attitude of Organized Labor." *Journal of Accountancy*, July, pp. 189–94.

Golembiewski, R. T. 1964. "Accountancy as a Function of Organization Theory." *Accounting Review*, April, pp. 333–41.

Golob, Eugene O. 1968. *The "Isms": A History and Evaluation*. Freeport, NY: Books for Libraries.

Goodloe, J. S. M. 1920. "Accountant's Report from the Standpoint of the Several Parties at Interest." *Journal of Accountancy*, August, pp. 91–103.

Gorbachev, Mikhail. 1991. "For the Record." *Washington Post*, June 7, p. A20.

Gordon, Myron J. 1963. "Cost Allocations and the Design of Accounting Systems for Control." *Accounting Review*, April, pp. 209–20.

Gordon, R. A., and J. E. Howell. 1959. *Higher Education for Business*. New York: Columbia University Press.

Gordon, Spencer. 1933. "Accountants and the Securities Act." *Journal of Accountancy*, December, pp. 438–51.

———. 1939. "Liability Arising from Accountant's Reports." In AIA 1939B, pp. 48–53.

Gore, E. E. 1901. "The Duties of an Auditor." *Commerce, Accounts and Finance*, January 12, pp. 6–8.

"Government Out of Place." 1916. *Journal of Accountancy*, May, pp. 365–66.

Governmental Accounting Standards Board. 1991. "Action Report." The Mission of the Governmental Accounting Standards Board, insert, June.

Grady, Paul. 1938. "Principles of Depreciation." In AIA 1938, pp. 13–16.

———. 1962. "The Quest for Accounting Principles." *Journal of Accountancy*, May, pp. 45–50.

———. 1965. *Inventory of Generally Accepted Accounting Principles for Business Enterprises.* ARS No. 7. New York: AICPA.

———. 1978. Written Contributions of Selected Accounting Practitioners, vol. 2. Urbana: CIERA, University of Illinois.

Granof, Michael H. 1973. "Operational Auditing Standards for Standards of Government Service." *CPA Journal*, December, pp. 1079–86.

Grant, Julia, ed. 1995. *The New York State Society of Certified Public Accountants: Foundation for a Profession.* New York: Garland.

Grant, Thornton. 1989. "GAO Report on Audits of Savings and Loans Associations." *Accounting and Auditing Bulletin*, February 28.

Grantham, Dewey W., Jr. 1964. "The Progressive Era and the Reform Tradition." *Mid-America*, October, pp. 227–51.

Graves, O. Finley, ed. 1991. *The Costing Heritage: Studies in Honor of S. Paul Garner.* Harrisonburg, VA: Academy of Accounting Historians.

Green, David. 1960. "Moral to the Direct Cost Controversy." *Journal of Business*, July, pp. 218–26.

———. 1966. "Evaluating Accounting Literature." *Accounting Review*, January, pp. 52–64.

Green, Fletcher. 1959. "Origins of the Credit Mobilier of America." *Mississippi Valley Historical Review*, September, pp. 238–51.

Green, Leon. 1937. "One Hundred Years of Torts." *Law: A Century of Progress.* Vol. 3. New York: New York University Press.

Green, Wilmer T. 1930. *History and Survey of Accountancy,* Brooklyn: Standard Text Press. Reprint, Nihon Shoseki, Osaka, 1974.

Greendlinger, Leo. 1923. *Financial and Business Statements.* New York: Alexander Hamilton Institute.

Greene, Thomas. 1897. *Corporation Finance.* New York: Putnam.

Greer, Howard C. 1928. "Where Teaching Lags behind Practice." *Accounting Review*, September, pp. 289–96.

———. 1931. "The Technique of Distribution Cost Accounting." *Accounting Review*, June, pp. 136–39.

———. 1932. "A Council on Accounting Research." *Accounting Review*, September, pp. 176–81.

———. 1937. "A Reply by Professor Greer." *Accounting Review*, March, pp. 79–82.

———. 1938. "To What Extent Can the Practice of Accounting Be Reduced to Rules and Standards?" *Journal of Accountancy*, March, pp. 213–23.

———. 1948. "Depreciation and Price Level." *Accounting Review*, April, pp. 129–31.

———. 1964. "The Corporation's Stockholder—Accountants' Forgotten Man." *Accounting Review*, January, pp. 22–31.

Greidinger, B. Bernard. 1942. "SEC Administrative Policy on Financial Statements." *Journal of Accountancy*, March, pp. 219–24.

Gressley, Gene M. 1971. *Bankers and Cattlemen.* Lincoln: University of Nebraska Press.

Groesbeck, John. 1884. *Practical Book-keeping.* Philadelphia: Eldredge & Brother.

Grundfest, J. 1987. "The New Technology of Finance." *DH & S Review,* October 12, p. 4.

Gundelfinger, S. 1924. "Principles Which Should Govern the Determination of Capital and Amounts Available for Distribution of Dividends in the Case of Corporations With Special Reference to the System of Capital Stock Without a Par Value." *Journal of Accountancy,* May, pp. 321–48; June, pp. 420–31; July, pp. 31–41.

Gynther, Reginald S. 1967. "Accounting Concepts and Behavioral Hypothesis." *Accounting Review,* April, pp. 274–90.

Habakkuk, H. J. 1967. *American and British Technology in the Nineteenth Century.* London: Cambridge University Press.

Hacker, Louis M. 1961. *Major Documents in American History.* Princeton, NJ: VanNostrand.

Hain, H. P. 1965. "History Tells . . ." *Australian Accountant,* Monthly feature, April 1964–October 1973.

———. 1972. "History Tells . . ." *Australian Accountant,* September, p. 355.

Hall, William D. 1987. *Accounting and Auditing: Thoughts on Forty Years in Practice and Education.* Chicago: Arthur Andersen & Co.

Hamman, W. D. 1914. "Efficiency in Municipal Accounting and Reporting." *Journal of Accountancy,* January, pp. 28–36.

Hammond, Theresa D. 1990. "The Minority Recruitment Efforts of the Major Public Accounting Firms in New York City: A Sociological Analysis." Ph.D. diss., University of Wisconsin.

Hammond, Theresa D., and D. W. Streeter. 1994. "Overcoming Barriers: Early African American Certified Public Accountants." *Accounting, Organizations and Society,* vol. 19, no. 3, pp. 271–88.

Hancock, M. Donald, and Gideon Sjoberg, eds. 1972. *Politics in the Post-Welfare State.* New York: Columbia University Press.

Hanson, Walter E. 1977. "Big Brother and the Big Eight." *Management Accounting,* April, pp. 15–19.

Harding, Warren G. 1920. "Less Government in Business and More Business in Government." *World's Work,* November, pp. 25–27.

Harlan, S. D., Jr. 1974. "Practical Interpretations of SAP No. 54 (The Auditors' Study and Evaluation of Internal Control)." *CPA Journal,* March, pp. 21–26.

Harris, Jonathan. 1936. *What Did You Earn Last Month?* New York: National Association of Cost Accountants.

Harwood, John. 1996. "Politics and Policy: Economic Insecurity is Widespread." *Wall Street Journal,* May 16, p. A20.

Haskell, John. 1939. "What Does the Investor Expect of the Independent Auditor?" In AIA 1939B, pp. 12–16.

Haskins, Charles Waldo. 1901A. "Accountancy and the Economic Association." *Commerce, Accounts and Finance,* January 5, p. 10.

———. 1901B. "Accountancy as a Profession." *Commerce, Accounts and Finance,* January 19, p. 17.

——. 1901C. "The Growing Need of Higher Accountancy." *Commerce, Accounts and Finance,* April 20, pp. 5–7.

——. 1901D. "Higher Commercial Education." *Commerce, Accounts and Finance,* October, pp. 7–9.

Haskins & Sells. 1901. *Report on the Methods of Accounting of the City of Chicago.* New York: Haskins & Sells.

Hasson, C. J. 1932. "The South Sea Bubble and Mr. Snell." *Journal of Accountancy,* August, pp. 128–37.

Hatch, F. S. 1923. "Budgetary Control of Manufacturing Burden—How We Do It?" *Official Publications,* April, pp. 38–42; "Discussion," pp. 43–46.

Hatfield, Henry Rand. 1909. *Modern Accounting: Its Principles and Some of Its Problems.* New York: Appleton.

——. 1913. Review of *Auditing Theory and Practice,* by R. H. Montgomery. *Journal of Political Economy,* November, p. 781.

——. 1915. "Some Neglected Phases of Accounting." *Electric Railway Journal,* October 16, pp. 799–802.

——. 1924. "Historical Defense of Bookkeeping." *Journal of Accountancy,* April, pp. 241–53.

——. 1927. "What Is the Matter with Accounting?" *Journal of Accountancy,* October, pp. 267–79.

——. 1928. Review of *How to Understand Accounting,* by H. C. Greer. *Accounting Review,* June, pp. 210–12.

——. 1934. "Accounting Principles and the Statutes." *Journal of Accountancy,* August, pp. 90–97.

——. 1939. "A Survey of Developments in Accounting." In AIA 1939B, pp. 5–11.

——. 1977. "Zwei Pfadfinder (Two Pathfinders)." *Accounting Historians Journal,* Spring, pp. 6–8.

Hausdorfer, Walter. 1986. *Accounting Bibliography: Historical Approach.* Palo Alto: Bay Books.

Hawkins, David F. 1963. "The Development of Modern Financial Reporting Practices among American Manufacturing Corporations." *Business History Review,* Autumn, pp. 135–68.

Haynes, Benjamin R., and Harry P. Jackson. 1935. *A History of Business Education in the United States.* Cincinnati: South-Western Publishers.

Hays, Samuel P. 1957. *The Response to Industrialists, 1885–1914.* Chicago: University of Chicago Press.

Heakel, Mohamed. 1968. "A Classification of the Schools of Accounting Thought." Ph.D. diss., University of Illinois.

Healy, Robert. 1938. "Next Step in Accounting." *Accounting Review,* March, pp. 1–9.

——. 1939. "Responsibility for Adequate Reports." *Controller,* June, pp. 196–99.

"Hearing Focuses on Accountants' Effectiveness." 1985. March 4, *CPA Letter,* vol. 65, no. 4, p. 1.

Heilbroner, Robert, ed. 1961. *The Worldly Philosophers.* New York: Simon & Schuster.

Hein, L. W. 1962. *The Impact of the British Companies Acts upon the Major Areas of the Practice of Accountancy in the British Isle.* Ph.D. diss., University of California,

Los Angeles. Reprint, 1978, retitled *The British Companies Act and The Practice of Accountancy: 1844–1962;* New York: Arno.

Hendricksen, E. S. 1982. *Accounting Theory.* Homewood, IL: Richard D. Irwin.

Henry, Robert S. 1945. "The Railroad Land Grant Legend in American History." *Mississippi Valley Historical Review,* September, pp. 171–94.

Herrick, Anson. 1911. "The Importance of the Municipal Budget as a Means of Control." *Journal of Accountancy,* April, pp. 414–18.

———. 1969. "I Remember When . . ." *California CPA,* October, pp. 27–29, 72.

Heuser, Forrest L. 1969. "The Question of Uniform Accounting Standards." *Management Accounting,* July, pp. 2–3.

Higgins, Thomas G. 1962. "Professional Ethics: A Time for Reappraisal." *Journal of Accountancy,* March, pp. 29–35.

———. 1965. *Thomas G. Higgins, CPA: An Autobiography.* New York: Comet.

———. 1969. "Arthur Young: 1863–1948." *Arthur Young Journal,* Summer, pp. 20–23.

Higgins, Thomas G., and Wallace E. Olson. 1972. "Restating the Code of Ethics: A Decision for the Times." *Journal of Accountancy,* March, pp. 32–39.

Higgs, Robert. 1992. "Wartime Prosperity? A Reassessment of the U.S. Economy in the 1940s." *Journal of Economic History,* March, pp. 41–60.

Hill, Henry P. 1956. "The Necessity for the Experience Requirement for Certified Public Accountants." *New York Certified Public Accountant,* March, pp. 196–99.

———. 1973. "Reporting on Uncertainties by the Independent Auditor." *Journal of Accountancy,* January, pp. 55–60.

Himmelblau, David. 1928. "Some Problems in Property Accounting." *Accounting Review,* June, pp. 149–60.

Hines, Ruth D. 1988. "Financial Accounting: In Communicating Reality, We Construct Reality." *Accounting, Organizations and Society,* vol. 13, no. 3, pp. 251–61.

———. 1989. "Social Political Paradigm in Accounting." *Accounting, Auditing and Accountability,* Spring, pp. 52–76.

Historical Highlights . . . John Deere's Contribution to Farm Mechanization. 1976. Moline, IL: John Deere Co.

Hoagland, Robert. 1991. "RICOs are Amazing and That's Redundant." Letter to the Editor. *Wall Street Journal,* July 5, p. A7.

Hockett, Homer C. 1936. *Political and Social Growth of the United States, 1492–1852.* New York: Macmillan.

Hoffman, Charles. 1956. "The Depression of the Nineties." *Journal of Economic History,* June, pp. 137–64.

Hofstadter, Richard. 1955. *Social Darwinism in American Thought.* Boston: Beacon.

———. 1963. *The Progressive Movement, 1900–1915.* New York: Simon & Schuster.

Hoke, D. 1989. "Product Design and Cost Considerations: Clock, Watch, and Typewriter Manufacturing in the 19th Century." *Business and Economic History,* pp. 119–28.

Holden, P., and W. Ford. 1928. "Waste and Its Elimination." *National Association of Cost Accountants,* March 5, pp. 803–12.

Holmes, Walter G. 1938. *Applied Time and Motion Studies.* New York: Ronald Press.

Holmes, William. 1974. "Wit and Wisdom from Some Early American Accountants." *World,* Summer, pp. 8–13.

———. 1975A. "Accounting and Accountants in Massachusetts." *Massachusetts CPA Review,* January/February, pp. 15–21; March/April, pp. 16–22; May/June, pp. 12–23.

———. 1975B. "CPAs Owe Much to Puritan 'Wrightings.'" *Boston Globe,* June 8.

———. 1976. "Digging in Boston's Accounting Dumps." *Accounting Historian's Journal,* Summer, pp. 1, 5.

Holmes, William, Linda Kistler, and Lou Corsini. 1978. *Three Centuries of Accounting in Massachusetts.* New York: Arno.

Homburger, R. H., and G. J. Previts. 1977. "The Relevance of 'Zwei Pfadfinder.'" *Accounting Historians Journal,* Spring, pp. 9–13.

Hooper, Ben W. 1923. "The Fantasy of the Living Wage." *Nation's Business,* June, pp. 16–18.

Hooper, L., and L. Berton. 1991. "IBM to Record Large Charge for New Rule." *Wall Street Journal,* March 29, p. A3.

Hopper, T., and Peter Armstrong. 1991. "Cost Accounting, Controlling Labour, and the Rise of Conglomerates." *Accounting, Organizations and Society,* vol. 16, nos. 5–6, pp. 405–38.

Hopper, T., J. Storey, and H. Wilmott. 1987. "Accounting for Accounting: Toward the Development of a Dialectical View." *Accounting, Organizations and Society,* vol. 12, no. 5, pp. 437–56.

Hopwood, Anthony G. 1983. "On Trying to Study Accounting in the Contexts in Which It Operates." *Accounting, Organizations and Society,* vol. 8, nos. 2–3, pp. 287–305.

Hornberger, D. J. 1923. "Some Aspects of Reserve Accounting." In *Papers and Proceedings of the American Association of University Instructors in Accounting—1923.* pp. 81–84. New York: Arno, 1980.

Horne, Henry A. 1940. "Accounting Procedure and Research." In AIA 1940, pp. 46–53.

Horngren, Charles. 1959. "Increasing the Utility of Financial Statements." *Journal of Accountancy,* July, pp. 39–46.

———. 1971. "Accounting Discipline in 1999." *Accounting Review,* January, pp. 1–11.

Horngren, Charles, and G. Foster. 1991. *Cost Accounting: A Managerial Emphasis.* Annotated Instructor's Edition. Englewood Cliffs, NJ: Prentice Hall, pp. 92, 150.

Horwitz, G. B. 1970. "EDP Auditing: The Coming of Age." *Journal of Accountancy,* August, pp. 48–56.

Hoskin, K., and R. Macve. 1987. "The Genesis of Accountability: The West Point Connections." *Accounting, Organizations and Society,* vol. 13, no. 1, pp. 37–73.

———. 1988. "The Genesis of Managerialism and Accountability: Springfield, Tyler, and West Point." *Collected Papers of the Fifth World Congress of Accounting Historians,* edited by A. T. Craswell. Sydney: University of Sydney Press.

Howard, Stanley E. 1931. "Charge and Discharge." *Accounting Review,* March, pp. 51–56.

Howard, T. W. 1930. "The Value to Industry of Association Work in Cost Accounting." *National Association of Cost Accountants,* November 1, pp. 381–88.

Hoxsey, J. M. B. 1930. "Accounting for Investors." *Journal of Accountancy,* October, pp. 251–84.

———. 1931. Letter to G. O. May, March 4, 1931. May Papers, AIA File 31. Price Waterhouse Library, New York.

———. 1939A. Letter to G. O. May, February 22. May Papers, AIA File 39. Price Waterhouse Library, New York.

———. 1939B. Letter to G. O. May, March 8. May Papers, AIA File 39. Price Waterhouse Library, New York.

Hubbard, E. K. 1925. "The Executive's Viewpoint in Reference to Cost Figures." *Paper Trade Journal,* August 6, p. 66.

Hudon, E. G., ed. 1969. *The Occasional Papers of Mr. Justice Burton.* Brunswick, ME: Bowdoin College.

Hughes, Hugh P. 1976. "The Contributions of Thomas Jones and Benjamin Franklin Foster." *Collected Papers,* AAA, Southeast Regional Group, pp. 93–98.

———. 1982. "Some Contributions of and Some Controversies Surrounding Thomas Jones and Benjamin Franklin Foster." *Accounting Historians Journal,* Fall, pp. 43–51.

Humphrey, Christopher, and Peter Mozier. 1990. "From Techniques to Ideologies: An Alternative Perspective on the Audit Function." *Critical Perspectives on Accounting,* September, pp. 217–38.

Hunt, H., and R. Hogler. 1990. "Agency Theory as Ideology: A Comparative Analysis Based on Critical Legal Theory and Radical Accounting." *Accounting, Organizations and Society,* vol. 15, no. 5, pp. 437–54.

Hunt, Margaret. 1989. "Time-Management, Writing, and Accounting in the Eighteenth-Century English Trading Family: A Bourgeois Enlightenment." *Business and Economic History,* vol. 18, 2d ser., pp. 150–59.

Hunter, G. S. 1985. "The Development of Bankers: Career Patterns and Corporate Form at the Manhattan Company, 1799–1842." *Business and Economic History,* vol. 14, 2d ser., pp. 59–77.

Hunt's Merchants' Magazine. 1839–65. Edited by Freeman Hunt. New York.

Hurdman, Frederick H. 1919. "Capital Stock with No Par Value." *Journal of Accountancy,* October, pp. 246–57.

———. 1940. "Proposed Revision of Rules of Professional Conduct." In AIA 1940, pp. 76–77.

Hurdman, G. C. 1939. "Services of Public Accountants to Public Bodies." *Journal of Accountancy,* September, pp. 157–61.

Hurley, Edward. 1916A. *Awakening of Business.* New York: Doubleday, Page.

———. 1916B. Letter to F. A. Delano, September 18, National Archives, RG 122, File 8306, p. 5.

Husband, George. 1937. "Accounting Postulates: An Analysis of the Tentative Statement of Accounting Principles." *Accounting Review,* December, pp. 386–401.

———. 1938. "The Corporate Entity Fiction and Accounting Theory." *Accounting Review,* September, pp. 241–53.

———. 1946. "That Thing Which the Accountant Calls Income." *Accounting Review,* July, pp. 247–54.

———. 1954. "Rationalization in the Measurement of Accounting Income." *Accounting Review,* January, pp. 3–14.

———. 1955. "Professor Dein, Mr. Alexander, and Supplementary Statement Number 2." *Accounting Review,* July, pp. 383–99.

Hyatt, J. 1970. "R. G. Barry Includes Its Employee Values on Its Balance Sheet." *Wall Street Journal,* April 3, p. 14.

Hylton, Delmar P. 1962. "Current Trends in Accounting Theory." *Accounting Review,* January, pp. 22–27.

Ihlanfeldt, W. J. 1991. "The Rule-Making Process: A Time for Change." *Financial Reporting and Standard Setting,* edited by G. J. Previts. pp. 25–34. New York: AICPA.

Ijiri, Yuji. 1975. *Theory of Accounting Measurement.* Studies in Accounting Research No. 10. Sarasota: AAA

———. 1989. *Momentum Accounting and Triple-Entry Bookkeeping: Exploring the Dynamic Structure of Accounting Measurements.* Studies in Accounting Research No. 31. Sarasota: AAA.

Ijiri, Yuji, and R. S. Kaplan. 1970. "The Four Objectives of Auditing: Representativeness, Corrective, Protective and Preventive." *Management Accounting,* December, pp. 42–44.

———. 1971. "A Model for Integrating Sampling Objectives in Auditing." *Journal of Accounting Research,* Spring, pp. 73–87.

———. 1972. "The Auditor's Sampling Objectives: Four or Two?—A Reply." *Journal of Accounting Research,* Autumn, pp. 413–16.

"The Income Tax Once More." 1871. *Commercial and Financial Chronicle,* January 7, p. 7.

Inoue, K. 1982. "Threefold Bookkeeping." *Accounting Historians Journal,* pp. 39–51.

Institute of Accountants in the United States of America. 1916. *1916 Year Book of the Institute of Accountants in the United States.* New York: American Institute of Accountants.

Institute of Accounts. 1896. "By-Laws." Reprint, New York: American Antiquarian Society, 1948.

Institute of Internal Auditors. 1947. "Responsibilities of the Internal Auditor." New York: Institute of Internal Auditors.

"Internal Revenue Tax upon Dividends of Corporations." 1871. *Commercial and Financial Chronicle,* April 1, p. 40.

Introducing Women Accountants, Past, Present and Future. 1958. Chicago: American Society of Women Accountants.

Jackson, B., and V. Milliron. 1989. "Tax Preparers: Government Agents or Client Advocates?" *Journal of Accountancy,* May, pp. 76–83.

Jackson, J. Hugh. 1928. "Teaching Auditing by the Case Method." *Accounting Review,* September, pp. 297–310.

Jackson, S. 1983. *J. P. Morgan: A Biography.* New York: Stein and Day.

James, Edwin P. 1969. "Certification of Cost or Price Data Under Defense Contracts." *Management Accounting,* April, pp. 47–51.

James, J. A. 1979. Review of *Finance and Enterprise in Early America: A Study of Stephen Girard's Bank, 1812–1831,* by D. R. Adams. *Business History Review,* Spring, pp. 135–36.

James, William. 1907. *Pragmatism.* New York: H. Holt.

Jameson, William J. 1956. "Cooperation between the Legal and Accounting Professions." *Journal of Accountancy,* November, pp. 273–75.

Jenks, Leland H. 1944. "Railroads as an Economic Force in American Development." *Journal of Economic History,* May, pp. 1–20.

Jennings, Alvin R. 1948. "Staff Training—Present and Future." *Accounting Review,* October, pp. 401–7.

———. 1957. "Speech at Annual Meeting of AICPA, October 28." Manuscript File. AICPA, New York.

———. 1958A. "Accounting Research." *Accounting Review,* October, pp. 547–54.

———. 1958B. "Present Day Challenges in Financial Reporting." *Journal of Accountancy,* January, pp. 28–34.

———. 1964. "Opinions of the APB." *Journal of Accountancy,* August, pp. 27–33.

Jennings, R. M. 1962. "Selection from a Pre-Revolutionary Accounting Record." *Accounting Review,* January, pp. 73–75.

Jensen, Michael. 1989. "Eclipse of the Public Corporation." *Harvard Business Review,* September/October, pp. 61–74.

Jensen, Michael, and W. Meckling. 1976. "Theory of the Firm: Managerial Behavior, Agency Costs and Ownership Structure." *Journal of Financial Economics,* October, pp. 305–60.

John Paul II. 1991. *Centesimus Annus: On the Hundred Anniversary of Rerum Novarum,* Washington, D.C.: United States Catholic Conference.

John, R. C., and T. J. Nissen. 1970. "Evaluating Internal Controls in EDP Audits." *Journal of Accountancy,* February, pp. 31–38.

Johns, R. S., and H. A. Wilkey. 1969. "Authoritative Accounting Guide for Colleges and Universities." *Journal of Accountancy,* March, pp. 55–59.

Johnson, H. Thomas. 1972. "Lyman Mills: Early Cost Accounting for Internal Management Control in the 1850's." *Business History Review,* Winter, pp. 466–74.

———. 1975. "The Role of Accounting History in the Study of Modern Business Enterprise." *Accounting Review,* July, pp. 444–50.

———. 1979. Review of *The Effect of Scientific Management on the Development of the Standard Cost System,* by M. J. Epstein, *Business History Review,* Winter, p. 574.

———. 1981. "Toward a New Understanding of Nineteenth-Century Cost Accounting." *Accounting Review,* no. 3. pp. 510–18.

———. 1987. "The Decline of Cost Management: A Reinterpretation of 20th-Century Cost Accounting History." *Cost and Management,* Spring, pp. 5–12.

Johnson, H. Thomas, and R. S. Kaplan. 1987. *Relevance Lost: The Rise and Fall of Management Accounting.* Cambridge: Harvard Business School Press.

Johnson, Hans V. 1976. "Merchant Accountants." *Management Accounting,* October, pp. 57–61.

Johnson, Joseph French. 1902. "The Relationship of Economic to Higher Accounting." *Commerce, Accounts and Finance,* February, pp. 6–9.

Johnson, Roxanne T. 1987. "An Analysis of the Early Record Keeping in the Du Pont Company 1800–1818." Ph.D. diss., Pennsylvania State University.

Jones, Edward T. 1796. *Jones's English System of Book-keeping,* Bristol: R. Edwards. Reprint, New York: Arno, 1978.

Jones, Ralph C. 1955. *Case Studies of Four Companies.* Columbus, OH: AAA.

———. 1956. *Effects of Price Level Changes on Business Income, Capital and Taxes.* Columbus, OH: AAA.

Jones, Sidney. 1989. *Demographic Trends in America: Squaring the Population Pyramid, Research Highlights.* Washington Forum, Washington, D.C., 20007.

Jones, Thomas. 1842. "Analysis of Bookkeeping as a Branch of General Education." *Hunt's Merchants' Magazine,* December, pp. 513–26.

———. 1859. *Bookkeeping and Accountantship.* New York: John Wiley.

Jones, Thomas F. 1933. *New York University, 1832–1932.* New York: New York University Press.

Joplin, J. Porter. 1914A. "Ethics of Accountancy." *Journal of Accountancy,* March, pp. 187–96.

———. 1914B. "Secret Reserves." *Journal of Accountancy,* December, pp. 407–17.

Josephson, Matthew. 1972. *The Money Lords.* New York: Weybright and Talley.

Kann, Peter. 1989. "Centennial Special Commentary." *Wall Street Journal,* January 9, p. A9.

Kaplan, Maurice, and Daniel Reaugh. 1939. "Accounting Reports to Stockholders and to the SEC." *Accounting Review,* September, pp. 203–36.

Kaplan, R. S. 1983. "Measuring Manufacturing Performance: A New Challenge for Managerial Accounting Research." *Accounting Review,* October, pp. 686–705.

———. 1984. "The Evolution of Management Accounting." *Accounting Review,* July, pp. 390–418.

Kapnick, H. 1977. "Corporate Internal Professionals Also Have Public Responsibilities." Address before the 16th Annual Corporate Counsel Institute of the Northwestern University School of Law, October.

Kasyan, Lorraine. 1975. "The Philosopher's Accounts." *Arthur Young Journal,* Spring, pp. 32–37.

Kataoka, Yasuhiko. 1989. "The Comparative Study of the Consolidated Financial Statements of the House of Mitsui and the House of Fugger." *Otsuki Tandai Ronshu,* no. 20, March, pp. 125–41.

Keating, P. J., and S. F. Jablonsky. 1990. *Changing Roles of Financial Management: Getting Close to Business.* Morristown, NJ: Financial Executives Research Foundation.

Kehl, D. 1939. "The Origin and Early Development of American Dividend Law." *Harvard Law Review,* vol. 53, pp. 36–67.

Keister, D. A. 1896. "The Public Accountant." *The Book-keeper,* July, pp. 21–22.

Kell, Walter. 1958. "The Commission's Long Run Goals." *Accounting Review,* April, pp. 198–205.

Keller, Wayne I. 1970. "Link between Management and Accounting." *Management Accounting,* June, pp. 36–40.

Kelley, Arthur. 1951. "Can Corporate Income Be Scientifically Determined?" *Accounting Review,* July, pp. 289–98.

————. 1958. "Comments on the 1957 Revision of Corporate Accounting and Reporting Standards." *Accounting Review,* April, pp. 214–16.

Kelley, William. 1939. "Testimony of William Kelley, Chief Counsel of the Federal Trade Commission," in *TNEC,* Verbatim Record, March 2, pp. 261–69.

Kelly, M. 1980. "New Annual Reports: Confusion Is the Game." *Cleveland Plain Dealer,* March 9, pp. E1, E12.

Kennedy, John T. 1921. "Federal Tax Laws and the Practice of Accountancy." *Pace Student,* October, pp. 161–63, 172–73.

Kent, E. J. 1975. "The Firm of S. D. Leidesdorf and Company, Certified Public Accountants." Typed memorandum, S. D. Leidesdorf & Co., New York.

Kerrigan, Harry D. 1959. "Recent Data on Accounting Majors and Programs." *Accounting Review,* April, pp. 262–65.

Kessler, Louis M. 1956. "Let's Build the Profession through Education." Address at the Annual Meeting of the American Institute of Accountants, September. Manuscript File. AICPA, New York.

Kester, Roy B. 1918. "Principles of Accounting." *Accounting Theory and Practice.* Vol. 1. New York: Ronald Press.

————. 1921. "Discussion." *Proceedings of the American Association of University Instructors in Accounting,* pp. 77–78.

————. 1936. "Education for Professional Accountancy." *Accounting Review,* June, pp. 99–108.

Kheil, Karl P. 1898. *Valentin Menher und Antich Rocha, 1550–1565.* Prague: Bursik und Kohut.

————. 1906. *Benedetto Cotrugli Raugeo [Erganzier Sonderabdruck aus der Oesterreichischen Zeitshrift für das Kaufmannishe Unterrichtswesen, 2 Jahrg.]* Vienna: Mannzshe Buchhandlung.

Kibbe, M. B. 1991. "The Laffer Curve in Reverse." *Wall Street Journal,* July 22, p. A8.

Kiker, B. F. 1966. "The Historical Roots of the Concept of Human Capital." *Journal of Political Economy,* October, pp. 481–89.

Kilduff, Frederick W. 1927. "Inventory Control." *NACA Bulletin,* January 1, pp. 477–92.

King, Earle. 1948. "Need for a Definite Statement of Accounting Principles." *Journal of Accountancy,* November, p. 369.

King, Willford Isbell. 1915. *The Wealth and Income of the People of the United States.* New York: Macmillan.

Kingwill, J. H. 1909. "The Colorado CPA Examination, 1908." *Journal of Accountancy,* pp. 287–94.

Kinney, W. R. 1972. "The Auditor's Sampling Objectives: Four or Two?" *Journal of Accounting Research*, Autumn, pp. 407–12.

Kirchner, Paul. 1961. "Theory and Research in Management Accounting." *Accounting Review*, January, pp. 43–49.

Kirk, D. J. 1981. "Concepts, Consensus, Compromise and Consequences: Their Roles in Standard Setting." *Journal of Accountancy*, April, pp. 83–86.

Kirkland, Edward C. 1946. "Comments on the Railroad Land Grant Legend in American History Texts." *Mississippi Valley Historical Review*, March, pp. 557–76.

———. 1967. *Industry Comes of Age*. Chicago: Quadrangle Books.

Kistler, L. H., and R. M. Jennings. 1969. "An Accounting Primer Circa 1831." *Accounting Review*, January, pp. 168–73.

Kistler, L. H., P. C. Clairmont, and B. Hinchey. 1984. "Planning and Control in the 19th Century Ice Trade." *Accounting Historians Journal*, Spring, pp. 19–30.

Kitman, Marvin. 1970. *George Washington's Expense Account*. New York: Simon & Schuster. (Reviewed in *Management Accounting*, December 1970, p. 60.)

Kittredge, Anson. 1901. "Balance Sheet." *Commerce, Accounts and Finance*, December, pp. 3–7.

Klammer, Thomas P. 1973. "Capital Budgeting Techniques and Firm Performance." *Accounting Review*, April, pp. 353–64.

Klebaner, B. J. 1979. "State Chartered American Commercial Banks, 1781–1801." *Business History Review*, Winter, pp. 528–38.

Klebaner, E. 1964. "Potential Competition and American Anti-Trust." *Business History Review*, Spring, pp. 163–85.

Klein, Joseph J. 1969. Interviews by Thomas Hogan. Typed transcripts, in authors' possession.

Klemstine, C. F., and M. W. Maher. 1984. "Management Accounting Research: 1926–1983." An annotated bibliography distributed by the Management Accounting Section of the AAA.

Knauth, Oswald. 1957. "An Executive Looks at Accountancy." *Journal of Accountancy*, January, pp. 29–32.

Knebel, Fletcher. 1974. *The Bottom Line*. Garden City, NJ: Doubleday.

Knights, D., and D. Collinson. 1987. "Disciplining the Shopfloor: A Comparison of the Disciplinary Effects of Managerial Psychology and Financial Accounting." *Accounting, Organizations and Society*, vol. 12, no. 5, pp. 457–77.

Knortz, Herbert C. 1976. "Salute to the Bicentennial." Paper delivered at the NAA International Conference, June 21.

Knowlton, Don. 1947. "A Brief Study of Balance Sheets." *Accounting Review*, October, pp. 360–67.

Kohler, Eric L. 1919. "Inadmissible Assets and Invested Capital." *Proceedings of the American Association of University Instructors in Accounting*, pp. 37–41.

———. 1926. "Tendencies in Balance Sheet Construction." *Accounting Review*, December, pp. 1–11.

———. 1934. "A Nervous Profession." *Accounting Review*, December, pp. 334–36.

————. 1939. "Some Old Rules Revised." *Accounting Review,* December, pp. 453–57.

————. 1940. "The Goal of Accounting Education." In AIA 1940, pp. 84–88.

————. 1945. "Contemporary Accounting." In *Eric Louis Kohler: A Collection of His Writings,* edited by W. W. Cooper, Y. Ijiri, and G. J. Previts. Tuscaloosa, AL: Academy of Accounting Historians, 1980.

————. 1948. "Depreciation and Price Level." *Accounting Review,* April, pp. 131–36.

————. 1953. "The Development of Accounting Principles by Accounting Societies." *Accounting Research,* 4, pp. 30–61. Reprinted in Backer 1955, pp. 177–206.

————. 1955. "Activity: Nerve Center of Management Accounting." *NACA Bulletin,* August, pp. 1627–33.

————. 1963. "Why Not Retain Historical Cost?" *Journal of Accountancy,* October, pp. 35–41.

————. 1970. *A Dictionary for Accountants.* 4th ed. Englewood Cliffs, NJ: Prentice Hall. pp. 6–7.

————. 1975. "In All My Years . . ." *Accounting Historians Journal,* Spring, pp. 4, 6.

Kohler, Eric L., and Paul Morrison. 1926. *Principles of Accounting.* Chicago: A. W. Shaw.

Kolko, Gabriel. 1963. *The Triumph of Conservatism: A Reinterpretation of American History, 1900–1916.* New York: Free Press.

Kornblith, G. J. 1985. "The Craftsman as Industrialists: Jones Chickering and the Transformation of American Piano Making." *Business History Review,* Autumn, pp. 349–68.

Kottke, Frank. 1959. "Mergers and Acquisitions of Large Manufacturing Companies, 1951–59." *Review of Economics and Statistics,* November, pp. 430–33.

Kozub, R. M. 1983. "Antecedents of the Income Tax in Colonial America." *Accounting Historians Journal,* Fall, pp. 100–116.

Krebs, William S. 1930. "Asset Appreciation, Its Economic and Accounting Significance." *Accounting Review,* March, pp. 60–69.

Kreiser, L., and P. Dare. 1986. "Shaker Accounting Records at Pleasant Hill: 1830–1850." *Accounting Historians Journal,* Fall, pp. 20–36.

Krekstein, I. H. 1972. "A Founding Partner's Story." *The Accountant,* no. 3, pp. 25–33.

Kreps, Juanita. 1978. "Why We Need a Regulatory Budget." *Business Week,* July 31, p. 14.

Kripke, Homer. 1970. "Conglomerates and the Moment of Truth in Accounting." *St. John's Law Review,* pp. 791–97.

Kristol, Irving. 1976. "The Republican Future." *Wall Street Journal,* May 14, p. 18.

Kroll, J. J. 1987. "Quote." *Cleveland Plain Dealer,* April 19, p. 2-E.

Kurtz, C. 1957. "The Cost of Human Depreciation: An Ostrich Liability." *Accounting Review,* July, pp. 413–18.

Labaton, S. 1991. "Wall Street's Ambitious Top Cop." *New York Times Magazine,* March 24, pp. 13, 15, 30–32.

Laeri, J. Howard. 1966. "Statement in Quotes." *Journal of Accountancy,* March, pp. 57–58.

Laidler, Harry W. 1932. *Concentration of Control in American Industry.* New York: Crowell.

Lamoreaux, N. R. 1985. *The Great Merger Movement in American Business, 1895–1904.* Cambridge: Cambridge University Press.

Landis, James M. 1933. "Federal Securities Act and Regulations Relating to the Work and Responsibility of the CPA." In *Addresses and Discussion Relating to the Federal Securities Acts.* New York: New York State Society of Certified Public Accountants.

———. 1935. Address before American Management Associates, October 9. Mimeographed. AICPA, New York.

———. 1936. "Address at the 25th Annual Conference of Investment Bankers Association." December 4. Manuscript File, 1939. AICPA, New York.

———. 1958. "The Legislative History of the Securities Act of 1933." *George Washington Law Review,* pp. 29–49.

Langenderfer, Harold Q. 1954. "The Federal Income Tax, 1861–1872." Ph.D. diss., Indiana University.

Langenderfer, Harold Q., and Jack C. Robertson. 1969. "A Theoretical Structure for Independent Audits of Management." *Accounting Review,* October, pp. 777–87.

Lauss, Arthur M. 1970. "A Fat Maverick Stirs Up the Accounting Profession." *Fortune,* December, pp. 96–99, 122–25.

"Laventhol Says It Plans to File for Chapter 11." 1990. *Wall Street Journal,* November 20, pp. A3, A8.

Law: A Century of Progress. 1937. 3 vols., New York: New York University Press.

Lawler, John. 1969. "The Current State of the Accounting Profession." Mimeographed. AICPA, New York.

Lawson, Thomas. 1905. *Frenzied Finance.* New York: Ridgeway Thayer.

Lazonick, W. 1988. "Financial Commitment and Economic Performance: Ownership and Control in the American Industrial Corporation." *Business and Economic History,* vol. 17, 2d ser., pp. 115–28.

Leder, L. H., and V. P. Carosso. 1956. "Robert Livingston (1654–1728): Businessman of Colonial New York." *Business History Review,* March, pp. 18–45.

Lee, C. 1797. *The American Accomptant; being a plain, practical and systematic compendium of Federal Arithmetic; in three parts: designed for the use of schools and specially calculated for the Commercial Meridian of the United States of America.* Lansingburgh, NY: W. W. Wands. Reprint, Tokyo: Yushodo Booksellers, 1982.

Lee, Geoffrey A. 1972. "The Oldest European Account Book: A Florentine Bank Ledger of 1211." *Nottingham Mediaeval Studies,* vol. 16, pp. 28–60.

———. 1975. "The Concept of Profit in British Accounting, 1760–1900." *Business History Review,* Spring, pp. 6–36.

Lee, Susan. 1988. "Efficient Market Theory Lives!" *Wall Street Journal,* May 6, p. 20.

Leech, S. A. 1986. "The Theory and Development of a Matrix-Based Accounting System." *Accounting and Business Research,* pp. 327–41.

"The Legal Liability of Auditors." 1910. *Journal of Accountancy,* March, pp. 380–81.

Lehman, C., and T. Tinker. 1987. "The Real Cultural Significance of Accounts." *Accounting, Organizations and Society,* vol. 12, no. 5, pp. 503–22.

Leinwand, Gerald. 1962. "A History of the United States Federal Bureau of Corporations: 1903–1914." Ph.D. diss., New York University.

Lenhart, Norman J. 1939. "Testimony before the Securities and Exchange Commission in the Matter of McKesson & Robbins Inc." U.S. Securities and Exchange Commission, Washington, D. C. pp. 221–69.

Lerner, Max. 1957. *America as a Civilization.* Vol. 1. New York: Simon & Schuster.

Lev, B., and A. Schwartz. 1971. "On the Economic Concept of Human Capital." *Accounting Review,* January, pp. 481–89.

Levitt, Arthur. 1996. Letter to J. Michael Cook, April 22. Securities and Exchange Commission, Washington, D. C.

Levy, L. S., and R. J. Sampson. 1962. *American Economic Development: Growth of the United States in the Western World.* Boston: Allyn and Bacon.

Lindbloom, Charles E. 1977. *Politics & Markets.* New York: Basic Books.

Lindsay, C. H. Forbes. 1908. "New Business Standards in Washington: Work of the Keep Commission." *American Review of Reviews,* February, pp. 190–95.

Link, Arthur S., with W. B. Catton. 1967. *The American Epoch.* New York: Knopf.

Linowes, David. 1968. "Development of Socio-Economic Accounting." *Journal of Accountancy,* November, pp. 37–42.

———. 1972/73. "Let's Get on with the Social Audit." *Business and History Society Review,* pp. 39–42.

Littleton, A. C. 1924. "Discussion of Principles of Valuation Related to the Balance Sheet." *Proceedings of the Annual Meeting of the American Association of University Instructors in Accounting,* pp. 14–15.

———. 1927. "Thomas Jones—Pioneer." *Certified Public Accountant,* June, pp. 183–86.

———. 1928. "What Is Profit?" *Accounting Review,* September, pp. 278–88.

———. 1929. "Value and Price in Accounting." *Accounting Review,* September, pp. 147–54.

———. 1932. "Capital and Surplus." *Accounting Review,* December, pp. 290–93.

———. 1933A. *Accounting Evolution to 1900.* New York: American Institute of Accountants.

———. 1933B. "Social Origins of Modern Accountancy." *Journal of Accountancy,* October, pp. 261–70.

———. 1935. "Value or Cost?" *Accounting Review,* September, pp. 269–73.

———. 1936A. "Contrasting Theories of Profit." *Accounting Review,* March, pp. 10–18.

———. 1936B. "The Professional College." *Accounting Review,* June, pp. 109–16.

———. 1939. "Memorandum—Unamortized Discount and Redemption Premium on Bonds Refunded." May. CAP Correspondence File. AICPA, New York.

———. 1941. "A Genealogy for 'Cost or Market.'" *Accounting Review,* June, pp. 161–67.

———. 1942. *Directory of Early American Public Accountants.* Bureau of Economic and Business Research Bulletin No. 62, Urbana, IL.

———. 1946. "Accounting Exchange." *Accounting Review,* December, pp. 459–63.

————. 1953. *Structure of Accounting Theory*. Urbana, IL: AAA.

————. 1956. "Choices Among Alternatives." *Accounting Review*, July, pp. 363–70.

————. 1958. "Accounting Rediscovered." *Accounting Review*, April, pp. 246–53.

Littleton, A. C., and V. K. Zimmerman. 1962. *Accounting Theory: Continuity and Change*. Englewood Cliffs, NJ: Prentice Hall.

Lively, Robert A. 1955. "The American System." *Business History Review*, March, vol. 29, no. 1, pp. 81–95.

Lockwood, Jeremiah. 1938. "Early University Education in Accountancy." *Accounting Review*, June, pp. 131–44.

Loeb, Stephen. 1971A. "Incompatible Occupations for CPAs: An Inquiry into Compliance." *New York Certified Public Accountant*, June, pp. 433–37.

————. 1971B. "A Survey of Ethical Behavior in the Accounting Profession." *Journal of Accounting Research*, Autumn, pp. 52–60.

————. 1972. "Enforcement of a Code of Ethics: A Survey." *Accounting Review*, June, pp. 1–10.

Loeb, Stephen, and Gordon S. May. 1976. *A History of Public Accounting in Maryland*. Baltimore: Maryland Association of Certified Public Accountants.

Loebbecke, J. K., and J. Neter. 1973. "Statistical Sampling in Confirming Receivables." *Journal of Accountancy*, June, pp. 44–50.

Loft, Anne. 1986. "Towards a Critical Understanding of Accounting: The Case of Cost Accounting in the UK, 1914–1925." *Accounting, Organizations and Society*, vol. 11, pp. 137–70.

————. 1991. "The History of Management Accounting: Relevance Found." In Ashton, Hopper, and Scapens 1991, pp. 17–37.

Loomis, Noel M. 1968. *Wells Fargo*. New York: Crown.

Lorig, Arthur N. 1937. "Comment." *Accounting Review*, December, pp. 401–3.

Loving, Rush, Jr. 1970. "The Penn Central Bankruptcy Express." *Fortune*, August, pp. 104–9, 154–71.

Lowi, Theodore J. 1969. *The End of Liberalism*. New York: Norton.

Lubar, S. 1984. "Managerial Structure and Technological Style: The Lowell Mills, 1821–1880." *Business and Economic History*, vol. 13, 2d ser., pp. 20–30.

Lybrand, William. 1908. "The Accounting for Industrial Enterprises." AAPA, *Year Book* 1908, pp. 255–90.

Lyon, Leverett S. 1924. "Accounting Courses in Universities." *Journal of Accountancy*, December, pp. 422–29.

Lyons, John. 1969. "Earnings, Can Anyone Believe the Numbers?" *Investment Banking and Corporate Financing*, Autumn, pp. 21–26, 80–86.

MacMillan, William R. 1939. "Sources and Extent of the Liability of a Public Accountant." Reprinted from *Chicago Kent Review*, December. New York: American Surety.

MacNeill, James H. 1968. "A Reply to The Common Body of Knowledge for CPAs: Some Problems in Analysis." *Journal of Accounting Research*, Autumn, p. 141.

MacRitchie, Kenneth. 1983. "FTC and SEC Proceedings under the Securities Act of 1933." MBA thesis, New York University.

Madden, J. T., R. A. Stevenson, and W. R. Gray. 1928. "The Place of Accounting in the Commerce Curriculum." *Accounting Review,* June, pp. 189–207.

Magee, Henry C. 1913. "The Accountant's Relation to Inventory." *Journal of Accountancy,* December, pp. 443–56.

Maggin, D. L. 1990. "Fictional Profits." *Cleveland Plain Dealer,* February 6, p. 5-B.

Magill H. T., and G. J. Previts. 1991. *CPA Professional Duties and Responsibilities: A Guide.* Cincinnati, OH: South-Western Publishing.

Main, Frank W. 1923. "President's Message." *Certified Public Accountant,* January, pp. 3–5.

Main, Lafrentz & Co. ca. 1974. *When the World Was Still Young.* New York: Main, Lafrentz & Co.

Mair, John. 1763. *Book-keeping Methodiz'd.* Edinburgh: Sands, Murray and Cochran.

———. 1768. *Book-keeping Moderniz'd.* 6th ed. Reprint, New York: Arno, 1978.

"Major Henry Harney, Incorporator." 1897. *Financial Record,* October 15.

Manchester, William. 1975. *The Glory and the Dream—A Narrative History of America, 1932–1972.* New York: Bantam.

Manne, Henry G. 1975. *The Economics of Legal Relationships: Readings in the Theory of Property Rights.* Saint Paul, MN: West Publishing.

Markowitz, H. M. 1991. "Markets and Morality." *Wall Street Journal,* May 14, p. A16.

Marple, Raymond P. 1963. "Value-Itis." *Accounting Review,* July, pp. 478–82.

———. 1965. *National Association of Accountants on Direct Costing: Selected Papers.* New York: Ronald Press.

Marsh, C. C. 1864. *The Theory and Practice of Bank Book-keeping and Joint Stock Accounts.* 4th ed. New York: Appleton.

Marshall, Alfred. 1964. *Principles of Economics.* 8th ed. London: Macmillan.

Marshall, Leon Carroll. 1926. "The Collegiate School of Business at Erewhon." *Journal of Political Economy,* June, pp. 289–326.

Martin, Albro. 1984. "Introductory Essay: Transportation and the Evolution of the American Economic Republic." *Business History Review,* Spring, p. 1.

Martin, J. W. 1979. "A Contemporary Review of the Evolution of Value Concepts." Working Paper No. 39, Academy of Accounting Historians.

Maslow, Abraham. 1965. *Eupsychian Management.* Homewood, IL: Irwin.

Mason, Perry. 1933. "Illustrations of the Early Treatment of Depreciation." *Accounting Review,* September, pp. 209–18.

———. 1956. *Basic Concepts and Methods.* Columbus, OH: AAA.

———. 1961. *Cash Flow Analysis and the Funds Statement.* ARS No. 2. New York: AICPA.

Mather, Charles E. 1948. "The Development of the Accounting Profession." In *Fifty Years of Service: 1898–1948,* pp. 7–9. Newark, NJ: New Jersey Society of Certified Public Accountants.

Mathews, George C. 1938. "Accounting in the Regulation of Security Sales." *Accounting Review,* September, pp. 225–33.

Mattessich, Richard. 1956. "The Constellation of Accountancy and Economics." *Accounting Review,* October, pp. 551–64.

———. 1957. "Toward a General and Axiomatic Foundation of Accounting." *Accounting Research,* October, pp. 328–55.

———. 1972. "Methodological Preconditions and Problems of a General Theory of Accounts." *Accounting Review,* July, pp. 469–87.

———. 1978. "What Effect Has the Time Period Assumption upon Disclosure? A Questionable Question and Its Meaningful Alternatives." *Accounting Research Convocation Proceedings,* 1978, University of Alabama, pp. 55–68.

———. 1984. *Modern Accounting Research: History, Survey, and Guide.* Vancouver British Columbia: Canadian Certified General Accountants' Research Foundation.

———. 1991. "Reading the Tea Leaves on Corporate Privatizations." *Wall Street Journal,* September 19, 1989, p. A31.

Matthews, J. B. 1981. Review of *Power and Morality: American Business Ethics, 1840–1914,* by S. Engelbourg. *Business History Review,* Spring, pp. 98–99.

Mautz, R. K. 1978. "Discussion." In *Accounting Research,* edited by Abdel Khalik and Wayne Keller, pp. 174–82.

Mautz, R. K., and Gary J. Previts. 1977. "Eric Kohler." *Accounting Review,* March, pp. 301–7.

Mautz, R. K., and Hussein Sharaf. 1961. *The Philosophy of Auditing.* Sarasota, FL: AAA.

May, George O. 1906. "The Proper Treatment of Premiums and Discounts on Bonds." *Journal of Accountancy,* July, pp. 174–86.

———. 1915. "Qualifications in Certificates." *Journal of Accountancy,* October, pp. 248–59.

———. 1916. "Reasons for Excluding Interest on Cost." *Journal of Accountancy,* June, pp. 401–9.

———. 1927. Letter to the Editor. *New York Times,* August 27.

———. 1932. "Influence of the Depression on the Practice of Accountancy." *Journal of Accountancy,* November, pp. 336–50.

———. 1933A. "Memorandum Regarding Securities Bill H. R. 4314." May Papers, SEC File. Price Waterhouse Library, New York.

———. 1933B. Transcript of speech before the Illinois Society of Certified Public Accountants, December 6. AICPA, New York.

———. 1934. "Position of Accountants under the Securities Acts." *Journal of Accountancy,* January, pp. 9–23.

———. 1936A. "The Influence of Accounting on Economic Development." *Journal of Accountancy,* January, pp. 11–22; February, pp. 92–105; March, pp. 171–84.

———. 1936B. *Twenty-Five Years of Accounting Responsibility.* Edited by Carleton Hunt. New York: American Institute of Accountants.

———. 1938. "Uniformity in Accounting." *Harvard Business Review,* Autumn, pp. 1–8.

———. 1939. "General Purpose of Financial Statements." Memorandum. CAP Correspondence File. AICPA, New York.

———. 1943. *Financial Accounting: A Distillation of Experience.* New York: Macmillan.

————. 1949. *Business Income and Price Levels: An Accounting Study.* New York: AICPA.

————. 1952. "Limitations on the Significance of Invested Cost." *Accounting Review,* October, pp. 436–40.

————. 1957A. "Business Combinations: An Alternate View." *Journal of Accountancy,* April, pp. 33–39.

————. 1957B. "Income Accounting and Social Revolution." *Journal of Accountancy,* June, pp. 36–42.

————. 1960. Letter to J. S. Seidman, June 10. May Papers. Price Waterhouse Library, New York.

May, Marvin. 1968. "The Earnings Per Share Trap." *Financial Analysts Journal,* May/ June, pp. 113–17.

May Papers. 1927–62. G. O. May Archival Collection. Price Waterhouse Library, New York.

Mayer, Caroline E. 1977. "Accountants—Cleaning Up America's Mystery Profession." *US News & World Report,* December 19, pp. 39–42.

Mayhew, Ira. 1875. *Mayhew's Practical Book-keeping.* Boston: Nichols and Hall.

McConnell, Grant. 1966. *Private Power and American Democracy.* New York: Knopf.

McCraw, Thomas K. 1975. "Regulation in America." *Business History Review,* Summer, pp. 159–83.

————. 1981. *Regulation in Perspective: Historical Essays.* Cambridge: Belknap.

————. 1984. *Prophets of Regulation.* Cambridge: Harvard University Press.

McCrea, Roswell C., and Roy B. Kester. 1936. "School of Professional Accountancy." *Journal of Accountancy,* February, pp. 106–17.

McCredie, H. 1957. "Theory and Practice of Accounting." *Accounting Review,* April, pp. 216–33.

McFarland, Walter B. 1961. "Research in Management Accounting by the National Association of Accountants." *Accounting Review,* January, pp. 21–25.

McGaw, J. A. 1985. "Accounting for Innovations: Technological Change and Business Practice in the Berkshire County Paper Industry." *Technology and Culture,* vol. 4, pp. 703–25.

McGladrey, I. B. 1933. "The Accountant as a Help to the Business Man." *Certified Public Accountant,* February, pp. 105–7.

McGrath, Kathryn. 1990. "Sage Advice from a Fund Warrior." *US News & World Report,* July 16, p. 64.

McGregor, Douglas. 1960. *The Human Side of Enterprise.* New York: McGraw-Hill.

McKee, T. E. 1979. "An 1870 Corporate Audit Committee." *Accounting Historians Journal,* Fall, pp. 61–68.

McKendrick, Neil M. 1970. "Josiah Wedgwood and Cost Accounting in the Industrial Revolution." *Economic History Review,* vol. 23, pp. 45–67.

McKenzie, Robert H. 1971. "A History of the Shelby Iron Company, 1865–1881." Ph.D. diss., University of Alabama.

McKinsey, James O. 1923. "Municipal Accounting." *Journal of Accountancy,* February, pp. 81–94.

———. 1924. "President's Address." *Proceedings of the American Association of University Instructors in Accounting,* pp. 59–64.

McMickle, P. 1984. *Abacus,* June.

McMickle, P., and R. Vangermeersch. 1987. *The Origins of a Great Profession.* Atlanta: Academy of Accounting Historians.

McNaught, Kenneth. 1966. "The American Progressives and the Great Society." *Journal of American History,* December, pp. 504–20.

McQuaid, Kim. 1986. *A Response to Industrialism: Liberal Businessmen and the Evolving Spectrum and Capitalist Reform, 1886–1960.* New York: Garland.

———. 1994. *Uneasy Partners: Big Business in American Politics, 1945–1990.* Baltimore: Johns Hopkins University Press.

McShane, Clay. 1995. [cmcshane@lynx.dac.neu.edu]. "H-Business Posting" [lists@cs.muohio.edu]. December 4.

Mead, George C. 1970. "A Managerial Approach to Governmental Accounting." *Journal of Accountancy,* March, pp. 50–55.

Meade, Edward. 1903. *Trust Finance.* New York: Macmillan.

Means, Gardiner. 1962. *The Corporate Revolution in America.* New York: Collier Books.

Mednick, R. 1984. "Call for New Standards for Attestation." *CPA Journal,* August, pp. 13–16.

———. 1996. "Licensure and Regulation of the Profession: A Time for Change." *Journal of Accountancy,* March, pp. 33–38.

Mednick, R., and G. J. Previts. 1987. "The Scope of CPA Services." *Journal of Accountancy,* May, pp. 220–38.

Melloan, G. 1987. "Fund Managers Were Edgy Long before Crash." *Wall Street Journal,* November 10, p. 31.

Mellon, Andrew. 1924. *Taxation: The People's Business.* New York: Macmillan.

"Memorandum of Luncheon Meeting at the Broad Street Club, May 28, 1935." 1935. May Papers, AIA File. Price Waterhouse Library, New York.

Mepham, M. J. 1988A. "The Eighteenth-Century Origins of Cost Accounting." *Abacus,* no. 1, pp. 55–74.

———. 1988B. "Matrix-Based Accounting: A Comment." *Accounting and Business Research,* pp. 375–78.

———. 1988C. "The Scottish Enlightenment and the Development of Accounting." *Accounting Historians Journal,* Fall, pp. 151–76.

Mepham, M. J., and W. E. Stone. 1977. "John Mair, M.A.: Author of the First Classic Bookkeeping Series." *Accounting and Business Research,* Spring, pp. 128–34.

Merino, Barbara D. 1975. "The Professionalization of Accountancy in America: A Comparative Analysis of Selected Accounting Practitioners, 1900–1925." Ph.D. diss., University of Alabama.

———. 1976. "Development of American Accountancy from 1876–1976." *CPA Journal,* June, pp. 31–36.

———. 1977. "The CPA Experience Requirement in Historic Perspective." *Accounting Journal,* Spring, pp. 51–60.

————. 1993. "An Analysis of the Development of Accounting Knowledge: A Pragmatic Approach." *Accounting, Organizations and Society,* vol. 18, no. 1, pp. 163–86.

Merino, Barbara D., and T. Coe. 1978. "Uniformity in Accounting: A Historical Perspective." *Journal of Accountancy.* August, pp. 62–69.

Merino, Barbara D., B. Koch, and K. MacRitchie. 1987. "Historical Analysis—a Diagnostic Tool for Events Studies: The Impact of the Securities Act of 1933." *Accounting Review,* October, pp. 748–62.

Merino, Barbara D., A. Mayper, and Ram Sriram. 1994. "An Examination of Auditor/Client Relationships in Publicly Traded Companies, 1927–1929." *Journal of Business Finance and Accounting,* July, pp. 619–42.

Merino, Barbara D., and M. D. Neimark. 1982. "Disclosure, Regulation and Public Policy: A Sociohistorical Reappraisal." *Journal of Accounting and Public Policy,* Fall, pp. 33–57.

Merritt, Rita Perine. 1925. *The Accountants' Directory and Who's Who.* New York: Prentice Hall.

Merritt, Walter G. 1922. "The Struggle for Industrial Liberty." *Textile World,* May 6, p. 184.

Middleditch, Livingston., Jr. 1918. "Should Accounts Reflect the Changing Value of the Dollar?" *Journal of Accountancy,* February, pp. 114–20.

Miller, Arthur S. 1969. "Corporate Gigantism and Technological Imperatives." Program of Policies Studies, reprint no. 6, George Washington University.

Miller, Herbert E. 1979. As quoted in *A History of Accounting in America,* by G. J. Previts and B. D. Merino. New York: John Wiley and Sons, p. 304.

Miller, Hermann C. 1937. "A Suggested Program of Education for the Accountant." *Accounting Review,* June, pp. 191–98.

Miller, M. H. 1991. "Leverage." *Journal of Finance,* June, p. 488.

Miller, M. and Lambert W. 1991. "Peat Marwick Cleared of Allegations that Bad Audit Caused Loan Defaults." *Wall Street Journal,* July 8, p. B6.

Miller, Peter, and Ted O'Leary. 1987. "Accounting and the Construction of the Governable Person." *Accounting, Organizations and Society,* vol. 12, no. 3, pp. 235–65.

Mills, Patti A. 1986. "Financial Reporting and Stewardship Accounting in Sixteenth-Century Spain." *Accounting Historians Journal,* Fall, pp. 65–76.

Mills, C. Wright. 1959. *The Power Elite.* New York: Oxford University Press.

"The Minimum Wage Decision." 1923. *Nation's Business,* June, p. 44.

Minton, R. W. 1976. "John Law's Bubble: Bigger . . . bigger and then BUST!" *Smithsonian,* January, pp. 93–98.

Mintz, M., and J. Cohen. 1976. *Power, Inc.* New York: Viking.

Mio, L. 1991. "Man of The Half-Century." *Cleveland Plain Dealer Magazine,* February 3, p. 4.

Miranti, P. J. 1986. "From Conflict to Consensus: The American Institute of Accountants and the Professionalization of Public Accountancy: 1886–1940." Ph.D. diss., Johns Hopkins University.

———. 1988. "Professionalism and Nativism: The Competition in Securing Public Accountancy Legislation in New York during the 1890s." *Social Science Quarterly*, June, pp. 361–80.

———. 1989. "The Mind's Eye of Reform: The ICC's Bureau of Statistics and Accounts and a Vision of Regulation, 1887–1940." *Business History Review*, Autumn, pp. 469–509.

———. 1990A. *Accountancy Comes of Age: The Development of an American Profession, 1886–1940,* Chapel Hill: University of North Carolina Press.

———. 1990B. "Measurement and Organizational Effectiveness: The ICC and Accounting-Based Regulation, 1887–1940." *Business and Economic History,* July, pp. 183–212.

Mitchell, Neil J. 1989. *The Generous Corporation.* New Haven: Yale University Press.

Mitchell, Wesley. 1918. "Human Behavior and Economic Theory." *Journal of Political Economy,* November, pp. 1–47.

Mobley, Sybil. 1970. "Challenges of Socioeconomic Accounting." *Accounting Review,* October, pp. 762–68.

Montgomery, Robert H. 1904. "The Importance of Uniform Practice in Determining Profits of Public Service Corporations Where Municipalities Have the Power to Regulate Rates." *Financial Record,* November 2, pp. 34–38.

———. 1905. "Value and Recent Development of Theoretical Training for the Public Accountant." *Business Man's Magazine,* September, pp. 417–19.

———. 1907. "Professional Ethics." *Journal of Accountancy,* December, pp. 94–96.

———. 1912A. *Auditing Theory and Practice.* New York: Ronald Press.

———. 1912B. "Federal Control of Corporations." AAPA, *Year Book,* pp. 193–211. See also *Journal of Accountancy,* October, pp. 272–90.

———. 1914. "Accountancy Laboratory—the Connecting Link between Theory and Practice." *Journal of Accountancy,* June, pp. 405–11.

———. 1919. "Discussion." AIA, *Minutes,* pp. 177–80.

———. 1927. "Accountants' Limitations." *Journal of Accountancy,* October, pp. 245–49.

———. 1937. "Curse of Balancing or Theory vs. Practice." *Journal of Accountancy,* April, pp. 279–81.

Montgomery, Robert H., and Walter Staub. 1924. *Auditing Principles.* New York: Ronald Press.

Moody, J. C. 1980. Review of *R. G. Dun & Co., 1841–1900: The Development of Credit Reporting in the Nineteenth Century,* by J. D. Norris. *Business History Review,* Spring, pp. 139–41.

Moody, John. 1904. *The Truth about Trusts.* New York: Moody Publishing.

———. 1916. *How to Analyze Railroad Reports.* 4th ed. New York: Moody's Investor Service.

Moody, Paul. 1845. *A Practical Plan of Bookkeeping by Double Entry.* Philadelphia: J. B. Lippincott.

Moonitz, Maurice. 1961. *The Basic Postulates of Accountancy.* ARS No. 1. New York: AICPA.

————. 1973. "The Beamer Committee: A Golden Opportunity for Accounting Education." *Journal of Accountancy*, August, pp. 64–67.

————. 1974. *Obtaining Agreement on Standards in the Accounting Profession*. Studies in Accounting Research No. 8. Sarasota, FL: AAA.

Moonitz, Maurice, and Carl Nelson. 1960. "Recent Developments in Accounting Theory." *Accounting Review*, April, pp. 206–17.

Moore, R. H. 1899. "Ethics of the Bookkeeper." *The Book-keeper*, May, pp. 34–37.

Moran, M., and G. J. Previts. 1984. "The SEC and the Profession, 1934–84: The Realities of Self-Regulation." *Journal of Accountancy*, July, pp. 68–83.

Morey, Lloyd. 1948. "Trends in Government Accounting." *Accounting Review*, July, pp. 227–34.

Morgan, E. S. 1958. *The Puritan Dilemma: The Story of John Winthrop*. Boston: Little, Brown.

Morris, Richard B. 1975. "Financial Wizards of the Revolution." *Ford Times*, August, pp. 32–37.

Morrison, Paul. 1935. "Reports to Stockholders." *Accounting Review*, March, pp. 77–83.

Most, Kenneth S. 1972. "Sombart's Proposition Revisited." *Accounting Review*, October, pp. 722–34.

————. 1976. "How Wrong Was Sombart?" *Accounting Historians Journal*, Vol. 3, pp. 22–29.

Mott, Frank L. 1954. "The Magazine Revolution and Popular Ideas in the Nineties." *Proceedings of the American Antiquarian Society*, vol. 64, pp. 195–214.

Mouck, Tom. 1989. "The Irony of the Golden Age of Accounting Methodology." *Accounting Historians Journal*, December, pp. 85–106.

Mowry, George. 1965. *The Urban Nation, 1920–1960*. New York: Hill and Wang.

Moyer, C. A. 1951. "Early Developments in American Auditing." *Accounting Review*, January, pp. 1–8.

"Mr. Boutwell and Fiscal Reform." 1871. *Commercial and Financial Chronicle*, January 28, pp. 102–3.

"Mr. McCulloch's Annual Report." 1867. *Commercial and Financial Chronicle*, December 7, pp. 709–10.

Mueller, G. 1989. Letter to Executive Committee of the American Accounting Association, January 9.

"Municipal Finances." 1891. *Commercial & Financial Chronicle*, July 11, pp. 35–36.

Murphy, G. J. 1975. "Historical Vignette: Benjamin Franklin on Accounting." *Accounting Historians Journal*, pp. 49–50.

Murray, David. 1930. *Chapters in the History of Bookkeeping, Accountancy & Commercial Arithmetic*. Glasgow: Jackson, Wylie.

Myer, John C. 1931. "Teaching the Accountant the History and Ethics of His Profession." *Accounting Review*, March, pp. 47–50.

Myers, John H. 1959. "The Critical Event and Recognition of Net Profit." *Accounting Review*, October, pp. 528–32.

Nash, N. C. 1988. "SEC Studies Changes On Private Placements." *New York Times,* October 26, p. D2.

National Association of Accountants. 1986. *The Common Body of Knowledge for Management Accountants.* Statement Number 1D, June 3, Statement on Management Accounting. Montvale, NJ: NAA.

National Association of Cost Accountants. 1921. "A Bibliography of Cost Books." *Official Publications,* April, New York, NACA.

———. 1924. *Industrial and Financial Investigations.* New York: NACA.

National Association of State Boards of Accountancy (NASBA). 1955. "Education and Uniformity." *Proceedings of the 1955 Annual Meeting,* October, pp. 22–24.

———. 1973. *NASBA: A Review of the History, Organization, Accomplishments, Policies and Other Activities of the National Association of State Boards of Accountancy.* New York: NASBA.

———. 1976. "Combination of Education and Experience Required for CPAs: Summary of State Laws and Regulations." New York: NASBA.

National Committee on Governmental Accounting. 1968. *Governmental Accounting, Auditing, and Financial Reporting.* Chicago: Municipal Finance Association.

National Commission on Fraudulent Financial Reporting. 1987. *Report of the National Commission on Fraudulent Financial Reporting.* October, Washington, D.C.

"National Federation of Accountants." 1902. *Commerce, Accounts and Finance,* December, pp. 17–18.

National Society of Public Accountants. 1966. "Rules of Conduct for Members in Tax Practice." *National Public Accountant,* June, pp. 12–13.

Navin, T. R., and M. V. Sears. 1955. "The Rise of a Market for Industrial Securities, 1887–1902." *Business History Review,* June, pp. 105–38.

Nelson, Carl. 1967. "An Accountant's View of Profit Measurement." *Profits in the Modern Economy,* edited by J. R. Nelson and H. W. Stevenson. Minneapolis: University of Minnesota Press.

———. 1976. "Statements to Make an Accountant See Red." *Business Week,* March 8, pp. 12–15.

Nelson, Charles A. 1976. "Is There a Past in Our Future?" *World,* Spring, pp. 2–3.

Nelson, Richard, and Sydney Winter. 1982. *An Evolutionary Theory of Economic Change.* Cambridge: Harvard University Press.

Neu, Dean. 1991. "Trust, Impression Management and the Public Accounting Profession." *Critical Perspectives on Accounting,* September, pp. 295–313.

Neuhaus, R. J. 1991. "The Pope Affirms the 'New Capitalism.'" *Wall Street Journal,* May 2.

Neumann, Fred L. 1968. "Independent Auditor's Concern with Unattested Data in Annual Reports." *New York Certified Public Accountant,* August, pp. 485–90.

New Jersey Society of CPAs (NJSCPA). 1948. *Fifty Years of Service, 1898–1948.* Trenton, NJ: NJSCPA.

Newlove, G. H. 1975. "In All My Years: Economic and Legal Causes of Changes in Accounting." *Accounting Historians Journal,* Winter–Fall, pp. 40–44.

Newman, Maurice. 1967. "Historical Development of Early Accounting Concepts and Their Relation to Certain Economic Concepts." Master's thesis, New York University.

New York State Society of Certified Public Accountants (NYSSCPA). 1897–1912. *Minute Books.* Handwritten in binders. NYSSCPA, New York.

———. 1907. *Ten-Year Book.* New York: NYSSCPA.

———. 1927. *Thirty-Year Book.* New York: NYSSCPA.

New York Stock Exchange. 1978. *Fact Book.* New York: NYSE.

Nichols, Herman. 1927. "Letter to Editor: Inventory Valuations." *Journal of Accountancy,* June, pp. 448–49.

Nicholson, J. Lee. 1913. *Cost Accounting: Theory and Practice.* New York: Ronald Press.

Nikitin, Marcy. 1990. "Setting-up an Industrial Accounting System at Saint-Gobain (1820–1888)." *Accounting Historians Journal,* December, pp. 73–93.

Nissley, Warren. 1935. "Education for the Profession of Accountancy." *Journal of Accountancy,* August, pp. 90–103.

———. 1937. "The Future of Professional Accountancy." *Journal of Accountancy,* February, pp. 99–114.

———. 1940. "Charges against Surplus." In AIA 1940, pp. 38–42.

"No Last Trumpet: Abe Briloff Still Leads the Crusade for Honest Accounting." 1976. *Barron's,* April 12, April 26.

Noble, Edward J. 1939. "Accountancy and the Nation's Business." In AIA 1939B, pp. 279–86.

Noble, H. S. 1927. "The Relation of Business Organization to Accountancy." *Journal of Accountancy,* September, pp. 232–36.

Noble, Paul L. 1950. "A Quantitative Analysis of Accounting Curricula." *Accounting Review,* April, pp. 163–69.

Norgaard, Corine. 1969. "The Professional Accountant's View of Operational Auditing." *Journal of Accountancy,* December, pp. 45–48.

———. 1972. "Extending the Boundaries of the Attest Function." *Accounting Review,* July, pp. 433–42.

North, Douglass C. 1956. "International Capital Flows and the Development of the American West." *Journal of Economic History,* December, pp. 493–505.

Norton, G. P. 1894. *Textile Manufacturers' Book-Keeping.* London: Simkin, Marshall, Hamilton, Kent.

Noyes, Alexander D. 1909. *Forty Years of American Finance.* New York: Putnam.

———. 1926. *The War Period of American Finance, 1908–1925.* New York: Putnam.

Nuawmalee, Prakong. 1957. "The Historical Development of Financial Statements in the United States Between 1900–1933." Master's thesis, University of Pennsylvania.

Oakey, Francis. 1915. "Standardization of Financial Statements." *Journal of Accountancy,* September, pp. 179–85.

Oddy, D. J. 1974. "Early Business History Seminar: Accounting in the Nineteenth Century." *Business History,* July, pp. 175–82.

O'Dell, George T. 1921. "The Federal Trade Commission Yields to Pressure." *The Nation,* January, pp. 36–37.

Okano, H. 1985. "Harrington Emerson and Standard Costing: His Critical Viewpoint on Cost Accounting." *Business Review* (Japan), November, pp. 85–104.

Olds, Leland. 1940. "Responsibility of Accountants in a Changing Order." In AIA 1940, pp. 116–23.

Oliver, Fred M. 1973. "Municipal Governments' Accounting for Federal Grants." *CPA Journal,* December, pp. 1073–78, 1102.

Olson, W. E. 1982. *The Accounting Profession: Years of Trial: 1969–1980.* New York: AICPA.

Ophir, Adi. 1989–90. "Beyond Good—Evil: A Plea for a Hermeneutic Ethics." *Philosophical Forum,* Fall–Winter, pp. 94–121.

Organization for European Economic Cooperation (OEEC). 1952. *Cost Accounting and Productivity: The Use and Practice of Cost Accounting in the USA.* Geneva: OEEC.

Owen, H. S. 1926. "Preparation and Administration of the Budget." *Paper Trade Journal,* December 9, pp. 51–53.

Pace, Homer. 1924. "Relation of the Accountancy Instructor to the Development of Professional Standards in the Practice of Accountancy." *Journal of Accountancy,* May, pp. 349–56.

Packard, S. S. 1868. *Manual of Theoretical Training in the Science of Accounts.* New York: published by the author.

———. 1881. "Philosophy in Book-Keeping." *The Book-Keeper,* December 6, pp. 131–32.

Packard, S. S., and H. B. Bryant. 1878. *The New Bryant and Stratton Common School Book-Keeping.* New York: American Book Company.

Pae, Peter. 1990. "Laventhol Says It Plans to File for Chapter 11." *Wall Street Journal,* November 20, pp. A3–A8.

Palen, Jennie. 1955. "The First Women CPA." *New York Certified Public Accountant,* August, pp. 475–77, 496.

Palmer, John R. 1976. "The Revolution Was Not in Accounting." *Tempo,* vol. 22, pp. 19–23.

Parker, Larry M. 1989. "The Reemergence of Cost Accounting Standards Board." *Research in Accounting Regulation,* pp. 219–27.

Parker, Lee D. 1986. "The Classical Model of Control in the Accounting Literature." *Accounting Historians Journal,* Spring, pp. 71–92.

Parker, R. H. 1965. "Lower of Cost or Market in Great Britain and the United States: An Historical Survey." *Abacus,* December, pp. 156–72.

———. 1986. *The Development of the Accountancy Profession in Britain to the Early Twentieth Century.* Monograph No. 5. Atlanta: Academy of Accounting Historians.

Parrington, Vernon L. 1930. *The Beginnings of Critical Realism in America, 1860–1920.* New York: Harcourt, Brace & World.

Parrish, Michael E. 1970. *Securities Regulation and the New Deal.* New Haven: Yale University Press.

―――. 1982. *Felix Frankfurter and His Times.* New York: Free Press.

Pateman, Carol. 1970. *Participation and Democratic Theory.* Cambridge: Cambridge University Press.

Paton, William A. 1917. "Theory of the Double Entry System." *Journal of Accountancy,* January, pp. 7–26.

―――. 1920A. "Depreciation, Appreciation and Productive Capacity." *Journal of Accountancy,* July, pp. 1–11.

―――. 1920B. "Discussion of Invested Capital." In *Proceedings of the American Association of University Instructors in Accounting,* pp. 46–49.

―――. 1921. "Assumptions of the Accountant." *Administration,* June, pp. 788–802.

―――. 1922. *Accounting Theory.* New York: Ronald Press.

―――. 1924. "Tendencies in the Accounting Literature." In *Proceedings of the American Association of University Instructors in Accounting,* pp. 64–69.

―――. 1931. "Economic Theory in Relation to Accounting Valuations." *Accounting Review,* June, pp. 89–96.

―――. 1932. "Accounting Problems of the Depression." *Accounting Review,* December, pp. 258–67.

―――. 1934. "Shortcomings of Present Day Financial Statements." *Journal of Accountancy,* February, pp. 108–32.

―――. 1935. *Corporate Profits as Shown by Audit Reports.* New York: National Bureau of Economic Research.

―――. 1937. "Presentation of Bond Discount." *Accounting Review,* September, pp. 285–90.

―――. 1938. "Comments on 'A Statement of Accounting Principles.'" *Journal of Accountancy,* March, pp. 196–207. See also "Correspondence," ibid., April, pp. 328.

―――. 1939A. "Objectives of Accounting Research." In AIA 1939B, pp. 229–33.

―――. 1939B. "Plant Write-Ups and Write-Downs and the Resulting Treatment of Depreciation." Typed memorandum, CAP Correspondence File. AICPA, New York.

―――. 1948. "Depreciation and Price Level." *Accounting Review,* April, pp. 118–23.

―――. 1953. "Statement of William Patton, University of Michigan, Ann Arbor," in U.S. Congress, House Committee on Ways and Means, Wednesday, July 22, pp. 699–704.

―――. 1963. "Accounting and the Utilization of Resources." *Journal of Accounting Research,* Spring, pp. 44–72.

―――. 1972. Foreword to the reissue of *The Philosophy of Accounts,* by Charles E. Sprague. Houston, TX: Scholars Book Co.

―――. 1973. "Financial Misrepresentation and Mismeasurement." *Financial Executive,* April, pp. 14–21.

Patton, William A., and A. C. Littleton. 1940. *An Introduction to Corporate Accounting Standards.* Columbus, OH: AAA.

Patton, William A., and Russell Stevenson. 1918. *Principles of Accounting.* 3d ed. New York: Macmillan.

Patten, Simon. 1907. *The New Basis of Civilization.* New York: Macmillan.

Peat, Marwick & Mitchell. 1977. "ARS 173—Review Committee Report." New York: Peat, Marwick & Mitchell.

Pedelahore, J. Earl. 1956. "Case for the Dissent—Report of the Commission on Standards of Education and Experience for CPAs." Typed manuscript. AICPA, New York.

Peloubet, Maurice E. 1928, "Current Assets and the Going Concern." *Journal of Accountancy,* July, pp. 18–22.

———. 1943. "Observations on Cost." *Accounting Review,* January, pp. 9–15.

———. 1955. "The Historical Background of Accounting," In Backer, 1955, pp. 7–39.

Pemberton, Jackson. 1976. "A New Message On the Constitution." *Freeman,* July, pp. 408–18.

Penney, Louis H. 1960. "Why Research?" *Accounting Review,* January, pp. 1–10.

———. 1962. "The American Institute of CPAs." *Journal of Accountancy,* January, pp. 31–39.

Pennsylvania Institute of CPAs (PICPA). 1905. *Fifth Annual Banquet.* Philadelphia: George H. Buchanan Co.

———. 1922. *Records of the Twenty-Fifth Anniversary Proceedings.* Philadelphia: PICPA.

Penrose, Edith. 1959. *The Theory of the Firm.* New York: John Wiley and Sons.

"People Are Capital Investments at R. G. Barry Corporation." 1971. *Management Accounting,* November, pp. 53–55, 63.

Peragallo, Edward. 1956. "Origin of the Trial Balance." *Accounting Review,* July, pp. 389–94.

Perkins, E. J. 1989. "The Entrepreneurial Spirit in Colonial America: The Foundations of Modern Business History." *Business History Review,* Spring, pp. 160–86.

Perry, Donald P. 1955. *Public Accounting Practice and Accounting Education.* Cambridge: Harvard University Press.

Persons, Stow. 1958. *American Minds.* New York: Henry Holt.

Phillippe, Gerald. 1963. "Corporate Management's Stake in the Development of Sound Accounting Principles." Collected Papers of the Annual Meeting, AICPA. New York.

Phillips, Susan, and J. R. Zecher. 1981. *The SEC and the Public Interest.* Cambridge: MIT Press.

Piaker, P. M. 1969. "Non Accounting for Goodwill: A Critical Analysis of Accounting Research Study No. 10." *New York Certified Public Accountant,* November, pp. 837–44.

Pierson, Franklin, et al. 1959. *The Education of American Businessmen.* New York: McGraw-Hill.

Pilcher, D. J. 1935. "Certain Historic Accounting Facts and Trends." *Certified Public Accountant,* March, pp. 134–41.

Pinchot, Amos. 1958. *History of the Progressive Party.* New York: New York University Press.

Pines, J. Arnold. 1965. "Securities and Exchange Commission and Accounting Principles." *Law and Contemporary Problems,* Autumn, pp. 727–51.

Pixley, Francis W. 1881. *Auditors: Their Duties and Responsibilities.* London: Effingham Wilson, Royal Exchange. Reprint, New York: Arno 1976.

———. 1904. "The Duties of Professional Accountants." *Financial Record,* November 2, pp. 28–34.

Porter, Dale L. 1981. *The Emergence of the Past.* Chicago: University of Chicago Press.

Porter, D. M. 1980. "The Waltham System and Early American Textile Cost Accounting, 1813–1848." *Accounting Historians Journal,* Spring, pp. 1–16.

Potts, James. 1976. "An Analysis of the Evolution of Municipal Accounting to 1835 with Primary Emphasis on Developments in the United States." Ph.D. diss., University of Alabama.

Powell, Weldon. 1923. "Accounting for No Par Value Stock." In *Proceedings of the American Association of University Instructors in Accounting.* pp. 114–34. New York, Arno, 1980.

———. 1959. "Report on the APB." AICPA, *Minutes,* pp. 50–57.

———. 1960. "Challenge to Research." *Journal of Accountancy,* February, pp. 34–41.

———. 1961. "Report on the Accounting Research Activities of the American Institute of Certified Public Accountants." *Accounting Review,* January, pp. 26–31.

Pratt, James W. 1973. "The Need for Attested Interim Statements of Public Companies and Attendant Implications." *CPA Journal,* May, pp. 390–95.

Previts, Gary J. 1972. "A Critical Evaluation of Comparative Financial Accounting Thought in America, 1900–1920." Ph.D. diss., University of Florida.

———. 1975A. "American Accountancy: An Overview, 1900–1925." *Business and Economic History,* vol. 5, pp. 109–19.

———. 1975B. "Pathways to a New Vista of Accountancy's Past." *Accounting Historians Journal,* Winter, pp. 3–5.

———. 1976A. "The Accountant in Our History: A Bicentennial Overview." *Journal of Accountancy,* July, pp. 45–51.

———. 1976B. "Origins of American Accounting." *CPA Journal,* May, pp. 13–17.

———. 1978. "The SEC and Its Chief Accountants: Historical Impressions." *Journal of Accountancy,* August, pp. 83–89.

———, ed. 1980. *Early 20th Century Development in American Accounting Thought.* New York: Arno.

———. 1984. "Frameworks of American Financial Accounting Thought." *Accounting Historians Journal,* Fall, pp. 1–17.

———. 1985A. "Pluralism and Professionalism: Issues for the 1990s." *Proceedings of the Accounting Research Convocation 1985,* School of Accountancy, University of Alabama, pp. 1–9.

———. 1985B. *The Scope of CPA Services: A Study of the Development of the Concept of Independence and the Profession's Role in Society.* New York: John Wiley and Sons.

———. 1990. "A Centennial Sketch of Accountancy Education in the United States."

In *Comparative International Accounting Educational Standards.* pp. 31–40. Urbana: CIERA, University of Illinois.

———, ed. 1991. *Financial Reporting and Standard Setting.* New York: AICPA.

———. 1992. "Financial Reporting in an Investor Fund Economy." *Research in Accounting Regulation,* pp. 201–10.

———. 1996. "The Politics of Disclosure." *Research in Accounting Regulation,* pp. 211–14.

Previts, Gary J., and Barbara D. Merino. 1979. *A History of Accounting in America.* New York: John Wiley and Sons.

Previts, Gary J., and Terry K. Sheldahl. 1977. "Accounting and 'Countinghouses': An Analysis and Commentary." *Abacus,* June, pp. 52–59.

———. 1988. "From Rote to Reason: The Development of American Accounting Thought from 1830 to 1880." In *Collected Papers of the Fifth World Congress of Accounting Historians,* edited by A. T. Craswell. Sydney: University of Sydney Press.

Price Waterhouse. 1976. *Cost Accounting Standards Board: A Guide to the Background, Objectives, Operations and Pronouncements of the Cost Accounting Standards Board.* New York: Price Waterhouse.

Prickett, A. L. 1931. "Labor Turnover Rate and Cost." *Accounting Review,* December, pp. 261–77.

Priest, D. 1991. "Whitten Opposing Chief Financial Officers Act." *Washington Post,* May 24.

"The Proposed Corporation Tax Bill." 1909. *Journal of Accountancy,* July, pp. 237–39.

Pryce-Jones, J. E., and R. H. Parker. 1974. *Accounting in Scotland: A Historical Bibliography.* Glasgow: Institute of Chartered Accountants of Scotland.

"Punters or Proprietors?" 1990. *The Economist,* May 5, pp. 5–20.

"A Radical Goal for Financial Statements." 1973. *Business Week,* October 6, pp. 46–48.

Putnam, B. H., and E. I. Stevens. 1991. "Management as a Liberal Art." *Chronicle of Higher Education,* July 24, p. B2.

Puxty, Anthony G. 1993. *The Social and Organizational Context of Management Accounting.* London: Academic Press.

Queenan, John W. 1962. "Current Problems and Opportunities of the CPA." Speech delivered at Omaha, Nebraska, June 18. AICPA, New York.

———. 1966. "The Development of Accounting Principles." In *Selected Papers 1966,* by Haskins & Sells. New York: Haskins & Sells.

———. 1977. Interview by B. Merino. March.

"Railroad Management and Its Bearing on the Value of Stocks." 1867. *Commercial and Financial Chronicle,* April 27, pp. 520–21.

Rappaport, A. 1990 "The Staying Power of the Public Corporation." *Harvard Business Review,* January/February, pp. 96–104.

Rappaport, Louis H. 1963. "Forces Influencing Accounting: The Stock Exchanges." *Lybrand Journal,* pp. 43–57.

Ratoff, Steven B. 1973. "Auditing Phase II Price Control Compliance." *CPA Journal,* February, pp. 115–19, 131.

Rautenstrauch, Walter. 1924. "The Budget as a Means of Industrial Control." *Chemical and Metal Engineering,* August 30, pp. 415–16.

Rayburn, F. R. 1986. "A Chronological Review of the Authoritative Literature on Interperiod Tax Allocation: 1940–1985." *Accounting Historians Journal,* Fall, pp. 89–108.

———. 1991. "The Cost Accounting Standards Board: Its Creation, Its Demise and Its Re-establishment." *The Costing Heritage,* edited by F. Graves. pp. 99–121. Monograph No. 6, The Academy of Accounting Historians.

Rayburn, Samuel. 1933. Letter to R. W. Morrison. Correspondence Files, Rayburn Library, Bonham, TX.

Raymond, Robert H. 1966. "History of the Flexible Budget." *Management Accounting,* August, pp. 9–15.

Razek, Joseph R. 1987. "Ante-Bellum Banking—a Case Study: The New Orleans Savings Bank in the 1930s." *Accounting Historians Journal,* Fall, pp. 19–39.

"Recent Court Decision Helps Put Out the Fire Burning Accounting Firms." 1990. *Public Accounting Report,* June 15, p. 6.

Reckitt, Ernest. 1953. *Reminiscences of Early Days of the Accounting Profession.* Chicago: Illinois Society of Certified Public Accountants.

Reed, Sarah A. 1989. "A Historical Analysis of Depreciation Accounting: The U.S. Steel Experience." *Accounting Historians Journal,* December, pp. 119–54.

"Reform of Federal Governmental Accounting." 1948. *Journal of Accountancy,* February, pp. 93–94.

Reich, Robert. 1989. *The Resurgent Liberal.* New York: Vintage Books.

Reid, J. M. 1988. "Legal Acceptance of Accounting Principles in Great Britain and the United States." *Accounting Historians Journal,* Spring, pp. 1–27.

Reighard, John J. 1932. "Earning Statements in Periods of Prosperity and Depression." *Accounting Review,* June, pp. 108–14.

Reigner, C. G. 1958. *Beginnings of the Business School.* Baltimore: H. M. Rowe.

Reiter, P. 1926. *Profits, Dividends and the Law.* New York: Ronald Press.

Remond, J. L. 1900. "Needs in Municipal Accounting." *Business,* October, pp. 464–65.

"Reorganization of the Accountants Examining Board." 1897. *Accountics,* November, p. 38.

"Report of the American Institute of Accountants Special Committee on Cooperation with the SEC." 1937. *Journal of Accountancy,* June, pp. 434–43.

"Report of the Committee on Behavioral Science Content of the Accounting Curriculum." 1971. *Accounting Review,* Supplement, pp. 260–84.

"Report of the Committee on Management Accounting." 1959. *Accounting Review,* April, pp. 207–14.

"Report of the Sub-Committee on Independent Audits and Audit Procedure of the Committee on Stock List." 1939. New York Stock Exchange, April 15.

"Reports on 'Introduction to Corporate Accounting Standards' and 'A Statement of Accounting Principles.'" 1940. *Journal of Accountancy,* October, pp. 48–57.

"Review and Outlook: Accounting's New Horizons." 1973. *Wall Street Journal,* October 30, p. 18.

R. G. Barry. 1969. *Annual Report of R. G. Barry Corporation.* Cincinnati: R. G. Barry.

Richardson, A. P., ed. 1913. *The Influence of Accountants' Certificates on Commercial Credit.* New York: AAPA.

Richardson, Mark. 1960. "Standards of Responsibility of CPAs in Tax Practice." *Journal of Accountancy,* January, pp. 29–33.

Richberg, Donald C. 1937. "The New Deal's Revolution Defended." *New York Times Magazine,* December 5. Reprinted in Degler 1970, pp. 220–33.

Rice, W. B. 1944. "Statistical Uses of Accounting Data." *Accounting Review,* July, pp. 260–66.

Ripley, William Z. 1927. *Main Street and Wall Street.* Boston: Little, Brown.

Rittenhouse, Charles F. 1921. "The Scope and Content of a Course in Accounting Systems." *Proceeding of American Association of University Instructors in Accounting,* pp. 79–88.

———. 1923. "President's Address." *Proceedings of American Association of University Instructors in Accounting,* pp. 59–65.

Robert, R. 1957. "Roman Accounting." *Accountant,* August 10, pp. 157–58.

Roberts, Alfred R. 1975. "American Accountancy: An Overview, 1875–1900." *Business and Economic History,* vol. 4, pp. 98–108.

Robbins, Carl. 1929. "Business Secrets." *Accounting Review,* June, pp. 65–79; September, pp. 155–66.

Robinson, J. S. 1925. "The Concept of Cost." *Proceedings of the American Association of University Instructors in Accounting,* pp. 72–79.

Robinson, Maurice H. 1909. "Accounting in Relation to Economics." *Journal of Accountancy,* February, pp. 282–94.

Ronen, Joshua, Simcha Sadan, and Charles Snow. 1976. "Income Smoothing: A Review." *Accounting Journal,* Winter, pp. 11–22.

Roosevelt, F. D. 1933. *Looking Forward.* New York: John Day.

Roosevelt, T. R. 1901. "Presidential Message." *Congressional Record–Senate.* Vol. 35, pt. 1, December 3, pp. 81–92.

———. 1904. *Address and Presidential Messages of Theodore Roosevelt.* New York: Putnam.

———. 1908. "Presidential Message." *Congressional Record–Senate.* Vol. 43, pt. 1, December 8, pp. 16–29.

Rorem, C. Rufus. 1928A. *Accounting Method.* Chicago: University of Chicago Press.

———. 1928B. "Social Control through Accounts." *Accounting Review,* September, pp. 261–68.

———. 1929. "Replacement Cost in Accounting Valuation." *Accounting Review,* September, pp. 167–74.

———. 1932. "The Costs of Medical Care." *Accounting Review,* March, pp. 38–41.

———. 1937. "Accounting Theory: A Critique of the Tentative Statement of Accounting Principles." *Accounting Review,* June, pp. 132–38.

———. 1981. *A Quest for Certainty: Essays on Health Care.* New York: Garland.

Rorty, Richard. 1982. *Consequences of Pragmatism.* Minneapolis: University of Minnesota Press.

Rosen, L. S., and D. T. DeCoster. 1969. "Funds Statement: An Historical Perspective." *Accounting Review,* January, pp. 124–36.

Rosenbaum, D. E. 1990. "Big Shortfall in Corporate Taxes Thwarts Key Goal of 1986 Law." *New York Times,* March 6.

Rosenkampff, A. H. 1921. "The Scope and Content of a Course in Accounting Systems." *Proceedings of American Association of University Instructors in Accounting,* pp. 88–100.

Rosenthal, H. F. 1989. "Judge Suspends Jail Terms, Orders Fine." *Cleveland Plain Dealer,* July 6, pp. 1A.

Ross, Edward A. 1916. "The Making of a Profession." *International Journal of Ethics,* October, pp. 67–79.

Ross, Frances E. 1974. "John Caldwell Colt." *Dividend,* Spring, pp. 17–19.

Ross, Howard. 1969. *Financial Statements: A Crusade for Current Values.* New York: Pitman.

Ross, Stephen. 1979. "Disclosure Regulation in Financial Markets: Implications of Modern Finance Theory and Signaling Theory." In Edwards 1979, pp. 180–298.

Ross, T. Edward. 1937. "Random Recollection of an Eventful Half Century." *LRB & M Journal,* January, pp. 7–25.

———. 1940A. *Pioneers of Public Accountancy in the United States.* Philadelphia: E. Stern Co.

———. 1940B. "What the Practitioner Looks for in the College Trained Accountant." In AIA 1940, pp. 89–90.

Rostow, W. W. 1971. *The Stages of Economic Growth.* Cambridge: Cambridge University Press.

———. 1975. *How It All Began.* New York: McGraw-Hill.

Roth, William. 1968. "Breaking the Tablets: A New Look at the Old Opinion." *Journal of Accountancy,* July, pp. 63–67.

Rousseas, Stephen. 1979. *Capitalism and Catastrophe.* London: Cambridge University Press.

Roy, Robert A. 1964. "The Common Body Study—Evidence and Opinions." *Journal of Accountancy,* August, pp. 78–82.

Roy, Robert A., and James MacNeill. 1967. *Horizons for a Profession.* New York: AICPA.

———. 1968. "A Reply to The Common Body of Knowledge for CPAs: Some Problems in Analysis." *Journal of Accounting Research,* Autumn, p. 142.

Royster, V. 1987. "The Revenue Act of 1987?" *Wall Street Journal,* January 14, p. 16.

Rublee, George. 1926. "The Original Plan and Early History of the Federal Trade Commission." *Annals of the American Academy of Political and Social Science,* January, pp. 115–17.

Rudd, George H. 1939. "Bases for Accounting Research." In AIA 1939B, pp. 245–52.

Ruml, F. 1928. "The Formative Period of Higher Education in American Universities." *Journal of Business,* April, pp. 238–63.

Rutledge, J. 1991. "Economic Outlook: Managing Capital in the Coming Decade." *US News & World Report,* April 22, p. 49.

Sack, Robert J. 1985. "Commercialism in the Profession: A Threat to Be Managed." *Journal of Accountancy,* October, pp. 125–34.

Safer, Karl. 1966. *Theory of Accounts in Double-Entry Bookkeeping.* Urbana: CIERA, University of Illinois.

Sakolski, A. M. 1909. "The Federal Corporation Law and Modern Accounting." *Yale Review,* February, pp. 372–89.

Salwen, K. G. 1991. "SEC to Air Short-Sales Registration." *Wall Street Journal,* June 7, p. C1.

Sampson, Roy J. 1960. "American Accounting Education, Textbooks and Public Practice Prior to 1900." *Business History Review,* Winter, pp. 459–66.

Samuelson, Paul A. 1962. "Economists and the History of Ideas." *American Economic Review,* March, pp. 1–18.

———. 1975. "U.S. Still the Richest?" *Newsweek,* August 18, p. 66.

Sanders, Thomas H. 1921. "A Graduate Course in Industrial Accounting." *Proceedings of American Association of University Instructors in Accounting,* pp. 88–100.

———. 1929. *Industrial Accounting: Control of Industry through Costs.* New York: McGraw-Hill.

———. 1933. Review of *Basic Standard Costs,* by Eric Cammon. *Accounting Review,* June, pp. 175–76.

———. 1937. "Comments on the Statement of Accounting Principles." *Accounting Review,* March, pp. 76–79.

———. 1939. "Introduction—Progress in Accounting Research." In AIA 1939B, pp. 227–29.

———. 1944. "Accounting as a Means of Social and Economic Control." *NACA Bulletin,* December, pp. 319–34.

Sanders, Thomas H., Henry R. Hatfield, and Underhill Moore. 1938. *A Statement of Accounting Principles.* New York: American Institute of Accountants.

Sargeant, James E. 1981. *Roosevelt and the Hundred Days.* New York: Garland.

Sass, S. A. 1982. *The Pragmatic Imagination: A History of the Wharton School, 1881–1981.* Philadelphia: University of Pennsylvania Press.

Saxe, Emannuel. 1971. "Accountants' Responsibility for Unaudited Statements: A Recent Case." *New York Certified Public Accountant,* September, pp. 651–60.

———. 1972. "Unaudited Financial Statements: Rules, Risks and Recommendations." *CPA Journal,* June, pp. 457–64.

Schaefer, W. G. 1988. "Lame 'Random Walk' Theory." Letters to the Editor, *Wall Street Journal,* January 6, p. 17.

Schein, Edgar H. 1972. *Professional Education: Some New Directions.* New York: McGraw-Hill.

Schlesinger, Arthur M., Sr. 1939. *Political and Social Growth of the United States, 1852–1933.* New York: Macmillan.

Schlesinger, Arthur M., Jr. 1956. *The Crisis of the Old Order, 1919–1933.* Boston: Houghton Mifflin.

———. 1959. *The Coming of the New Deal.* Boston: Houghton Mifflin.

———. 1995. "The Talk of the Town: Camelot Revisited." *New Yorker,* June 5, p. 33.

Schluter, William. 1933. "Accountancy under Economic Self-Government." *Accounting Review,* December, pp. 278–84.

Schmidt, Fritz. 1930. "The Importance of Replacement Value." *Accounting Review,* September, pp. 235–42.

———. 1931. "Is Appreciation Profit?" *Accounting Review,* December, pp. 289–93.

Schmidt, L. B. 1939. "Internal Commerce and the Development of the National Economy before 1860." *Journal of Political Economy,* December, pp. 798–822.

Scholfield, A. G. 1880. *Essay on debit and credit, embodying an elementary and practical treatise on book-keeping.* Providence: Press of J. A. and R. A. Reid.

———. 1890. *The Key to Success in Business.* Providence: Scholfield's Commercial College.

Schroeder, R. G., L. D. McQullers, and M. Clark. 1987. *Accounting Theory.* New York: John Wiley and Sons.

Schultz, J. J., ed. 1989. *Reorienting Accounting Education: Reports on the Environment, Professoriate and Curriculum of Accounting,* Accounting Education Series No. 10. Sarasota, FL: AAA.

Schumpeter, J. A. 1942. *Capitalism, Socialism, and Democracy.* New York: Harper & Row.

———. 1946. "The American Economy in the Interwar Period." *American Economic Review,* May, pp. 1–10.

Schur, Ira. 1976. Interview by B. Merino, December.

Scott, DR. 1931A. *The Cultural Significance of Accounts.* Lawrence, KS: Scholars Book Club, 1976.

———. 1931B. "Unity in Accounting Theory." *Accounting Review,* June, pp. 106–12.

———. 1933. "Veblen Not an Institutional Economist." *American Economic Review,* June, pp. 274–77.

———. 1937A. "The Tentative Statement of Principles." *Accounting Review,* September, pp. 296–303.

———. 1937B. "Trends in the Techniques and Tools of Management." *Accounting Review,* June, pp. 130–45.

———. 1939. "Responsibilities of Accountants in a Changing Economy." *Accounting Review,* December, pp. 396–401.

———. 1941. "The Basis for Accounting Principles." *Accounting Review,* December, pp. 341–49.

Scovill, Hiram T. 1924. "The Relation of Accounting Instructors to Professional Associations." *Proceedings of the American Association of University Instructors in Accounting,* pp. 49–54.

"Scrapbook—Elijah Watt Sells." Haskins & Sells Archival Collection, New York.

SEC (U.S. Securities and Exchange Commission). 1939. *United States of America before the Securities Exchange Commission in the Matter of McKesson Robbins: Testimony of Expert Witnesses.* Washington, D.C.: GPO. Reprint New York: Garland, 1982.

"SEC Seeks Control of Unaudited Companies." 1946. *Journal of Accountancy,* August, pp. 93–95.

"Secret Reserves." 1915. *The Accountant,* March 13, pp. 335–36.

Seidler, Lee J. 1972. "The Chaos in Financial Accounting: Will It Continue?" *Financial Analysts Journal,* March–April, pp. 88–91.

———. 1973 . "The Financial Accounting Standards Board: Goldfish in a Pool of Sharks." *Accountants Magazine,* October, pp. 558–66.

———. 1975. "No Accounting for Conspirators." *Business Week,* June 23, p. 10.

Seidler, Lee J., and Lynn L. Seidler. 1975. *Social Accounting: Theory, Issues and Cases.* Los Angeles: Melville.

Seligman, Eustace. 1934A. "Amend the Securities Act." *Atlantic Monthly,* March, pp. 370–80.

———. 1934B. "An Analysis of the Securities Act Amendments." *New York Times,* June 6.

Seligman, Joel. 1982. *The Transformation of Wall Street: A History of the Securities and Exchange Commission and Modern Corporate Finance.* Boston: Houghton Mifflin.

Sells, Elijah Watt. 1906. "Inaugural Address." *Journal of Accountancy,* November, pp. 39–41.

———. 1908. *Corporate Management Compared With Government Control.* New York: Press of Safety Systems.

———. 1922. "Causes of Examination Failure." *Journal of Accountancy,* March, pp. 232–33.

Shanks, Alexander Graham. 1964. "Sam Rayburn and the New Deal." Ph.D. diss., University of North Carolina.

Shannon, F. A. 1951. *America's Economic Growth.* New York: Macmillan.

Shaw, R. 1991. Editorial. *Columbia,* March.

Sheldahl, T. K. 1985A. "America's Earliest Recorded Text in Accounting: Sarjeant's 1789 Book." *Accounting Historians Journal,* Fall, pp. 1–42.

———. 1985B. Review of *Three Centuries of Accounting in Massachusetts,* by W. Holmes, et al. *Accounting Historians Journal,* Fall, pp. 138–41.

———. 1988. "Accounting Education in the Eighteenth Century America." In *Dedication Seminar of the Accounting History Research Center: Proceedings,* edited by N. X. Dressel, E. L. Slocum, and A. R. Roberts, pp. 82–130. Atlanta: Academy of Accounting Historians.

———. 1989. *Accounting Literature in the United States Before Mitchell and Jones 1796.* New York: Garland.

Shelton, R. C. 1961. "Accounting and the Unauthorized Practice of Law: Balance Sheet or Brief." *Kentucky Law Journal,* Summer, pp. 542–51.

Shenkir, William. 1974. "Efforts by Authoritative Bodies to Establish a Conceptual Framework for Financial Reporting." Typed memorandum. FASB.

Shenkir, William, G. A. Welsch, and J. A. Baer, Jr. 1972. "Thomas Jefferson: Management Accountant." *Journal of Accountancy,* April, pp. 33–47.

Sherman, W. Richard. 1986. "Where is the 'r' in Debit?" *Accounting Historians Journal,* Fall, pp. 127–43.

Sheys, B. 1818. *The American Book-keeper; etc.* New York: Collins. Reprint, Tokyo: Yushodo Booksellers, 1982.

Simon, Herbert. 1947. *Administrative Behavior.* New York: Macmillan.

Simpson, Kemper. 1916. "Prospectuses of the New Industrials." *Journal of Accountancy,* October, pp. 265–69.

————. 1921. *Economics for the Accountant.* New York: Appleton.

Sinclair, Andrew. 1981. *Corsair: The Life of J. Pierpont Morgan.* Boston: Little, Brown.

Sinclair, Upton. 1911. *"The Principles of Scientific Management;* A Criticism." With an answer by F. W. Taylor. *American Magazine,* March, p. 243.

Sivkumar, K., and G. Waymire. 1994. "Voluntary Interim Disclosures by Early 20th Century New York Stock Exchange Industrials." *Contemporary Accounting Research,* Spring, pp. 673–98.

Skinner, R. M. 1987. *Accounting Standards in Evolution.* Toronto: Holt, Rinehart.

Slocum, E., and A. Roberts. 1980. "The New York School of Accounts: A Beginning." *Accounting Historians Journal,* Fall, pp. 63–70.

Smalls, I. S. 1973. "Hospital Cost Controls." *Management Accounting,* March, pp. 17–20.

Smith, Alexander. 1912. "The Abuse of Audits in Selling Securities." AAPA, *Year Book,* pp. 169–80. See also *Journal of Accountancy,* October, pp. 243–53.

Smith, E. H. 1971. *Charles Carroll of Carrollton.* Reprint of the 1942 ed. New York: Barnes & Noble.

Smith, Frank P. 1955. "Progress Report of Commission on Standards of Education and Experience for Certified Public Accountants." *NASBA 1955 Proceedings,* pp. 28–29.

Smith, K. A. 1972. "The Relationship of Internal Control Evaluation and Audit Sample Size." *Accounting Review,* April, pp. 260–69.

Smith, M. R. 1977. *Harpers Ferry Armory and the New Technology.* Ithaca: Cornell University Press.

————. 1984. Review of *The Coming of Industrial Order: Town and Factory Life in Rural Massachusetts, 1810–1860,* by Jonathan Prude. *Business History Review,* Autumn, pp. 428–30.

Smith, Willis A. 1973. "The Revised AICPA Rules of Conduct: To Serve the Public Interest." *CPA Journal,* November, pp. 963–68.

Sobel, Robert I. 1965. *The Big Board.* New York: Free Press.

————. 1968. *The Great Bull Market.* New York: Norton.

Solomons, David. 1961. "Economic and Accounting Concepts of Income." *Accounting Review,* July, pp. 374–83.

————. 1965. *Divisional Performance Measurement and Control.* Ontario: Irwin Dorsey.

————. 1968. "The Historical Development of Costing." *Studies in Cost Analysis,* edited by David Solomons. Homewood, IL: Irwin.

————. 1987. "The Twilight of Income Measurement: Twenty-Five Years On." *Accounting Historians Journal,* Spring, pp. 1–6.

Sombart, Werner. 1924. *Der moderne Kapitalismus.* 6th ed. Munich and Leipzig: Duncker & Humblot.

Sorter, George. 1969. "An Events Approach to Basic Accounting Theory." *Accounting Review,* January, pp. 12–19.

Sorter, George, and Charles Horngren. 1962. "Asset Recognition and Economic Attributes: The Relevant Costing Approach." *Accounting Review,* July, pp. 391–99.

Soulé, George. 1911. *Soulé's New Science and Practice of Accounts.* 9th ed. New Orleans: published by the author.

Soulé, George. 1924. "The Safety Razor Views Society." *New Republic,* October 1, pp. 5–6.

———. 1967. *Planning USA.* New York: Viking.

Sowell, Elliott. 1973. *The Evolution of the Theories and Techniques of Standard Costs.* Tuscaloosa: University of Alabama Press.

Spacek, Leonard. 1953. "Statement of Leonard Spacek, Managing Partner, Arthur Andersen, Chicago." U.S. Congress, House Committee on Ways and Means, Thursday, July 3, pp. 733–34.

———. 1956. "Are Industrial Common Stocks Selling at Fictitious Earnings?" Address before Financial Analysts of Philadelphia. Chicago: Arthur Andersen Library.

———. 1958A. "Can We Define Generally Accepted Accounting Principles?" *Journal of Accountancy,* December, pp. 40–47.

———. 1958B. "The Need for an Accounting Court." *Accounting Review,* July, pp. 368–79.

———. 1964A. "A Suggested Solution to the Principles Dilemma." *Accounting Review,* April, pp. 275–84.

———. 1964B. "Are Double Standards Good Enough for Investors but Unacceptable to the Securities Industry?" *Journal of Accountancy,* November, pp. 67–72.

Sprague, Charles E. 1880. "The Algebra of Accounts." *The Book-Keeper,* July 20, pp. 2–4.

———. 1901. "The General Principles of the Science of Accounts." *Commerce, Accounts and Finance,* February, pp. 1–2.

———. 1906. "Premiums and Discounts." *Journal of Accountancy,* August, pp. 294–96.

———. 1908. *The Philosophy of Accounts.* New York: published by the author.

———. 1978. "Income and Outlay." *Accounting Historians Journal,* Fall, pp. 79–84.

Sprouse, Robert T. 1963. "Historical Costs and Current Assets—Traditional and Treacherous." *Accounting Review,* October, pp. 687–95.

———. 1964. "The 'Radically Different' Principles of Accounting Research Study No. 3." *Journal of Accountancy,* May, pp. 63–69.

Sprouse, Robert T., and Maurice Moonitz. 1963. *A Tentative Set of Broad Accounting Principles for Business Enterprises.* ARS No. 3. New York: AICPA.

Staats, Elmer B. 1968. "Information Needs in an Era of Change." *Management Accounting,* October, pp. 11–15.

———. 1969. "Uniform Cost Accounting Standards in Negotiated Defense Contracts." *Management Accounting,* January, pp. 21–25.

———. 1972. "The Role of the Accountant in the 1970s." *Management Accounting,* April, pp. 13–14, 19.

Stamp, Edward. 1981. "Why Can Accounting Not Become a Science Like Physics?" *Abacus,* Vol. 17, No. 1, pp. 13–27.

Starkey, Rodney. 1935. Letter to G. O. May, June 28. May Papers, SEC File 35. Price Waterhouse Library, New York.

———. 1938. "Statement." AIA, *Minutes,* pp. 82–83.

Staub, E. Elmer. 1912. "Municipal Cost Accounts." *Journal of Accountancy,* February, pp. 99–108.

Staub, Walter A. 1904. "Mode of Conducting an Audit." *Financial Record,* November 2, pp. 40–43.

———. 1939. "Uniformity in Accounting." In AIA 1939B, pp. 3–7.

———. 1942. *Auditing Developments during the Present Century.* Cambridge: Harvard University Press.

Staubus, George J. 1957. *Activity Costing and Input/Output.* Homewood, IL: Irwin.

———. 1958. "Comments on 'Accounting and Reporting Standards for Corporate Financial Statements—1957 Revision.'" *Accounting Review,* January, pp. 11–24.

———. 1959. "The Residual Equity Point of View in Accounting." *Accounting Review,* January, pp. 3–13.

———. 1971. *Activity Costing and Input Output Accounting,* Homewood, IL: Irwin.

———. 1987. "The Dark Ages of Cost Accounting: The Role of Miscues in the Literature." *Accounting Historians Journal,* Fall, pp. 1–18.

Stedry, Andrew. 1960. *Budget Control and Cost Behavior.* Englewood Cliffs, NJ: Prentice Hall.

Stempf, Victor H. 1944A. "The Post War Challenge." In AIA 1944, pp. 1–8.

———. 1944B. "Some Problems of Professional Advancement." *Canadian Chartered Accountant,* April, pp. 204–14.

Sterling, Robert. 1967A. "Elements of Pure Accounting Theory." *Accounting Review,* January, pp. 62–73.

———. 1967B. "Reviewer's Corner: A Statement of Basic Accounting Theory." *Journal of Accounting Research,* Spring, pp. 95–112.

———. 1971. *Asset Valuation and Income Determination.* Lawrence, KS: Scholars Book Club.

———. 1973. "Accounting Research, Education and Practice." *Journal of Accountancy,* September, pp. 44–61.

———, ed. 1974. *Institutional Issues in Public Accounting.* Lawrence, KS: Scholars Book.

———. 1976. "Accounting at the Crossroads." *World,* Spring, pp. 51–56.

Stern, Joel M. 1972. "Let's Abandon Earnings Per Share." *Wall Street Journal,* December 18, p. 14.

Sterrett, Joseph E. 1904. "Chairman's Address." *Official Record of the Congress of Accountants,* pp. 23–33.

———. 1905. "Education and Training of a Certified Public Accountant." *Journal of Accountancy,* November, pp. 1–15.

———. 1906. "The Profession of Accountancy." *Annals of the American Academy of Political and Social Science,* July, pp. 16–27.

———. 1907. "Professional Ethics." AAPA, *Year Book,* pp. 108–33. See also *Journal of Accountancy,* October, pp. 407–31.

———. 1908. "Present Position and Probable Development of Accountancy as a Profession." *Proceedings of the Annual Meeting of the American Economic Association,* pp. 85–96.

———. 1913. "Interest Not Part of Cost of Production." *Journal of Accountancy,* April, pp. 241–44.

———. 1916. "Comparative Yield on Trade and Public Service Investments." *American Economic Review,* March, pp. 1–8.

Stevens, W. S. 1926. "Stockholders' Voting Rights and the Centralization of Voting Control." *Quarterly Journal of Economics,* May, pp. 353–401.

Stevenson, H. W., and J. R. Nelson, eds. 1967. *Profit in the Modern Economy.* Minneapolis: University of Minnesota Press.

Stevenson, W. C. 1900. "Development of Principles of Debit and Credit." *Business,* July, pp. 305–7.

Stidger, William L. 1923. "Henry Ford's Ideal: People Before Profits." *Outlook,* May 9, pp. 845–46.

Stone, Williard E. 1960. "Can Accounting Meet the Challenge of Liberalized Business Education?" *Accounting Review,* July, pp. 515–20.

———. 1973. "An Early English Cotton Mill Cost Accounting System: Charlton Mills, 1810–1889." *Accounting and Business Research,* Winter, pp. 71–78.

———. 1975. "Accounting Woes, Pilgrim Style." *Massachusetts CPA Review,* November–December, pp. 7–8, 36.

———. 1979. "1794 Middletown, Delaware—from Accounting Records." *Accounting Historians Journal,* pp. 39–52.

———. 1982A. "Editor's Preface." *Book-keeping in the True Italian Form,* by W. Jackson. 1801. Reprint ed., Tokyo: Yushodo Booksellers.

———. 1982B. "Editor's Preface." *The American System of Practical Book-keeping,* by J. Bennett. 1820. Reprint ed. Tokyo: Yushodo Booksellers.

———. 1982C. "Editor's Preface." *Book-keeping and Accountantship,* by Thomas Jones. 1859. Reprint ed. Tokyo: Yushodo Booksellers.

———. 1982D. "Editor's Preface." *Agricultural Book-Keeping: Being a Concise and Scientific System of Keeping Farm Accounts,* by W. D. Cochran. 1858. Reprint ed. Tokyo: Yushodo Booksellers.

———. 1982E. "Editor's Preface." *The American Book-keeper,* by B. Sheys. 1818. Reprint ed. Tokyo: Yushodo Booksellers.

———. 1986. "The Boston Bookkeeping Schools: Comer's Commercial College." Unpublished manuscript.

Storey, Reed K. 1959. "Revenue Realization, Going Concern and Measurement of Income." *Accounting Review,* April, pp. 232–38.

———. 1964. *The Search for Accounting Principles.* New York: AICPA.

Suffern, Edward L. 1909. "Corporation Tax Law." *Journal of Accountancy,* October, pp. 397–400.

Suffern, Ernest S. 1909. "Are CPA Examinations Always Fair?" *Journal of Accountancy,* March, pp. 384–89.

————. 1910. "Accountant as a Financial Advisor." *Moody's Magazine,* June, pp. 437–44.

————. 1911. "Safety First." AAPA, *Minutes,* 164–70.

————. 1912. "Accountant: What He Is, What He Does and the Place He Occupies in the New Economics of Business." *Canadian Chartered Accountant,* October, pp. 112–17.

————. 1922. "Twenty-Five Years of Accountancy." *Journal of Accountancy,* September, pp. 174–81.

Summers, E. L. 1977. "Academic Opportunities Related to MAS in the CPA Profession." In *Emerging Issues,* Proceedings of the Alabama Accounting Research Convocation, 1976, pp. 91–111.

Suojanen, Waino. 1954. "A Theory of Large Corporations." *Accounting Review,* July, pp. 391–98.

Supreme Court of the United States. 1984. *United States v. Arthur Young & Co. et al.* Syllabus and Opinion, March 21, I-III; 1–15; 82–687.

Swanson, G. A., and J. C. Gardner. 1986. "The Inception and Evolution of Financial Reporting in the Protestant Episcopal Church in the United States of America." *Accounting Historians Journal,* Fall, pp. 55–63.

Swanson, Theodore. 1972. "Touche-Ross: A Biography." *Tempo,* Special Anniversary Issue.

Sweeney, Charles T. 1937. "Comment." *Accounting Review,* December, pp. 403–6.

Sweeney, Henry W. 1930. "Maintenance of Capital." *Accounting Review,* December, pp. 277–87.

————. 1931. "Stabilized Depreciation." *Accounting Review,* September, pp. 165–78.

————. 1932. "Stabilized Appreciation." *Accounting Review,* June, pp. 115–21.

————. 1933A. "Capital." *Accounting Review,* September, pp. 185–99.

————. 1933B. "Income." *Accounting Review,* December, pp. 323–35.

————. 1934. "How Inflation Affects Balance Sheets." *Accounting Review,* December, pp. 275–99.

Swisher, C. B. 1958. *Historic Decisions of the Supreme Court.* New York: Van Nostrand.

Sylla, R. 1985. "Early American Banking: The Significance of the Corporate Form." *Business and Economic History,* pp. 105–23.

"A Symposium on Appreciation Prepared by Graduate Students at the University of Illinois with Comments by Andrew Barr, C. C. Carpenter, E. R. Dillavou, Irving Fisher, Louis O. Foster, Henry Rand Hatfield, and John R. Wildman." 1930. *Accounting Review,* March, pp. 1–59.

Taft, William H. 1909A. "Presidential Message." *Congressional Record–Senate.* Vol. 45, pt. 1, December 9, pp. 25–33.

————. 1909B. "Special Message on Federal Incorporation." *Congressional Record–Senate.* Vol. 45, pt. 1, December 9, pp. 381–83.

Taggart, Herbert. 1934. Relation of Cost Accounting to the NRA Code. *Accounting Review,* April, pp. 149–77.

————. 1949. "1948 Revision of the American Accounting Association's Statement of Principles and Comparison with the 1941 Statement." *Accounting Review,* January, pp. 54–60.

Tawney, R. H. 1926. *Religion and the Rise of Capitalism.* New York: Harcourt, Brace.

"Tax Relief and Tax Repeal." 1872. *Commercial and Financial Chronicle,* March 2, pp. 278–79.

Taylor, Frederick W. 1895. "A Piece Rate System Being a Step Toward a Partial Solution of the Labor Problem." *Transactions,* American Society of Mechanical Engineers, pp. 856–903.

———. 1903. *Shop Management.* New York: Harper.

———. 1911A. "Letter to the Editor—An Answer to Criticism." *American Magazine,* vol. 72, p. 244.

———. 1911B. "Principles and Methods of Scientific Management." *Journal of Accountancy,* June,, pp. 117–24; July; pp. 181–88.

Taylor, Jacob B. 1938. "Valuation of Fixed Assets and Principles Related to Write Ups and Write Ins." In AIA 1938, pp. 17–20.

Tedlow, R. S. 1985. Comments on *The Coming of Managerial Capitalism,* by A. D. Chandler and R. S. Tedlow. *Business History Review,* Summer, pp. 312–13.

Teichmann, M. M. 1901. "National Accountancy Legislation." *Business,* June, pp. 205–10.

Temporary National Economic Committee. 1939. *Verbatim Record of the Proceedings of the Temporary National Economic Committee.* Washington, D.C.: GPO.

Testimonial Banquet to S. S. Packard. 1896. Program of Speeches by his friends on the occasion of Packard's Seventieth Birthday, April 28. New York: privately printed.

"Testimony of Expert Witnesses at SEC Hearings." 1939. *Journal of Accountancy,* April, pp. 199–220; May, pp. 279–97; June, pp. 350–63.

Theiss, Edwin L. 1932. "Budgetary Procedure as a Means of Administrative Control." *Accounting Review,* March, pp. 11–21.

———. 1935. "Accounting and Budgeting." *Accounting Review,* June, pp. 156–61.

———. 1937. "The Beginnings of Business Budgeting." *Accounting Review,* March, pp. 43–55. Reprinted in *Reading on Accounting Development,* edited by S. P. Garner and M. Hughes. New York: Arno, 1978.

Thelan, David P. 1969. "Social Tensions and the Origins of Progressivism." *Journal of American History,* September, pp. 323–41.

"The Theory and Objects of Taxation." 1888. *Commercial & Financial Chronicle,* February 18, p. 213.

Thomas, Arthur L. 1964. "Value-itis: An Impractical Theorist's Reply." *Accounting Review,* July, pp. 574–81.

———. 1965. "Amortization Problem: A Simplified Model and Some Unanswered Questions." *Journal of Accounting Research,* Spring, pp. 220–32.

———. 1969. *The Allocation Problem in Financial Accounting Theory.* Sarasota, FL: AAA.

Thorton, Frank W. 1928. "Teaching Them How to Think." *Journal of Accountancy,* August, pp. 81–85.

Tinker, Anthony. 1984. "Theories of the State and the State of Accounting: Economic Reductionism and Political Volunteerism in Accounting Regulation Theory." *Journal of Accounting and Public Policy*, vol. 3, no. 1, pp. 55–74.

———. 1988. "Panglossian Accounting Theories: The Science of Apologising in Style." *Accounting, Organizations and Society*, vol. 13, no. 2, pp. 165–89.

Tinker, Anthony, Barbara Merino, and Marilyn Neimark. 1982. "The Normative Origins of Positive Theories." *Accounting, Organizations and Society*, vol. 7, no. 2, pp. 167–200.

Tinsley, James A. 1962. *Texas Society of Certified Public Accountants: A History*. Houston: Texas Society of Certified Public Accountants.

Tipson, F. S. 1901. "The Profit and Loss Account." *Business*, November, p. 434.

Tobey, J. R. 1925. "The Preparation and Control of a Budget." *NACA Bulletin*, September, pp. 36–48.

Tondkar, R. 1983. "An Empirical Investigation of Financial Analysts' Use of Data Required by FASB No. 33." *Southwest Business and Economic Review*, August, pp. 8–20.

"Top 60: Revenue Breakdown." 1989. *Accounting Today*, September 25, p. SS4.

Torres, C. 1991. "Big Board Plans to Start 1/2 Hour Earlier." *Wall Street Journal*, p. C1.

Touissant, J. R. 1970. "The Problem with Hospital Accounting." *Management Accounting*, November, pp. 37–40.

Towns, Charles H. 1940. "Internal Check and Control." In AIA 1940, pp. 10–15.

"Treasury Figures in a New Form." 1891. *Commercial & Financial Chronicle*, May 9, pp. 696–97.

"Treasury Statements Under the New Form." 1891. *Commercial & Financial Chronicle*, July 4, pp. 4–5.

Trueblood, Robert. 1963. "Education for a Changing Profession." *Journal of Accounting Research*, Spring, pp. 88–94.

———. 1966. "Accounting Principles: The Board and Its Problems." In *Empirical Research in Accounting: Selected Studies*. pp. 183–91. Chicago: Institute of Professional Accounting, University of Chicago.

———. 1969. "Ten Years of APB: One Practitioner's Appraisal." Speech at American Accounting Association, privately printed.

Truman, Harry S. 1955. *1945: Year of Decision. Memoirs*. New York: Signet Books.

———. 1956. *Years of Hope and Triumph, 1946–1952. Memoirs*. New York: Signet Books.

"Trying to Do Too Much." 1991. Editorial. *Accounting Today*, July 22, p. 22.

Tucker, B. M. 1981. "The Merchant, the Manufacturer, and the Factory Manager: The Case of Samuel Slater." *Business History Review*, Autumn, pp. 297–313.

Tucker, J. J., III. 1994. "Initial Efforts of Kenneth W. Stringer to Develop a Statistical Sampling Plan." *Accounting Historians Journal*, June, pp. 223–54.

Tuckerman, John R. 1970. "Some Aspects of the Development of Accounting Prior to 1900." Master's thesis, University of Sydney.

Turner, Thomas. 1804. *An Epitome of Book-Keeping by Double Entry*. Portland: Jenks & Shirley. Reprint, Tokyo: Yushodo Booksellers, 1982.

Tyson, T. 1988. "The Nature and Function of Cost Keeping in a Late Nineteenth-Century Small Business." *Accounting Historians Journal,* Spring, pp. 29–44.

———. 1990. "Accounting for Labor in the Early 19th Century: The U.S. Arms Making Experience." *Accounting Historians Journal,* June, pp. 47–59.

"Uniform Accounts." 1905. *Chronicle,* November 18, 1905, p. 1463.

U.S. Congress. 1898. House. *Public Act 141.*

———. 1900. House. *Preliminary Report on Trusts and Industrial Combinations.* H. Doc. 476. 56th Congress, 1st sess.

———. 1901A. House. *Report of the Industrial Commission on Transportation.* H. Doc. 178. 57th Congress, 1st sess.

———. 1901B. House. *Report of the Industrial Commission on Trusts.* H. Doc. 182. 57th Congress, 1st sess.

———. 1902. House. *Final Report of the Industrial Commission.* H. Doc. 380. 57th Congress, 2d sess.

———. 1913. House. *Economy and Efficiency Reports.* H. Doc. 104. 62d Congress, 3d sess.

———. 1933. Senate. Committee on Banking and Currency. *Hearings on the Securities Act.* 73d Congress, 1st sess.

———. 1953. House. Committee on Ways and Means. *Hearings on General Revenue Revisions.* 73d Congress, 1st sess. Washington, D.C.: GPO.

———. 1957, 1958. Committee on the Judiciary. *Administered Price Hearings.* Washington, D.C.: GPO.

———. 1976. House. *Federal Regulation and Reform, Report by the Subcommittee on Oversight and Investigation of the Committee on Interstate and Foreign Commerce.* 94th Congress, 2d sess. Washington, D.C.: GPO.

———. 1977. Senate. *The Accounting Establishment: A Staff Study, Prepared by the Subcommittee on Reports, Accounting and Management of the Committee on Governmental Operations.* 94th Congress, 2d sess. Washington, D.C.: GPO.

U.S. Executive. 1912–14. "Reports of the President's Commission on Economy and Efficiency: Correspondence with Public Accountants." National Archives Manuscript Division, RG 51, Sec. 311. Washington, D.C.

U.S. General Accounting Office. 1972. *Standards for Audit of Governmental Organizations, Programs Activities and Functions.* Washington, D.C.

———. 1989. *CPA Audit Quality: Status of Actions Taken to Improve Auditing and Financial Reporting of Public Companies.* GAO/AFMD-89-38. March, Washington, D. C.

U.S. Securities and Exchange Commission. 1939. *United States of America Before the Securities and Exchange Commission in the Matter of McKesson Robbins.* Washington, D.C.: GPO. Reprint New York: Garland, 1982.

U.S. Treasury. 1794. *An Account of the Receipts and Expenditures of the United States for 1793.* Philadelphia: John Fenno.

———. 1911. *Constructive Recommendations with Respect to Forms of Expenditures to be Used by Several Departments.* Circular No. 35, May 6. Washington, D.C.: GPO.

———. 1946. "Study of Stockholders Reports of Unlisted Companies." *Official Decisions and Releases. Journal of Accountancy,* August, pp. 167–82.

Van Wyhe, Glenn. 1993. *The Struggle for Status: A History of Accounting Education.* New York: Garland.

Vanderbilt, A. T., II. 1989. *Fortune's Children.* New York: Morrow.

Vangermeersch, R. 1979. "Comments on Accounting Disclosures in the Baltimore and Ohio Annual Reports from 1828 to 1850." Working Paper Series No. 38. Harrisonburg, VA: Academy of Accounting Historians.

———. 1986. *The Contribution of Alexander Hamilton Church to Accounting and Management.* New York: Garland.

Vatter, Harold G. 1963. *The U.S. Economy in the 1950s.* New York: Norton.

Vatter, William J. 1945. "Limitations of Overhead Allocation." *Accounting Review,* April, pp. 163–76.

———. 1947. *The Fund Theory of Accounting and Its Implication for Financial Reporting.* Chicago: University of Chicago Press.

———. 1950. *Managerial Accounting.* New York: Prentice Hall.

———. 1962A. "Another Look at the 1957 Statement." *Accounting Review,* October, pp. 660–69.

———. 1962B. "Fund Theory View of Price Level Adjustments." *Accounting Review,* April, pp. 189–207.

———. 1963. "Postulates and Principles." *Journal of Accounting Research,* Autumn, pp. 188–97.

Vaughan, A. 1975. *American Genesis: Captain John Smith and the Founding of Virginia.* Boston: Little, Brown.

Veblen, Thorstein. 1897. *The Theory of the Leisure Class.* New York: Macmillan.

———. 1904. *The Theory of Business Enterprise.* New York: Scribner.

———. 1918A. "The Modern Point of View and the New Order." *The Dial,* October 19, pp. 349–55; November 2, pp. 289–93; November 16, pp. 409–14; December 28, pp. 605–11.

———. 1918B. "The Modern Point of View and the New Order: Free Income." *The Dial,* November 30, pp. 482–88.

———. 1918C. "The Modern Point of View and the New Order: The Vested Interests." *The Dial,* December 14, pp. 543–49.

———. 1919. "The Captains of Finance and the Engineers." *The Dial,* June 14, pp. 599–606.

———. 1950. *The Portable Veblen.* New York: Victory.

Ver Steeg, Clarence L. 1959. "The American Revolution Considered as an Economic Movement." *Huntington Library Quarterly,* August.

Voke, Albert F. 1926. "Accounting Methods of Colonial Merchants in Virginia." *Journal of Accountancy,* July, pp. 1–11.

Vollmers, Gloria. 1993. "An Analysis of the Cost Accounting Literature of the United States from 1925 to 1950." Ph.D. diss., University of North Texas.

Wallace, Wanda. 1980. *The Economic Role of the Audit in Free and Regulated Markets.* New York: Touche Ross.

Walsh, Lawrence M. 1960. "Accounting Education in Review." *Accounting Review,* April, pp. 183–89.

Walton, Seymour. 1909. "Earnings and Income." *Journal of Accountancy,* April, pp. 452–69.

———. 1915. "Fixed Assets at Cost or Market." *Journal of Accountancy,* November, pp. 482–83.

———. 1917. "Practical Application of Theoretical Knowledge." *Journal of Accountancy,* October, pp. 276–88.

Walton, Seymour, and H. A. Finney. 1918. "Increased Values of Fixed Assets." *Journal of Accountancy,* November, pp. 392–93.

Wasserman, Max J. 1931. "The Regulation of Public Accounting in France." *Accounting Review,* December, pp. 249–60.

Watson, Max. 1921. "Interview with Joseph E. Sterrett." *New York Post,* January 18.

Watts, Ross. 1990. "The Evolution of Economics—Based on Empirical Research in Accounting." *Accounting History,* vol. 2, no. 1, pp. 1–5.

Watts, Ross, and Jerold Zimmerman. 1986. *Positive Accounting Theory.* Englewood Cliffs, NJ: Prentice Hall.

"The Way It Was on the Eve of the Revolution." 1976. *US News & World Report,* June 21, pp. 54–56.

Webster, Norman E. 1944. "Some Early Accounting Examiners." *Accounting Review,* April, pp. 142–50.

———. 1954. *The American Association of Public Accountants: Its First Twenty Years, 1886–1906.* New York: American Institute of Accountants.

Weidenhammer, Robert. 1933. "The Accountant and the Securities Act." *Accounting Review,* December, pp. 272–78.

Weinstein, G. W. 1987. *The Bottom Line: Inside Accounting Today.* New York: New American Library Books.

Wellington, C. O. 1936. "Comments of Chairman of the Committee on Cooperation with the Securities and Exchange Commission." AIA, *Minutes,* pp. 48–53.

Wells, M. C. 1970. "A Pulseless, Inanimate and Boneless Thing." *Abacus,* September, pp. 88–90.

———. 1974. Review of *The Evolution of the Theories and Techniques of Standard Costs,* by E. M. Sowell. *Abacus,* December, pp. 178–79.

———. 1976. "A Revolution in Accounting Thought." *Accounting Review,* July, pp. 471–82.

———. 1978A. *Accounting for Common Costs.* Monograph 10. Urbana: CEIRA, University of Illinois.

———. 1978B. *American Engineers' Contributions to Cost Accounting.* New York: Arno.

———. 1991. "The Nature of Activity Costing." In *Costing Heritage,* edited by F. Graves. Monograph No. 6, Academy of Accounting Historians, pp. 128–37.

Werntz, William A. 1939A. "Subjects for Accounting Research." In AIA 1939B, pp. 234–44.

———. 1939B. "What Does the Securities and Exchange Commission Expect of Independent Auditors?" In AIA 1939B, pp. 17–26.

———. 1958. "Accounting in Transition." *Journal of Accountancy,* February, pp. 33–36.

———. 1959. "History of the Accounting Procedure Committee From the Final Report." *Journal of Accountancy,* November, pp. 70–71.

———. 1961. "Accounting Education and the Ford and Carnegie Reports." *Accounting Review,* April, pp. 186–90.

Weschler, D. 1989. "A Peculiar Beauty Contest." *Forbes,* July 10, p. 43.

West, Cornel. 1989. *The American Evasion of Philosophy.* Madison: University of Wisconsin Press.

Wettergreen, John A. 1989. "The Regulatory Policy of the New Deal." In Eden, 1989, pp. 199–213.

Whalen, R. J. 1958. "The Mess at Atlas Plywood." *Fortune,* January, pp. 234–36.

———. 1965. "The Big Skid at Yale Express." *Fortune,* November, pp. 146–49.

"What are Earnings? The Growing Credibility Gap." 1967. *Forbes,* May 15, pp. 28–39.

"The Wheat Commission Report." 1972. *Journal of Accountancy,* May, pp. 35–36.

Wheat, Francis M. 1972. "Recommendation on the Study on Establishment of Accounting Principles." Official Releases. *Journal of Accountancy,* May, pp. 66–71.

"Wheat Panel Drafts Program." 1972. *Journal of Accountancy,* July, p. 14.

Wheeler, George. 1973. *Pierpont Morgan and Friends: The Anatomy of a Myth.* Englewood Cliffs, NJ: Prentice Hall.

Wheeler, J. R. 1907. "The Idea of College and University." *Columbia University Quarterly,* December, pp. 1–13.

White, Hayden. 1978. *Tropics of Discourse: Essays in Cultural Criticism.* Baltimore: Johns Hopkins University Press.

White, L. J. 1991. "Another Financial Regulation Disaster." *Wall Street Journal,* February 22, p. A10.

Whitney, Jack M. 1963. "Address Before the Washington Society of Investment Analysts." February 5, typescript. AICPA, New York.

"Why Accountants Need to Tell a Fuller Story." 1971. *Business Week,* February 6, pp. 36–37.

"Why Foreign Investors Turn Their Eyes toward America." 1977. *US News & World Report,* April 18, pp. 92–93.

Wickersham, George W. 1909. Correspondence with Public Accountants. Haskins & Sells Archival Collection. New York.

Wiebe, Robert. 1958. "Business Disunity and the Progressive Movement. " *Mississippi Valley Historical Review,* March, pp. 664–85.

Wiesen, Jeremy. 1978. *The Securities Acts and Independent Auditors: What Did Congress Intend?* New York: AICPA.

Wildman, John R. 1911. *Cost Accounting.* New York: Accountancy Publishing.

———. 1914. "Depreciation from a Certified Accountant's Point of View." *Electric Railway Journal,* April, pp. 332–33.

———. 1924. "The Educational Program of the Institute." *Proceedings of the American Association of University Instructors in Accounting,* pp. 33–36.

——. 1925. "Favorite Methods of Business Crookdom." *Proceedings of the American Association of University Instructors in Accounting*, pp. 127–29.

——. 1927. "Significant Developments Relating to No Par Stock." *Haskins & Sells Bulletin*, June, pp. 42–44.

——. 1928A. "Appreciation from the Point of View of the Certified Public Accountant." *Accounting Review*, December, pp. 396–406.

——. 1928B. "Diversity of No Par Stock Statutes Create Problems for the Accountant." *American Accountant*, February, pp. 19–21.

Wildman, John R., and Weldon Powell. 1928. *Capital Stock without Par Value*. Chicago: A. W. Shaw.

Wilkinson, George. 1903. *The CPA Movement*. New York: Wilkinson, Reckitt & Williams.

——. 1904. "The CPA Movement and the Future of the Profession of the Public Accountant in the United States of America." *The Accountant*, October 22, pp. 464–71.

——. 1928. "The Genesis of the CPA Movement." *Certified Public Accountant*, September, pp. 261–66, 279.

Williams, H. M. 1979. "Corporate Accountability and Corporate Power." Carnegie Mellon University Fairless Lecture Series, October 24, 1979, p. 20.

Williams, J. R. 1988. *A Framework for the Development of Education Research*. Accounting Education Series No. 8. Sarasota, FL: AAA.

Williamson, H. F. 1952. *Winchester: The Gun That Won the West*. New York: A. S. Barnes.

Williamson, Oliver F. 1981. "The Modern Corporations Origins: Evolution and Attributes." *Journal of Economic Literature*, pp. 1537–68.

——. 1983. "Organizations Form, Residual Claimants and Corporate Control." *Journal of Law and Economics*, June, pp. 351–63.

Willmott, Hugh. 1991. "The Auditing Game: A Question of Ownership and Control." *Critical Perspectives on Accounting*, March, pp. 109–22.

Winjum, James O. 1970. "Accounting in Its Age of Stagnation." *Accounting Review*, October, pp. 743–61.

——. 1971. "The Journal of Thomas Gresham." *Accounting Review*, January, pp. 149–55.

Winter, S. G. 1928. "The Next Decade in Accounting." *Accounting Review*, September, pp. 311–22.

Wisconsin State Bar. 1961. "Statement of Principles and Agreement between the Wisconsin Society of CPAs and the State Bar of Wisconsin." *Wisconsin Bar Bulletin*, April, pp. 69–72.

Wise, T. A. 1982. *Peat, Marwick, Mitchell & Co*. New York: Peat, Marwick, Mitchell.

Witte, John M. 1985. *The Politics and Development of the Federal Income Tax*. Madison: University of Wisconsin Press.

Wolk, H. I., J. R. Francis, and M. G. Tearney. 1984. *Accounting Theory*. Boston: Kent.

Woodruff, William. 1966. *Impact of Western Man: A Study of Europe's Role in the World Economy, 1750–1960*. London: Macmillan.

———. 1971. *The Emergence of an International Economy, 1700–1914*. London: Fontana.

———. 1975. *America's Impact on the World: A Study of the Role of the United States in the World Economy, 1750–1970*. London: Macmillan.

Woodside, Byron. 1964. "Government-Accountants Relations." *Journal of Accountancy*, September, pp. 67–68.

Woodward, P. D. 1956. "Depreciation—the Development of an Accounting Concept." *Accounting Review*, January, pp. 71–76.

Wormser, I. Maurice. 1931. *Frankenstein Incorporated*. New York: Whittesey House.

Wren, D. A. 1983. "American Business Philanthropy and Higher Education in the Nineteenth Century." *Business History Review*, Autumn, pp. 321–46.

Wyatt, Arthur. 1963. *A Critical Study of Business Combinations*. ARS No. 5. New York: AICPA.

———. 1983. "The Efficient Market Theory and Its Impact upon Accounting." *Journal of Accountancy*, February, pp. 56–65.

Wyllie, Irvin G. 1959. "Social Darwinism and the Businessman." *Proceedings of the American Philosophical Society*, October, pp. 629–35.

Yamey, Basil S. 1940. *Functional Development of Double Entry Bookkeeping*. London: Gee & Co.

———. 1964. "Accounting and the Rise of Capitalism: Further Notes on a Theme by Sombart." *Journal of Accounting Research*, pp. 117–36.

———. 1976. Letter to G. J. Previts, dated October 5.

———. 1978. Introduction to Cronhelm's *Double Entry by Single*. Reprint ed. New York: Arno.

———. 1989. *Art and Accounting*, New Haven: Yale University Press.

Yates, J. 1986. "The Telegraph's Effect on Nineteenth Century Markets and Firms." *Business and Economic History*, vol. 15, 2d ser., pp. 149–63.

Yerak, Rebecca. 1990. "A Chat with a Local Legend." *Cleveland Plain Dealer*, February 4, p. E-1.

Yu, S. 1957. "Macroeconomic Accounting and Some of Its Basic Problems." *Accounting Review*, April, pp. 264–72.

Yu, S., and J. Neter. 1973. "Stochastic Model of the Internal Control System." *Journal of Accounting Research*, Autumn, pp. 273–95.

"A Yuppie's Guide to Keeping What's Yours." 1989. *Wall Street Journal*, September 20, p. A23.

Zald, M. 1968. "The Common Body of Knowledge for CPAs: Some Problems in Analysis." *Journal of Accounting Research*, Autumn, pp. 130–40.

Zecher, J. R. 1986. "An Economic Perspective of SEC Corporate Disclosure." In *The SEC and Accounting: The First 50 Years*. Arthur Young Professors' Roundtable. New York: North-Holland, pp. 69–77.

Zeff, Stephen A. 1962. "Replacement Cost: Member of the Family, Unwelcome Guest or Intruder." *Accounting Review*, October, pp. 611–25.

———. 1972. *Forging Accounting Principles in Five Countries: A History and Analysis of Trends*. Champaign, IL: Stipes.

————, ed. 1976. *Asset Appreciation, Business Income and Price Level Accounting.* New York: Arno.

————. 1988. *The U.S. Accounting Profession in the 1890s and Early 1900s.* New York: Garland.

————. 1996. "A Study of Academic Research Journals in Accounting." *Accounting Horizons,* September, pp. 158–77.

Zuckerman, M. B. 1991. "The Professoriate of Fear." *US News & World Report,* July 29, p. 64.

Index

Page numbers for photographs are in italics.

**Historical Perspectives
on Business Enterprise Series**

Mansel G. Blackford and K. Austin Kerr, Editors

The scope of the series includes scholarly interest in the history of the firm, the history of government-business relations, and the relationships between business and culture, both in the United States and abroad, as well as in comparative perspective.

The Passenger Train in the Motor Age: California's Rail and Bus
Industries, 1910–1941
  Gregory Lee Thompson

Rebuilding Cleveland: The Cleveland Foundation and Its Evolving Urban
Strategy
  Diana Tittle

Daniel Willard and Progressive Management on the Baltimore & Ohio
Railroad
  David M. Vrooman